Frank Buchholz—Janet Robinson—Joe Robinson

The Great War Dawning

Frank Buchholz—Janet Robinson—Joe Robinson

THE GREAT WAR DAWNING

Germany and its Army at the Start of World War I

Verlag Militaria

www.militaria.at, verlag-militaria@aon.at

ISBN 978-3-902526-65-6

DEDICATION

To Almighty God, who made this possible.

"Come now, and let us reason together, saith the LORD. . ."

Isaiah 1:18

TABLE OF CONTENTS

APPENDICES

FOREWORD

During recent years a positive flood of books concerning the First World War and the period leading up to it has been written for the Anglophone market. However, one strange associated point is the fact that this outpouring of work is remarkably one sided. In fact it is most unusual for the German army to receive anything other than a passing mention and, even when it does, careful examination of bibliography and footnotes tends to reveal that little has been included beyond that which may be obtained from a study of the notes on the German army contained in the volumes of the British Official History. There are probably several reasons for this. The devaluing of the study of foreign languages is undoubtedly one. As a result, a generation of mono-lingual historians has emerged, unable or unwilling to devote the time needed to achieve the mastery of a second or third language, which is an essential tool for the researcher. A further problem arises from the general, but false, assumption that, following the destruction of huge quantities of records during the Second World War, little of value remains in the surviving archives in Germany; that the potential returns do not justify the effort involved.

Of course there are honorable exceptions. The brilliant scholarship of Professor Christopher Clark of Cambridge University, England, is a case in point. His work on the history of Prussia and the convoluted lead up to the outbreak of war in 1914 is quite outstanding and likely to remain standard reference for many years to come. In terms of pure military history, a trickle of work relating to the old German army during the First World War is starting to appear as the centenaries of these events approach. In that context, the books of Terence Zuber are worthy of mention. He is an assiduous researcher and very knowledgeable historian, who may not set out to be controversial, but succeeds in being so; his provocative approach forces us to think more deeply about the subjects he discusses. This is precisely what this excellent book does. Whereas Zuber tends to be systematically laudatory of the fighting ability of the old German armies, seeing only the positive aspects of their performance and attributing their undoubted tactical successes in 1914 to superior organization and training, the authors have set out to answer the question, 'If that is the case, what caused the entire strategic undertaking to unravel so swiftly?'

In undertaking this quest, they set out to place the development of the various contingents of the German army in their political, social and historical context. They are fully aware that 19th and early 20th century Germany is more or less a closed book to the modern reader; that the appreciation of German cultural and scholarly achievements, so common amongst our forbears one hundred years ago, has been lost in the noise of 20th century conflict. In response, they have taken enormous care to fill in some of the gaps, to guide the reader through the complexities of pre-war German society as a whole and the role and position of the German army within it, in particular. Not content merely with straightforward explanations and the provision of numerous informative tables and charts, they devote a great deal of space to describing, not only the successful aspects of the development of the German armies post-1870, but also the negative ones. In so doing, they highlight matters such as the tension between traditionalists and modernizers and the way that failure to face up to structural anomalies and fundamental contradictions in areas such as battlefield logistics, command and control, and the training and management of cavalry operations, led directly into major problems and, ultimately, failure, soon after the massive invasion of France and Belgium began in August 1914.

This timely and authoritative book should be on the shelf of every serious student of the First World War. I commend it highly and hope that it will be widely read.

Jack Sheldon
Vercors, France
August 2013

ACKNOWLEDGMENTS

Our thanks go out to many who made this work possible. Included in that group are Brett Butterworth, Andreas Bauer, Jim Turinetti, Georg Ortenburg, Rony Kastoun, Sam Wouters, and Dr. Rolf Wirtgen of the *Wehrtechnische Studiensammlung*, Koblenz, who contributed outstanding pictures from their personal and official collections. And, to Mattias Hoffman who found and scanned several key source books. Dr. Nancy Gillard, Professor Carol Ann Britt and Jackson Bockus proofread and offered many common sense suggestions for the manuscript.

Glenn Jewison and Paul Hederer made suggestions and corrections to the drafts. All of these additions added greatly to the finished product. Larry Stewart and Kristiaan Cornelis helped with a nagging Franco-Prussian War picture problem. We could not have done this without them. I am sure there are still mistakes that are ours alone, but these friends and scholars have reduced that number significantly.

The late Georg Ortenburg was a great mentor and aided our efforts. We wish him eternal peace and can only wish that he were here to read the book. Jack Sheldon was our "*lektor*" and gave great suggestions for the entire manuscript. Thank you for your time, patience, and comments that helped bring the entire book together.

There are no words to thank Jack Sheldon for all that he has done. His main purpose was to make this a readable text, and he far exceeded that. We learned so much from him, both style and content. There is no question why he is the premier professional historian concerning this subject.

The Robinsons would like to thank Col. (Ret.) Merle Tiedemann whose knowledge of logistics gave rise to many discussions and the original idea that we needed to explore a serious logistical problem. We would also like to thank Col. (Ret.) Barbara Eager and Jane Bockus, who supported and listened to us, when sometimes we couldn't see the forest for the trees.

Much of this manuscript was put together using Dragon Dictate voice software for the Macintosh. We need to thank the makers of that software that allowed an author to create much of this book even though typing was beyond him.

INTRODUCTION

The Great War Dawning is a study in the English language about the birth of imperial Germany and its army from the German point of view. Although countless books in English about World War I have contributed to the general knowledge, each in their own way, there is a continuing gap in understanding not only of imperial Germany, but also its World War I army as it entered the war in 1914. What the reader is going to discover is that this world was significantly different than the one we live in, and that peacetime cultural, doctrinal, and organizational cracks in the military machine led directly to Germany's failure in the early days. What you are not going to see is a regurgitation of the same old historical lessons of British-centered histories that pointed fingers and avoided blame. We are offering a completely different view on why the war did not go well on the Western Front in early 1914. We will address several examples that show a flawed army structure. These include the disaster of the *Höhere Kavallerie-Kommandeur* (HKK), logistical shortfalls, and leadership issues. All three are organizational and structural flaws that could have been addressed prior to launching the war. We also present the only English-language explanation of the role of German general staff officers of which we are aware. This book is not a rewrite of the history of the Marne, but an explanation of how the culture and the army structure led to problems in doctrine and execution.

For a very long time, we have been told that the army that Germany fielded in 1914 was the best military force in German history, and that the General Staff was the best in its profession worldwide. We have learned they were faithful to the teachings of Schlieffen, and that they passed the sure European war victory blueprint to the German military elite in 1914.[1] Looking back at the 1914 mobilization, historians have admired the precision of this military machine as it evolved from peace to war. The implication is that everything had been thought through, everything had been foreseen, forecasted, and planned. And, what resulted was a well-trained, perfectly motivated, and well-equipped military force that went into the field superior to its foes in operational and tactical doctrines, ordnance, and fighting spirit. It follows then, that Germany deliberately risked starting the war to make use of its superior military force. This popular thought leads to a critique of Germany's assumed militarism. Very few historians have questioned the efficiency of the war machine itself. During the 1920s, the Schlieffen disciples in the *Reichsarchiv* invested a lot of effort to make us believe that the weak Helmuth v. Moltke the Younger had watered down the blueprint of victory that his predecessor Schlieffen had bequeathed him. Moltke's messenger, Lt. Col. Hentsch, by conveying wrong and panic-driven decisions to the forces fighting at the Marne, had spoiled

[1] (Storz, 1992), pp. 19–20.

the sure victory. This has been the leitmotif of the historical debate for decades. It was even the theme of the Schlieffen Plan debate triggered by Terence Zuber in 2002.

There may have been other reasons leading to the miracle of the Marne. For example, the various contingents that made up the German Army had severe systemic cracks as far as leadership, logistics and in the operational methodology pertaining to cavalry forces in 1914 were concerned. Our analysis shows that these cracks seriously demythologize the German army of 1914, and that these cracks may have had such a severe impact upon German military performance that the miracle of the Marne was made possible.

This is not a discussion of any nation's actions or reactions to military operations. Rather, it is an analysis of how these identified cracks affected the German military. In the miracle of the Marne, the French and British were only one-half of the equation. This is not about that much-discussed one-half. This book is about how deficiencies in the German army structure affected the outcome even without the pressures of enemy action.

The following 17 chapters introduce imperial Germany well before the Great War. The first chapters set the stage and provide a general understanding of the political, social, and economic situation in imperial Germany and its many states. This discussion leads to the training, organization, and doctrine of the pre-war army. Obvious flaws and weaknesses are discussed. Finally, we provide a concrete discussion of the results of flaws and fissures pointed out in earlier chapters, when the army was put to the test in battle.

"Wars produce many stories of fiction, some of which are told until they are believed to be true."[2] Not only is it true for "war stories," but also it is true for wartime self- and critical analysis. Self-analysis by the imperial German leaders did not always lead to the true causes of failure, but rather it emphasized the failure of someone else. And, in many instances, critical analyses of the German Army have been repeated and repeated until they have become conventional wisdom.

Why cover topics that range from social and cultural aspects to mobilization and war? What the reader will discover is that imperial Germany was a nation in conflict. The well-established, traditional society was evolving into a more universal, constitutional, and reformed system. At the start of the 20th century, the monarchy and aristocracy held sway. A rural economic system and a traditional conservative political system were bolstered by a non-universal voting system. Also, a traditional religious system permeated an even more traditional military. Population, urban economics, socialist political systems, and multi-confessional religions all demanded change. Within the military, the tug-of-war affected force structure, assignments, doctrine, and, as a consequence, results. Even within the highest levels of government, secrecy and competition between the Great General Staff and the War Ministry caused fundamental problems that ultimately led to failure; when these traditional systems were tested at the opening of the Great War, they were found wanting. Attempting to understand the Great War using a modern framework, not only leads to misunderstandings but also frustration.

Why is the Western Front in 1914 so important? Because of the horrific casualties incurred later in the war, the significance of 1914 is frequently misunderstood. In point of fact, it was by far the deadliest year of the war. Even compared with the big battles of the Somme and Verdun, 1914 produced the highest death rates. Imperial Germany lost 116,000 men killed and 400,000 men wounded on the Western Front in 1914. Compare that with the 43,000

---

[2] Quote by Ulysses S. Grant (Shafritz, 1990), p. 253.

men lost during the entire Franco-Prussian War. In August and September 1914 alone, Germany suffered 29 percent of all of the war casualties it would receive on the Western front.[3]

Events in Europe in the 19th century had encouraged many Germans to think of creating a single state in which all Germans could be combined. This mindset contributed to the lyrics of their national hymn, *Deutschland, Deutschland über Alles*, written by Heinrich Hoffman von Fallersleben in 1841. The words seemed threatening when translated into English as "Germany, Germany over all," but to those who heard it in the 19th century, it meant they should put aside their parochial feelings as Bavarians or Saxons or Prussians and think of themselves as Germans above all else.[4]

In 1871, Germany became a country. This simple statement underlines the fact that prior to 1871 there was no Germany, no German army, and no German officer corps. Though it is convenient to call it "Germany" at the start of the First World War, there was still no united Germany, no imperial German army, and no unified German officer corps. This is just an opening salvo to allow the reader to understand a significant difference from what has become a dogmatic conventional wisdom view of imperial Germany.

Heretofore, different authors have addressed different aspects—collectors, historians, and educators all have their own area of expertise, as do the authors. Dr. Buchholz is German and Secretary of the highly regarded *Deutsche Gesellschaft für Heereskunde*. Col. Joe Robinson retired from the US Army, where he was a Division G3 in a combat zone; he has written several thousand operational orders. Col. Janet Robinson retired from the US Air Force and has an undergraduate degree in German language and history and a master's degree in strategic studies. This book is not an academic tome; the authors are not professional historians; they are students of the Great War.

Americans historically have studied World War I history from a British perspective. From middle schools to the U.S. Army War College, histories repeat the facts as well as the errors of previous English-language works. Popular authors such as Barbara Tuchman have added greatly to this body of "facts;" however, many of her statements from the 1960s are now openly questioned. One commenter called her work a "novel." Unfortunately her "facts" have been often repeated as facts. A classic and highly readable British account of the early weeks of the war is *Mons* by John Terraine—a clear example of the English-sided treatment of American education. Terraine says,

> The information contained in this book is drawn from many sources . . . A special mention must, however, be made of the following works on which all else rests: *The Official History of the War*, compiled by Brig. Gen. J. E. Edmonds; *Liaison 1914*, by Sir Edward Spears; *The Memoirs of Marshal Joffre*; *1914* by The Earl of Ypres; *Memories of Forty-Eight Years of Service* by General Sir Horace Smith-Dorrien; *The War in the Air*, by Walter Raleigh; *The Wilson Diaries*, edited by Maj Gen Sir C. E. Callwell; and *Alarms and Excursions* by Lt. Gen. Sir Tom Bridges.

No German sources were included! Were the Germans not one-half the experience? If one examines the index of Terraine's book, you will see that there is no mention of any German formations lower than army; whereas, on the British side, there are dozens and dozens of entries right down to individual battalions and gun batteries. This kind of bias has dominated

---

3 (Neiberg, 2011), pp. 173–174.
4 (Shafritz, 1990), p. 180.

the American understanding of the Great War as well. The Allied side of the story has found its way into tradition, and the German story has been forgotten. History belongs to the victor. By reading and interpreting many primary and second-source references, both in German and English, the authors have made judgments and taken sides. The outcome is a balanced synthesis of a variety of sources.

Often, secondary sources are interpreted through the eyes of current historical thought. New books are published and existing thought changes to match extant reality. During the 1950s, Gerhard Ritter influenced prevailing thought with his premise that Europe had accidentally slid into a war that was not all Germany's fault and that Adolf Hitler was an accident or an aberration of history.[5] The 1961 book by Fritz Fischer, *Germany's Aims in the First World War,*[6] postulated a relatively novel idea at that time that the pre-1914 German belief in European hegemony was a major cause of the war. This thought further evolved in 1973, when Hans-Ulrich Wehler wrote *The German Empire 1871–1918.*[7] He discussed the methods used to govern imperial Germany and focused on internal politics. In his view, the "élites" tried to hold on to power by means of an expansionist foreign policy.

More recent history focuses on German social issues and attempts to rehabilitate the imperial German Empire and the Third Reich. These recent authors discuss *Sonderweg,* a philosophy that attempts to explain that common western patterns of social and political development were not applicable to Germany. Otto v. Bismarck ordered the revolution from above rather than having it foment from the bourgeoisie below. The justification of Hitler's rise to power occurred because politics and society were not in synchronization. Two observations: German historical thought is evolving, and most English language history books have only a distinctly English or British view of the war. The points-of-view of France, Russia, Germany, and Austria-Hungary provide different insights but have not been widely read by American students of the Great War. This one-sided portrayal has confused amateur historians for decades. Occasionally, the authors found that some well-accepted "facts" are really myths.

For example look at the first picture in the picture block. This is a well-known picture that has been used in various forms in many schoolbooks, academic articles, and general histories for decades. It is asserted that it is a picture of German soldiers advancing in Belgium or France in August of 1914. There is nothing startling or new about the picture except the provenance is a myth. This picture appeared on the front page of a Prussian newspaper dated September 1913. Debunking myths also has been part of our focus.

We also include, for the first time, parts of a previously unpublished and little-known *Handbook of the General Staff Officer.* These officers had great influence on every military organization and had a guidebook that was issued to them individually. Its distribution was very limited and very few copies exist today. Sometimes, what is not in this handbook is as telling as what it actually contains.

Time has marched on and imperial Germany is no more. A world of quality was replaced by a world of quantity. With the end of this era, stories and pictures faded behind a glass frame. It is difficult to put it all together, especially from an American viewpoint as the media has historically vilified the opponents of the American military; therefore, imperial Germany and its Kaiser were automatically evil. The German Army was too small. Despite the fact that the 1906 infantry regulation demanded some sort of acquiescence to extended order tac-

[5] (Retallack, 1996), p. 8.
[6] (Fischer, 1968)
[7] (Wehler, 1985)

tics, many leaders ignored those changes. Different army corps had different methods. That misapplication alone has been accused of adding 10 percent to the German casualty lists in August 1914.[8] There were coordination problems between the different branches, especially artillery and infantry. This failure led to fratricide and was caused in part by a deep-rooted social misunderstanding of what a soldier was supposed to do. Based on tradition and social perceptions, the cavalry at Haelen charged its way into disaster. There was not only a failure of aviation assets in reconnaissance, but also a failure to understand the technology and for commanders to rely upon the reports of mounted patrols. There was a conflict of culture and means that led to uncertain outcomes

Research is never-ending. New questions arise and the answers frequently point in different directions. To that end, a line must be drawn in the sand. In the final analysis, we are left still scratching our heads as to why most of the cavalry was not originally placed on the right flank if indeed the idea was to turn the flank with the right. Did this have something to do with the leadership ideology of *Vernichtungsschlacht*—the battle of annihilation? There will be those who will criticize every effort made here. As Saint Augustine said, "For those who think I have said too much or too little, I beg pardon."

8 (Brose, 2001), pp. 202–203.

CHAPTER 1

THE MAKING OF IMPERIAL GERMANY

THE GERMANIC CONFEDERATION AND THE ZOLLVEREIN

There is general agreement that the First Reich was the Holy Roman Empire, and the Third Reich was Nazi Germany. In 1923, a German fiction writer named Arthur Moeller van den Bruck coined the term "Second Reich" to tag the years between 1871 and 1918; however, German-language historians rarely, if ever, use the term Second Reich. If not the Second Reich, what then was imperial Germany? Was it Wilhelmine Germany, based on the reign of Wilhelm II, the last German Kaiser, who came to the throne on his father's death in 1888 and abdicated in November 1918? Is the end of the Franco-Prussian War in 1871, the beginning of imperial Germany? In fact, these arbitrary dates define what is called imperial Germany too narrowly. The beginnings of a German cultural identity begin much earlier.

The Germanic Confederation was born after the Napoleonic Wars and the Congress of Vienna. It replaced the Holy Roman Empire, which Voltaire had already declared neither Holy, nor Roman, nor an Empire. Napoleon's conquests had previously reduced the independent state status of the Holy Roman Empire from 380 entities to 39 that included 35 different monarchies.[1] This Confederation (also known as the *Deutsche Bund*) was more of a cultural concept than a political reality. Membership was not clearly defined and most often centered on a particular monarch, who defined the state's identity.[2] Prussia benefitted substantially from this reorganization. Its territory expanded into the Rhineland, while Saxony suffered, because of its earlier alliance with Napoleon Hanover became a kingdom and Württemberg prospered.

Not all monarchs were bound by the provisions of the Confederation. The King of England, who owned Hanover; the King of Holland, who owned Luxembourg; and the King of Denmark, who owned Holstein were exempt from mutual defense. The Germanic Confederation included both the Habsburg (Austrian) and the Hohenzollern (Prussian) dynasties, while Austria provided the president of the Bund. Some British observers have referred to this organization as that of the "Germanys."[3]

Eventually, the remaining members of the Bund were held together through a loose series of treaties that had little in the way of teeth. The principal cause of inefficiency was a rivalry between the two leading states of Austria and Prussia. Because the Habsburg dynasty (Aus-

1 (Feuchtwanger, 2001), p. 1.
2 (Green, *Fatherlands*, 2001)
3 (White, 1996), p. 137.

tria) included both Germanic and non-Germanic peoples, the boundary of the Germanic Confederation ran through the middle of the Habsburg Empire.

Supporters of unification inside the Germanic Confederation boundaries endorsed a concept called *Großdeutschland*. It would include all German-speaking peoples, Austria would lead the organization, and the Habsburg Empire would be divided.[4]

Those on the other side of the unification argument supported a concept called *Kleindeutschland*. This organization would include all Germanic states, excluding Austria. Prussia would be the dominant state and lead this unification. In 1848–49, the years of liberal revolutions in Europe, the Germanic Confederation's left-leaning parliament adopted a *Constitution of the German Empire* in something known as St. Paul's Parliament. This constitution excluded Austria, and the German Emperor's crown was offered to Frederic William IV of Prussia, who declined to accept it, because he did not wish to go to war with Austria.

There was another abortive attempt by Prussia to take the lead in a treaty among three kingdoms known as the *Dreikönigsbund*, but the States of Hanover and Saxony hesitated and the Dreikönigsbund became a short-term side note. Despite this maneuvering, Austria continued to dominate the Germanic Confederation.[5]

It was then that Otto von Bismarck emerged on the scene and began moving Prussia towards German unity and a German Empire. Bismarck used an existing organization called the *Deutsche Zollverein* founded in 1834. Prussia pressured its neighbors to join the organization that allowed tariff-free trade among the members. This move went a long way to make Kleindeutschland a reality. As tariffs represented about 50 percent of a state's income, Prussia surrendered a substantial income but gained dominance in foreign policy.

The smaller states also prospered from membership in the Zollverein; consequently, most states wanted to join. Saxony, which had suffered after the 1815 Congress of Vienna, recovered substantially as a member. By 1854, all states of the Germanic Confederation were members of the Zollverein except the three Hanseatic cities,[6] the Mecklenburgs, Holstein, and Austria. Austria's growing economic isolation would soon take its toll as Prussia continued to control the Zollverein. A common cliché was that there was a fictitious Germany called the Confederation (really dominated by Austria) and a working Germany called the Zollverein (run by Prussia).[7]

The Zollverein was a major influence in German's industrialization. It fostered trade among members and created interdependence. Green, in his book *Fatherlands,* points out that Saxony was dependent on Prussian grain. Baden and Württemberg imported Prussian coal and iron. Prussia imported wine and tobacco from Hesse-Darmstadt.[8] Leaving the Zollverein simply was economically not feasible so, through increased interdependence, Prussia gained support for its economic leadership.

The Zollverein itself was not enough of a stimulus to ensure German unification, nor did unification complete the Zollverein. Hamburg did not join until 1881, nor Bremen until 1884.[9] What came next was a series of wars of German pre-unification. The war with Denmark in 1864 and the war with Austria in 1866 were indeed steps towards the unification of Germany, but not all agree that the ultimate goal of those wars was to achieve unification.

4 (Krüger, 1915), pp. 13–17.

5 (Krüger, 1915), pp. 17–18.

6 Bremen, Hamburg, Lübeck

7 (Green, *Political and Diplomatic Movements, 1850–1870, 2004*), pp. 70–76.

8 (Green, *Fatherlands*, 2001), p. 229.

9 (Pounds, 1996), p. 17.

Our interpretation suggests that there was no grand design for unification; rather that Bismarck exploited a series of events that led in that direction.

THE DANISH WARS

Two German-Danish Wars intervened to influence the make-up of the German Confederation. In 1815, the province of Holstein was admitted to the German Confederation because the population was ethnically German, despite the fact that the King of Denmark owned it. Schleswig, in contrast, was 50 percent Danish, had never been part of the Holy Roman Empire, and was considered to be an integral part of the Danish kingdom. A third province, Lauenburg, was often considered a small add-on to Holstein. There was a pre-1850 minority movement within Denmark to create an independent state named Schleswig-Holstein. The King of Denmark objected, offered independence to Holstein, but insisted that Schleswig remain closely tied to Denmark and give up its autonomy, thereby losing home rule and linguistic privileges. In 1850, the German Confederation asked Prussia to police Danish notions of hegemony in the region; they were successful until pressed to conclude a truce. The three provinces remained part of Denmark while retaining their local autonomy.[10]

When the King of Denmark, Frederick VII, died in 1863, the Schleswig-Holstein crisis gained in significance. The new Danish king, Christian IX of Schleswig-Holstein-Sonderburg-Glücksburg, a junior branch of the House of Oldenburg, announced his intent to annex Schleswig. Based on the Treaty of the First Danish War in 1850, the duchies were to belong to the new Danish king provided he did not annex them. The Germanic Confederation offered a plan to name Prince Friedrich of Augustenburg as the new Duke of Schleswig-Holstein. While most of the members of the Germanic Confederation supported a new smaller state, Austria and Prussia demanded that Denmark abide by its treaty obligations and not annex any land.

When King Christian of Denmark sent troops into the duchies and attached Schleswig directly to Denmark, Austria and Prussia went to war without the approval of the Confederation because, as has been mentioned, the Confederation supported Prince Augustenburg as Duke.[11] Although the war was originally intended to re-establish home rule in Schleswig, when Denmark lost the Danes ceded Schleswig, Holstein, and Lauenberg jointly to Austria and Prussia.

With Denmark out of the way, Austria and Prussia agreed to the Gastein Convention. This agreement awarded Schleswig to Prussia and Holstein to Austria. Austria also agreed that any dispute about the provinces would be handled purely as a matter for Prussia and Austria to resolve. The Austrian-dominated German Confederation would not be involved. Austria agreed to sell Lauenburg to the Prussians and to allow Prussia the use of Holstein's roads and telegraph facilities.[12]

A popular notion is that Bismarck went to war against Denmark in 1864 to engineer unification of the Confederation. When Denmark lost, Bismarck was able then to contrive a war between Prussia and Austria over the governance of the newly acquired provinces. While some believe this stratagem was his intent, it was a complex issue made even more so because of the number of players. Most agree that it would have been difficult for one man to engineer the outcome.

[10] (Wawro, 1998), pp. 40–41.
[11] (Green, *Political and Diplomatic Movements, 1850–1870, 2004*), pp. 81–84.
[12] (Wawro, 1998), pp. 41–42.

THE AUSTRO-PRUSSIAN WAR OF 1866

The Gastein Convention was short-lived. Austria violated the agreement to settle any disputes directly with Prussia when it took its disputes about Holstein directly to the German Confederation. Prussia then threatened to invade Holstein. On 14 June 1866, Austria asked the German Confederation to join with their armies to punish the Prussians. Contrary to popular opinion and many sources, not all states of the Confederation jumped at the opportunity to fight Prussia. Prussia attacked Austria, as well as the warring states of the German Confederation and won the War of 1866 (also known as the Seven Weeks War).[13] This conflict was to prove by far the most significant struggle for the establishment of a German Empire and far more important than the Franco-Prussian War that was yet to come.[14]

There is confusion as to who was on which side, because many secondary sources say that most states sided with Austria. The conventional thought is that when the German Confederation asked for mobilization, everyone responded. This assumption is not true. Prussia's allies were the King of Italy (who wanted Venetia), Mecklenburg-Schwerin, Mecklenburg-Strelitz, Oldenburg, Anhalt, Brunswick, Saxe-Altenburg, Saxe-Coburg and Gotha, Lauenburg, Lippe-Detmold, Schwarzburg-Sondershausen, Waldeck-Pyrmont, Bremen, Hamburg, and Lübeck.

Austria had fewer allies, but they were more powerful and included: the Kingdoms of Bavaria, Hanover, Saxony, and Württemberg, as well as Baden, Hesse-Darmstadt, Nassau, Hesse-Kassel, Saxe-Meiningen, Reuß Senior Line, Schaumburg-Lippe, and Frankfurt. Six other members of the German Confederation stayed neutral: Limburg, Liechtenstein, Luxembourg, Reuß Junior Line, Saxe-Weimar-Eisenach, and Schwarzburg-Rudolstadt.[15]

Under the terms of the Treaty of Prague that ended the war on 23 August 1866 (and was mediated by Napoleon III),[16] the Austrian Emperor recognized the dissolution of the German Confederation and consented to the new formation of German states in which the imperial state of Austria would have no part. Pope Pius IX greeted the news with the comment, "the world has collapsed."[17]

The war had lasted only seven weeks but at its conclusion, the balance of power shifted from Austria to Prussia, and the concept of Kleindeutschland began to come to fruition. No territorial claims were made of Austria in exchange for 30 million silver florins (about $405 million) worth of Austrian indemnity payments that allowed Bismarck to balance the Prussian budget. Bismarck also secured an agreement with Austria to allow Prussia to annex Schleswig, Holstein, the kingdom of Hanover, Hesse-Kassel, Nassau, and the free city of Frankfurt-am-Main, thus disregarding the rights of the existing imperial houses. These annexations created a physical bridge between the eastern and western parts of the Prussian kingdom.[18] This was also important because the armies from the states that were absorbed became part of the Prussian army and politically many legislative votes went with this territory.[19]

---

13 (Perris, 1912), pp. 225–229.

14 (*Großer Generalstab, Kriegsgeschichtliche Abteilung I., 1867*)

15 (Generalstab, 1867)

16 (*The Free Dictionary* by Farlex)

17 (Feuchtwanger 2001), p. 43.

18 (Wawro, 1998), p. 277.

19 (Krüger, 1915), pp 18–19. A side note on the confusing name of Hesse. Hesse-Kassel was absorbed along with Frankfurt, Nassau, and Hanover to become the Prussian State of Hesse-Nassau. This should not be confused with Hesse-Darmstadt, (which most know as Hesse) that maintained its statehood, even though it lost some land after 1866. Hesse-Homburg was absorbed by Hesse-Darmstadt just before the war because Hesse-Homburg's bloodline had died out. Hesse-Homburg was ceded to Prussia as part of the indemnity process.

Those that had sided with Austria fared little better. Bavaria was given an indemnity of 23 million Florins ($303 million). Saxony had more to pay (10 million Talers) reducing that kingdom to almost a vassal. The Kingdom of Württemberg had to pay 8 million Guilders, Baden 6 million Guilders, Hesse-Darmstadt 3 million Guilders, and the principality of Reuß 100,000 Talers.[20] Frankfurt-am-Main, which had been a free city, had its indemnity reduced from 25 million to 6 million Florins when the city voted itself out of existence and incorporated into Prussia.[21]

These actions essentially sounded the death knell for Austria. Emboldened by Austria's loss in 1866, the Hungarians made a play for semi-independence. Austria reached a compromise with Hungary known as the *Ausgleich* in 1867. Austria ceased to exist, and in its place, Austria-Hungary was born. Prussia had annexed and absorbed the armies of half of the German Confederation and entered into military convention with most of the states that had joined the North German Confederation. This introduced Prussian conscription into the North German Confederation and 800,000 more soldiers were pressed into Prussian service.[22]

THE NORTH GERMAN CONFEDERATION

The North German Confederation was created in 1867 and primarily centered north of the Main River. Prussia led the 22 member states.

- Prussia (incl. Lauenburg)
- Saxony
- Mecklenburg-Schwerin
- Saxe-Weimar
- Mecklenburg-Strelitz
- Oldenburg
- Brunswick
- Saxe-Meiningen
- Saxe-Altenburg
- Saxe-Coburg-Gotha
- Anhalt
- Schwarzburg-Rudolstadt
- Schwarzburg-Sondershausen
- Waldeck
- Reuß (Elder Line)
- Reuß (Younger Line)
- Schaumburg-Lippe
- Lippe-Detmold
- Lübeck
- Bremen
- Hamburg
- The parts of the Grand Duchy of Hesse that were north of the River Main [23]

---

[20] Prior to unification, there were several different types of currency. Most currencies were linked to something called *Vereinsthaler*. This was a currency based on silver. When the exchange was made, the general rate was three gold marks to one Vereinsthaler. Southern Germany's use of the Gulden was valued at 1.71 Marks.

[21] (Wawro, 1998), p. 277.

[22] (Wawro, 1998), pp. 281–283.

[23] (Howard, 1906), pp. 6–7.

The southern German states of Bavaria, Hesse (the northern enclave of Hesse-Darmstadt was part of the North Germanic Confederation, while the southern enclave was not), Baden, and Württemberg already were tied to the North German Confederation through the Zollverein. They officially petitioned to join the North German Confederation and became members in November 1870 through a series of individual treaties.[24] When the southern states were added to the North German Confederation, they reserved some rights or *Sonderrechte* for themselves. As a result, the southern states of Baden, Württemberg, and Bavaria are sometimes called the Sonderrechte states.[25]

FRANCO-PRUSSIAN WAR 1870–1871

France felt it had lost its primacy over central Europe during the 1866 war. Tensions between France and the North German Confederation mounted steadily, causing France to embark on a hasty program of rearmament. In 1868–1869, Prince Leopold of Hohenzollern-Sigmaringen (the Catholic branch of the Hohenzollern family) emerged as a strong candidate for the Spanish throne. Queen Isabella II had been overthrown, and Spain was looking for a suitable Catholic king. Bismarck encouraged Leopold to accept the offer believing that a German king of Spain would offer security against French aggression. On Bismarck's initiative the *Norddeutsche Allgemeine Zeitung* (one of Germany's biggest newspapers) leaked the *Emser Depesche,* a secret account of the meeting between King Wilhelm I and the French ambassador in Bad Ems. Bismarck was responsible for the leak that he released without the king's consent. The document swung public opinion in Germany in favor of the war against France and triggered the Franco-Prussian War.[26]

France demanded reassurances from Prussia that no such candidacy would happen, or they would use force to resolve the issue. Even though Leopold withdrew, France declared war on Prussia in July 1870. Napoleon III initially led the French troops with Moltke the Elder as head of the Prussian forces. The French had expected support from the Italians, but the Italians used the occasion of the withdrawal of French troops in September 1870 to take over the Papal States.[27]

Because of their military alliances with the North German Confederation, the southern German states participated in the war against France. Feelings of a national Germanic community outweighed fears of Prussian ascendancy. Germany was victorious at the Sedan in France (Napoleon having been captured) only a few weeks after the war began. At last, Kleindeutschland would become a reality.

All of the North German Confederation (of course without Austria) went to war against France during the Franco-Prussian War of 1870–1871. The Treaty of Frankfurt ended the war and gave French Alsace and part of Lorraine to Germany. At the conclusion of the war, the princes of the States declared Germany to be an empire. Bismarck engineered a letter from Ludwig II, King of Bavaria that suggested that the King of Prussia become the Emperor or Kaiser.[28] This letter ensured that decree, rather than the people, would establish the monarchy. Now referred to as "imperial Germany," it included the North German

---

24 (Krüger, 1915), pp. 20–21.
25 (Howard, 1906), p. 17.
26 (Naujoks, 1968), pp. 85–118.
27 (Feuchtwanger 2001), p. 57.
28 (Green, *Political and Diplomatic Movements, 1850–1870, 2004*), pp. 88–90.

Confederation and the states of southern Germany. Most of the North German Confederation's constitutional precepts became part of the constitution of the unified Germany. The Kaiser was crowned on 16 April 1871.

Imperial Germany

Imperial Germany consisted of the following:
- Prussia (incl. Lauenburg)
- Bavaria
- Württemberg
- Saxony
- Baden
- Mecklenburg-Schwerin
- Saxe-Weimar
- Mecklenburg-Strelitz
- Oldenburg
- Brunswick
- Saxe-Meiningen
- Saxe-Altenburg
- Saxe-Coburg-Gotha
- Anhalt
- Schwarzburg-Rudolstadt
- Schwarzburg-Sondershausen
- Waldeck
- Reuß (Elder Line)
- Reuß (Younger Line)
- Schaumburg-Lippe
- Lippe-Detmold
- Lübeck
- Bremen
- Hamburg
- Imperial Territory (*Reichslande*) of Alsace-Lorraine[29]

The initial effect of unification was a resounding boon to the imperial German economy. It adopted a common currency, boundaries, and weights and measures. Internal tariffs were completely eliminated. Coal and steel production increased, as did railroad construction. An industrial imperial Germany that had not existed prior to unification was suddenly a major player in the world markets and was on its way to becoming the industrial giant of the continent.

The indemnity that France paid for the loss of the war in 1871 fueled a great deal of this growth. With prosperity, the population grew from 41 million in 1871 to 65.3 million in 1911. The agricultural workforce shrank from 49 percent of the population at unification to 35 percent by 1907. The industrial workforce grew from 31 percent to 40 percent during the same timeframe. Urban centers in the Ruhr and major cities like Berlin grew at staggering rates.[30]

---

29 (Howard, 1906), p. 19.
30 (Howard, 1906), p. 19.

There was no "Big Bang" in imperial German industrialization although there is significant disagreement among authorities as to when the German Industrial Revolution actually began. There is even more disagreement as to the date when the Industrial Revolution ended. We do know that it happened.[31] Anglo-Saxon or English industrialization was significantly different than continental industrialization. Private capitalism and the state united on the continent. Funding was private in England. There was either state ownership or significant state investment in railways. This state investment is one reason why the debt of the Prussian state more than doubled between the 1840s and 1865 (Remember that Bismarck used Austrian War reparations after 1866 to deal with this deficit).[32] There was even a word for the great expansion and unification of imperial Germany known as the *Gründerboom*.[33]

Some believe that despite the initial boom, imperial Germany suffered a major economic depression from 1873–1879.[34] Current economic historians generally do not accept this thought even though a modern academic proposed it. The general view now is that the two major depressions that imperial Germany suffered from 1873–1879 and later from 1890–1895 were actually slowdowns in the growth rate of the Gründerboom.

By one estimate the growth rate was four and one-half percent per year. During the depressions, the rate slowed to three percent per year. The myth of the depression started with scholars at the time, who felt it was a depression; however, to modern economic and social historians, it was not.[35] The slowdown hit suddenly in October 1873 with a massive price collapse of industrial goods

The effect on wages based on the price deflation was severe and some workers at Krupp saw their wages halved between 1873 and 1878. There was an upturn of sorts in 1883 but, between 1884–1887 and 1891–1895, there were other downturns. This was not comparable with the devastating 1929 crash because growth was consistent. On the other hand, unemployment and deflation were not nearly the equivalent of the 1929 downturn.[36]

During this same time, there was a growing patriotism in that the population looked forward to the nation-building process that would unite all German states and principalities into one nation. Under the leadership of Prussia, (some Southern Germans would say under Prussian dominance) the war against France became the constituting event in forging the nation. Previously, there had been no clear national identity. There were not even any common holidays. So patriotism had to be based on the Franco-Prussian war and the Germanic victories there. Sedan Day was now celebrated.[37] What is called the Franco-Prussian War in English is called *Deutsch-französischer Krieg* (German-Franco War) in Germany. Within this new state, people could have different home regions, called *Heimat* in German. The Heimat (an original local region) was celebrated as a distinct part of a larger nation. A Heimat might have its own dialect, foods, or discernible landscapes, but the concept of regionalism did not enter the German vocabulary until the 1920s.[38]

After 1871, this newly-developed patriotism slowly developed into nationalism that tended to span both class and religious barriers. Catholics and Jews both considered themselves German. Workers would sing both patriotic and socialist songs. One large exception

31 (Tipton, 1996), p. 63.
32 (Blackbourn, 2003), p. 141.
33 (Berghahn, 1994), pp. 5–13.
34 (Blackbourn, 2003), p. 147.
35 (Berghahn, 1994), pp. 4–12.
36 (Feuchtwanger, 2001), pp. 67–70.
37 (Confino, 1997), pp. 27–30.
38 (White, 1996), pp. 131–132.

seemed to be the Poles living inside Germany.[39] Frederick Nietzsche wrote in 1873, "Up until now there has been no original German culture."[40] The increasing influence of societies like the Pan-German-League (*Alldeutscher Verband*), the Navy League (*Deutscher Marinebund*) and the Colonial Society (*Deutscher Kolonialbund*) turned the patriotism of the *Gründerzeit* (founding years) into a growing nationalism and militarism going far beyond the patriotic attitude of the founding years of the German Empire.

The more these nationalist organizations and societies dominated the public discussion on colonial and military issues and on issues of foreign politics, the more the undertone moved to nationalism. Soon these nationalistic societies slipped out of the control of the political elites and started to develop a life of their own. Subjects like the "superiority of the Germanic race over Romanic and Slavic races," a subliminal anti-Semitism and a "*Deutschland über alles*" (Germany above all) rhetoric became predominant.[41]

The more the patriotic pride of this newly formed nation turned into nationalism, the more the other European nations felt unsettled and alienated. The imperial newcomer that was Germany sought Great Britain's acceptance and to be on par in the global power game. This desire led to a growing antagonism with England. England felt challenged by this newcomer and was determined to maintain its global supremacy by beating Germany in a naval arms race. Germany could not win the naval race and that became one of the driving forces for Europe sliding into the Great War in 1914.[42]

---

[39] (Blackbourn, 2003), pp. 322–323 and 332–334.
[40] (Applegate, 2008), p. 107.
[41] (Förster, 1985), pp. 80–91.
[42] To learn more about this fatal antagonism, turn to the analysis by Robert K. Massie: *Dreadnought–Britain, Germany and the Coming of the Great War*, first published in 1992.

CHAPTER 2

THE GOVERNMENT AND CONSTITUTION

THE CONSTITUTION OF 1871

There are fundamental differences between how Americans understand government and the way that the German Empire functioned. The German Empire was a federation of 25 states not "united states." This was not an empire composed of 65 million people, but a union of 25 individual members. Neither was it a league of princes; rather, it was a federation constructed of divergent states. Upon joining the German Empire, the individual states gave up their sovereignty, but they retained a wide range of powers to govern their internal affairs. This ability was an extension of their rights that existed before they joined the Empire. The central government had specific rights, and while these rights were quite extensive, they had definite limits; anything not covered by the constitution was a matter for the states.[1]

Article 4 of the Imperial Constitution gave the empire specific powers:

1. Regulations relating to domicile, settlement, and citizenship (except in Bavaria),
2. Legislation pertaining to customs, commerce, and their taxes,
3. Regulation of weights, measures, and coinage,
4. Banking regulation,
5. Patents and inventions,
6. Protection of intellectual property,
7. Protection of trade in foreign countries, the high seas, and consular representation,
8. Railway matters (some reservations to Bavaria),
9. Waterways and navigation,
10. Postal and telegraph matters (with some reservations to Bavaria and Württemberg),
11. Regulations pertaining to the execution of judgments in civil matters,
12. Authentication of public documents,
13. Legislation concerning civil and criminal law,
14. Military establishment of the Empire and the Navy,
15. Regulation of the medical and veterinary police,
16. Regulation of the press and the right of association[2]

---

1 (Howard, 1906), pp. 20–21. For further details about the political, social, and economic system in Wilhelminian Germany see: Mommsen, Wolfgang J., *Bürgerstolz und Weltmachtstreben 1890–1918,* Propyläen-Verlag, Frankfurt a.M. and Berlin 1995. See Appendix A.

2 (Howard, 1906), pp. 21–22. See Appendix A.

States, on the other hand, determined the laws of succession, internal administration of their own budgets, police regulations, fire and building regulations, water rights, road laws, credit, forestry, mines, public instruction, agriculture, and the relationship between church and state. Municipalities shared the responsibility for care of the poor, education, urban planning, public hygiene, utilities, hospitals, local roads, and transport.[3]

Of course, not all states were equal. The southern states were added to the North German Confederation with certain reserved rights.[4] These were the Sonderrechte states. Individual treaties with each southern state determined these rights. Most of the treaties dealt with the taxation on beer, brandies, and some telegraph and post issues, but Bavaria received the advantage of six votes in the *Bundesrat* instead of four. Bavaria also maintained the right to send an Ambassador to the Vatican. The four kingdoms had permanent seats on the Committees on Army, Fortifications, and Foreign Affairs.[5]

Another fundamental difference between imperial Germany's government and that of America is that the states were required to enforce the imperial laws. State officials, not officials of the empire, levied imperial customs and taxes. In matters pertaining to foreign affairs, as well as the Navy and fortifications, the control of the empire was supreme. Ambassadors to foreign lands were imperial officers, while the consuls and officials in the protectorates were imperial appointees.

There was a dual arrangement with the Army. The empire directly regulated all the activities of the officers in command. On the other hand, the subordinate officers were under the control of the states and the whole system of military organization, instruction, religious care, and justice was left in the hands of the states. The army inspectors were imperial, the commanding generals and the ministers of war were state officials.[6]

This confederation was not a parliamentary government, as we know it. A chancellor, whom the Kaiser handpicked and appointed, headed the imperial government. The chancellor decided what legislation would be drafted, and then the ministers drew up the legislation for Parliament's approval. There were two kinds of laws—general laws and regulations.[7] Unlike the Constitution of the United States, constitutional amendments were relatively common and were considered general laws. There were 11 constitutional amendments by 1914. There were also several laws that had the effect of amending the Constitution.[8]

In the Imperial Parliament, there were two houses—the *Bundesrat* and the *Reichstag*. (Individual states had different kinds of parliaments and franchises that are discussed in Chapter 3.) Most legislation was introduced in the Bundesrat and then sent to the Reichstag. In the case of a tie, Prussia's vote in the Bundesrat decided the matter. However, under the Constitution, legislation could be introduced into either or both houses so there was not an upper house and a lower house.[9]

---

[3] (Hewitson, 2008), pp. 44–45.
[4] (Howard, 1906), p. 17.
[5] (Howard, 1906), pp. 26–27.
[6] (Krüger, 1915), pp. 42–44.
[7] (Krüger, 1915), p. 110.
[8] (Krüger, 1915), pp. 25–28.
[9] (Howard, 1906), pp. 100–101.

THE POSITION OF THE KAISER AND THE CIVIL CABINET

All of the powers that the Kaiser enjoyed under the Imperial Constitution were originally found in the Constitution of the North German Confederation but under three different designations:

1) As the King of Prussia, he was the chief magistrate of the State of Prussia.
2) As *Bundesfeldherr*, he commanded the Imperial Navy and was responsible for the regulation and organization of the Army and was also given complete military authority over the North German Confederation.
3) In the capacity of the *Präsidium*, he opened and closed the legislative bodies, published federal laws, appointed the chancellor, and supervised the federal administration. The powers of the King of Prussia, the Bundesfeldherr, and the Präsidium were combined into the powers of the Kaiser in the 1871 Imperial Constitution.

There was no change whatsoever in the relationship between the King of Prussia and the other states and monarchs of the Confederation. The title of Kaiser had no powers that he did not already have in Northern Germany except a purely personal right to the specific title of Kaiser and to imperial arms and a standard. There was never the notion of elevating the King of Prussia to the position of Monarch of Imperial Germany. The title Imperial German Kaiser carried with it no idea of territorial domination. The title was carefully chosen to be Imperial German Emperor, not Emperor of Germany or Emperor of the Germans.[10] The Kaiser was a monarch in the Empire, but not over the Empire.[11] It is incorrect to characterize the government as headed by the Kaiser as a monarch of the Empire and the Bundesrat as the upper house and the Reichstag the lower house of parliament.[12]

The position of the Kaiser in a unified Germany allowed him considerable power. He had control over all common foreign policy. He had supreme command over the military. He had the right to appoint a chancellor, who would run the government. He had the right to both summon and disband parliament, as well as to interpret the constitution as he saw fit. He also had the right to declare martial law.[13] There was even a law that prohibited insulting the Kaiser. This injunction once led to the incarceration of a left liberal academic, who compared Wilhelm II to the Roman Emperor Caligula.[14] There were some interesting legal twists and studies made in the case of regency. The consensus was that a Prussian regent would be the regent of the Empire also.[15]

The Kaiser's "iron fist" was the army. The idea of ensuring that the army was loyal and not subject to inappropriate influences became the key to keeping the Kaiser and his associates in power. As far as the other kingdoms were concerned, being in the Saxon military, for example, and then transferring to the Prussian army was a way to get ahead. As we later will see in detail, the army had three separate leadership elements. The Kaiser had no one single military point of contact. So although supreme command of the military might sound good; in fact the Kaiser had to give the supreme command to three separate individuals. Those three were the Chief of the Great General Staff, the War Minister, and the Chief of the Military Cabinet. [16]

---

[10] (Pounds, 1996), p. 13.
[11] (Howard, 1906), pp. 28–39.
[12] (Krüger, 1915), p. 37.
[13] (Howard, 1906), pp. 39–47.
[14] (Hewitson, 2008), p. 48.
[15] (Howard, 1906), pp. 36–37.
[16] (Kitchen, 1968), p. 20.

The Kaiser was absolutely determined to lead "his" army. Kaiser Wilhelm II was known for interfering in petty ways without having the skill to be constructive. Kaiser Wilhelm II's involvement in annual maneuvers became a major distraction. The Kaiser insisted on leading one side and winning with a massive cavalry charge. Troops were structured and moved around to satisfy this end. One pundit complained in 1904 that they were now struggling with the 37th change of uniform since the Kaiser had taken the throne.[17]

When citizens joined the army, they swore allegiance to the Kaiser if they were Prussian or to the king of their state. So, for example, soldiers from Saxony swore an oath to serve their king faithfully during their period of military service and to offer obedience to "His Majesty the Kaiser and the Laws of War." The situation was similar in other contingents, though the oath might also be to the senate of a Hanseatic Town, a duke, or, in the case of men from Alsace and Lorraine, direct to the Kaiser.[18] Therefore, in all cases there was a personal bond between the soldier and his ruler. This was an ethical bond that linked the individual to the position. Direct allegiance, or oath of obedience was to the Kaiser, not to Wilhelm II.[19] The Kaiser exercised his command through those individuals who had immediate access to him. Originally, that had been the Minister of War and the commanding generals of the Army Corps. In 1883, the Chief of the General Staff was added to the group and eventually those with immediate contact with the Kaiser amounted to 40 generals within the army alone. With 25 corps commanders, there was significant rivalry among those who would have immediate access to the Kaiser. There was also a military entourage consisting of aides (*Flügeladjutanten*), adjutants, and guards amounting to 44 people in 1914.[20]

The Kaiser was honorary Colonel in Chief of these regiments:

- *Garde du Corps*
- *Leib Garde Husaren Regiment*
- *Regiment Königsjäger zu Pferde Nr. 1*
- *Leib Kürassier Regiment Grosser Kurfürst (Schlesisches) Nr. 1*
- *Leib Husaren Regiment Nr. 2*
- *Leib Husaren Regiment Königin Viktoria von Preussen Nr. 2*. (From 1909, Wilhelm's daughter Princess Viktoria Luise was deputy Colonel-in-Chief.)
- *Königs Ulanen Regiment (1.Hannoverisches) Nr. 13*
- *Kgl. Bayerisches 1. Ulanen Regiment Wilhelm II, Deutscher Kaiser und König von Preussen*
- *1.Garde Feld Artillerie Regiment*
- *Garde Regiment zu Fu.*
- *Grenadier Regiment König Friedrich Wilhelm IV (1. Pommersches) Nr. 2*
- *Leib-GR König Friedrich Wilhelm III (1. Brandenburgisches) Nr. 8.*
- *GR König Friedrich Wilhelm I (2. Ostpreuß.) Nr. 3*
- *Königs Infanterie Regiment (6. Lothringisches) Nr. 145.*
- *IR Kaiser Wilhelm (2. Grossherz. Hessisches) Nr. 116*
- *IR Kaiser Wilhelm, König von Preußen (2. Württembergisches) Nr. 120*
- *Kgl. Bayerisches 6. IR Wilhelm, Deutscher Kaiser und König von Preußen*
- The British 1st Royal Dragoons 1894–1914

17 (Mombauer, 2003), p. 18.
18 (Stein, 1984), pp. 88–89.
19 (Mombauer, 2003), p. 21.
20 (Mombauer, 2003), pp. 22–24.

- The Austro-Hungarian Husaren Regiment Wilhelm II, Deutscher Kaiser und König von Preußen Nr. 7
- The Austro-Hungarian Infanterie Regiment Wilhelm I, Deutscher Kaiser und König von Preußen Nr. 34 (the name was carried permanently to honor Wilhelm's grandfather, who died in 1888.)
- The Russian Saint Petersburg Lifeguards Regiment (The German Emperor, Friedrich III's Regiment until 1914.)
- The Russian 3rd Pernov Grenadier Regiment, King Friedrich Wilhelm IV's Regiment until 1914.
- The Russian 85th Vyborg Infantry Regiment, the German Emperor Wilhelm II's Regiment until August 1 1914.
- The Russian 13th Narva Hussar Regiment, the Emperor of Germany and King of Prussia Wilhelm II's Regiment until August 1 1914.
- The Portuguese 4th Cavalry Regiment

THE CHANCELLOR AND THE ADMINISTRATION

The Chancellor was the only official of the Empire provided for in the Constitution; therefore, he was the supreme officer of the Empire. He was also the Prussian prime minister and chairman of the Bundesrat.[21] However, he was responsible to the Reichstag and could be questioned and asked to give an account of his actions.[22] As head of imperial administration, he counter-signed decrees and ordinances from the Kaiser. He was responsible to the Kaiser alone and had no recourse but to resign if he could not agree with the policies of the Kaiser. Bismarck was the first and most famous of the chancellors. He was present at the founding of the Empire up through the beginning of Wilhelm II's reign until he was fired on 20 March 1890.[23]

Count Caprivi, the commander of X Corps replaced Bismarck. Not known as strong-willed or independent, the octogenarian governor of Alsace-Lorraine, Prince Hohenlohe-Schillingsfürst, replaced him in 1894 and was chancellor until 17 October 1900. He was often considered simply a caretaker. His successor was Prince Bernhard v. Bülow who resigned on 14 July 1908. Other than Bismarck, v. Bülow lasted longer in the job than anyone after 1890. His successor was Dr. v. Bethmann-Hollweg,[24] who was known as an office-bound bureaucrat and called by at least one notable, "the leech."[25] After Bethmann-Hollweg, there were a series of short-term chancellors prior to the end of the Empire.

---

21 There were two short periods of time under Bismarck and Caprivi, where the offices were separated. (Krüger, 1915), p. 108.

22 (Feuchtwanger 2001), p. 45.

23 (Krüger, 1915), pp. 97–102.

24 (Krüger, 1915), pp. 100–108.

25 (Blackbourn, 2003), p. 307.

THE BUNDESRAT

The Bundesrat (Federal Council) consisted of deputies from each of the states. The aristocratic ruler of the state (or elected official in the Free Cities) appointed deputies. With the exception of those three city republics, each of the German states were monarchies (though not all kingdoms) and aristocratic in nature. They were sovereign entities with the right to appoint representatives to the Bundesrat. As a result, again with the exception of the three republics, the members were delegates of the reigning princes. Imperial Germany was not a monarchy in theory, but an aristocratic polyarchy.[26] There were 58 votes, as shown by Article 6 of the Constitution that stated:

> The Federal Council shall consist of the representatives of the States of the Confederation, among whom the votes shall be divided in such a manner as that Prussia (including the former votes of Hanover, the Electoral-Hesse, Holstein, Nassau, and Frankfurt am Main.) shall have 17 votes; Bavaria, 6 votes; Saxony, 4 votes; Württemberg, 4 votes; Baden, 3 votes; Hesse, 3 votes; Mecklenburg-Schwerin, 2 votes; Saxe-Weimar, 1 vote; Mecklenburg-Strelitz, 1 vote; Oldenburg, 1 vote; Brunswick, 2 votes; Saxe-Meiningen, 1 vote; Saxe-Altenburg, 1 vote; Saxe-Coburg-Gotha, 1 vote; Anhalt, 1 vote; Schwarzburg-Rudolstadt, 1 vote; Schwarzburg-Sondershausen, 1 vote; Waldeck, 1 vote; Reuß (Elder branch), 1 vote; Reuß (younger branch), 1 vote; Schaumburg-Lippe, 1 vote; Lippe, 1 vote; Lübeck, 1 vote; Bremen, 1 vote; Hamburg, 1 vote.[27]

A couple of points are worth discussing on this division of votes. There was a constitutional amendment on 31 May 1911 that admitted three representatives of Alsace-Lorraine, under certain circumstances. Prior to 1911, Alsace-Lorraine had been the province of the Empire and there was no representation in the Bundesrat. Once Alsace-Lorraine became a quasi-state in 1911, Prussia appointed the administration and therefore controlled the votes. Also, Waldeck had ceded its administration to Prussia as of 2 March 1887. That means there was an independent state of Waldeck but that Prussia controlled the vote.[28]

The Bundesrat was generally conservative and not controversial for the Kaiser and other princely rulers. Prussia dominated, so if you controlled the Prussian provincial legislature you controlled the Bundesrat. While either house could introduce legislation, the imperial ministers originated the great majority of bills in the Bundesrat. The Kaiser could not introduce legislation; however, he could introduce bills through his Prussian delegates in the Bundesrat.[29]

---

[26] (Krüger, 1915), p. 38.
[27] (Howard, 1906), p. 407.
[28] (Krüger, 1915), p. 64.
[29] (Krüger, 1915), p. 111.

THE REICHSTAG

Members of the Reichstag were elected every three years using universal suffrage. All males who were citizens of any state and over the age of 25 and were neither criminals nor debtors were eligible to vote. All of the votes counted equally. Women were not included; in fact, an 1851 Prussian law forbade women from attending meetings where politics were discussed.[30] Universal male suffrage was a foreign concept in Prussia but was the norm in Bavaria and most of the other states of Imperial Germany. The idea had taken root in St. Paul's Parliament in 1849, but in 1867, it was still considered very radical. Even Karl Marx opposed universal male suffrage. Bismarck supported it, because he saw that the conservative rural population would vote the way he wanted.[31]

The Reichstag voting resulted in a 397 member split: Prussia, 235; Bavaria, 48; Saxony, 23; Württemberg, 17; Baden, 14; Hesse, 9; Mecklenburg-Schwerin, 6; Saxe-Weimar, 5; Mecklenburg-Strelitz, 1; Oldenburg, 3; Brunswick, 3; Saxe-Meiningen, 2; Saxe-Altenburg, 1; Saxe-Coburg-Gotha, 2; Anhalt, 2; Schwarzburg-Rudolstadt, 1; Schwarzburg-Sonderhausen, 1; Waldeck, 1; Reuß (Elder branch), 1; Reuß (younger branch), 1; Schaumburg-Lippe, 1; Lippe, 1; Lübeck, 1; Bremen, 1; Hamburg, 1; Lauenburg, 1; Alsace-Lorraine, 15.[32]

Of the 397 members (also called deputies) in the Reichstag, more than half came from Prussia. The Reichstag had the right to overturn or approve any legislation. While the Reichstag did not create the legislation itself, the Kaiser, who was used to absolute power, still had to go through that civilian branch of government to decree legislation. While most legislation was introduced in the Bundesrat, the approval of the Reichstag was necessary for loans, the budget, and treaties. If a budget were to require a deficit or a credit, the Reichstag held the keys.[33]

The representation in the Reichstag changed over time, based on its membership. The number of seats and their assignments to various districts did not. Originally, representatives were selected on the basis of one deputy for every 100,000 people. If you had 50,000 or more, you rounded up to another representative.[34] Population migration altered the distribution. As the population moved into cities and other urban areas, one district had one representative based on a population of 219,000, another based on 339,000, and a third based on 163,000. Yet some rural districts had only 13,000 or 15,000 qualified voters, but as the population migrated, the number of representatives was not adjusted.

This unbalance was a major cause of friction between the government and conservative forces, who believed that the Reichstag should represent the different classes, while the liberal Social Democrats believed the Reichstag representation should be based on an arithmetical exactness. By 1912, the Conservative Party had 74 deputies supporting 1,933,000 voters. By contrast, the Socialists had 110 representatives supported by 4,250,000 voters. Of the 397 districts, 243 were rural with the majority of the population living in communities of less than 2,000 inhabitants. The Social Democrats controlled only 24 of those districts. Of the 154 urban districts, the conservative groups controlled only five. While the North German Confederation Parliament had a majority of noble members, there were only 57 noble Reichstag members in 1912. Eighty deputies had reserve commissions. 189 members had served in the army.[35]

30 (Shaser, 2008), p. 141.
31 (Krüger, 1915), pp. 46–48.
32 (Krüger, 1915), p. 48.
33 (Krüger, 1915), p. 45.
34 (Howard, 1906), pp. 84–87.
35 (Krüger, 1915), pp. 48–62.

Reichstag Deputies were elected using the dual ballot system. In a district where candidates from multiple parties ran, and no one candidate obtained 50 percent of the vote, there was a second ballot run-off between the top two candidates. The Reichstag Deputy election would often be decided by an alliance between groups of political parties. A high number of votes short of 50 percent, with no allies, would doom that candidate. The Social Democratic Party, having few allies, almost always lost in runoff elections. By 1912, 190 deputies were elected by run-off elections.[36]

Under Article 24 of the Constitution, the Bundesrat could dissolve the Reichstag with the consent of the Kaiser. This tool was used several times to close the Reichstag and install new representatives in an effort to pass stalled legislation. The Kaiser had to establish an election date at the time of dissolution and assemble the new Reichstag within 90 days.[37]

[36] (Feuchtwanger, 2001), p. 60
[37] (Howard, 1906), pp. 90–91. See Appendix A.

CHAPTER 3

ROYALTY, THE REICH AND ITS STATES AND PROVINCES

ROYALTY

In the early years of the 20th century, the European sovereign was "the personification of the state, the symbol of continuity, the emblem of permanence, the magnet of all loyalties, the embodiment of the past history and the present identity of the nation."[1] Bismarck wrote, after many years of German unification, that Germans were, in fact, strong supporters of monarchies, more so than any of the European countries.[2] To the Germans, their monarchs provided a national focus and basis for unity.

However, the German royal families were intertwined with those of other European nations through familial relationships, financial investments and business ventures. Intermarriage protected property, finances and political interests, but it also pressured the families and created insurmountable problems when monarchs could not or would not separate their personal feelings from sound political decisions or when the political reality forced a choice against family.

For example, Queen Victoria and her nine children were related through blood or marriage to the German Kaiser, the Tsar of Russia and the kings of Spain, Portugal, Bulgaria, Romania and Belgium. Albert, Queen Victoria's husband, was a prince of Saxe-Coburg-Gotha and her first cousin. Their son, King Edward VII, married Alexandra, who was linked to the royal families of Greece, Denmark and Norway.[3] This created a familial and political issue when Germany annexed Schleswig and Holstein. Edward supported his wife's father, King Christian IX, of Denmark, against his mother's wishes.

The Kaiser's family is a further example of intertwined bloodlines. Friedrich III, the Kaiser's father, was married to Queen Victoria's oldest child, Victoria (Vicky) and, as a result, Kaiser Wilhelm was Queen Victoria's first grandchild. The Queen wrote to Augusta of Prussia (Saxe-Weimar-Eisenach), "Our mutual grandson binds us and our two countries even closer together!"[4] Wilhelm, who spoke fluent English, spent long periods of time in England and held

1 (Aronson, 1986), p 3.

2 "On the one hand, he saw the German dynasties as the 'glue' which held a disparate nation together; on the other hand, he recognized that they were the source and focus of centrifugal forces within Germany, the point around which the German drive for separatism crystallizes." (Green, Fatherlands, 2001) p. 62.

3 (Shaw, 1999) p. 68.

4 (Bolitho, 1938) p. 104

a deep admiration for England and its navy. Family connections ran deep, but cultural convictions were often at odds.

The Hohenzollern and Romanov families had also intermarried and appeared to genuinely like each other on a personal level.[5] Tsar Alexander II of Russia had married Marie of Hesse-Darmstadt and their son, Tsar Alexander III, married Marie of Denmark. The wife of Nicholas II, the last tsar, was Alexandra of Hesse-Darmstadt, Queen Victoria's granddaughter.[6]

It is little wonder that members of the British, Russian, and German royal families often visited one another in private or state visits. King Edward VII, who considered himself European, met with his nephew the Kaiser on five different occasions, although they were not all particularly cordial, as political exigencies precluded a close relationship. After Edward's death, the Kaiser attempted to advise George V on a number of issues. The two had, in fact, signed a treaty of alliance in 1905, which provided a momentary feel-good union, but it did not stand up to the political realities of the times.[7]

Further, George V met with the Kaiser on at least three subsequent occasions, one of which in 1913 was the wedding of the Kaiser's daughter, Viktoria Luise to Ernest Augustus, heir to the title of Duke of Cumberland and grandson of Christian IX of Denmark.[8] Nicholas II also attended this family affair and spent private time with George V, much to the consternation of the Kaiser, who was concerned that they might be conspiring against him.[9]

Politics won out over blood in the relationship between Britain's George V and the Kaiser. Unlike his father, George had always identified more with Britain than with Europe. Some have gone so far to say that he detested foreigners.[10] Nonetheless, rumors and speculation were widespread that he secretly supported the Kaiser. H.G. Wells spoke out against George, as did many members of the media.[11] As political events unraveled in 1917, George ordered all family members to renounce any German titles, and he changed his own family's name from Saxe-Coburg-Gotha to Windsor.[12] Nicholas, upon hearing this, allegedly said that Shakespeare's play "The Merry Wives of Windsor" should be changed to "The Merry Wives of Saxe-Coburg-Gotha."[13]

It was during that same year that George, after vacillating, refused to grant asylum to Tsar Nicholas II and his family. Wilhelm was likewise distressed. Initially, Britain agreed to grant the family asylum, and Wilhelm agreed to their safe passage through Germany. Again, political realities superseded bloodlines. George finally chose to show his unequivocal allegiance to country over heritage.

What George and Wilhelm were slow to understand was that the hereditary monarchies were changing, losing ground in their once revered position in society. The industrial revolution with its innovations and the explosion of science and art were negating the influence of the monarchs, though some would argue that the British sovereigns, constitutional monarchs since 1689, had been well aware for many years of the limitations to their power. After the Napoleonic era, monarchs searched for ways to strengthen their rule but were

5 (Carter, 2010), p. 6.
6 Please see the second picture in our picture block depicting the Royal Mob meeting at Coburg in April 1894.
7 (Aronson, 1986), p. 57.
8 (McLean, 2007), p. 193.
9 (Aronson, 1986), p. 62.
10 (Green, *Fatherlands*, 2001), p. 35.
11 (Aronson, 1986), p. 152.
12 (John A Hutcheson, 2005), p. 470.
13 (Green, Fatherlands, 2001), p. 154.

forced to anchor their power in the constitutions of their states, in which they voluntarily limited their own power.[14]

Genetic Legacy

Intermarriage among royals had long been encouraged as a means of keeping the bloodlines pure. Marrying first cousins was not condemned as shown in the examples above.[15] Unfortunately, the cost of this intermarriage among Victoria's offspring played out in two specific health issues–hemophilia and porphyria. Hemophilia is a malfunction of the X chromosome that is carried by women and passed to their sons. Perhaps the most well-known case of hemophilia was that of Tsar Nicholas' and Victoria's granddaughter's son, Alexi. After his bones were unearthed in 2007, an analysis found a genetic mutation on the X chromosome that indicates he did indeed have hemophilia B. A further analysis showed that not only his mother, Alexandra, was a carrier, but also his sister, Anastasia.[16]

The issue of how hemophilia entered the royal family is open to speculation. There was once a suggestion that perhaps Victoria was not her father's daughter as there had been no earlier reported cases of hemophilia;[17] an example of how the view of history changes over time. Victoria's son, Leopold, eventually died from the "Royal Disease," as did other descendants of Queen Victoria; two of her daughters, Alice and Beatrice were carriers.[18] Alice married the Grand Duke of Hesse. Of her seven children, Alice's only son, Friedrich, died from the disease. Her daughter, Irene, married her first cousin, Prince Henry of Prussia, who was Queen Victoria's eldest daughter's son and brother to Kaiser Wilhelm II. Two of her three sons inherited the disease.[19] And, Beatrice had two sons who were hemophilic. Her daughter, Ena, married King Alphonso XIII of Spain, thus introducing the disease into the Spanish royal family. The royal house of Britain, Russia, Spain and Germany were eventually affected.[20]

A second genetic defect was porphyria, which can cause debilitating illness, insanity and death. It is genetic but not linked to a particular chromosome so both parents can pass on the disease. It manifests itself in purple urine and other "attacks," such as heart palpitations, sun allergies, the flu and mental confusion. Acute attacks can lead to severe abdominal distress, fevers and chills, paralysis of the limbs, brain damage, coma and death.

Although porphyria is a lesser-known malady, "The Madness of King George III" is most likely attributed to porphyria. In their 1998 book, *Purple Secret: Genes, 'Madness' and the Royal Houses of Europe*, the authors provide exhaustive research into the probability that Queen Victoria exhibited symptoms of the "Royal Malady" and probably passed it to her children, particularly her daughter, Vicky, as well as Vicky's daughter, Charlotte, and her daughter, Feodora.[21] There is also ample evidence that the Tsarina, Alexandra, had porphyria. Current thought is that the disease may have originated with Mary Queen of Scots. Research continues.

---

14 (Green, Fatherlands, 2001), p. 64.
15 (Martinez, 2011) Location 263.
16 (Price, 2009)
17 (Rushton, 2008), p. 31.
18 (Israel, 2009)
19 (*English Monarchs*, 2004)
20 (Shaw, 1999), p. 73.
21 (Rohl, 1998), p. 148.

THE REICH

It is important to understand the individual provinces and states that constituted Imperial Germany. Imperial Germany was composed of many dialectical cultures and customs; therefore, its social history is not just that of Prussia, or "Germany," it is a conglomerate of all the provinces and states. Most sources give readers this information only in part and organize it by reference to the monarchies and nobility; differentiating for instance, kingdoms and grand duchies. A simple alphabetical listing of provinces and states can be confusing to readers, but provides an easy reference.

That which follows is designed to give the reader a reference to the most frequently discussed areas and state names. There were other provinces such as Lichtenstein, but the following chart shows a quick summary of each in a slightly different organizational pattern. First on the list are the four kingdoms (two of which were southern Sonderrechte states); then one additional southern state; followed by the eight states that are known as Thuringen; the three city states known as Hanseatic Cities; and the nine other states of the North German Confederation that comprised the 25 states in total of Imperial Germany. Following that group is a list of the other states that ceased to exist before 1867. Finally a separate section on Alsace-Lorraine is included.

States and Territories of Imperial Germany after 1871

Province	Form of Government	Internal Parliament	Population & Religion
The Four Kingdoms in the Empire			
Kingdom of Prussia Capital: Berlin	Hereditary constitutional monarchy—house of Hohenzollern	Upper chamber, *Herrenhaus,* Lower house, *Abgeordnetenhaus*	42.1 million 68% Protestant
Kingdom of Bavaria (Sonderrechte) Capital: München	Hereditary constitutional monarchy—house of Wittelsbach	Upper house *Kammer der Reichsräte,* Lower house (*Kammer der Abgeordneten*	7.1 million 70% Catholic
Kingdom of Saxony Capital: Dresden	Hereditary constitutional monarchy—house of Wettin the junior Albertine line	Two chambers known as the *Ständekammer*	5 million 94% Protestant
Kingdom of Württemberg (Sonderrechte) Capital: Stuttgart	Hereditary constitutional monarchy—house of Württemberg	Two chambers known as the *Kammer*	2.5 million 65% Protestant
The Additional Southern Sonderrechte State of Baden			
Grand Duchy of Baden Capital: Karlsruhe	Hereditary constitutional monarchy	Two chambers	2.14 million 66% Catholic
The Thüringian States of the North German Confederation			
Principality of Reuß Junior Line Capital: Gera	Hereditary constitutional monarchy	One chamber known as the *Landtag*	157,000 95% Protestant

Province	Form of Government	Internal Parliament	Population & Religion
Principality of Reuß Senior Line Capital: Greiz	Hereditary constitutional monarchy	One chamber known as the *Landtag*	74,000 98% Protestant
Duchy of Saxe-Altenburg Capital: Altenburg	Hereditary constitutional monarchy	One chamber known as the *Landtag*	222,000 98% Protestant
Duchy of Saxe-Coburg-Gotha Capitals: Gotha and Coburg	Hereditary constitutional monarchy	Two separate parliaments, one for the Duchy of Coburg and another for the Duchy of Gotha	266,000 98% Protestant
Principality of Saxe-Meiningen Capital: Meiningen	Hereditary constitutional monarchy	One chamber known as the *Landtag*	287,000 98% Protestant
Grand Duchy of Saxe-Weimar-Eisenach Capital: Weimar	Hereditary constitutional monarchy	One chamber known as the *Landtag*	442,000 98% Protestant
Principality of Schwarzburg-Rudolstadt Capital: Rudolstadt	Hereditary constitutional monarchy	One chamber known as the *Landtag*	103,000 98% Protestant
Principality of Schwarzburg-Sondershausen Capital: Sondershausen	Hereditary constitutional monarchy	One chamber known as the *Landtag*	93,000. 98% Protestant
Principality of Saxe-Gotha	Extinct 1826		
Principality of Saxe-Hildburghausen	Extinct 1826		
The Hanseatic Cities of the North German Confederation			
Free Hanseatic City of Bremen	A republic	Two chambers known the *Senat* and the *Bürgerschaft*	270,000 93% Protestant
Free Hanseatic City of Hamburg	A republic	Two chambers known the *Senat* and the *Bürgerschaft*	1.1 million 85% Protestant
Free Hanseatic City of Lübeck	A republic	Two chambers known the *Senat* and the *Bürgerschaft*	122,000 98% Protestant
The Other North German Confederation States			
Duchy of Anhalt Capital: Dessau	Hereditary constitutional monarchy	One chamber known as the *Landtag*	330,000 95% Protestant
Duchy of Brunswick Capital: Brunswick	Hereditary—limited constitutional monarchy	One chamber known as the *Landtag*	500,000 95% Protestant
Grand Duchy of Hesse-Darmstadt Hessen und bei Rhein Capital: Darmstadt	Hereditary constitutional monarchy	Two chambers known as the *Kammer*	1.33 million 63% Protestant
Principality of Lippe-Detmold Capital: Detmold	Hereditary constitutional monarchy	One chamber known as the *Landtag*	154,000 95% Protestant
Grand Duchy of Mecklenburg-Schwerin Capital: Schwerin	Hereditary monarchy	No parliament	648,000 97% Protestant

Province	**Form of Government**	**Internal Parliament**	**Population & Religion**
Grand Duchy of Mecklenburg-Strelitz Capital: Neustrelitz	Hereditary monarchy	No parliament	108,000 97% Protestant
Grand Duchy of Oldenburg Capital: Oldenburg	Hereditary constitutional monarchy	One chamber known as the *Landtag*	516,000 83% Protestant
Principality of Schaumburg-Lippe Capital: Bückeburg	Hereditary constitutional monarchy	One chamber known as the *Landtag*	48,000 94% Protestant
Principality of Waldeck-Pyrmont Capital: Arolsen	Hereditary constitutional monarchy administered entirely by Prussia	One chamber known as the *Landtag*	63,000 98% Protestant
States that ceased to exist prior to the 1871 unification			
Free City of Frankfurt	Annexed in 1866		
Kingdom of Hanover	Annexed in 1866		
Electorate of Hesse	Annexed in 1866		
Landgraviate of Hesse	Ceded to Prussia in 1866 by Hesse Darmstadt		
Principality of Hohenzollern-Hechingen	Incorporated into Prussia, 1849		
Principality of Sigmaringen	Incorporated into Prussia, 1849		
Duchy of Holstein	Annexed in 1866		
Duchy of Lauenburg	Purchased by Prussia in 1865		
Duchy of Limburg	Incorporated into the Netherlands in 1866		
Duchy of Nassau	Annexed in 1866		
Duchy of Schleswig	Annexed in 1866		
The Reichslande-Imperial Territory			
Alsace-Lorraine	Imperial Appointee	From 1911 two chambers known as the *Landtag*	1.9 million 79% Catholic

THE FOUR KINGDOMS

When Germany unified there were four kingdoms, Prussia being the most powerful. The other kingdoms were Bavaria, Saxony, and Württemberg. Napoleon had elevated these last three to kingdoms as a reward for joining the Rhine Alliance *(Rheinbund)*. Bismarck used to facetiously refer to them as Kingdoms of Napoleon's Mercy. Each had its own king, its own army, and its own war minister.

Prussia

(1618–1871: *Preußen*)

Prussia was the largest of the German kingdoms, the most populous, and the most important state of the German Empire. The Hohenzollerns were the ruling family. In 1618, the merger of the Markgraviate (*Markgrafschaft*) of Brandenburg and the Duchy of Prussia, led to the formation of the double state, the Electorate of Brandenburg and the Duchy of Prussia, the latter renamed in 1701 as the Kingdom of Prussia. The Brandenburg Hohenzollerns joined the reformation as Lutherans and later turned to Calvinism.[22] Prussia was a member state of the German Confederation from 1815 to 1866. After the Austro-Prussian War, Prussia became the leading member state of the North German Confederation in 1867 and then a member state of the Imperial German Empire in 1871.

It is easy to get confused when discussing the kings of Prussia. Remember that Prussia had a hereditary monarchy along the male line of the Hohenzollerns. As you follow the generations, you will also see that the Hohenzollerns were related by marriage to many of the royal families in the other German states. Fredrick the Great (Fredrick II) ruled from May 1740–August 1786 and was married to Elisabeth Christine of Brunswick-Bevern.

He was followed by his nephew, Friedrich Wilhelm II (August 1786–November 1797), whose love life was legendary. His son, Friedrich Wilhelm III succeeded him (November 1797–June 1840). Friedrich Wilhelm III had ten children with Louise of Mecklenburg-Strelitz; their daughter was the Tsarina Alexandra. After Louise's death, he entered into a morganatic marriage with Auguste von Harrach. It was Friedrich Wilhelm III who led Prussia during the Napoleonic Wars.

Friedrich Wilhelm IV (the son of Friedrich Wilhelm III) was king from June 1840–January 1861. He was married to Elisabeth Ludovika of Bavaria and was a member of the Lutheran Church. He created a new constitution with two chambers, but retained much of the power to himself.

Wilhelm I, the second son of Friedrich Wilhelm III (and Friedrich Wilhelm IV's brother), became regent for Friedrich Wilhelm IV (who had suffered a stroke) from October 1858 until the monarch's death in 1861. Wilhelm I was King of Prussia during the wars against Denmark, Austria, and France and was married to Princess Augusta of Saxe-Weimar-Eisenach. Their only daughter became Louise, Grand Duchess of Baden. He was declared the first German Kaiser in 1871 and ruled until 9 March 1888. This was the grandfather of the wartime Kaiser and was declared "Wilhelm the Great" by his grandson.

His son, Friedrich III, who had been Crown Prince for 27 years, ascended the throne as the second Kaiser for only 99 days, 9 March 1888–15 June 1888, succumbing to throat cancer. His famous saying, "*Lerne Leiden ohne zu klagen*," roughly translated was, "Learn to suffer without complaining." Friedrich III had married Princess Victoria, the oldest daughter of Queen

---

[22] *(Hohenzollern Dynasty, 2011)*

Victoria. Both shared a liberal and England-friendly ideology, and there has been much speculation that the Great War could have been avoided had he reigned for a longer time.

Friedrich III's son, Wilhelm II (Friedrich Victor Wilhelm Albert Hohenzollern), became the third and last Kaiser and King of Prussia. He took over 15 June 1888 and abdicated 9 November 1918. Wilhelm was the eldest child of Friedrich III and Victoria, and during a breech birth he suffered an injury to his left arm. There is some speculation that he may have suffered light brain damage as well.[23] Any pictures of him are posed to hide the deformity. Wilhelm was married to Auguste Victoria, Princess of Schleswig-Holstein-Sonderburg and they had seven children—six sons and one daughter.[24] Upon his abdication, the family fled to the Netherlands, where he lived until his death. During their exile, Auguste Victoria died after suffering through her youngest son's divorce and subsequent suicide. Wilhelm II then married Princess Hermine Reuß of Greiz. She was the daughter of Heinrich XXII, Prince of Reuß-Greiz and his wife, Princess Ida of Schaumburg-Lippe.[25] Attempts to extradite him and try him for war crimes did not succeed.[26]

Prussia had two houses of parliament. The king alone exercised the executive power, had the supreme command of the army, and was head of the protestant church; however, the king shared the legislative power with the Prussian parliament. The legislative assembly or *Landtag* consisted of two chambers. The consent of both houses, as well as the king, was required before a measure could pass. The chambers had control of the finances and controlled taxes. The upper chamber, *Herrenhaus,* contained both hereditary and non-hereditary members. The hereditary members were the adult princes of the house of Hohenzollern, the important princes and counts of the old imperial nobility, and the heads of the great territorial nobility. The non-hereditary members were chosen for life by the king from the ranks of the rich landowners and manufacturers. The elevation into the Herrenhaus was usually accompanied by granting the honorary title of a *Kommerzienrat* (Commercial Counselor); sometimes elevation to nobility followed soon after. The lower house, or *Abgeordnetenhaus,* consisted of 433 members who were elected for periods of five years by indirect suffrage that included all male citizens who were at least 25.[27] This system used the Prussian three-tier system of elections. Based on the election of 1908, if all of the votes had been of equal value, the Social Democrats would have had 113 of 443 seats. With the three-tier system, the SPD won only seven.[28]

It is essential to remember that the Kingdom of Prussia and the German Empire were separate entities. The King of Prussia was at the same time German Emperor, and the Prime Minister of Prussia was also the imperial Chancellor. The ministries of war and foreign affairs were the same as those of the empire. It was sometimes difficult to determine which hat the individual was wearing. The imperial government administered the customs, postal, and telegraph services. Prussia had 17 votes in the *Bundesrat* and sent more than half of the members to the *Reichstag*. Many individuals were deputies of both the imperial and Prussian parliaments. The imperial Reichstag and Prussian *Landtag* were often in session at the same time, and legislation in the Kingdom was often accorded a lower priority[29] The Empire and the Kingdom of Prussia often shared diplomats.[30]

23 (Carter, 2010). p. 3.
24 (Tice, 2010), p. 3.
25 (Royal Musings, 2008)
26 (BBC History)
27 (Krüger, 1915), p. 312.
28 (Perris, 1912), p. 482.
29 (Krüger, 1915), p. 312.
30 (Hilger, 1905), pp. 115–116.

The population in 1914 was 42.1 million, of whom 68 percent was Protestant. Prussia comprised 12 separate provinces that were internal parts of the Kingdom of Prussia. Frequently they are confused with separate states. This is especially true of the Prussian state of Saxony, which was adjacent to the Kingdom of Saxony.[31] The kingdom was 348,657 km². The capital of the Kingdom of Prussia was Berlin.[32]

Bavaria

(1813–1871: *Bayern*)

The Kingdom of Bavaria, a German state since the 10th century, became a member state of the German Confederation between 1815 and 1866 and was considered the second most important state in Imperial Germany after Prussia. Because of its size and special status, it was certainly atypical and not as representative of Prussian dominated Germany as were smaller states such as Saxony and Württemburg. Bavaria fought on Austria's side in 1866, lost, and gave up a small enclave in Thuringia called Kaulsdorf, the Bezirksamt Gersfeld, the Landgerichtsbezirk Orb and an indemnity of 30 million guilders. After the 1866 war, Prussia, opposed the suggestion that the southern states should join the North German Confederation in order not to alarm France. However, there was an offensive and defensive alliance between Bavaria and Prussia. Bavaria no longer had "a need of France," and in the War of 1870–71, the Bavarian army joined Prussia, under the command of the Prussian Crown Prince, against France.

The Bavarian parliamentary chambers ratified the incorporation treaty on 21 January 1871, and Bavaria became a state of the German Empire, though not without considerable opposition.

However, the kingdom reserved certain separate privileges (Sonderrechte) in respect to the administration of the army, the railways, the mail, and the excise duties on beer, the rights of domicile and the insurance of real estate. The King of Bavaria was the supreme head of the Bavarian army. Though Bavaria became an integral part of the new German Empire, it reserved a larger measure of sovereign independence than any of the other constituent states. Thus, retaining a separate diplomatic service, military administration, postal, telegraph and railway systems.

Bavaria had a military treaty with Prussia from 23 November 1870. Prior to that, there was a mutual defense alliance that placed the Bavarian army under the Prussian king during time of war. What made Bavaria significantly different than the other states was that Articles 61–68 of the North German Confederation Constitution did not apply to Bavaria. As these were the military clauses, Bavaria maintained significant independence in military matters. Section IX of the Imperial German Constitution specifically references the treaty.

Ludwig I reigned as King of Bavaria from 1825–1848. The celebration of his marriage to Therèse of Saxe-Hildburghausen was the first *Oktoberfest*. That union produced three daughters and four sons. Ludwig I was well-educated and enjoyed literature, both classical and modern so much that he visited with Johann Wolfang von Goethe.[33] Bavaria enjoyed many successes during his time as king. He actively supported a Bavarian constitution and was considered a moderate. He supported Greece in its war for independence and even

---

31 The 12 States were: Brandenburg, Hannover, Hessen-Nassau, East Prussia, Pommern, Posen, Rheinland, Saxony, Silesia, Schleswig-Holstein, Westfalen, and West Prussia.

32 (*Kaiserliches Statistisches Amt, 1914*)

33 (Hashagen, 2011), Loc 2.

loaned money from his private resources. His second son, Otto, was elected King of Greece in 1832, but was forced to abdicate in 1862.[34]

As with many royal figures, Ludwig had a string of lovers. Perhaps the most famous was his Irish-born mistress, Eliza Gilbert, known by her stage name Lola Montez. When they met, he was 60 years old and she just 25. He spent millions remodeling a house for her and even tried to make her a Countess, something the Council of Ministers refused to endorse. Rather than remaining discreet, Lola began demanding more and more from Ludwig, including favors for those who had sought her patronage. She particularly abhorred Jesuits and the Catholic Church. When she convinced Ludwig to close the Catholic university, a riot ensued. Ludwig's entire cabinet resigned, and she had to flee to Switzerland. Ludwig was forced to abdicate in 1848, but continued his love for her until he died. She died at age 40 in 1861, and it is said that her mother traveled to New York City, where Lola had been living, to see if she could perhaps acquire some of the jewels that Ludwig had given her.[35] Maximilian, Ludwig's oldest son, succeeded him.

Maximilian II was studious and well read. He admired Hans-Christian Andersen, who often visited him. His marriage to Marie Friederike Hedwig, daughter of Prince William of Prussia (the fourth and youngest son of Friederich Wilhelm II), produced two sons, Ludwig II (sometimes referred to as "Mad King Ludwig") and Otto. Unfortunately, the frequent intermarriage on both sides of the family contributed to Otto's insanity. He was not alone in his infirmity. Alexandra, Maximilian's sister, was convinced that she had swallowed a glass piano, which was, of course, quite uncomfortable. She also was so obsessed with cleanliness that she would only wear white so that she could see any flecks of dirt.[36]

Ludwig II, on the other hand, was withdrawn and often lived in an imaginary world where he built castles and other grand structures.[37] When his father died in 1864, he was anything but ready to rule. Shortly after assuming power, he met Richard Wagner.[38] Ludwig installed him in a home close to him, but Ludwig's advisors and subjects did not appreciate their close relationship. When Prussia and Austria moved toward war, Ludwig escaped to visit his friend Wagner.

When the time came to marry, Ludwig proposed to his cousin, Sophie, but his thoughts were with Wagner, so much so that Ludwig broke the engagement. Not long after, he began the 20-year construction of Neuschwanstein Castle, much of it inspired by Wagner's operas, whose characters form the basis of much of the internal decoration.[39] There is speculation that Ludwig was torn between his alleged homosexuality and the Catholic Church, of which he was a member.

In 1870, Bismarck suggested to Ludwig that he recommend King Wilhelm I to serve as Kaiser. This proposal was important from Bismarck's perspective that the Kaiser should be "recommended" by one of the "princes," rather than the Parliament. As an incentive, Bismarck also donated a large sum of money for Ludwig's building projects.[40] Realizing he would not be considered for Kaiser, Ludwig began construction on his second castle, Linderhof; the building of Herrenchiemsee followed that. This continued building frenzy left him bankrupt, as he had used personal funds, not those of Bavaria.

34 (Hashagen, 2011), Loc 43.
35 (Mahon, 2007)
36 (Braun, 2012)
37 (Braun, 2012), p. 7.
38 (Roach, 2000) Loc 819.
39 (Braun, 2012), p. 47.
40 (German History Docs)

Prime Minister Lutz felt the time right for removing Ludwig from the throne. He met with Maximilian's brother Prince Luitpold. Luitpold was concerned for the House of Wittelsbach and for the financial dealings with Ludwig's creditors. Lutz then created a commission to determine Ludwig's sanity with Dr. Gudden as chair. Gudden had been retained to provide psychiatric care for the royal family. Four doctors concurred that Ludwig's behavior gave the impression of insanity, which was enough to remove him as king. Ludwig was imprisoned at Neuschwanstein and then moved to Berg. Late one afternoon, Ludwig asked to walk with Gudden on the grounds. Neither returned alive and both bodies were found in the lake under mysterious circumstances.[41]

Otto became King of Bavaria upon his older brother's death in 1886, but never truly ruled as King and was by some accounts not even aware that he had become King. Even as a child, he suffered hallucinations.[42] Ludwig had confined Otto to Nymphenburg Palace when he was in his 20s. He often spent weeks not removing his boots and barking like a dog. In his 30s, he was officially declared insane (by the same doctor who later declared Ludwig insane) and was moved to Fürstenried, where he lived within padded walls and screamed at all hours of the day.[43] But he was indeed king for 30 years. He died in 1916. Otto's uncle, Prince Luitpold of Bavaria, served as Prince Regent for Otto until Luitpold's death. Luitpold's son Ludwig then became the next Prince Regent.

The constitution of Bavaria was amended on 4 November 1913 to include a clause specifying that if regency for reasons of incapacity lasted for ten years with no expectation that the king would ever be able to reign, the regent could proclaim the end of the regency and assume the crown himself. The following day, his cousin, Prince Regent Ludwig, deposed Otto and assumed the title Ludwig III. Otto was permitted to retain his title and honors, which he did until his death in 1916. Ludwig III reigned until the end of the Great War.

Bavaria had six votes in the Bundesrat and sent forty-eight deputies to the Reichstag. The Wittelsbach dynasty was the hereditary ruling family. The Kingdom was a hereditary constitutional monarchy and the Parliament had two chambers. The upper house of the Bavarian parliament (*Kammer der Reichsräte*) was composed of various royalty, bishops, and appointees. The lower house (*Kammerder Abgeordneten*) or chamber of representatives consisted of 159 deputies, based on a population split of the census of 1875.[44] Voting was universally secret and direct.

The Prussian *Kulturkampf* increased the hostility toward Catholics, as did the 1870 Dogma of Papal Infallibility. Bavaria proclaimed a federal law that expelled the Jesuits on 6 September 1871, and it was extended to the Redemptorists in 1873. Bavarian Sonderrechte, founded on traditional racial and religious antagonism to the Prussians, continued, but was seen officially only in the limitation to display only the Bavarian flag on public buildings on the emperor's birthday; a provision which was modified to allow the Bavarian and imperial flags to be hung side by side.

The population in 1914 was 7,100,000 of which 70 percent was Catholic.[45] The kingdom was 75,780 km². The capital was Munich. Bavaria had its own army and army corps system. Soldiers were assigned to the Bavarian army corps numbers I through III. Similar to the other kingdoms of Saxony and Württemberg, there were two Bavarian infantry regiments

---

[41] (Braun, 2012), p. 108.

[42] (Braun, 2012), p. 11.

[43] (Braun, 2012), p, 80.

[44] (Krüger, 1915), p. 312.

[45] (*Kaiserliches Statistisches Amt, 1914*)

garrisoned in Lorraine. However, due to the treaty of 1870, these were under control of the Bavarian II Corps in peacetime, rather than the corps area in which they were stationed. The Bavarian army formed a separate portion of the army of the German Empire, with a separate administration. Bavarian regiments did not participate in the sequential numbering of the Prussian army. The regulations applicable to other sections of the whole German army were observed.[46]

Saxony

(1813–1871: *Sachsen*)

The Kingdom of Saxony, a German state since 1180, was a member of the German Confederation from 1815 to 1866. Prior to that, the Wettin dynasty had split in 1547 and the junior Albertine line took over Saxony. The senior line ruled the Thüringian area. In the Austro-Prussian war of 1866, Saxony declined Prussia's offer of neutrality, and the Saxon army joined the Austrians. The Prussians occupied the entire kingdom. On the conclusion of peace, Saxony lost no territory, but had to pay a war indemnity of 10 million Thalers, and was compelled to enter the North German Confederation. The military, postal and telegraph systems were placed under Prussian control. The Saxon military became a contingent of the Prussian army on 7 February 1867. Saxony became a member state of the German Empire in 1871.

King George of Saxony died on 15 October 1904; his son, as King Friedrich Augustus III, succeeded him until his abdication in 1918. Friedrich served in the Royal Saxon Army until his coronation and commanded several units. Friedrich Augustus III was the only German royal who renounced his own rights for the throne, but not his family's rights. The 800-year plus reign of the House of Wettin ended with his abdication. Frederick Augustus III's son, Crown Prince George of Saxony gave up his succession rights to become a Jesuit priest in 1923.

Saxony's royal scandal involved the Crown Princess Louise's (the wife of Friedrich August) flight in December 1902 with André Giron, who had been the French tutor to her three children. When Louise (Princess of Tuscany) and Friedrich August married, he was the Crown Prince. She was very popular in Saxony, as she did not follow the etiquette at the court, and her foibles did not endear her to her father-in-law. On 9 December 1902, pregnant with her youngest daughter (some say Giron's child), she left Saxony with Giron but without her children. She was divorced 11 February 1903 by royal decree. Her last child was sent to Dresden to live at the court. Louise's Italian father awarded her the title of Countess of Montignoso. The relationship with Giron did not last and on 25 September 1907, she married the musician Enrico Toselli in London. They were divorced five years later. She died in poverty in Brussels in 1947.

Saxony was a hereditary constitutional monarchy with four votes in the Bundesrat and 23 deputies in the Reichstag. Saxony was known as the "Red Kingdom," when in 1903 with universal suffrage, 22 of 23 Reichstag deputies were Social Democrats. The parliament of the kingdom had two chambers known as the *Ständekammer*. The upper chamber consisted of princes, certain members of the nobility and prominent men appointed by the King. The lower chamber consisted of 43 members from the towns and 48 from the country, who were elected for six-year terms. All male citizens 25 years and older, who paid three marks per annum in taxes, had the vote. The number of Social Democratic delegates in the Kingdom's

---

[46] (Krüger, 1915), p. 312.

parliament increased steadily. As a result, in 1896 a new electoral law was passed, introducing indirect elections and a franchise based on a three-tier system. In 1901, this change eliminated the Socialists from the Kingdom's parliament but, by 1903, the Social Democrats were the overwhelming majority in the Imperial Reichstag.[47] This majority changed further in 1909 with plural voting of between one and four votes determined by the amount paid in direct taxation.[48]

In 1914, the population of Saxony was 4,986,000. Saxony was the most densely populated state in the empire, and its population increased at a more rapid rate than any of the larger German states. No kingdom had so large a proportion of urban population, forming 52.97 percent of the whole. About 94 percent of the inhabitants were Protestants; about 12,500 were Jews; and about 4.7 percent, including the royal family, were Roman Catholics. There was a neighboring Prussian province of Saxony that had the same name.[49] The Kingdom was 14,993 km². The capital was Dresden. Saxon soldiers were concentrated into two Army Corps: the XII and XIX Army Corps. However, the 105th Infantry Regiment and the 12th Foot Artillery Regiment were located in Alsace-Lorraine.

Württemberg

(1813–1871)

The Kingdom of Württemberg, a German state since 1083, was a member state of the German Confederation until 1866. Württemberg fought on the side of Austria in 1866, but three weeks after the battle of Königgrätz, her troops were decisively beaten at Tauberbischofsheim. Württemberg paid an indemnity of 8,000,000 Gulden, and at once concluded a secret offensive and defensive treaty with Prussia. The Württemberg military became a contingent of the Prussian army by convention in November 1870. In this convention, the Kingdom of Württemberg was treated similarly to the Kingdom of Saxony from their 1867 agreement. When Württemberg became a member of the German empire in 1871, it retained control of its own post office, telegraphs and railways. In 1904, the railway system was united with that of the rest of Imperial Germany.

Friedrich I was King from 1805 until 1816. Previously, as Duke Friedrich II, he joined Napoleon against Prussia and even married his daughter, Catherine, to Napoleon's youngest brother. Much was written about Friedrich and his girth. Napoleon allegedly commented that, "God had created the Prince to demonstrate the utmost extent to which human skin could be stretched without bursting."[50] Friedrich I's first wife was Augusta of Brunswick, whose mother was the elder sister of George III of Great Britain. Her younger sister was the wife of George IV of the United Kingdom. Her sister-in-law, Friedrich's sister Sophie, was married to Paul, the future Emperor of Russia.

Augusta and Friedrich's marriage was not a happy one, and she sought refuge in St. Petersburg. The Empress of Russia, Catherine II, offered Augusta the use of one of her estates, and Augusta became pregnant. She went into premature labor and subsequently died. She was buried in an unmarked grave in the vicinity of Tallinn, Estonia in 1788. Friedrich then married Princess Charlotte, daughter of King George II of Great Britain. They had no surviving children.

---

47 (Krüger, 1915), p. 312.
48 (Hewitson, 2008), p. 49.
49 (*Kaiserliches Statistisches Amt*, 1914)
50 (Van der Kiste, 2003), p. 130.

Friedrich entered into a treaty with Metternich in 1813 and joined the German Confederation. He died three years later and was succeeded by his son, Wilhelm I, who led an adventurous life. Before ascending to the throne, Wilhelm I ran away to Paris with his mistress and was introduced to some of the more liberal political views of the time. As he matured, his ruling style became more conservative and he advised his son to understand clearly the limits of his constitutional authority.[51] Wilhelm was married three times. His first wife was Princess Charlotte of Bavaria, daughter of King Maximilian I. They were divorced after six years, and he married his first cousin, the Grand Duchess Catherine Pavlovna of Russia. He then became king. Upon her death, he married another first cousin, Pauline Therèse of Württemberg. Wilhelm I ruled until 1864 and was succeeded by his son Charles, whose mother was Pauline. Charles and his wife, Olga Nikolaevna, had no children (it was rumored he was homosexual), and when he died suddenly, his nephew Wilhelm II (not to be confused with Kaiser William II) succeeded him. Wilhelm II was the fourth and final King of Württemberg.

Wilhelm II married twice; first to Princess Marie of Waldeck and Pyrmont and upon her death, he married Princess Charlotte of Schaumburg-Lippe. She was the last queen of Württemberg as well as any German state. Neither King Wilhelm nor his protestant relatives had sons and, as a result, the succession passed to a Roman Catholic branch of the family.

The Württembergs produced a plethora of interesting royals. A number of morganatic marriages ensued between grandsons of King Frederich; perhaps the most famous was the marriage between Franz, Duke of Teck, and Princess Mary of Cambridge (his father's third cousin) that produced the future British Queen Mary. Another grandson, Paul Wilhelm, visited the United States several times and met Sacagawea's son, Jean Baptiste, whom he invited to Germany. Jean Baptiste spent five years in Europe before returning to the United States.[52]

Württemberg had a hereditary constitutional monarchy with four votes in the *Bundesrat* and 17 deputies in the Reichstag. The parliament consisted of two chambers known as the Kammer. The upper chamber was appointed and contained various noble, religious, and educated subjects. The lower house had 92 members, with 69 being elected by universal, direct, and secret ballot by all male citizens over 25 years of age. The other 23 members were elected based on proportional representation.[53]

The population in 1910 was 2,437,000, of which 65 percent was Protestant. The kingdom was 19,508 km². The capital was Stuttgart. Most of the soldiers of this kingdom were concentrated in the XIII Army Corps. Similar to Saxony, Württemberg Infantry Regiment 126 was assigned to XV Army Corps in Alsace-Lorraine, unlike the other Württemberg troops that became Army Corps XIII of the Prussian army with its own War Ministry but under the leadership of a Prussian commanding general. [54]

---

51 (Green, *Fatherlands*, 2001), p. 70.

52 (Martinez, 20110) Location 123.

53 (Krüger, 1915), p. 312.

54 The 8th Württemberg Infantry Regiment no. 126 (Straßburg) was under the tactical command of XV Army Corps, but still remained an integral part of the XIII Army Corps. The "Rangliste 1914" marked the regiment as "*abkommandiert zum XV AK.*" With mobilization this regiment also served with the XV Army Corps.

THE SONDERRECHTE GRAND DUCHY OF BADEN

Baden had been a German state since the 12th century and was a member state of the Germanic Confederation between 1815 and 1866, during which time it quadrupled in size.[55] Due in part to its close alliance with France over the years, Baden was one of the centers of liberal, radical activities in 1848; in fact, it became a republic for a short time.[56] Leopold, the Grand Duke of Baden, joined with Bavaria and asked Prussia to invade. Prussia successfully eliminated the revolution. Prince Wilhelm (later Wilhelm I) led the invasion.

Leopold died in 1852 and his second son, Frederick, succeeded him. His elder son, Louis II, had a number of mental health issues. Grand Duke Friedrich I reigned from 1858 until 1907. Frederick was married to Louise, the only daughter of German emperor Wilhelm I and Augusta—yet another example of the interrelationships in European royalty. Friedrich's mother was a daughter of King Gustav IV of Sweden. His daughter, Victoria, married King Gustaf V of Sweden. His son, Frederick II, the last Grand Duke of Baden, succeeded him but abdicated in 1918.

Baden fought on the side of Austria during the 1866 war, and consequently, paid Prussia an indemnity of six million guilders. Beginning in 1867, Friedrich I placed a Prussian general in command of Baden's troops and all Baden forces were trained according to the Prussian model. The military became a contingent of the Prussian Army on 25 November 1870. Frederick reserved the exclusive right to tax beer and spirits, but Prussia controlled the army, the post-office, railways, and the conduct of foreign relations. In addition to the Kingdoms of Bavaria and Württemberg, the Grand Duchy of Baden, also a Sonderrechte state, joined the German Empire in 1871.

The government of Baden was a hereditary constitutional Grand Duchy with a parliament of two chambers. The upper chamber was composed of all princes of the reigning family, certain members of the nobility, and eight members nominated by the Grand Duke. The lower chamber consisted of 73 popular representatives, the burgesses of certain towns elected 24, while the rural communities elected 49. Every male citizen of 25 years of age had a vote and balloting was secret. The elections were indirect, the citizens nominating the deputy electors (*Wahlmänner*), and the Wahlmänner electing the representatives.[57] The 1904 introduction of direct secret voting changed this system and led to a left-leaning alliance of liberals and socialists that controlled the Catholic vote.[58]

The internal politics of Baden centered on religion. The signing of a concordat with the Holy See, which placed education under the oversight of the clergy, led to a constitutional struggle, which the Protestants won. In 1867, a law was passed to compel all candidates for the priesthood to pass government examinations. The archbishop of Freiburg resisted, and on his death in April 1868, the See remained vacant. The Kulturkampf raged in Baden and lasted throughout the 1870s. Not until 1880 was there reconciliation with Rome. In 1882, the position of the Freiburg archbishopric was finally filled.[59]

The population in 1910 was 2,142,000, 66 percent of which was Catholic. The area was 15,081 km^2. The capital was Karlsruhe. Most of the soldiers of this Grand Duchy were concentrated in XIV Army Corps of the Prussian army.

---

55 (White, 1996), p. 135.
56 (Grand Duchy of Baden)
57 (Krüger, 1915), p. 312.
58 (Hewitson, 2008), p. 49.
59 (Perris, 1912), pp. 290–302.

THE THURINGIAN DUCHIES AND PRINCIPALITIES

Thuringia was not a state in the sense of a common political entity, but rather a geographical area. It is common to hear them referred to as the Thuringian states, the Thuringian Duchies, or the Saxon Duchies even though they were not all duchies.[60] This area was once part of the Kingdom of Saxony, but the senior line of the House of Wettin took Thuringia and the junior line took what became known as the Kingdom of Saxony. The tradition of splitting the inherited properties among the male heirs led to the emergence of these small enclaves.

Reuß Junior Line

(1813–1871: *Reuß jüngere Linie*)

The Principality of Reuß Junior Line, (sometimes called Reuß Gera) a small German state in Thuringia since 1673, was a member state of the German Confederation from 1815 to 1866. The principality remained neutral during the Austro-Prussian war. Later it became a member state of the North German Confederation in 1867. The Reuß military became a contingent of the Prussian army on 26 June 1867. It became a member state of the German Empire in 1871.

The princely family of Reuß had the unique custom of naming all its male members Heinrich, in honor of the Holy Roman Emperor Heinrich VI, from whom they received their lands in the 13th century. A complicated system of numbering was developed into two different forms: the Elder line followed a sequence from 1 to 100 and then returned to 1; the Younger line numbered the first Heinrich to be born in the century as number 1 and followed the sequence until the end of the century, then began again with the new century. There were several notable family members. Augusta Reuß, daughter of Heinrich XXIV was grandmother to both Queen Victoria and Prince Albert. She was also grandmother to Empress Carlota of Mexico and Leopold II of Belgium. Heinrich XXVII ruled the principality until he abdicated in 1918.

The form of government was a hereditary constitutional monarchy.[61] There was one chamber in parliament known as the Landtag. The 16 members of the Landtag had 12 members, who were elected by all taxpayers; three by the highest paying taxpayers; and one appointed by the Prince.[62]

The population was 157,000 of whom 95 percent was Protestant in 1914. The principality was 827 km². Its capital was Gera. The soldiers were concentrated among other small states in 7. thüringisches Infanterie-Regiment Nr. 96 of the Prussian army.

Reuß Senior Line

(1813–1871: *Reuß ältere Linie*)

The Principality of Reuß Senior Line, (sometimes called Reuß Greiz) a small German state in Thuringia since 1673, was a member state of the German Confederation from 1815 to 1866. The principality allied with Austria in 1866, and barely escaped annexation with an indemnity of 100,000 Thalers. After the Austro-Prussian War, it became a member state of the North German Confederation in 1867. The Reuß military became a contingent of the Prussian army on 26 June 1867. It became a member state of the German Empire in 1871.

---

[60] Although they are located in Thuringia they were usually referred to as the "Saxon Duchies." Particularly XI Army Corps consisted of regiments and battalions coming from these principalities.

[61] Despite not being a kingdom, monarchy was the type of government of these smaller states.

[62] (Krüger, 1915), p. 315.

Prince Heinrich XXII died in 1902, and his son Heinrich XXIV was judged mentally incapable of ruling the principality. A regent, Heinrich XXVII, was appointed from the Junior Line and ruled all of Reuß until the end of the war.

The form of government was a hereditary constitutional monarchy. There was one chamber of parliament known as the Landtag. The 12 members of this chamber included three who were appointed by the monarch; the landowners universally elected seven; and two were elected from the clergy.[63] The principality electors were known as a difficult group in the Bundesrat. The conservative principality frequently went against the Prussian party line.

The population was 74,000 in 1914, and 98 percent was Protestant. The capital was Greiz. The principality was 223 km². The soldiers were concentrated among other small states in 7. thüringisches Infanterie-Regiment Nr. 96 of the Prussian army.

Saxe-Altenburg

(1813–1871: *Sachsen-Altenburg*)

The Duchy of Saxe-Altenburg, a German state in Thuringia since 1602, was a member state of the German Confederation from 1815 to 1866. After the Austro-Prussian War, when the duchy allied with Prussia, it became a member state of the North German Confederation in 1867. The Saxe-Altenburg military became a contingent of the Prussian army on 26 June 1867, and it became a member state of the Imperial German Empire in 1871.

Duke Ernst I served for 55 years until 1908. Ernst II was the last reigning Duke of Saxe-Altenburg; his father's death left him first in line when his uncle, Ernst I, died without a surviving male son. During WWI, he was offered an honorary appointment to the Kaiser's headquarters, but turned it down to enter the army as a colonel and ended his military career as a division commander.

Saxe-Altenburg was a hereditary constitutional monarchy. The parliament had one chamber called the Landtag consisting of 32 members. The franchise was even more restrictive than Prussia with nine Landtag members elected only by the highest taxpaying section and the other 23 by all males over 25 years of age who paid taxes according to the Prussian three-tier system. Saxe-Altenburg had one vote in the Reichstag and one in the Bundesrat.[64]

The population was 222,000, 98 percent of which were Protestant. The capital was Altenburg. The Duchy consisted of two detached and almost equal sections, as well as 12 small enclaves. The duchy was 1323 km². The soldiers were concentrated among other small states in 8. thüringisches Infanterie-Regiment Nr. 153 of the Prussian army.

Saxe-Coburg-Gotha

(1815–1871: *Sachsen-Coburg-Gotha*)

Saxe-Coburg-Saalfeld and Saxe-Gotha became a combined double state in 1826 named the Duchy of Saxe-Coburg-Gotha. In addition to the two almost equal sized parts, there were a number of small enclaves. The small Thuringian state was a member state of the German Confederation until 1866. After the Austro-Prussian War, during which it allied with Prussia, it became a member state of the North German Confederation in 1867. The Saxe-Coburg-Gotha military became a contingent of the Prussian army on 26 June 1867. It became a member state of the German Empire in 1871.

[63] (Krüger, 1915) p. 315.
[64] (Krüger, 1915), p. 314.

Saxe-Coburg-Gotha's first duke was Ernest I; his younger brother was Leopold I, the King of the Belgians. In 1817, Ernst I married Princess Louise of Saxe-Gotha-Altenburg and they had two children, Ernest II and Albert, who later married Queen Victoria. Ernest I was a noted philanderer and his marriage ended in divorce, which created a political challenge. Louise's uncle was the last duke of Saxe-Gotha-Altenburg. Ernst would have been next in line to inherit Gotha, but there was disagreement on the succession. A compromise was reached. Unfortunately, Louise died shortly thereafter. Ernest I then married Duchess Marie of Württemberg, his sister's daughter, making her Albert's cousin and stepmother.

Ernest II succeeded his father and married Alexandrine of Baden and they had no children. This lack of progeny proved problematic, as the line of succession was then to Albert's line. This transfer meant that a British sovereign would also become a German sovereign and neither Queen Victoria nor Albert supported this turn of events. In 1855, Albert agreed to renounce his right of succession.[65] The succession passed to Alfred, the second son of Albert and Queen Victoria. When Alfred died, the line of succession passed to Charles Edward, a Prince of the United Kingdom, whose father was Prince Leopold (the fourth son of Queen Victoria). He reigned until 1918. After the war, he had to give up all British titles and honors.

Saxe-Coburg-Gotha was a hereditary constitutional monarchy. There were two separate parliaments, one for the Duchy of Coburg and another for the Duchy of Gotha. The Coburg diet consisted of 11 members and the Gotha diet numbered 19 members. Common issues were decided by a joint session. The franchise was given to all male taxpayers who were at least 25 years of age. The united duchy was represented in the Bundesrat by one member and in the Reichstag by two members, one for each duchy. The Duke of Saxe-Coburg-Gotha was quite rich as Duke Ernest I sold the principality of Lichtenberg to Prussia for a large sum of money.[66]

The population was 226,000 in 1914 of which 98 percent was Protestant. The capital was both Gotha and Coburg (summer). The duchy was 1977 km^2. The soldiers were concentrated in the 6. thüringisches Infanterie-Regiment Nr. 95.

Saxe-Meiningen

(1813–1871: *Sachsen-Meiningen*)

The Principality of Saxe-Meiningen, or more correctly Saxe-Meiningen-Hildburghausen, a German state in Thuringia since 1680, was a member state of the German Confederation from 1815 to 1866. In 1826, it absorbed Saxe-Hildburghausen in exchange for Saxe-Gotha-Altenburg.

Bernhard II, Duke of Saxe-Meiningen, succeeded his father, Georg I when he was but three years old. His mother served as regent until 1821. Shortly thereafter, he married Marie Frederica of Hesse-Kassel. During the Austro-Prussian War of 1866, Saxe Meiningen allied with Austria and was then occupied by Prussian troops. In September 1866, Duke Bernard abdicated and was succeeded by his son George II, who had supported the Prussians. George II immediately made peace with Prussia.

George II married three times, the first for love. His first wife was Charlotte Frederica of Prussia, a niece of Frederick William IV. They spent much time in Berlin and Potsdam but had to return to Meiningen for the birth of their four children. Their second son, George died young, and Charlotte died shortly thereafter, giving birth to their fourth child.

---

65 (Royal Musings, 2008)
66

Her death left George distraught. His second wife, Feodora, was his second cousin and a niece of Queen Victoria. It was believed he married to find a mother for his two children. He and Feodora had three additional children. Fedora died of scarlet fever in 1872.Their eldest son, Bernhard III, succeeded his father.

George and Feodora's second son's (Fredrick Johann's) daughter, Adelheid, would later marry the Kaiser's third son, Prince Adalbert.[67] There is early evidence that Adelheid suffered porphyria symptoms as a girl, and they grew worse with age. She did not die until 1971, and her obituary referenced that she died of an illness bravely born.[68]

George's third wife was Ellen Franz, a former actress; it was a morganatic marriage that angered Kaiser Wilhelm. George and Ellen devoted themselves to the arts and Meiningen became well known for its patronage of the theater. Johannes Brahms and Richard Strauss both performed for them. George was succeeded by his eldest son, Bernard III, who was the last Duke of Saxe-Meiningen.

Saxe-Meiningen was a hereditary constitutional monarchy. There was one chamber in the parliament known as the Landtag. The parliament consisted of 24 members who were elected by three different groups. Four members were elected by the largest landowners, four members by those who paid taxes up to a certain level, and 16 by all of the citizens in a direct secret election. Voting was by all males over 25 years of age who paid taxes. Saxe-Meiningen had one vote in the Bundesrat and two deputies in the Reichstag.[69]

The Saxe-Meiningen military became a contingent of the Prussian army on 26 June 1867 and George became a lieutenant general in the Prussian army. Saxe-Meiningen subsequently joined the North German Confederation in 1867. It became a member state of the German Empire in 1871.

The population was 287,000 in1914, of which 98 percent was Protestant. The capital of the duchy was Meiningen. The soldiers were gathered in 2nd Battalion 6. thüringisches Infanterie-Regiment Nr. 95.

Saxe-Weimar-Eisenach

(1813–1871: *Sachsen-Weimar-Eisenach*)

The Grand Duchy of Saxe-Weimar-Eisenach, a German state in Thuringia since 1566, was a member state of the German Confederation from 1815 to 1866. The Saxe-Weimar family was the oldest branch of the Ernestine line, and therefore, the entire House of Saxony. It was the largest of the Thuringian states, and comprised the three detached districts of Weimar, Eisenach, and Neustadt, along with 24 scattered enclaves. In 1877, it officially changed its name to the Grand Duchy of Saxony (*Großherzogtum Sachsen*), but this name is rarely used in modern sources. In 1896, the order of the colors for the flag and the cockades was changed to black-yellow-green. Prior to that time, the color order was black-green-yellow.[70] After the Austro-Prussian War, when it allied with Prussia, it became a member state of the North German Confederation in 1867. The Saxe-Weimar-Eisenach military became a contingent of the Prussian army on 26 June 1867. It became a member state of the German Empire in 1871.

Karl Alexander reigned as duke from 1853 until 1901. He was a close friend of Hans Christian Andersen until the Danish War in 1849. Throughout his reign, he supported the arts and

67 (Tice, 2010), p. 11.
68 (Rohl, 1998), p. 62.
69 (Krüger, 1915), p. 314.
70 (Hilger, 1905), p. 134.

was a protector of Richard Wagner and Franz Liszt. Wilhelm Ernst, his grandson, succeeded him, as his father had died previously. Wilhelm was in line for the Netherland's throne as he was the grandson of Princess Sophie. Queen Wilhelmia gave birth to a daughter, thus ensuring that the crown remained in the Netherlands. He was an interesting ruler, rumored to be a sadist, who was told, when he abdicated, that he was the most unpopular prince in Germany and had better run for it.[71] His first wife died mysteriously in 1905. Natural causes and suicide were both rumored. He remarried and lived until 1923.

Saxe-Weimar-Eisenach was a hereditary constitutional monarchy. The parliament consisted of one chamber known as the Landtag with 38 members. There was a four-tier voting system with five members chosen by the largest landholders, five by high-paying taxpayers, five by the University of Jena, and 23 by the rest of the inhabitants. The franchise was rather more liberal than some and included all male citizens over 21 years of age. The Grand Duchy was represented by one vote in the Bundesrat and by two members in the Reichstag.[72]

The population in 1914 was 442,000 who almost entirely were Lutherans.[73] The capital was Weimar. The total area of the grand duchy was 3,609 km^2. The soldiers were gathered into the Infanterie-Regiment Großherzog v. Sachsen (5. Thuringisches) Nr. 94.

Schwarzburg-Rudolstadt

(1813–1871)

The Principality of Schwarzburg-Rudolstadt, a German state in Thuringia since 1711, was a member state of the German Confederation from 1815 to 1866. Schwarzburg-Rudolstadt and Schwarzburg-Sondershausen originally were joined by family lines. Similar to the Reuß family, all of the male descendants had a common name, in this instance Günther, such as Günther XL, who died in 1552. Schwarzburg-Rudolstadt was the junior line. After the Austro-Prussian War, where they allied with Prussia, Schwarzburg-Rudolstadt became a member state of the North German Confederation in 1867. The Schwarzburg-Rudolstadt military became a contingent of the Prussian army on 26 June 1867. It became a member state of the German Empire in 1871.

On the death of Charles Günther of Schwarzburg-Sondershausen in 1909, the two Schwartzberg principalities were united in a personal union under Günther Viktor of Schwarzburg-Rudolstadt. He still ruled two separate states inside the German Empire. Günther Viktor was fond of calling the joint principality Schwarzburg. They were not united in a constitutional sense and were always two separate states having two distinct votes in the Bundesrat.

Schwarzburg-Rudolstadt was a hereditary constitutional monarchy. The parliament consisted of one chamber called the Landtag and was only summoned every three years. The parliament consisted of 16 members, four chosen by the highest assessed taxpayers, the others by universal secret and direct elections. The principality had one vote in the Reichstag and one in the Bundesrat.[74]

---

[71] (*The Most Unpopular Prince in Germany: Grand Duke Wilhelm Ernst of Saxe-Weimar-Eisenach, 1999*)

[72] (Krüger, 1915), p. 313.

[73] (*Kaiserliches Statistisches Amt, 1914*)

[74] (Krüger, 1915), p. 315.

The capital was Rudolstadt; the population was 103,000 in 1914, and almost all were Lutheran.[75] The principality was only 103 km² in size. The soldiers were concentrated in 3 Battalion 7. thüringisches Infanterie-Regiment Nr. 96 of the Prussian army.

Schwarzburg-Sondershausen

(1813–1871)

The Principality of Schwarzburg-Sondershausen, a German state in Thuringia since 1697, was a member state of the German Confederation from 1815 to 1866. After the Austro-Prussian War where she allied with Prussia, Schwarzburg-Sondershausen became a member state of the North German Confederation in 1867. It became a member state of the German Empire in 1871.

Prince Charles Günther succeeded his father on 17 July 1880 when his father renounced the throne due to eye disease. With the death of Prince Charles Günther in 1909, the Sondershausen line ended and the prince of Schwarzburg-Rudolstadt ruled both states.[76]

Schwarzburg-Sondershausen was a hereditary constitutional monarchy. The parliament had one chamber known as the Landtag. There was a three-tier appointment system where of the 18 members of parliament, six representatives were appointed by the highest taxpayers, six by universal secret and direct election, and six were appointed for life by the prince. The principality had one vote in the Reichstag and one in the Bundesrat.[77]

The population was 93,000 in 1914 and they were almost all Lutheran.[78] The capital was Sondershausen. The principality was 862 km² in size. The soldiers were concentrated in 3 Battalion 7. thüringisches Infanterie-Regiment Nr. 96 of the Prussian army.

THE HANSEATIC CITIES OF THE NORTH GERMAN CONFEDERATION

The name Hanseatic really referred to a league of trading cities that dated back to the 13th century. By the late 1800s, the meaning, as far as imperial Germany was concerned, was limited to the German cities of Hamburg, Bremen, and Lübeck. There were also other members of the Hanseatic League in other countries from the furthest reaches of the Baltic to the North Sea.

Bremen

(1813–1871)

The Free Hanseatic City of Bremen, a German state since 1646, was a member state of the German Confederation between 1815 and 1866. After the Austro-Prussian War, it became a member state of the North German Confederation in 1867.[79] In 1869, Prussia granted territory to Bremen to give it control of Bremerhaven at the mouth of the Weser River and

75 *(Kaiserliches Statistisches Amt, 1914)*
76 (Hilger, 1905), p. 141.
77 (Krüger, 1915), p. 315.
78 *(Kaiserliches Statistisches Amt, 1914)*
79 (Hilger, 1905), p. 87.

some other small ports along the river.[80] It became a member state of the German Empire in 1871.[81]

The government was a republic with a two-chamber parliament—the Senate and the *Bürgerschaft*. The Senate was composed of 16 life members elected by the Bürgerschaft. Their colleagues elected two of the Senators as mayor (*Bürgermeister*), who presided over the republic in succession for a year at a time. The Bürgerschaft consisted of 150 representatives, chosen by the citizens for six-year terms, who formed the legislative body. The most educated citizens (university graduates) of Bremen elected 14 members. Forty members were elected by the merchants, 20 by the manufacturers and artisans, and 48 by the other citizens. For the remaining representatives, the towns of Bremerhaven and Vegesack, provided 16 and the rural districts furnished 12. As a member of the German Empire, the State of Bremen had one vote in the Bundesrat and had one deputy in the Reichstag. Bremen joined the Zollverein quite late in 1888 with the exception of two small free districts in Bremen and Bremerhaven.[82]

In 1914, the population was approximately 326,000 of which 93 percent was Protestant, six percent Roman Catholic, and only two percent Jewish. The republic was 256 km² in size. The soldiers were concentrated in Infanterie-Regiment Bremen (1. hanseatisches) Nr. 75. Strictly speaking the garrisons towns were: Bremen (HQ, 1st and 2nd Bns) and Stade (3rd Battalion) but really the whole regiment was linked to Bremen.

Hamburg

(1813–1871)

The Free and Hanseatic City of Hamburg was a German state since 1618. It was a member state of the Germanic Confederation between 1815 and 1866. After the Austro-Prussian War, it became a member state of the North German Confederation in 1867. Hamburg became a member state of the German Empire in 1871.[83]

Hamburg was a republic with the parliament having two chambers, the Senate and the *Bürgerschaft*. The Senate, which exercised the greater part of the executive power, was composed of 18 life members. The Bürgerschaft elected the members of the Senate for life. There were two mayors. However, a chief Bürgermeister, called “Magnificence,” was chosen annually in secret ballot and had a two-year term limit. The Bürgerschaft consisted of 160 members who were elected using a unique three-tiered system. Eighty members were elected by secret ballot of all tax-paying citizens, 40 members by the owners of real estate within the city, and the “notables” directly elected the remaining 40 for a period of six years. The senate could veto all legislation except taxation; if the two bodies differed, the issue was referred to a court of arbitration. Hamburg had one representative in the Bundesrat and three deputies in the Reichstag.[84]

In 1914, the population was approximately 1,099,000 of which 85 percent was Protestant. The republic was 415 km² in size. The soldiers were concentrated in Infanterie-Regiment Hamburg (2. hanseatisches) Nr. 76.[85]

---

80 (Pounds, 1996), pp. 16–17.
81 (Hilger, 1905), p. 82.
82 (Krüger, 1915), p. 316.
83 (Hilger, 1905), pp, 91–92.
84 (Krüger, 1915), p. 316.
85 (*Kaiserliches Statistisches Amt, 1914*)

Lübeck

(1813–1871)

The Free and Hanseatic City of Lübeck, a German state since 1226, was a member state of the Germanic Confederation from 1815 to 1866. There is some confusion because there is a principality of Lübeck, which is a province of Oldenburg, and also a separate entity, the Free City of Lübeck. After the Austro-Prussian War, Lübeck became a member state of the North German Confederation in 1867. It became a member state of the German Empire in 1871.[86]

The Free State was a republic and Parliament consisted of two chambers. The Senate consisted of 14 life members, who were elected by a joint session of the Senate and the lower house. The Senate was presided over by the *Oberbürgermeister* who, during his two-year term of office, was called "Magnificence" and was also considered the president of the Senate and the head of the republic. All citizens possessing four-year longevity elected the lower house (Bürgerschaft) of 130 members under a unique two-class property system of those who paid income tax. The Bürgerschaft had the right of initiating legislation, including that relative to foreign treaties.[87]

In 1914, the population of 122,000 was nearly all Lutheran. The republic was 297 km^2 in size. The soldiers were concentrated in Infanterie-Regiment Lübeck (3.hanseatisches) Nr. 162.[88]

THE OTHER NORTH GERMAN CONFEDERATION STATES

Anhalt

(1813–1871, *Anhalt-Dessau* until 1863)

The Duchy of Anhalt-Dessau, a German state since the 17th century, was a member state of the Germanic Confederation in 1815. In 1863, the duchies of Anhalt-Bernburg and Anhalt-Köthen were united and renamed the Duchy of Anhalt. The country consisted of two larger portions—Eastern and Western Anhalt, separated by the interposition of a part of Prussian Saxony and of five enclaves surrounded by Prussian territory. During the Austro-Prussian War of 1866, Anhalt sided with Prussia. Anhalt became a member state of the North German Confederation in 1867. The military became a contingent of the Prussian army on 28 June 1867. Anhalt became a state of the German Empire in 1871.

There was a whirlwind of succession in Anhalt with three rulers during World War I. Frederick II, Duke of Anhalt, reigned until April 1918, when he died without issue. His younger brother, Eduard succeeded him. He lived only five months longer and was succeeded by his eldest son, Joachim Ernst. As Joachim Ernst was only 17, Aribert, the fourth son of Frederick I, was appointed regent. Aribert was widely rumored to be homosexual. His marriage to Princess Marie was termed null and void in 1900, and she obtained a British title. Ostensibly, the marriage ended with her abandonment of her husband. In reality, she had found Aribert with another man. She believed that he married her under false pretenses and could not even consummate the marriage, but his family disowned her while she was out of the coun-

86 (Hilger, 1905), p. 99.
87 (Krüger, 1915), p. 316.
88 (*Kaiserliches Statistisches Amt, 1914*)

try. He divorced her without her consent and allowed word to spread that it was because she couldn't have children.[89]

The duchy was a hereditary constitutional monarchy. There was one chamber in the parliament.[90] The parliament was comprised of 36 members, of whom the duke appointed two; eight were representatives of landowners paying the highest taxes, two were the highest taxpayers of commerce and industry, 14 from the towns, and 10 from the rural districts.[91]

In 1914, the population was approximately 333,000 of which 95 percent were Protestant and members of the Evangelical (Union) Church.[92] The capital was Dessau. The duchy was 2,294 km² in size. The soldiers were concentrated in Anhaltisches Infanterie-Regiment Nr. 93.

Brunswick

(1813–1871: *Braunschweig*)

The Duchy of Brunswick, a German state since the 10th century, was a member state of the Germanic Confederation between 1815 and 1866. Brunswick allied with Prussia during the 1866 war against Austria. After the Austro-Prussian War, Brunswick became a member state of the North German Confederation in 1867. It became a member state of the German Empire in 1871. Brunswick was comprised of three larger and six smaller portions of territory. A portion of the Harz Mountains was, until 1874, common to Brunswick and Prussia (Hanover) and known as the Communion Harz. In 1874, a partition was agreed to, but the mines were still worked in common, four-sevenths of the revenues going to Prussia and the remaining three-sevenths to Brunswick. The destiny of this Duchy is intertwined with the history of the Kingdom of Hanover.

The question of the succession to the Brunswick throne was acute after the 1866 war. Duke William of Brunswick was unmarried, and according to the existing conventions, upon the extinction of the elder line, the duchy would pass to the younger line headed by George, King of Hanover, who had just been deprived of his kingdom by the King of Prussia.

In 1879, Duke William of Brunswick, with the active support of Prussia, concluded an arrangement for a temporary council of regency to take over the government on his own death. Moreover, according to the arrangement, should the rightful heir be unable to take possession of the Duchy, the council was empowered to appoint a regent. Duke William died on the 18 October 1884, and the senior branch of the House of Guelph became extinct.

There had been strong Prussian pressure against having George V of Hanover or his son, Ernest, the Duke of Cumberland, succeed to a member state of the German Empire, without swearing loyalty to the Imperial German Constitution. Ernest, Duke of Cumberland, claimed Brunswick and promised to respect the Imperial German Constitution. This claim was disregarded by the council of regency, and the Bundesrat declared that the accession of the Duke of Cumberland would be a threat to the peace and security of the empire. The Council of Regency chose Albert, Prince of Prussia, as regent. Albert died in September 1906, and after some perfunctory negotiations with the Duke of Cumberland, the Brunswick parliament chose Duke Johan Albert of Mecklenburg-Schwerin as regent in 1907.

Agitation between the two royal houses of Prussia and Hannover continued, and Prussia looked for a way to make a deal. In 1912, when King Frederik VIII of Denmark died, the Duke

[89] (King, 2007), p. 58
[90] (Hilger, 1905), p. 73.
[91] (Krüger, 1915), p. 314.
[92] (*Kaiserliches Statistisches Amt, 1914*)

of Cumberland sent his eldest son, George Wilhelm, as a representative to the funeral. The heir died in a car accident while driving through Germany. The Kaiser sent two representatives to George Wilhelm's funeral. In thanks, the Duke of Cumberland sent his second son, Ernst August III to Berlin to thank the Kaiser. While at court, Ernst fell in love with the Kaiser's only daughter, Viktoria, and they were married in 1913. The Duke of Cumberland then renounced his claim to Brunswick in favor of his youngest son. The new Duke of Brunswick swore allegiance to the German Empire and was allowed to ascend to the throne of the duchy in November 1913.[93] Both he and his father were deprived of British titles derived from Hannover in 1919, for "bearing arms against Great Britain."

The constitution was a limited monarchy. The throne was hereditary in the house of Braunschweig, (Brunswick)-Lüneburg (Welfisch in German–Guelph in English) but should that line go extinct, the throne would go to the House of Hanover. The parliament of the duchy consisted of one house of 48 deputies, of whom communities elected 30, while the remainder represented the Evangelical church, the large landed proprietors, manufacturers and the professions.[94]

The capital was Braunschweig. The population in 1914 was 500,000 of which 95 percent was Protestant. The religion was primarily Lutheran evangelical, and there was a large Roman Catholic community centered on the bishopric of North Germany. The Jews had several synagogues, with a rabbinate in Brunswick.[95] The soldiers were concentrated in the famous Braunschweigisches Infanterie-Regiment Nr. 92 as well as the Braunschweigisches Husaren-Regiment Nr. 17.

Hesse-Darmstadt

(1813–1871: *Hessen (-Darmstadt)*)

The Grand Duchy of Hesse-Darmstadt was a German state beginning in 1567. The *Landgraf* of Hesse-Darmstadt became the Grand Duke of Hesse (*Großherzog von Hessen*) in 1806, after being forced to join Napoleon I's Rhine Alliance. After Napoleon's army had been defeated in 1815, Hesse-Darmstadt's territory was enlarged to include cities near the Rhine River, such as Mainz. The official title was changed from Hesse-Darmstadt to "Hesse and the Rhine" (*Hessen und bei Rhein*). It was a member state of the Germanic Confederation between 1815 and 1866. Hesse-Darmstadt sided with Austria during the war in 1866. After the Austro-Prussian War, it became a member state of the North German Confederation. It was known until 1866 as Hesse-Darmstadt. After Prussia annexed Hesse-Cassel and Hesse-Homburg in 1866, Hesse-Darmstadt remained the only independent part of Hesse, and it became known as Hesse. Not only were the inhabitants known as Hessians, but also the inhabitants of the former states of Hesse and the new Prussian province of Hesse-Nassau were considered Hessians. Hesse-Darmstadt became a member state of the German Empire in 1871. It consisted of two main parts, separated from each other by a narrow strip of Prussian territory. The northern part was the province of Oberhessen; the southern consisted of the contiguous provinces of Starkenburg and Rheinhessen. It is a common misconception that Hesse-Darmstadt lost no land as a result of royal connections after the war of 1866. While doing far better than many of its neighbors, it still lost a great deal of land north of Wetzlar.

[93] (Opfell, 2001), p. 45
[94] (Hilger, 1905), pp. 84–85.
[95] (*Kaiserliches Statistisches Amt, 1914*)

In 1862, the Grand Duke Louis IV married Queen Victoria's second daughter, Alice, who was a carrier of hemophilia. Their daughter, Alexandra, princess of Hesse Darmstadt, married Nicholas II of Russia and thereby introduced the genetic disorder into the Russian royalty.[96] Their son, Friedrich suffered from hemophilia and died from a fall. Alice died in 1878, and in 1884 the duke entered into a morganatic marriage. His oldest son, Ernst Louis, succeeded him.

In 1894, Ernst Louis married Victoria of Saxe-Coburg Gotha, his first cousin. This marriage was not a happy one, and the death of their daughter Elisabeth, and the birth of a stillborn son, did nothing to help their relationship. Victoria Melita's (Ducky's) fights with the passive Ernst were legendary and included the throwing of china and glassware. They were divorced in 1901, after the death of Queen Victoria, who previously would not permit the divorce. There is controversy today whether the Grand Duke was gay or bisexual, or if Victoria Melita created this rumor maliciously. He married again in 1905 and had two sons.

The Hessian military became a contingent of the Prussian army on 7 April 1867. Even though only the northern part of Hesse joined the North German Confederation, the entire military was integrated into the Prussian army. There were some significant variances with other conventions and there was even a separate War Minister for Hesse. A further convention was signed in June 1871 maintaining more control over uniforms and other functions than most of the other small states. The Grand Duke retained the right to order any changes in the uniform, which may be found in later imperial orders.

The form of government was a hereditary constitutional monarchy. There were two legislative chambers in the parliament both called Kammer. The upper consisted of princes of the grand-ducal family, heads of noble houses, the Bishop of the Roman Catholic Church, the superintendent of the protestant church, the chancellor of the university, two elected representatives of the land-owning nobility, and 12 members nominated by the Grand Duke. The lower chamber consisted of 50 members who were indirectly elected by deputy electors. The voting right was offered to all taxpayers and was secret and direct.[97]

There were 1,333,000 inhabitants in 1914 of which 63 percent was Protestant.[98] The capital was Darmstadt. The grand duchy was a total of 7,688 km². The soldiers were concentrated in the 25th Infantry Division of the Prussian XVIII Army Corps.

Lippe-Detmold

(1813–1871)

The Principality of Lippe-Detmold, a German state since the 12th century, was a member state of the Germanic Confederation from 1815 to 1866. Lippe allied with Prussia during the 1866 war against Austria. After the Austro-Prussian War, it became a member state of the North German Confederation in 1867. It became a member state of the German Empire in 1871.

There were arguments over the succession in this house. Woldemar, Prince of Lippe died in 1895. His brother Alexander, the last of the senior line (Detmold), succeeded him. Alexander was hopelessly insane, single, and had been declared incapable of ruling. A struggle over the succession ensued between the regents, Adolf of Schaumburg-Lippe and Ernst of Lippe-Biesterfeld. The Bundesrat requested that the Chancellor of the Empire refer the question of the succession to a special court of arbitration. This court was presided over by King Albert of Saxony, who determined in 1897 that Count Ernst of Lippe-Biesterfeld was the rightful

96 (Packard, 1998), p. 340
97 (Krüger, 1915), p. 313.
98 (*Kaiserliches Statistisches Amt, 1914*)

successor and was sole regent of the principality. The Schaumburg-Lippe's family launched a counter-offensive by challenging Count Ernst's marriage, attempting to declare it morganatic. Count-Regent Ernst died in 1904 and his eldest son Leopold became regent. The Kaiser especially objected to Leopold, as his grandmother was an American. The Kaiser refused to recognize him as regent and once again, the issue of who was the legitimate regent raged. It was so contentious that the Kaiser ordered the officers of the Prussian regiments stationed in Lippe not to provide the customary salute and bowing to any of the Countesses of Lippe.[99] The Biesterfeld line assumed sovereign status on the extinction of the Detmold line in 1905, when the insane Prince Alexander died and the Court of Justice declared that the descendants of Count-Regent Ernst were entitled to the crown. Leopold, who had a morganatic marriage, was named the regent. He remained as regent, and the court of arbitration declared the marriage in question to be equal; thus, Leopold (b. 1871) became Prince of Lippe.

Lippe-Detmold was a hereditary constitutional monarchy. The constitution called for a parliament of 21 members, known as the Landtag. The franchise for electoral purposes was similar to the Prussian three-tier system except for that the vote was secret. The population was divided into three classes based on taxation, each of which sent seven members to the Landtag. Lippe-Detmold had one vote in the German Reichstag, and also one vote in the Bundesrat.[100]

There were 154,000 inhabitants in 1914. More than 95 percent of the population was Protestant. The capital was Detmold.

Mecklenburg-Schwerin

(1813–1871)

The Duchy of Mecklenburg-Schwerin was formed in 1701 and it became a Grand Duchy in 1815. It was a member state of the Germanic Confederation from 1815 to 1866. Mecklenburg-Schwerin sided with Prussia during the 1866 war, and afterward became a member state of the North German Confederation in 1867, and then a member state of the imperial German Empire in 1871. Despite conventions with Prussia dating back to 1849, the formal convention between Mecklenburg-Schwerin and Prussia about the military was not ratified until 2 January 1873. Special note was taken in the convention to ensure that cost differentials between Mecklenburg uniforms and Prussian uniforms were accounted for. After the reunification of Germany in 1990, Mecklenburg became part of the new state of Mecklenburg-Vorpommern.

Friedrich Franz III succeeded his father Paul Frederick and served as the Grand Duke from 1883 until his mysterious death in 1897. Some say it was an asthmatic attack, others suicide. He was openly homosexual but was married to Anastasia Mikhailovna of Russia. They had three children, the youngest of whom, Cecile, married the Kaiser's son, Wilhelm, the Crown Prince.[101] His son, Frederick Francis IV, followed him and was the last Grand Duke of Mecklenburg-Schwerin.

The grand duchy was a monarchy limited by the representation of two estates. There was no parliament. Mecklenburg was the closest thing to medieval serfdom in Germany. Mecklenburg was so backward that Bismarck once said, "If one day the world will be destroyed, I'll move to Mecklenburg because there everything happens at least a hundred years later." Serfdom was eliminated in Mecklenburg in 1820. However, it was replaced by a citizenship

99 (Koenig, 2010)
100 (Krüger, 1915), p. 316.
101 (Tice, 2010), p. 5.

system that was very similar.[102] Under the old feudal system, landowners were responsible for the workers when they became old or disabled. Under the new system, landowners were only responsible to those workers who had been granted a "right of establishment" by the landowner. As a result, landowners kept few permanent workers, and granted the right of establishment to few.

It was not a right of all residents of Mecklenburg, but rather a privilege granted by the landowner. A side result of this system was that residents were not citizens of Mecklenburg as much as they were citizens of the city or village in which they obtained their right of establishment. Residents who did not have the right of establishment could not get married, start a permanent home, or have children. The ruling class refused to grant the right of establishment to a large part of the population, who were temporary laborers for their entire lives. They were given only a limited right to residence, only for as long as they had work. As a result, it was fair to say that many Mecklenburgers were homeless inside their own country.

The byproduct was that Mecklenburg had the third highest emigration rate in Europe. 261,000 Mecklenburgers left their home country (the Grand Duchies of Mecklenburg-Schwerin and Mecklenburg-Strelitz) between 1820 and 1890. Without the right of establishment, the lower classes did not have any prospects for the future in Mecklenburg.

Between 1850 and 1890, approximately 146,000 Mecklenburgers emigrated overseas, most going to the United States of America. This loss of population was most apparent in the rural farmland. Eighty-eight and one-half percent of all emigrants came from rural areas, most from the manor houses of noble and titled major landowners. Despite the emigration, the total population grew between 1830 and 1850. New births could not make up for the high number of emigrants between 1850 and 1905 and the population in the rural areas dropped by 25,000. After 1871, the number of people who moved overseas decreased and internal migration increased. More people willing to emigrate went to cities and industrial towns outside of Mecklenburg, such as the areas around Berlin. Almost one-third of the people who were born in Mecklenburg lived outside of their home state.

There were 648,000 people living in Mecklenburg-Schwerin in 1914 of which 97 percent was Protestant.[103] The capital was Schwerin. The grand duchy was a total of 13,161 km². The soldiers were concentrated in the 17th Infantry Division of the Prussian IX Army Corps.

Mecklenburg-Strelitz

(1813–1871)

The Grand Duchy of Mecklenburg-Strelitz was a member state of the German Confederation from 1815 to 1866. It consisted of two detached parts, the duchy of Strelitz to the East of Mecklenburg-Schwerin, and the principality of Ratzeburg in the West. Mecklenburg-Strelitz attempted to stay neutral during the war of 1866 until Bismarck pressured the Grand Duke by threatening occupation; shortly afterward, they joined Prussia. A military convention was signed 9 November 1868 and a further convention was concluded in December 1872. A strange anomaly existed, called the Grand Ducal Military Department in Neustrelitz, which provided a quasi-War Ministry that gave the Grand Duke some sense of sovereignty. After the Austro-Prussian War, it became a member state of the North German Confederation in 1867. Mecklenburg-Strelitz was a member state of the German Empire in 1871.

---

102 (Krüger, 1915), p. 313.
103 (*Kaiserliches Statistisches Amt, 1914*)

Adolph VI, the Grand Duke, was the cousin of the Grand Duke of Mecklenburg-Schwerin, Friedrich-Franz. Adolph, a 35-year-old bachelor, mysteriously killed himself several months before the end of the war (Feb 1918) when his long-term love affair with Mafalda Salvatini was discovered. She was an Italian opera singer, with whom he had two illegitimate sons. The next in line, Duke Karl-Michael, hated Germany, lived in Russia, and served in the Army of the Tsar. So, when the war ended there was no Grand Duke; therefore, the cousin (Fredrick Franz IV of Mecklenburg Schwerin, the regent) abdicated from both Mecklenburg Schwerin and Mecklenburg-Strelitz. Karl-Michael renounced his claim in a letter in 1914 but it did not get delivered until 1919 due to the Russian revolution. Eventually, Karl-Michael was allowed to adopt an heir and the line lives on.

The form of government was a monarchy limited by a representation of estates, and like Mecklenburg-Schwerin, there was no parliament. Mecklenburg-Strelitz maintained feudal serfdom in a way very similar to Mecklenburg-Schwerin.[104]

The population was 108,000 residents in 1914 of which 97 percent was Protestant. The capital was Neustrelitz. The grand duchy was a total of 2,930 km².[105] The small military contingent was concentrated in Second Battalion Großherzoglich Mecklenburgisches Grenadier-Regiment Nr. 89 and a battery of artillery.

Oldenburg

(1813–1871)

The Duchy of Oldenburg was a member state of the German Confederation from 1815 to 1866 and in 1829 was renamed, the Grand Duchy of Oldenburg. The Grand Duchy consisted of three widely separated portions of territory: the Duchy of Oldenburg, the Principality of Lübeck, and the Principality of Birkenfeld close to Trier. In 1866, Oldenburg sided with Prussia against Austria and after the Austro-Prussian War, became a member state of the North German Confederation in 1867. The Oldenburg military became a contingent of the Prussian army on 15 July 1867. Oldenburg became a member state of the German Empire in 1871.

The first child of Grand Duke Friedrich August and his first wife, HRH Princess Elisabeth of Prussia was Sophie Charlotte, who married the Kaiser's second oldest son, Eitel Friedrich. She was considered the best looking and wealthiest of the Kaiser's daughters-in-law. They first met at the wedding of the Crown Prince to Cecile.[106] They had a rocky relationship with multiple accusations of infidelity. There were no children born of the union that ended in divorce.

Oldenburg was a hereditary constitutional monarchy and was considered one of the most liberal in Germany. Parliament consisted of one chamber of 40 members known as the Landtag and direct secret voting was open to all taxpayers. Provincial councils of 15 members each governed the local affairs of Birkenfeld and Lübeck. Interestingly, the finances of each constituent state of the grand duchy were kept and managed separately.[107] Oldenburg had one vote in the Bundesrat and three members in the Reichstag. Oldenburg was by and large a protestant country, and the Grand Duke was required to be a member of the Lutheran Church.[108] It was also largely agricultural, though many rural residents moved to the cities.

[104] (Krüger, 1915), p. 313.
[105] (*Kaiserliches Statistisches Amt, 1914*)
[106] (Tice, 2010)
[107] (Krüger, 1915), p. 313.
[108] (Sacher, 1911)

The population of the three combined areas was 516,000 in 1914 of which 83 percent was protestant.[109] The capital was Oldenburg. The grand duchy was a total of 6,428 km². The soldiers were concentrated in Oldenburgisches Infanterie-Regiment Nr. 91 of the 19th Infantry Division, which formed part of the Prussian X Army Corps. Oldenburgisches Dragoner-Regiment Nr. 19, served initially in 1914 with 9th Cavalry Division under HKK 2.

Schaumburg-Lippe

(1813–1871)

The Principality of Schaumburg-Lippe, a German state since 1280, was a member state of the Germanic Confederation from 1815 to 1866. In 1854, Schaumburg-Lippe joined the Prussian Customs Union (Zollverein). In 1866, Schaumburg-Lippe sided with Austria against Prussia during the Austro-Prussian War. In 1867, Schaumburg-Lippe joined Prussia in a military union. After the Austro-Prussian, it became a member state of the North German Confederation in 1867 and a member state of the German Empire in 1871.

Adolf I served as Prince of Schaumburg-Lippe until 1893. His son George (who married Princess Marie Anne of Saxe-Altenburg) succeeded him. George's younger brother, Adolf, married the Kaiser's sister, Victoria (also known as Moretta). He was not her first love, but her relationship with Prince Alexander of Battenberg was politically unacceptable to both the Kaiser and Bismarck. A second prospect fell through when she would not convert to Catholicism to marry the Crown Prince of Portugal. She then left for England to spend time with her grandmother, Queen Victoria. Despairing of finding true love, Moretta agreed to the marriage to Adolf, much to her brother's relief.

Moretta suffered a miscarriage early in the marriage, and they had no further children. She contemplated divorce, as she believed she was in love with Adolf's nephew. Prince Adolf died in 1916 and she asked the Kaiser's permission to marry the nephew. He denied the request. Some sources indicate that Moretta may have suffered from porphyria also, as her sister Charlotte had inherited the disease.

The reigning prince at the end of the war was Adolph II, George's son. After the war and the fall of the German Empire, Moretta was allowed to live in Germany and she moved to a castle in Bonn. In 1927, when she was 62, she met a young Russian refugee and professional waiter, Alexander Zubkov, who was 27 years old. He had passed himself off as a noble Russian émigré, but was in fact, a penniless con man. She married him in November of that year. Her family was shocked with the news of her marriage, and they broke off relations with her. She did not care, and she defended her marriage, "Nobody's consent—not even the Kaiser's—is required for my marriage. It is incorrect to say that he has refused consent as such a step would be unnecessary, owing to the fact that the Kaiser is not head of the Schaumburg Lippe family. In fact nobody's consent is required." Moretta was scorned and ridiculed throughout Europe after the marriage. Zubkov delighted in the money he could make by staging photo-ops and granting interviews as the Kaiser's brother-in-law. He quickly spent her fortune, and she had to auction her belongings. Zubkov was exiled from Germany and Moretta filed for divorce, but died on 13 November 1929 before the case came to court. Zubkov was on his way to attend his wife's funeral when he was arrested for violating a law expelling all Russian parvenus from German soil. He died in poverty in Luxembourg in 1936.[110]

---

[109] (*Kaiserliches Statistisches Amt, 1914*)
[110] (Royal Musings, 2008)

The principality was a hereditary constitutional monarchy whose constitution called for a parliament of one house. This consisted of 15 members with two appointed by the Prince, two elected by the clergy, one by the professors, three by cities, and seven in rural communities. The vote was universal, direct, and secret. Schaumburg-Lippe sent one member to the Bundesrat and one deputy to the Reichstag.[111]

Schaumburg-Lippe was the smallest of the independent states with a population of about 48,000 in 1914. The great bulk of the population, 94 percent, was Lutheran. [112] The capital was Bückeburg, and the tiny principality was made up of 340 km². The principality had a limited ceremonial function with the Westfälisches Jäger Batallion Nr. 7 of the Prussian army.

Waldeck-Pyrmont
(1813–1871)

The Principality of Waldeck-Pyrmont, a German state since 1625, was a member state of the Germanic Confederation from 1815 to 1866. Waldeck-Pyrmont consisted of two separated areas. The smaller of the two, Pyrmont, was a mere 67 km². In 1866, the principality sided with Prussia against Austria. Waldeck-Pyrmont was governed by Prussia as the result of a treaty started in 1867 and renewed every 10 years with the proviso that it could be canceled on two-year's notice. A Prussian appointed *Landesdirector* conducted the government in the name of the prince. The officials of the State took an oath of allegiance to the King of Prussia. The Prince of Waldeck reserved very few rights and was restricted to paying off his debt that was accruing with an interest rate of 32 percent.[113] After the Austro-Prussian War, it became a member state of the North German Confederation in 1867 and agreed a convention with Prussia the same year. It became a member state of the German Empire in 1871.

George Victor was the Prince until 1893. His son Prince Friedrich, the last prince of Waldeck-Pyrmont, succeeded him. George Victor's sister, Helena, married Queen Victoria's youngest son. They were married for only two years before Leopold died from a fall; he was a hemophiliac. She and their two children continued to live in England.

Waldeck-Pyrmont was a hereditary constitutional monarchy whose parliament had one chamber known as the Landtag. There were 15 members of the Landtag, three of whom represented Pyrmont. Waldeck-Pyrmont had one vote in the Bundesrat and one in the Reichstag.

The population in 1914 was 63,000. The population was almost wholly (98 percent) Protestant.[114] The capital was Arolsen. The area was 1121 km². There was no special military relationship between this principality and any unit.

---

[111] (Krüger, 1915), p. 316.
[112] *(Kaiserliches Statistisches Amt, 1914)*
[113] (Krüger, 1915), pg. 315.
[114] *(Kaiserliches Statistisches Amt, 1914)*

STATES THAT CEASED TO EXIST PRIOR TO 1871

Frankfurt am Main.

(1813–1866)

The Free City of Frankfurt, a German state since the 14th century, was a member state of the Germanic Confederation between 1815 and 1866. In 1815 after the Congress of Vienna, Frankfurt again became a free city and in 1816 was made the seat of the German Confederation Parliament. The city joined the German *Zollverein* in 1836. In the war of 1866, Frankfurt was on the Austrian side. On July 16, the Prussian troops, under General Vogel von Falkenstein, entered the town. A fine of 25,000,000 florins was exacted. Rather than pay in full, the city voted itself out of existence and into a union with Prussia, which reduced the fine to 6 million florins. On 18 October, it was formally incorporated into the Prussian state. In 1871, Prince Bismarck and Jules Favre signed the treaty that concluded the Franco-German War in the Swan Hotel (*Hotel zum Schwan*), and it is consequently known as the Peace of Frankfurt.[115]

The population of Frankfurt steadily increased throughout the 19th century. The numbers shown in 1817 were 41,458; in 1840, 55,269; in 1864, 77,372; in 1875, 103,136; in 1890, 179,985; and in 1905, including the incorporated suburban districts, 334,951, of whom 175,909 were Protestants, 88,457 were Roman Catholic and 21,974 were Jewish.

Hanover

(1813–1866: *Hannover*)

The Electorate of Hanover (*Hannover*) was a German state originating from the 15th century Principality of Calenberg-Göttingen. In 1714, George Louis of Hanover became George I, who ruled both Great Britain and Hanover. Four successive monarchs ruled both Great Britain and Hanover. After the fall of Napoleon, it was renamed the Kingdom of Hanover in 1814. The ruling family was the Guelphs. The friction between the Guelphs and the Prussian royal house was felt in every aspect of life—land, religion, and politics. Hanover was a member state of the Germanic Confederation between 1815 and 1866. There was a personal union (where the ruler of two houses or states is the same person) between Hanover and the United Kingdom. As a member of the British royal family, the King of Hanover was also the Duke of Cumberland. This union ended in 1837 on the accession of Queen Victoria because the succession laws (Salic Laws) in Hanover prevented a female inheriting the title of King of Hanover, if there was any surviving male heir. This separated the crowns of Great Britain and Hanover after a union of 123 years and brought Ernest August, Duke of Cumberland, to the Hanoverian throne. He acted quickly to annul the constitution. The Göttingen Seven (two of whom were the brothers Grimm) actively argued against any changes.[116]

In 1849, after the failure of St. Paul's Parliament at Frankfurt, the King of Hanover joined with the sovereigns of Prussia and Saxony to form the "Three Kings' Alliance." This union with Prussia was a short-term failure, and the King of Hanover and the King of Saxony soon transferred their support to Austria and became a member of the "Four Kings' Alliance." Hanover joined the *Zollverein* in 1851.

---

[115] (Wawro, 1998), p. 277. Hotel zum Schwan was one of the oldest and best-known hotels in Germany. Run as a hotel between 1592 and 1919, the building was destroyed in an air raid in 1944 and never rebuilt after the Second World War.

[116] (Hettinga, 2001), p. 149.

George V, the new King of Hanover (1851), was totally blind and tried to sweep away the constitution of 1848.[117] He knew the Hanoverian parliament would resist, so the king appealed to the Germanic Confederation in 1855. The diet of the German Confederation declared the Hanoverian constitution of 1848 to be invalid. Hanover supported the German Confederation during the wars with Denmark.

As war approached in 1866, George V vacillated between Prussia and Austria. Over the objections of his parliament, he threw his lot in with Austria. The decision was made after the Diet of the German Confederation voted to mobilize against Prussia on 14 June 1866. Prussia requested Hanover remain neutral during the war but King George refused. Prussian troops then crossed his frontier, but the Hanoverians were victorious at the ensuing battle of Langensalza on 27 June 1866. Langensalza is of particular interest since it is one of the very few battles where an army equipped with muzzle-loaded rifles won over the Prussian army equipped with breech-loaded Dreyse rifles. The arrival of overwhelming reinforcements from Prussia compelled Hanover to capitulate two days later. What is regularly glossed over is that the Prussians came at them from two sides. Prussia geographically surrounded Hanover and classically out-maneuvered the armies of King George.[118]

By the terms of this surrender, the king was not to reside in Hanover; his officers were to take no further part in the war; and his stores became the property of Prussia. Prussia saw a great opportunity to connect their Eastern lands to their Western possessions. Prussia could be geographically contiguous, but a few pieces of real estate stood in the way, and Hanover was the biggest. The decree of 10 September 1866, formally annexed Hanover to Prussia. King George appealed in vain from exile in Austria to the powers of Europe to restore his kingdom. In 1867, King George V of Hanover agreed to accept Prussian bonds as compensation for the confiscation of his estates in Hanover. In 1868, due to his continued hostility to Prussia, the Prussian government sequestrated this property. Known as the *Welfenfonds,* or *Reptilienfonds,* it was employed as a secret fund to combat the intrigues of the Guelphs in various parts of Europe. In 1892, it was arranged that the interest should be paid to the Duke of Cumberland. It was this secret fund that Bismarck used in 1871 to bribe the Bavarian King Ludwig II to write to Wilhelm I of Prussia and urge him to take the imperial crown.[119]

Reptilienfonds is still used today in German language as a kind of nickname for secret funds spent by the government beyond Parliamentarian control and the control of auditors. It is said that Bismarck himself, (who wanted to use the money to "chase the reptiles back into their caves") defined the name.[120] Bismarck used parts of these funds to bribe journalists and to systematically swing public opinion—not only against the Guelphs, but also other political enemies. It was well-known that Bismarck had systematically bribed the biggest news agencies of Imperial Germany, *Wolffs Telegraphisches Bureau* (W.T.B.).

Many of the Hanoverians remained loyal to their Hanoverian sovereign. A substantial political party in the Imperial Reichstag, the Guelph party, continued to agitate and to hope for a restoration. This nostalgia and loyalty failed to bring about the return of the king to Hanover. George died in June 1878. His son, Ernest August III maintained his claim to the crown of Hanover. He refused to reconcile with Prussia. Consequently, the imperial German government refused to allow him to take possession of the Duchy of Brunswick, which he inherited on the extinction of the elder branch of his family in 1884. The Empire also refused

[117] The King of Hanover was also the Duke of Brunswick and Duke of Cumberland.
[118] (Horsetzky, 1905), Tafeln XXXI.
[119] (Feuchtwanger, 2001), p. 58.
[120] (Nöll v. d. Nahmer, 1968)

to allow him to take possession of the Duchy of Brunswick when Prince Albert of Prussia, the Regent, died. You always see pictures of Hanoverian male royalty wearing the uniform of Austria until Ernest August married the daughter of Kaiser Wilhelm II, Princess Viktoria Luise on 13 May 1913. Ernest August swore his oath of allegiance to the Kaiser, was promoted to the rank of a Rittmeister and took command over the 4th squadron of Husaren-Regiment von Zieten (Brandenburgisches) Nr. 3, a regiment, which one was under the honorary command of his grandfather King George V.

The Kingdom contained an area of 38,511 km^2 and the total population, was approximately 3,000,000 in 1914. The proportion of urban to rural population was roughly three to one. Religious statistics show that 84 percent of the inhabitants belonged to the Evangelical Lutheran Church, 15 percent to the Roman Catholic, and less than one percent to the Jewish communities.[121] Hanover as a province of Prussia had 19 members in the *Reichstag* and 36 in the Prussian parliament (*Landtag).*

Hesse-Cassel

(1813–1866: *Hessen (-Cassel)Kurhessen*)

The Electorate of Hesse, a German state since 1567, was a member state of the German Confederation from 1815 to 1866. Frederick William, the Elector of Hesse, joined the North German Confederation. In 1848, he dissolved the parliament and placed the country under martial law. Having major problems with the military that had sworn allegiance to the constitution, the Elector appealed for aid to the German Confederation diet, which passed a decree of "intervention." In 1850, an Austrian and Bavarian force occupied the electorate.

Prussia objected violently to the occupation because it had an agreement with the Electorate of Hesse-Cassel to have use of the roads to connect Prussia's eastern and western provinces. Prussian troops also entered the electorate. Shots were actually exchanged, but Prussia was in no condition to press the issue, and the diplomatic contest that followed became the Austrian triumph at Olmütz (1851). In 1866, the elector allied with Austria; the Prussians occupied the electorate and the elector was taken prisoner. By the treaty of Prague, Hesse-Cassel was annexed to Prussia and Frederick William was guaranteed his personal property. The property was sequestered in 1868 because of Frederick William's intrigues against Prussia; part of the property's income was paid to other relatives, and part, together with certain castles and palaces, was assigned to the towns of Philippsthal and Philippsthal Barchfeld.

Hesse-Homburg

(1813–1866: *Hessen (Homburg)*)

The Landgraviate of Hesse became a German state in 1708. It was a member state of the German Confederation between 1815 and 1866. It was comprised of two parts: the district of Homburg on the east side of the Rhine and the district of Meisenheim, which was added in 1815, on the west side of the same river. When the last ruler (Ferdinand) died on 24 March 1866, Louis III, Grand-Duke of Hesse-Darmstadt, inherited Hesse-Homburg. Louis was forced to cede his new possession to Prussia in restitution, as Hesse-Darmstadt had fought on the side of Austria during the war between Austria and Prussia.

---

121 (*Kaiserliches Statistisches Amt, 1914*)

Hohenzollern-Hechingen

(1813–1849)

The Principality of Hohenzollern-Hechingen, a German state since 1576, became a member state of the Germanic Confederation between 1815 and 1849. In 1849 after the abdication of Prince Frederick William, the principality was incorporated into Prussia. It is often confused as part of Hohenzollern-Sigmaringen, when in reality it was part of the province of Rhineland. The family of Hohenzollern-Hechingen became extinct in 1869.

Hohenzollern-Sigmaringen

(1813–1849)

The Principality of Sigmaringen, a German state since 1576, became a member state of the Germanic Confederation between 1815 and 1849. In 1849, it was incorporated into Prussia, not as an independent province, but as a governmental district of the province of the Rhineland. This branch of the royal family was Catholic.

Hohenzollern was the name of a castle that stood on the hill of Zollern just south of Hechingen and gave its name to the Kaiser's family. Due to the political troubles of 1848, Prince Frederick William of Hohenzollern-Hechingen and Prince Charles Anton of Hohenzollern-Sigmaringen abdicated their principalities in favor of the King of Prussia. There was a serious proposal to raise Prince Leopold of Hohenzollern-Sigmaringen (1835–1905) to the Spanish throne. This initiative was the alleged cause of the Franco-Prussian War.[122] In 1908, the head of this branch of the Hohenzollerns was called simply Prince of Hohenzollern. In 1866, Prince Charles of Hohenzollern-Sigmaringen was chosen Prince of Rumania, becoming king in 1881. As this territory was Prussian, the 114th Infantry Regiment from Baden provided a castle guard company.

Holstein

(1815–1866)

A fiefdom of Denmark since the 15th century, the Duchy of Holstein was a member of the Germanic Confederation from 1815 to 1864; therefore, the King of Denmark was a member of the German Confederation during that time. The King of Denmark attempted to incorporate the Duchy of Schleswig into Denmark as the result of a dispute about ownership of that duchy. This action led to the second Danish war in 1864. The victorious Austria was awarded administration of Holstein and agreed to give Prussia free access on the roads and railroads to the Prussian administrated province of Schleswig. The province came under dispute during the 1866 war and was awarded to Prussia and incorporated into that kingdom at the end of the war.

Lauenburg

(1848–1865)

The Duchy of Lauenburg was a duchy of Denmark that Prussia purchased after 1865. In 1848, during the first war between Prussia and Denmark, Lauenburg was occupied at her own request by some Hanoverian troops and was then administered for three years under the Germanic Confederation. Denmark incorporated the duchy in 1853. After the war of 1864, between Denmark and Prussia/Austria, Lauenburg was ceded with Schleswig and Holstein to Prussia/Austria. By the peace treaty of Gastein in 1865, Austria sold her claim over

122 (Perris, 1912), pp. 243–244.

Lauenburg to Prussia for £300,000. Lauenburg entered the North German Confederation in 1866 and the Imperial German Empire in 1871 as part of Prussia. Lauenburg retained its constitution and its special privileges until 1876, when it was completely incorporated into the kingdom of Prussia. Due to this semi-autonomous status, Prussia is referred to as the Kingdom of Prussia and Lauenburg, as noted in Art. I of the Imperial Constitution.[123]

Limburg

(1839–1866)

The Duchy of Limburg was part of the Dutch province of Limburg until the Treaty of London in 1839. This treaty split the province between Belgium and the Netherlands. Due to cultural and language differences the smaller Duchy of Limburg on the eastern side of the province was added to the Germanic Confederation. Limburg was held in personal union with the ruler of the Netherlands, and therefore, the ruler of the Netherlands was part of the Germanic Confederation. This union ended in 1866 when the second Treaty of London made Luxembourg and Limburg integral parts of the Kingdom of the Netherlands, and withdrew any connection with the Germanic Confederation.

Nassau

(1813–1866)

The Duchy of Nassau was a member state and an independent and sovereign duchy of the Germanic Confederation from 1815 to 1866. In 1866, Duke Adolph joined the Austrian cause, sent his troops into the field, and asked the Landtag for money after-the-fact. The two chambers of parliament refused and Adolph became a fugitive who fled from the Prussian troops. On 3 October 1866, Nassau was formally incorporated into the kingdom of Prussia. In 1867, the deposed Duke Adolph entered into an agreement with Prussia by which he retained a few castles and received an indemnity for renouncing his claim to the Duchy of Nassau. In 1890, he became the Grand-Duke of Luxemburg.

This duchy should not be confused with a province of Prussia, Hesse-Nassau, that was formed in 1867–1868 out of the territories which accrued to Prussia after the war of 1866, namely, the Landgraviate (*Landgrafschaft*) of Hesse-Cassel and the Duchy of Nassau, in addition to the greater part of the territory of Frankfurt-on-Main, parts of the Grand-Duchy of Hesse Darmstadt, and the territory of Hesse Homburg. In 1864, the duchy contained 468,311 inhabitants, of whom 242,000 were Protestants, 215,000 Roman Catholics, and 7,000 Jews. The province had an area of 15,700 km^2, and a population in 1914 of 2,323,000.[124] The province had 14 representatives to the Reichstag.

Saxe-Gotha

(1813–1826: *Sachsen-Gotha*)

The Principality of Saxe-Gotha, also known as Saxe-Gotha-Altenburg, was a German state in Thuringia beginning in 1572, was a member state of the German Confederation in 1815, and in 1826 it merged with Saxe-Coburg into Saxe-Coburg-Gotha when the original royal family died without heirs.

---

123 (Howard, 1906). See Appendix A.

124 (*Kaiserliches Statistisches Amt, 1914*)

Saxe-Hildburghausen

(1813–1826: *Sachsen-Hildburghausen*)

The Principality of Saxe-Hildburghausen, a German state in Thuringia from 1680, was a member state of the German Confederation in 1815. In 1810, a princess of Saxe-Hildburghausen, Therese, was married to Crown Prince Ludwig of Bavaria, who became king of Bavaria 15 years later; this event is the reason for the Oktoberfest, held annually in Munich. In 1826, it was ceded to Saxe-Meinigen and became part of it.

Schleswig

(1864–1866)

A fiefdom of Denmark since the 11th century, Denmark attempted to integrate the Duchy of Schleswig into the Danish kingdom in 1848; this caused a swift and immediate reaction from Prussia and led to the First Danish War. While Prussia won the war, all territory was returned with the promises of autonomy. Denmark tried again in 1864, which led to the Second Danish War, this time between the Germanic Confederation and Denmark. Prussia and Austria were given control of the provinces of Schleswig and Holstein respectively. This province was disputed in the War of 1866, and after the war, the Duchy was incorporated into the Kingdom of Prussia.

THE REICHSLANDE-IMPERIAL TERRITORY

Alsace-Lorraine

(*Elsaß-Lothringen*)

This territory, also known as the *Reichslande*, was a prize seized from France after the Franco-Prussian war of 1871. It was a Reich's province until it became a quasi-state in 1911, but never an actual state of the German Empire. The Kaiser appointed the head administrator, who was called the *Reichsstatthalter*. The province was split into three sections: upper Alsace (which was the most southern), lower Alsace that was the more northern, and Lorraine, which included the fortress city of Metz. Lorraine was the most culturally French of the areas, and French was the primary language. The majority of the population did speak some German or an Alsatian dialect of German. Historically and realistically, there was no Alsace-Lorraine prior to the Franco-Prussian War. A common myth asserts that there was someone known as an Alsace-Lorrainer. There was Alsace, and there was Lorraine and they were joined for political expediency, but there was no Alsace-Lorrainer. The populations were not homogeneous. Alsace often held sway over Lorraine due to the immigration of German middle classes into Alsace.[125] In 1913, the president of Stanford University noted that the region was tied to France by culture, to Prussia by government, and to Bavaria by economics.[126]

There were problems with this area from a constitutional perspective. The peace treaty of 1871 ceded all of France's rights to the title and territory of Alsace-Lorraine to the German Empire, but the imperial Constitution made no provision for the disposition and administration of such a territory. [127] The imperial Constitution assumed that, between the individual territories and the imperial power, a state power was interposed to execute many laws and

[125] (Silverman, 1972), pp. 6–8.
[126] (Neiberg, 2011), p. 59.
[127] However, the railroad was not included and was eventually purchased by Germany.

functions. Alsace-Lorraine was not a state. The attempted solution was to make the Kaiser the head of state for Alsace-Lorraine and to make it an imperial territory. The Kaiser appointed the Statthalter as his personal representative. The powers of the Statthalter were attached to the person not to the office. Prior to statehood, an emasculated territorial committee existed in place of a parliament. They had 15 representatives in the Reichstag, but zero in the Bundesrat.[128]

There was much outcry and confusion about citizenship immediately after unification, when Alsace-Lorraine moved from French control to imperial German control. The residents of Alsace-Lorraine were given the option to retain French citizenship, but they had to declare their intent and to move to French territory by 1 October 1872. Those who did not leave were automatically granted German citizenship. A group of 100,000, called the optants, had declared their intent to leave but for various reasons did not. This issue was never resolved, thus creating 100,000 individuals who had no citizenship. Many minors returned to France to avoid service in the German military. Forty-five percent of the French Foreign Legion between 1882 and 1908 originally was from Alsace-Lorraine. It is estimated that in the first 15 years of German rule, 156,000 individuals left the Reichslande for France. As French citizens moved out, imperial German citizens from numerous states moved in. Many of these German citizens took jobs as civil servants for the empire in Alsace-Lorraine. By 1910, 12 percent of the population was German, and had immigrated into the Reichslande. This population percentage increased in the larger cities where between 30 and 41 percent of the population were immigrant Germans.[129]

In American terms, this area was Indian country. There was an eternal dilemma facing the Germans—should they govern Alsace-Lorraine as a conquered territory for national security purposes, or should they integrate Alsace-Lorraine into the German Empire? The Germans, who thought originally that Alsatians would welcome them as long-lost German brothers, found many parts of the population to be anti-German. Many aristocratic authorities and especially the military considered all people from Alsace-Lorraine to be highly untrustworthy and called them *Wackes*.[130] Draft evasion was a telling metric. In 1872, 20,000 out of 32,000 draftees failed to appear. By 1879, the draft evasion had dropped to 25 percent and by 1904 to 10 percent.[131] There were several reasons not to serve in the Prussian military. Much of them were economic, some religious. There was an urban–rural divide as well as a native–German immigrant divide; yet, some native inhabitants of Alsace and Lorraine embraced Germany. Many Germans came to view the Alsatians and those from Lorraine as disloyal Germans.

In May 1911, the rules were changed for Alsace-Lorraine as it moved closer to statehood. There was a constitution, yet it was not a state. Many historians overlook this fact. The Landtag for Alsace-Lorraine was to consist of two houses. In the upper house the Kaiser appointed one-half of the 36 members. Others were members by virtue of holding certain offices. The lower house had 60 members elected by secret ballot based on universal suffrage. These two chambers made the laws, but the Kaiser had an absolute veto. Alsace-Lorraine was represented in the Bundesrat by three votes, but they would not be counted if they provided a majority for Prussia; the territory elected 15 members to the Reichstag, but these were not allowed to vote on issues concerning the Reichslande.[132]

[128] (Silverman, 1972), pp. 36–64.
[129] (Silverman, 1972), pp. 65–69.
[130] (Kramer, 1997), p. 109. Wackes was a colloquial pronunciation of the word vagabond.
[131] (Silverman, 1972), p. 72.
[132] (Silverman, 1972), pp. 144–147.

Another myth is that the German government used a repressive program of coercion to impose its will on the people from Alsace-Lorraine. In fact, the empire vacillated between coercion and conciliation and never really determined which was the right approach. There was a reasonable chance of German success in integrating the province into the German Empire until the Zabern affair of 1913–1914.[133]

That event tested the German imperial system and made it incredibly clear that Alsace-Lorraine was a second-class part of the imperial territory.[134] Zabern was a garrison town of 9,000 (mostly Catholic) in lower Alsace that since 1890 had housed the mostly Lutheran 2. Oberrheinisches Infanterie-Regiment Nr. 99. The major protagonist was 20-year old Lieutenant Günther Freiherr v. Forstner, who had been educated at the upper Prussian cadet school. While he retained airs of aristocratic privilege, the townspeople thought of him as a buffoon. He made disparaging remarks about his recruits from Alsace-Lorraine and the French Foreign Legion. He referred to the local population as *Wackes*.[135] The claim was that during his instruction hour, he offered his recruits ten mark instead of three months in prison, should they stab a rowdy *Wackes*. The paper published this incident and soon mobs threatened Lieutenant Forstner. Both the Commander of the Infantry Regiment 99 and the Burgomaster were involved unsuccessfully, and the fire brigade was ordered to drive off the crowd with hoses, which they did neither enthusiastically, nor successfully. A company of soldiers from the garrison arrived on the scene and arrested those who refused to leave.[136]

Lieutenant Forstner was reprimanded, but on the very next day, he and several other officers had an alcohol-induced altercation with some local youths, and one of the officers, a Lieutenant Schad, called out the guard with fixed bayonets. This situation continued to simmer until 29 November when the same Lieutenant Forstner went shopping for chocolates with four armed soldiers. Some of the locals made fun of him, and the same Lieutenant Schad started arresting locals. The regimental commander, Colonel von Reuter, deployed 60 men and ordered them to load rifles and barked commands with drums beating.[137]

Lieutenant Forstner was transferred to Infanterie-Regiment Graf Schwerin (3.Pommersches) Nr. 14, and he was killed in action on the Eastern Front in 1915. Lieutenant Schad was transferred to Füsilier-Regiment Königin (Schleswig-Holsteinisches) Nr. 86, and while he survived the war, he was not promoted beyond *Oberleutnant*.[138]

The key issue revolved around the rights of the local people versus those of the army. Did the army have the right to act as police in arresting citizens and quelling unrest? Who had the right to discipline members of the army? Should the local authorities and local courts have jurisdiction? Could the Kaiser and the army maintain their personal authority in this matter? As it turned out, the army whitewashed and sidestepped the constitutional question.[139] The residents of the Reichslande learned without question that their constitution had little value. While the war interrupted the outcome of this incident, it certainly exposed nerves.[140] However, the Reichstag made the first vote of censure against a sitting government in German history. They condemned the behavior of the German government with a vote

---

[133] (Silverman, 1972), p. 1–3.

[134] (Macky, 1991)

[135] "Wackes" was a very negative slang word derived from "vagabond" and suggesting that all "native" people in Alsace and Lorraine would be little more than begging and stealing "underclass" proletariats.

[136] (Macky, 1991), pp. 29–37.

[137] (Macky, 1991), pp. 37–39.

[138] (Lundström, 2009)

[139] (Blackbourn, 2003), pp. 285–286.

[140] (Macky, 1991)

of 293–54. As a result of this "Zabern Affair," many Reichstag deputies further protested by not rising when the Kaiser came to the chamber to ceremonially close the annual session.[141]

Their military superiors generally considered the soldiers from Alsace-Lorraine unreliable. Those who were considered a significant problem were transferred to the Eastern front against the Russians and away from the French. It became a self-fulfilling prophecy: the sense among the soldiers that the Reich had rejected them tended to increase their unreliability. Large-scale transfers to the Eastern front were disastrous to unit morale because loyal troops from Alsace-Lorraine considered themselves humiliated. By the same token, desertion was very rare within the remainder of the German forces with a rate of only one per 10,000 soldiers. Compare this rate to July 1917, when the desertion rate for soldiers from Alsace-Lorraine was 80 per 10,000.[142]

The capital was Straßburg (Strasbourg in French), the 24th largest city in the empire and was multicultural and bilingual. Catholics outnumbered Protestants 1.5 million to 400,000. The old French regime had given the Catholic clergy significant power. Total population in 1914 was approximately 1,900,000.[143] The land area had a total size of 14,522 km^2.

COLONIES

On 24 April 1884, Bismarck announced that the coast of southwest Africa was under the protectorate of the German Empire. The colonies eventually included: German Southwest Africa (today Namibia), German East Africa (much of present-day Tanzania), Togoland, (integrated into Ghana and the current Togo), Cameroon (divided after the war into French and British colonies), German New Guinea (now Papua, New Guinea,) Samoa, and Kiautschou (leased from China).[144] Over time, purchases and leases enlarged the size of many of these territories. Contrary to many myths, German involvement in its colonies was not significantly different than other imperial powers. Internally, it had a significant public impact. Some of the citizens reasoned that colonies indicated the nation's arrival as a great power. Many believed that colonial involvement would increase economic activity and enrich the homeland. For that reason, the belief was more important than the colonies themselves.[145] The truth is that colonialism had had little economic impact on Imperial Germany.

Historical assessments of German colonialism have varied widely. Fritz Fischer tied the colonies into Germany's war aims.[146] Hans-Ulrich Wehler focused on economics and Bismarck's attempts to unify support of the Junker-dominated political system. Wehler's views championed a great plan to reassure the bourgeoisie while using colonialism to divert the revolutionary tendencies of the proletariat. The colonies could be used to even out the eco-

---

141 (Neiberg, 2011), p. 61.

142 (Kramer, 1997), pp. 111–112.

143 (*Kaiserliches Statistisches Amt*, 1914)

144 *Kiautschou* (*Jiao Zhou*) in China was not really a colony but a *Schutzgebiet*, a kind of a protectorate directly under the command of the Navy and headed by a Navy governor with the rank of a commander (*Kapitän z.S.*). Therefore the 3rd Naval Infantry Battalion (3. *See-Bataillon*) in Qingdao and the Eastern Asian naval detachment in Beijing and Tianjin belonged to the Navy, whereas all other colonies belonged to the Imperial Colonial Office (*Reichskolonialamt*) and the occupation forces were named *Kaiserliche Schutztruppen* (Imperial Protection Forces). (*Kriegsministerium*, 1914), pp. 1348–1355. (*Kaiserliche Schutztruppen*) and *Marine-Kabinett* (Ed.) (*Kriegsministerium*, 1914), pp. 93–95 (*Schutzgebiet Kiautschou* including 3rd naval inf bn).

145 (Lerman, 2008), p. 33.

146 (Fischer, 1968)

nomic impact of downturns in the business cycle.[147] Today's accounts put more emphasis on the autonomy of ideology and politics.[148]

Why did imperial Germany involve itself in colonialism? Bismarck was originally opposed to the concept but changed his mind. He was not convinced that any colonies would be worth the expense and was concerned that the colonies would lead to undesirable international tension. Internal politics, the colonial movement inside Germany, and the splitting of the Liberal leadership seem to have convinced him to reconsider. Private German merchants entered into signed treaties with local rulers in East Africa. While Bismarck was reluctant to embrace these actions, he did not wish to alienate the German Colonial Association (1884: *Deutscher Kolonialverein*, renamed in 1887: *Deutsche Kolonialgesellschaft*). Consequently, he found himself in an unanticipated rivalry with Britain.[149]

Most Germans expected a colonial empire to be a moneymaker. Minimally, they anticipated that trading would produce profits for Germans in the homeland and that the colonies would be self-sufficient from a tax perspective. Unfortunately, the colonies were far from profitable.[150] Of the colonies, only Togo and Kiaochow were able to cover their expenses out of tax revenue on a consistent basis. Most merchants were not willing to follow-up their accepted concessions with investments until the government created adequate infrastructure. With the exception of the two colonies listed above, each colony required a substantial annual subsidy from the Reich. Not only were colonies expensive, but also there was an added intangible cost of damage to international relations with other colonial powers.[151]

England and Germany actually worked out their boundary disputes and there was an era of cooperation between England and Germany over the colonies in the 1890s. In 1890, there was a Helgoland-Zanzibar Treaty between imperial Germany and Great Britain. Germany agreed to abandon all claims concerning Zanzibar, Uganda and on the Kenyan and Somali coast. Wituland and Zanzibar became British in exchange for the tiny North Sea island of Helgoland. In addition, German South-West Africa (Namibia) obtained access to the Zambezi River through the Caprivi Strip.

Contrary to some notable myths, many of the indigenous people resisted efforts to transform them into capitalist peasant farmers. In 1904, there was a significant revolt in Southwest Africa and another one in East Africa in 1905. By the end of 1907, the revolts were crushed with enormous loss of African lives. In particular, the war against the Herero tribe in Southwest Africa may be considered a kind of systematic genocide. The need to dispatch a military force and the outbreak of the rebellions themselves provided fodder for criticism of the German colonial movement. In 1906, the opponents of colonialism defeated an appropriations request in the *Reichstag*. This resulted in Chancellor Bülow dissolving the Reichstag and holding a new election that became known as the 1907 Hottentot election. This election opened the door for reform of the colonial movement and the bourgeois support of the colonies.[152] Interesting to note, after the war, when the victorious powers stripped Germany of her colonies, the ostensible reason given was the unusually abusive German actions toward their colonial subjects.[153] Helgoland was the only new German territory that survived the Versailles Treaty of 1919.

[147] (Wehler, 1985), pp. 173–176.
[148] (Smith, 1996), pp. 430–432.
[149] (Smith, 1996), pp. 442–445.
[150] (Smith, 1996), pp. 440.
[151] (Smith, 1996), pp. 433–436.
[152] (Smith, 1996), p. 445.
[153] (Smith, 1996), p. 449.

CHAPTER 4

THE SOCIAL, POLITICAL, AND ECONOMIC STRUCTURE OF THE REICH

LINGUISTIC ANOMALIES

The first thing to understand when referencing German texts is that the German language in imperial Germany was not standardized. Just as the individual states retained much of their unique cultural foundations, so did the language. The myth that one could just look things up in a standardized dictionary was far from the truth. There were a slew of dictionaries and official languages that followed state or dialectic (*Mundart)* lines such as the *Wörterbuch der Elsässischen Mundarten*.

In 1876, Prussia tried to bring the dialects together, but the various states rejected the attempt. In 1879, Bavaria published its own grammar guide, followed by Austria and Prussia one year later. Using the Bavarian and Prussian rules, Konrad Duden published a more widely accepted dictionary. Its use spread slowly and only Württemberg accepted it.[1] Today the term "*Duden*" refers to the standardized dictionary of German language.

The General German Language Association was not founded until 1885, well after the foundation of the empire.[2] In June 1901, in order to make sure uniform grammar and spelling were adopted in all German-speaking states (including Austria and Switzerland), a second conference was called to promote spelling and grammar reform (*Beratungen über die Einheitlichkeit der deutschen Rechtschreibung).* Better known as *II Orthographische Konferenz,* the results of the conference gained a much wider acceptance and, in 1901, a lot of "th's" were abolished and replaced by a simple "t" (e.g., *Thal* became *Tal* or *Fürstenthum* that became *Fürstentum*). In several words and names, "k" replaced "c" except in Cassel and Cöln. Many other letter "c's" in words with a French background were turned into "z's," "ie" replaced the "i" that had a long pronunciation. These standards were generally accepted and turned into official regulations by December 1902.

The Kaiser initially opposed the changes and demanded that official documents be written in both forms until 1911. Many publishers did not adopt the changes because they did not wish to change their typeset. In theory, the Study Group for German Word Research (*Arbeitsgemeinschaft für deutsche Wortforschung*) did not reconcile this until 1939. That is why there are different spellings in texts written between 1871 and 1918. Additionally, there was

1 (Wikipedia, 2009).
2 (White, 1996), p. 131.

an unbelievably convoluted way for alphabetization that is often encountered where certain letter groups such as "sch" were treated as a single letter.

There is also confusion in abbreviations for the units themselves. You will often see the letter "J" substituted for the letter "I." This change was only done at the beginning of the word and was done to minimize the confusion with the letter "L." This convention was commonly found on signs, titles, and papers. A classic English language confusion is that J.R. means *Jäger* regiment; in fact, it stands for infantry regiment. (Please check postcard on picture page 51.)

THE POPULATION

There are many long-held misconceptions about the nature of the imperial German population. One of the most common-held mental pictures includes a middle-class farmer with a nuclear family and stout health. He lived on a well-stocked farm that had been in the family for generations. Some over-privileged and amazingly wealthy aristocrats ruled over him. He was inevitably Protestant. Nothing could be further from the truth. As was previously discussed, imperial Germany was a divergent patchwork of cultures. To understand this cultural diversity within the imperial German population, one needs to consider class structure, population movement, and religious preference. Membership in each of these classifications impacted the individual's views on such diverse issues as inheritance, voting, education, employment, and the government.

Class Structure

From a class-structure perspective, imperial German society was divided into three categories: the aristocracy, who were those with titles; the bourgeoisie, who were further sub-divided, but generally referred to as the middle class; and the proletariat, who were at or just below the poverty level—the manual laborers.

The Aristocracy—Nobility belonged to the *Adelstand*, which was divided into *Uradel*, or "old" nobility and *Briefadel*, or "patent nobility" (commoners elevated into the German nobility). Only a few German nobles could grant these patents. There were also various non-hereditary titles of nobility granted to members of certain orders. There were further subdivisions and a distinct pecking order such as *Hochadel* vs. *niederer Adel* (higher nobility vs. lower nobility).

Marriages were often considered unequal even though both parties came from noble families because they were from different levels of the nobility. Not everyone with a "von" in his or her name was noble. For the most part, if you wanted to differentiate noble families from the non-nobility, the "von" in noble names was abbreviated "v.," while it was left as "von" for non-nobles. Numerically, the aristocracy was a very small group consisting of between 15,000 and 17,000 families, many sharing a common last name.[3]

Historically, the aristocracy ranked with the monarchy. While many were impoverished; others had inherited great wealth. Landowners in the eastern parts of Prussia became quite wealthy after leveraging their estates. By 1911, the top 10 percent of the Prussian population owned 63 percent of the assets. Industry offered greater profitability than agriculture, as

---

[3] (Mommsen W. J., 1995), p. 114.

land ownership was only profitable around the margins of expanding cities. The aristocracy was invested in land, but the higher profit margin in industry meant that the aristocracy had to adapt. Because of the huge investments in mortgages and land costs, some 5,000 estates went into bankruptcy between 1885 and 1900.

Individuals who had invested in industry did extremely well. There were almost 10,000 millionaires by 1911. Some 21,000 Prussians allegedly made an annual income of over 100,000 marks.[4] Keep in mind that the aristocracy represented approximately one percent of the total population, while 70 percent of the officer cadets came from this one percent.[5]

Imperial Germany's national identity was built on the nobility. The noble families east of the Elbe River originally founded Prussia. Collectively, they became known as Junkers, a well-worn word that few people truly understand. They were the landed nobility—people who generated their income from the land and the estates that they owned. They had many privileges including a great deal of control over of the accession of officers into the military.

The three-tiered system of voting that the Junkers wielded inside the kingdom of Prussia was enormously influential. Basically, all male voters over the age of 25 were divided into three classes based on the amount of tax revenue they provided. The richest five percent, which included the Junkers, was Class One. The next richest 15 percent was Class Two. The remaining 80 percent was Class Three. Each class had an equal share of the vote for representatives to the Landtag or Prussian territorial parliament—the top five percent had as much clout as the bottom 80 percent; however, only 20 percent of the possible voters in Class Three turned out to vote.

Obviously, the Junkers were not willing to cede this advantage, as the Landtag was responsible for legislation covering commerce, tariffs, and banking. They benefited disproportionately from the tariff protectionism especially in the 1890s. The three-tiered system of voting kept the Class One members in charge of the Kingdom of Prussia. In exchange for these privileges, the Junkers were to give blind loyalty and fealty to the King of Prussia. When the King of Prussia became the Kaiser under the *Kleindeutschland* unification, the power of the Junkers grew. In 1894, these estate holders did support the founding of an agrarian league, but they supported neither socialism nor the mechanized wonders of the Industrial Revolution. As rural landowners, they distrusted workers in the big cities.[6]

Central to the power of the aristocracy was their belief in the constitutional role of the army. Collectively, the Kaiser, the Junkers, and the military leaders believed there was a direct tie between the Kaiser and the army. They considered the military separate from the population. The Prussian members of the military swore their loyalty to the Kaiser—not to Prussia. The loyalty of those from other states such as Saxony and Württemberg was to their own king; to the Kaiser they promised only obedience and, in the case of Bavaria, during wartime only. Nevertheless, it followed from this that only the most trusted citizens, those who believed in the Kaiser's authority could be allowed to become officers. Civilian authority had little influence when dealing with the army. But, constitutionally, there was a question as to who was in charge of the army. This question never came to a head, but it is the central point in understanding much of what transpired in Imperial Germany.

Many historians have overestimated the number of Junkers. By 1895, there were only 317 noble family names in Germany. No longer were all members of the aristocracy owners

[4] (Berghahn, 1994), pp. 6–7.
[5] (Frevert, 2004), p. 155.
[6] (Fairbairn, 2008), pp. 70–72.

of large estates. Many of those estates were heavily mortgaged, about a third of them were handed down through inheritance, some were sold, and a few were auctioned. The aristocratic mindset was that financial issues were below them. Re-payment of debts was not a major concern to them; nonetheless, in 1885, the aristocracy still owned more than two-thirds of the largest estates in eastern Prussia. By 1900, only one-third of the largest estates in the six eastern Prussian provinces would still belong to nobility.[7] Even though migrant workers provided the labor, the estate owners oversaw them. This method was significantly different than southern Germany where the aristocracy did not cultivate the land but rather lived off rents from small peasant farmers.[8]

The Bourgeoisie—The bourgeoisie made up approximately 30 percent of the population.[9] The term bourgeoisie originally denoted a wide range of individuals, from substantial business owners to small shopkeepers, from unbelievably rich non-titled individuals to those just above the poverty level. As members of the middle class, they had always been a substantial part of the modern German economic system. They tended to believe in property, hard work, achievement, recognition and rewards, and the importance of rules. The bourgeoisie considered themselves a *Bildungsbürgertum* or "élite built on education." They were defined by the institution of the family. The male figure was expected to have a public working life; his spouse to devote herself to domesticity and teaching values to the next generation. Women and children had specific subordinate roles—*Kinder, Küche, Kirche (*children, cooking, church*).*[10]

The term *Mittelstand* eventually evolved to include only the "lower" or "petty" bourgeoisie and consisted primarily of small shopkeepers, clerks and supervisors, who existed on the margins. The Mittelstand prided themselves on titles, badges, and status that separated them from the working class.[11] The Mittelstand was politically far to the right of the Socialists and the proletariat. Marxism preached the elimination of the bourgeoisie, which made the socialist political party the "enemy."[12] Even in today's Germany, Mittelstand has a special meaning: there is a common belief that the economic success of the country is not based upon big industry and big business, but upon many successful and innovative companies of the Mittelstand (*mittelständische Industrie*). Usually these are family owned companies that are very often market leaders of their businesses or industry and have enormous success in exporting innovative machinery or chemical goods.

Likewise, there was a divide between the bourgeoisie and the peasants in the countryside. Even the richest peasants were set apart from the bourgeoisie because they performed manual labor and were not as well educated. The divide was important for the Mittelstand. The small shopkeepers and artisans of the Mittelstand, who had been protected by regulations in the old towns, became known as the old Mittelstand. The white-collar workers were the new Mittelstand, and they saw themselves as a class above the proletariat even though their economic circumstances were very similar. Looking at the average wages of different bourgeois workers, you can see where the Mittelstand was squarely located.

---

7 (Clemente, 1992), p. 17.
8 (Feuchtwanger 2001), p. 8.
9 (Berghahn, 1994), p. 9.
10 (Blackbourn, 2003), pp. 157–162.
11 (Blackbourn, 2003), pp. 163–165.
12 (Feuchtwanger 2001), pp. 100–102.

Annual Wages in marks in 1913

- Craftsmen 1,163
- White-collar workers 3,753
- Educators 2,607[13]

In 1882, 60 percent of the employment came from small enterprises of five or fewer employees. That number shrank to 31 percent by 1907. The largest industries of 1,000 employees or more remained fairly constant at five percent. As a result midsize enterprises provided most of the employment.[14]

When looking at economic reality versus the class understanding, about a third of the master artisans in Friedberg lived at the edge of poverty. And about half of this group employed no one but themselves: 55 percent of the masters did not own their own shops in 1913; over a quarter were so poor that they paid no municipal taxes. This state of affairs was clearly a proletarianization of the crafts.[15]

Although life expectancy was increasing, the average number of children in the bourgeoisie actually shrank from four to two by 1914. Bourgeois women faced a separate problem known as the spinster emergency. Middle-class fathers were finding it more and more difficult to find suitable husbands for their daughters. A good bourgeois father would not allow his "surplus daughters" to find a future husband among the "surplus sons of the proletariat."[16]

It was far less common in imperial Germany to move from the bourgeoisie to the nobility than it was in Britain. Some of the most powerful bourgeoisie declined titles; instead, the title of Commercial Councilor (Kommerzienrat), or its parallel councilor titles in professional fields, was highly prized, as were reserve commissions in the army.[17]

The Proletarians (*Proletariat*)—About two-thirds of the population made up the proletariat, split between agricultural workers and the urban manual laborers. Half of them made less than 900 marks annually; most had no assets and were at or below the poverty level.[18] The proletariat existed entirely on the margin of society. Mobility between classes was very poor, with little hope of self-employment.[19] The lack of capital to fall back on or invest in a business created a society that was barely capable of survival. Unemployment and job insecurity were rampant, with a third of the workforce expected to be unemployed at some time during the year. For the urban poor, lockouts or strikes contributed to this insecurity.

Individuals in the proletariat began working at age 15, after they finished *Volksschule*. Marriage regularly happened in a worker's late 20s, coinciding with the period when his wage earning ability peaked. Income for the household increased when children, who still lived at home, worked. By the age of 40, a worker's earning power and health was in a major decline. Poverty was a huge problem for the aged, and old age began very early by our standards. Widows represented the largest single group of extremely impoverished individuals.[20]

---

[13] (Berghahn, 1994), p. 302.
[14] (Fairbairn, 2008), p. 78.
[15] (Chickering, *The Great War and Urban Life in Germany*, 2007), p. 29.
[16] (Shaser, 2008), p. 145.
[17] (Blackbourn, 2003), pp. 279–280.
[18] (Berghahn, 1994), p. 9.
[19] (Blackbourn, 2003), pp. 273–274.
[20] (Blackbourn, 2003), pp. 168–169.

Agricultural workers made even less money than their urban counterparts. By 1913, the average agricultural wage was 682 marks a year;[21] however, both household servants and agricultural laborers generally received free room and board even though it was often substandard.[22] Research has shown that some estate owners spent more on their pigs than on their hired hands. Agricultural laborers employed by the larger estates accounted for 40 percent of the working-class. As more workers moved to urban locations, chronic labor shortages among the peasants made family life difficult and resulted in the extensive use of child labor. Workweeks of 100 to 120 hours were common. To compensate for the labor shortages, 500,000 migrant workers from the Polish province came to Germany annually. The migrants returned to Czarist Russia at the end of the season, causing social and financial prejudices against the Polish migrant workers.[23]

Circumstances were not significantly different for the agricultural workers in Prussia. When serfs were freed on the large estates in eastern Prussia, it was a simply a business deal. The serfs were tenants in the agriculturally used areas of the estates, and each had small individual plots for his own subsistence. The emancipation of the serfs meant that the serfs bought out their obligations to work on their lords' land. To do this, they mortgaged or sold their individual holdings. This sale made the estate holders more powerful and made agriculture dependent on hired labor. Agricultural issues were not the same throughout imperial Germany. The institution of divided inheritance in Sonderrechte states required the division of farm holdings into smaller plots, resulting in fewer laborers, available for hire.[24]

A number of laws further disadvantaged agricultural peasants. Until 1843, it was illegal for a peasant to be in debt. That meant that peasants were largely dependent upon private credit from moneylenders, many of whom were Jewish, that often resulted in high interest rates and indebtedness, which led in turn to anti-Semitic movements. While estate owners and non-agricultural peasants could all organize and take part in cooperatives, the law specifically excluded farm workers. Not until 1918 could farm laborers unionize. Further, laws excluded farm workers from obligatory health insurance, and they were not included until 1911. While insurance starting in 1884 covered other workers, farm workers were not covered by accident insurance until 1886 and by old age insurance until 1889.[25]

During the time of industrialization in German society, the population morphed from being predominantly rural to an urban majority. By 1892, the agricultural society along with their dependents represented 42 percent of the total workforce, compared with 35 percent in industry, and 20 percent in commerce. Just three years later in 1895, industry was the largest single sector and, by 1907, it had reached 42 percent, matching the agricultural percentage of 25 years earlier.[26]

Urban workers of the proletariat differed from the craftsmen of the Mittelstand, as they were paid fixed wages, while a craftsman could enter into contracts for the delivery of specific goods. The urban working-class was a fluid workforce. Industrial personnel turnover rates of 50 to 100 percent were not uncommon. There was a core of skilled workers that the

---

[21] These earnings are very difficult to pin down. During Imperial Germany, weekly money earnings tripled and hourly earnings quadrupled. Real earning did not grow nearly as fast. The authors chose a point close to the start of World War I. (Tipton, 1996), p. 75.

[22] (Berghahn, 1994), p. 9.

[23] (Berghahn, 1994), pp. 23–24.

[24] (Aldenhoff, 1996), pp. 27–28.

[25] (Aldenhoff, 1996), p. 45.

[26] (Fairbairn, 2008), pp. 66–70.

employers wanted to keep, and a "floating" labor force augmented them. Unemployment seemed to vary between 8 and 15 percent.[27]

The average workweek for the urban proletariat was 75 hours as late as 1870. In certain industries, the week was even longer. Eventually, the urban workday fell from 12 hours to 9 ½ hours just prior to World War I. The six-day workweek was common, and legislation as far back as 1875 banned work on the Sabbath, but the laws were circumvented easily and employers openly abused the Sabbath. Not until 1892 did the government establish stricter laws requiring Sunday as a resting day for the working class. Working-hour legislation protected children and women; however, male workers were not so fortunate.[28] Life expectancy for a man born in the 1870s was less than 37 years. For women it was 38 ½ years. By the first decade of the 20th century, the life expectancy had risen to 45 and 48 for men and women respectively.[29]

The proletariat lived in residential segregation and feared layoffs or any change in circumstances that would affect their ability to earn wages. Between 1870 and 1885, rents increased an estimated 63 percent in the industrialized cities. In 1875 in Berlin, one-half of the houses had only one heated room and 20 percent of the city's inhabitants lived at least five people to a room. Overcrowding, dampness, lack of proper ventilation, and primitive sanitary conditions all led to frequent outbreaks of infectious diseases such as cholera, consumption, pneumonia, and typhus. An epidemic of tuberculosis was responsible for nearly half of the deaths of 15 to 40-year-olds in the 1880s.

To the poor, something as significant as the height of the buildings in which they lived meant everything. Buildings in every neighborhood had occupants from a variety of different social backgrounds. Not having to climb the stairs was an indication of class status. The lower floors were the residences of choice. The upper floors that lacked plumbing and possibly lighting were reserved for the poorest. An example of the class divisions would be a rich widow living on the first floor, an insurance company employee and his wife on the second level, a retired couple on the third floor, and a mechanic on the fourth level.[30]

The infant mortality rate also escalated; in the large cities it was often higher than one-third.[31] Some industrial districts had infant mortality rates as high as 40 percent as late as 1911.[32] Economic necessity dictated that already overcrowded families often had to take in lodgers. Twenty-five percent of those involved were female. In the same way as male workers, they often rented a bed from families for certain hours of the day, which meant that the family could rent the same bed to workers on different shifts.

The German criminal code of 1871 contained no penalties for cohabitation, but the pressure to legalize a living situation as a marriage was intense. Individual states declared co-habitation to be punishable if it caused a public nuisance. A vengeful spouse or neighbor only had to report a couple in order to show that they constituted a public nuisance. Homelessness was also a major issue, with 200,000 men a year accommodated by the Berlin Homeless Shelter Association. [33]

Families spent one-half to two-thirds of their income on food. The remainder went for housing and utilities. Another set of statistics shows that families spent 52 percent of their

[27] (Tipton, 1996), p. 75.
[28] (Abrams, 1992), p. 22.
[29] (Blackbourn, 2003), pp. 165–168, 266–269.
[30] (Chickering, *The Great War and Urban Life in Germany*, 2007), p. 32.
[31] (Blackbourn, 2003), pp. 151–157.
[32] (Fairbairn, 2008), pp. 64–65.
[33] (Shaser, 2008), pp. 134–139.

income on food with an additional 33 percent on housing, heating, light, and clothing. The same study says that a family typically spent at least a quarter of their food budget on bread alone.[34]

Working-class urban districts were violent places where major riots took place in 1906 and 1910 over increases in beer prices. Prussians moving to an urban area from the east initially bought a watch and then a gun. Many locations had a Wild West reputation. In rural areas, there were pitched battles to drive out gypsies and for servants to revenge themselves on former employers. In some areas, both crimes against property and violent crime rates doubled in the decade before the war. Nonetheless, the murder rate was about 20 times lower than that of Italy or Spain and of the 30–40 murders in Berlin annually, half of them were infanticide.[35]

As a result of endemic poverty, some workers became involved in the labor movement and left-wing socialist parties, but it would be a mistake to equate the Socialists with the proletariat. By 1914, only about 25 percent of the working class belonged to trade unions or the socialist parties.[36]

The majority of the German working class did not have the luxury of looking to the future. They were driven by short-term need. Most did not have stable jobs, appeared aimless, and wandered from company to company doing a variety of unskilled jobs. This group consisted primarily of young single men who epitomized a culture of poverty.[37] The biggest vulnerability of the proletariat was that the labor market was a buyer's market. Population was increasing and laborers were interchangeable. Employers and markets were comparatively free of rules.[38]

Working Women

In bourgeois circles, the typical family managed to maintain its gender-specific roles. This was not true for the other classes. In general, the Great War opened a variety of new employment opportunities for women. There was still a high demand for clerical workers, but opportunities in industry also opened. In Great Britain, nearly two million women entered the work force in jobs previously held by men. In Russia, the number of women working in industry rose by nearly 20 percent.[39] This was not true in imperial Germany. The increase in the number of working women between 1907 and 1925 did not increase substantially.[40] Many of the openings were in the skilled labor area, and factories preferred to get deferments for their male workers rather than train unskilled women. Further, knowing that they would lose their jobs after the war, German women did not flock to war industry jobs; they had no desire to be simply "place-holders." In any case, men such as Hindenburg discouraged their active participation in the workplace.

Family Aid, a program that was instituted to provide financial support to dependents of soldiers, did not provide an adequate income and if women earned additional income, their Family Aid could be reduced. The recipients did not look for factory jobs, but did sewing at home on piece rates (in some instances for the army), took in laundry and ironing for a

---

34 (Fairbairn, 2008), p. 64.
35 (Blackbourn, 2003), pp. 282–283.
36 (Abrams, 1992), p. 5.
37 (Abrams, 1992), p. 5.
38 (Fairbairn, 2008), p. 63.
39 (Wilde)
40 (Ute, 1989), p. 276.

fee, and if possible, sublet rooms where they were living to boarders.[41] This enabled them to earn extra money and yet be available to care for dependents in their charge. One half of all women who were employed worked in agriculture. A third of working women were domestic servants and no more than one-sixth worked in factories.

During this time, working women suffered disproportionately higher rates of illness and industrial accidents than did their male counterparts. Life on the home front was painful, difficult, and often resulted in psychological scarring. Some statistics indicate that women's rates of industrial diseases were 25 percent higher than those of their male counterparts. Deaths from childbirth and lack of medical care rose over the war years by 60 percent.[42]

The Importance of Social Insurance

The most remarkable and long-lasting achievement of Bismarck's last years was the introduction in 1883 of social insurance. Imperial Germany was far ahead of its European counterparts in the area of social insurance. Employers paid two-thirds of the cost for their employees, who received both free medical care and weekly payments when ill. Farm workers did not receive health insurance until 1911 and, as was mentioned earlier, farm laborers could not unionize until 1918, the assumption being that in the countryside patriarchal relationships existed between employers and employees.

In 1884, the government passed accident insurance into law with employers paying all contributions. It was extended to farm workers two years later.[43] In addition to the costs, the insurance legislation included a limit on working hours. Employers partially funded the insurance and, as such, it was more industry-oriented than state-oriented.[44]

The 1889 old-age and infirmity insurance provided for a split premium between employees and employer with the employer paying for only a small amount; old-age insurance was liberalized in 1899, when recipients could collect upon reaching age 70.[45] These programs were expanded in 1900. Accident insurance covered 15 million workers and medical insurance covered 28 million workers.[46]

As they did not own any property, these insurances tied the proletariat closer to the government and away from the Social Democrat Party. People on a pension understandably developed loyalty toward the monarchial state. Social historians believe that the state-offered insurance kept the Social Democrat Party a reform rather than a revolutionary organization. The insurance is also credited for a huge patriotic surge in 1914. Health insurance payments were small but they replaced a system where they had been zero. By 1917, basically all wage earners were covered by this system.

In 1891, the insurance legislation was supplemented by prohibiting child labor in factories, restricting night shifts for women and youths, and work on Sundays. The legislation was expanded in 1903, prohibiting child labor on building sites; in 1905, it limited the workday to eight and one-half hours for miners; and in 1911, it included an insurance program for widows and orphans.[47] The big gap in the social net was unemployment insurance. The municipalities and charities had to provide whatever support they could.[48]

41 (Blackbourn, 2003), p. 168.
42 (Higonnet, 1999), p. xx.
43 (Aldenhoff, 1996), p. 45.
44 (Feuchtwanger, 2001), pp. 85–87.
45 (Fairbairn, 2008), p. 77.
46 (Hewitson, 2008), p. 48.
47 (Hewitson, 2008), p. 48.
48 (Fairbairn, 2008), pp. 77.

Population Migration

In general, the population began shifting from rural to urban life; from the East and the South up to the Northwest and West. By the Great War, 54 percent of the population no longer lived where they were born.[49] Emigration was the first major drain on the population; however, emigration decreased the competition for work and actually helped the growth rate as workers who remained were in demand.

A quick look at migration shows that several waves left Germany in the 1850s, 1860s, and 1880s. Most of the emigrants moved to the United States. In 1880, about one-third of the German-born population in America was employed in agriculture, and two-thirds had moved to urban areas. As many as 30 percent of New York's population were German-born immigrants. The United States received 85 to 90 percent of the 4.5 million German immigrants between 1847 and the First World War. Brazil was a very distant second with 86,000.[50]

Internal population movement within imperial Germany was rapid. In 1871, less than five percent of the population lived in cities of over 100,000 inhabitants. By 1910, this number had grown to 21 percent.[51] This influx was one of the many advantages of constitutional guarantees—almost everybody became a citizen of the state where he or she lived and citizenship allowed individuals to move.[52] It would seldom be a one-way journey or a once-and-for-all migration. In Düsseldorf, 25,000 of the 29,000 new arrivals left within 12 months. As much as 25 percent of the city's population rotated out of the city annually.[53] Between 1850 and 1870, population doubled in Berlin, tripled in Hanover, and quadrupled in Dortmund and Essen. By 1910, Berlin had gained another 250 percent. In 1912, 60 percent of Berliners were born outside of the city.[54]

Urbanization did not mean the immediate disruption of a rural population. Internal migration provided seasonal agricultural laborers to the farms of the empire. There was also seasonal migration seeking urban employment. Many rural workers found jobs in the industrial belt, returning to their villages just twice a year.

When workers attracted to urban sites left the Prussian State Mines, the owners, in turn, had to recruit workers from the surrounding rural areas. In 1875, a full one-third of the Saar miners commuted weekly. The normal routine was to walk to work on Monday morning and return home on a Saturday evening. These working conditions were far from ideal. As a result, heavy burdens fell upon women, children, and the elderly. Men were strangers in their hometowns and were scorned and poorly housed where they worked.[55] Young, unmarried, and unskilled male workers accounted for 90 percent of the transient workers in some cities.[56]

The urbanization of smaller cities followed similar patterns and population migration brought social ills. The charming medieval town walls were destroyed to make room for the first urban suburbs. As growing towns expanded, they annexed neighboring towns and incorporated them before basic services were established. Sewage systems also lagged behind and cities utilized open gutters. By the turn-of-the-century, 60 percent of the Prussian population still drew water from wells. Many major cities lacked a central water supply. By 1900,

---

49 (Berghahn, 1994), pp. 43–46.
50 (Blackbourn, 2003), pp. 147–149
51 (Tipton, 1996), p. 74.
52 Not all states had constitutions. See the section on Mecklenburg.
53 (Abrams, 1992), p. 15.
54 (Neiberg, 2011), p. 93.
55 (Blackbourn, 2003), pp. 149–151.
56 (Abrams, 1992), p. 16.

97 percent of the population was on central water; in contrast, in Posen only 11 percent of the population enjoyed the same service.[57]

As drinking water was generally unhygienic, beer became the replacement drink, and its major nutritional properties were touted. Despite the cost, alcohol consumption remained high and a culture of public houses developed. Employers generally discouraged workplace drinking and eventually helped to enforce laws regulating the purity of water and soft drinks. But it was normal for the man of the house to escape to the public house at night as a method of finding some peace from crowded living conditions.[58] Between 1899 and 1913, records reported a 25 percent reduction in the consumption of alcohol. Both city administrators and employers were trying to improve conditions for a shifting population.[59]

There was always a housing shortage in industrializing towns. Companies sometimes provided lodging houses for single men and these often housed up to 1,200 workers. Women were generally restricted to boarding with resident families, and overcrowding was a major problem. Despite the conditions, the men believed that working conditions were better in the city: hours were shorter, and pay was significantly higher.[60] The army also contributed to the migration. Soldiers who were stationed in garrisons in urban areas often would not return to the countryside unless they had an existing relationship or were due to inherit some land.

Up until the 1880s, the working population was split. Agriculture represented 35 to 40 percent of the economy, whereas industry amounted to 30 to 35 percent. Just before the war, agriculture had decreased to 25 percent of the economy and industry (include mining) had risen to 45 percent. There was always a commercial and service sector that was constant at about 30 percent.[61] Constitutionally, it was fairly easy to move between geographic locations and places of employment, but movement between the class structures was not.[62]

In the latter part of the 19th century, Prussia experienced a strong Polish national movement that threatened to drive back the boundaries of Germanism in the eastern provinces of Prussia. In 1831, the "Congress" Kingdom of Poland was fully absorbed and integrated into Russia. So the Polish people were either Prussian citizens, Russian citizens, or citizens of Austria-Hungary.[63] Historically the most important social class in Posen had been the Polish nobles, many of whom were very poor. On the other hand, the economic development of the country had created a comparatively wealthy Polish middle class that threatened German ascendancy more seriously than had the traditional nationalism of the nobles.

To combat this perceived problem with the Polish population, the Prussian government enforced a policy of compulsory "Germanization" of the Polish population. In 1872, an administrative ordinance made the German language mandatory in the schools. In April 1888, the Prussian parliament passed a law establishing a commission for the purpose of buying all Polish land in Posen and West Prussia for the German colonists to use. Under the 1907 Public Meetings Bill, German was the only acceptable language used in any public meetings. German settlers were able to buy property under very favorable terms, but

57 (Berghahn, 1994), p. 326.
58 (Abrams, 1992), p. 23.
59 (Abrams, 1992), pp. 63–86.
60 (Frevert, 2004), p. 191.
61 (Berghahn, 1994), p. 2.
62 (Retallack, 1996), pp. 93–104.
63 (Pounds, 1996) p. 15.

there were specific criteria restricting the settler's freedom in movement and disposal of the property.[64]

In 15 years, an area of nearly 1,554 km^2 of land was purchased from the Poles and more than 4,000 German families settled there. The Prussian Landtag enacted legislation in 1908 that allowed the expropriation of land from unwilling Polish peasants. In spite of this policy, however, the number of Polish peasants increased due to immigration.[65]

The language policy in Alsace-Lorraine was much more tolerant and liberal. The Lithuanians and Masurians suffered little discrimination. A map included in the picture section of this book shows the large area inside the Reich where German was not spoken. The Polish speaking territories on the eastern border with Russia were immense. In addition, the Polish peasants provided unskilled labor throughout the empire. From about 1890, the Germans received 1.2 million foreign workers or four percent of the industrial labor force. By 1914, this percentage had grown to eight percent of workers in agriculture alone.[66]

Religion

During the 19th century, religious tolerance began to get a foothold, particularly in Roman Catholic countries. Consider that when Austria (primarily Catholic) ceded its power to Prussia (primarily Protestant) in 1866, from a religious standpoint a considerable change in power occurred. The balance of power in Germany now lay with the Protestants.[67] As a result, there were deep religious differences within imperial Germany. The notion that imperial Germany had a Catholic population in the South and Protestants in the north is a misconception. So is the thought that the population was generally deeply religious, churchgoing and tolerant of one another. Bismarck's *Kulturkampf* dispelled this myth.

The Germans adopted a strong anti-Catholic program known as the Kulturkampf starting in 1873. This policy was one of Bismarck's schemes to bring the Catholic faction more in line with the ruling aristocracy. It implied that Protestants had "culture" while the Catholics did not. The religious division, in many minds, threatened the unity of the new imperial Germany. Escalating disputes between protestant liberals and the more conservative Catholics eventually became open warfare. The government could prosecute priests for undermining perceived public order under a new law called the "pulpit paragraph." Catholics no longer had the right to supervise their own religious teaching, and Germany expelled the Jesuit order. In Prussia, the law of 1873 enabled the state to supervise the training of priests as well as their certification, and the state had the right to veto ecclesiastical appointments.

The Pope counterattacked with threats of excommunication and many bishoprics and parishes remained vacant. The Catholic Center Party received 28 percent of the vote in 1874 and became the largest opposition party to the government administration.[68] There was even an effort to keep Catholics out of public office, while the imperial government tried to force the Kulturkampf throughout the empire.

In many places, the Catholic clergy simply failed to abide by the new laws. The protestant authorities countered by imposing ineffective sanctions that ranged from imprisonment to fines and exile. When the Catholic clergy did not pay the fines, the authorities would confiscate the property and sell it at public auctions. Loyal Catholics would then rally and

---

64 (Aldenhoff, 1996), p. 51.
65 (Silverman, 1972), p. 89.
66 (Tipton, 1996), p. 74.
67 (McManners, 2001), p. 357.
68 (Feuchtwanger, 2001), pp. 63–67.

manage the auction to ensure that the property was sold at the lowest possible price and then returned to the clergy. When imprisoned priests were released, they returned home as heroes.

In 1874, the Expulsion Law, which sent priests and bishops to remote locations, counteracted the clergy's resistance. The favorite location for expulsion was the island of Rügen in the Baltic. Rügen became incredibly difficult to police, and while hundreds of priests were exiled between 1875 and 1879, the politically acceptable successors were entirely rejected by the Catholic population. Perhaps the most telling result of the failure of Kulturkampf was that while 23 percent of the Catholics voted for the Center Party in 1871, by 1874, that number had risen to 45 percent. The Catholic Center Party became a huge voting bloc.[69] The Kulturkampf failed and left deep scars and mistrust between the Catholics and Protestants. It died out officially around 1878 with the death of Pope Pius IX. Slowly the anti-Catholic laws were revoked.[70]

Almost all references point to the *Dogma of Papal Infallibility of 1870* as the cause of the problems that imperial Germany had with the Catholics and the papacy. This Dogma asserted that the Pope, when speaking *ex cathedra* on questions of faith and morals, was indeed infallible, but only then. Infallibility was nothing new, but this act codified it as dogma for statements concerning faith or morals. Why would Germany declare Catholics as enemies of the Empire when the Pope issued policy only on matters of faith and morals?

There was a deeper issue. In 1864, the Vatican issued *The Syllabus of Errors*. This document was a collection of 80 propositions that rejected the separation of church and state, declared the church supreme over civil laws, and demanded control of education and cultural affairs. It also rejected any alignment of the Pope with progress and modern civilization. *The Syllabus of Errors* was unacceptable, but the *Dogma of Papal Infallibility* issued some six years later was the trigger point.

Remember that imperial Germany was now a protestant country, and it was not alone in the rejection of the Syllabus and the Dogma. Even catholic countries objected. Italy occupied Rome and declared it as the capital of the Italian monarchy. Austria canceled its concordant with the Catholic Church.[71] Until 1870, there were still Papal States that the Pope directly governed. This was not a small papal enclave like today's Vatican City. The Papal States were sizable and politically active. Thoughts and memories of the political power of the papacy were alive in the minds of both Catholics and non-Catholics. When the Catholic politicians requested that the Kaiser militarily restore the Papal States, mass misunderstandings and reaction arose. The lasting effects of the Kulturkampf were a strengthened Catholic thought and militancy.

Regardless of religious strife, there was a strong sense of national identity throughout the Empire. However, Protestants, Jews, and Catholics—each had a significantly different sense of what it was to be German. There were liberal and conservative factions in all religions. Imperial German protestant churches generally called themselves "evangelical" not "protestant" and were broadly divided between liberal and conservative or orthodox wings. The liberal movement had a sense of social mission and morality and attempted to adapt Christianity to modern scientific ideas. Traditional Lutherans and Calvinists became the more orthodox Protestants.

---

69 (Clark, 2008), pp. 88–90.
70 (Blackbourn, 2003) pp. 223–226.
71 (Dürr, 1985), pp. 8–9.

The situation in the Kingdom of Prussia was rather more complex. King Frederick William III forced a union between the Reformed (Calvinist) and the Lutheran churches in 1817. The new church was called *Evangelische Kirche in Preußen*, later renamed *Evangelische Landeskirche in Preußen,* and finally known as *Evangelische Landeskirche der älteren Provinzen Preußens*. The King of Prussia was head of both the Reformed and the Lutheran churches in his country and referred to as *Summus episcopus* (Latin) meaning highest bishop. In the Kingdom of Prussia, the Kaiser was not only the sovereign of the state but was also the supreme bishop for the protestant faith.

Until 1918, their respective monarchs headed the different protestant Landeskirchen, much as today the Queen of England is head of the Church of England. But this union in Prussia was mainly administrative in nature. In matters of theology, parishes remained Lutheran, Reformed, or found a united position, unlike in some southern areas where in the Palatinate and Baden the churches made real theological unions.

The urban bourgeoisie fell away from church attendance as did the proletariat, among whom attendance fell to between one and three percent. Nonetheless, there was a middle class feeling of "cultural Protestantism" that encompassed Prussia. The German throne and the German ethos were protestant.[72]

There was significant decrease in church attendance between 1880 and 1914. Religion maintained its position as an academic topic and at least one-eighth of all the books published in the 1870s in Germany were religious in nature. Authors such as Karl von Hase (Dietrich Bonhoeffer's great-grandfather), Friedrich Naumann and Max Weber published during this time.

One of the reasons for falling Protestant observance was a lack of churches and pastors. Migration to the cities caused parishes in Berlin to be as large as 50,000 people. The transformation of smaller towns into dormitory cities also influenced church attendance. In particular, the protestant church's perceived relationship with the state became problematic as workers viewed the pastor as a government supporter.[73]

Church attendance was far higher in rural environments due to the influence of the family. However, when the peasants began migrating to urban areas, those remaining had to work in the fields on Sundays. The aristocracy, of course, was primarily protestant and attended church. Altogether two-thirds of churchgoers were women. There were also orthodox and liberal factions within the Catholic Church; the orthodox conservative faction was vastly superior in size. Supremacy of the orthodox conservative Catholics meant a strong support of the primary position of the Pope. The small liberal faction was less dedicated to the Pope in Rome. The liberals tended to be more bourgeois, whereas the mass of the peasantry was very orthodox. Pope Pius IX, who was the Pope for 31 years until 1878, dominated the church. He was a very active political and religious spokesman and was the last ruler over the Papal States. His French supporters were defeated in battle by the Italians in 1860. French troops remained in Rome until 1870.

Catholic Church attendance remained relatively high because the priests were of a lower social status than the protestant pastors and the workers could identify with them. Catholic workers tended to work for protestant bourgeoisie employers. There was less of a social gap in the Catholic Church. Because they were the minority, the Catholics tended to band together.[74]

---

[72] (Blackbourn, 2003), pp. 219–221.
[73] (Blackbourn, 2003), pp. 220–222.
[74] (Blackbourn, 2003), pp. 226–227.

The Jewish population was a small but important minority, making up between one and two percent of the population. The Jewish population generally was divided between Orthodox Judaism and the more liberal Reform Judaism. In Reform Judaism, dietary prescriptions and head coverings were far less common. There was more assimilation to German culture and the army. Larger urban areas tended to be more reform oriented, while the small town communities in the rural areas were more orthodox. [75]

Anti-Semitism became a significant part of the German subculture starting after the economic crisis of the 1870s. The term anti-Semitism was coined in 1879. The Jewish population was blamed for making money off the "poor workers." A dichotomy of criticism arose where, because of racial characteristics, the Orthodox Jewish population was incapable of assimilating into the mainstream German population. On the other side, there was also criticism that Jews had assimilated all too well and were hidden in the population. Caricatures of Jewish racial characteristics were normal in the print media.[76]

The illegitimate birth rate in imperial Germany was high. By 1914, the estimate was 350,000 illegitimate births a year. In heavily Catholic Munich, the estimate of illegitimate births was 31 percent. But in the western Catholic area of Cologne, the rate was less than 10 percent.[77] Abortions were common because women reached childbearing maturity by age 15, but often did not marry until 10 years later. This was not a reflection of morals, but rather a reality of the time.[78]

Over time, the schism between the Catholics and Protestants lessened slightly and interfaith marriages increased. In Prussia, the rate of mixed marriage more than doubled between 1840 and 1900 from 3.7 to 8.4 percent. The empire as a whole reached 10.2 percent mixed marriages by the time the war started in 1914. Such marriages were most common in the industrialized cities. In 1896, mixed marriages represented 34 percent of all marriages in Frankfurt, but even in areas that were more religiously pure, such as rural Alsace, there was a gradual increase from 8.4 percent in 1818 to 12 percent in 1912.[79]

Like most things associated with the government, the army was heavily protestant. After the *Kulturkampf,* the Prussian army actually introduced Catholic chaplains, but if Catholics were stationed outside of Catholic regions, they normally did not attend services. Soldiers were only forced to attend their own denominational church services when they were celebrating a major holiday such as the Kaiser's birthday; then Catholics were obliged to go to protestant services. In general, church attendance was low. Sunday was supposedly free time although there were a number of drills and cleaning parties scheduled during "The Lord's Day." Thirty-four percent of Catholic soldiers and 23 percent of Protestants attended church.[80]

---

[75] (Blackbourn, 2003), pp. 214–218.

[76] (Blackbourn, 2003), p. 231–233.

[77] (Berghahn, 1994), p. 71. At first, this number seemed incredible. But the author listed Dresden at 20.5% and Berlin at 12.3%. His figures about the numbers of prostitutes in those cities also raise an eyebrow.

[78] (Berghahn, 1994), pp. 65–74.

[79] (Clark, 2008), pp. 94–95.

[80] (Frevert, 2004), pp. 186–188.

THE EDUCATION SYSTEM

Schools

The German school system provided the road to adulthood. The Constitution of both the North German Federation and imperial Germany delegated the control of public education to the states.[81] Unlike the American system, German boys and girls began *Volksschule* at age 6 and continued to age 14. Paid for by the government, this education was free to students and contributed to a literacy rate that was nearly 100 percent. These eight years (age 6–14) of education completed the education for many and was noted by the student's confirmation.[82] The decision had to be made whether or not the student was going to secondary school, which was not free. If the child was going to attend secondary school, he transferred into a private secondary school at age 9–10. Parents of these students had to start paying for this education from age nine until they no longer supported the child. There were of course private preparatory schools, which also were not free. Only a few students continued on to secondary schools or university. Most girls continued their education at home.

In 1885 for example, there were 7.5 million children in elementary schools, but only 238,000 attended secondary schools. Rural families needed their children to work on the farm so they seldom attended secondary school. In practical terms, only children from bourgeois or noble families had any hope of going to secondary school. Approximately 500,000 part-time students attended continuation schools at the age of 14, but these were primarily for apprentices in the Guild Associations.[83] The percentage of children that attended the secondary schools seems to vary from source to source but in general between three and five percent of the children had the opportunity.[84]

Primary schools were denominational. "Simultaneous schools," in which children of different religions were taught together, were the exception until the Great War created teacher shortages.[85] As late as 1906, 95 percent of protestant children and 90 percent of Catholics attended schools of their own religious denomination. But in Baden where there were state-controlled the schools, simultaneous schools were compulsory from 1876.[86] Truancy in the Volkschule was a huge problem in urban areas. In one year alone in Düsseldorf, the police contacted more than 13,000 parents out of the total population of 91,000 about truancy. More than 1,000 children had a daily police escort to school.[87]

There were three types of secondary schools—six-year schools, nine-year schools, and cadet schools. Chapter Nine contains a full discussion on the Cadet Schools. The focus of this discussion is on six- and nine-year schools. There were three types of six- and nine-year schools: the *Gymnasium*, the *Realgymnasium*, and the *Oberrealschule*. Each of these had both a six-year and nine-year school equivalent. Girls attended separate secondary schools. The Gymnasium was considered the best of these and was the guardian of classical studies. German society considered graduates to have both education and culture. The Realgymnasium was a compromise between the Latin and Greek of the Gymnasium and the technical

---

[81] (Albisetti, 2006), p. 244.
[82] (Shaser, 2008), p. 133.
[83] (Tipton, 1996), p. 76.
[84] (Donson, 2010), p. 4.
[85] (Shaser, 2008), p. 133.
[86] (Albisetti, 2006), p. 248.
[87] (Blackbourn, 2003), pp. 290–291.

side of the Oberrealschule. The Oberrealschule taught a more technical curriculum for engineers, chemists and the like. There were 388 total nine-year schools in 1900 consisting of 277 Gymnasien, 85 Realgymnasien, and 26 Oberrealschulen. In 1900, 66 percent of students attended the gymnasium, with much emphasis on humanism and the classics.[88]

The names of the different classes in the secondary schools are shown on the chart. The six-year schools were the same as the nine-year schools, but without the top three additional classes. Civilian schools offered an opportunity to move into the army directly from civilian schooling and enter the commissioning process as a *Fahnenjunker* (potential active duty officer) or to continue in civilian education through the university. Cadet schools offered the opportunity to switch to civilian schools or continue on into the higher cadet school with a clear goal of joining the army.

Different Classes of Secondary Schools

Class	Age Approx.	Name	Civilian School	Cadet School
VI (5th grade)	10–11	Sexta		Voranstalt
V	11–12	Quinta		Voranstalt
IV	12–13	Quarta		Voranstalt
UIII	13–14	Untertertia		Voranstalt
OIII	14–15	Obertertia		Voranstalt
UII	15–16	Untersekunda	One-year Certificate*	One-year Certificate
OII	16–17	Obersekunda	Primareifezeugnis**	Fähnrich-Examen
UI	17–18	Unterprima		
OI	18–19	Oberprima	Abitur	Abitur
Selekta	17–18	Selekta		

(Moncure, 1993), pp. 150–151.

* Proof of educational qualification for "One-Year Volunteer" service also taken at conclusion of Untersekunda class by cadets.

** Proof of fitness for attendance at the Unterprima/Oberprima classes of a Prussian Gymnasium or Realschule and the minimum acceptable educational qualification for non-cadet entrance as a Fahnenjunker.

Opportunities abounded for students in the higher classes of secondary school. The very top students would take an examination known as the *Abitur*. It was a voluntary test; however, holders of the Abitur certificate had a monopoly on higher state positions and university enrollment prior to the turn-of-the-century. Having the certificate of successful completion, the *Abiturreifezeugnis*, ensured the holder of a successful financial life. There was no higher educational accomplishment than the Abitur. Approximately one-third of the Prussian Gymnasium students successfully passed the Abitur.

There was one disturbing trend among secondary students. Two percent of rural students from the Volksschule were near-sighted and had to wear glasses. Urban Volksschule students

88 (Shaser, 2008), p. 133.

were from four to nine percent myopic. The percentage of near-sightedness rose to 44 percent for clerks, merchants, and bookkeepers. Fifty-eight percent of Realgymnasium students needed glasses, and the figure rose to 65 percent for gymnasium students.

Another issue was the overall shortage of secondary school teachers. Teachers received a major pay raise in 1909 that in Prussia made them equal to judges in civil service. After this improvement, their income placed them in the top four percent of wage earners, which helped to alleviate the shortage to some degree. Even so, the shortage worsened during and after the war.[89] Societal norms prepared all German citizens to enter the army. Schoolteachers were civil servants, many of whom had reserve commissions and were known for pushing patriotism. The entire school system was designed to prepare the best and brightest for service in the army.[90]

Secondary education for girls was available only at schools for young ladies (*höhere Töchterschulen*), available to very well-to-do families; they had neither a formal curriculum, nor textbooks. In general, girls did not study classical languages, but they did learn foreign languages, conversation, music, and needlework. There were no final examinations, making it difficult to judge the quality of the schools. This was the pinnacle of all schooling for girls; there were no qualification certificates and the goal was to find a suitable husband. In 1901, there were 213 state-run and 656 private secondary schools for girls.[91]

The German secondary school system was influenced by economic pressure. Graduation rates in secondary schools varied significantly. The longer a student stayed in school, the more potential benefits would accrue. Conversely, the longer the period of schooling, the higher the economic burden was to the family supporting the student. There was a definite incentive for students to graduate and start earning their way. As a result, students began leaving the secondary schools to enter the workforce after the *Untersekunda* (6th secondary) year as they weighed the costs and benefits of remaining in school. Catholic students were generally poorer and were less likely to go into secondary school, and far less likely to attend university.[92]

Receiving a reserve commission was the single most sought-after goal of any student, even those with the Abitur. Because students were also liable for conscription, the law gave the educated student an alternative. Young men could earn the One-Year Certificate and could elect to serve just one-year of compulsory military service on active duty to avoid delaying university education or other employment, provided that they had the means to pay all their own expenses. They were known as one-year volunteers (OYVs, or *Einjährig Freiwillige*). A student could earn a one-year certificate at the end of the Untersekunda year through an examination. Students in the six-year schools could take this examination, as well as students after their sixth class of the nine-year school. Only one-third of those eligible and possessing a one-year certificate continued on into the military; most were rejected for medical reasons. Students sought the OYV examination certificate, as some employers would hire only those who held one. So a certificate holder at the age of 16 could qualify to bypass two years of active service, and do it in one year. One-year volunteers had the potential to become reserve officers. Secondary school students could continue their education and try to become an active duty officer. At the end of the Obersekunda year, students could take

89 (Albisetti, 2006), p. 255.
90 (*Wehrordnung des Deutschen Reiches*, 1888)
91 (Shaser, 2008), pp. 133–134.
92 (Clark, 2008), p. 93.

the *Primareifezeugnis* examination and qualify to take the top two Prima years in the Gymnasium or enter the army and serve as a Fahnenjunker.[93]

Between 1890 and 1914, imperial German university enrolment exploded from 28,000 to 60,000 students. The increase in size was largely unplanned, unregulated, and led to many worries about an oversupply of university trained graduates. From the mid 1890s, women were allowed to attend university classes, but could not enroll for courses leading to graduation until 1909. By 1914, there were 4,000 women in German universities. However, these numbers meant that imperial Germany had taken the first step towards opening universities to the middle class.[94]

University Student Societies

It is common to see photographs of young men in fantastic dress armed with dueling sabers. These were members of student fraternities. With the exception of military officers, almost every prominent man in German public life belonged to a student fraternity, from the Chancellor on down. These fraternities were male bastions where one could prove oneself and show that one was not afraid of bodily harm and would not flinch when one's honor was tested in a sword duel. There is a traditionally American view of what dueling is all about. A pistol duel is visualized with two antagonists, each one trying to harm or even kill the other. Sword duels can be seen as two antagonists dancing back and forth in a ballet of thrusts. What the student dueling societies did was something entirely different.

In dead earnest, the students entered into a duel—something known as the *Mensur*. The Mensur consisted of two antagonists from different fraternities. This match was seldom conducted to overcome some slight, but rather to fulfill the requirements the fraternities placed on dueling. In fact, the two antagonists often became close friends after the duel. Each participant was known as *der Herr Paukant*. The dueling ground was called *Paukboden*. The sword was known as the *Schläger* and typically had a blade about 85 cm long and at least 1 cm wide (the last 20 cm sharpened). It had a conspicuous "basket grip" that protected the hand and was typically decorated in the colors of the student *Burschenschaft* to which the Paukant belonged.

In swordplay, there are basically two types of damage systems: "impact" fencing (use of a blade to pierce mortally) and "blow" fencing (use of a blade to strike). The weapons used for the evolved form of blow fencing (*Schlägefechten*), known as the Mensur, commonly came to be known in Germany as *Racqueten*. The dueling sword differed from the Mensur racquet only in the nature of the blade, which on the former was curved and somewhat heavier. These two parallel forms of individual sword interaction grew largely side-by-side. The first consisted of actual dueling with sharp, pointed saber blades; the other consisted of the Mensur (or ritualized fencing), with the "basket racquet" (*Korbschläger*) or the "bell racquet" (*Glockenschläger*). During a Mensur duel, there were no foot movements, only that of the sword arm.

The Paukant also wore protective clothing that included reinforced leather aprons, arm coverings, neck protection, and steel goggles to protect the eyes. The head and face were left totally unprotected. The left hand was placed behind the back, and the right hand held up in one of two general positions, both of which protected the right side of the face. For a student and German society in general, the badge of courage was the *Schmiß* (the dueling scar,

93 (Clemente, 1992)
94 (Retallack, 1996), p. 55.

or sometimes called the *Renommierschmiß*, or bragging scar), mostly on the left side of the face, where blows would fall from a right-handed duelist. This scar was born by a generation of doctors, jurists, professors, and officials, certifying the owner's claim to manly stature. The dueling scar was certain to attract attention because it signified courage and breeding. There are stories that students would resort to self-infliction with a razor. Those who received their Schmiß in this less honorable way would frequently enhance it by pulling the wound apart and irritate it by pouring in wine or sewing horsehair into the gash.

Dueling was a social institution in Germany. The nobility had to maintain its honor code. Wilhelm II declared that he would punish any officer who fought a duel, but would dismiss from the army anyone who refused to do so. Participation in dueling showed the world that you had no fear but were honorable. Student societies could trace their roots back to the Middle Ages. While there were many different types of clubs and fraternities, this discussion is limited to three kinds of student fraternities extending from the mid-1800s to the start of World War I.

It should be remembered that few went to the university. Of those that did, about 25 percent were in fraternities. The others were "savages." The expense was immense and the requirements demanding. While at university, students would join a group of fellows known as a *Burschenschaft* that took on three general forms. The first was a *Landsmannschaft.* They tended to be regional fraternities based on geographic location and were politically more liberal. The second kind was a more normal Burschenschaft. These were national in nature and tended to be politically right wing. The third kind was called a *Korps*. These tended to be more aristocratic in nature, and the discussion of politics was strictly prohibited. The use of the terms Landsmannschaft, Burschenschaft, and Korps are often mistakenly used interchangeably in literature. Among these three groups were dueling and non-dueling fraternities. Generally, the Catholic fraternities did not duel.

The different groups were identifiable based on their style of uniform, hat, and a brightly colored sash worn in the colors of that fraternity, but all three had several things in common. First, there were generally three kinds of members. Membership was life-long and alumni played an active role in the chapter. The first type of member was an irregular member. Irregular members were those who were physically unable to participate in a Mensur or whose parents refused to allow them to participate. The second type of member was a novice, also known as a pledge in American fraternities. The novices were also known as Foxes (*Fuchs* in German language), as they had not yet earned the right to participate in a Mensur. Typically, a new fox had to complete one-and-a-half to two terms of study that included one hour of fencing study daily that was instructed by the Burschenschaft "fencing master." Some Burschenschaften had a shorter novice period. The third kind of member, or Burschen, was a full-fledged Korps student, eligible to become an officer. One of the members took charge of each novice, and it was his duty to keep the novice out of trouble and to serve as a role model. In addition, there was a position known as "Fox-Major" (*Fuchsmajor*). This individual was in charge of all of the novices and provided instruction about the fraternity on a weekly basis. This individual wore a distinctive headpiece regularly adorned with fox accouterments and could forever use the initials "FM" after his signature.

Fraternity life consisted of many jovial gatherings. There were ritual meetings and methods for drinking beer. A *Salamander* was a common device. The top officer would open meetings with a salamander, where members slid beer mugs along the table and then pounded them in unison three-times. This method was used for opening and closing meetings as well as numerous toasts. There were also such things as beer duels where two opponents chugged beer and whoever emptied their glass first was declared the winner. The President could order any member to drink a quantity of beer as a punishment. Any full member could direct a novice to do the same thing. (As a side note, most fraternity houses had something called a *Kotzbecken* or puking sink. This practical device came up to just under chest level and had support bars on the wall to hold a man up.) The same devices could be found in most army or navy officers' clubs as well. Singing was another indispensable part of every regular meeting. All members had songbooks, and the songs tended to be patriotic. The songbooks were called *Kommersbücher* in German.

The real purpose of these societies was to impress the aristocratic code of honor into the educational system and the sons of the rich bourgeoisie. The intent was to bind the future middle-class to the pre-industrial aristocratic ruling groups. In addition, the fraternities provided a very functional "good old boys" network that provided great connections into all manner of work. In addition, there was a direct connection to the ability to become a reserve officer.[95]

INTERNAL POLITICAL PARTIES

Political parties were an outgrowth of universal suffrage. While parties had existed previously, now voters could have a direct effect on the Reichstag and national policy. Universal suffrage applied to every male German citizen who was over the age of 25. By law, active military service disqualified the voter—this was to reduce any political involvement—as did imprisonment, bankruptcy, being a welfare recipient, or having a guardian.[96]

Participation rates in Reichstag elections grew from 55 to 84 percent by 1912. Ninety-three percent participation levels were often found at the local level, which is higher than the amount usually found currently in Great Britain.[97] While women's suffrage has already been discussed, the Association Law of 1908 superseded the various state laws and allowed women to join political parties and participate in political meetings. Prior to 1908, only the Socialists had addressed political equality for women.[98] Universal male suffrage made the effect of urbanization and the aspirations of the Socialists more important. The Social Democrats (who were primarily from urban areas) and the Left Liberals were considered to be the enemy of conservatism. The term "from the left" or "leftist" comes from the seating arrangements of certain European parliaments. The German Reichstag was no exception, with the liberal or more socialist parties arranged on the left and the conservatives on the right.[99]

[95] (Wehler, 1985), pp. 124–127.
[96] (Krüger, 1915), p. 50.
[97] (Blackbourn, 2003), p. 312.
[98] (Shaser, 2008), p. 145.
[99] (Krüger, 1915), pp. 52–54.

Distribution of Seats in the Reichstag 1887–1912

Party	1887	1890	1893	1898	1903	1907	1912
German conservatives	80	73	72	56	54	60	43
Free conservatives	41	20	28	23	21	24	14
National Liberals	99	42	53	46	51	54	45
Catholic Center	98	106	96	102	100	105	91
Left Liberals	32	76	48	49	36	49	42
Social Democrats	11	35	44	56	81	43	110
Minorities	33	38	35	34	32	29	33
Right Wing Splinter Parties	3	7	21	31	22	33	19
Total	**397**	**397**	**397**	**397**	**397**	**397**	**397**

(Fife Jr., 1916), pp. 119–129.

The history of political parties in imperial Germany is based on disagreements, division, and reorganization. Bismarck drove a wedge into the Liberal party dividing it into two parts—the National Liberals, who gravitated towards conservatism, and the German Radicals, who split again and became two radical groups—the Social Democrats and the Left Liberals. The National Liberals came to stand for those industrial interests that demanded a strengthening of the national power. The German and Free Conservative parties tended more and more to represent agrarian interests. There were actually many parties, each one having an individual program and each claiming to represent more or less important interests. Generally, these can be divided into four more or less well-defined groups. Sometimes there is little difference between the parties except for the personalities of the leaders. The four groups were:

- Conservative (agrarian)
- Center (Catholic)
- Liberals (middle-of-the-road)
- Socialist or Social Democrats (proletarian)[100]

The Catholic Center Party and the Liberals dominated until the turn-of-the-century. Then the Social Democrats started making major headway.[101] Between the years 1890 to 1912, the conservatives oscillated between 13 and 18 percent, the Catholic Center Party between 23 and 27 percent, and the Liberals between 11 and 13 percent.[102]

The conservatives consisted of the German Conservative and the Free Conservative Party. The former was the old Prussian party of feudal landholders. The latter, while defending feudal interests, accepted and approved the absorption of Prussia into the German Empire; they tended to be strongly nationalistic. The Free Conservatives tended to submerge Prussian interests into the interests of the Empire. In the 1890s, this group became anti-Semitic and appealed to the prejudices of money-borrowing landlords and peasants. These were the defenders of autocratic and military power. They were largely Prussian, defending Prus-

[100] (Fife Jr., 1916), pp. 119–129.
[101] (Abrams, 1992), p. 14.
[102] (Hewitson, 2008), p. 46.

sia's prestige in federal affairs rather than that of imperial Germany. Religiously, they were strongly Lutheran and ultraorthodox.[103]

The clerical or Center Party began life as a representative of the Roman Catholic Church. They had a conservative attitude in religious and educational matters and were occasionally anti-national in military and colonial affairs. They drew great support from the Rhine area, eastern and southeastern Prussia, and the strongly Catholic south. The Center Party often allied with small anti-national factions such as some Guelph patriots who never accepted Prussia's rule over Hanover; Danes disenfranchised by the wars of 1864 and 1866; and Poles from West Prussia, Posen, and Silesia. Additionally, there were also the representatives from Alsace-Lorraine who refused to be subsumed into Germany's political system.[104]

The liberal parties had an historical foundation in the effort to create an English-style parliamentary government. Economically they represented the industrial system, which favored a strong national policy. Many professionals belonged to this group and as time went on this group became more closely aligned with the government.[105] The Left Liberal or radical group was born through a series of splits and suffered from selfish leaders. The National Liberals started to move more and more to the right and came to represent the great commercial class with sensitivity toward international trade and a desire for direct taxation. The liberal parties would often ally with the Social Democrats to fight for matters of taxation.[106]

In theory, the Social Democratic Party (SPD) represented the working and un-propertied classes that opposed the government and were classified as enemies of the State or *Reichsfeinde*. Theoretically, the Social Democrats were pledged to a program that included the overthrow of the capitalistic state.[107] Even though the Kulturkampf was ineffective, in 1878 the government targeted the Socialists in much the same way.[108] This focus led to anti-socialist laws passed between 1878 to 1890. The impetus for these laws came from an assassination attempt on the Emperor by a socialist named Hödel.[109] The resulting laws created unity among those who considered themselves persecuted. When the laws were repealed in 1890, the Social Democratic Party (SPD) had 100,000 members. By 1907, they had grown to a half a million and by 1914 over one million members. By comparison, this number was more than the combined membership of the largest socialist parties in Austria, Belgium, Denmark, France, Italy, Holland, Norway, Sweden Switzerland, and Great Britain.[110] Still it was not unanimous. At the start of the war, only 25 percent of the proletariat belonged to the SPD or trade unions. Most of these were skilled laborers. In general, the party disregarded unskilled laborers and used a derogatory term *Lumpenproletariat* when describing them.[111]

Despite the increasing size of this party, no other party was willing to make an alliance with them. As a result, the number of Social Democrat deputies in the Reichstag remained low as the socialist candidates could not generally win the runoff of a second ballot election.[112] Bismarck blamed the socialists for a series of assassination attempts against the Prussian king. As a result, the party was forced to operate for a number of years as an ille-

---

[103] (Fife Jr., 1916), pp. 120–122.
[104] (Fife Jr., 1916), pp. 122–123.
[105] (Fife Jr., 1916), pp. 123–124.
[106] (Fife Jr., 1916), pp. 124–125.
[107] (Fife Jr., 1916), pp. 125–126.
[108] (Hewitson, 2008), p. 42.
[109] (Perris, 1912), p. 311.
[110] (Blackbourn, 2003), pp. 312–313.
[111] (Abrams, 1992), p. 5.
[112] (Feuchtwanger, 2001), pp. 70–72.

gal entity. While still allowing candidates to run for election, authorities were empowered to prohibit meetings and publications that supported the socialists.[113] Civil service and postal workers were disciplined for voting for a socialist. It was no wonder that there was limited growth in the Social Democrat Party.[114]

It is instructive that an Army doctor quizzed a group of recruits in 1903–04 with such questions as, "What are Social Democrats?" Answers included: "They are the ones who don't want a Kaiser," "They don't believe in anything," "They want to get rid of the Church and the Army," and "They insult the German army." The recruits gave the impression of being well-informed on issues such as social insurance that affected their life, but could not tell the difference between Kaiser Wilhelm I and Kaiser Wilhelm II. They had heard of Bismarck; 25 percent read the paper regularly, but did not know the name of the current Chancellor; and they did not know the difference between state and national parliaments.[115]

They were not just a common group of recruits. They had been designated for a Silesian Cavalry Regiment. Of the 174 recruits, 147 of them had come from agricultural backgrounds and 44 percent of them were voluntary enlistees. The results may have been significantly different had they come from an urban background. The Social Democrats in urban areas had been focusing on youth clubs for those under 18 because they had been banned from political meetings.[116]

The SPD was very effective at winning the primary elections and turning out the vote. The party received 10 percent of the national vote while the antisocialist laws were in effect; 20 percent of the national vote immediately afterwards; and by 1912, one third of all votes cast. While this party was the largest in national parliamentary vote, the party represented three quarters of the vote in Berlin, 60 percent in Saxony, and 50 percent of all cities with a population over 10,000.[117]

NEWSPAPERS

Given today's world of communication and information flow, it is hard to understand that the only dissemination of information to the population of imperial Germany was through newspapers. Newspapers had fierce political leanings and could be directly tied to a party. In 1914, all political parties had their official newspaper. The SPD had *Vorwärts*; the other left wing liberals had the *Frankfurter Zeitung, Berliner Tageblatt*, and *Vossische Zeitung*; the National Liberals had the *Kölnische Zeitung* and *Magdeburgische Zeitung*; the Center Party had the *Kölnische Volkszeitung* and the *Kreuzzeitung*; Conservatives had the *Neue Preußische Zeitung;* agrarians had the *Deutsche Tageszeitung*; and the Pan-Germans had the *Täglische Rundschau*. *Norddeutsche Allgemeine Zeitung* presented the official government view and a great deal of the provincial press.[118] Once the war started, the official government bulletins were viewed with skepticism. They continually reported stunning victories that brought no peace.[119]

---

113 (Feuchtwanger, 2001), pp. 70–78.
114 (Feuchtwanger, 2001), pp. 104–105.
115 (Frevert, 2004), pg. 195.
116 (Frevert, 2004), pp. 195–196.
117 (Blackbourn, 2003), pp. 313–314.
118 (Verhey, *The Spirit of 1914*, 2000), pp. 15–16.
119 (Chickering, *The Great War and Urban Life in Germany*, 2007), pp. 78–79.

It was primarily members of the middle or upper-middle class who wrote the newspapers. This also applied to socialist periodicals; the lowest classes were insufficiently educated to write and print newspapers. These writings carried through to diaries and memoirs as well—those who left such works were from the middle and upper-middle-class not the lowest class.[120] There was also the issue of government control and censorship.

MILITARISM AND OTHER GROUPS

There were also agricultural and nationalist organizations. Not only were these groups or societies important to the government, but they also grew significantly during the imperial period. A man needed to own land to belong to an agricultural society. Although peasants with large, middle, and small land holdings could participate along with the estate owners, the three million agricultural hired workers could not. The example of West Prussia was extreme, but it shows that 57 of the 62 members of the Prussian state Landtag were members of the Agrarian League.[121]

The Pan-German League (*Alldeutscher Verband*) was the best known and the most notorious of the nationalist organizations; its members seemed obsessed with both internal and external enemies. It began as a revolution of members of the Colonial Society (*Deutsche Kolonialgesellschaft*), who were furious that the government had signed away a great deal of East African territory to Great Britain in exchange for the island of Helgoland in the North Sea.[122] It was a male-dominated organization that considered enemies from within imperial Germany to include homosexuals and women. While the Pan-German League was rather small, one of its nationalist cousins, the Navy League (*Deutscher Marinebund*) was quite large. Most of the nationalist organizational support came from Protestants in larger cities. By 1904, the Pan-German League was openly anti-Semitic. Their caricatures of Jewish people became commonplace. German racial purity and the Aryan ideal were themes of this organization. Other groups also demonized successful Jewish middlemen or department store owners; especially vitriolic was the Bavarian Peasant League. The Mittelstand tended to denounce Jews with the generally accepted politically correct term of "unfair competition."[123] Heinrich Class, the leader of the Pan-German League, blamed the Jewish population for nearly every ill facing imperial Germany in his 1912 book, *If I Were the Kaiser*. The government employed 54 percent of the members of the Pan-German league. In other right wing societies, that percentage was even higher. Conservatives were an educated minority.[124]

---

[120] (Verhey, *The Spirit of 1914*, 2000), pp. 12–13.
[121] (Aldenhoff, 1996), p. 40.
[122] (Chickering, *Militarism and Radical Nationalism*, 2008), p. 209.
[123] (Blackbourn, 2003), pp. 324–325.
[124] (Chickering, *Militarism and Radical Nationalism*, 2008), pp. 210–211.

THE ECONOMY

Industrialization, Trade and Railroads

Historically Germany was rural. As industrialization expanded there was a constant shift from rural to urban areas. The share of agricultural GNP shrank from 55 to 40 percent in 1880 to about 25 percent in 1913.[125] Until 1861, the large feudal estates in Prussia were totally exempt from taxation. The tax burden on the lower classes was oppressive. There was no clear method for a common standard of assessment. As a result, corruption of the civil servant was widespread. Despite efforts at tax reform by 1893 the exemption of taxes for the large feudal estates basically returned. Taxation became a uniform application of taxes versus a progressive income tax.[126]

Protective tariffs kept other nations' agricultural products from entering into the market. Extremely high excise fees went directly into the state coffers. The disparity in the development of income distribution resulted from constant favors bestowed upon the top incomes. Industrial workers' share of the national income shrank by 55 percent between 1870 and 1900. At the same time, the share of agrarian income dropped as expressed by growth rates. So, while industrial workers were earning less each year, the growth of agricultural income was also small. Yet national income continued to rise, especially in periods of economic boom. Literally, the rich were getting richer and the poor were getting poorer.[127]

Industrialization began later in Germany than in Britain, and the German economy was not a significant part of the world economy until late in the 19th century. Germany's industrialization started with the building of railroads in the 1840s and 1850s and the subsequent development of coal mining and iron and steel production; activities that made up what is called the First Industrial Revolution. In Germany, the Second Industrial Revolution—that is, the growth of chemical and electrical industries—followed the enormous expansion of coal and steel production so closely that the country can be said to have experienced the two revolutions almost simultaneously.

The political interests of the Zollverein were discussed in Chapter 1. However, it really is impossible to discuss the Zollverein without discussing the development of railroads. They were described as Siamese twins. Railway construction not only connected different regions and cities, but also played a crucial role in what has been termed the dual revolution: the twin processes of industrialization and national unification. Primarily the Zollverein was an economic institution. Between 1850 and 1860, the railroad network doubled in length from 6,000 to 11,500 km. By 1870, there was almost 20,000 km of track. From a tonnage perspective, the volume of rail freight increased 21 times between 1850 and 1870.[128]

This union encouraged the economic interdependence of the various member states. States received the majority of their funds from indirect taxation such as tariffs. Previously, internal trade between states could be taxed up to ten different times. The idea now was to support trade between the different members by removing tariff barriers inside the German states. These tariffs had resulted from the fragmentation of the states present in the Holy Roman Empire. Customs barriers of member states were leveled, and a uniform tariff was instituted against non-members. The customs at foreign frontiers were collected into a joint

[125] (Berghahn, 1994), p. 2.
[126] (Wehler, 1985), pp. 138–141.
[127] (Wehler, 1985), pp. 142–143.
[128] (Wehler, 1985), pp. 16–17.

account, and the proceeds were distributed in proportion to the population and resources of the member states. It was incredibly profitable for the member states, and members could not afford to leave this Prussian-dominated union. In the early 1860s, Bismarck was able to use the Franco-German trade treaty as a means to further isolate Austria. This pact made the economic isolation permanent. As an example of the profitability, Württemberg's share of the combined tariffs went from 7.4 percent of the budget to 14.6 percent after joining the union.[129]

The overwhelming need in this trade frenzy and the trade revolutions was to connect markets. Technology came to the front and provided railroads that could not only connect burgeoning industry with natural resources but also could make more isolated markets such as agricultural goods, more readily available. Because of size, the capital markets in Germany were not well developed enough to finance privately huge railway construction projects, as was the case in Britain. The state became involved as a company struggled, and most German states included both state-run railroads and private companies. Eventually the state became the primary source for funding railroad construction, and many states borrowed huge amounts of money in the form of railway loans. The states had several choices—either they could give some sort of financial concession, such as guaranteeing the interest on railroad shares, or they could build the railroads themselves. Smaller states tended to use private investment and larger states opted for state railways. Medium-sized states such as Baden, Bavaria, and Württemberg were overwhelmingly state run.[130] Prussia nationalized its railways in 1880 in an effort both to lower rates on freight service and to equalize those rates among shippers. Instead of lowering rates as far as possible, the government ran the railways as a profitmaking endeavor, and the railway profits became a major source of revenue for the state. The nationalization of the railways slowed the economic development of Prussia because the state favored the relatively backward agricultural areas in its railway building. Between 1880 and 1889, most of the private lines were nationalized.

Unlike other Western more uniform economies, the smaller German states needed to prove themselves through railway policy. It was a more state-centered network than a federal structure. Territorial fragmentation created not a single German national railway as much as a conglomeration of state networks. The individual railways acted as if they were independent operations and developed their own rolling stock. The smaller states feared they would be cut off from their traditional trade flows with their neighbors if they did not connect by rail.[131]

Finances

Imperial Germany's fiscal year ran 1 April to 31 March. Under budgetary law, money not spent by the end of the fiscal year had to be returned to the Minister of Finance. For this reason, money necessary for ships was approved in installments. Orders for ships were not paid for in full when the ships were delivered, rather advances were paid during construction. Only the states levied direct taxes. States provided contributions to the imperial budget by "Matricular Contributions," which were provided from the states to the Empire based on

[129] (Green, *Fatherlands*, 2004), pp. 238–240.
[130] (Green, *Fatherlands*, 2004), pp. 240–241.
[131] (Green, *Fatherlands*, 2004), pp. 238–244.

population, not on the size or value of their economies.[132] This amount changed every year through legislation between the Reichstag and the Bundesrat.[133]

Prior to unification there were several different types of currency. While different states had different currencies, most of them were linked to something called *Vereinsthaler*. This was a currency based on silver—a large amount of silver. When the exchange was made, the general rate was three gold marks to one Vereinsthaler. Southern German states generally used the *Gulden,* which was worth 1.71 *Mark*.[134] From 1876, a common currency was created based on the gold standard. This currency was called the *Goldmark,* which differentiated it from paper currency. The official exchange was 1 Mark=358 mg of gold. The United States was also on the gold standard at this time, and the official exchange was approximately $0.25 for a Goldmark.

Tax officials tended to be rich landowners who hid their own taxable assets. Historically, tax revenue in Southern Germany was a type of capital gains tax. Northern Germany tended to adopt personal income taxes that were class oriented, with the primary burden of taxation falling on the lower classes. It was not until after the formation of the Empire that a graduated income tax replaced taxes based on class.[135] In 1891, Prussia adopted a progressive income tax. This progressive measure provided for incredibly low taxes compared with post-war or modern taxes. There was a top rate of four percent for income greater than 100,000 marks. People earning less than 900 marks per year were exempt from taxation. While this saved a great deal of money for the lower class, it also affected the voting franchise when this was based on the amount of taxes paid.[136]

The income of the empire derived heavily from customs' duties or tariffs. At times almost half of the operating income came from these sources (47 percent in 1913). A series of commercial treaties were concluded and tariffs were always a hot topic of discussion in the legislatures. Another huge source of income was the excise tax or consumption tax levied on brandy, beer, cigarettes, sugar, and salt. Many of these taxes were kept by the South German states as a condition of their joining the Prussian-led Confederation. There was also stamp duty paid on playing cards, bills of exchange, foreign banking notes, shares, deeds, mortgages, bills of sale, bills of lading, tickets, and licenses among other things. Empire property, such as railroads, post offices, and telegraphs were run like any public corporation; their profits were added to the imperial revenue.

In 1914, between 52 and 65 percent of monetary circulation was coinage. For most transactions, the government endeavored to discourage the use of coins and other forms of cash. Whenever possible, the central bank preferred paper money to coins. Both checks and interbank transfers were encouraged to keep liquidity higher. While the amount of imperial assets was small, there was a fund known as the Imperial War Treasury that contained 120 million marks in gold intended to cover the costs of mobilization.[137] Under the terms of the treaty between Germany and France in 1871, France paid a significant indemnity. Not only was the war treasury established, but also a large-scale disabled veterans' fund. The railroads in Alsace-Lorraine were actually purchased from France for 325 million francs in 1871.

---

[132] (Feuchtwanger, 2001) p. 62.
[133] (Aldenhoff, 1996) p. 47.
[134] This is only a rough guide; there were many exceptions, especially in the independent cities.
[135] (Wehler, 1985), pp, 137–141.
[136] (Hewitson, 2008), p. 47.
[137] (Krüger, 1915), pp. 134–140.

There were also leftover funds used for the administration of the empire. France paid off this indemnity much faster than anyone in imperial Germany had imagined.[138]

Army appropriations were different from normal budgetary appropriations. From 1867 to 1874, the army operated under something known as the "Iron Budget." This budget strongly favored the army. The military budget, which made up over 90 percent of the imperial budget, provided a fixed sum for every soldier, whose numbers were determined as fixed percentage of the population.[139] A compromise with the Reichstag was reached in 1874 that allowed a seven-year cycle of military budget appropriations. This compromised much of the Reichstag's power because, in so doing, it accepted a peacetime force structure that was fixed for longer than the three-year term of office of the Reichstag Deputies.[140] Eventually this cycle was changed to a five-year cycle of appropriations. This cycle was significantly different from the pattern followed by the imperial Navy. The Navy went through an annual scrutiny by the Reichstag beginning in 1898.

While military bills were the most hotly contested legislation in imperial Germany, they never failed to pass. There were times when extraordinary measures were taken to pass such a budget, such as the 1887 "war scare" or the dissolution of the Reichstag by Caprivi in 1893.[141] The *Wehrbeitrag*, or defense contribution, was a one-time capital gains tax in 1913 to fund an increase in the army, necessitated by imperial German knowledge of secret agreements between its enemies. This levy was a direct property tax on estates exceeding 10,000 marks. There was also an increase in the stamp duty and sugar taxes.[142]

Financial control of the military budgets changed dramatically in May 1873, when the property of all the military administrations was transferred to the Empire. With the exception of the Navy, the Chancellor became responsible for all the military budgets. This role brought the ministers of war of the four contingents under the financial supervision of the Chancellor.[143] Bavaria was different in that its part of the budget was received as a lump sum annually, and Bavaria determined how to use it.[144] Although it is not simple to understand, Bavaria administered its army at its own expense, but in accordance with the general regulations for the rest of the German army.[145]

[138] (Howard, 1906), pp. 251–259.
[139] (Feuchtwanger, 2001), p. 46.
[140] (Förster, 2006), p. 461.
[141] (Blackbourn, 2003), p. 308.
[142] (Krüger, 1915), pp. 143–144.
[143] (Krüger, 1915), p. 32.
[144] (Krüger, 1915), pp. 144–145.
[145] (Howard, 1906), p. 249.

Tax Revenues of Imperial Germany 1913

	Revenues—1913	
Death Duties	43.6	
Capital Gains	2.8	
Property Tax	0	
Stamp Duties	183.1	
Tariffs	560.8	
Consumption Tax	775.8	Beer, liquor, tobacco, sugar
Matricular Contribution	51.9	
Wehrbeitrag (1913 only)	637.4	
Post Office/Railroad	43.6	
Other	118.3	
Total	**2417.3**	
	Expenditures—1913	
Armaments	2406.4	
Administration	176	
Social insurance	87.9	
Total	**2670.3**	

(Howard, 1906), p. 249.

CHAPTER 5

NATIONAL SERVICE

THE ONE PERCENT RULE AND THE ARMY (QUINQENNAT BUDGETS)

There was a constant three-way struggle over the size of the army. The Reichstag wanted to limit the cost of the army. The Chief of the General Staff wanted to enlarge the army for operational reasons. The War Minister wanted to maintain the high quality and reliability of both the officer corps and the enlisted soldiers. While the original compromise of seven-year budgets and three-year service commitments limited the control of the Reichstag, it also provided a tool that allowed the Army to limit recruiting intake to acceptable circles that came from primarily rural locations. While the aim of the Kaiser, the army leadership, and Bismarck was to limit the influence of civilian politicians, there was always conflict with the liberal parts of the Reichstag.

Right-wing theoreticians might have favored military spending, but the conservatives balked when asked to pay.[1] Compromise was reached between the Kaiser's right to fix the peacetime strength of the army and the counterbalancing right of the Reichstag to approve the military budget. While Article 57 of the Constitution provided for universal conscription, that really did not happen because of limits placed on the size of the army. Conscription was never truly universal, because the army was limited in size and could not accept all fit men as recruits. Originally, Article 60 of the Constitution set the peacetime strength of the army at one percent of the population. Changes to this limit had to be fixed by law. In 1874, Bismarck tried to make this percentage permanent, but the Reichstag rejected it, as that would have eliminated their influence on military budget, and as a result, 90 percent of the Empire's budget.

The original compromise fixed the peacetime strength in seven-year increments, known in 1874 as the *Septennat*.[2] There was a second Septennat in 1880 and a third one in 1887. As the growth of foreign armies and Franco-Russian rapprochement meant that a larger army was needed. In 1890, the War Minister worked out a plan to increase the army size by 150,000 men. The Reichstag rejected this increase, and a second attempt was made, limiting the increase to 72,000. When this effort also ran into opposition from the Reichstag, it was dissolved and Chancellor Caprivi submitted a smaller increase of 60,000 men to the new Reichstag. The key changes also included a reduction in service commitment to two years

1 (Showalter D., 2000), p. 687.
2 (Förster, 2006), pp. 460–462.

and a reduction in the budget length from seven to five years. These last two changes offered the Reichstag more control but increased the number of individuals in the army, thereby increasing the army's exposure to the more populated urban areas, and the Social Democratic Party.[3]

The army budget came under greater pressure after 1897 once the decision was made to enter into a massive naval buildup. In 1890 and 1900, the Reichstag approved a shipbuilding program that was to produce 45 capital ships by 1920. The army acquiesced to smaller budgets and sizes in favor of the navy until around 1910. With political backing, the army again started expanding, this time against the inclination of the War Minister, who was attempting to limit the increase, so as to prevent dilution in the quality of officers and noncommissioned officers at a high level. By 1913, Admiral Tirpitz abandoned the navy's priority of budgeting to the army, based on the imminence of an impending war.[4]

Army strength, which had started at 400,000 in the 1870s, jumped to 600,000 by 1900. After the large expansion of 1911 through 1913, the peacetime strength stood at 770,000. There was a special authorization for three years in 1890. The budget timing then moved to five years in 1893, 1899, 1905, and in 1911. There were special one-year increases in 1912 and 1913.[5]

Growth of the Army between 1871 and 1914

	1871	1881	1887	1891	1893	1899	1904	1905	1911	1912	1913
Auth. (000's)	402	424	468	487	479	496	496	506	551	544	662
Sep.Auth. NCOs (000's)	0	0	0	0	77.8	81.9	81.9	847	88.5	94.9	110
Infantry battalions	469	503	534	538	711	625	633	633	634	651	699
Cavalry squadrons	465	465	465	465	477	482	510	510	510	516	550
Field artillery batteries	300	340	364	434	494	574	574	574	592	633	633
Foot artillery battalions	29	31	31	31	37	38	40	40	48	48	55
Engineer battalions	18	19	19	20	24	26	29	29	29	33	44
Verkehrs-truppen battalions	0	0	0	0	2	11	12	12	17	18	31
Train battalions	18	18	18	21	21	23	23	23	23	25	26

(Staatsbürger Bibliotek, 1913), pp. 15–80. It should be noted that field artillery figures are in batteries not battalions.

3 (Förster, 2006), pp. 470–473.
4 (Förster, 2006), pp. 472–479.
5 (Staatsbürger Bibliotek, 1913), pp. 14–78.

TWO OR THREE YEARS OF SERVICE?

Every man in Germany, with the exception of some royalty and criminals who had served custodial sentences, was liable for military service. This was stipulated in imperial German law (*Wehrordnung*) in 1888.[6] The individual state governments carefully guarded the granting of full citizenship. With citizenship came responsibility for service in the military. This statement can be very misleading. Had every fit man in Germany served in the army, the German military would not have had a manpower shortage in completing the Schlieffen Plan. Some believe that all Germans entered the army and learned from the "school of the nation" all things German. This is another myth. Germany drafted only about 35 percent of its available manpower, of which only 20 percent actually served in the active army. France drafted about 50–60 percent. The Chief of the General Staff wanted to enlarge the numbers of men drafted, but the War Minister was against it. A future leader from the General Staff, Erich Ludendorff estimated that in 1912 alone, 540,000 adult Germans avoided any kind of military service with their class.[7]

The recruiting numbers below from 1907 shows that not everyone served:

- Number of men liable 556,772
- Physically unqualified 35,802
- Voluntarily enlisted before required age 57,739
- Sent to Navy 10,374
- Available as army recruits 452,857
- Assigned to active military service 212, 661
- Assigned to Landsturm 240,196.[8]

While the top line continued to grow, the percentage of soldiers needed varied by year's requirements for replacements and maneuvers. The population had grown from 56 million to 67 million from the turn-of-the-century to 1913. Yet in 1912, only 212,000 were assigned to active military service, and in 1913, 305,000 were assigned to active military service.[9] In May 1914, the Chief of Staff lamented that 38,000 qualified young men annually were evading the draft because of a shortage of funds.[10]

MUSTERUNG

To facilitate conscription, all citizens were categorized by annual class year designated by the year in which they were born (*Jahrgang*). For example, the class of 1892 would enter the recruiting process in 1912 when their *Jahresklasse* reached the age of 20. This process is often confused because the French system used the year in which they reported. Recruiting was a yearlong cycle. Between the first of January and the middle of February, a list of

[6] (*Wehrordnung des Deutschen Reiches*, 1888)
[7] (Strachan, *The First World War*, 2003), p. 46.
[8] (Harrell, 1983), p. 12.
[9] (Berghahn, 1994), p. 43.
[10] (Herwig H. , 2009), p. 45.

service-eligible young men from the subject class year was assembled. The lowest recruiting committee considered requests for exemption from service.[11]

Though the list was prepared, the class would be mustered or assembled at one location for each recruiting committee. This annual spring event was called Musterung. Four different groups of men went to a medical examination at Musterung:

1) The Jahrgang class in question,
2) *Restanten*—men who were required to repeat the examination from the two previous years,
3) A few older men who had been allowed to postpone their service for various reasons,
4) Younger men allowed in before their Jahrgang class—primarily these were enlistees.

The examination was a large event attended by many families as the young men went through medical and psychological testing.

There was also a period when a candidate could list the reasons why he should not serve or should be deferred for a year. The doctors had a specific list of criteria for fitness. Recruits were supposed to be of a certain height, and weak men were deferred one year at a time for up to three years. There was a process of requesting exemption that was often granted in cases where the recruit was the sole breadwinner, or if he were indispensable in his place of work.[12] After the tests, specific individuals were crossed off the list. Those removed from the list included one-year volunteers, two-, three-, or four-year volunteers, enlistees, those who had not shown up, and those physically, morally, or mentally unfit.[13]

Each man undergoing the examination was given one of four rankings:

- K.V. (*kriegsverwendungsfähig*)—fit for active service.
- G.V. (*garnisonsverwendungsfähig*)—fit for garrison duty in Germany or along the lines of communication.
- A.V. (*arbeitsverwendungsfähig*)—fit for labor employment only.
- D.U. (*dienstunfähig*)—permanently unfit.[14]

Recruiting tended to be done geographically and along regimental lines. A wartime reserve infantry regiment usually drew its members from the recruiting areas of two peacetime infantry regiments, and a reserve field artillery unit from the recruiting area of a peacetime infantry division. An engineering company drew its members from the recruiting area of a peacetime army corps. The units of the Prussian Guard drew their recruits—and thus their reservists—from the entire recruiting area of the Prussian army.

In the provinces that were not ethnically German, there was resistance to being enlisted—especially by the bourgeoisie. The residents of Alsace-Lorraine were culturally used to the French system where one could “buy” a replacement. This substitution was not allowed under the German system.[15] It is surprising then that Alsace stood first among all German provinces in the ratio of draft eligible men, who were found fit and passed the test with 66.7 percent. Lorraine was fourth with 58.9 percent and was exceeded only by East and West Prussia.[16]

---

11 (U.S. Army War College, 1917), p. 28.
12 (Frevert, 2004), pp. 49–50.
13 (Stubbs, 2004), p. 33.
14 (*The General Staff*, 1918), p. 13.
15 (Frevert, 2004), p. 52.
16 (Silverman, 1972), p. 73.

For those candidates who remained and were qualified, lots were drawn to determine who should serve and who would not if there were more candidates than spaces required. This lottery number remained with the candidates and soldiers throughout their lives. After the Musterung, chosen candidates would be sent to various units. The various arms and services had different minimum standards. For instance, infantry had to be 1.54 m tall, and engineers were somewhat taller—1.57 m. Guard infantry were supposed to be 1.7 m tall. Railway troops were not allowed to be colorblind. This entire operation was completed by the first of May each year. Those selected in the Jahrgang class began their *Dienstpflicht*.[17]

There was also a small ritual in the days prior to reporting for duty. Those selected would march through town beating drums and demanding money from folks to pay for a last drink. The local ladies would tie bright ribbons to the hats of the soldiers-to-be. This ritual lasted two or three days and was often funded by those not selected.[18]

The increase in army strength after 1912 is very evident. The majority of the *Landsturm Contingent I* and *Ersatz Reserve* was selected from those who were examined for the third and last time—the 22 year olds. Rejected men were not liable for any form of military service. Those rejected amounted to five or six percent of the total mustered number. Restanten were released from service after three Musterung and entered into the Landsturm's second contingent.[19]

From Musterung to Conscription 1911–1913

	Total going to *Musterung*	Posted to *Landsturm* 1st ban	Posted to *Ersatz Reserve*	*Dienst-pflicht*	Total including volunteers, Navy, and rejections	*Restanten* for next year
1911 20 year olds	563,024	16,680	6,141	106,249	565,520	705,864
21 year olds	367,688	13,925	4,817	53,185		
22 year olds	289,098	102,821	77,486	62,510		
Older and younger	51,574	8,881	3,699	1,981		
Total	**1,271,384**	**142,307**	**92,143**	**223,925**		

1912 20 year olds	557,608	15,022	5,969	112,624	572,168	717,700
21 year olds	385,163	12,366	4,621	57,757		
22 year olds	294,825	101,475	73,243	67,261		
Older and younger	52,272	9,059	3,873	2,075		
Total	**1,289,868**	**137,922**	**87,706**	**239,717**		

17 (Hein, 1901), p. 74.
18 (Frevert, 2004), pp. 171–173.
19 (*The General Staff*, 1918), p. 10.

	Total going to *Musterung*	Posted to *Landsturm* 1st ban	Posted to *Ersatz Reserve*	*Dienst-pflicht*	Total including volunteers, Navy, and rejections	*Restanten* for next year
1913 20 year olds	587,888	12,825	5,521	125,001		
21 year olds	380,331	10,371	4,439	80,767		
22 year olds	305,619	87,189	73,064	97,371	622,360	705,659
Older and younger	54,181	7,915	3,887	2,536		
Total	**1,328,019**	**118,300**	**86,911**	**305,675**		

(The General Staff, 1918), p. 10.

The Quality of Recruits: Rural vs. Urban

While clearly the requirement to recruit existed, there was a major controversy as to the source of the recruits. Reforms required recruits generally to reflect the make-up of society. The prevailing thought was that soldiers from the countryside were healthier and less likely to be socialists. Recruits from an urban background were less likely to be healthy and more likely to be involved in socialism. But, the population pressures of internal immigration took its toll. Before 1850, most of the recruiting took place in rural areas, but after the formation of the Empire, more and more recruits made their living as wage earners in factories. In the 1890s, the source of these recruits became a major subject of political debate. One economist, Lugo Brentano, made the case that two-thirds of the recruits actually came from an urban background.[20] The very emotional opposing view claimed that two-thirds of the recruits were from rural areas. In 1911, just six percent came from the large cities. There is still disagreement as to whether this was a leadership decision or the result of poor health of the urban recruits.[21] In 1904, the War Minister admitted that the aim was to avoid training members of the Social Democrats in weaponry and that the loyalty of soldiers was more important than their quality. There was a famous quote by War Minister Karl v. Einem, "I prefer a monarchist and religious soldier to a Social Democrat, even if he is not as good a shot."[22] The various methods used to control conscription and limit the influence of the Social Democrats took a major blow in 1892. Then Chancellor Caprivi agreed to shorten the three-year active service requirement to two years in order to gain Social Democrats' support for his rearmament program. The physical number of individuals entering the army skyrocketed, requiring more to be drawn from the growing urban areas under social democratic influence.[23]

Dienstpflicht

There were basically two divisions of manpower: active military service (Dienstpflicht and *Landwehr*) and the *Landsturm*. In theory, this was supposed to cover the ages of 17 through 45. Walter Bloem, author of *The Advance from Mons,* was a reserve captain at the age of 46

[20] (Frevert, 2004), pp. 191–192.
[21] (Blackbourn, 2003), p. 288.
[22] (Förster, *Der doppelte Militarismus*, 1985)
[23] (Förster, 2006), pp. 465–466.

in 1914; so, as usual, there were exceptions for officers.[24] The generally accepted idea was that foot soldiers served two years in the active force before joining the reserve. Mounted soldiers, like the cavalry or field artillery, would serve three years of active service.

Since the Napoleonic Wars, the Germans had had two kinds of armies: a professional army, and a people's army known as the Landwehr. The conservative aristocracy favored a professional army officered by the aristocracy, who swore direct allegiance to the king. The more liberal middle class and lower classes preferred a Landwehr, officered by the middle class and regulated by parliament. The system changed over time and provided 40 years of peace that incorporated all classes.[25]

Active military service was known as Dienstpflicht (often this is referred to as *Dienstzeit*, but that word primarily addressed the active years of the class). There are two further divisions; the active army and the reserve forces (both part of Dienstpflicht). The total time served in both equaled seven years. The second group was the first and second ban (the word ban is often exchanged for the word levy) of the Landwehr.

The start date of active service is interesting. For clarity, we will refer to the standard service soldier as a draftee (this is not a proper German term). Most young men left the *Volksschule* at the age of 14. Required active service started at the age of 20. Between the ages of 17 and 20, young men were not part of the Dienstpflicht. They actually were assigned to the Landsturm. A student who passed the one-year volunteer exam could delay entry until he was 20. Conversely, a one-year volunteer could join at the age of 17. Once he was in the army, a normal draftee served two years in the infantry or three years in the cavalry or horse artillery.

While generally true, there were exceptions. Soldiers who went to train battalions could serve much shorter periods of active duty. Prussian and Bavarian train soldiers could serve for one or two years and Saxons for two years. For the remaining years, up to a total of seven, soldiers then became part of that unit's reserve. During the period of reserve commitment, the soldier was called up twice for training. Lengths of training times seem to have been variable, but did not exceed eight weeks. At the end of his active time, if a soldier wanted to stay in the army, he could stay on as a professional called a *Kapitulanten* or enlistee. An interesting piece of trivia is that the Kapitulanten Gefreiter actually was paid about 50 percent more than the normal draftees. They were also given a monetary inducement to re-enlist.[26]

Recruits reported in October and were assigned to their regiments. Their regiment further assigned them to a specific company based on height. The tallest recruits were sent to the first company of each battalion or the fifth and ninth companies. The shortest recruits were sent to companies four, eight, and twelve. Uniforms and equipment were issued at the company or battalion level.[27] The oath of loyalty, or *Fahneneid*, was administered to the recruits several weeks after joining the regiment. The oath was administered one of three ways during a major ceremony: the soldier's left hand was placed either on the colors, the point of an officer's sword, or an artillery piece, and then he raised his right hand. Sometimes this was done in small groups, and sometimes at a larger formation.[28]

---

[24] (Bloem, 2004)
[25] (Frevert, 2004), pp. 155–157.
[26] (Rabenau, 1914), pp. 20–21.
[27] (Bartsch, *Deutsches Soldatenleben*, 1907), pp. 25–38.
[28] (Bartsch, *Deutsches Soldatenleben*, 1907), pp. 37–38.

> The oath in Prussia was: I (name) swear to God the Omniscient and Omnipotent one bodily oath to His Majesty the King of Prussia (Alsace-Lorraine, "the Emperor"), Wilhelm II, my most gracious sovereign, that I will, in any and all circumstances and places, wherever they may be on land and at sea, in war and peace time, serve you faithfully and truly; that I will, Most Highest, uphold all that is best and beneficial to you, avoiding all that is disadvantageous or damaging; that I will obey and follow precisely the Articles of War, which have been read to me, together with all regulations and orders given to me and will conduct myself always as an honest, fearless, dutiful and honorable soldier should., *So wahr mir Gott helfe durch Jesum Christum und sein heiliges Evangelium!* [So help me God, through Jesus Christ and his Holy Gospels!] (Jewish Soldiers: "*So wahr mit Gott helfe!*") [29]

The oaths used in other states were broadly similar, though the oath of allegiance was to the particular sovereign involved; to the Kaiser was pledged only a duty of obedience to his orders, this undertaking being further restricted in Bavaria to obedience during time of war. For the Hanseatic Cities the oath was given to . . . the high Senate and the free and Hanseatic state of ________.

Another type of Dienstpflicht was volunteers or *Freiwilliger*. There were two different types of Freiwilliger—multi-year and one-year. Multi-year Freiwilliger were basically enlistees. They applied to a specific unit and if they had parental permission and assurances that the family could do without them, they could apply for two-, three- or four-year status. The *Unteroffiziere* would vote to accept them or not. This was not comparable to a one-year volunteer and the family was not required to pay for the equipment and sustainment. While there is much about the volunteers, 96 percent of all soldiers were draftees.[30]

[29] Translated by Jack Sheldon with a note: The Prussian oath is a complex statement, including numerous expressions that were archaic even before the Kaiser ascended to the throne.

[30] (Frevert, 2004), p. 170.

CHAPTER 6

THE PEACETIME MILITARY

THE HIGHER LEADERSHIP

The German Army had four distinct elements: Prussian, Württemberg, Saxon and Bavarian armies. Because they were separate armies, the terminology used by each is often confusing. Even Otto v. Bismarck was confounded by the varying references. He admitted that it was not constitutionally correct, but rather than name each individual army, as a Prussian, he elected to use the expression "Imperial Army" for the sake of succinctness. *Reichsheer* was the term favored by the Kaiser.

According to the imperial Constitution, the empire covered the expenses of the Prussian, Württemberg, and Saxon components. Bavaria had to cover the peacetime expenses of its army from its own resources. Only upon mobilization did Bavaria receive financial support from the *Reichstag*. Article 53 of the Imperial Constitution declared that the navy of the Empire was united and under the Supreme Command of the Kaiser. It was written, in part, because of all the 25 states, only Prussia had a navy prior to the Constitution. The navy was an internal indivisible organization set forth in the constitution.

Article 63, on the other hand, stated: "The entire land force of the Empire shall constitute a united army, which in war and in peace shall be under the command of the Kaiser." It was legal language, but had many loopholes. There was no united imperial Army but simply contingents of the member states. The army was a collective unit and its unity did not cancel the existence of state contingents. The term "imperial German Army" is an improper collective phrase that is, nevertheless, often used through ignorance or simply as a type of shorthand.[1]

When the states joined the German Empire, they ceased to be sovereign but did not cease to be states. Nowhere did the states give up sovereignty more completely than in military affairs. Most states had their own armies but each army was recruited, organized, equipped, and drilled not in conformity with state regulations but rather by the rules of the empire, which in turn were determined by Prussia. Formally, the state possessed military supremacy, but the content and extent of that supremacy was determined by the military conventions between the states and Prussia.[2]

1 (Howard, 1906), p. 429 and (Pflugk-Hartung, 1896), pp. 67–68.
2 (Howard, 1906), pp. 19–27, 429.

The Hanseatic Cities and four principalities did not form their own military.[3] Rather, Prussia had units stationed in their capital cities and often those Prussian units have been erroneously considered units of the hosting state; however, they were not—they belonged directly to the Prussian army. The conscripts from these states entered directly into the Prussian army through separate military conventions. This was really a holdover from the North German Confederation, i.e., the *Militärkonvention zwischen dem Norddeutschen Bunde und Hamburg vom 23 Juli 1867.* This made sense at the time; however, these agreements froze regimental structure and eventually led to a very convoluted recruiting and naming system. For instance, in 1871, *Infanterie-Regiment Graf Bose (1. Thüringisches)* Nr. 31 moved from Erfurt in Thuringia to Altona, a suburb of Hamburg and lost any connection to Thuringia except in name.[4]

The states that had no contingents had links to particular units and formations. Third Battalion Infanterie-Regiment Graf Bülow v. Dennewitz (6. Westfälisches) Nr. 55, for example, was associated with the Principality of Lippe. The Principality of Schwarzburg-Sonderhausen was associated with First Battalion 3. Thüringisches Infanterie-Regiment Nr. 71. The Principality of Waldeck was associated with Third Battalion Infanterie-Regiment von Wittich (3. Kurhessisches) Nr. 83. The Principality of Schaumburg-Lippe was associated with Westfälisches Jäger Batallion Nr. 7. The Hanseatic city of Hamburg was associated with Infanterie-Regiment Hamburg (2. Hanseatisches) Nr. 76. The Hanseatic city of Lübeck was associated with First and Second Battalion Infanterie-Regiment Lübeck (3.Hanseatisches) Nr. 162. The Hanseatic city of Bremen was associated with First and Second Battalion Infanterie-Regiment Bremen (1. Hanseatisches) Nr. 75.[5]

All states eventually entered into military conventions with Prussia. These conventions ceded to the King of Prussia what constitutional powers the states may have had relative to military matters. Unlike the North German Confederation, each of the armies was placed under the Kaiser in the event of war. The King of Saxony and the King of Württemberg could appoint officers within their contingents; however, the appointment of generals was only with the consent of the Kaiser. The Kaiser personally approved the appointment of every army corps commander. The King of Bavaria had no such restrictions; he still had the right to appoint commanding generals of the Bavarian army corps without endorsement by the Kaiser. Their sovereignty over the military was in name only. The rulers did retain military honors and the right to appoint aides-de-camp.

The small states paid a certain price to the Prussian treasury for each soldier absorbed into the Prussian army. Prussia then paid the men, promoted them, and received their oath of allegiance. Officers of the small states were normally required to provide a written document to their ruler reinforcing their faith as loyal subjects, but then submerged themselves in the Prussian army. In many cases, the rulers of the small states, published farewell greetings to their troops.[6]

So why was Prussia so dominant? In addition to great success in the wars of the 19th century, when the 22 states of the North German Confederation united, Prussia represented

---

3 This is certainly true for Lübeck, where the 162nd Infantry was a completely Prussian regiment. But the 75th and 76th Infantry in Bremen and Hamburg were distinct Hanseatic regiments based on the tradition of the Hanseatic *Bürger-Militär*.

4 At the time of the convention Hamburg had a population of fewer than 290,000. Hamburg's population increased 279 percent by 1914. Hamburg only contributed one regiment to the Prussian army according to the convention and this did not increase by WW1.

5 (Ulrich Herr & Jens Nguyen, 2008), p. 18.

6 (Times, 1871)

80 percent of the total population and 85 percent of the total area. (Of that population of 30 million, 24 million were Prussian; 2 million were Saxon, leaving 4 million to be divided among the other 20 members.) Article 61 of the North German Confederation Constitution gave Prussia the power of having all military legislation immediately introduced into the entire territory of the union. It was the same with the change of words from "the entire territory of the union" to "the empire." Prussia gained the constitutional right to dictate military regulations and instructions; other legislation had to be adopted immediately by all contingents in the empire. By 1914, 19 of the 25 army corps were from Prussia and 75 percent of the Army was Prussian.[7]

The Kaiser's total control of the military, explained in the Constitution, was controversial because the Reichstag did not support that amount of power lying solely in the hands of the Kaiser. The Kaiser split this control of the army into three separate groups that led to an unbelievably convoluted chain of command that often revolved around who had the most access to the Kaiser.

First there was the War Minister, plus the ministries of the Bavarian, Saxon, and Württemberg armies and the Corps Commanders. Next was the Chief of Staff, who was in charge of the Great General Staff. The third group was the Kaiser's Military Cabinet that also held a leading position for the other contingents except Bavaria.

There were also the following—sometimes-competing—command and control bodies:

- Navy Office,
- General Staff of the Bavarian and Saxon general staffs,
- Admiralty Staff of the Imperial Navy,
- Navy Cabinet,
- Civil Cabinet,
- Imperial Headquarters with its aides-de-camp.

These parallel and, to a certain degree, redundant structures made any efficient co-ordination of military efforts, particularly between army and navy, very difficult, if not impossible. From a strategic point of view, the gigantic efforts to build up a blue water navy (*Hochseeflotte*) after 1898 were quite useless since a future war was supposed to be decided on the continent.

The Chief of Staff and the Great General Staff were responsible for military strategy, mobilization, and the readiness of the army. The War Minister, who was really the Prussian War Minister, was responsible for doctrine, ostensibly the corps commanders, and the structure of the Army. He was also directly responsible for the size of the army and obtaining annual financial support from the Reichstag. The Military Cabinet was directly responsible to the Kaiser, independent of both the Great General Staff and the Ministry of War and made all the personnel appointments in the Army.[8]

This is the crux of the split command issue. The Chief of Staff determined the requirement for the size of the army. The War Minister drafted the legislation and submitted the budget to the Reichstag that funded the size of the army. The Military Cabinet determined what key officers would be in position to make it all happen. This agreement and competi-

7 (Howard, 1906), pp. 427–428. See Appendix A.

8 (Mombauer, 2003), p. 14.

tion among these three groups, especially the War Minister and Chief of Staff, would lead to a disconnect between requirements and resources.

In addition, the army corps commanders, the so-called Commanding Generals, held very special positions since they had the right of immediate access (*Immediatvortragsrecht*) to the Kaiser. Around 1910, there were about 40 positions with the right of immediate access to the Kaiser (*Immediatstellen*):[9]

- Prussian War Minister,
- General Adjutants,
- Chief of Military Cabinet,
- Commanding Generals (and comparable positions),
- Commanders of the army inspections and of the general inspections of cavalry, foot-artillery, engineers and fortresses, and of the military transportation branch,
- *Befehlshaber in den Marken,*
- Chief of General Staff (since 1883).

The imperial Navy held a comparable number of positions with immediate access.

THE WAR MINISTRY

Founded by Gerhard v. Scharnhorst, in 1809, the War Ministry was the central command and control body of the Prussian Army. When Scharnhorst started his reforms after the devastating defeat of 1807, he wanted to have a centralized command organization equipped with the necessary power and responsibilities. He blamed decentralization and pluralism of military power together with a weak king, who hesitated to make quick and strong decisions. Originally, the ministry was responsible for the entire military administration, and the minister, a high-ranking general, was the king's highest and most senior military advisor. The Ministry of War did not maintain its central power for long. In 1821, with the appointment of a separate Chief of General Staff of the Army, a process of separation began. In 1824, a department for personal matters (*Abtheilung für die persönlichen Angelegenheiten*) was founded within the Ministry leading to a further erosion of centralized power.[10]

During the Danish War of 1864, War Minister Albrecht v. Roon was still the King's central and most powerful adviser, but this position shifted to Helmuth v. Moltke after the battle of Königgrätz in 1866. After 1871, the responsibilities of the Ministry were further reduced, as the General Staff and the Military Cabinet asserted themselves and claimed increasing shares in the Ministry's power and responsibilities.

Basically the War Ministry remained responsible for the army's organization, equipment, armament, budget, and related matters. The War Ministry was responsible for organizational issues, ordnance (rifle testing committee (*Gewehr-Prüfungskommission*)), artillery testing committee (*Artillerie-Prüfungskommission*), training (inspectors of the different arms (*Inspizienten der Waffengattungen*)), manuals and regulations, officer and NCO training schools, uniforms and equipment. In short, the War Ministry was an administrative

---

[9] Immediatvortragsrecht or Immediatrecht specifies the right of having immediate access to the Kaiser and presenting an issue to him without anybody else being present. All positions having this right of immediate access to the Kaiser were called *Immediatstellen*.

[10] (Mombauer, 2003), pp. 25–28.

body with shrinking political influence, which explains why Schlieffen was so welcome; he was a Chief of General Staff without any political ambitions—particularly in comparison to Waldersee. In cooperation with the General Staff, the War Ministry was responsible for training manuals and setting of standards for troops and non-commissioned officers (NCOS) as well as commissioned officers. While the General Staff took responsibility over operational planning, the War Ministry kept responsibility for strength, ordnance and mobilization issues.[11]

In fact, the Ministry assumed a more political role. It had to present the military budget to the Reichstag on behalf of the Kaiser following the One Percent Rule and had to administer it. To the Reichstag, the Minister did not just act as a Prussian minister but as a kind of an imperial War Minister (*Reichskriegsminister*). The General Staff informed him of its demands and requirements, but it was up to the War Minister to decide, in conjunction with the Kaiser, which army or navy increases were really needed and how the Reichstag would fund them. The Chief of the General Staff and the Chief of the Military Cabinet could not accept the influence of the War Minister, so they attempted to curb the Minister's power in the 1880s and 1890s. Particularly during Alfred von Schlieffen's tenure as Chief of the General Staff, there were never enough troops available to carry out Schlieffen's ambitious operational plans. The debate over army increases between the General Staff and the Ministry of War was of crucial importance for the build-up of active and reserve formations between the 1890s and 1914.

The War Minister was not the War Minister of the Empire. He was the War Minister of Prussia, who had to be a Prussian general and was obliged by oath to obey the King of Prussia. Bavaria, Saxony, and Württemberg each had their own War Ministers who were, in theory, of the same rank. But the Prussian War Ministry acted as a kind of imperial War Ministry taking the lead over the ministries in the other kingdoms. Luckily, there seemed to have been a positive relationship among the different war ministers and, therefore, a minimum of friction. Constitutionally, Prussia was dominant; this could have been a problem but it never became one.[12] Fortunately, the ministers had a positive personal relationship and worked together well in direct correspondence with each other, so that this unresolved and potentially troublesome situation had no negative consequences for the army.[13]

The War Minister's responsibility to present his issues to the Kaiser created some difficulties. As an officer, he had sworn an oath of obedience to the Prussian King, while as a Prussian minister he was bound by the Constitution of 1850 and obliged to object to orders that were in opposition or in conflict with the constitution. If he was caught between these positions and the conflict became irreconcilable, the only option was to resign. It is for that reason that the position of the Minister of War changed more frequently than any other of the top military positions. Only the Chancellor had a position as difficult as the Minister of War, who had to balance the competing demands of the Kaiser, Military Cabinet, the Commanding Generals and the Chief of General Staff vs. the Secretary of the Imperial Treasury and the Reichstag.[14]

---

[11] (Kriegministerum, 1909)

[12] (Mombauer, 2003), pp. 29–30. To compare with War Ministry organization in the 1890s, please see (Pflugk-Hartung, 1896), pp. 69–72.

[13] (Rüdt von Collenberg, 1922), p. 9.

[14] (Mombauer, 2003), p. 30.

Peacetime Organization of the War Ministry as of 6 May 1914

War Minister: Gen. Lt. v. Falkenhayn

1st Adjutant: Major Milchling v. Schönstadt
2nd Adjutant: Hptm. v. Steuben

Medical Department (Medizinal-Abteilung *MA*)
Head: Generalstabsarzt Prof. Dr. v. Schjerning

Horse Mobilization Inspection (Remonte-Inspektion *RJ*)
Head: Obstlt. Haack

Central department (Zentral-Departement *ZD*)
Director: Oberst Schëuch
Adjutant: Hptm. Henrici

Minister's office (1. Ministerial-Abteilung *Z1*)
Head: Obstlt. Hoffmann

Intendance Department (2. Intendantur-Abteilung *Z2*)
Head: Wirkl. Geh. Kr. Rat OLt. d.L. a.D. Dr. Meyer

Archive Department (Archiv-Verwaltung *Av*)
Head: Wirkl. Geh. Kr. Rat Lt. d. Res. Lehmann

Library (Bücherei-Verwaltung *Bv*)
Head: Major z.D. Frantz

Manual Administration (Druckvorschriften-Verwaltung *Dv*)
Head: Obstlt. z.D. Lehmann

General War Department (Allgemeines Kriegs-Departement *AD*)
Director: Gen. Maj. Wild v. Hohenborn
Adjutant: Hptm. Baron v. Ardenne

Secret War Chamber (Geheime Kriegs-Kanzlei *GKK*)

1st Army Department (1. Armee-Abteilung *A1*)
Head: Obstlt. v. Wrisberg

2nd Infantry Department (2. Infanterie-Abteilung *A2*)
Head: Obstlt. v. Wodtke

3rd Cavalry Department (3. Kavallerie-Abteilung *A3*)
Head: Oberst v. Lenthe

4th Field Artillery Department (4. Feldartillerie-Abteilung *A4*)
Head: Obstlt. v. Schwerin

5th Foot Artillery Department (5. Fußartillerie-Abteilung *A5*)
Head: Oberst Jung

6th Engineer Department (6. Ingenieur- und Pioner-Abteilung *A6*)
Head: Obstlt. Gundelach

7th Traffic and Transportation Department (7. Verkehrs-Abteilung *A7*)
Head: Obstlt. Meyer

In summer of 1914, it was broken up into the motor transport department and the air force department. Motor transport department was renamed *A7V* then, which provided the name for the first German tank introduced in 1918.

Airforce Department (Luftfahrt-Abteilung *A7L*)
Head: Obstlt. Oschmann

8th Factory Department (8. Fabriken-Abteilung *A8*)
Head: Major Giebe, later: Major Weidlich
Shifted as department B5 to the administration department in summer 1914.

9th Personnel Replacements Department (9. Ersatzwesen-Abteilung *A9*)
Head: Obstlt. Ritter v. Braun

Inspection of the infantry schools
Machinegun inspection
Rifle testing committee (Gewehr-Prüfungskommission)
Artillery testing committee (Artillerie-Prüfungskommission)
. . . and many more small departments . . .

Administration department (Armee-Verwaltungs-Departement *BD*)
Director: Gen. Maj. v. Schöler
Adjutant: Hptm. v. Oertzen

1st Treasury Department (1. Kassen-Abteilung *B1*)
Head: Wirkl. Geh. Kr. Rat OLt. d.L. a.D. Dr. Wrubel

2nd Supply Department (2. Verpflegungs-Abteilung *B2*)
Head: Wirkl. Geh. Kr. Rat OLt. d.L. a.D. Selle
Broken up into wartime supply department (1. Kriegsverpflegungs-Abteilung *B1*) and peacetime supply department (2. Friedensverpflegungs-Abteilung *B2*).

3rd Garment Department (3. Bekleidungs-Abteilung *B3*)
Head: Obstlt. v. Feldmann

4th Barracks Department (4. Unterkunfts-Abteilung *B4*)
Head: Oberst Friedrich
Broken up into barracks department East (*U1*) and West (*U2*) later.

5th Training Center Department (5. Übungsplatz-Abteilung *B5*)
Head: Obstlt. v. Oven

6th Construction Department (6. Bau-Abteilung *B6*)
Head: Geh. Ob. Baurat Andersen
Provisional construction department (*U5*) added later.

During a re-organization in summer 1914 the departments *B1*, *B4*, *B5* and *B6* were taken out of the administration department and put into a new **Accomodation facilities department (Unterkunfts-Department (*UD*)** as departments *U1*, *U2*, *U3*, *U4* and *U5*.

Payment and Legal Department (Versorgungs- und Justiz-Departement *CD*)
Director: Gen. Maj. Frhr. v. Langermann u. Erlencamp
Adjutant: Hptm. v. Freyhold

1st Pensions Department (1. Pensions-Abteilung *C1*)
Head: Obstlt. v. Aschoff

2nd Payment Department (2. Versorgungs-Abteilung *C2*)
Head: Obstlt. Fischer

3rd Legal Department (3. Justiz-Abteilung *C3*)
Head: Wirkl. Geh. Kr. Rat Hptm. d.L. a.D. Müller

Several departments were headed by *Militär-Beamten*. Since their ranks—*Wirklicher Geheimer Kriegsrat* or *Geheimer Ober-Baurat*—cannot be translated, the titles are given in the German language here. Similar to the General Staff, the names and reporting lines of departments were subject to frequent changes. Therefore different sources very often give at least slightly different names and structures. Peacetime structure given here is based upon the Rangliste 1914 (as of 6 May 1914).[15]

The War Ministry of Prussia was divided into four major departments:
1) ZD (Zentral-*Departement*—Central Department), responsible for dealing with the Reichstag and the press;
2) AD (*Allgemeines Kriegs-Departement*—General War Department.), responsible for military affairs and divided into seven sections correlating to the branches of the army;
3) BD (*Armee Verwaltungs-Departement*—Administration Department.), the army administration department, which handled administration and justice; and

15 (Kriegsministerium, 1914), pp. 8–15, (Buchholz, *Gab es einen Schlieffenplan?*, 2009), (Schmidt-Richberg, 1979), pp. 64–65.

4) CD (*Versorgungs- und Justiz-Departement*—Payment and Legal Department.), pensions and general legal matters.[16]

In the summer of 1914, there were other changes. It is unclear if this was caused by mobilization or due to existing plans. Changes are reflected in the list above.

The War Ministry was responsible for organization, administration, and legislative affairs. Remember that the legislation began with the appointed government ministries, and it was the War Minister that provided this link to the army. This also provided the administrative link between the government and the other armies of the Reich. Once the Great General Staff established independency from the War Minister, the War Minister started operating in the dark. Under Wilhelm II, he received no information about the Great General Staff strategic planning even though the War Minister was still responsible for armament policy.[17]

THE GENERAL STAFF AND GENERAL STAFF OFFICERS

Before 1914, it was commonly said that Europe was home to five reputedly perfect institutions: the Roman Curia, the British Parliament, the Russian Ballet, the French Opera, and the Prussian General Staff. The Great General Staff was the organizational center of the German armies.[18] In Berlin, the General Staff building address–*Königsplatz* 6–was directly opposite of the Reichstag building and seemed covered by a veil of secrecy.[19]

In theory, the General Staff was subordinate to the War Ministry; however, in 1883, the Chief of the General Staff gained immediate access to the Kaiser.[20] Traditionally the Chief of General Staff could only execute his right of immediate access when the War Minister and the Chief of the Military Cabinet were also present. The General Staff neither appeared in public, nor did it take a political role. Except for Alfred v. Waldersee, the Chiefs of General Staff dedicated themselves to their military profession and did not develop any political ambitions. Due to his strict neutral political stance, Schlieffen appeared to be an ideal Chief of General Staff to follow Waldersee. Waldersee was well acquainted with the Kaiser. Both had served in the 1st Foot Guards Regiment, where Prince Wilhelm served as a Second Lieutenant in the 6th Company of that regiment and became company commander of the life company (1st Company) in 1880. That gave Waldersee an enormous political influence, even beyond military issues and it extended to such matters as Bismarck's dismissal, the appointment of Verdy du Vernois to the position of Minister of War, and the dismissal of Bronsart v. Schellendorff. His final step was the appointment of General v. Kaltenborn-Stachau to Minister of War.

The General Staff was divided into 13 departments each controlled by a field grade officer (Major, Lieutenant Colonel, or even Colonel). *Oberquartiermeister* (senior quartermaster) oversaw six groups of departments. The 6th Department (*Kaisermanöver*) reported directly to the Chief of the General Staff together with the central department. Section IIIb of the General Staff, dealing with political issues, directly reported to the General Quartermaster, who was the Deputy Chief of General Staff at the same time.[21]

16 (Kitchen, 1968), p. 10. (Pflugk-Hartung 1896), pp. 69–72.
17 (Förster, 2006), p. 462.
18 (Mombauer, 2003), p. 34.
19 The general staff building was completely destroyed in 1945; today the Federal German Chancellery can be found approximately at the same place.
20 (Kitchen, 1968), p. 1.
21 (Kitchen, 1968), p. 6.

General Staff work happened under strict secrecy and behind closed doors. The general public would only recognize General Staff work during the autumn maneuvers and the Kaisermanöver, through the publications of the General Staff itself[22] or the publications of the departments for military history (*Kriegsgeschichtliche Abteilungen).*[23]

Peacetime Organization of the Great General Staff as of 1 May 1914

Chief of General Staff: Generaloberst v. Moltke
1st Adjutant: Major Tieschowitz v. Tieschowa
2nd Adjutant: Hptm. Köhler

Central Department (administration and personnel issues)
Head: Oberst v. Fabeck

Section IIIb (political issues, military intelligence)
Head: Oberst v. Bartenwerffer

6th Department (Kaisermanöver)
Head: N.N.

General Quartermaster (Generalquartiermeister): N.N., later Gen. Lt. v. Stein
Adjutant: N.N.

Senior Quartermaster (Oberquartiermeister) I: Gen. Lt. Schmidt v. Knobelsdorff
Adjutant: Hptm. Wahl

2nd Department (mobilization and deployment department)
Head: Obstlt. Tappen (following Oberst Ludendorff)
K.S. Obstlt. Hentsch (joining July 1st), Major Wetzell (joining Aug. 1st)

Railroad Department
Head: K.W. Obstlt. Groener

Section Ia (review of military transportation regulations)

4th Department, merged with 7th Department (foreign fortresses)
Head: Oberst Buchholtz

Senior Quartermaster (Oberquartiermeister) II: Gen. Lt. v. Bertrab
Adjutant: Major v. Poncet

3rd Department (France including Maroc; England including Egypt, Afghanistan)
Head: Oberst v. Kemnitz

---

22 *Viertelsjahreshefte für Truppenführung und Heereskund,* a quarterly magazine on military leadership and military sciences, published between 1904 and 1914.

23 *Kriegsgeschichtliche Einzelschriften*—studies on military history, *Studien zur Kriegsgeschichte und Taktik*—studies on military history and tactics, publications on the wars of Frederick the Great, the liberation wars, the wars of 1864, 1866 and 1870–71 and "contemporary" wars.

9th Department (Italy, Belgium, The Netherlands, Switzerland, Portugal, both Americas, German colonies)
Head: Oberst Bauer

Senior Quartermaster (Oberquartiermeister) III: Gen. Maj. (Georg) Graf v. Waldersee
Adjutant: Hptm. v. Hammerstein-Equord

5th Department (training and operational studies)
Head: Oberst v.d. Heyde

8th Department (War Academy and general staff service)
Head: Obstlt. v. Winterfeldt

Senior Quartermaster (Oberquartiermeister) IV: Gen. Maj. v. Kuhl
Adjutant: Hptm. v. Rundstedt

1st Department (Russia, Nordic states, East Asia, Persia, Turkey)
Head: Oberst Gr. v. Posadowsky

10th Department (Austria-Hungary, Balkan states)
Head: N.N.

Senior Quartermaster (Oberquartiermeister) V: Gen. Maj. v. Redern (following Gen. Lt. v. Freytag-Loringhoven)
Adjutant: Hptm. Weyland

Military History Department I (contemporary military history starting from mid 19th century)
Head: K.W. Obstlt. Renner

Military History Department II (older military history up to Napoleonic wars)
Head: Gen. Maj. v. Friedrich

Military Archive

Chief Cartography (Chef Landesaufnahme): Oberst Weidner
Adjutant: N.N.

Trigonometrical Department (Trigonometrische Abteilung)
Head: Obstlt. Scherenberg

Topographical Department (Topographische Abteilung)
Head: Obstlt. Launhardt

Mapping Department (Kartographische Abteilung)
Head: Obstlt. Launhardt

Picture and Air Picture Library

Colonial Section [24]

Day-to-day work in the Great General Staff was surprisingly basic. Due to the high level of secrecy, there were hardly any enlisted men (EM) or non-commissioned officers (NCOs) assigned to it. Officers were required to do even the basic work of typing and filing, since most issues were considered top secret and could only be handled by general staff officers. That resulted in an extremely high workload. Working tools were rare and up until 1914, the railroad department had only one typewriter available to it.[25] Besides the telephone on the desk of the Chief of the General Staff, there was only one additional telephone available in one of the corridors that was used by all the other general staff officers. Further, some Chiefs of the General Staff had particular idiosyncrasies. Graf Schlieffen, for example, was a widower, who lived with his daughters after his young wife passed away. Looking for company, he sent a messenger to his direct subordinates, delivering a war game exercise to them on Christmas Eve afternoon. Accompanying it was an invitation to have coffee with him on Christmas afternoon for the presentation of results.[26]

The limitations of the General Staff's responsibilities are as important as the tasks it did perform. The General Staff was the Kaiser's tool to lead the army. Its mission was to advise and prepare, not to command. Even after mobilization, the Chief of General Staff, who changed his title to *Chef des Generalstabes des Feldheeres,* could only issue orders on behalf of the Kaiser (*Seine Majestät befiehlt . . .*). The staff had neither the responsibility for the training of or the commanding of troops, nor the task of compiling field regulations. This was done either by the Ministry of War or the corps commanders. In 1914, the staff consisted of 625 officers divided between the Great General Staff in Berlin and the Troop General Staff that provided officers for corps and divisions.[27] There were three general staff officers per army corps staff and one per divisional staff. It is instructive to know that small unit commanders would go to "The General Staff Officer" to find out what was going on inside the division.[28]

The corps staffs, eventually grew to four general staff officers known as the Ia, Ib, Ic, and Id led by a *Chef des Stabes,* usually abbreviated as the "Chef," who were known as *Truppengeneralstab*, headed by a colonel. In wartime army staffs, there would also be the ordinance

---

[24] (Buchholz, *Gab es einen Schlieffenplan?*, 2009,) Bundesarchiv/Militärarchiv PH 3/124. Compare with the organization of the General Staff in the 1890s (Pflugk-Hartung, 1896), pg. 77–79. See also (Schmidt-Richberg 1979), p. 70. Due to confidentiality reasons the organization of the Great General Staff was not reflected by the Rangliste as detailed as the organization of the War Ministry. Please also refer to the Appendix F to see the transformation into the OHL upon mobilization.

[25] The Railroad Department was one of the departments with the highest workload due to the set-up of the annual mobilization plan with its complex railroad timetable. However, it was less prestigious than the departments dealing with operations, fortresses, and foreign countries. When General Wilhelm Groener was assigned to the railroad department, he felt being he felt he was shunted away. (Stoneman, 2006), p. 68.

[26] (Rochs, 1921), p. 30.

[27] Beginning around 1810, all brigades and fortress governors were assigned a permanent general staff officer. On the one hand supporting the commanding officer, but on the other hand acting as a kind of extension of the Berlin General Staff into all military formations. (Model, 1968), p. 12.

[28] (Mombauer, 2003), pp. 34–36.

officers IIa, IIc, etc. The Chef had a direct reporting line to the Great General Staff in Berlin. Divisions only had one Ia officer—roughly comparable to contemporary G3 officers. Due to their direct line to the Great General Staff, they often worked behind the back of their own commanders.[29] This seemingly insignificant fact becomes very important as World War I approaches.

Since the officers in General Staff were considered to be the absolute elite of army officers, there was heavy competition to become a General Staff Officer. The first step was to take a voluntary War Academy Entrance Examination. Applicants for the exam had to have held a commission for three years and were not supposed to be eligible for promotion to captain for five more years. The regimental commander of each applicant had to submit an evaluation, which covered, the applicant's duty experience and expertise, his suitability for advanced academic study, his health, his conduct and character, and his financial situation.[30]

Annually there were 400 test takers and about 25 percent were admitted to the War Academy in Berlin. In the last few years before the war, these numbers grew to 800 candidates, with about 150 to 160 young officers actually attending the War Academy. To create equal opportunities for all officers going through this entry examination, there was an intense preparation course held by general staff officers from the Troop General Staff. This preparation covered subjects such as tactics of a reinforced infantry brigade, topography, engineering, and ordnance. Tactics were divided into formal tactics and applied tactics. The applicants were responsible for their own preparation in languages, geography, and military history. There was abundant literature available to help in preparation for these examinations including comments concerning the entrance examination exercises of the previous year.[31]

In 1859, the former *Allgemeine Kriegsschule* was renamed "Military Academy" to underline the high level of applied military training. The academy was located in "*Dorotheenstrasse*" in Berlin and was as legendary as the General Staff Building at Königsplatz 6. The course of study was three years long (*Coetus* I–III) and Prussia, Saxony, and Württemberg sent officers to the same academy.[32] The following outline of the study plan of Coetus I to III in 1912 provides an understanding of the content and intensity of training:

Coetus I

Subject	Hours per week
Tactics	4
Military history	4
Ordnance	1
Fortification	2
Naval war	1
Military health care and hygiene	1
Military law	1

[29] (Kitchen, 1968), p. 6.

[30] (Stoneman, 2006), p. 56 and (Krafft H. , 1903), pp. 30–36.

[31] (Guderian Generaloberst a. D., 1951), pp. 412–418, (Berlin, 1904); (Griepenkerl, 1901); (Krafft H., 1903); (Krafft M., 1912), (Krafft M., 1910). These last four sources are books reflecting the entrance examinations of the respective years, exercises, and solutions.

[32] Coetus is a Latin word meaning "annual class," so Coetus I–III were the three classes, which had to be completed during War Academy studies.

Subject	Hours per week
General history	3
Geography	1
Arithmetic or French, English or Russian language	6
Japanese, if taken instead of other language	10

Coetus II

Subject	Hours per week
Tactics and general staff service	6
Military history	4
Fortification	2
Trigonometry and plan sketching	1
Logistics	2
General history, constitutional law and governmental administration	3
Civil law and economy	1
Arithmetic or French, English or Russian language	5
Japanese, if taken instead of other language	6

Coetus III

Subject	Hours per week
Tactics and general staff service	6
Military history	4
Fortification	3
General history	2
Trigonometry or French, English or Russian language	4
Japanese, if taken instead of other language	6

(Blumentritt, 1959), pp. 670–672.

Hours not covered by the study plan could be either dedicated to self-study, (particularly during Coetus III, in preparation for the final examination) or spent attending lectures at the Berlin University.

The later commander of the German armored forces, *Generaloberst* Heinz Guderian, who attended the War Academy in 1913, gave us a unique insight into the conduct of general staff training before the war:

> Lessons in the Prussian War Academy Dorotheenstrasse in Berlin were handled quite generously. In 1913 the director of the Prussian War Academy was Lieutenant General v. Gündell, a very capable and competent officer of the old Prussian Army. As much as him, probably even stronger, was the impression left by a member of the director-

> ate, Colonel v.d. Goltz, who earned his reputation during the war by his expedition to Finland and his operations in the Baltic states in 1919. He had a very strong educational influence upon the young officers. The teachers for tactics and military history came from the Great General Staff; whereas, the teachers for all other military subjects came from the Troop General Staff. Teachers for general subjects such as law, languages and arithmetic usually were professors at the Berlin University, coming to the War Academy to deliver their lectures. The entire teaching staff had quite a high intellectual level.
>
> The trainees came from all contingents of the German Army except Bavaria, which had its own War Academy. In general, there was good fellowship and teamwork. But there was very little contact during private time after the training hours, except between those who knew each other from before, or those who made friends during the course.
>
> During the first year, focus was on expanding and deepening knowledge. During the second and third year, the focus changed more to applied general staff training, first on divisional level, later also on army corps level. The most important subject was tactics; all other subjects came clearly behind. In military history, the Seven Years War of Frederick the Great was the major topic—particularly the opening phase in 1756. Then the focus changed to the campaign of 1805. The lectures were done as applied lessons, but there was no connection to the lessons in tactics.
>
> The lessons in general history delivered by Professor Höniger were about the Thirty Years War. Those lessons were also not connected to the lessons in military history. At the end of each coetus, the officer trainees were assigned to other arms during summer. The infantry and cavalry officers for example were assigned to artillery formations . . . At the end of the three years training the trainees joined a final staff ride, where the basis was laid for the final decision about course results and future military assignments.[33]

Bavaria had its own academy.[34] Almost the entire course of study was book learning but at the end, there was a three-week staff ride. Generally, the entry examination and the following training course were quite similar in Bavaria and in Prussia—the Prussian War Academy had been the role model for Bavaria to erect its own academy. Differences lay in details: in Bavaria the entry examination was not only written but also included an oral examination. The course design was likewise similar and included military subjects such as tactics, engineering, field fortification and ordnance; however, in Bavaria there was a larger emphasis on scientific topics and the students also attended lectures at Munich University. Attendance at these lectures was obligatory in Bavaria, unlike at the Prussian War Academy, where attending university lectures was expected but not required.

Around 1900, there were further attempts to turn the Prussian War Academy into a pure general staff academy by reducing the influence and importance of general scientific content and emphasizing applied military content. Only the Chief of General Staff, Graf Schlieffen, dared to openly resist this effort that was supported by the Kaiser. To Schlieffen, the general

---

33 Excerpt from a study about the history of the German General Staff, written by Generaloberst a.D. Heinz Guderian in 1948 as an unpublished manuscript. Quoted and translated into English after Model, Generalstabsoffizier, p. 16.

34 (Hackl, 1989)

academic and scientific training of future general staff officers seemed to be more important than pure military professionalism.[35]

There was one further considerable difference between the Prussian and the Bavarian War Academy. Whereas the Prussian academy put a high emphasis on training tools to support the military leader (*Führergehilfenausbildung*), the Bavarians focused more upon the art of war itself (*Kriegskunst*). The failure rate for the examination ending this course was between 66 and 75 percent. As a result, only 25 to 35 officers per year graduated from the War Academy. The graduates spent a year or more of probation in a unit before joining the Great General Staff in Berlin. The washout rate of probation was significant with only about ten officers per year actually being accepted as General Staff officers.[36]

The Chief of General Staff, Helmuth v. Moltke, a future de-facto Chief Erich Ludendorff, along with the Army League, were responsible for the massive Army Bill in 1913, which greatly expanded the German army and led to the introduction of the first direct federal taxation.[37]

The General Staff was deeply involved in planning and thinking about the use of railroads, which were considered an offensive tool. Railroads encouraged the development and use of timetables that were so intricate and exacting that they could not be changed easily. Between the momentum of mobilization and the intricacies of the railroad timetables, any changes could be momentous.

The development of railroads allowed them to be used as strategic instruments. They were used militarily in the Franco-Prussian war to move men and equipment; this capability was sharpened over the next four decades. There were improvements in track reliability and communications that allowed for more precise timing and control of train movements. The bureaucracy of the railroad lent itself to cooperation with the military authorities in making war plans.

On 1 August 1914, banking on hopes of British neutrality, the Kaiser wanted to move all his forces against Russia. The Chief of the General Staff responded that that change would create chaos and was not possible. Nevertheless, after the war, a general officer from the railroad section of this staff went to great pains to show that in his opinion, such a shift would have been possible.

The second strategic offense offered by the railroads was the creation of spurs and sidings in locations needed by the military and a huge increase in trans-Rhine capacity.[38] The primary reason that the Malmedy section of the empire was lost after the end of World War I was because of the nexus of rail spurs in that area.

In case of war, the General Staff was also broken up into the field headquarters (*Großes Hauptquartier*) and the *Stellvertretender Generalstab* (Replacing General Staff) left behind in Berlin. Moltke took over the function of Chief of Replacing General Staff after his dismissal over the Marne disaster in 1914.

Upon mobilization in August 1914, the Prussian and Bavarian War Academies were closed and the course attendees were transferred into junior Troop General Staff positions, often of Reserve, Landwehr and Ersatz formations. When it became clear that the war would take longer than expected, even former War Academy trainees who had failed to pass the final examination, were used as general staff officers. Eventually, even these officers were not

---

[35] (Zwehl, General der Infanterie a.D., 1923), p. 8.

[36] (Mombauer, 2003), p. 37.

[37] (Chickering, *Militarism and Radical Nationalism*, 2008), pp. 213–214.

[38] (Showalter D. , 2000), pp. 699–701.

sufficient to replace losses of general staff officers or to staff newly mobilized formations. Therefore, by the end of 1916, an abbreviated "General Staff Course at Sedan" (*Generalstabslehrgang Sedan*) was introduced, where distinguished field officers with war experience were trained to be general staff officers. Usually regimental or brigade adjutants with experience in tactical leadership were selected for these courses in 1917 and 1918.

Before the start of courses in Sedan, these officers were assigned to other arms for a couple of months, Then they served in divisional, corps, or army staffs, either as support to the first general staff officer (Ia), or even as third general staff officer (Ic) and carried out an actual general staff function. After completing approximately one and a half years of a probationary period and practical experience, these officers were called to four weeks of classroom training in Sedan. The usual quota of 20 participants in each course was divided into two classes, each of them lead by an experienced general staff officer. As probation preceded Sedan, the first general staff officers so trained were appointed in 1917.

Special emphasis was put on decision-making and developing strong military traits and personalities. During these four weeks, the workload was continually increased until during the last weeks the trainees had to work virtually day and night. Upon successful completion of the course, the participants—usually in the rank of a captain—were immediately used in Troop General Staff functions. Mostly they became second general staff officers (Ib) in divisional staffs, but they were sometimes appointed as general staff officers in corps or army staffs.

Although these officers had received only a very short training compared with their comrades who had gone through the pre-war general staff training, they were fully accepted as general staff officers due to their practical war experience. They were allowed to wear the same general staff uniform that the older general staff officers wore.[39]

THE MILITARY CABINET

Originally founded in 1809 as 1st Department of the War Ministry, the Military Cabinet (*Generaladjutantur)* was always responsible for personnel issues. As the "Department for Personal Matters," this institution had existed within the Prussian Ministry of War since 1824. The Military Cabinet, which was founded in spring 1871, was an entirely aristocratic organization.[40] The Kaiser appointed the Military Cabinet for Prussia, and it was responsible for all matters of personnel, except for appointment to the ranks of the highest positions within the army. The Military Cabinet had access to the Kaiser that neither the General Staff nor the War Ministry enjoyed, although the official status of immediate access (*Immediatstelle*) was only granted in 1883. There was no clear-cut understanding of the position of the Military Cabinet. The Military Cabinet prepared the Kaiser's orders and dealt with requests directed towards the Kaiser. As the old name indicates, it was the general adjutancy of the Kaiser. All officer positions were filled according to its suggestions. The Military Cabinet, without ministerial countersignature, could pass all military appointments, promotions and demotions of officers.

---

[39] Hans Felber, *General der Infanterie* in an unpublished study from 1949 about selection and training of German general staff officers during the war and during peacetime. Quoted after Model, Generalstabsoffizier, pp. 19–20. These unpublished documents are based upon studies and interviews made by the Historical Division of the U.S. Army after 1945.

[40] (Kitchen, 1968), p. 7.

On behalf of the Kaiser, the Military Cabinet executed the imperial command power concerning legal issues, the code of honor for officers, petitions for mercy, awards and decorations, promotions of officers, transfers of officers and retirements. Although the Military Cabinet was a Prussian institution, it was finally responsible for the entire army. The commanding generals, having direct access to the Kaiser (*Immediatvortragsrecht*), also had a direct approach to the Military Cabinet.[41]

The Chief of the Military Cabinet's domain was primarily in the area of appointments and promotions. The Military Cabinet's power was dependent upon personality. Many people in the Reichstag believed that because the Military Cabinet was appointed, it superseded the War Minister and was unconstitutional. No officer in the military wanted to enter the Military Cabinet as it could ruin a career.[42] With regard to the very powerful *Chef des Militärkabinetts* under Kaiser Wilhelm I (Emil v. Albedyll), there was a saying among Army officers waiting for promotion: "This year I'm going to be promoted—'*so Gott will und Albedyll*'" (if the Holy Lord and Albedyll agree).

The Kaiser thought the cabinet was his own domain. But he didn't follow the advice of the Military Committee for every promotion. Perhaps the most important case was his appointment of the younger Moltke to the position of Chief of General Staff, which occurred against the clear advice of Graf v. Hülsen-Haeseler, the Chief of the Military Cabinet.[43] Interestingly, the dissolution of the Military Cabinet was a key postwar reform requirement in November 1918, demanded by the central "Workers and Soldiers Council."

The Military Cabinet did not have any influence upon operational planning and decision making, which were the Chief of Staff's domain. The only point of potential conflict was the appointment of army commanders and army chiefs of staffs: for example, when it came to selecting the personalities leading the German armies into the war in 1914. But the Kaiser felt more than able to make his own decisions, even against the advice of his closest and most trusted advisors.

From the General Staff's point of view the Military Cabinet was an unwelcome rival. Together with the Civilian Cabinet and the Naval Cabinet, it was part of the Kaiser's system of personal reign. The chiefs of the cabinets could make themselves much more easily available than any ministers by accompanying the Kaiser on his journeys and having more regular access to him than those responsible to the Reichstag.[44] The Kaiser regarded this cabinet as his personal institution and a means by which he tried to escape the ties of constitutionalism. It was soundly criticized because the Kaiser executed officers' promotions without countersignature from the War Minister.

Georg Graf v. Waldersee outlined how the younger Moltke's work had been impeded because of the "sad chapter" of appointing the "right" personalities into military command positions.[45] The Military Cabinet, Waldersee complained, had allowed Moltke only very modest influence upon appointments and had frequently opposed General Staff suggestions. Compared with positions with constitutional responsibility, the Chiefs of the Military Cabinet changed very infrequently. There were only four such Chiefs between 1888 and 1918: Wilhem v. Hahnke from 1888–1901, Dietrich Graf v. Hülsen-Haeseler from 1901–1908, then

---

41 (Pflugk-Hartung, 1896), pp. 68–69.

42 (Kitchen, 1968), p. 11–12.

43 Hülsen-Haeseler even tried to influence the Kaiser not to select Moltke by employing War Minister v. Einem and the Reichskanzler v. Bülow to give the same advice.(Schmidt-Richberg, 1979), p. 68. (Mombauer, 2003), p. 33.

44 (Mombauer, 2003), p. 32.

45 (Waldersee, 1927), p. 444.

Moritz Frhr. v. Lyncker until July 1918, followed by Ulrich Frhr. v. Marschall until the end of the war.[46]

In peacetime, the Military Cabinet, on behalf of the Kaiser, worked out clear guidelines that officer candidates should come only from either aristocratic families or from families with a "desirable social background" (*erwünschte Kreise*). Even after officer losses went up during the war, the Military Cabinet did not significantly change this policy, leading to a junior officer manning shortage during the war.[47] Even during the war, promotions were controlled very carefully, so officers usually advanced not more than two ranks during the war. Rather than losing their control over appointments, the Military Cabinet preferred that majors lead regiments at the end of the war and that deputy officers (*Offiziersstellvertreter)* lead companies.

Here we can see a significant difference from the *Wehrmacht* in the Second World War. The Nazis called themselves national-socialists and therefore, executed a rather socialist officer promotion policy. During the late war years, a worker's background could be advantageous.[48] Hitler had a particular dislike for aristocratic officers, which was reinforced by the assassination attempt on 20 July 1944. Officer careers from captain to major general during the war were possible if the right performance and political attitude was shown.

The Military Cabinet was also responsible for the transferring of manpower from one army to another. Remember that there were four separate armies, as well as separate small army units from the smaller states within the Prussian army. Again, there were only four separate armies: Prussia, Bavaria, Württemberg, and Saxony. All the rest of the contingents were part of the Prussian army. Württemberg had a very close relationship with the Prussians and was the least independent of the contingents. Until 1893, the two armies were quite separate, but then Württemberg and Prussia concluded the so-called "Bebenhausen convention" (*Bebenhäuser Konvention*), aligning the promotion rules of Prussian and Württemberg officers. The Württemberg officers were included in the Prussian seniority list (*Dienstaltersliste*). Prussian or Württemberg officers who were assigned to regiments of the other state were formally transferred and were no longer listed as being "à la suite."[49] A Württemberg officer was assigned to the Prussian military cabinet to join in on decisions about Württemberg officers or Württemberg formations. After that, officers could move freely between the two—not so in Bavaria or Saxony; the Württemberg Rangliste became part of the Prussian army list in 1893 (though they continued to print one of their own).[50]

Bavaria was the most independent of the contingents and while the royalty favored a more complete separation, the Bavarian army did not have a particularly separatist philosophy. The Bavarian officer corps was considered to be the bearer of imperial feelings. Separation from Prussia within any army was neither practical nor desired.[51] The Prussian War Ministry would task the other armies for personnel to help the Prussian army and serve in key positions. This was considered an honor as opposed to a drain of manpower, because it gave an opportunity for minor contingents to put their best foot forward and impress the Prussians.

---

46 (Schmidt-Richberg, 1979), p. 67.

47 (Bald, 1982), pp. 38–42 and pp. 85–92.

48 This led to a very cynical dictum starting in 1944, when these typical national-socialist junior officers were called VOMAG—*Volksoffizier mit Arbeitergesicht* (People's Officer with a Workers Face) by the elder, more traditional, and often aristocratic officers.

49 (Kitchen, 1968), pp. 13–15.

50 (Pflugk-Hartung, 1896), pp. 68–69.

51 (Kitchen, 1968), p. 12.

Individual officers would sometimes apply for transfers to specific armies in the hope of speeding their promotions or correcting problems with their records. The War Ministry of the minor kingdoms controlled the transfers into their armies. Prussia was far less scrupulous and would often transfer the commission of black sheep into the minor kingdom armies. The number of transfers was not large, averaging four or five per army per year. Bavaria and Saxony had separate promotion lists for officers.[52] Within their own budgets the smaller contingents very often offered more favorable conditions to their officers. In Bavaria and Saxony, for example, officers could be promoted faster than in Prussia.

Officers were also posted to the minor kingdom armies and into the Prussian army without having their commission transferred. As a side note, the transferred officer wore the uniform of the officer corps to which he was attached. Records from Württemberg show that in 1914, six generals, 24 staff officers, 28 captains, and 20 lieutenants were posted from Württemberg to Prussia. Likewise, three generals, 15 staff officers, and 19 captains were posted from Prussia to the Württemberg army. Moves between the Saxon, Württemberg, and Bavarian armies were—as far as we know—unusual, if not impossible.

Postings promoted integration and placed Prussians within the separate armies of the Reich. This ensured that Prussia would have a dominant role. The armies of the different kingdoms were not the real problem; rather this was due to the confused and undefined division of the leadership of the army into three jealous factions. We hear the term "the School of the Nation" when referring to the German army. It was, in fact, the task of the School of the Nation to teach unification in the framework of a Prussian-dominated national identity.

THE OBERKOMMANDO IN DEN MARKEN

The tradition of this supreme command body can be traced to the beginning of the Prussian kingdom. *Oberkommando in den Marken* could be roughly translated as "Supreme Command in the Border Areas" and was on par with an army command. The commander usually carried the rank of a *Generaloberst* or even a field marshal. Traditionally, the *Oberbefehlshaber in den Marken* was also governor of the fortress of Berlin. Although this position was one of the most senior positions of the Prussian Army, it was more of an honorific sinecure at the end of a career, a few years before retirement. The Oberkommando in den Marken was on an equal level with army inspections (*Armeeinspektionen*) but without having any army corps assigned for inspection.[53]

Because the Oberbefehlshaber had direct access to the Kaiser, his influence should not be underestimated. As a member of the National Defense Committee (*Landesverteidigungskommission*) that was founded in 1873, the Oberbefehlshaber was one of the personal advisors to the Kaiser, giving suggestions about erecting and sighting fortresses.[54]

Permanent members of the National Defense Committee were the Chief of General Staff, the Inpector-General (*General-Inspekteur*) of the foot artillery, the Chief of the Engineer and Pioneer Corps, the Fortress Inspector, the Oberbefehlshaber in den Marken, and the Director of the General War Department of the War Ministry. The committee was usually headed by a senior general officer who was also a member of the royal family. Extraordinary members were the Commanding General of the III Army Corps and additional officers appointed by the Kaiser.

---

52 (Kitchen, 1968), pp. 13–14.
53 (Alten G. v., 1911), p. 478.
54 (Pflugk-Hartung), p. 83.

MILITARY CONVENTIONS

The military issues of the German empire were regulated in section XI of the Imperial Constitution. Articles 57–62 stipulated conscription, peacetime strength, military legislation, and distribution of the financial burdens of the German army. Article 63 is the main military part of the Constitution. There were reserved rights for the southern states of Bavaria, Baden, and Württemberg. With the end of the war against Austria in 1866, Prussia began entering into conventions between the kingdom and other principalities with the intent militarily to solidify Prussian domination. Most states transferred the bulk of their constitutional military rights to the King of Prussia (not to the empire!).

Articles 64 and 65 explained that all German troops were to unconditionally observe and follow imperial orders. This direction was included in the oath of allegiance of all contingents. Further, the commanders of all contingents could be only appointed by the Kaiser or with imperial endorsement. This also applied to the governors and commandants of fortresses.

> Article 66 stated that where it was not otherwise provided for by special convention, the heads of the German states and free cities were to appoint the officers of their contingents. These officers were the heads of all the troops belonging to their territory and were to enjoy the honors connected therewith. They particularly had the right of inspection at any time and to receive notices of changes about to take place. They were also to receive timely information about promotions and appointments regarding their troops, in order that the state could issue the necessary publication of those actions.[55]

The *Sonderrechte* states of Bavaria and Württemberg had exceptions applied in the final provision of section XI of the Constitution:

> The provisions contained in this section are to be applied to Bavaria in conformity with the more detailed stipulations of the Treaty of Alliance of 23 November 1870 (Bundesgesetzblatt 1871, p. 9) under III. § 5, and to Württemberg in conformity with the more detailed stipulations of the Military Convention of 21–25 November 1870 (Bundesgesetzblatt 1870, p. 658).

Saxony had already concluded a military convention with Prussia in 1867; the other German states concluded similar conventions around the time of the Franco-Prussian War. The legal validity of the military convention with Saxony was disputed, because it had been concluded before the founding of the North German Confederation and was neither sanctioned by the Constitution of the Federation nor by the Constitution of the German Empire. This dispute never led to any kind of actual problem.

The final provisions of section XI practically negated most stipulations of the Imperial Constitution for Bavaria. Articles 57, 58, and 60 of the Imperial Constitution (distribution of costs, conscription and national service, peacetime strength) were not legally binding. The same applied to Articles 64 (oath of allegiance, appointment of supreme commanders, appointment of governors, and commandants of fortresses), 65 (erection of fortresses), 66 (commission of officers), 67 (reductions of military budget), and 68 (declaration of war).

[55] See Appendix A.

Saxony and Württemberg kept their own military administration (Ministry of War). With this single exception, they did not enjoy the same rights as Bavaria.

Based upon its November 1870 alliance with Prussia and the provision of section XI of the Constitution, the Bavarian army was a homogenous block within the German armies and had its own administration and functioned under the supreme military authority of the Bavarian King.[56] Only after declaration of war and mobilization did the Bavarian army come under the supreme command of the Kaiser. In return, Bavaria committed itself to structure, arm, equip, and train its army in close accordance with the other contingents. Bavaria had its own general staff, war academy, etc. The obligation to follow the orders of the Kaiser in wartime—in the contract named *Bundesfeldherr* (Federal Commander)—was included into the oath of allegiance. But until 1918, all officers of the Bavarian army were appointed by the Bavarian King (or the prince regent) without any Prussian influence. To negotiate military issues with Prussia, a military plenipotentiary from Bavaria, Saxony, and Württemberg went to Berlin.

According to Article 62, the costs of the military budget had to be born by the entire German Empire. The Reichstag passed the budget, but the costs of the Saxon and Württemberg armies were specified and allocated to the respective royal war ministries. Bavaria received a lump sum allowance according to the size of its army, and then the Bavarian parliament and military administration had to decide how to use these funds. This process enabled the social-democratic party in the Bavarian parliament (*Landtag*) to collaborate during this decision making process.[57]

Prussia and the states linked to Prussia by military conventions had their military administration "imperialized" (*verreichlicht*). In practical terms—but not legally—the Prussian War Minister acted as the Imperial War Minister (*Reichskriegsminister*). Only Bavaria had a certain amount of independence. Bavaria could allocate officers to any existing or newly formed military institution or installation of the Empire. In Bavaria, only the King (not the Kaiser) had the right to assign Bavarian troops. In practical terms this required cooperation with the Prussians and the Bavarian military administration that agreed to locate the 1 and 8 Bavarian infantry regiments Kgl. Bayr. 1. Infanterie-Regiment König and Kgl. Bayr. 8. Infanterie-Regiment Großherzog Friedrich II. von Baden, 3 and 5 Chevaulegers regiments Kgl. Bayr. 3. Chevaulegers-Regiment Herzog Karl Theodor and Kgl. Bayr. 5. Chevaulegers-Regiment Erzherzog Friedrich von Österreich, together with 2 Foot Artillery regiments in the Reichslande.

Württemberg and Saxony did not enjoy a comparable level of independence. They formed their own army corps within the Prussian system (XIII Army Corps from Württemberg, XIV Army Corps mainly from Baden, XII and XIX Army Corps were the 1 and 2 Saxon Corps) and enjoyed several limited regional "modifications" on the basis of their military conventions. The Kings of Württemberg and Saxony passed only those rights to the Kaiser or the Prussian King that they were obliged to do based upon the Imperial Constitution. They retained the right to commission officers and to appoint civil servants of their contingents and they kept the legal control (*Rechtshoheit*) over their contingents. In Württemberg the supreme commander was only appointed with the endorsement of the Kaiser and was usually a Prussian general.

---

[56] Bavaria did not conclude a military convention with Prussia but instead concluded an alliance making sure that Bavaria would remain on an equal level with Prussia.

[57] Due to their supportive role, which was way different from the role of the Social Democrats in the Reichstag before 1914, they were jokingly named "Royal Bavarian Social Democrats" (*Königlich Bayerische Sozialdemokraten*).

Saxony was in an unfavorable situation when negotiating its convention with Prussia in 1867 because of its pro-Austrian position in the War of 1866. The Saxon senior commander was always appointed directly by the Kaiser. The Saxon King with the endorsement of the Kaiser appointed other Saxon generals. Those generals had to sign a letter guaranteeing their full loyalty to the Kaiser.

Saxony and Württemberg retained their own war ministries and administration, but participated in several key military institutions under Prussian control. These included the Great General Staff and the War Academy. Saxony had its own cadet corps. A well-known joke among Saxon officers was that the basic function of the Saxon War Minister was to countersign orders issued by the Prussian War Minister with the sentence: "This order is also valid in Saxony." As far as uniforms and accouterments were concerned, some regional distinctions were allowed for the Saxon and the Württemberg armies.

In peacetime, Württemberg formations were based only in Württemberg. Non-Württemberg troops could be based in Württemberg only with the endorsement of the King of Württemberg—except for the fortress of Ulm, where the Kaiser reserved his right of assigning troops. The issues of the Ulm fortress were regulated in a specific contract between Prussia, Bavaria, and Württemberg.

Saxony was promised that the Kaiser would execute his right of troop relocation only after Saxon endorsement and only if the redeployment was in the interest of the entire Empire and not just Prussia. The 8. Württembergisches Infanterie-Regiment Nr. 126 Großherzog Friedrich von Baden, Kgl. Sächs. 6. Infanterie-Regiment Nr. 105 "König Wilhelm II. von Württemberg," and Kgl. Sächs. Fußartillerie-Regiment Nr. 12 were relocated to the Reichslande.

With the exception of the kingdoms, the conventions of the remaining states stipulated that the respective contingents were to be fully integrated into the Prussian army for command, control, and administrative structures and functions. Some of the states reserved privileges for their contingents. For example, Hesse kept its contingent together within 25th Infantry Division that was exclusively based within Hesse. Both Mecklenburg duchies assigned units to the 17th Infantry Division; Baden kept its formations within the XIV Army Corps. Other principalities either completely disbanded their formations or fully integrated them into the Prussian army. Hessian and Mecklenburg officers were called "Grand Ducal" (*Großherzoglich*) officers only while serving within their own contingents. They received their patents from the military cabinet in Berlin; therefore a "Großerzoglich Hessischer Major a.D." never existed. Several uniform privileges were kept—the green color for Hesse dragoons or the "Golden" battalion of Strelitz. As far as military legislation and jurisdiction were concerned, several privileges were still granted; however, the relocation power went to the Kaiser (e.g. the Großherzoglich Mecklenburgisches Jäger Bataillon Nr. 14 was relocated to Colmar in the Reichslande in 1890).

In Baden the empire-minded Grand Duke (*Großherzog*) did not ask for such privileges. Although the Baden formations were absorbed completely into the XIV Army Corps, they only kept the addendum "Badisch" to their regimental number, which followed the Prussian numbering system; they were not called "Großherzoglich Badisch." Relocation only within Baden was promised.

The conventions of Prussia with Sachsen-Weimar, Coburg-Gotha, Altenburg, Meiningen, both Reuß, and Schwarzburg-Rudolstadt almost follow the exact same wording and were concluded at the same time. Oldenburg is very similar. The former contingents of Schwarzburg-Sondershausen, Waldeck, Lippe-Detmold, Schaumburg-Lippe, and the Hanseatic Cities were completely disbanded. Only unit traditions such as those of the Westfälisches Jäger Bataillon Nr. 7 commemorated the past of those contingents. Prussia took over the military obligations of these states, which received garrisons of Prussian military formations, together with the promise that these formations would be restricted to their garrisons except during "special events." The barracks of these formations usually displayed the national emblems of the former contingents.

For the non-kingdom contingents only honorary rights remained (e.g. consideration of personal wishes for appointments, conferring of orders, and other decorations, reports, inspections). The princes of those states usually dealt with their contingents as though they were commanding generals and executed respective disciplinary rights as well as their honorary rights. These military stipulations of the military conventions were usually not executed and were only considered as an act of courtesy. Also the honorary rights of the Senates of the three Hanseatic Cities were never touched. The right to commission officers or to appoint officers into certain positions was never taken away from these princes. Usually they delegated this right to Prussia but retained the right to appoint officers "à la suite," who were paid out of the respective prince's budget.

In addition to the convention, Baden and Hesse concluded special agreements concerning their gendarmerie corps. Although the members of the gendarmerie corps were considered military personnel (*Personen des Soldatenstandes*), they were paid out of regional Hesse and Baden funds, and the Grand Dukes had the right to appoint their officers.

The right to appoint officers à la suite was used many times (e.g., juvenile Oldenburg princes were promoted to the rank of "Großherzoglich Oldenburgische Leutnants" à la suite Oldenburgisches Infanterie-Regiment Nr. 91). In Mainz, the quite aged Grand Ducal District President (*Großherzoglicher Regierungs-Präsident*), Frhr. v. Gagern, was a second lieutenant à la suite in the Hesse cavalry together with a well-known factory owner from Worms. These officers appeared in the annual pocket-Rangliste of the XVIII Army Corps together with the officers of the gendarmerie, but not in the official Prussian "Rangliste." Appointments "à la suite" were quite common with aides-de-camp (Flügeladjutanten) who were not taken into Prussian service.[58]

Prince Henry XXII of Reuß senior line had never fully accepted the foundation of the German empire. During ceremonies and official occasions, he used to wear his old Reuß uniform, as did his aide de camp. In 1879, he appointed the former Austrian hussar officer Frhr. Titz v. Titzenhofer into this position and appointed him to the rank of a captain à la suite of the former Reuß contingent. When the prince passed away in 1902, Reuß junior line took over regency and the aide de camp went into the service of the Reuß court.

All contingents of the German army were subject to inspection by the Kaiser. The Kaiser frequently executed this right but never used it as a means of control. This can be seen from the fact that the Fourth Army Inspection was commanded by Crown Prince Rupprecht of Bavaria, the Sixth Army Inspection by Duke Albrecht of Württemberg and the Fifth Army Inspection by the Grand-Duke of Baden. The Bavarian, Württemberg, and Baden troops were parts of the respective inspections.

Only Brunswick did not conclude a military convention immediately; it was not concluded until the last Welph Duke had passed away in 1884. It was formulated on the basis of the conventions agreed to between Prussia and the Thuringian states. In 1867, Brunswick signed an alliance with Prussia laying the groundwork for military cooperation. In the 1867

[58] Check Fiebig, "*Flügeladjutanten*" in the Zeitschrift für Heereskunde 1937. See also (Herr, 2012), pp. 13–15.

agreement, the Brunswick troops came under Prussian command concerning peacetime training and tactical drill. However, the Duke reserved certain rights, such as the commissioning and dismissal of officers and the right to maintain a completely different uniform. Prussia had the command authority to relocate the Duchies' troops. The "Black Regiment" (Braunschweigisches Infanterie-Regiment Nr. 92) was relocated to the poorest garrisons of the Reichslande after the Franco-Prussian War. First they were located in Marsal, later in Metz. Only after concluding the convention in 1886, did the regiment come back to Brunswick, at which point the Brunswick formations appeared in the Rangliste of the Prussian army.[59]

Thanks to shared installations such as the war academy, military sporting institutions, and the general staff, cooperation between Prussia, Saxony, and Württemberg was much closer than that with Bavaria. The cooperation with Bavaria was improved, however, through joint exercises, staff rides, and operational plans, although Bavaria reserved more privileges for itself than any other state. The border did not only exist in the minds of military people—the 2nd class waiting room of the Aschaffenburg train station and pub were separated in two areas: one for local people and the other for "foreigners." Foreigners had to pay two *Pfennig* more per glass of beer.

[59] *Militärkonvention zwischen dem Norddeutschen Bunde (bzw. Preußen) und Sachsen vom 7 Februar 1867.*
Militärkonvention zwischen dem Norddeutschen Bunde und Hessen vom 13 Juni 1871 (Ersatz für die vom 7 April 1867).
Militärkonvention zwischen dem Norddeutschen Bunde und Mecklenburg-Schwerin vom 19 Dezember 1872 (Ersatz für die vom 24 Juni 1868).
Militärkonvention zwischen dem Norddeutschen Bunde und Mecklenburg-Strelitz vom 23 Dezember 1872 (Ersatz für die vom 9 November 1867).
Militärkonvention zwischen dem Norddeutschen Bunde und Oldenburg vom 15 Juni 1867.
Militärkonvention zwischen dem Norddeutschen Bunde und Braunschweig vom 9–18 März 1886.
Militärkonvention zwischen dem Norddeutschen Bunde einerseits und Sachsen-Weimar-Eisenach. Sachsen-Altenburg, Sachsen-Coburg-Gotha, Sachsen-Meiningen, Reuß ältere Linie, Reuß jüngere Linie und Schwarzburg-Rudolstadt vom 15 September 1873.
Militärkonvention zwischen dem Norddeutschen Bunde und Anhalt vom 16 September 1873 (Ersatz für die vom 28. Juni 1867).
Militärkonvention zwischen dem Norddeutschen Bunde und Schwarzburg-Sondershausen vom 17 September 1873 (Ersatz für die vom 28 Juni 1867).
Militärkonvention zwischen dem Norddeutschen Bunde und Lippe vom 14 November 1873 (Ersatz für die vom 26. Juni 1867).
Militärkonvention zwischen dem Norddeutschen Bunde und Schaumburg-Lippe vom 25 September 1873 (Ersatz für die vom 30 Juni 1867).
Militärkonvention zwischen dem Norddeutschen Bunde und Waldeck vom 24 November 1877 (Ersatz für die vom 6. August 1867).
Militärkonvention zwischen dem Norddeutschen Bunde und Lübeck vom 27 Juni 1867.
Militärkonvention zwischen dem Norddeutschen Bunde und Bremen vom 27 Juni 1867.
Militärkonvention zwischen dem Norddeutschen Bunde und Hamburg vom 23 Juli 1867.

CHAPTER 7

ARMY ORGANIZATION

This chapter describes the army organization in the late 1800s as well as in imperial Germany. The discussion begins with the command authorities (*Kommandostellen*) from the top down, starting with armies and army groups and ending with brigades. Regimental and battalion staffs will be discussed later in detail when describing the arms.

The next section will be about the different arms, starting with the combat troops of infantry, machinegun formations, light infantry, and cavalry. A discussion of combat support troops beginning with the artillery follows. Logistical and support formations, such as artillery or garment depots, concludes the chapter.

COMMAND AUTHORITIES IN PEACETIME AND AFTER MOBILIZATION

The army corps were distributed among eight army inspections in peacetime.

- I Army Inspection (Danzig, General Inspector Generaloberst v. Prittwitz und Gaffron) oversaw I, XVII, and XX Army Corps, mobilized as 8th Army Command (AOK 8).
- II Army Inspection (Berlin, General Inspector Generaloberst v. Heeringen) oversaw Guard Corps, XII, and XIX Army Corps, mobilized as 3rd Army Command (AOK 3).
- III Army Inspection (Hanover, General Inspector Generaloberst v. Bülow) oversaw VII, X, and IX Army Corps, mobilized as 2nd Army Command (AOK 2).
- IV Army Inspection (Munich, General Inspector Generaloberst Rupprecht Prinz v. Bayern) oversaw I Bav., II Bav., III Bav., and III Army Corps, mobilized as 6th Army Command (AOK 6).
- V Army Inspection (Karlsruhe, General Inspector Generaloberst Großherzog Friedrich II. v. Baden) oversaw VIII, XIV, and XV Army Corps, mobilized as 7th Army Command (AOK 7
- VI Army Inspection (Stuttgart, General Inspector Generaloberst Prinz Albrecht v. Württemberg) oversaw IV, XIII, and XI Army Corps, mobilized as 4th Army Command (AOK 4).
- VII Army Inspection (Saarbrücken, General Inspector Generaloberst v. Eichhorn) oversaw XVI, XVIII, and XXI Army Corps, mobilized as 5th Army Command (AOK 5).
- VIII Army Inspection (Berlin, Generaloberst v. Kluck) oversaw II, V, and VI Army Corps[1], mobilized as 1st Army Command (AOK 1).[2]

1 (Pflugk-Hartung, 1896), p. 85.
2 (Jany, 1967), p. 297.

In peacetime, General Inspectors (*General-Inspekteure*) commanded the army inspections, who had to inspect the army corps they oversaw and to report directly to the Kaiser. They had no power of command. The army inspections were not considered Prussian, Bavarian, Saxon, or Württemberg commands, but Reich commands during peacetime. To a certain extent, they already represented the build-up of a German field army (*Deutsches Feldheer*) upon mobilization.[3] The staffs of the armies after mobilization were built upon the existing army inspections with the General Inspectors becoming army commanders of their inspections—armies in most cases.[4]

There were other higher army-wide bureaucracies that oversaw various functions, i.e., the Prussian army had inspections for the various arms. There was a General Inspector of the cavalry with four inspections, a field-artillery inspection, and a general inspection of the foot artillery with two inspections. A general inspection of the engineer, the pioneer corps, and the fortresses had four engineer and three pioneer inspections. There was an inspection of the transportation and communication formations (*Verkehrstruppen*), a train inspection and an inspection of the light infantry (*Jäger* and *Schützen*). Bavaria had its own inspection of the cavalry, an inspection of the engineer corps, and one of the fortresses. Besides their peacetime function, most generals sitting in those positions had pivotal mobilization assignments.

Different from the infantry, the cavalry had four cavalry inspections plus the Bavarian cavalry inspection in peacetime that oversaw training, battle drill and cavalry exercises:

- 1st Cavalry Inspection in Posen,
- 2nd Cavalry Inspection in Stettin,
- 3rd Cavalry Inspection in Straßburg (Elsaß),
- 4th Cavalry Inspection in Saarbrücken.

The cavalry inspectors had the rank of division commanders. The Prussian cavalry inspections reported to a general inspection (*Generalinspekteur*) of the cavalry. The General Inspector of the cavalry became one of the *Höhere Kavallerie-Kommandeure* (HKK), and each of the four cavalry inspectors took over a cavalry division. The General Inspector closely cooperated with the cavalry department and had immediate access to the Kaiser (like a commanding general of an army corps), and was the Kaiser's top advisor on all cavalry issues.

Like the army inspections, these inspections checked and inspected the arms they oversaw and reported about the current status to the War Minister, but they had no power of command. They were responsible for the development of tactical doctrines and suggested reviews and new versions of training manuals to the War Minister. The inspections cooperated closely with the respective departments of the War Ministry.

Army Commands (*Armee-Oberkommandos*)

Upon mobilization the army inspections were turned into fielded armies and their organizational structure was heavily inflated. The army HQs, operating under a Chief of General Staff (usually a lieutenant general or a major general), a Senior Quartermaster (*Oberquartiermeister*) (acting as a kind of an army G4 officer), and a Deputy Chief of General Staff (usually a colonel or major general) were divided into four sections:

---

3 (Alten G. v., 1911), pp. 478–479.

4 Some of the commanders were changed according to the mobilization plan. Please check appendix F.

- I, general staff. Within the general staff the general staff officers were organized by their order: Ia was the first general staff officer, Ib the second officer, Ic the third, and Id the fourth.
- II, adjutancy/orderly officers. The adjutants were organized by their order: IIa, IIb and, etc.
- III, military jurisdiction.
- IV, administration and intendancy.

For details of the different function, please refer to the structure of an army corps staff that was structured similarly but smaller. Since army staffs did not exist in the peacetime organization, army corps staffs built a kind of a reference or model organization, and the higher staffs were built after or upon mobilization.

In the *Großes Hauptquartier* another level of confusion was added: in the respective departments (e.g., *Operations-Abteilung, Nachrichten-Abteilung*) sections like Ia or Ic were named "O Ia" or "N Ia" to clarify for which department the respective officers worked. Here department II usually had to support department I in carrying the biggest workload.

Army Groups (*Heeresgruppen*)

Going back to Frederick the Great, the regiments represented the highest organizational level of the Prussian army. Higher formations were only created during wars. Starting with the defeat of 1806, the Prussian army rebuilt its organizational structure following the French model by permanently introducing divisions and army corps. The King usually commanded his army directly. The commanding generals of the army corps, with their right of direct access to the King, played a pivotal role within the army. Traditionally, only detached groups of formations were put under a separate command. This separate command was traditionally taken either by the Duke of Brunswick or by Prince Heinrich, the brother of Frederick the Great. The size of armies during the unification wars made it necessary to establish army commands as an additional leadership layer between the corps and the royal commander. This additional level made it possible to keep such big military forces under control. This development increased the distance between the King and his soldiers and gave King Wilhelm I a feeling that he was no longer in full control. The armies of 1870–71 consisted usually of some three to five army corps and one or two cavalry divisions.

The armies of 1914 were even bigger, and the size of the war theaters they would cover made it even more likely that operations would slip out of control. Telegraph formations and radio stations attempted to keep the *Oberste Heeresleitung (OHL)*—Supreme Army Headquarters in touch with its armies. The necessity of covering even greater distances made the situation worse. During peacetime exercises, this problem had not occurred because staffs could make use of the existing civilian telephone and telegraph infrastructure. For the defenders—such as the German Eighth Army in eastern Prussia and the French forces in 1914—this system also worked well. For the German forces advancing into Belgium and France, the communications between armies and OHL turned out to be disastrous. With the growing distances, the advancing First and Second Army on the right wing slipped out of the control of the OHL that remained in Luxembourg.

Heavy radio stations had a theoretical maximum range of about 150 km, requiring several relay stations between the right wing army commands and the OHL; this system combined with telegraph lines to link the armies to the OHL. Together with encryption and decryption, these processes took hours to send messages. As those messages were kept short to avoid misunderstandings, an exchange of viewpoints about the operative intentions of the OHL between Moltke and his right wing army commanders was virtually impossible. Due to shorter communications lines, an army group command leading the three German right wing armies could have radically improved implementation of operative decisions—particularly given the strong-willed if not stubborn personalities of the commanders of the First and Second Army. The lack of army group commands between OHL and field armies certainly was a major factor contributing to the Marne disaster in 1914.

Army Corps and Their Districts

Underneath the hierarchy, the army itself was organized into corps. There were 22 corps that were active in the Prussian army by 1914. In addition, Bavaria maintained its own corps structure with three army corps, while the armies of Saxony and Württemberg became part of the Prussian army corps structure. The Saxon army was concentrated in XII Corps and XIX Corps, while the Württemberg army was in XIII Corps. The Guard Corps was separate and did not have its own district. The corps commanders were extremely powerful individuals who administered and recruited from their regions and reported directly to the Kaiser, or the King of Bavaria, Württemberg, or Saxony in the case of the non-Prussian corps. Communication went through the War Minister in most cases, but the chain of command was from the Kaiser to the corps commander.[5]

The corps areas changed four times during the time of imperial Germany. These changes corresponded to enlargements of the army and the subsequent reorganization of the units inside the corps. Starting with 11 army corps in 1871, expansion took place in 1889, 1898, 1905, and 1914 and corresponded to the increase in the number of corps. In 1888, there were 18 corps with 468,000 soldiers. In 1897 (before the next expansion), there were 20 corps and 480,000 soldiers. In 1904 prior to the next expansion, there were 23 army corps and 506,000 soldiers. Finally, on the eve of the Great War in 1914, there were 25 army corps and 661,000 soldiers. As these dates and numbers are for budgeting years, you will find some difference between these years and the actual execution of the all-highest cabinet orders (*Allerhöchste Kabinetts-Ordre–AKO*).[6]

These geographic corps areas were known as military districts. Military districts usually operated beside civilian bureaucracies but did not yield to the jurisdiction of the public structures. The boundaries of military districts did not always correspond to the boundaries of state governments. Fifteen military districts crossed the geographic boundaries of state governments. Many others encompassed two or more states while the XI Army Corps covered eight of the smaller states as well as a Prussian area.[7]

In case of war, each army corps fielded its army corps command and also formed a replacement general command *(Stellvertretendes Generalkommando)* in its home base that was concerned with personnel replacement, supplies, equipment, and taking over command functions in the corps area. In peacetime, the commanders were the commanders of the active corps; however, when those corps deployed, control of the military district fell to the deputy commanding general (*Kommandierender General des stellvertretenden*

---

5 You need to be very careful when looking at maps of the Army Corps areas. Very frequently, even in well-respected references, the area in the map does not match the date given. This inaccuracy is particularly true of 1914 Army Corps areas.

6 (Turinetti, James D.; O'Connor, John Albert, 2006), p. xvii.

7 (Chickering, *Imperial Germany and the Great War, 1914–1918,* 2004), p. 33. See also (Pflugk-Hartung, 1896), p. 90.

I.

25—8—24—4.

2.		1.	
4.	3.	2.	1.
7.	5.	3.	1.
8.	6.	4.	2.
		R. K. J. 1.	

D. 1.	U. 1.

2.				1.			
4.		3.		2.		1.	
II. (F.)	I.	II.	I.	II.	I.	II. (F.)	I.
I. (F.) M. K.	I. M. K.	I. M. K.	I. M. K.	I. M. K.	I. M. K.	I. (F.) M. K.	I. M. K.
S. K. 2.	D. Br. 2.	3./Pi. 1.	2./Pi. 1.	S. K. 3.	S. K. 1.	D. Br. 1.	1./Pi. 1.

I./1.

I. M. K.

Fl. A. 1.

Fernsp. A. 1.

(Einführung 1915 beendet.)

Scheinwerfer-Zg. Pi. 1.

Munitions-Kolonnen.

Fuß-A. I./1.	II.	I.
1—8	9 (F.). 8 (F.). 7. 6. 5. A. 4. 3. J.	4 (F.). 3. 2. 1. A. 2. 1. J.

Trains.

K. Br. 1.	II.	I.
	12. 11. 10. 9. 8. 7. F. L.	6. 5. 4. 3. 2. 1. F. L.
	6. 5. 4. Pr. K.	3. 2. 1. Pr. K.*)
2. 1. F. B. K.	2. Pf. D. 7. 6. 5. 4. Fp. K.	1. Pf. D. 3. 2. 1. Fp. K.

Organizational chart of a mobile Army Corps from the General Staff Officer's Handbook.

Generalkommando). He, in turn, was responsible only to the Kaiser. Therefore, the deputy commanding officers became rulers of independent areas. They could and did resist attempts by both military and civilian authorities to impose policies or common practices.[8]

The army corps controlled recruiting and usually followed regional regimental assignments.[9] Generally, the army did not trust residents of Alsace-Lorraine or the indigenous Polish population within Germany; therefore, recruiting exceptions for many organizations were widespread. Soldiers from Alsace-Lorraine were frequently found in units stationed on the Eastern front during World War I, but they were also present in XIV, XV, XVI, and XXI corps areas. Specifically, XXI and XV recruited heavily in Westphalia and the Rhineland. The Polish population was scattered throughout V and VI Corps districts. Because they labored in the mines, the Polish population was also found in VII and VIII Corps districts.[10]

Prior to 1914, the biggest peacetime formation of German armies was the army corps lead by a Commanding General (Kommandierender General) usually with the rank of *General der Infanterie*, *General der Artillerie,* or *General der Kavallerie*. The army corps consisted of two divisions, each division having two infantry brigades (with two regiments of three battalions and a machinegun company each), a field artillery brigade (with two field artillery regiments of two to three battalions each depending on whether they were equipped with field guns or with field howitzers), and a cavalry brigade (with two regiments). Besides these brigades, the army corps of 1914 had one Jäger battalion (the organization chart of the XV Army Corps with its two Jäger battalions shows an anomaly), one machinegun battalion (again the organization chart of the XV army corps shows an anomaly listing the fortress machinegun units of the Strasbourg fortress (*Festung Straßburg*) that were attached to infantry regiments of the corps), one engineer (*Pionier*) battalion, and one or two foot artillery regiments. The only supply unit in the peacetime organization chart was the train battalion of the army corps.[11]

During mobilization, this army corps structure changed as the cavalry brigades were eliminated as a corps unit, leaving behind only one cavalry regiment to be broken up as divisional cavalry between the two infantry divisions of the army corps. The cavalry brigade headquarters were used to form headquarters of the cavalry divisions and the cavalry (HKK)[12] that were created during mobilization. Horse artillery battalions were taken from their regiments and assigned to cavalry divisions. To increase combat strength, each cavalry division also got a Jäger battalion and machinegun battalion after mobilization. To keep up with the pace of the cavalrymen, these Jäger battalions usually had one company mounted on bicycles.[13]

The army corps engineer battalion was divided between the divisions and assigned by the company. Also, the foot artillery was broken up, usually leaving only one battalion with the army corps and pooling the other battalions as heavy artillery of the army. During mobilization, the infantry regiments were brought up to war strength, increasing the number from 140 to 150 men per company and up to 250 men by absorbing reservists. Additionally, each infantry regiment usually erected one, sometimes two, replacement (*Ersatz*) battalions to be left behind in the home garrison for training of new recruits who would replace losses in

[8] (Chickering, *Imperial Germany and the Great War, 1914–1918,* 2004), pp. 33–34.
[9] For further details please check the paragraph on personnel replacements.
[10] (The General Staff, 1918), p. 16.
[11] (Buchholz, Emails, 2009)
[12] Here we need a healthy dose of caution. Cavalry corps were not like infantry corps. When you think of Army Corps area—the cavalry did not have any such area. They might have been wrongly considered a corps, especially in the English language, but they were not the same.
[13] (Buchholz, Emails, 2009)

the field.[14] Field howitzer battalions traditionally were assigned in a way that each division got one battalion.

Upon mobilization the Order of Battle of an average army corps was changed as follows:
- The Jäger battalion was assigned to one of the two infantry divisions; the bicycle companies were usually assigned to a cavalry division.
- With each division, from three to five squadrons remained as divisional cavalry.
- The horse artillery batteries of the field artillery regiments were transferred from the army corps to cavalry divisions.
- Each field artillery regiment mobilized two light ammo columns.
- The army corps received one battalion of heavy artillery, usually of 21 cm heavy howitzers together with a respective light ammo column.
- Each division got one engineer or pioneer company and mobilized a divisional bridging train.
- A corps telephone detachment was mobilized.
- Each division usually got three medical companies.
- Four infantry and eight field artillery ammo columns were mobilized. The fourth and eighth field artillery ammo column usually transported ammo for the light field howitzer battalions.
- Eight separate foot artillery ammo columns were mobilized.
- The train battalion was heavily reinforced.
- Airship, airplane battalions, telephone and radio detachments were mobilized. (Check details given below.)[15]

Army corps staffs did not change too much upon mobilization. The Chief of the Corps General Staff managed the operations of the corps staff. Like the Chief of General Staff in an army HQ, he acted as the main advisor of the commander. Over his staff, the Chief of Staff executed disciplinary power comparable to a regimental commander.

In section I, an army corps staff usually had four general staff officers:[16]
- Ia (1st general staff officer) was responsible for operational orders (reconnaissance, marches, fights, bivouac, and defense against enemy air reconnaissance). The Ia was responsible for keeping in touch with the army HQ and the neighboring corps. He updated the corps staff about the tactical situation and the intentions of the commander. The Ia reported to the Chief of Staff and usually joined him when he reported into the commander. Id had to support Ia during regular staff work. Ia filled in for the Chief of General Staff during absences.[17]
- Ib (2nd general staff officer) was responsible for logistics and for orders addressed to the heavy baggage, the ammo columns, and the train formations. He had to create all logistical inserts to the corps orders worked out by the Ia. He was also responsible for any kind of war booty or prisoners and had to arrange the mop-up of battlefields after action. Ib reported to the Chief of Staff and was filled in for by the Ic during absences.[18]

[14] In 1914, many of these Ersatz battalions were mobilized and fielded in Ersatz divisions.
[15] (Rabenau 1914), pp. 136–137.
[16] (Pflugk-Hartung, 1896), p. 80.
[17] The Ia is most similar to a G3 in modern NATO terminology.
[18] Only for general comparison, the Ib is closest to a G4 in modern NATO terminology.

- Ic (3rd general staff officer) was responsible for military intelligence. He updated Ia and the Chief of Staff about the enemy situation and enemy estimates. He had to interrogate captured enemy officers and made sure that all prisoners were interrogated. He was also responsible for proper telephone, telegraph, and radio connections and directed the use of airplanes for recce operations. Ic reported into the Chief of General Staff and was replaced in absence by the Ib. Although he was the third general staff officer, the Ic was usually regarded as coming after the Ia in hierarchy. In staff organizational charts, the sequence is usually given as Ia, Ic, Ib and Id.[19]
- Id (4th general staff officer) initially had to work for the Ia. Id got his tasks assigned by the Ia. Usually he was responsible for getting orders and reports typed and printed and had to keep the war log. Id had to provide maps and other information material to the corps staff and to the assigned divisions. The IIa substituted for the Id. The Id filled in for the Ia during short absences. Very often Id officers were used as messengers for important messages and orders.

In section II, an army corps had three adjutants, two orderly officers (*Ordonnanzoffiziere*), and numerous other functions:

- Orderly officers supported other general staff officers, mainly Ic and Id. They were available also as messengers to the combat troops.
- IIa (1st adjutant) was responsible for administering disciplinary issues. He had to manage the day-to-day service of the corps and was responsible for dislocation of corps staff and the detached forward command post of the corps staff. IIa had to support the commandant of the corps HQ with deployment and bivouac issues.
- IIb (2nd adjutant) was the personal adjutant of the commanding general and had to support the Ic, particularly when dealing with foreign officers. In the forward command post, the IIb was responsible for maintenance and correct placement of the scissor scope.
- IIc (3rd adjutant) was responsible for any kind of bookkeeping and accounting, keeping personnel lists, loss lists, horse lists, etc. updated and was responsible for personnel and horses replacements, and replacements of lost and destroyed arms and equipment. He had to carry out ammo supply and other supply orders prepared by Ib.
- H.Q. was the commandant of the army corps HQ.
- St.W. (*Stabswache*) was the commander of the corps staff guards, made-up of infantry and cavalry detachments (platoon strength). St.W. reported to H.Q.
- G. (*Gendarmerie*) was the commander of the military police.
- M. (*Munition*) was the commander of all ammo columns. He had to cooperate closely with Ib and IIc.
- T. (*Train*) was the commander of the army corps trains. He had to closely cooperate with Ib, IIc, IVa, IVb, and IVc.
- Pi. (*Pionier*) was the commander of the engineer formations.
- Fsp. (*Fernsprecher*) was the commander of all radio, telegraph, and further communications functions.

In section III, the military jurisdiction was represented by the following:

- III, *Kriegsgerichtsrat*, chairing the courts martial of the army corps and counseling the commanding general on all legal issues.

[19] Again, only for a broad comparison, the Ic is closest to a G2 in modern NATO terminology.

Section IV was the corps intendancy:

- IVa was the corps intendant (*Korps-Intendant*). Usually a military official, he was responsible for managing all financial and administrative issues of the army corps and for overseeing all supply issues, food supply columns, bakery columns, etc. He had to set-up warehouses and distribution points for supply goods to make sure there was a working logistical and supply chain among the army and *Etappe* warehouses and the fighting formations of the army corps. Close cooperation with Ib was required to implement the logistical orders of the Ib.
- IVb was the chief medical officer (*Korpsarzt*) of the army corps.
- IVc was the chief veterinarian (*Korpsveterinär*) of the army corps.
- Po. was the field postmaster of the army corps, closely cooperating with the Ib.[20]

Cavalry Corps (Höherer Kavallerie-Kommandeur: HKK)[21]

Although serving in a cavalry regiment was a higher status for officers than other regimental assignments, the cavalry found it more difficult to adapt to the needs of modern warfare than did the infantry and artillery. In our chapter on doctrine, the reader might recognize that cavalry leaders before 1914 were generally more traditional than infantry or artillery leaders. This conservative attitude resulted in manuals and operational concepts that were unsuitable to meet the demands of modern warfare in 1914. Ironically, the experiences of 1866 and 1870–71 (where the cavalry bodies formed upon mobilization and did not fully meet the expectation of General Staff and War Ministry) were repeated in 1914.

After the war of 1870–71, three cavalry divisions with their divisional staffs were included in the peacetime structure of the Army: the Guard Cavalry Division, the cavalry divisions of the I Army Corps, and of the XII (1st Saxon) Army Corps. In 1887 and 1890, all but the Guard Cavalry Division were dismantled; the highest peacetime formation was again the cavalry brigade.[22] Cavalry divisions were only formed temporarily during the autumn exercises; cavalry corps were only formed for one day during the autumn exercises in 1905, 1909, and in 1912. Due to high costs and the collateral damage caused to countryside and farmland, the participation of bigger cavalry formations was reduced every year. In 1909, seven cavalry divisions and a cavalry corps were assembled during the exercises. In 1912, only two divisions and a corps were assembled. In the same year, the War Ministry clearly refused to allow four or six cavalry division to exercise in the open countryside by pointing to the high costs caused by collateral damage (*Manöverschaden*). The cavalry inspectors usually led the cavalry divisions during exercises.[23]

Although the General Inspection of the cavalry clearly saw the problems caused by a lack of leadership experience for the commanders of cavalry divisions, neither the War Ministry nor the Chief of General Staff opposed the permanent introduction of peacetime divisional commands for the cavalry. By filing an aide memoire to the War Minister on 4 August 1908, the General Inspector of the cavalry, General d. Kav. v. Kleist, asked for the formation of six permanent cavalry divisions—besides the Guard Cavalry Division (one Bavarian, one Saxon, and four Prussian). The proposal was turned down and Kleist waited until 1912 before he

20 (*Großer Generalstab*, 1914), pp. 25–33.

21 The German wording *Höherer Kavallerie-Kommandeur*—higher cavalry commander—makes it clear that these commanders were not on par with the Commanding Generals of Army Corps. The HKK was a corps sized unit but it was not an army corps. Many mistaken works refer to these as cavalry corps. That is an easy but inexact English translation. Some works used the word *Heeereskavalleriekorps*.

22 (Blau, 1934), p. 24.

23 (Blau, 1934), pp. 27 and 33.

used his right to immediately approach the Kaiser (*Immediatvortragsrecht*) to raise his point again. Kleist wrote to the Kaiser that he found the role of a cavalry division commander one of the most difficult roles to fill—certainly more complex and more difficult than the role of an infantry division commander. Without proper peacetime training and without being personally familiar with the performance and the leadership style of his regimental and brigade commanders, Kleist felt that these division commanders would fail at war.[24]

In early 1913, the General Staff finally started planning to mobilize a cavalry command structure above divisional level. This command structure operationally should lead the assigned divisions and give directives to the cavalry divisions directly—like cavalry corps had already done during previous exercises—but without interfering with the authority of the Supreme Command (*Oberste Heeresleitung*). The idea of HKK created an extremely difficult situation for their leaders, who were taking over an organization with no peacetime practice and leading cavalry divisions that were formed only upon mobilization.

Ironically, Moltke discussed the general idea of the HKKs with the General Inspector of the Cavalry, Gen. Lt. Georg v.d. Marwitz, but he refused to inform Marwitz about the intended operational details of the mobilization plan. After receiving a request for further information, Moltke answered Marwitz:

> Regretfully, I will not be able to meet Your Excellency's wishes to be briefed about the tasks of the big cavalry formations upon mobilization. But during the winter war games led by me and during the general staff rides, similar tasks of the cavalry will be analyzed. In case Your Excellency wishes to join personally or to send a delegate on your behalf, it would be my pleasure to follow this wish.[25]

The introduction of the HKKs into the mobilization plan of 1914–15 seemed to be the exclusive initiative of the General Staff. The cavalry department of the War Ministry still opposed the idea of the HKKs in an aide memoir (*Zur Frage der Höheren Kavalleriekommandeure*) written in January 1913. The War Ministry did not want mobilization plans higher than cavalry divisions. While the General Staff wanted bigger cavalry formations, they also wanted to make sure that these cavalry formations carried out the missions of the OHL—even if that meant a bypass of the army commands. The War Ministry, on the other hand, wanted to have cavalry divisions operating under the direct command of their Armies, therefore only under the indirect control of the OHL. The General Staff succeeded in getting its cavalry corps but at the expense of watering down command structures among armies, HKKs, and the OHL.

In direct contrast to the regular army corps, cavalry corps possessed neither command nor corps troops, and no train or columns. Instead, the cavalry corps consisted of two or three cavalry divisions. The divisions were equipped with a small staff that covered all necessary functions and departments. The HKKs did not even have a staff. As a result, the commander was not designated as a commanding general but rather a senior cavalry commander. This designation meant that his authority extended only into the area of tactics and strategy. The corps chief of staff was assigned to the HKK staff, but had no logistical role—logistics was all at the division level. So, the HKK was a reporting headquarters that established tactical and

---

24 (Blau, 1934), p. 31. Emphasis by author.

25 Files of the General Inspector of the Cavalry, letter by Moltke from 4 November 1913, found in (Blau, 1934), p. 35.

strategic guidance. Within that umbrella, the division commanders had to provide for their own supply and administration.[26]

There is little information on the structure of the HKK. It is not even mentioned in the General Staff Officer's Pocket Book.[27] This reference told the general staff officer everything about everything—except the HKK (and the super-heavy artillery). Writing after the war, even General Maximilian v. Poseck in his seminal work on the German cavalry, did not discuss the structure.[28] The only source that mentioned the mobilization of HKKs is the cavalry reconnaissance manual from 1914 (issued before mobilization) that was not issued by the War Ministry, but by the General Inspection of the Cavalry with permission of the War Ministry. This limited information again illustrates the political struggle about the mobilization of cavalry corps that was fought within the military. In this manual, the role of the HKK is described as a weak intermediate command position with the function to coordinate the operations of several cavalry divisions that were temporarily formed to accomplish a joint mission. The HKK commander (here again named commander and not commanding general) had a purely coordinating function that was only possible if he joined one of his cavalry division staffs and then made use of their staff command and communications infrastructure.

The task of the HKK commander was to keep the operations of the cavalry in line with the overall situation of the army they supported and to follow the intentions of the army commander. The manual emphasized that this role was not to slow down the delivery of reconnaissance results to the army commanders. If necessary, important messages were to be delivered from the cavalry divisions directly to the army commands bypassing the HKK. These HKK commanders found themselves in a weak and ambiguous position when operations started in 1914.[29]

When looking at the last peacetime assignment of the HKK and cavalry division commanders, there are some interesting insights. Following are the pre-war cavalry inspections and cavalry brigade commanders in the 1914 *Rangliste*[30] and in the 1913 and 1914 *Militärhandbuch Bayern*; their last peacetime assignment is in parentheses:[31]

- HKK 1—Gen. Lt. Frhr. v. Richthofen (commander 6th Infantry Division).
- HKK 2—Gen. Lt. v. d. Marwitz (Generalinspekteur der Kavallerie).
- HKK 3—K.B. Gen. d. Kav. Ritter v. Frommel (Bavarian Cavalry Inspection, retired to z.D. in 1913).
- HKK 4—Gen. Lt. Frhr. v. Hollen (commander 21st Infantry Division).
- Garde-Kavallerie-Division—Gen. Maj. v. Storch (15 cav. Brig.), the peacetime commander Gen.Lt. v. Pelet-Narbonne, who passed away on 14 June 1914.
- 1. KD[32]—Gen. Lt. Brecht (1st Cavalry Inspection).
- 2. KD—Gen. Maj. Frhr. v. Krane (39 Cavalry Brigade).
- 3. KD—Gen. Lt. v. Unger (20 Cavalry Brigade).
- 4. KD—Gen. Lt. v. Garnier (2nd Cavalry Inspection).
- 5. KD—Gen. Lt. v. Ilsemann (39 Cavalry Brigade).
- 6. KD—Gen. Lt. v. Schmettow (4th Cavalry Inspection).
- 7. KD—Gen. Lt. v. Heydebreck (3rd Cavalry Inspection).

26 (Cron, Imperial German Army 1914–1918, 2002), p. 94.
27 (Großer Generalstab, 1914)
28 (Poseck M. v., 1921)
29 (Generalinspektion der Kavallerie, 1914), pp. 4–5.
30 (Kriegsministerium, 1914)
31 (Kriegsministerium K., 1914)
32 KD is the abbreviation for Kavallerie Division.

- 8. KD—Gen. Lt. Graf v.d. Schulenburg (2 Saxon Cavalry Brigade no. 24).
- 9. KD—Gen. Maj. Graf v. Schmettow, Eberhardt (Leib-Husaren-Brigade).
- Bavarian Cavalry Division—K.B.—Gen.Lt. v. Stetten (Bavarian Cavalry Inspection, successor of Ritter v. Frommel).

Obviously, there is a trend: commanders of HKKs were either division commanders or (general) inspectors of the cavalry—whether in Prussia or in Bavaria. Cavalry division commanders were either commander of cavalry inspections or of cavalry brigades before mobilization. The disbanded cavalry brigade staffs (made redundant by assigning their regiments as divisional cavalry) were used in the same way as cadre around which to form cavalry division staffs upon mobilization.

Divisions

Infantry Divisions

Like army corps staffs, divisional staffs did not change much upon mobilization. Most officers were used to working with each other. Also, in the staff of an infantry division, section I was the general staff section:

- Ia (1st general staff officer) was responsible for operations and all tactical issues. For all issues, he reported directly to the division commander. The Ia kept the division's war log.
- O. (*Ordonnanz-Offizier*) acted as the main support of the Ia; he was responsible for all issues covered by Ib and Ic in a corps HQ. The Ordonnanz-Offizier had to substitute for the Ia during absence.[33]

In section II the divisional HQ had two adjutants and the commandant of the HQ:

- IIa (1st adjutant) managed the day-to-day routine jobs of the division HQ and managed disciplinary issues and personnel files of the officers of the division. He handled legal issues together with the III. IIa also had to keep the divisions files.
- IIb (2nd adjutant) was responsible for personnel, horses, ammo, arms, and equipment replacements.
- St.Q. was commandant of the division staff quarter.

Section III consisted of the following:

- III was the military jurisdiction officer who acted as the main legal advisor of the divisional commander.

Section IV consisted of the following:

- IVa, the divisional intendant, managed all supply issues of the divisions in close cooperation with the Ia.
- IVb was the chief medical officer (*Divisionsarzt*) of the division.
- IVc was the chief chaplain (*Feld-Divisionsgeistlicher*) of the division.
- Po. (*Post*) was the field-postmaster of the division.
- Gr.B. (*Große Baggage*) was the leader of the heavy baggage of the division.[34]

Reserve divisions had division staffs like active divisions.

---

33 (Pflugk-Hartung, 1896), p. 81.
34 (Großer Generalstab, 1914), pp. 13–15.

Cavalry Divisions

Cavalry divisions were generally assembled upon mobilization. Their staffs were built-up around the existing peacetime brigade staffs. An exception was the Guard Corps, in which a Guard Cavalry Division existed in the peacetime structure. In cavalry divisions, section I was the general staff section. Different from infantry divisions, the cavalry divisions had two general staff officers:

- Ia (1st general staff officer) was responsible for operations and all tactical issues. The main tactical advisor of the division commander reported directly to the division commander. Ib substituted for him.
- Ib (2nd general staff officer) was responsible to liaise with the HKK and the army HQ and was also responsible for information and intelligence and for all supply issues. Due to the absence of a supply infrastructure on corps level, it was obviously necessary to have a general staff officer responsible for supply issues in the division staff. He supported the Ia and reported to the Ia.

1. 0—24—3.

3.	2.	1.
U. 1.	H. 1.	D. 1.
U. 2.	H. 2.	D. 2.

Nachr. A.
m. f. Funk. St. 1, 2
» l. » » 1, 2
Pi. A.
1.
M. 1.
l. M. K.
Kav. Kw. Kol. 1.

Organizational Chart of a cavalry division after mobilization from the General Staff Officer's Handbook. The footer line to this chart, which reads in English "By mobilization of higher cavalry commands the uniform lead of several cavalry divisions is already prepared," is the only hint in the 1914 general staff officer's handbook that points to the planned formation of HKKs.

In section II, the cavalry division had two adjutants:

- IIa (1st adjutant) managed the day-to-day routine jobs of the division HQ and had to manage disciplinary issues and personnel files of the officers of the division. He handled legal issues together with III. IIa also had to keep the divisions files.
- IIb (2nd adjutant) was responsible for personnel, horses, ammo, arms, and equipment replacements.
- St.Q. was commandant of the division staff quarter.

Section III consisted of the following:

- III was the military jurisdiction officer who acted as the main legal advisor to the divisional commander.

Section IV consisted of the following:

- IVa was the divisional intendant, managing all subsistence supply issues of the division in close cooperation with the Ia.
- IVb was the chief medical officer (Divisionsarzt) of the division.
- IVc was the chief chaplain (Feld-Divisionsgeistlicher) of the division.
- Po. was the field-postmaster of the division.
- Gr.B. was the leader of the heavy baggage of the cavalry division.[35]

Brigades

Peacetime infantry divisions consisted of two (sometimes three) infantry brigades, a cavalry brigade, and an artillery brigade. Brigades were the biggest formations consisting of only one arm, not the very modern term of "combined arms." This organizational structure is probably the biggest difference when comparing brigades to current German or American armies. Brigade drills were the largest formal drills and were usually carried out at the start of the training period in the corps training center (*Truppenübungsplatz*). For infantry and artillery brigades, this brigade drill was the formal close of the formal drill period starting with the drill of the individual soldier. On brigade level, this formal drill was replaced by tactical training. But for cavalry brigades, there was a certain amount of brigade drill required in the tactical manual even up to 1914.

Two (sometimes three) infantry regiments made up a brigade commanded by a major general. He commanded the brigade, supervised the regimental training and supervised the disciplinary affairs of the regiments. Brigade staffs were very small; besides the brigade commander, they had a regimental adjutant—usually a first lieutenant or captain or a *Rittmeister* in cavalry brigades. Two NCOs served as staff assistants. Planning of brigade maneuvers was a real challenge to the work capacity of such tiny staffs. Upon mobilization, a brigade staff was reinforced by an *Ordonnanz-Offizier*, usually a reserve officer, who had to support the adjutant. Artillery brigades also had a *Feuerwerk-Offizier*, who had to supervise the supply of ammunition.

Every three years, the brigade commander inspected the uniform stocks of the regiment and supervised the presumed economic affairs (*Wirtschaftsbetrieb der Regimenter*).[36] Besides this job, he was responsible for recruiting within the brigade district in cooperation with the *Bezirkskommandos*. Usually, two Bezirkskommandos controlled the recruiting business within a brigade district. This rule did not apply for the Guards Corps and within regions controlled by *Landwehrinspektionen*.[37]

Whereas infantry brigade commands were involved in the recruiting business, cavalry and artillery brigades had pure command and control functions over their assigned regiments.

[35] (Großer Generalstab 1914), pp. 37–40.
[36] (Pflugk-Hartung, 1896), p. 49.
[37] (Alten, 1911), pp. 538–540

THE ARMS

Infantry

The infantry was considered as the most important arm based on firepower and the bravery of its men when attacking. The 1906 infantry manual wrapped up this importance as follows:

> The infantry is the most important arm. Together with the artillery, her role is fighting the enemy. The infantry alone can break the last enemy resistance. She carries the main burden of the battle and endures the heaviest losses; therefore, she will also gain the greatest glory. The infantry has to strive for attack; all her actions must be determined just by one thought: forward and on the enemy, regardless what price that may cost.[38]

Infantry regiments had three battalions of four companies each. Companies 1–4 were battalion I, companies 5–8 were battalion II, and battalion III had companies 9–12. A regiment with a high peacetime budget (*hoher Etat*) had approximately 1,700 men and a company had approximately 180 men. Upon mobilization, this number increased to more than 250 men per company, so more than 3,300 men in total.[39] There were companies with a low budget (*niedriger Etat*) that had four officers (the company commander and the three platoon commanders), 18 non-commissioned officers (NCOs), and 142 Enlisted Men (EM), including musicians. In a high budget company, there were four officers, 19 NCOs, and 160 EM, including musicians. Usually the army corps in border areas (East Prussia and Alsace-Lorraine) and the Guards Corps had high budget companies; most other corps were on a small budget.

During the 1890s, most regiments also had a fourth battalion (a so-called half-battalion) consisting of only two companies. It was formed to cover guards' services and other military duties during basic training periods in the battalions I–III.[40] Those IV battalions were really inefficient and were dissolved to build the pool of surplus formations for the build-up of new army corps in 1897–99.

The regimental staff consisted of the following positions: commander (colonel), vice-commander (lieutenant colonel), and three staff officers (majors or senior captains), adjutant (first lieutenant), regimental paymaster (*Regimentszahlmeister*—the regimental paymaster was in fact an official and not an officer, but was considered equal with a commissioned officer), regimental doctor (*Oberstabsarzt*—comparable with the rank of a medical major),[41] two doctors (*Stabsärzte*—comparable with the ranks of medical captains) and four assistant doctors, as well as 49 other ranks (37 of whom were in the regimental band and doubled as stretcher bearers). It also had 16 horses, an entrenching and construction equipment wagon, and a baggage wagon. The regimental commander was the disciplinary superior of all officers, NCOs, and EM of his battalion; he could transfer officers, NCOs, and men within his regiment, promote NCOs and EM, and suggest officers for promotion. He adjudicated formal complaints (*Beschwerden*) of NCOs and EM. The regimental commander could act as chair-

---

38 (Kriegsministerium, 1906), p. 81. Translated by the author.

39 A mobilized and fully stocked infantry regiment had a so-called ration strength (*Verpflegungsstärke*) of 3,390 in total (Großer Generalstab, 1914), pp. 18–19.

40 (Pflugk-Hartung, 1896), p. 46.

41 Formally, all medical doctors in the regiment belonged to the regimental staff, but each battalion had a doctor permanently assigned. The regimental doctor (Oberstabsarzt) was also the battalion doctor of the first battalion.

man of instant military courts (*Standgericht*) after mobilization. He was responsible for uniforming and equipping his regiment.

The staff of each battalion had a commander, usually a major, a captain (so-called staff captain), the battalion adjutant (usually a second lieutenant), four company commanders (captains), four first lieutenants, eight second lieutenants,[42] a battalion-doctor (*Stabsarzt*), an assistant doctor, the Paymaster (*Zahlmeister*) and 1054 other ranks.[43] The three "staff" captains of the battalions, together with the vice commander of the regiment and the three staff officers of the regimental staff, were active officers of the reserve to take over commanding roles in reserve and Landwehr formations upon mobilization. After mobilization, many active officers could be found with reserve formations, and many reserve officers were mobilized to serve with active formations. This pattern was one of the secrets that gave reserve formations a combat value comparable with active formations.

The battalion had 58 horses and 19 wagons. The four ammunition wagons, the medical wagon, and the four field kitchens were considered fighting baggage (*Gefechtsbaggage*). They belonged to the companies. The other 10 baggage wagons were counted as heavy baggage (*Große Baggage*). This heavy baggage consisted of two staff baggage wagons, five food wagons, and three battalion ammo wagons. The companies had four wagons each. The company ammo wagon carried 14,400 rounds of rifle ammo as each soldier carried 150 rounds of so-called pocket ammo; the field kitchen; the engineer equipment wagon that carried 100 small spades, 10 small and five big axes, 4 wire-cutters to cut wire up to 5mm; and a baggage wagon called the *Kompaniepackwagen*.[44]

There was an unappreciated, secret advantage that German active units had over their opponents. This advantage was a horse-drawn wagon that was actually a mobile field kitchen with a 200 liter cooking kettle and a coffee maker. Through local requisitioning, a series of ingredients including meat could be made into a stew while the mobile field kitchen marched with the company. When the company stopped, the troops could simply line up and be served hot food. Known as a *Gulaschkanone,* not all units were equipped with one. For instance, the artillery, the cavalry, and the Landwehr formations did not have them. The Gulaschkanone allowed the infantry to cover greater distances. In the French army, cooking was a squad function. This expectation of squad food preparation was not only time-consuming, but it often resulted in no food when the soldiers had to march out leaving the food half prepared.

With the introduction of the machinegun company (whose company commander was a captain), a first lieutenant and two second lieutenants had to be added to the third battalion. By calling up reservists, the active companies grew from approximately 150–180 officers and men up to 250–270, including four cyclists, a communications detachment, and four stretcher bearers (the former musicians).

In July 1860, the Prussians began numbering their regiments, but modified the structure in 1861. After the War of 1866, the states that Prussia annexed had their armies integrated into the numbering system. Bavaria had its own numbering system that was completely separate from that of Prussia. There appears to have been no standardization to the numbering. So, you had the integration of the Hanseatic States, Hanoverian regiments, the old electoral Hesse (Kurhessen), Schleswig-Holstein, and Nassau. That accounted for regiment numbers

[42] These were the four officers in a company. The company commander and three platoon commanders—first platoon (first lieutenant) doubled as the vice company commander—and the platoon commanders of second and third platoons (second lieutenants).

[43] (Pflugk-Hartung, 1896), pp. 45–46.

[44] Compare to battalion structure in the 1890s (Pflugk-Hartung, 1896), pp. 46–47.

up to 88. In 1867, the other states of the North German Confederation and Saxony joined the numbering system, but it was not continuous nor did it follow any particular chronology. The order was the Mecklenburg Grand Duchies, Oldenburg, Brunswick, Anhalt, Saxe-Weimar, the Saxon duchies, and the other Thuringian states, covering numbers 89 to 96. The numbers for infantry regiments 97–99 were reserved for future Prussian units, which were not created until 1881. Saxony added their regiments to the mix beginning at number 100. This military convention preceded the convention of some other states—*Militärkonvention zwischen dem Norddeutschen Bunde und Sachsen vom 7 Februar 1867*. Baden's numbering started at 109 with *Militärkonvention zwischen dem Norddeutschen Bunde und Baden vom 25 November 1870*. Hesse and Württemberg followed—*Militärkonvention zwischen dem Norddeutschen Bunde und Hessen vom 13 Juni 1871*. *Militärkonvention zwischen dem Norddeutschen Bunde und Württemberg vom 25 November 1870*. Both the regimental numbers and the seniority of the regiments were combined. Hanoverian regiments retained their original founding date, while other regiments traced their founding date to their parent organization. An analysis of regimental names and the movement of regiments led to some interesting anomalies. For example, infantry regiment 67 (*4. Magdeburgisches Infanterie-Regiment Nr. 67*) was originally from Prussian Saxony and called "Magdeburgisch." It later relocated to Metz and drew its recruits mainly from the Rhineland that had nothing to do with Prussian Saxony.

Machinegun Formations

During the 1880s, the weapon testing commission (*Gewehr-Prüfungskommission*) tried available multi-barrel machineguns. Either Gatling or Nordenfeldt designed them, and they were intended for fortress use. Although having immense firepower, the trials were not successful. After the machinegun designed by the American engineer Hiram Maxim was introduced, the commission ordered practical field trials and, in 1898, two mounted machineguns were tried by 1st Battalion Infantry Regiment 146 in Königsberg. These trials were successful, and a further six infantry battalions received machineguns for extended field trials, with another six trial formations in 1900. On 26 March 1901, the Maxim gun was accepted as the *Maschinengewehr 01*. These had the same caliber as the infantry rifle and fired the same ammunition. Machine guns provided an immense increase in infantry firepower. Together with accepting the machinegun model 01, the trial formations were turned into six machinegun detachments of six guns each (Guards and no 1–5); another five detachments were soon to follow. In 1906, 15 detachments existed, which meant that the entire German field army had 91 machineguns in total. An additional 80 machineguns were installed across numerous fortresses. These figures alone show the traditionalists' reluctance to use machinegun formations.[45]

Those detachments (*Maschinengewehr-Abteilungen*) consisted of four officers, 14 NCOs, one trumpeter, and 76 enlisted men. They had 60 horses, six mounted machineguns, one reserve machinegun and three ammo wagons. Upon mobilization, they were increased to 130 men, 90 horses, and 14 wagons. Most of the wagons were assigned for baggage and ammunition. A mobilized machinegun detachment consisted of a gun detachment (*Gefechtsabteilung*) with six mounted guns and three ammo wagons, organized into three platoons, a fighting baggage of one big four-horse ammo wagon, one material wagon and 11 surplus horses, and a heavy baggage of one two-horse baggage wagon, one food wagon, and

[45] (Storz 1992), p. 297.

one wagon with horse rations.[46] To provide a real superiority in infantry firepower, each infantry regiment had to be equipped with its own machinegun detachment.

With the introduction of the Maschinengewehr *08* a 13th (machinegun) company with six mounted machineguns, organized in three platoons of two guns each, was added to infantry regiments. Machinegun companies of infantry regiments had their guns mounted on two-horse carriages. The guns could only be fired when dismounted. Machine gun battalions had six guns mounted on horse-driven carriages. But four horses each towed their carriages making them faster and more mobile to keep pace with cavalry units. The guns of MG-battalions could also be fired when mounted on their carriages.

Since each infantry regiment, each Jäger battalion, the infantry marksmanship schools, and the infantry training and demonstration battalion (*Infanterie Lehr-Bataillon*) had their own machinegun companies, there were 182 Prussian, 26 Bavarian, 19 Saxon, and 10 Württemberg companies in 1914. Multiplied by six guns each, this number of weapons was an enormous increase in firepower compared to the situation only 10 years earlier.

With infantry regiments, the machinegun companies formed a 13th company and usually belonged to the 3rd Battalion. Peacetime strength was about four officers, 10 NCOs, plus one medical NCO, and 60 EM. The company had 22 horses, six machineguns mounted on two-horse carriages, and three ammo carriages. Mobilization strength increased up to 96 men, 40 horses, and 12 wagons.

On 1 October 1913, 15 fortress machinegun detachments were established; this organization put the machineguns of the fortresses under uniform tactical command. These companies also consisted of six guns, four officers, 16 NCOs, and 70 men with 22 horses. They had fewer baggage wagons than the machinegun companies that were fielded with infantry regiments.[47] During the war, machinegun formations were heavily reinforced until at the end each infantry battalion had its own machinegun company.

Jäger and *Schützen* (Light Infantry)

Included as part of the infantry, were the Jäger and Schützen battalions. These were considered somewhat elite and competition to join was keen. There were many volunteers for these battalions as participation within was a requirement for a subsequent civil service positions in the forestry service. Originally, they consisted of four companies, each having 23 officers, two medical officers, 70 NCOs (named *Oberjäger instead of Unteroffizier*), and 570 men. However, in 1913 this number grew to six companies, which included a machinegun and a bicycle company. Bavaria only increased to five companies, which were bicycle companies. Jäger battalions were considerably stronger than regular infantry battalions; they were able to cover more difficult or demanding tactical missions because of higher firepower and better training,

Originally, Jäger formations fought in more open tactical formations (see details in the Chapter 12 about infantry doctrine). Their major task was either reconnaissance or acting as a flank guard of line infantry bodies. They were not trained to fight in line with other infantry units; instead, they were trained to accomplish their own missions. In general, this formation required better-trained men with a higher understanding of the tactical situation and with a higher level of marksmanship than regular infantrymen.

---

46 (Rabenau, 1914), p. 54.

47 (Rabenau, 1914), pp. 55–56.

With enlisted men and NCOs usually coming from families with hunting or forestry background, marksmanship played a bigger role. Although shooting in the same exercises as the regular infantrymen, the Jäger put a higher emphasis upon high levels of marksmanship. The regular men were better trained with their rifles that resulted in their own *Kaiserpreis* contest. Competition ran within the Jäger battalions and not between Jäger and infantry. Since they were very often attached to cavalry formations upon mobilization and during exercises, Jäger were trained to fulfill their task more independently. Most had at least some hunting experience and had more experience in taking advantage of natural cover and camouflage. While the regular infantryman was used to advance in dense lines without too much concern for cover, the average Jäger was trained differently.

Since Jäger and Schützen units were considered elite, they had their own uniforms, wearing shakos instead of spiked helmets and green jackets instead of royal blue.[48] They traditionally also used their own rifles. When *Dreyse* needle-fire rifles were issued to the infantry during mid 19th century, the Jäger battalions got special Jäger rifles model 1865, which were 10 cm shorter than infantry rifles. These had a heavy and more precise octagonal barrel along with a hair trigger. The last particular Jäger rifle was issued with the model 1871 systems. The Jäger battalions did not get their own model 1871–84 rifles (just the sling was slightly different compared to that issued to the line infantry gun); when they were re-armed with 8mm model 1888 rifles, they were absolutely identical with the respective infantry rifles. When model 98 rifles and carbines replaced the model 1888 rifles, the Jäger formations received rifles instead of carbines.

Before the war, a clear doctrine different from the regular infantry doctrine did not exist. Up through 1914, the Jäger were either assigned to cavalry divisions or held back as a special reserve of a Commanding General of the army corps.[49] Beginning in 1915, Jäger formations were used to build *Sturmbataillone* that specialized in trench raiding. Only these very elite formations were allowed to get the too-long model 98 rifles replaced by shorter carbines.

Cavalry

In 1914, there were 110 active cavalry regiments, 33 reserve cavalry regiments, two Landwehr cavalry regiments, one mobile Ersatz cavalry Regiment, and 38 self-standing Landwehr cavalry squadrons. Cavalry regiments were authorized five squadrons, but several of them had only four. Functionally, by 1901, they were all equipped and employed in a similar fashion but had different uniforms and histories.

After 1900 and the introduction of machineguns, the role of the cavalry shifted from a "battle cavalry" (deciding battles by mass attacks like in the Kaisermanöver) to a reconnaissance cavalry. This development also blurred the differentiation between all the different branches of cavalry towards an *Einheitskavallerie* (uniform cavalry). Taking the tradition of hussars, uhlans, cuirassiers, and dragoons into consideration, together with the egotistical noble tradition of many regiments, one might imagine how painful this process must have been.

Cavalry regiments consisted of four to six (usually five) squadrons (*Eskadrons*). Peacetime strength of a squadron was about four officers (one of them a captain (*Rittmeister*)) including the squadron commander, while three others acted as troop leaders. Eighteen NCOs, three musicians, and 127 EM and 145 horses made up a squadron. This designation resulted

48 Even after issuing field grey uniforms, the "Jäger" and the machinegun formations had a more greenish field grey than the regular infantry.

49 (Mattuschka, 1979), p. 164.

in an average regiment of 740 men and 726 horses. A lieutenant colonel or a colonel usually commanded cavalry regiments. The regimental staff consisted of a major and a captain. Two regiments made up a cavalry brigade led by a colonel or a major general. In the peacetime structure, the cavalry brigades were usually assigned to a division, except the Guards Corps, in which the existing four cavalry brigades were merged into a cavalry division.[50]

The horses were recruited through mounting committees (*Remontierungskommissionen*): five Prussian, one Bavarian, one Saxon, and one from Württemberg. Newly-bought horses were put into mounting depots (*Remontierungsdepots*) for one or two years for training.[51] There were 19 depots in Prussia, four in Bavaria, four in Saxony, and one in Württemberg. All mounted formations requested horses from the IIb department of the army corps, who liaised with the War Ministry for further orders. The mounting inspection of the War Ministry (*Remonteinspektion*) assigned the necessary number of trained horses to each formation.

Regiments used their horses for at least two years and issued them to the officers of the mounted formations as official horses (*Chargenpferde*). After at least four years, they became the personal property of the officers, who were allowed to sell them. Mounted officers received financial compensation (*Pferdegeld*) for their personally-purchased horses. This Pferdegeld was calculated on the base of 1,500 *Mark* per young horse for all lieutenants and first lieutenants. The Pferdegeld was written-off with an eight-year depreciation and was paid out at 15.62 Mark per month. More senior officers received a higher compensation. Regimental commanders received 600 Marks per year. All other staff officers and captains received 300 Mark per year. Military veterinarians and blacksmiths took care of the horses.[52] Upon mobilization, the five-squadron regiment was usually broken up into four active squadrons of 180 officers and men and 180 horses, each with three wagons and a replacements squadron (*Ersatz-Eskadron*) that remained in the garrison or mobilization station to take in and train further reservists.

Cavalry regiments had a fighting baggage of the following:

- 58 replacement horses;
- two medical aid horses;
- two bridge wagons with two steel pontoons and four bridge elements (four meters long and one meter wide) each. This equipment could build either a small footbridge of 1 meter width and 20 meters length; a small bridge, 2 meters wide and 12 meters long; a wide bridge of 3 meters and 8 meters length; or a pontoon ferry of about 16 sq m;
- each bridge wagon also carried 32 demolition charges also to destroy bridges;
- one telegraph wagon carrying up to 15 km of field telephone line plus 350 meters of waterproof telephone line;
- and in addition, each regiment had two communications detachments.

Heavy baggage consisted of the following:

- one baggage wagon for the regimental staff,
- four wagons for the squadrons,
- five food wagons,
- five forage wagons.[53]

---

50 (Pflugk-Hartung, 1896), pp. 50–52.
51 (Pflugk-Hartung, 1896), p. 92.
52 (Rabenau, 1914), p. 58
53 (Rabenau, 1914), pp. 64–66.

Upon mobilization each division had about three to five (usually four) squadrons; the bulk of the cavalry went into the higher cavalry organizations (HKK).

Field Artillery

The battery was the smallest unit of the field artillery and was commanded by a captain; it was comparable to a company in infantry formations. A battery usually had six horse-drawn 7.7 cm field cannons—M/96 new model. In 1914, it was subdivided into three platoons (of two guns each) and had an observation wagon carrying a shielded observation platform with a scissor scope that could be elevated. Batteries also had one ammo wagon per gun. On low budget, a battery had four officers and 124 NCOs and EM, plus 75 horses. On high budget, a battery had four officers and 143 NCOs and EM, plus 100 horses. Batteries were increased to 150 EM, 135 horses, and 17 wagons upon mobilization.[54]

If unlimbered in firing position, one ammo wagon was beside each gun. Each gun carried 36 shrapnel rounds; each ammo wagon carried another 90 shrapnel rounds, plus 36 high explosive (HE) rounds in the first ammo wagon of each battery. Shrapnel rounds were designed to be used as either real shrapnel or as light HE rounds. Use depended upon the setting of the fuse. The batteries had 756 rounds of shrapnel plus 36 rounds of HE with them as combat load. Very soon, this ratio was changed to fewer (quite inefficient) shrapnel rounds and more HE rounds.

Batteries of field artillery were either riding or driving. In the riding batteries of the horse artillery,[55] six horses, plus four extra horses towed the limbered gun, with the entire crew of five gunners and the command NCO on horseback. In addition, an ammo carriage accompanied each gun with another four soldiers running the supply chain between the ammo train and the gun. Driving batteries did not have the four extra horses per gun. Three gunners sat on the limber and two gunners on the gun carriage riding with the gun; only the commanding NCO was on his own horse. The other crewmen rode on the gun team horses

Three batteries formed a battalion (Abteilung) commanded by a major. Two battalions formed a regiment commanded by a lieutenant colonel or a full colonel. The battalion staff also had a military veterinarian, whereas the regimental staff had an extra field grade officer and two extra captains. Like the infantry, those extra officers were usually assigned to reserve or Landwehr units upon mobilization. The 1st Guard Field Artillery Regiment; the Field Artillery Regiments nos. 1, 3, 5, 8, 10, 11, 15, and 35; the Saxon Field Artillery Regiment 12 and the Bavarian Field Artillery Regiment 5 had a third battalion of horse artillery (reitende Artillerie) with three batteries of four guns each. Those horse artillery batteries had four officers, 19 NCOs, 116 EM, 144 horses, four ammo wagons, and one observation wagon. Upon mobilization, the horse batteries were increased to 130 EM, 170 horses, and 13 wagons—most of them were ammo wagons (high budget—low budget not listed here). The horse artillery battalions were designed to join the cavalry divisions and cavalry corps upon mobilization as a fast moving element of artillery firepower.[56]

Each battery had fighting baggage consisting of the spare horses and one supply wagon. The heavy baggage consisted of one supply wagon carrying 38 big spades, 31 big axes, 33 hatchets, seven small axes, and a hand-saw as entrenchment tools; horse batteries had about

---

[54] (Pflugk-Hartung, 1896), pp. 53– 55

[55] The word "riding battery" is directly translated from the German word *reitende Batterie* to be distinguished from driving batteries (*fahrende Batterie*); the corresponding English phrase for riding battery would be "battery of horse artillery."

[56] (Pflugk-Hartung, 1896), pp. 55–57.

30 percent fewer tools. Additionally, there was one wagon with food and another wagon with horse fodder.

Two field artillery regiments formed a field artillery brigade, commanded either by a full colonel or by a major general. Each division had one field artillery brigade. One battalion per brigade was equipped with 10.5 cm field howitzer M/98 new model instead of field cannons. Each field howitzer carried 24 rounds per limber and 34 rounds per ammo wagon, together 516 rounds—326 of them shrapnel, and 190 HE as the combat load.

For each field artillery battalion (cannon, howitzer, or horse artillery), a light ammo column was mobilized, consisting of about 190 officers, NCOs and men, 180 horses, 24 wagons—21 of them ammo supply wagons, one food wagon and one wagon with horse food. The columns also had a small baggage wagon with entrenchment tools: 50 big spades, 50 hatchets, 52 small axes, 25 big axes and a handsaw. The unit load (*Grundbeladung*) was the ammunition stock carried by the batteries and battalions themselves. This unit load was further divided into the combat load (*Gefechtsbeladung*) carried by the gun and its limber and into the basic load (*Truppenbeladung*), and the stocks the ammo columns of the battalions and regiments carried with them.[57]

In cannon battalions, the ammunition columns were subdivided into two shrapnel groups of three platoons, with two wagons each and one HE group with three platoons of three wagons each. Each wagon was loaded with 90 rounds—altogether 1,890 rounds, 1,080 of them shrapnel and 810 HE—that came up to 105 rounds per gun (calculated per battalion of three batteries with six guns each).[58] In howitzer battalions, the ammo column had one shrapnel platoon and one HE platoon. Each wagon carried 58 rounds, altogether 1,218 rounds. 174 of them were shrapnel and 1,044 HE—that came out to 68 rounds per gun. This amount was the basic load, which together with the combat load should be sufficient ammunition to supply the batteries for one day of battle (*Schlachttag*).

Horse artillery formations mobilized light ammo columns of the cavalry divisions with 150 officers, NCOs, and EM; 200 horses; and 25 wagons. Besides artillery rounds, some of their wagons also carried infantry ammo. Cavalry divisions had an extra load of entrenchment tools. These ammo columns of the field artillery battalions and regiments and of the cavalry divisions were called light ammo columns. The army corps also mobilized regular ammo columns: two battalions of ammo columns with two infantry and four artillery columns each. An infantry column had 186 officers, NCOs, and EM; 197 horses; and 28 wagons. An artillery column had 185 officers, NCOs, and EM; 192 horses; and 28 wagons—21 of them ammo wagons carrying about 1,900 rounds. The 4th and 8th ammo column carried ammo for howitzers.[59]

Prior to the campaign in 1914, all of the ammunition combined through the army corps was estimated to sustain (a very optimistic calculation) four days of heavy fighting called "days of battle." These figures given by Rabenau (see footnote below) are obviously based upon calculations of the War Ministry that were the calculation base for the capacity layout of ammo trains and columns. The calculations of the General Staff were based upon higher consumption estimates obviously influenced by evaluations of the Balkan Wars that the War Ministry had not included yet. A day of battle was an approximation for estimated average ammunition consumption during a major action based upon historical experience and evaluation of the latest wars abroad. In field gun battalions, this supply number meant 168 rounds

[57] Or by the individual soldier or trooper as far as infantry or cavalry were concerned.
[58] (Rabenau, 1914), p. 73.
[59] (Rabenau, 1914), pp. 68–74.

of shrapnel or HE as a combat load and 105 rounds as a basic unit load—together with 273 rounds of shrapnel or HE per gun for one battle day. In howitzer battalions, the estimates were even lower: 58 rounds of shrapnel or HE as combat load and 68 rounds as unit basic load—together 126 rounds per gun for a battle day.

In the *Handbook for General Staff Officers*, the calculations based upon an estimated average rate of fire during a major combat action were even lower. By using their combat loads, a field gun battery could sustain seven hours of fire during a major combat action; a light field howitzer battalion could fire for four and one-half hours and a heavy field howitzer battalion for three and one-half hours. The basic load would last for another six hours in cannon battalions, four hours for light field howitzers, and two and three-quarter hours for heavy field howitzer batteries. The ammo stocks carried by the ammo columns of the army corps would allow another seven hours of fire for cannon batteries, five hours for light field howitzers, and fifteen and one-quarter hours for heavy field howitzers. If the entire ammo stock carried by an army corps were used, the field cannon batteries of this corps could keep firing for 20 hours; the light field howitzers could keep firing for 13 ½ hours; and the heavy field howitzers could keep firing for 21 ½ hours. After using up these stocks, the army corps had to order new ammunition supply trains through their army commands to refill the stocks of their train and columns.[60] Bear in mind that these figures do not represent a precise after-action evaluation; they are approximations to enable calculations for resupply. The differences resulted in the different calculations between the War Ministry and the General Staff. When this basic load had been used up, the battalions had to be resupplied by the ammo columns of the corps. As we will see in the Chapter 14 on doctrine, the French were stronger in field artillery due to their modern, mobile, and highly efficient guns and their early adoption of indirect fire. But the Germans had the advantage in howitzers and heavy artillery.

Foot Artillery

During peacetime, foot artillery regiments had two battalions of four batteries each. Each battery had four guns. Prior to November 1908, the batteries in foot artillery formations were known as companies. The regiments were commanded by either lieutenant colonels or full colonels and had one to two extra field grade officers and one extra captain—again assigned to reserve formations upon mobilization. On a high budget, a battery had approximately 20 officers, 84 NCOs, and 464 EM—depending on the type of guns with which they were equipped. Besides the so-called "fighting batteries," the foot artillery battalions had extra limbering detachments, usually commanded by a captain with the disciplinary role of a company or battery commander. Those limbering detachments were separated from the batteries to keep the foot artillery units more mobile. The purpose of these limbering detachments was to allow the foot artillery to be broken up into battalions and assigned to army corps or divisions.[61]

Initiated by Schlieffen, the number of heavy artillery formations was increased massively before 1914. There were three Prussian foot artillery inspections with six brigades and a Bavarian foot artillery brigade. The Saxon regiments belonged to Prussian brigades. In 1914, 19 Prussian, three Bavarian, and two Saxon foot artillery regiments existed, plus the demonstration regiment (*Lehr-Regiment*) of the foot artillery school that was created in 1912.[62] This heavy artillery played a very special role in overcoming the Belgian and French fortifi-

[60] (Großer Generalstab, 1914), pp. 58–59.
[61] (Pflugk-Hartung, 1896), pp. 59–60.
[62] (Mattuschka, 1979), p. 176.

cations. In peacetime, three to four foot artillery regiments made up a foot artillery brigade; a foot artillery inspection oversaw two brigades each as well as the Bavarian brigade. Due to their significant intended tactical role, the foot artillery regiments were dual-hatted: one reporting line went to their army corps, while the other went into the foot artillery inspections. The inspections had a particular role in overseeing the tactical drill and live firing of the foot artillery.

When the war started, the foot artillery regiments were essentially divided, and 32 of the 57 foot artillery battalions were assigned to the army corps as heavy corps artillery. Foot Artillery Regiments 9 and 17 were assigned to coastal defense purposes upon mobilization. The bulk of those battalions were equipped with the 15cm heavy field howitzer M/02 (abbreviated *s:FH*, some of them with 21cm heavy mortars, some others with 10 M/04, and 13 had obsolete 15 cm guns. Upon mobilization, a howitzer battalion consisted of four batteries of four howitzers each with 960 officers, NCOs, and EM; 520 horses; and 80 wagons. A battery consisted of 230 officers, NCOs, and EM; 120 horses; and 19 wagons and was divided into two platoons of two howitzers each. A heavy mortar battalion had two batteries of four guns with 570 officers, NCOs, and EM; 320 horses; and 50 wagons. The battery had 270 officers, NCOs, and men; 150 horses; and 23 wagons. Since the mortar battalions should act as siege artillery, their army corps had so called "park companies" with light field railroad equipment.[63]

Engineers and Pioneers

Pioneer battalions had four companies of five officers, 20 NCOs, and 140 EM each. Those battalions that had a searchlight company had an additional two officers, four NCOs, one blacksmith, 22 enlisted engineers, 11 wagon drivers, and 25 horses. Usually each army corps had one or two engineer battalions; upon mobilization, the battalions were broken up and assigned to the divisions, with one or usually two engineer companies per division.

In addition, each division had a divisional bridging train and, after mobilization, the army corps had one corps bridging train. Each divisional bridging train consisted of 60 officers, NCOs, and EM; 100 horses; and 21 wagons. Among them were 15 wagons with bridging equipment to either build a footbridge of 63 meters in length, a small bridge of 41 meters, a wide bridge of 34.5 meters or a heavy bridge of 21 meters. A corps bridging train had 145 officers, NCOs, and men; 240 horses; and 39 wagons, 28 of which carried bridging equipment to build bridges between 153 and 75 meters in length. In addition, each corps bridging train had an extra engineer detachment of 70 officers, NCOs, and EM.[64]

Cavalry divisions mobilized engineer detachments of 40 officers, NCOs, and EM; they also had a baggage wagon loaded with entrenchment tools and explosives. Four reserve formations, reserve or Landwehr engineer companies, and reserve divisional bridging trains were mobilized. For special purposes like intended attacks on forts or fortresses, engineer regiments were mobilized. They consisted of an engineer battalion with three companies—altogether 810 officers, NCOs, and EM; 70 horses; and 17 wagons. The regiments had an engineer siege train with 310 officers, NCOs, and EM; 160 horses; and 59 wagons. Such siege trains were especially equipped with entrenchment tools (4,000 big spades, 4,000 axes of different sizes, and more than 8,000 explosive charges) adding up to 1.68 tons of explosives.[65]

---

63 (Rabenau, 1914), pp. 74–87.
64 (Pflugk-Hartung, 1896), p. 62.
65 (Rabenau, 1914), pp. 92–95.

Supply and Train Formations

Sufficient supplies with ammunition, subsistence, and horse rations were essential to keep the million-men-armies of the early 20th century combat ready. During the Thirty-Years-War, armies could live off the land, but Frederick the Great implemented an infrastructure of warehouses and depots to keep his army moving and combat ready. On the one hand this logistical infrastructure did keep Frederick's army well supplied and combat ready. On the other hand it created certain inflexibility and restricted operations to an area within reach of these warehouses. Napoleon tried to have his armies live off the land to achieve higher operational freedom.

His armies were relatively small, but even under Napoleon, living off the land led to undersupplied armies and to underfed soldiers and horses. This was evident not only during the campaign in Russia in 1812, but also during the campaigns against Allied forces in Spain. Here the British army setup a considerable logistical infrastructure of depots and warehouses, while the French forces suffered from a poor supply chain. As for resupplying ammunition, for the armies using muzzle-loaded arms, it was not a real issue. Bullets could be easily cast in lead; black-powder would fit the enemy's rifles as well as the own rifles, so war booty could be used easily. Both sides had rifles featuring approximately the same caliber.

This situation drastically changed around the mid-19th century, when breech loaded rifles and artillery pieces required a different and more complex supply with ammunition and when armies outgrew the size that could be fed off the country. During the Unification Wars a sufficient supply via railroad and by a constantly growing tail of trains and columns trailing behind the army corps turned out to be inevitable. This applied even more when the armies outgrew a million men on each side and had to be supported with an ever growing number of supply goods, ammunition for light and heavy artillery, infantry, engineers and food for men and rations for horses for huge troop bodies. Supply became an outstanding success factor. This is particularly true for the German Army, which at least since Schlieffen, followed a more and more offensive Blitzkrieg doctrine, bidding victory in a future war on a short campaign of six to eight weeks to beat the French Army in the West before fighting against the slower mobilizing Russians in the East. Different from all other armies it could be expected from the German Army that supply, logistics and technical formations were organized in a perfect way to support such doctrine.

In the following paragraphs and in the Chapters 15 and 17, we will see that this is not the case. In a nutshell, serving in logistical formations was less attractive to officers. While combat formations promised fighting experience, fame and a good reputation to young officers, supply formations as well as technical formations were denoted as a kind of shipping company in uniform or as a kind of plumber's battalion. The logistical war games starting around 1910 to train the intendancy officials were internally called "flour rides" to differentiate them from the more "important" tactical war games and staff rides. In the following paragraphs we will learn about the comparatively weak logistical formations of the German Army in peacetime, and in Chapter 15 we will see how these quite small units were heavily inflated to a huge apparatus of trains and columns trailing behind the army corps. The same applies to technical formations such as automobile and aircraft formations. Only railroad formations were prepared in a more thorough way and based upon the experience of the Unification Wars. Logistics were certainly one of the weak points of the German Army going to field in 1914.

In peacetime, one train battalion per army corps was assigned. There was one anomaly, prior to 1901: the Train Battalion 18 was known as the Train Battalion 25. These battalions consisted of four companies with a total reduced peacetime strength of 466. Each train battalion mobilized numerous subsistence and ammunition transport columns, two field hospitals, and a horse depot.[66] Usually an army corps had four heavy and two light subsistence columns. Light columns had food wagons carrying fewer loads and were able to move faster and better to follow tactical operations. A light subsistence column had four officers, 125 NCOs, and EM; 183 horses; 36 food wagons carrying 750 kg of food each; and two supply wagons. A light column could carry up to 27 tons of food. Heavy columns had four officers, 99 NCOs and men; 27 wagons carrying 1,000 kg of food each; and two supply wagons. A light column built a marching column of 575 meters in length—a heavy column of 450 meters in length.[67]

The train battalion would mobilize a park column consisting of wagons requisitioned from civilian sources in the operational area. A park column had five officers, 97 NCOs and EM; 139 horses; and 48 wagons, which could carry about 1,200 kg of load each. The train battalions were usually armed with revolvers before they were equipped with the carbine M/88 in 1893 and rearmed with the carbine 98 in 1911. At the same time, the marksmanship required for the train was tightened. The intent was that train formations should be able to defend themselves against surprise or cavalry attacks.

The horse depot of the battalion had three officers, 63 NCOs, and EM; 107 horses; and two supply and forage wagons. The battalion had two field bakeries (one per division) with 12 mobile baking ovens and 13 supply wagons. A bakery had 190 officers, NCOs, and EM and 100 horses. When operating in shift service, each bakery could bake about 23,000 portions of bread per day; both field bakeries could meet the bread demand of an army corps even during highly mobile operations. Under favorable conditions one field bakery had an output of 23,000 bread rations in 24 hours (1 loaf of 1.5 kilograms equaled 2 bread rations). Thus a field bakery could furnish a one-day's supply of bread to an infantry division with a few trains and ammo columns attached. During moves, this rate went down significantly.[68]

Upon mobilization, those train battalions expanded in strength like the ammo columns of the army corps. Numerous new formations were mobilized. Medical companies were assigned to the divisions; each division received one or two medical companies. A medical company consisted of three officers: one Medical Major (*Oberstabsarzt*), one Chief Apothecary (*Oberstabsapotheker,*) and one paymaster officer. Further, it consisted of 20 NCOs, 16 privates, 206 stretcher-bearers, one cyclist, nine medical NCOs, eight military nurses, and 36 train soldiers. A further eight military doctors (*Assistenzärzte*) were assigned per company. Certainly such a medical company was one of the most diverse formations the army had. A medical company was equipped with eight ambulance wagons carrying seven to nine stretchers each, two wagons with medical equipment, two baggage wagons, one food wagon and a field kitchen. Altogether the company had 53 horses. Medical companies could run between one and two field hospitals; theoretically they could be tactically separated but were ideally to be used as one hospital. The field hospitals run by these medical companies were permanently assigned to the divisions. Upon mobilization, the army corps built up their own medical infrastructure. A mobile army corps could run up to 12 separate small field hospitals. Usually they were merged to fewer but bigger and more efficient hospitals.

Further, each train battalion mobilized all the wagon drivers for all wagons of infantry, engineer, and artillery formations. The train battalions had to care about the huge heavy baggage of the division, and they had to mobilize all the rear area train and supply formations

66 A column was comparable to a company, led by a captain or a Rittmeister.
67 (Pflugk-Hartung, 1896), pp. 66–67.
68 (Kuhl, 1929), p. 141.

populating the so-called rear operations area. This responsibility included the warehouses and depots, reserve train columns, stretcher-bearer transport companies, and reserve hospitals. No other arm had such a high share of reserve officers and reserve NCOs.[69] Including the ammo columns already described in the sections on infantry and artillery, an army corps had four ammo columns for the infantry, eight columns altogether for the field artillery, and eight columns for the heavy artillery. These ammo columns organized into three battalions upon mobilization, two battalions of ammo columns *(Munitionskolonnen-Abteilungen)* with two infantry ammo columns, four field artillery columns each, and a heavy artillery ammo battalion (*Fußartillerie Munitionskolonnen-Abteilung*) with eight columns.[70] The trains were comprised of six subsistence companies, seven heavy supply companies, two horse depots, two field bakeries, and the corps bridge train.

A major challenge for mobile operations was the length the road space required for moving formations. (*Marschtiefe*). An infantry regiment had a marching column 1,520 meters long including the fighting baggage, in addition to 390 meters of heavy baggage. The road space of the fighting troops of an infantry division was 15 km and that of an army corps marching on one road was 31 km. The trains of an infantry division covered 3 km, whereas those of an army corps required 7 km of road space.[71] An infantry ammo column was 600 meters long. Artillery ammo columns were 650 meters long. The ammo columns of an army corps had a marching length of 4 km, when marching in double row. Including foot artillery and other columns, an army corps had about 21 km of columns, trains, and baggage moving behind it.[72] Knowing these figures, one might imagine the logistical challenge the Ib officers of the 1st Army were confronted with during the Ourcq battle in 1914, when army corps were thrown from a southbound direction to a westbound direction moving 50 to 60 km overnight.

Gendarmerie

There were three different types of military police: the *Landgendarmerie*, the *Feldgendarmerie,* and the *Leibgendarmerie*.[73] The Landgendarmerie existed in peacetime as a special police force patrolling the countryside, particularly around big garrisons and towns. It belonged to the military, and its members were considered *Militärpersonen*. The War Ministry's infantry department (A2) oversaw and budgeted for the Landgendarmerie; officers and NCOs were recruited from the army; and NCOs who had a flawless service record could sign-up with the Landgendarmerie after at least nine years of military service. Concerning their police task, the Ministries of the Interior in Prussia, Württemberg, and Bavaria oversaw the Landgendarmerie. In Saxony, the Gendarmes were civil servants (*Beamten)* instead of members of the military. In Württemberg, they were called *Landjäger*; in Bavaria, the *Gendarmeriekorps*. Only in Saxony, did the Gendarmerie have no military status. The imperial Governor in Straßburg commanded the *Gendarmeriebrigade* in Alsace and Lorraine. Each corps district had a *Landgendarmerie-Brigade,* which had strength of about 300. The Landgendarmerie were listed in the Rangliste.[74]

Feldgendarmerie was not a peacetime formation and was only mobilized from former Landgendarmerie personnel. The Feldgendarmerie were classical military police, who

[69] (Rabenau, 1914), pp. 121–125.
[70] (Kuhl, 1929), pp. 126–127
[71] (Kuhl, 1929), p. 2
[72] (Großer Generalstab, 1914), pp. 30–32.
[73] Although the Leibgendarmerie was the Imperial lifeguard directly recruited from army officers and NCOs, they were counted as a kind of police.
[74] (Mattuschka, 1979), p. 189.

secured the rear operations area behind the armies advancing into enemy territory. Members could be easily identified by their special collar ornamentation *Ringkragen* made of white metal.

The Leibgendarmerie belonged to the Imperial Entourage and had to protect the Kaiser himself. This special Leibgendarmerie had a police role, belonged to the military like the Landgendarmerie did, and was commanded by a general adjutant. It was subdivided into two platoons: the first platoon acted as the lifeguard of the Emperor, the second platoon acted as the lifeguard of the Empress. This Leibgendarmerie can be seen as an early form of today's bodyguards.

Railroad Formations

The railroad formations had to operate all field railroad installations in the operations area. They had to repair and operate all tunnels, bridges, and railroad stations that were of any importance for the operating armies. They had to either operate existing railroads with normal pre-war civilian rails (about one meter wide, so called standard-gauge railways (*Vollbahn*)), or they had to be able to build field railroad lines with rails 60 cm wide (*Feldbahn*), the so-called small-gauge railways.[75]

The railroad formations had their own locomotives and coaches to operate either Vollbahnen or Feldbahnen. The three peacetime railroad regiments mobilized numerous railroad, railroad reserve, Landwehr railroad, railroad operating, and railroad building companies in either the Prussian or the Bavarian army.

Railroad formations cooperated closely with the Railroad Section of the Great General Staff. Since railroads took a crucial role both during mobilization and as a force multiplier for fast troop movements between different war theaters, the railroad formations went through a massive build-up upon mobilization.

Telegraph and Communications Formations

In 1899, telegraph formations were separated from the engineer corps and established as their own arm. Prior to 1914, there were 10 telegraph battalions—among them two from Bavaria and one from Saxony. Each battalion had three (the Saxon Battalion no. 7 only two) telegraph, field telephone, or radio companies. Telegraph battalion no. 4 had an extra Württemberg company. Peacetime strength of a telegraph company was about five officers, 195 NCOs and EM, and 40 horses. Peacetime strength of a radio company was about eight officers, 140 NCOs and EM, and 90 horses. In general, the telegraph formations recruited their own officer candidates, but since there were obviously not enough candidates, the bigger arms such as infantry, cavalry, and field artillery frequently detailed young lieutenants for one-year assignments into telegraph battalions.

Besides these field formations, each fortress usually had its own fortress telephone company (*Festungsfernsprechkompanie*) operating the radio equipment of the fortress. Since almost all military communication lines to the War Ministry were telephones, they intended to change the name of all telegraph formations into telephone formations. In 1914, communication was done through radio stations and by telephone. Communication by telegraph and Morse code messages, that had been the elder Moltke's preferred communication tools, were abandoned in 1910. All military formations were equipped with a military telephone that could be used for connections through field-telephone wire, but that also could tap into

---

[75] For details about railroad regiments and railroad battalions see (Pflugk-Hartung, 1896), pp. 64–65.

the civil telephone network.[76] Upon mobilization, the following formations were activated—one telephone detachment per army corps (*Korpsfernsprechabteilung*) with four platoons each. The peacetime telegraph platoon per army corps was assigned to these detachments as a fifth platoon. Altogether, such Korpsfernsprechabteilung had a field strength of about 200 officers, NCOs, and EM; 160 horses; 30 wagons; 60 field telephones; and about 120 km of field telephone wire. One kilometer could be built within 20 minutes.[77]

There were also army telephone detachments building the communications lines between the army HQs, the rear operations area (*Etappengebiet*), and the military installations back in Germany. While the corps telephone detachments usually laid their lines directly on the ground, the army telephone detachments placed their lines on wooden poles.

In addition to this communications infrastructure, there were numerous field and fortress radio stations, radio relay stations, light (cavalry) radio stations, and zeppelin radio communications stations. Army commands (AOK), cavalry divisions, and fortresses got one heavy radio station each. In addition, cavalry divisions also got one light radio station each. Army corps, HKKs, and lower did not get any radio equipment and had to fully rely upon field telephone or upon signaling by flag or light signal. In general, the range of radio stations was relatively low. Messages had to be forwarded through a chain of relay stations that led to significant delays in time and had a high potential for misunderstandings. Only short radio messages could be transmitted and received, since messages had to be encrypted before radio operators sent them. After receiving a message, someone had to decrypt it and hand it to the receiving officer as a written note. Radio talks between commanders wherein they could exchange ideas about reconnaissance results or tactical problems were virtually impossible.

Aircraft, Zeppelin and Automobile Formations

The modern reader might find it astonishing that aircraft, zeppelin, and motor transport formations are together under one heading. These modern technical branches were quite young in 1914 and were jointly lumped together under the headline of transport and communications formations (*Verkehrstruppen*).

Zeppelin and Airship Formations

In the English language, airships were commonly called zeppelins. In the German language the correct name was *Luftschiff* (airship)—airships did not fly, they sailed like ships. The same language rules applied to balloons. Only those airships, which were built by the *Zeppelin* factory, were called Zeppelins. Another famous brand was *Schütte-Lanz*, which followed different construction principles than Zeppelin airships. Usually the airships were named according to their type, Z plus number or SL plus number. Both the Zeppelin and the Schütte-Lanz airships were built around aluminum fixtures and had fixed gondolas for passengers and engines. Semi-fixed airships had some wooden or aluminum elements to keep their shape. The third category was "unfixed" (*unstarre*) airships that were considerably smaller than the Zeppelin or Schütte-Lanz models. After emptying the gas, they were just big fabric bags with an engine and passenger gondola, making them easily transportable by wagon or train. The Parseval factory usually built this third brand of ship.

---

76 (Schmidt, 1923), pp. 198–199.
77 (Rabenau, 1914), pp. 110–113.

There were six airship battalions (including one Bavarian) for a total of 17 companies. Each company had four officers, 14 NCOs, 150 EM, and about eight civilian airship specialists and mechanics. A company operated one or two airships and an airship hall. Besides the airship battalions, there were field airship detachments *(Feldluftschiffabteilungen)* operating observation balloons. They were 190 officers, NCOs, and EM; 120 horses; and 20 wagons. Divided into two platoons, each platoon had one balloon and six gas wagons with spare gas. An observation balloon that carried one person could climb up to 1,000 meters; with two people aboard, it could climb up to 500 meters.

The observers sat in a basket-like structure connected to the ground by a telephone line. It took about 20 minutes to get one balloon into the air. Getting it back to ground from about 1,000 meters took about the same time. Manning observation balloons became pretty unpopular in 1915 after the British and the French built fighter aircraft able to fire machineguns right through the propeller blades (like the Fokker planes). From then on, the balloon crews were exposed targets for enemy fighters and had to be protected by German fighter planes. Starting in 1915, the balloon crews were equipped with simple parachutes in case their balloons were hit by enemy fire.

Aircraft Formations

The youngest arm of the German army was the aircraft unit. Created in 1913, there were five active aircraft battalions including one Bavarian—in total 14 companies. Each active army corps had an aircraft formation (*Feld-Flieger Abteilung*); the reserve corps had none (with the exception of the Guards Reserve Corps, which also had an aircraft battalion).

These battalions mobilized the following field-aircraft-battalions. No. 1 mobilized the Field Aircraft Battalions 1, 7, 11, 12, and 30 in Döberitz and the Battalions 23, 24, and 29 in Großenhain. The 2nd Battalion mobilized Field Aircraft Battalions 13, 14; Fortress Aircraft Battalion 4 in Posen; Field Aircraft Battalions 16 and 17; Fortress Aircraft Battalion 6 in Graudenz Field; Aircraft Battalions 14 and 15; and Fortress Aircraft Battalions 5 and 7 in Königsberg. No 3 mobilized Field Aircraft Battalions 9 and 10; Fortress Aircraft Battalion 3 in Cologne; Field Aircraft Battalions 21, 22, and 28 in Hannover; and Field Aircraft Battalions 6, 18, and 27 in Darmstadt. No 4 mobilized Field Aircraft Battalions 3 and 4; Fortress Aircraft Battalion 2 in Straßburg; Field Aircraft Battalions 2, 5, and 8; Fortress Aircraft Battalion 1 in Metz; and Fortress Aircraft Battalions 20, 25, and 26 in Freiburg. In Bavaria, the Field Aircraft Battalions 1, 2, and 3 and the Fortress Aircraft Battalion Germersheim were mobilized.[78]

After mobilization, each field aircraft battalion consisted of 15 officers and 117 NCO and EM and operated six aircraft. Upon mobilization, there were 12 different types of aircraft, including Rumpler-Taube, several Albatros, Aviatik, A.E.G., and Gotha models. In general, they had mostly 100 hp Mercedes-Benz (or Argus) engines that allowed them to fly between 80 and 100 km/h. With a ceiling of 2,000 to 2,400 meters, they would ideally operate at an altitude of 800–1,000 meters. This altitude left them exposed to infantry and machinegun fire. Being able to fly for a maximum of four hours, their range was about 300 km.[79] Planes were not armed; the pilots only carried their pistols 08 or long pistols 08, and later their Mondragon or Mauser self-loading carbines. Only after Fokker invented a mechanism that

78 (*Kriegsgeschichtliche Abteilung der Luftwaffe*, 1939), p. 104.
79 (Kriegswissenschaftliche Abteilung, 1939), p. 105.

allowed a machinegun to fire right through the propeller blades did the Fokker E1 become the first really efficient fighter plane.

The mounted orderly or messenger was still the primary method of transmitting orders and reports, not aircraft. Aerial reconnaissance was considered a good complement to the cavalry reconnaissance, especially behind enemy lines in a war of position. "On the other hand, it is only the powerful cavalry units which are able to give the reconnaissance the necessary persistence and drive, capable of sweeping back the enemy reconnaissance organs and thus achieving a superiority on the advanced battlefront."[80] This argument was included in an endeavor to keep aviation assets out of the cavalry corps and assigned directly to the army command. Compared to the French army, the Germans started late building up their air power, and when the war came, they were comparatively weak.

Automobile Formations

The automobile battalion was another very young arm that had 24 officers and 700 NCOs and EM; it was organized into four companies. The battalion also had a Saxon and a Württemberg detachment. Bavaria had its own automobile company. Before 1914, there was a defined military truck (*Armeelastzug*) with a trailer. The truck could carry up to four tons of cargo—the trailer up to two tons. The engine was about 35 hp strong; with one tank of gas, a fully loaded truck could travel up to 120 km. In flat countryside, the average range was about 100 km. This distance decreased to either 60 or 80 km if the truck had to climb hills. Nine fully loaded trucks could carry the entire food consumption of an army corps per day—about 54 tons, making them as efficient as two food columns. Also, when carrying ammo, nine trucks could carry as much load as two infantry or two artillery ammo columns. This capacity made trucks much more efficient than horse-drawn columns.[81]

Motor transport columns were planned only for the cavalry divisions and the rear communication zone upon mobilization. Each cavalry division had a cavalry motor transport column (*Kavallerie-Kraftwagenkolonne*) with 15 light trucks, carrying a load of about three tons. The motor transport columns of the communications zone (*Etappen-Kraftwagenkolonne*) consisted of approximately 17 military trucks with trailers.[82] Before 1914, the German government funded private purchases of military standard trucks by civilians. In return, the owners had to agree that their trucks and drivers were available for army service upon mobilization for the next five years without further financial compensation. A driver, a co-driver, and a braking aid for the trailer operated each army truck. There were only 9,639 registered trucks in Germany by 1914, which was certainly no basis for abandoning the horse.[83] After 1914, the number of truck-operated supply and transport formations exploded.

Personnel Replacements

The army corps district was responsible for the recruiting, equipping, and training of a certain number of troops. Upon mobilization, different branches left behind a cadre to provide it with reinforcements. These were known by different names for different types of units. An *Ersatz* (replacement) battalion was the cadre left behind in an infantry or foot artillery regiment. An Ersatz company was the cadre left behind for a Jäger or pioneer battalion.

---

80 (v. Poseck M., 1921), p. 231.
81 (Rabenau, 1914), pp. 113–118.
82 (Kuhl/Bergmann, 1929), p. 71
83 (Stoneman, 2006), p. 116.

For peacetime recruiting, each army corps had one big replacement district (*Ersatzbezirk*). Each corps replacement district had four or five brigade replacement districts. Each brigade district was further subdivided into two or three *Landwehrbezirke*. Each Landwehrbezirk had a small permanent staff. The corps commander was responsible for tactical (not technical) training of the soldiers in his region. Each corps was administered independently. In Prussia alone, there were 212 *Bezirkskommando* (or Landwehrbezirke) with assigned personnel of about 6,000 people. Landwehrbezirke were either subordinated to an infantry brigade headquarters or a *Landwehrinspektion*.[84] Landwehrinspektionen were alternative higher headquarters that replaced brigade headquarters in the more populous (and popular) areas of the empire. The commander of the Landwehrinspektion was a *Generalmajor*. Each Landwehrbezirk consisted of several replacement districts (*Aushebungsbezirke*).

The replacement organization had four different levels:

- The ministerial level (*Ministerialinstanz*) consisted of the respective departments of the War Ministry and other higher authorities.
- The level III replacement organization (*Ersatzbehörde III. Instanz*) consisted of the Commanding General of the Army Corps and the administrative head of the respective province (*Oberpräsident*).
- Level II replacement organizations, called *Oberersatzkommissionen*, consisted of the respective brigade commander and a senior administration officer.
- Level I replacement organizations consisted of the commander of the respective Landwehrbezirk and an administration officer; in Prussia either the head of police (*Polizeipräsident*) or the chief administrative officer of the county *(Landrat*). Level I replacement organizations were also called the replacement committee (*Ersatzkommission*).[85]

Each Landwehrbezirk also had an assessment committee for One Year Volunteers (OYV) called *Prüfungskommission für einjährige Freiwillige*.

An Ersatz *Eskadron* was the cadre left behind for a cavalry regiment. An Ersatz *Abteilung* was used for a field artillery regiment. Many of the active regiments had two Ersatz battalions. These were used not only for recruits but also for forming new units. Occasionally, recruits were sent to different regiments than their original Ersatz battalion. While active infantry regiments had two Ersatz battalions, reserve and Landwehr regiments had only one each.[86] Each Ersatz battalion normally had three or four Ersatz companies, a convalescent company, a company of men fit only for garrison duty, and one or two recruit depots (*Rekruten Depots*). Untrained recruits were initially sent to the recruit depot. After a preliminary course, they were moved into an Ersatz company regularly of 100 to 200 men.[87]

This system stayed in place only until the beginning of 1915. Until that time, recruits moved directly from their regimental depot to the units at the front. A new organization known as a field recruit depot (*Feld Rekruten Depot*) became an advanced replacement center at the front. After one to three months training at home in the Ersatz battalion, recruits were sent to the field recruit depot where their training was completed. From there they moved to the front. Wounded soldiers returning to the front would also pass through the field recruit depot to learn the latest techniques. There were times when entire recruit companies

84 (The General Staff, 1918), p. 15.
85 (Pflugk-Hartung, 1896), p. 28.
86 (The General Staff, 1918), pp. 16–17.
87 (The General Staff, 1918), p. 17.

were used to fill the gap in the line during critical times. Most field recruit depots were associated with divisions. Recruits arrived as a combined draft from the home depots and were distributed as required among the regiments. Therefore, you can easily see how someone who trained with regiment A in the homeland could easily be assigned to regiment B in the field.[88]

Most of the group pictures that you see are training classes held in the depot system. A German platoon was made of eight *Gruppen* that consisted of eight to 10 men. Two Gruppen were known as a *Korporalschaft*. An *Unteroffizier* led a Korporalschaft; therefore, a platoon had four Korporalschaften. What was called Korporalschaft in infantry and engineer units was called *Beritt* in mounted units such as cavalry, field artillery and train. Once they were in a *Kaserne* (barracks), a group of recruits would live in a single large *Stube*. Trainees had one Korporalschaft for each Stube. Many of those pictures show a Korporalschaft or a Stube. Often the soldiers in the wartime pictures were wearing older blue uniforms; this attire was normal as the older blue uniforms had to be used.

The Feldzeugmeisterei

Another organization controlled by the General War Department of the War Ministry was the *Feldzeugmeisterei,* which could be roughly translated as "field equipment and ordnance department." The Feldzeugmeisterei controlled the manufacturing and storage of all major field equipment and ordnance of the army. In the earlier description of the War Ministry, this type of organization is referred to as "administration of armories." The Saxon and Bavarian armies had their own Feldzeugmeisterei. The Artillery Testing Commission and the Rifle Testing Commission were responsible for the design, development, and testing of new weapons. The Feldzeugmeisterei controlled their production. Weapons and ammunition were manufactured either in privately owned factories such as *Mauser* in Oberndorf, Württemberg; the *Deutsche Waffen- und Munitionsfabriken* (DWM) in Berlin; the Krupp factories in Essen; *Rheinmetall* in Düsseldorf; or in state-owned armories named *Militärtechnische Institute* in general.

Those Militärtechnische Institute could be armories like the Prussian rifle factories (*Gewehrfabriken*)—where all types of handguns and rifles were manufactured—in Spandau, Erfurt, and Danzig and the Bavarian armory in Amberg. If not armories, they could be so-called "powder factories" (*Pulverfabriken*) or other kinds of ammo and field equipment factories. A director, who was usually a field grade officer, headed each military-technological institute. A civilian administrative director, a civilian administrative committee, and several officers assigned from military formations supported the director.[89] The Feldzeugmeisterei was founded in 1898 to oversee all state-owned armories (rifle factories), maintenance workshops, and depots in one organization. A lieutenant general who had immediate access to the Kaiser (*Immediatvortragsrecht*) headed the Meisterei. Following the Prussian example, Bavaria and Saxony had their own Feldzeugmeisterei.

The following administrations belonged to the Feldzeugmeisterei:

- The Inspection of Armories and Ammo factories (*Inspektion der Gewehr- und Munitionsfabriken)* originally founded in 1856 as *Inspektion der technischen Institute der Infanterie* oversaw the infantry weapons development office (*Infanterie-Konstruktionsbüro*) in Spandau, the ammunition factory in Spandau, and the armories in Spandau, Danzig, and Erfurt.

---

88 (The General Staff, 1918), pp. 17–18.
89 (Pflugk-Hartung, 1896), p. 93.

- The *Inspektion der technischen Institute der Artillerie* oversaw the Artillery Weapons Development Office (*Artillerie-Konstruktionsbüro*) and the artillery factory in Spandau, as well as the other technical institutions of the artillery. The technical institutes included the ammunition factory in Spandau, and the artillery repair and maintenance workshops in Danzig, Lippstadt, Spandau, and Straßburg. Not only were guns repaired here, but also any kind of ordnance and field equipment such as military horse wagons, cavalry lances, gun limbers, ammo carriages, etc. The cannons that were not manufactured by Krupp or Rheinmetall were made in the artillery factory (*Geschützgießerei*). In the ammunition factories in Spandau and Siegburg, handguns and artillery were made. The powder factories in Hanau and Spandau supplied powder to the ammunition factories. The biggest civilian factory for infantry ammo was Polte in Magdeburg. In Bavaria there were similar technical institutes in Ulm and Ingolstadt.
- The *Artilleriedepot-Inspektion* was founded in 1898, with its four *Artilleriedepot-Direktionen* in Spandau, Stettin, Kassel, and Darmstadt.
- The *Traindepot-Inspektion* was erected in 1860 with *Direktionen* in Berlin and Kassel. Each army corps had a train depot storing the equipment of all formations that had to be created upon mobilization—particularly that of all the train formations and columns.
- The *Militärversuchsamt* was created in 1890 to conduct tests of any kind of explosives.[90]

Orders for weapons, ammunition, or field equipment were channeled through the army corps and the General War Department to the Feldzeugmeisterei, who distributed such orders to the respective technical institutes or privately owned factories according to available budgets.

All weapons, ordnance, and field equipment had to go through a very rigid acceptance process after manufacturing. While the acceptance process was very rigid in state-owned factories, it was a little more liberal in privately owned factories. It was well known that Mauser, Krupp, and the DWM delivered fine quality, which was documented by inspector-officers leaving their proof marks and acceptance stamps on the accepted weapons. If you compare Luger pistols made in the Erfurt armory with DWM-made pistols, you will find considerably more proof marks on the Erfurt pistols than on the DWM pistols.

The manufacturing process also resulted in a phenomenon called "matching numbers" by modern collectors. In Germany, gun parts were manufactured according to templates, and the machines used were considerably less precise than the machines that factories like Colt or Smith & Wesson used. Therefore, the individual parts of a particular gun had to be fit together manually to guarantee an absolutely perfect fit. To avoid any later confusion of parts, those parts had to be stamped with at least the last two digits of the serial number. This numbering applied even to screws! NCOs had to make sure that each gun had only matching numbers upon re-assembly after field stripping and cleaning.

Artillery Depots

After manufacturing weapons—whether handguns or cannons—the weapons were stored in artillery depots. Those depots stored replacement guns to cover wear and tear of peacetime use. They received damaged and dented guns from military formations, delivered them to one of the technical institutes or privately owned factories for repair and maintenance, and replaced them with well-maintained guns. Usually each army corps and each fortress had at least one artillery depot storing the spare and replacement weapons of the respective army

[90] (Mattuschka, 1979), pp. 186–187.

corps and of the reserve and Landwehr units to be mobilized within the army corps district. Artillery depots usually had an infantry department, a field artillery department, and a foot artillery department. A field grade officer *"zur Disposition"* headed artillery depots.

Garment Departments and Garment Depots

Each army corps had its own garment department *(Bekleidungsamt)* responsible for the manufacturing of boots, uniforms, and other items of individual field equipment. They either produced items by themselves, such as boots in workshops operated by the army corps, or they arranged manufacturing of these uniforms and helmets by privately owned factories in the corps area. Usually, the Bekleidungsamt called for tender among the regional industry based upon sealed samples issued by the War Ministry.

After production and upon delivery, the Bekleidungsamt checked the produced items and sealed them with their acceptance mark, usually "B.A." (Bekleidungsamt), followed by the number of the army corps in Roman figures, and the year of acceptance in Arabic figures.

There was some share of responsibilities among the Bekleidungsämter. The garment department of the Guard Corps, for example, handled all demands for sword knots, lances, and signal instruments for the entire Prussian army. The garment department of the V Army Corps negotiated the demand for underwear and sports suits for the entire army. The VI Army Corps negotiated the demand of linen and cotton fabrics. The VII Army Corps negotiated all major pieces of field equipment and the XV Army Corps handled all demands for aluminum-made items such as tent poles. They were also responsible for tarpaulin tent-squares and bread bags. The garment department of the War Ministry negotiated for either blue or field-grey fabrics for uniforms, and the respective quantities were assigned to the army corps for manufacturing of uniforms by private factories.

After 1901, most army corps beginning with the VI and VII Army Corps increased their military workshops by employing numerous civilian workers and craftsmen (*Ökonomie-handwerker*). Beginning in 1897, the garment departments had their own officer corps of *Bekleidungsoffiziere*. Upon mobilization, each army corps took over responsibility for manufacturing of uniforms and equipment by themselves; they were also allowed to source beyond borders of their corps district. The garment department of an army corps consisted of 90 officers and approximately 3,000 NCOs, EM, and drafted workers.[91]

Uniforms, boots, and other items of field equipment were stored in garment depots of the army corps after acceptance by the Bekleidungsamt and delivered to the regiments and battalions from there. NCOs and EM received their equipment from the garment stores of their formations (*Bekleidungskammer*). Officers had to equip themselves at their own expense, but they had the right to purchase pieces of equipment from their units for considerably lower prices.

Finally, the uniforms were stored in the Bekleidungskammer of the individual company, battery or squadron. Usually five sets of uniforms were stored per soldier:

1st set—not used and only issued upon mobilization,

2nd set—like new and only used upon mobilization and for parade purposes,

3rd set—issued for inspections by senior officers,

4th set—worn on guard, during vacations, and on Sundays,

5th set—worn during field exercises and formal drill.

---

[91] (Rabenau 1914), pp. 23–26.

Very often, there was also a 6th and sometimes even a 7th set that was to be used during field exercises and formal drill.[92]

The companies had their own garments' budget—the so-called company economy (*Kompaniewirtschaft*), which meant that they could save money for other purposes not supported by an official budget, i.e., the equipment of the officer's club. The better they managed storage, mending, and repairing of older sets of uniforms, the more they were able to keep them years beyond their estimated and budgeted service lifetime. Spiked helmets, for example, had an estimated lifetime of about 15 years.

This system resulted in soldiers who looked relatively non-professional as they wore really old and worn out uniforms during their regular service. When field-grey uniforms were issued after 1907, it became obvious that the new uniforms were being saved, since usually only the first and second sets were field-grey uniforms; the rest of the uniforms were still the old blue tunics. Blue uniforms were used by replacement and training formations until the end of the war. When enlisted soldiers finished service and were discharged, the company had to equip them with military uniforms if those soldiers had no proper civilian clothes. The companies were not eager to discharge them with the 4th or 5th set uniforms but used the surplus 6th or 7th set uniforms that were obviously worn out and heavily mended. Garment Repair Workshops (*Bekleidungs-Instandsetzungs-Ämter (BIA)*) were established at the end of 1914, when clothes and uniforms were so worn that they had to be mended and repaired before being reissued. Like the *Bekleidungsämter,* the army corps organized the Bekleidungs-Instandsetzung-Ämter. Repaired pieces received a stamp mark BIA together with the number of the respective army corps. A letter "F" indicated that those pieces were field serviceable and could be reissued to field units again.

Special functions

The following specialists were responsible for overseeing their technical arms and functions:

- ***Ingenieurkorps*** and ***Festungbau-Offizierskorps***—ensured the construction and maintenance of the fortifications.
- ***Zeug-Offizierskorps***—managed the holdings of the artillery depot that protected material in the forts.
- ***Feuerwerks-Offizierkorps***—had the wartime completion and supervision of artillery ammunition under them.
- ***Reitendes Feldjägerkorps***—were used for the transport of important dispatches, instructions and commands between the emperor and his authorities, mainly abroad.
- ***Sanitätskorps***—responsible for the medical health of the Army.
- ***Veterinär-Offizierkorps***—responsible for the health of horses.
- ***Intendantur***—responsible for the pay, clothing, and food for the troops. The paymaster of the troops was under the *Intendanturbehörden.*
- ***Kriegs- und Oberkriegsgerichtsräte***—practiced the administration of justice.
- ***Militärgeistlichkeit***—responsible for the pastoral care of the troops.
- ***Armee-Musikinspizienten***—ensured the smooth handling of the rules in music matters in the army.

[92] (Rabenau 1914), pp. 21–22.

CHAPTER 8

ARMY RESERVE, LANDWEHR, LANDSTURM, AND ERSATZ-RESERVE

What distinguished the German army in 1914 from the allied armies was that the reserve corps were successfully integrated into the active army corps during the campaign. Reserve divisions of the French army were used as a second echelon force, but did not operate alongside active units at the beginning of the campaign. A broader explanation of second-line formations is necessary for the understanding of the German army in 1914, since no other army fielded so many reserve, *Ersatz, Landwehr,* and *Landsturm* formations. In contrast to the French, who only assigned a single reserve division per active corps, the German army fielded complete reserve corps with good results. In the east, an entire Landwehr corps was mobilized. Created by Generaloberst v. Moltke after 1906, the German reserve corps were organized similar to the active army corps but were considerably weaker in artillery pieces and supply units. Reserve corps usually only had one reserve field artillery regiment with two battalions of field guns per division and no foot artillery. The artillery of reserve corps had less than half the firepower compared to the artillery of the active corps. In addition, only a few reserve corps had a reserve *Jäger* battalion.[1]

RESERVE UNITS

Even active units were not fully manned in peacetime. Reservists filled them in time of mobilization. The deployed strength of an active infantry company on paper was 250 NCOs and men. When Walter Bloem first addressed his company (2nd Company, 1st Battalion, Grenadier-Regiment Prinz Carl v. Preußen (2. Brandenburgisches) Nr. 12) early in the mobilization of 1914, he had 14 NCOs and 162 men, of whom 50 were reservists who had already reported.[2] Once a soldier had completed his active military service, he had a further liability of five more years in the reserves. When the war broke out, the active-duty soldiers were those who had turned 20 in 1912 and 1913 (i.e., those who were born in 1892 and 1893). The reservists were drawn from the previous five classes: 1891, 1890, 1889, 1888, and 1887. There were more reservists than there were positions in the active regiments. Remaining reservists formed or filled out other units.

1 (Buchholz, Emails, 2009)
2 (Bloem, 2004)

THE LANDWEHR

After a soldier's seven years of Dienstpflicht (eight for mounted artillery and cavalry), his class passed into the Landwehr (usually at the age of 27) and command-and-control changed. Landwehr soldiers were no longer affiliated with a particular regiment—whether reserve personnel of an active regiment or a reserve regiment; rather they served under control of the reserve and personnel replacement organization (*Landwehrbezirkskommando*). The Bezirkskommando mobilized not only the reserve regiments, but also a number of Landwehr and Ersatz formations, depending upon the number of available reservists.

The controlling body of the replacement organization was the Army Corps District, which was further sub-divided into brigade districts and then into Landwehr districts or Bezirks-kommandos (Landwehrbezirk). The district was further grouped into either a first or second contingent. Men were assigned to the first contingent for five years. In general, there were two training periods during the first contingent, each lasting from one to two weeks. Cavalry and horse artillery soldiers, plus men who had voluntarily served three years with the colors, were liable for three years service in the first contingent. Reservists passed into the second Landwehr contingent at about age 32 until age 39. There was no training requirement during this period. There were 96 Landwehr regiments, but not all of these had the same number of battalions.

Landwehr units were issued whatever equipment was left over from either the active or reserve units. For instance, in 1914, there were no platoons of machinegunners and no field kitchens in the Landwehr units. Many units were issued the 88/05 old-style rifle and as many as 20 percent of the units still wore blue uniforms. The shortage of equipment was especially marked in those Landwehr regiments assigned to fortress duty. In peacetime, no Landwehr cavalry units existed, although Landwehr officers of the cavalry branch remained on the books of their respective Landwehrbezirk. Landwehr cavalry squadrons were formed on mobilization.[3]

THE DEVELOPMENT OF LANDWEHR REGIMENTS, RESERVE REGIMENTS, RESERVE DIVISIONS, AND RESERVE CORPS PRIOR TO 1914

To understand the 1914 organizational structure of reserve units and other second-line units, it is important to look briefly at the development of these units before 1914. In Prussia and the other German states, Landwehr (called *Seewehr* in the Navy) and reserve formations were always distinguished from the line formations and were regarded as second-line formations. In Austria-Hungary, Landwehr formations were traditionally first-line units. In addition to the "*k. und k.*" (*kaiserlich und königlich*) Austro-Hungarian units, there were two additional unit groups—"*k.k.*" (*kaiserlich-königlich*) Austrian and "*k. ung.*" (*königlich ungarisch*). This was Royal Hungarian, called *Honvéd* in Hungarian. All three formations were first-line formations; however, each had its own chain of command and ministry of war. In other words, in Austria-Hungary prior to 1914, three different ministries of war existed in parallel.

3 (Busche, 1998), p. 44.

Foundation of the Landwehr in 1813

The history of the Landwehr dates back to the War of Liberation against Napoleonic occupation. On parallel initiatives, General Gerhard v. Scharnhorst and the Prussian minister, Count Friedrich zu Dohna, joined with General Johann v. Yorck and the Prussian King Friedrich Wilhelm III to mobilize a Landwehr in the provinces of Eastern Prussia, Brandenburg, and Silesia as a reinforcement of the small regular army formations. This mobilization was ordered simultaneously with the active army on the declaration of war against France on 13 March 1813.

This Landwehr was mobilized by the cities of Berlin, Breslau, and Königsberg and by the counties of the provinces. The Landwehr accepted men without any military training—both volunteers and young men drawn by lot. Recruits had to be between 17 and 40 years old. The Prussian state issued the weapons. Originally only 55,000 muskets were available, so training began without weapons. Later, the Russian Czar gave 15,000 muskets to the Eastern-Prussian Landwehr; 5,000 muskets came from British supplies; and additional muskets came from Austrian stocks. Eventually, many thousands of muskets that were captured from the French were used. Finally, the Prussian Landwehr was equipped with five different types of muskets that had different calibers and fired different kinds of ammunition.

Most Landwehr formations were of very little military value, lacked training and discipline, and had a high level of desertion—particularly during marches. Exceptions were found in Eastern Prussia and in the regions of Kurmark and Neumark. Those regions had suffered under French occupation and had developed a fighting spirit to drive the French out of the country. Due to its very limited value, the Landwehr was unpopular with the people and out-of-favor with the military leaders. In the beginning, the Landwehr not only suffered from a lack of muskets, but also from a lack of uniforms and equipment. In early 1813, the only available uniform was a shako-style cap featuring a cross that was made of iron sheet with the motto: "*Mit Gott für König und Vaterland*" (With God for King and Country). This cross was similar to the Iron Cross created by King Friedrich Wilhelm III when he declared war against Napoleon. The Landwehrkreuz became the distinctive mark of the Landwehr and reserve personnel until 1918.

At the 1814 armistice, the Landwehr comprised 149 battalions of infantry and 113 ½ squadrons of cavalry. The numbers increased to 168 battalions and 136 cavalry squadrons during the last part of the Napoleonic wars in 1815. Battalions had four companies, each with 150–200 men. A cavalry regiment had about four squadrons, each with 70–95 troopers on average. Four battalions of infantry plus a cavalry regiment were merged into a Landwehr brigade, which was renamed a Landwehr regiment after 1815.

Value Under Fire

At the end of the Napoleonic wars, the Landwehr was still considered to have limited value and definitely not to be on par with line formations due to the following reasons:

- Lack of discipline,
- Lack of training,
- Low marching performance,
- High rate of illness,
- Poor steadiness under fire.

But compared to 1813, the Landwehr of 1815 had already significantly improved. In 1815, a few Landwehr battalions that had been mobilized in 1813 were almost comparable to line formations; whereas battalions mobilized in 1815 showed the same teething problems that the veterans had back in 1813. Landwehr formations were considered useful for defensive tasks or for small operations. They were nearly worthless for attack, and any kind of retreat generally led to complete disorganization and break-up. If Landwehr formations performed well, it was generally because experienced officers, who served as professional role models, led them based upon their decades of experience. All in all, Landwehr formations did not play a decisive role during the liberation wars.[4]

Development after 1814

In the Military and Conscription Act (*Wehrgesetz*) of 3 September 1814, military service was restructured to seven years of service in the active army, then seven years in the first contingent (*I. Aufgebot*) of the Landwehr, followed by another seven years in the second contingent (*II. Aufgebot*), and retirement at the age of 39. The first contingent of the Landwehr was a mix of trained reservist from active duty and untrained men who had been previously physically rejected or had not been selected by lot. (Prussia had more potential recruits than were needed, so recruits were chosen by lot). Untrained Landwehr recruits had to undergo three months of basic training that gave them a basic knowledge of military drill. For members of the first contingent, two annual exercises of one week each were obligatory; for members of the second contingent, only one annual exercise was required.

Additionally in 1815, a Landwehr regulation (*Landwehrordnung*) was issued that outlined the Landwehr's role as second-line formations and provided reliable structure. Each Landwehr regiment was assigned a fixed recruitment area, which was divided into two battalion areas. Each regiment had to mobilize two first-contingent battalions of infantry, two squadrons of cavalry and, ideally, an artillery company. For each administrative region (*Regierungsbezirk*), either a general or a Landwehr inspector (*Landwehrinspecteur*) with the rank of a senior staff officer was appointed to oversee the training and exercise of his Landwehr formations. He was also responsible for the necessary weapons and material. The inspector drew up the mobilization plans for his units and checked them during annual exercises. Between 1816 and 1818, further Landwehr formations, including Guard Landwehr battalions, were established. Permanent skeleton staffs and personnel (*Stammpersonal*) for each first contingent Landwehr formation were included in the budget. In the 1819 Rangliste, 36 Landwehr regiments of two battalions were listed.[5]

Landwehr officers could either be former active officers who transferred to the Landwehr or those who were trained one-year volunteers. A third category comprised former active NCOs who had particularly good performance marks and were domiciled in the recruitment area of the respective Landwehr regiment. Soon after the liberation wars, a Landwehr myth about the role of the Landwehr in the victory over Napoleon grew and made service in the Landwehr more and more popular. On the other hand, many conservative generals remained critical over its value in any future war. General Kleist v. Nollendorff, who had influence with the king, was especially critical of the military value of the Landwehr. He supported the Landwehr only for budgetary reasons. Under the cover of the Landwehr, he could bypass the Reichstag and create 36 additional regiments upon mobilization (which had to be staffed with skeleton staffs in peacetime).

---

4 (Alten G. v., 1913), p. 820.

5 (Kriegsministerium, 1819)

After 1815, the military value of the Landwehr again declined. As more veterans with war experience left once they turned 39, Landwehr units morphed into typical peacetime formations. The short basic training of Landwehr recruits was not enough to keep them on a par with line soldiers. Only when active soldiers transferred to the Landwehr were they provided with some semblance of professionalism.

This led to the Landwehr reform of 1819:

- Each Landwehr regiment had three battalions and had to mobilize one first-contingent and one second-contingent regiment.
- Each Landwehr cavalry regiment comprised six squadrons drawn from both contingents.
- Former Landwehr inspections were turned into Landwehr brigades; one Landwehr brigade was assigned per active division.

Landwehr officers were by now almost exclusively one-year volunteers.

During the coming years, this reform was watered down for budgetary reasons. The basic training of Landwehr recruits was reduced from three months to four weeks, and the number of exercises was drastically reduced. From 1837 until 1856, conscription for active infantry recruits was reduced to two years. This reduction meant a higher share of potential recruits were drafted, trained, and eventually transferred to the Landwehr after their active service. Despite this, only about 25 percent of the enlisted Landwehr men came from active service units.

In the 1838 Rangliste, a variety of different Landwehr formations are listed:[6]

- Infantry regiment 33–40 (also called 1–8 Reserve Regiment) each with three battalions plus one Landwehr battalion.
- 1–4 Guard Landwehr Regiment (1 in Eastern Prussia, 2 in Berlin and surrounding areas, 3 in Silesia, 4 in Westphalia) each with three Landwehr battalions.
- 32 (1–32) Landwehr regiments—so-called provincial Landwehr—each with three Landwehr battalions.
- Eight Landwehr battalions assigned to the eight reserve regiments.

Here, for the first time, may be seen the threefold structure of active units, reserve units, and Landwehr units that made up the standard reinforcement structure of the army in the future.

The next challenge came with the revolution of 1848–49, when once again the Landwehr failed to meet expectations. Landwehr units were unreliable when operating against revolutionaries; some Landwehr battalions even refused to follow orders. In Baden, a Landwehr battalion ran under fire. In 1852, the Landwehr brigades were disbanded and the Landwehr regiments were merged together with an active line regiment to form a brigade. But this mix of active and Landwehr units turned out to be disastrous during the mobilization of 1859 when active army formations had to follow their much slower Landwehr formations so as to keep the brigades together.[7]

---

6 (Kriegsministerium, 1838)

7 1859 was the war between France and Austria-Hungary in Northern Italy. France took the side of the Italians unifying their nation against Austro-Hungarian occupation and resistance. Prussia remained neutral but mobilized her army. Moltke considered this mobilization as a kind of test-mobilization for the Prussian army after decades of peace.

In the 1851 Rangliste, the following Landwehr units are listed:

- Infantry regiment 33–40 (also called 1–8 Reserve Regiment) with three battalions each, plus one Landwehr battalion.
- Guards Reserve Infantry (Landwehr) Regiment.
- 1–4 Guard Landwehr Regiment, each with three Landwehr battalions.
- 32 (1–32) Landwehr provincial regiments, each with three Landwehr battalions.
- Eight Landwehr battalions assigned to the eight reserve regiments.[8]

Reorganization and the Unification Wars

All the above fed into the 1860 reorganizations initiated by war minister, Count Albrecht v. Roon and supported by Crown Prince Wilhelm I, the regent of the Prussian kingdom (on behalf of his ill brother, Friedrich Wilhelm IV). Wilhelm was an extremely conservative prince, who was known as the grapeshot prince (*Kartätschenprinz*) due to his brutal and violent crushing of the 1848 Revolution in Berlin. He tried to roll back any kind of democratic movement and intended to cut the parliamentary power over the military budget. Therefore, the 1860 military reform was not only a military reform, but also a power struggle among the Crown Prince and the Parliament (*preußischer Landtag*) and his cabinet—known as the constitutional conflict.

The 1859 war between France and Austria-Hungary led Prince Wilhelm to mobilize 32 Landwehr regiments. He kept them under arms after the formal end of the confrontation. In 1860, these 32 Landwehr regiments were turned into active regiments, almost doubling the size of the Prussian army. The active army was officially named the operational army and the Landwehr and reserve formations became the occupational army (*Besatzungsheer*). These units were no longer called second-line formations, but followed the operational army into the field. There they secured the logistical lifelines of the operations and were prepared to join the fighting line as reinforcements.

The 1860 reorganizations paved the way for a conversion of the Landwehr and reserve formations from a kind of a militia with limited value to highly efficient units that were intended, after some field training, to be on par with the active units. There was little change after 1860 except that the first and second contingents were eliminated in 1867, and Landwehr service was reduced to five years. The Landwehr performed very well during the unification wars, particularly in France during the long winter of 1870–71. Turning the Landwehr into a highly professional reserve force instead of keeping it a semi-professional militia was important if such units were intended to operate alongside the active army.

In the war of 1866, two Landwehr divisions deployed with the operational army without actively fighting. During the initial phase of the war, Landwehr formations guarded the North Sea coast while the 1st Reserve Division, made up of Landwehr battalions, assembled close to Berlin. The 1st Guard Landwehr Division marched behind the army of the Elbe. Landwehr formations manned the fortresses along the Western border to free active formations for the operations in Bohemia. The Landwehr also occupied the kingdom of Saxony.[9] Only two Landwehr cavalry regiments and a few Landwehr battalions came into fighting contact with the enemy. Most Landwehr units remained in their garrisons and did not enter the operational theater.

---

8 (Kriegsministerium, 1851)

9 For details please check (Großer Generalstab, *Kriegsgeschichtliche Abteilung I.*, 1867).

In the Franco-Prussian war of 1870–71, the Guard Landwehr Division and four provincial Landwehr divisions were mobilized and sent into the field. Again the Landwehr had to guard the North Sea coast against expected French landing operations. To bolster those Landwehr divisions, active regiments were assigned to them. The Landwehr progressed beyond the initial tasks of forming a personnel pool to replace losses from the active regiments and of guarding the coast and rear areas. Landwehr formations fought against French *franc-tireurs* operating behind the German lines receiving about 1,000 casualties (2nd Landwehr Division). They also operated together with first-line formations. The 3rd Landwehr Division, with a majority of Landwehr and some active formations, reinforced the army of Prince Friedrich Karl in August 1870. 1st and 4th Reserve Divisions, both made up of Landwehr, took part in the siege of Belfort. After the occupation of Strasbourg, the 1st Reserve Division was left behind as an occupational force.[10]

In 1870–71, 140 out of 169 mobilized Landwehr battalions operated in French territory. Seventeen Landwehr cavalry regiments were also used in France—often against French mobile guards that were threatening the German communication lines.

In the Rangliste 1870–71, the following Landwehr structure can be found:[11]
- Guard Landwehr Regiment,
- Grenadier Guard Landwehr Regiment,
- 1–32 Landwehr Infantry Regiments,
- 33–40 Reserve Landwehr Infantry Battalions,
- 41–96 Landwehr Infantry Regiment,
- Five Baden Landwehr regiments.

Landwehr regiments were formed with two battalions each.

Baden had placed its units under Prussian command. Therefore, they were listed in the Prussian Rangliste. Under the Military Act of 30 January 1868, Bavaria introduced the Landwehr and designated 32 Landwehr areas, approximately two per active regiment. Bavarian Landwehr regiments were comprised two battalions, each battalion being mobilized by one Landwehr area. Eight Bavarian Landwehr battalions were fielded against France; the rest remained in their garrisons. However, no Bavarian Landwehr units were employed in combat actions in 1870–71. Saxony did not have a Landwehr until 1870. In Württemberg, the Landwehr was structured similar to that of Prussia. Württemberg fielded four Landwehr battalions that basically served as a personnel replacement pool for the active field units

Here the future double-role of the Landwehr could be seen: on the one hand, they filled the classical role of an occupational army, and on the other hand, they were a highly efficient reserve force used to fill the gaps in active line formations. From this time on, the Landwehr was on a positive development track, further accelerated by the Military Act (*Wehrgesetz*)[12] of 11 February 1888, when the first and second contingent was re-introduced and Landwehr service was once more limited to the age of 39. A little later the Landwehr regiments and battalions were disbanded and their active skeleton staffs turned into regional Landwehr

[10] (Janke, 2011), pp. 48–55. For details please check (Großer Generalstab, *Kriegggeschichtliche Abteilung I.*, 1874–1881).

[11] (Kriegsministerium, *Geheime Kriegs-Kanzlei* (Red.), 1871.

[12] The Wehrgesetz provided the legal basis for the Wehrordnung. The Wehrordnung, Heeresordnung, and Marineordnung were military manuals formulating in detailed requirements.

commands that were responsible for recruiting and mobilization planning. From then on, the story of the reserve formations began.

The *Landwehrbezirkskommando* was responsible for a Landwehr battalion area. The active brigades that were responsible for recruiting were usually assigned several Landwehr areas. Those Landwehr areas were often, but not always, identical with the borders of political counties. Such a Landwehr area was commanded by a Bezirkskommando, who was usually a reactivated staff officer z.D. The exceptions were Landwehr areas Berlin I–IV, which were usually under the command of active staff officers equal in rank to a regimental commander. The Landwehr area officers (*Bezirksoffiziere*) were usually reactivated officers z.D. One Bezirksoffizier was normally responsible for the cooperation with one or more civilian registration offices. In addition, each Landwehr area had one active officer serving as adjutant to the commander (*Bezirksadjutant*) and an active sergeant major (*Bezirksfeldwebel*) doing a similar job that of a company sergeant major in an active unit.

Landwehr and Reserve Units between 1888 and 1914

With the restructuring of 1888, the era of the elder Moltke also ended. Count Alfred v. Waldersee, who had already acted as General-Quartiermeister and Moltke's deputy, assumed the position of Chief of the General Staff. At the same time, the political élite changed and, in 1890, Bismarck was pushed into resignation with the help of Waldersee. The former war minister, Bronsart v. Schellendorf, was dismissed and was replaced by Verdy du Vernois. But even Verdy showed too much political ambition and was replaced by General Hans v. Kaltenborn-Stachau in October 1890.

The year 1888 was the "Three Emperors' Year." When Wilhelm I passed away, his son and successor Friedrich III assumed the throne, but was already suffering from cancer. After a little more than three months, Friedrich III passed away and his young son took over as Willhelm II. This meant not just a dynastic change, but also a change in policy: the German Empire was transformed into an imperialistic power demanding its "place in the sun" (*Platz an der Sonne*) by occupying colonies, violating French and British interests, and jeopardizing peace and stability in Europe. Starting in 1898, the massive build-up of the German fleet by Admiral Alfred v. Tirpitz led to increasing tension with Great Britain.[13] While Count George Caprivi and Prince Hohenlohe were still acting cautiously in foreign policy, the new chancellor, Bernhard v. Bülow, claimed a more dominant role for Germany in the world and defined what was called *Weltpolitik*.

These changes could also be felt within the Prussian-German army. While Moltke's strategic planning was basically focused on defense—although defense could also mean attacking or counter-attacking into enemy territory—Waldersee envisioned pre-emptive strikes and saw the need for fast and decisive mobilization. Under Waldersee and Schlieffen, who assumed the position of Chief of the General Staff in 1891, the focus of mobilization changed from the Eastern Theater to the West. The French ability for rapid mobilization and quick offensive was considered more threatening than the slowly mobilizing Russian giant. Waldersee and Schlieffen started dealing with the two-front dilemma in a much more offensive and pre-emptive way than had the elder Moltke and this required additional, stronger military forces. Starting in 1894, the Franco-Russian alliance led to huge French investments in Russia and the Russian railroad system, thereby speeding up Russian mobilization and forward deployment. In 1904, the Entente Cordiale between France and England further reinforced

---

[13] (Massie, 1992)

this alliance. This was mainly an initiative of the French foreign minister Delcassé and it intensified the German perception of encirclement by superior powers.

From the time of Waldersee, the General Staff prepared two mobilization plans in parallel: Deployment Plan I (*Aufmarsch I*) focused on the West and Deployment Plan II (*Aufmarsch II*) on the East. The reality of a two-front threat threw up the thorny issue that Germany possessed too few formations for both theaters. Reinforcing the operational army by just a few Landwehr and reserve formations would no longer be enough, particularly if Landwehr formations were basically planned as an occupational army, i.e., second-line formations, not to be used together with active formations. Furthermore, the army was still suffering from budget restrictions allowing only 35–55 percent of the available recruits to be drafted into active service. France, on the other hand, was able to draft about 80 percent of her available recruits. Schlieffen, as *Generalquartiermeister* and Waldersee's deputy, drew the Emperor's and the war ministers' attention to this fact in an aide memoire filed on 25 August 1889, in which he suggested a massive increase in the number of Landwehr, reserve, and replacement (*Ersatz*) formations in case of mobilization. Walter Bronsart von Schellendorff (Minister of War) strongly opposed these suggestions, fearing that such a rapid build-up of second-line formations would weaken the entire structure of the army.

The War Ministry planned mobilization of Landwehr and reserve formations very slowly. Luckily, in 1888, the new small caliber (8 mm) infantry rifle model 88 using smokeless (cordite) powder was introduced and issued to the infantry regiments, thus rendering obsolete the previous model 71/84 repeating rifles that fired 11 mm black-powder rounds. With the issue of the model 88 rifles, hundreds of thousands of redundant model 71/84 and model 71 rifles and carbines still using black-powder were available to equip reserve and Landwehr formations in case of mobilization. General v. Kaltenborn-Stachau, the new War Minister (who assumed his position in October 1890), was less traditional than Bronsart and Verdy; therefore, he was more inclined to support Schlieffen's ideas. Given these conditions, the massive build-up of reserve and Landwehr formations began in the 1890s. Since the Landwehrbezirkskommandos handled recruitment issues (in cooperation with the active brigades) as well as mobilization issues, the build-up of Landwehr and reserve formations could be managed in parallel. In case of mobilization for each army corps, one reserve division and two Landwehr brigades also had to be mobilized.

Unfortunately, after 1889, the Landwehr formations generally disappeared from the Rangliste making it difficult to trace the history of these formations today. Reserve formations never appeared in the Rangliste. In the 1897 Rangliste, dated 4 May 1897, there were the following:

- Guard Landwehr Regiment 1(I[st] Bn in Königsberg, II Bn in Graudenz),
- Guard Landwehr Regiment 2(I[st] Bn in Berlin, IInd Bn in Stettin),
- Guard Landwehr Regiment 3(I[st] Bn Hannover, IInd Bn Schleswig),
- Guard Landwehr Regiment 4 (I[st] Bn Magdeburg, IInd Bn Cottbus),
- Guard Fusilier Landwehr Regiment (I[st] Bn Frankfurt a.M., IInd Bn Wiesbaden),
- Guard Grenadier Landwehr Regiment 1(I[st] Bn Görlitz, IInd Bn Lissa),
- Guard Grenadier Landwehr Regiment 2 (I[st] Bn Hamm, IInd Bn Cassel),
- Guard Grenadier Landwehr Regiment 3(I[st] Bn Breslau, IInd Bn Liegnitz),
- Guard Grenadier Landwehr Regiment 4(I[st] Bn Coblenz, IInd Bn Düsseldorf),
- *Garde-Landwehr-Jäger* Battalion,
- *Garde-Landwehr-Schützen* Battalion,
- Guards Landwehr cavalry (structured into 1st and 2nd contingents but without naming regiments),

- Guard Landwehr field artillery and Guard Landwehr foot artillery, (both also structured into two contingents, but without regiments),
- Further listed were Guard Landwehr engineers, a Landwehr railroad brigade, and Guard Landwehr train.

It can be assumed that most of these formations had been formed either into two Guard Landwehr divisions or even a Guard Landwehr corps upon mobilization. Regretfully, further sources are missing. Since the Guard Landwehr infantry regiments had two contingents, it can be assumed that mobilization of further Guard Landwehr or Guard Landsturm formation was planned.[14]

Until 1897, the Guard Landwehr (not the line Landwehr) formations were listed, since they still had very small active skeleton staffs. Reserve officers were listed by their active regiments in an extra chapter of the Rangliste.[15] For each reserve officer, the Landwehrbezirkskommando to whom he belonged was listed, because it was not clear if he would join "his" regiment in case of mobilization, or if he would join another active or reserve regiment as set out in the annually changing mobilization plan.[16] Landwehr officers were only listed with the first or second contingent of their Landwehrbezirkskommando; they were mobilized with Landwehr formations and usually not with reserve formations.

On mobilization, the Landwehr formations kept their own numbering system—based upon the active regiments mobilizing them; whereas, the numbering of the reserve formations was oriented to the numbering system of the active brigade to which the Landwehr area belonged. This system can be quite misleading and confusing as several authors called the reserve formations with same numbers "sister regiments" of the respective active regiment. This grouping was not always true because the reserve regiments were mobilized with reservists provided by the Landwehr areas and cadre personnel coming from active regiments. Sometimes they had the same number, but usually not. There was no correlation between active regiments and reserve regiments that had the same numbers. Similarities in numbering were coincidental and not systematic.

For example, the active 28 Infantry Brigade (Düsseldorf) of the 14th Reserve Division (VII Reserve Corps) comprised 9 Füsilier-Regiment (Niederrheinisches) Nr. 39 (Düsseldorf) and 8 Lothringisches Infanterie-Regiment Nr. 159 (Mülheim a.d.Ruhr). The 28 Reserve Infantry Brigade belonged to the 13 Reserve Division (VII Reserve Corps) and consisted of the Reserve Infanterie-Regiment Nr. 39 (mobilized in Düsseldorf in August 1914) and the Reserve Infanterie-Regiment Nr. 57 (mobilized in Wesel–Friedrichsfeld in August 1914). Weapons, uniforms, helmets, and other equipment of these reserve regiments were stored together with the stock of the Landwehr Infanterie-Regiment 53 (Essen) in the artillery depot in Wesel and in the sub-depot in Düsseldorf (sub-depot for reserve personnel called in to join active units). Although the personnel of these formations came from Düsseldorf, Essen, Mülheim, and other surrounding cities, the units were finally formed and entrained for deployment in Wesel and Friedrichsfeld.

---

14 (Kriegsministerium, 1909), pp. 752–764

15 These were the regiments they had joined as one-year volunteers. Usually they conducted their annual reserve exercises with these regiments.

16 If an officer had completed his one-year volunteer training with a certain regiment but, in fact, lived in a place apart from the garrison of this regiment, he was not only listed with his regiment but also has the Landwehrbezirkskommando who administered him listed behind his name.

From the 1890s, care was taken to have a good mix of active and reserve officers and NCOs in reserve units to bolster these units and increase their military value. Upon mobilization, the deputy commanders of active Regiments or staff officers of the rank of Oberstleutnant generally moved to command reserve regiments. In addition, several active officers and senior NCOs were assigned to reserve formations (not necessarily within their "home" brigade) and their reserve officers and NCOs filled positions. About 50–70 percent of the officers and NCOs in reserve formations were reserve officers and NCOs (*Beurlaubtenstand*); all others came from active formations. Initially about 100 percent of the enlisted men in reserve formations were reservists and 1st contingent Landwehr reservists. In active units the number of enlisted men increased dramatically, e.g., from 150 enlisted men in a peacetime infantry company to about 250 men.[17]

After his appointment to Chief of the General Staff on 2 February 1891, Schlieffen came up with a second aide memoire, stating that with a future mobilization, hundreds of thousands of reservists with previous military training in an active unit and *Ersatzreservisten* without such training would be mobilized—far more than the army could absorb with her active, prepared reserve, and Landwehr formations. Schlieffen suggested forming replacement battalions (*Ersatzbataillone*) and replacement brigades (*Ersatzbrigaden*) to support the army corps during operations. Again the Ministry of War strongly opposed such an employment of makeshift formations that lacked proper training and cohesion. For such Ersatz formations, neither enough weapons nor equipment, nor support and supply units such as artillery, trains, etc. could be made available. There was also a lack of officers and NCOs. Even the War Minister v. Kaltenborn came to the conclusion that the operational use of such formations would certainly lead to a disaster—and the operational army would at the same time lose its personnel replacement pool.

Driven by the ever-present problem of the two-front dilemma and realizing that the current number of active, reserve, and Landwehr formations would be much too few to conduct operations successfully on both Western and Eastern fronts simultaneously, Schlieffen again approached the Kaiser with an aide memoire, asking for the following:

- Each army corps should mobilize with as many reserve battalions and Landwehr battalions as could be staffed with available men;
- Each corps should form one reserve division and at least one Landwehr division upon mobilization out of these formations;
- Reserve and Landwehr artillery and reserve and Landwehr train formations should be prepared to provide these reserve divisions the necessary sustainability for extended operations;
- Staffs of reserve brigades should be taken out of the reserve divisions to reduce the numbers of officers and staff officers needed. Reserve brigade staffs that were saved should be used to command further reserve and Landwehr divisions.

Again the War Ministry opposed these plans and successfully advised the Kaiser not to follow Schlieffen's suggestions. But Schlieffen continued pushing, presenting a fourth aide memoire to the Kaiser on 11 December 1893. This memoire focused on the defense of Eastern Prussia to shield his intended offensive operations in the West. This is when what was later called the Schlieffen plan became visible. With reference to the French revolution and to the success of the French armies against other more traditional European armies, Schlief-

[17] For details in 1914, please check Chapter 16.

fen wanted a *levée en masse* of trained and untrained Landwehr and Landsturm units that were armed and equipped from numerous small depots spread along the border. This levée en masse was intended to shield Eastern Prussia against Russian cavalry and reconnaissance, and behind this shield the active and reserve formations of Eastern Prussia could be mobilized and deployed for systematic defensive action against the attacking Russians. Finally, in 1897, Schlieffen suggested an increase in the number of active army corps of the German field armies from 20 (Guard Corps, I–XI and XIV–XVII Prussian—including the Baden Army Corps—XIII Württemberg Corps, I Saxon, I and II Bavarian Army Corps) to 27. However, at the same time, Tirpitz was proposing a massive naval build-up to the Kaiser. That being the case it was obvious that there would be hardly any budget to support Schlieffen's plan.

Despite the parallel naval build-up, Schlieffen partly succeeded in 1899, when the formation of three further active corps (XVIII Prussian, II Saxon, and III Bavarian) was endorsed by the Kaiser and budgeted for by the Reichstag. This authorization increased the number of active army corps to 23. Schlieffen also managed to increase the number and quality of reserve and Landwehr formations. In 1902, Schlieffen also convinced the Ministry of War to form five so-called war corps (*Kriegskorps*) to be formed from reserve formations and surplus active formations.[18] These war corps were in fact already reserve corps (Guard Reserve Corps, and XX–XXIII Corps) and were comparable to the reserve corps mobilized in 1914. In 1903, War Minister Karl v. Einem reduced the number of these war corps to three (Guard Reserve Corps, XX and XXI Army Corps). Einem strictly opposed this massive build-up of the army because he feared a dilution of quality if numbers became too large.[19] In 1910, the existing 27 reserve divisions were formed into 13 reserve corps ready for mobilization. With the massive build-up of 1912, the XX and XXI Kriegskorps were finally turned into active army corps. By 1914, the number of reserve corps was increased to an equivalent of 17 corps (Guard Reserve Corps, I–X, XII, XIV, and XVIII Reserve Corps; I Bavarian Reserve Corps plus 3, 30, 33, and 35 Reserve Divisions—made up of Landwehr regiments—being deployed to fortresses and therefore not being part of a reserve corps). The Guard Reserve Corps commanded the active 3rd Guard Infantry Division and the 1st Guard Reserve Division, and was, in fact, considered as an active corps. Second Guard Reserve Division and 19th Reserve Division were merged in the X Reserve Corps. Several reserve divisions were composed of three reserve regiments and one active regiment as some active divisions also contained a reserve regiment.

Two, sometimes three, infantry regiments made up a brigade commanded by a Generalleutnant or Generalmajor as the brigade commander. He was responsible for recruiting within the brigade district in cooperation with the *Bezirkskommandos*. Usually two Bezirkskommandos controlled the recruiting within a brigade district. This rule did not apply for the Guards Corps and within regions controlled by *Landwehrinspektionen*. Two to three brigades formed one division together with a cavalry and a field artillery brigade. This formation changed during mobilization. Usually there was one Bezirkskommando per brigade area. In densely populated areas like Berlin, Hamburg, Munich, Frankfurt, and the Rhine-Ruhr area, Landwehr inspections were in charge of the Bezirkskommandos. In the small town of Minden (Eastern Westphalia), recruiting was controlled by a Bezirkskommando reporting to the 26 Infantry Brigade (13th Division, VII Army Corps). In the city of Essen, the center of the densely populated industrial area at the river Ruhr, a Landwehrinspektion reporting

18 Several infantry brigades consisted of three regiments. The third regiment was regarded as being surplus and assigned to one of these war corps upon mobilization.

19 (Storz, *Kriegsbild und Rüstung vor 1914*, 1992), p. 323.

directly into the VII Army Corps, was in charge of recruiting and mobilization. Essen had two Bezirkskommandos reporting into the Landwehrinspektion Essen. Berlin had six Bezirkskommandos (nos. I–VI) reporting into the Landwehrinspektion Berlin, which then reported into the III Army Corps. Usually Landwehrinspektionen were commanded by a *Generalmajor z.D.*, sometimes a Generalleutnant z.D. with the rank of a division commander.

Landwehr-Inspektion Berlin appears for the first time in the 1904 Rangliste—not yet staffed with a commander; in 1905, it was Gen. Lt. v. Hoepfner, later promoted to General d. Inf. but still commanding the Landwehr-Inspektion Berlin. In the 1908 Rangliste, there were three inspections: Berlin (Gen. d. Inf. v. Hoepfner), Dortmund (Gen. Maj. v. Gersdorff), and Essen (Gen. Maj. v. Lueder). In the 1914 Rangliste, there were already seven in Prussia—Berlin, Breslau, Bromberg, Dortmund, Düsseldorf, Essen, and Insterburg, all of them commanded by either an active Generalmajor or an active Generalleutnant. There is a possibility that the Landwehr-Inspektionen were assigned to play a distinctive role during mobilization by building either reserve division or reserve corps staffs. This assumption is still a matter of research.

There were also confusing exceptions. In rather sparsely populated regions like Pomerania and Eastern Prussia, there were Landwehrinspektionen to facilitate recruiting and mobilization. In Pomerania, it was the Landwehrinspektion Bromberg (created 1 October 1913), reporting into the 4th Division of the II Army Corps that controlled the Landwehrbezirken Bromberg, Deutsch-Krone, Gnesen, Hohensalza, Neustettin, and Schneidemühl. In Eastern Prussia, it was the Landwehrinspektion Bartenstein (created 1 October 1913), reporting into the 2 Division of the I Army Corps that controlled the Landwehrbezirke Bartenstein, Goldap, Gumbinnen, Rastenburg and Tilsit. This exception was introduced to facilitate the formation of the new XVII Army Corps, together with the mobilization preparation of numerous reserve and Landwehr formations during the last armament push before the war.

A Major or an Oberstleutnant z.D. with the rank of a battalion commander usually commanded a regular Bezirkskommando. Some larger Bezirkskommandos such as I Bremen and I Breslau were commanded by an Oberst z.D. with the rank of a regimental commander and assisted by one or two additional z.D. field officers.[20] Uniquely, the Berlin and München Bezirkskommandos were commanded by officers holding the rank of an active Oberst, again with the authority of a regimental commander and assisted by two or three z.D. field officers. The Bezirkskommando was assisted by an active lieutenant or second lieutenant acting as the adjutant to the commander and called the Bezirksadjutant. Furthermore, each Bezirkskommando had additional reserve or Landwehr officers acting as district (company) officers or Bezirksoffiziere. Each company-sized district also had a Company Sergeant Major—the Bezirksfeldwebel. Additionally, several NCOs and enlisted men were assigned for the purpose of administrative support. Some of the larger Bezirkskommandos had a non-active medical officer, usually in the rank of an Oberstabsarzt z.D., to carry out medical examinations during the *Musterung* of new recruits. The smaller Bezirkskommandos would call upon the assistance of a neighboring unit to provide this medical support.[21]

---

[20] z.D. is the abbreviation of "zur Disposition gestellt." These were semi-retired officers who were receiving their regular pensions, but still being actively used in positions not really requiring an active officer to cover them. Usually officers z.D. were also assigned to positions in reserve or Landwehr formations.

[21] (Friedag, *Führer durch Heer und Flotte 1914, 1914*), pp. 177–194.

LANDSTURM

The Landsturm was introduced as a third-line militia in 1813 and consisted of all men under the age of 45 who belonged neither to the active army nor to the Landwehr. The Landsturm was to be mobilized by the cities and counties of a province only in case of an immediate threat by an enemy. With few exceptions, the Landsturm did not participate in any military action during the liberation wars. Later the Landsturm comprised all untrained men up to age of 45 and of trained reserve soldiers, transferred after 19 years of service in the active army, reserve formations, and/or Landsturm to the second contingent (*zweites Aufgebot*) of the Landwehr. This second contingent was usually a mobilization pool for Landsturm. All conscripts not drafted by lot or rejected for physical reasons automatically belonged to the Landsturm and received a Landsturm certificate (*Landsturmschein*). After 1815, the Landsturm was neither trained nor mobilized; during the unification wars the Landsturm was never used nor mobilized. In 1914, the Landsturm was mobilized for the first time. By the end of 1914, 334 Landsturm infantry battalions were mobilized and 142 of them fielded either in Belgium to secure communication lines or in the East for occupation purposes or to secure the German border. By 1918, 834 Landsturm infantry battalions had been mobilized, 492 of them were fielded in Belgium and France or behind the Eastern front.[22]

In the Wehrordnung of 1888, the Landsturm was divided into two separate and distinct contingents based on age. [23] The Dienstpflicht and Landwehr were one and the Landsturm was the second. Those between the ages of 17 and 20 who had not yet entered service and had no training were enrolled in the first contingent of the Landsturm. They were not organized into standing units and were listed for reporting purposes. The second contingent of the Landsturm included all soldiers and untrained individuals between the ages of 39 and 45. Second contingent Landwehr soldiers joined at age 39.[24] This group was a really rough militia that had no training requirement. They were a home guard at best. This arrangement ensured, however, that individuals were accounted for throughout their time of military commitment. Not only were the reserve and Landwehr controlled by the Bezirkskommando, but also the army corps district controlled the Landsturm in the same way.

There were 334 Landsturm battalions. Of these, 142 were considered mobile. Landsturm brigade organization is really a bit of a misnomer as there was no commander or staff. They were grouped into brigade organizations only because they were administered by the army corps district that was itself further divided into brigades. It becomes even less clear because the battalions were administered through the Bezirkskommando, just as were soldiers of the Landwehr. Some battalions did not fall under a Landwehr Bezirkskommando. There was no such organization as a Landwehr inspection that took the place of the missing Bezirkskommando in some instances—mostly in larger towns.

---

22 (Friedag, 1914), p. 817. (Busche, 1998), p. 260.

23 (Wehrordnung des Deutschen Reiches, 1888).

24 (Wehrordnung des Deutschen Reiches, 1888).

ERSATZ RESERVE

Not everybody was selected for Dienstpflicht. The 1907 statistics show that 240,000 of 556,000 eligible males never entered Dienstzeit. They had failed the Musterung physical for one reason or another and many of the reasons were extremely minor. There simply were not enough slots. There were also exceptions made for family emergencies. If a soldier was one of those excused service, but was in every other way fit and suitable for the active army, he was entered into the Ersatz Reserve for a period of 12 years. These civilians were trained in administrative (not armed) duties three times during a 12-year time period. These training periods could be quite long, but could not exceed 20 weeks in total; if that period is divided by three, the time involved comes close to seven weeks per activation. That was a long time and apparently not everyone completed it. After 12 years, if they had completed their training, the class went to the second contingent of the Landwehr. If the training had not been completed, they went to the first contingent of the Landsturm.[25]

Members of the Ersatz Reserve served in small battalions at mobilization that were built around brigade headquarters. Initially there were over 90 such battalions. One of Schlieffen's ideas was to use these battalions as maneuver units with no service support establishment. They were purely men with rifles and had few officers and with no supply, medical, or other essential support elements. The purpose of an Ersatz battalion was to give replacements to their regiments. If an Ersatz battalion became a maneuver unit, it could not perform this function. Nonetheless, they were needed by 1914, and eventually there were Ersatz divisions. Initially these were used close to the German border, mainly with the Sixth and Seventh Armies. In the next chapter we are going to analyze the officer corps, which provided the leadership for all these first and second-line formations.

[25] (Sigel, 1900)

CHAPTER 9

THE OFFICER CORPS

On 1 October 1913, the German Army numbered 30,029 officers (23,346 from Prussia, 3,322 from Bavaria, 2,247 from Saxony and 1,114 from Württemberg). This total did not include the 222 officers in supernumery positions. Just one year later that total number had grown to 76,000—26,000 of whom were regular officers and 25,000 from the reserve.[1] There were several types of officers, although this chapter concentrates on combatant officers. In this category were three grade groups: general officers; field grade officers or *Stabsoffiziere* (major, lieutenant colonel, colonel); and regimental officers, usually in the ranks of captain and lieutenant (*Dienstgradgruppen*). In addition to the combat arms, there were various technical officers. These officers were graded on a scale that paralleled the ranks of combatant officers. There were medical officers (*Sanitätsoffiziere*); veterinary officers (*Veterinäroffizier*); ordnance and artificer officers (*Zeug und Feuerwerksoffiziere*), (seldom promoted above captain); and fortress construction officers (*Festungsbauoffiziere*).

Historically, these officers had been from the nobility, but the wartime build-up required additional manpower. This change in status created a conundrum. There were three classes of people within imperial Germany—the nobility and the traditional old officer families, the middle class or bourgeoisie (some were quite rich, but their families were without the benefit of nobility), and the lower class or proletariat. In a key order dated 29 March 1890, Kaiser Wilhelm II opened the door to an expanded officer corps with what he termed *erwüncshte Kreise* (desired personal/social background).[2] This change provided imperial guidance for the selection of officers and an admission that the numbers of blood nobility were insufficient to meet the task at hand.[3] The commonly held belief was that the nobility were of good solid stock and could be counted on when loyalty was paramount. Expansion of the army mandated that imperial Germany begin accepting others into the fold, so the nobles had to find ways to restrict entry, and they did so by admitting only those who had the "right attitude."[4]

This policy was not a totally new idea. As early as 1786, when Frederick the Great died, 10 percent of the officers were members of the middle class. In 1861, a little more than 40 percent of the army was non-noble. One of the great military theoreticians of the time, Colmar von der Goltz, repeatedly argued that an aristocratic background was required as

1 (Clemente, 1992), p. 205.
2 (Bald, 1982), pp. 25 and 85. (Demeter, 1963), p. 27.
3 (Moncure, 1993) pp. 65–66.
4 (Kitchen, 1968), pp. 22–23.

aristocrats were in the habit of commanding others. He believed fewer nobles would lead to a breakdown in military discipline and the blurring of the line between enlisted and officer ranks. Furthermore, only aristocrats would have the tie to the Kaiser, and only they could be relied upon. The following table indicates how matters stood in 1861. As is shown, the Prussian aristocracy favored the cavalry and infantry guards.[5]

Share of Nobility

Types of Regiments	Percentage of Nobles
Infantry Guards	95
Infantry Line	67
Cavalry Guards	100
Cavalry Line	95
Artillery Guards	67
Artillery Line	16
Engineers	16

The nobility's feelings toward the other branches were really historic in nature. One historian of renaissance Italy referred to the artillery as "this pestilential armament."[6] As to the pioneers or engineers (middle class soldiers), historically they were not soldiers at all. They had been civilians who were hired to dig and construct the siege works.[7]

Prussia was the most obdurate of the contingents, but understood that the need to fill officer vacancies was of paramount concern. The other contingents more readily accepted officers from the middle class. In Saxony after 1866, for instance, some members of the Guelph aristocracy from the former Kingdom of Hannover joined Saxon service. This policy led to a concentration of aristocracy within certain Saxon regiments.[8] A bad joke was often told that it was never clear if any given toast to His Majesty the King went to the King of Saxony or the King of Hannover. By 1890, Saxony had only 19 percent nobility in its officer corps. Württemberg had only 25 percent nobles after unification.[9] Bavaria, the most liberal-minded state, had only 15 percent nobles in its officer corps. In that army only the *Abitur* was a prerequisite for a regular Army commission as of 1890.[10]

Although the change was a necessity, the Prussian nobility simply would not integrate with the middle class, so élite regiments were formed. Initially, all nobles went to cavalry regiments, but not all could afford the extra expense of maintaining a horse, so Foot Guard Regiments were formed. Unlike the élite Foot Guard Regiments, middle class soldiers were found in Pioneer and Foot Artillery Regiments. As more and more middle class officers with better skills and test scores entered the ranks, instructors were given greater leeway to give extra credit to candidates with a good attitude (noble upbringing). A non-passing score could be rescued by deportment. Likewise, if a proletarian had managed to enroll in an officer's

5 (Clemente, 1992), p. 16.
6 (Moncure, 1993), pp. 26–27.
7 (Clemente, 1992), p. 3.
8 Infantry Regiments 100, 101, 108, Jäger Battalions 12 and 13, and some cavalry regiments.
9 (Clemente, 1992), p. 18.
10 (Clemente, 1992), p. 41.

course, a superb score could be made into a fail by his "attitude." However, even this reluctant willingness to accept middle class officers did not fix the shortages. Eight percent of the infantry officer requirements were unfilled in 1889. Fifty-six infantry regiments received no applications for commission in 1902.[11]

By 1913, 70 percent of the Prussian officers came from middle-class families, but regimental exclusiveness did not end.[12] In 1913, 80 percent of cavalry officers, 48 percent of infantry officers, and 41 percent of field artillery officers were from noble families. A few middle class individuals known as "Concession Joes" (*Konzessionschulzes*) made it into the Guard regiments but were not very welcome.[13] There was a lack of prestige in technical schools, despite the fact that these schools made greater demands on their students. By 1913, 48 percent of the generals were middle class. When promoted to the position of commanding general of an army corps, bourgeois generals became nobility "automatically."[14]

The aristocracy also favored regiments that were located in major urban areas. In 1913, 61 percent of the regiments in the Prussian Army were more than 50 percent noble and 16 regiments were exclusively aristocratic. The 3. Garde-Regiment zu Fuß had 67 aristocrats and no non-nobles. Infanterie-Regiment Graf Bose (1. Thüringisches) Nr. 31 in Altona had 47 nobles and six non-nobles; Braunschweigisches Infanterie-Regiment Nr. 92 in Brunswick had a split of 44 nobles and 10 from the middle class. By comparison, 8. Ostpreußisches Infanterie-Regiment Nr. 45 east of the Elbe had two aristocrats and 50 non-nobles. Most cavalry regiments were entirely noble; however, Dragoner-Regiment Prinz Albrecht von Preußen (Litthauisches) Nr. 1 in Tilsit had a split of three nobles and 24 non-nobles. Field artillery regiments in large cities, such as Feldartillerie-Regiment von Peucker (1. Schlesisches) Nr. 6 in Breslau had a split of 29 nobles and six middle class; whereas, Feld Artillerie-Regiment Prinz August von Preußen (1. Litthauisches) Nr. 1 in Gumbinnen and Insterburg had a split of three nobles and 40 non-nobles. Foot artillery was almost entirely non-noble including the Guards Foot Artillery whose split was 10 noble and 37 non-nobles. Pioneers were also considered technical, and pioneer battalions in large cities routinely had no nobles.[15] Regiments that relocated their garrisons would often lose their nobles, such as Schleswig-Holsteinisches Ulanen-Regiment Nr. 15 when it relocated to a frontier garrison; it went from a split of 25 nobles and three non-nobles to seven nobles and 17 non-nobles.[16] The General Staff was usually not noble and valued professional efficiency above all.[17] Eighty-three percent of the officers were Protestant as opposed to 62 percent of the population.[18]

Service with the I (Eastern Prussia) and XVI (Metz) Army Corps was particularly undesirable. Their regiments were located in less attractive garrisons close to the Russian and French borders, and that resulted in more drills, alarms, and exercises. Additionally, for many years, both army corps had very demanding commanding generals leading to a well known rhyme among army officers: "*Gott bewahr mich vor der Grenze—vor Gottlieb Haeseler und August Lentze!*" (May God protect me from serving at the border—with Gottlieb v. Haeseler and August v. Lentze).

[11] (Clemente, 1992), p. 207.
[12] (Frevert, 2004), p. 158.
[13] (Clemente, 1992), p. 206.
[14] (Clemente, 1992) p. 205.
[15] (Kitchen, 1968), p. 24.
[16] (Kitchen, 1968), p. 24.
[17] (Förster, 2006), p. 465.
[18] (Frevert, 2004), p. 229.

The striking thing about the German officer corps is its youth. Far younger than any of their western counterparts, many officer aspirants were only 17 years old. Young Germans rushed to obtain commissions that started the clock on seniority, despite a lack of maturity and education. Officers could choose the academy cadet route or the *Fahnenjunker* officer candidate civilian route. The source of commission was nearly as important as noble birth. France only accepted cadets who had passed the first half of their baccalaureate, somewhat equivalent to the German Abitur. Cadet ages at the St. Cyr Military Academy in France ranged from 17 to 21. Although perhaps a gross generalization, people get the impression that young Germans were commissioned as lieutenants at the age when French youngsters entered their Military Academy.[19]

CADET SCHOOLS

Cadet schools were completely separate from the *Volkschule* and *Gymnasium* discussed in Chapter 4. A man could enter a lower cadet school (*Voranstalt)* and remain within the cadet system until he graduated from the upper cadet school. Movement between civilian schools and cadet schools certainly happened in both directions.[20] There were eight Prussian lower cadet schools located in Bensberg, Köslin (formerly Culm), Karlsruhe, Naumburg, Oranienstadt, Plön, Potsdam, and Walstadt. There was also a lower cadet school in Dresden, Saxony and one in lower Bavaria. The Prussian upper cadet school was called the *Hauptkadettenanstalt* (HKA) and was located at Gross-Lichterfelde. Not only Prussian, but also Württemberg and some Saxon cadets, aspired to attend the Prussian upper cadet school.[21] Bavarian cadet schools stood alone and arguably were always better. The Abitur was a prerequisite for commissioning in the Bavarian army.

Cadets were an interesting group. By 1910, two-thirds of the cadets were non-noble.[22] The major investiture was the quasi-formal clothing ceremony. Prussian lower cadets did not wear helmets, but each school had a unique uniform. If the uniform was too large, the cadet had no recourse but to grow into it.[23] Cadet life seemed to revolve around efforts to find food, as their normal fare was inadequate.

There were never many cadets. A Voranstalt had 200 or fewer students. The HKA at Gross-Lichterfelde had 1,000 cadets and produced about 240 officers per year. These cadets mostly entered the army as officer candidates shortly before commission, in the rank of *Fähnrich*. The number of civilians entering the active army with Fahnenjunker status varied from twice as many cadets to about the same number.[24] As to religion, while 38 percent of Germans were Catholic, less than four percent of the cadets were Catholic. This disparity shows the religious discrimination in the selection process as well a requirement that the Prussian officers raise their children as Protestants.[25]

---

19 (Moncure, 1993), pp. 216–217.
20 See chart in Chapter 4, Schools.
21 (Clemente, 1992), p. 83.
22 (Clemente, 1992), p. 111.
23 (Clemente, 1992), p. 115.
24 (Clemente, 1992), pp. 257–258.
25 (Moncure, 1993), p. 76.

The cost of schooling was a major issue. One of the attractions of cadet school was that scholarships to the "Kings Cadets" could be quite substantial. Reduction or elimination of tuition fees was available. This was granted almost automatically for the sons of officers, as well as for certain non-commissioned officers, civil servants, and gendarmes.[26] The emancipation of students became a major concern of families. Commissioning and self-sufficiency were urgent considerations. Families had to decide very early (when the boy was age nine) whether to bear this expense or not. The student graduation year, seniority, and long-term benefits differed between the cadet schools. There were three distinct methods of leaving the cadet schools. The fastest and most direct method, and the one that applied to most cadets, was to leave the HKA after the *Obersekunda* year and enter a regiment as a *charakterisierter* (brevet) Fähnrich (at age 17). Option two was to be selected as a *Prima* cadet gaining the Abitur (at age 19). Option three was for a very élite group called the *Selekta*, which was in charge of the other cadets for the period of one year (at age 18).

At the end of six cadet years or at the age of 17, the cadets took the Fähnrich exam and those that left the Academy merged into the commissioning process. The cadet was a little different because he was a *charakterisierter* Fähnrich. There were exceptions, as some 10 percent of the cadets left the academy with some advanced training and were considered *Patent* Fähnrich. If a cadet did really well on the Fähnrich exam, he could be selected as a Selekta cadet and remain at the school. Selekta became cadet non-commissioned officers and "ran" the non-senior cadets in the following year. This position was prestigious; if the individual passed the officer's exam, he was commissioned. There was no need for the officers of the regiment to vote on Selekta.[27] A cadet could also compete to be a Prima cadet. This policy was selective and could lead the candidates to continue at the HKA for two years, with the goal of gaining the Abitur (at age 19). Being a Selekta cadet helped him for the rest of his military life. The Abitur was a civilian life advantage.[28] As such, the number of military Abitur holders grew steadily from one-third in 1880 to two-thirds in 1912. The number of middle class officers who saw the lifelong civilian advantages of the Abitur became dominant.[29]

Inside the cadet corps, social class was non-existent. One anachronistic institution existed that ran counter to this classless society. The Corps of Pages was open only to the children of nobles. By an order of 1878, pages were drawn from the two highest classes of the HKA. A page had to be successful in his own right and had to have been selected to enter the ranks of the Prima or the Selekta. Thirty cadets were chosen as *Leibpagen* and 30 additional cadets were chosen as *Hofpagen*. Leibpagen directly served a member of the royal family. Hofpagen performed general duties at the imperial Court. When on official duties, the pages dressed in 18th century uniforms with the Leibpagen having a more ornate dress. Those cadets who had exposure to royalty and the court were highly successful. Forty-seven percent of those Selekta who were pages became generals.[30]

---

26 (Moncure, 1993), pp. 90–92.
27 (Clemente, 1992), p. 94.
28 (Clemente, 1992), p. 101.
29 (Clemente, 1992), p. 209.
30 (Moncure, 1993), pp. 136–141.

THE STEPS TO BECOMING AN ACTIVE OFFICER

The steps to becoming an officer were aimed at ensuring that the right personnel were accepted. As with all things related to commissioning, there were, of course, exceptions. Sometimes, it may appear that there were more exceptions than rules, but these 10 steps outline the basics. The route to commissioning was similar for the civilian Fahnenjunker and the Fähnrich from the cadet schools, but there were exceptions. Rabenau, a German military author of the time, identified six different steps. These steps were designed for active officers. Reserve officers took a different track that is explained under the one-year volunteer scheme. In addition to the exceptions, there were many differences in the length of time devoted to commissioning, including the cost and the final educational level. Dates of rank varied significantly.[31]

Step 1—Select a Regiment to Join
All guard and cavalry regiments actively recruited nobles to keep the regiments as "pure" as possible. A variety of methods was used to lure young noblemen, including fancy uniforms and depot locations near fashionable, large towns. Guard and cavalry units could expect additional income of 1,000 *Mark* per month from these candidates who would pay to belong to the units. The more remote, lower-regarded regiments often had problems attracting new recruits. Despite this difficulty, they insisted on a rigid class and social selection process.[32] This maintenance of high social standards resulted in a shortage of officers. Officially, the blame was placed on the middle-class for not wanting to wade through the army's prejudices.[33] Even until 1918, regiments tried to keep up the illusion of a "noble" officer corps with a personal relationship to the Kaiser.

Step 2—Get a Regimental Colonel to Sponsor You
Sponsorship was key and perhaps the most difficult step on the ladder. Both the candidate and his family were scrutinized carefully. The candidate had to have a sufficient income because the regimental commander and the current officers did not want to accept men who might get into financial difficulty. Vera von Etzel tells a touching story about how Artur v. Klingspor made it into the *Kürassier-Regiment von Seydlitz (Magdeburgisches) Nr. 7*. The clothing and equipment was very expensive at that time and a burden even for his father, Lieutenant General Leo v. Klingspor. Artur's father underwrote him, and he received his commission, but the support came only after his younger brother, Hans Arvid, died while at the academy. Perhaps the loss of a son persuaded his father to ensure that his surviving son was in the best regiment. [34]

After selecting a regiment, the candidate's father introduced him to the regimental commander, who approved every volunteer applying to the regiment. The enormous cost of a premier regiment would keep the regiments populated by the more affluent—the "vons." The father of the candidate and his son went to a dinner to be seen by all in a one-night precursor to Step 8.The commander then determined whether or not to accept the new officer candidate, called either *Offiziers-Aspirant* or *Avantageur*.[35] Then the officer candidate had

[31] (Rabenau, 1913), pp. 298–305.
[32] (Clemente, 1992), p. 64.
[33] (Clemente, 1992), p. 207.
[34] *Wehrmacht*-Awards thread, Prussian commissioning, 28 Jul 2004 Posted by Brian S.
[35] (Kriegsministerium, 1905), pp. 2–3.

Die Wochenschau

Nr. 37 | 13. September 1913 | 5. Jahrgang

Von den diesjährigen Kaisermanövern in Schlesien.

Der Schauplatz der diesjährigen Kaisermanöver befindet sich in Schlesien am Ostabhang der Jauerschen Berge und des Eulengebirges. Am 6. September rückten die beiden Parteien in die Anfangsaufstellung, wie sie ihnen durch die Manöverleitung angegeben worden war. Es fochten das 5. Armeekorps unter dem General der Infanterie von Strantz (Generalstabschef Oberstleutnant Meister) gegen das 6. Armeekorps unter General von Pritzelwitz (Generalstabschef Oberstleutnant von Derschau). Oberschiedsrichter ist der Generalfeldmarschall Frhr. v. d. Goltz.

Kaiser Wilhelm, der am 7. September abends auf dem Bahnhof ı Salzbrunn eintraf, nahm als Gast des Fürsten von Pleß während drei Manövertage im Grand Hotel zu Salzbrunn Wohnung, das ıgentum der fürstlich Pleßschen Badeverwaltung ist. Ebenda hatten .uch König Konstantin von Griechenland, der Schwager des Kaisers, und der griechische Kronprinz ihr Quartier. — In Freiburg in Schlesien hatte die Manöverleitung Quartier genommen: der Chef des Generalstabes der Armee Generaladjutant General der Infanterie von Moltke. Hier wohnten auch der Chef des Generalstabes der österreichisch-ungarischen Armee General der Infanterie Frhr. v. Hötzendorff, der Chef des Generalstabes der italienischen Armee Generalleutnant Pollio und der vom Kaiser zu den Manövern eingeladene Graf Zeppelin Der preußische Kriegsminister Generalleutnant v. Falkenhayn mit seinem Stabe hatte Quartier in Schweidnitz. Der König von Sachsen nahm auf Schloß Sibyllenort Wohnung.

Die eigentlichen Bewegungen begannen am 8. September in den frühen Morgenstunden, doch trat der Kriegszustand bereits am 7. September abends 9 Uhr ein; von diesem Zeitpunkt an mußten sich die einzelnen Unterkunftsorte kriegsgemäß sichern.

Infanterie nimmt eine Anhöhe mit Sturm. Gebr. Haeckel, Berlin.

Wochenschau September 1913. This is a well-known picture that has been used in various forms for decades. It is asserted that it is a picture of German soldiers advancing in Belgium or France in August of 1914. There is nothing startling or new about the picture except the provenance is a myth. This picture appeared on the front page of a German newspaper dated September 1913.

An extended Royal Family gathering at Coburg in April 1894. Note the three Emperors/Cousins. How similar they look

Danish King Christian IX.

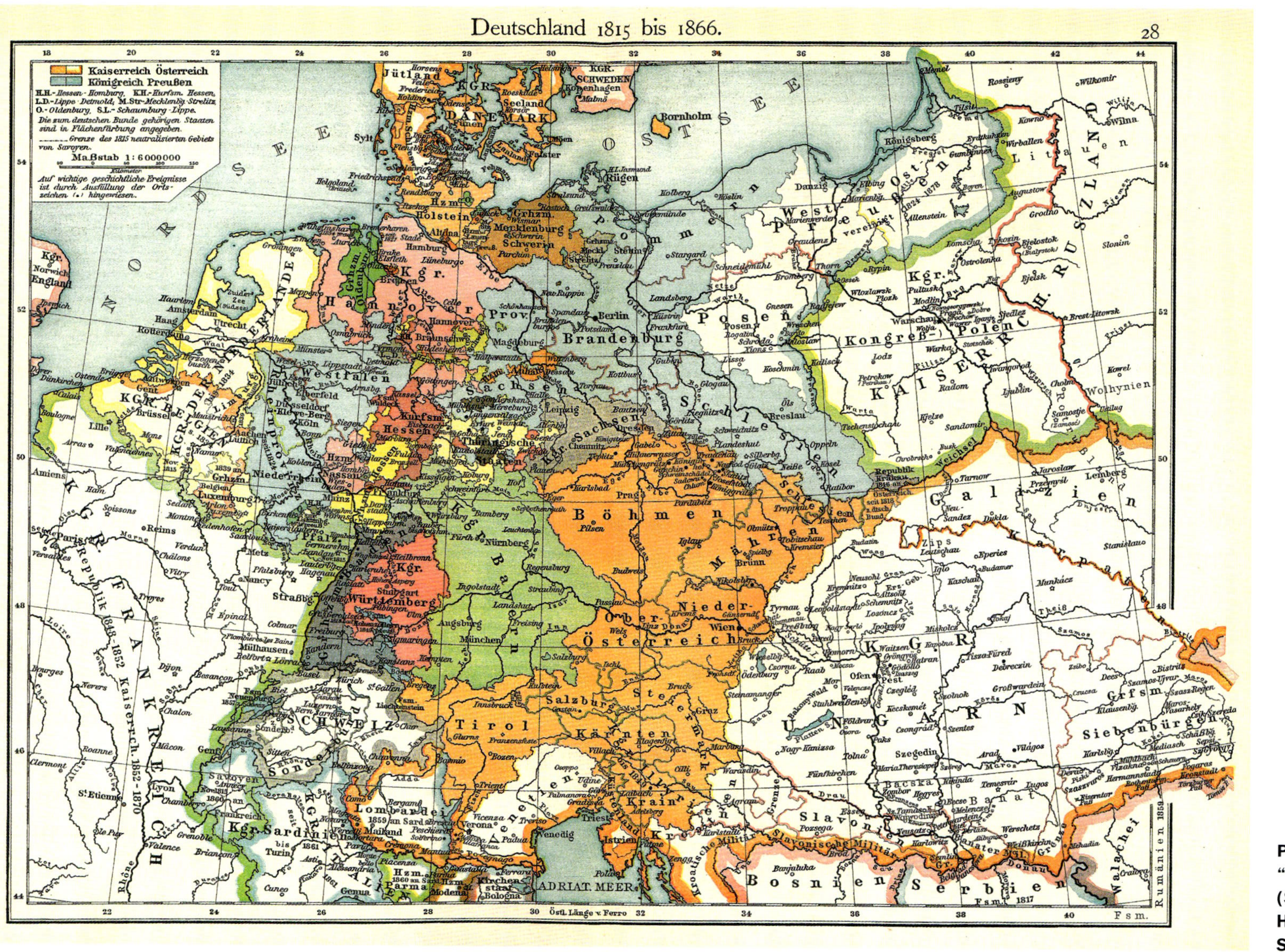

Post 1815–
"The Germanys."
(Source: Putzgers
Historischer
Schul-Atlas 1903)

Prussian Jäger attacking Austrian infantry at Königgrätz. (Courtesy of Wehrtechnische Studiensammlung, Koblenz. Copyright: WTS/BAAINBw.)

Typical dense infantry firing line in 1870.

Proclamation of Kaiser Wilhelm I in the Hall of Mirrors in Versailles.

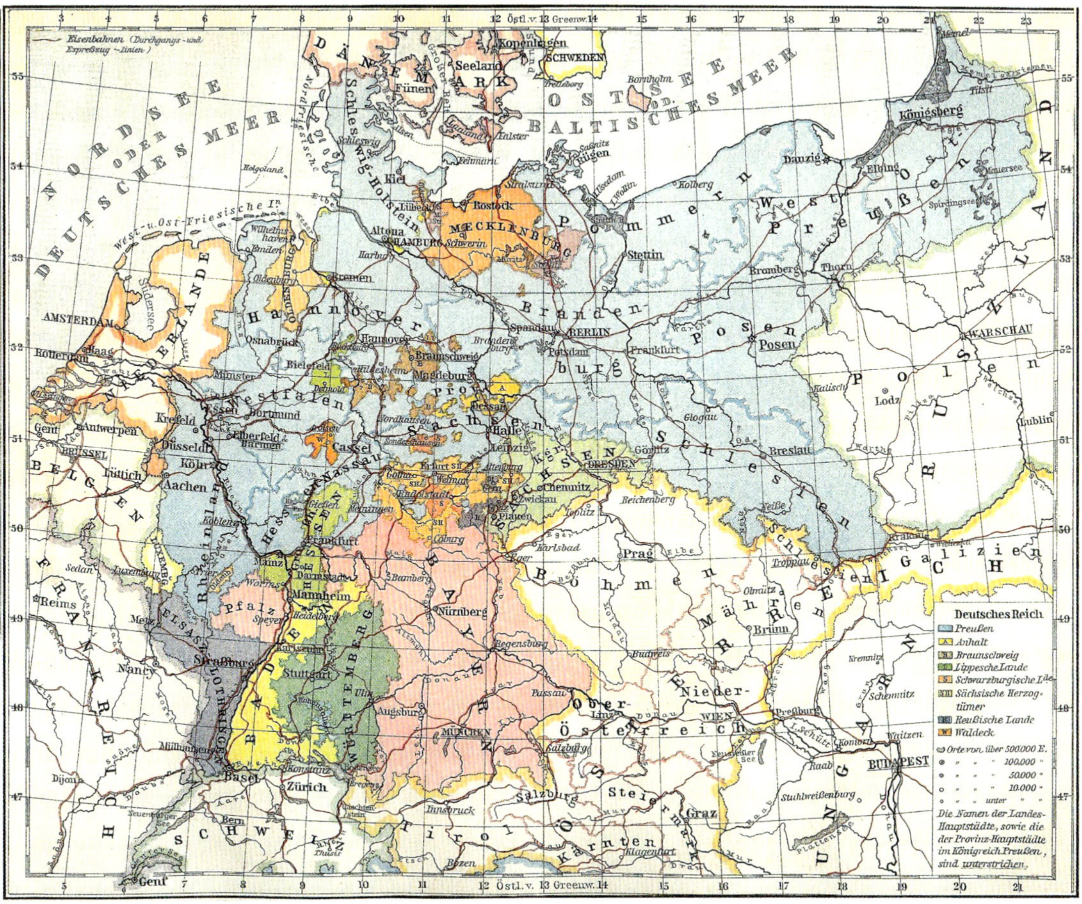

Map of the German Empire in 1900. (Source: Meyers Konversations-Lexikon, 6. Edition, Leipzig 1902)

Kaiser Wilhelm I.

Kaiser Wilhelm II.

Kaiser Friedrich Wilhelm III.

Chancellor Otto Fürst v. Bismarck.

Chancellor Leo Graf v. Caprivi.

Chancellor Berhhard Fürst v. Bülow.

Chancellor Theobald v. Bethmann-Hollweg.

The Reichstag Building.

Reichstag session with Chancellor v. Bülow.

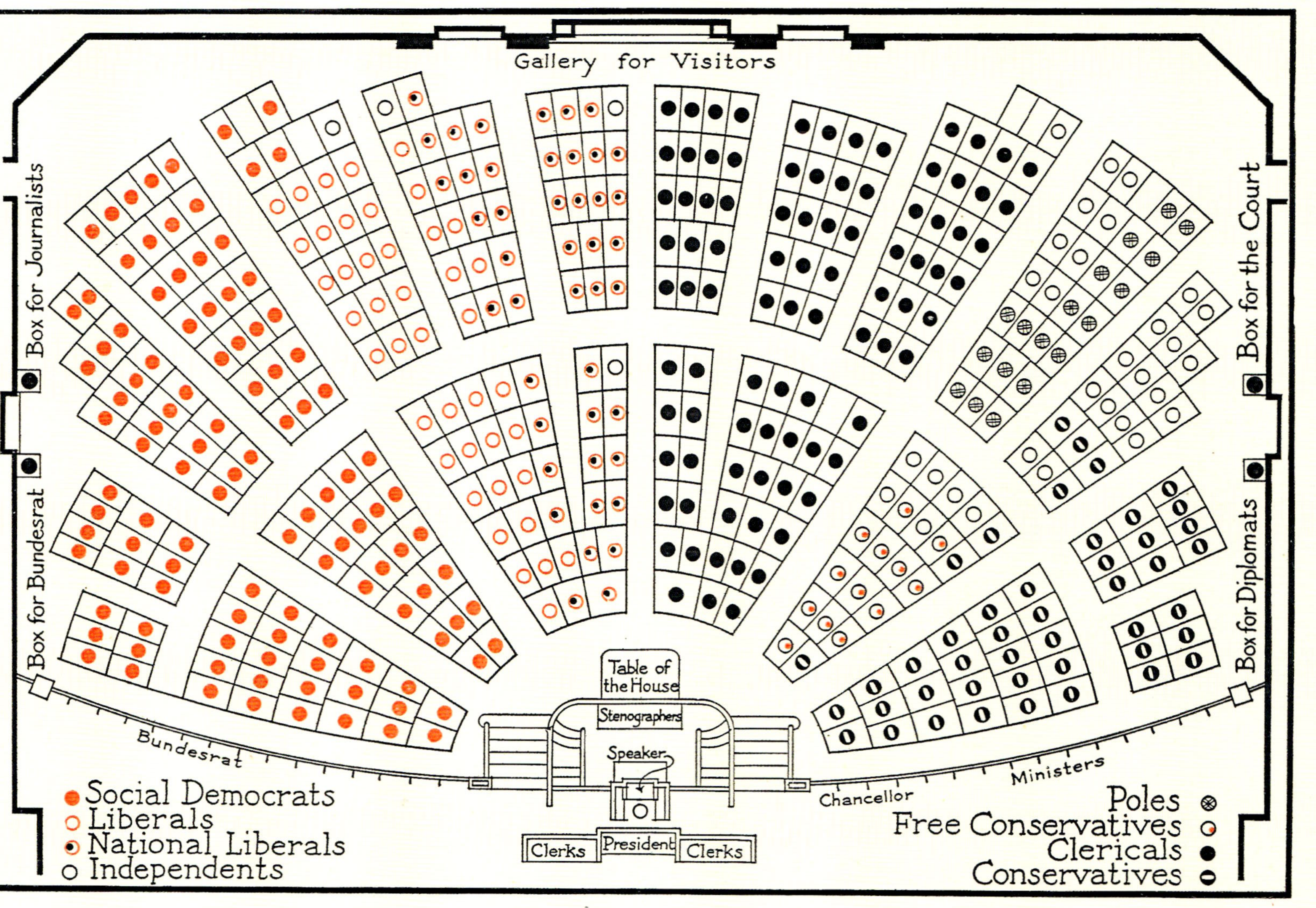

Reichstag chamber after the 1912 Reichstag election. Note the 110 Seats of the Social Democrat Party.

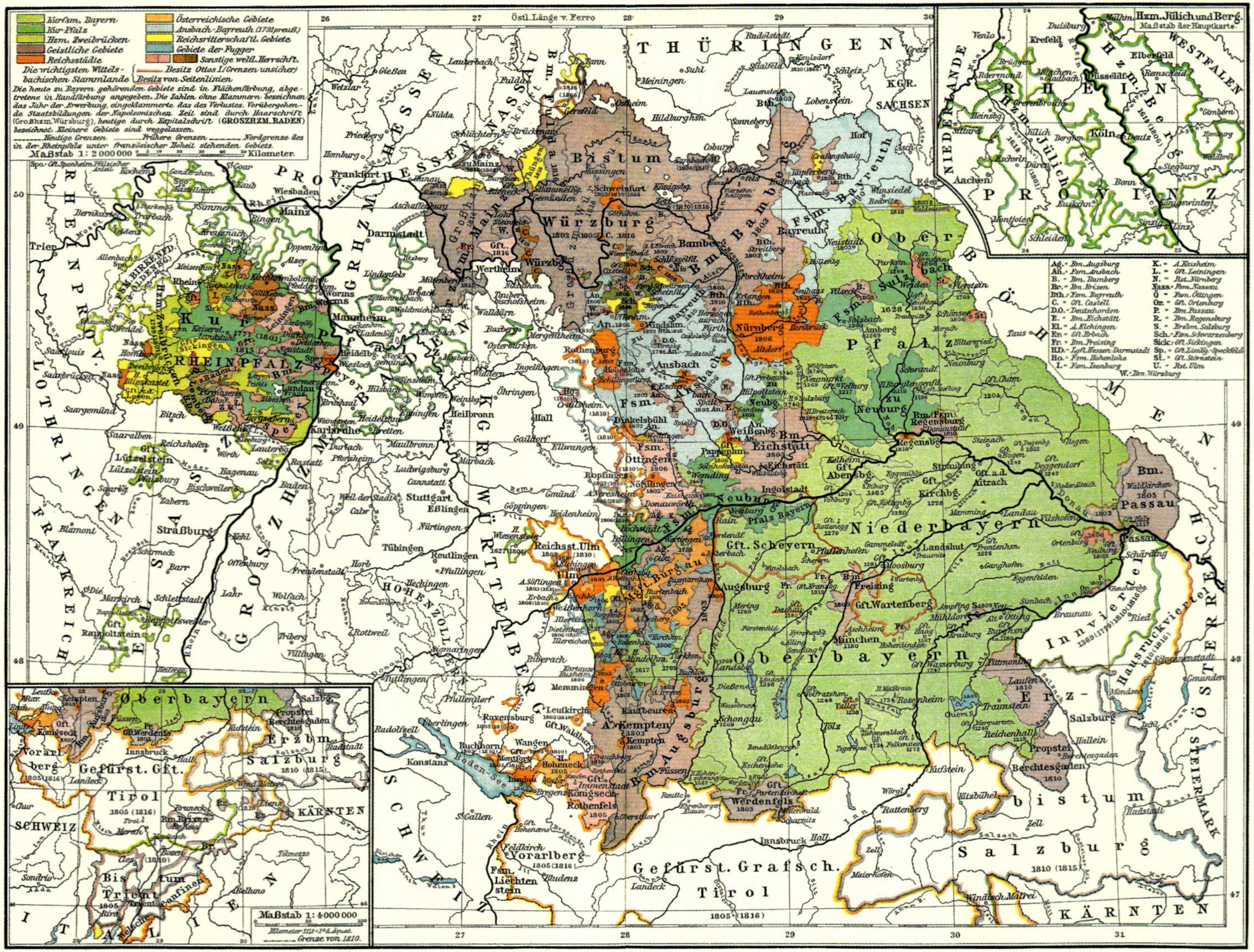

Map of Bavaria.
(Source: Putzgers
Historischer Schul-
Atlas 1903)

King Ludwig II and the later King Otto.

Prince-Regent Ludwig, the later King Ludwig III.

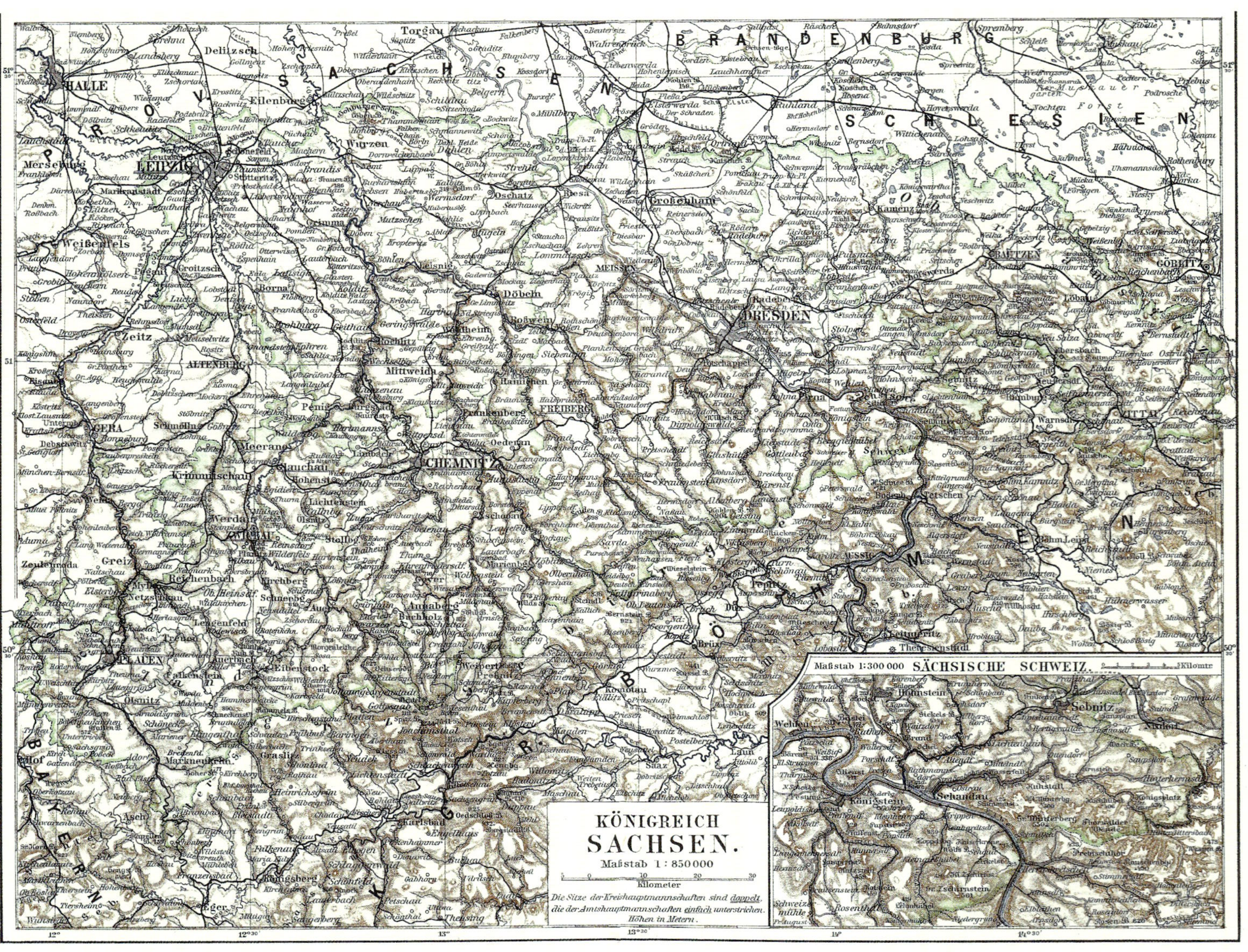

Map of Saxony.

Prince Friedrich August, later King Friedrich August III.

Saxon Crown
Princess Louise.

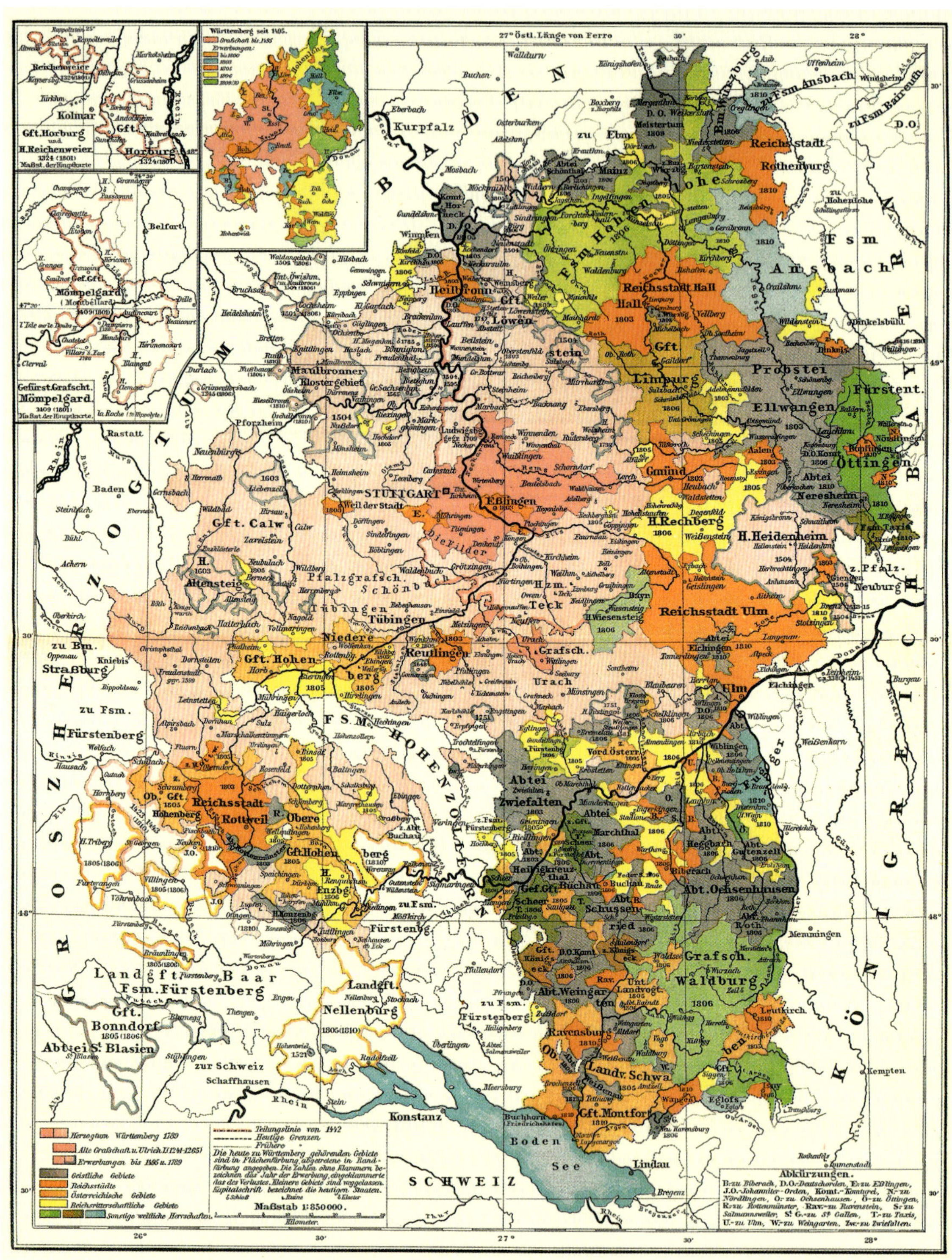

Map of Württemberg. (Source: Putzgers Historischer Schul-Atlas 1903)

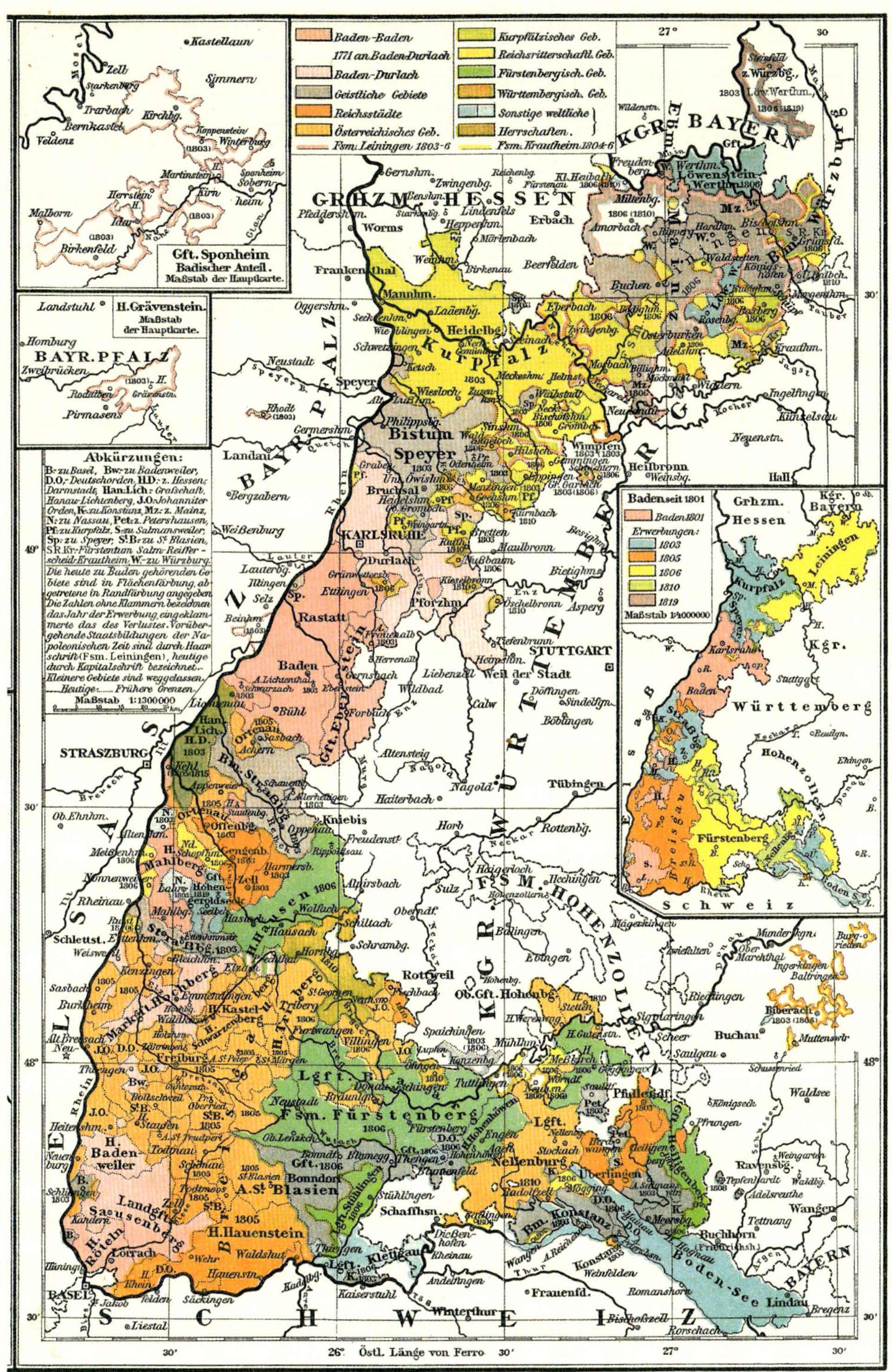
Baden-Baden
1771 an Baden-Durlach
Baden-Durlach
Geistliche Gebiete
Reichsstädte
Österreichisches Geb.
Fsm. Leiningen 1803-6
Kurpfälzisches Geb.
Reichsritterschaftl. Geb.
Fürstenbergisch. Geb.
Württembergisch. Geb.
Sonstige weltliche
Herrschaften.
Fsm. Krautheim 1804-6
Gft. Sponheim
Badischer Anteil.
Maßstab der Hauptkarte.
H. Grävenstein.
Maßstab
der Hauptkarte.
BAYR. PFALZ
Abkürzungen:
B: zu Basel, Bw: zu Badenweiler, D.O.: Deutschorden, H.D.: z. Hessen-Darmstadt, Han.Lich.: Grafschaft Hanau-Lichtenberg, J.O.: Johanniter Orden, K.: zu Konstanz, Mz.: z. Mainz, N: zu Nassau, Pet.: z. Petershausen, Pf.: zu Kurpfalz, S.: zu Salmansweiler, Sp.: zu Speyer, S.B.: zu St. Blasien, S.R.Kr.: Fürstentum Salm-Reifferscheid-Krautheim, W.: zu Würzburg.
Die heute zu Baden gehörenden Gebiete sind in Flächenfärbung, abgetretene in Randfärbung angegeben. Die Zahlen ohne Klammern bezeichnen das Jahr der Erwerbung, eingeklammerte das des Verlustes. Vorübergehende Staatsbildungen der Napoleonischen Zeit sind durch Haarschrift (Fsm. Leiningen), heutige durch Kapitalschrift bezeichnet. Kleinere Gebiete sind weggelassen.
Heutige ..... Frühere Grenzen
Maßstab 1:1300000
Baden seit 1801
Baden 1801
Erwerbungen:
1803
1805
1806
1810
1819
Maßstab 1:4000000
GRHZM. HESSEN
KGR. BAYERN
BAYR. PFALZ
KGR. WÜRTTEMBERG
FSM. HOHENZOLLERN
ELSASS
SCHWEIZ
Kurpfalz
Bistum Speyer
KARLSRUHE
STUTTGART
STRASZBURG
Fsm. Fürstenberg
Boden-See
Östl. Länge von Ferro

Map of Baden.

King Wilhelm II of Württemberg.

Grand Duke Friedrich II of Baden.

Map of Saxon and Thuringian Duchies. (Source: Putzgers Historischer Schul-Atlas 1903)

Prince Heinrich XXXIII of Reuß younger line.

Prince Heinrich XXIV of Reuß elder line.

Carl Eduard, Duke of Saxe-Coburg-Gotha.

Bernhard III, Duke of Saxe-Meiningen.

Wilhelm Ernst, Grand-Duke of Saxe-Weimar-Eisenach.

Günther, Prince of Schwarzburg-Rudolstadt.

Aribert, Prince of Anhalt,
abdicated November 1918.

Edward, Prince of Anhalt, September 1918.

Friedrich, Hereditary Prince of Anhalt, April 1918.

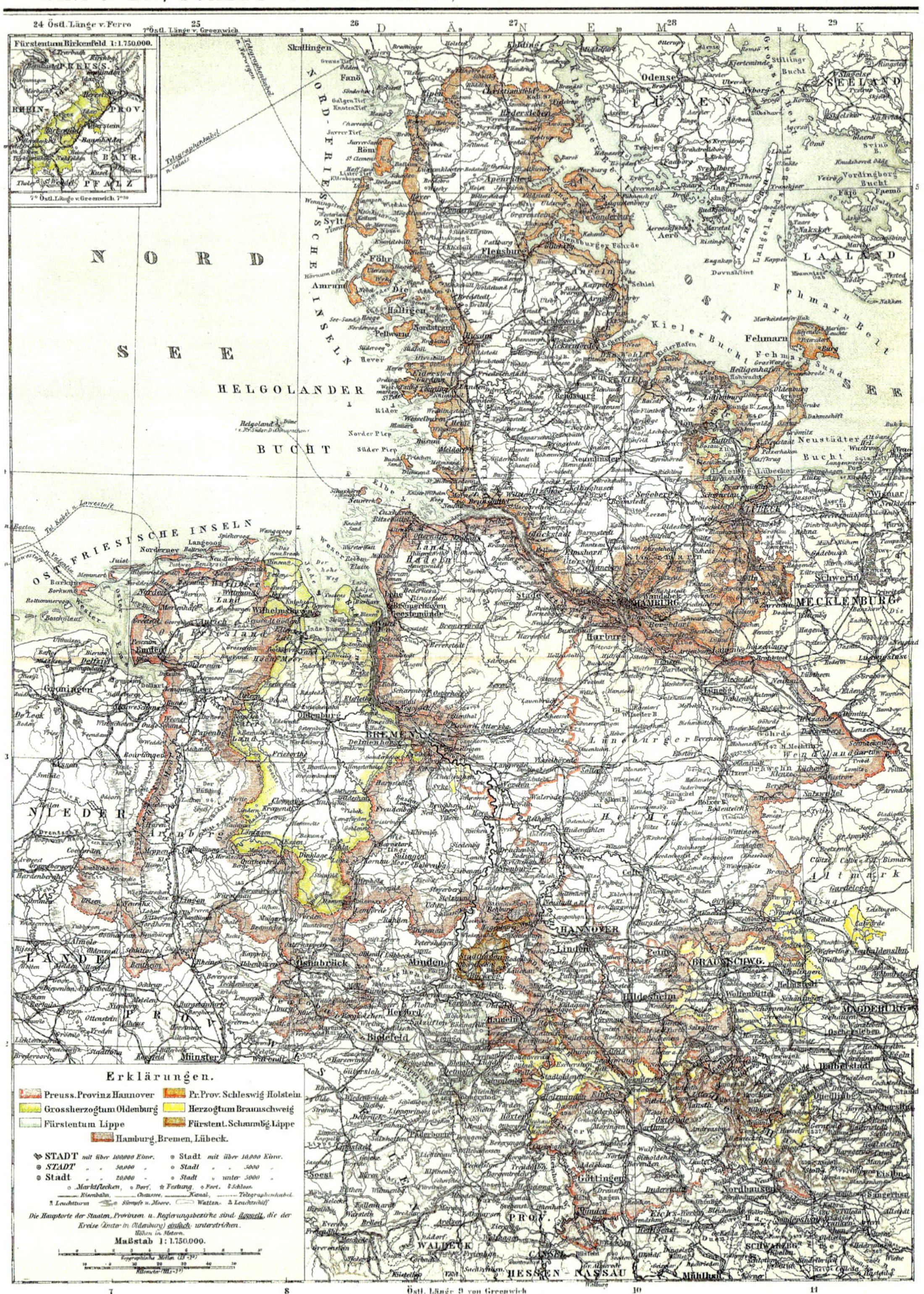

Map of Northern Germany, showing the territories of Oldenburg, Schleswig-Holstein, Brunswick, and Hanover. (Source: Meyers Konversations-Lexikon, 6. Edition, Leipzig 1902)

King George V of Hanover, who was blind.

Ernest the Duke of Cumberland and Duke of Brunswick and Lüneburg. Note the Austrian uniform worn in defiance of Prussia.

Grand-Duke August of Oldenburg.

The Regent of Brunswick, Duke Johann Albrecht of Mecklenburg and his wife Elisabeth.

Prince Adolph II of Schaumburg-Lippe.

Prince Leopold of Lippe-Detmold.

Prince Friedrich of Waldeck and Pyrmont.

Grand-Duke Friedrich Franz IV of Mecklenburg-Schwerin.

Grand-Duke Adolph Friedrich VI of Mecklenburg-Strelitz, who died on 24 February 1918.

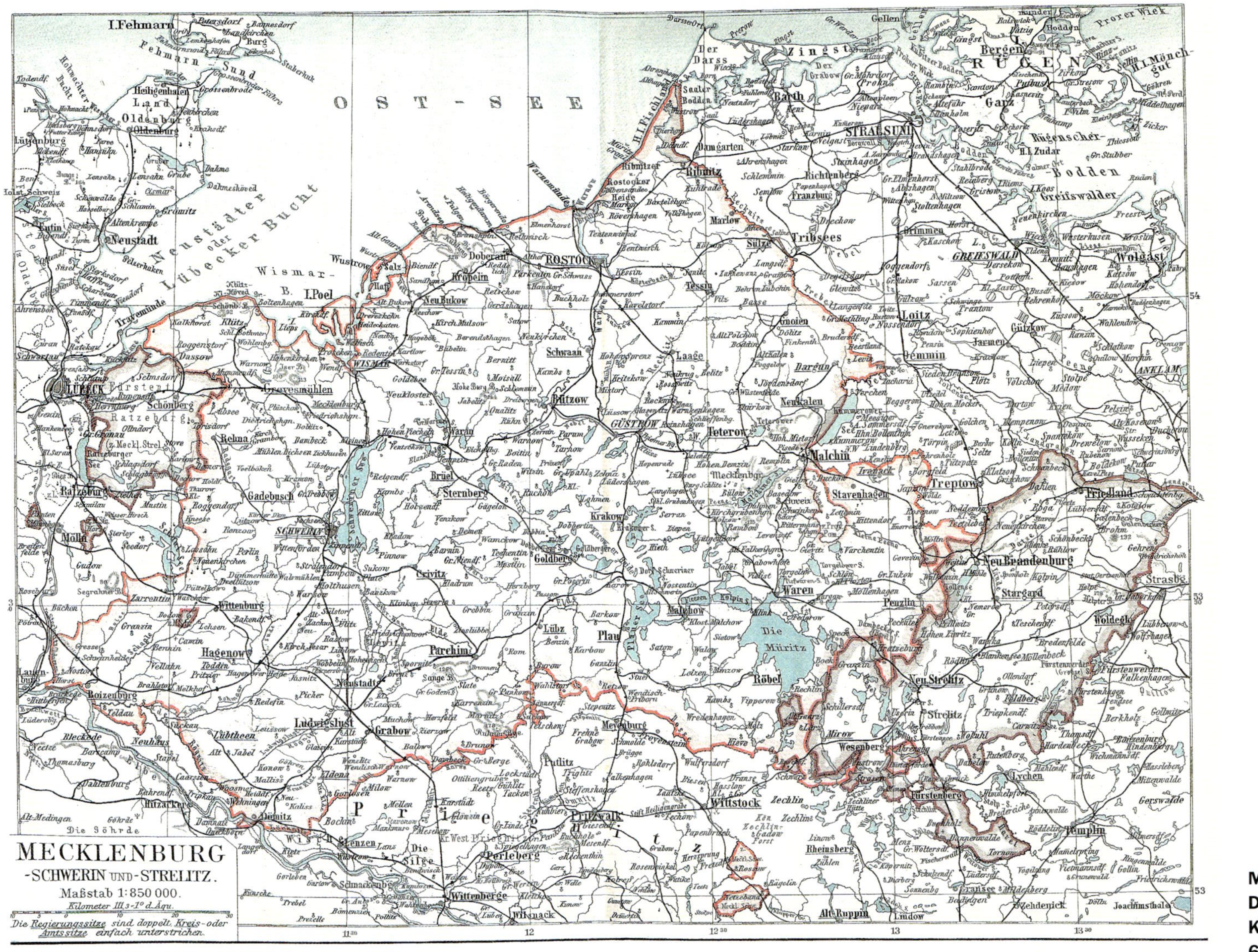

Map of the Mecklenburg Duchies. (Source: Meyers Konversations-Lexikon, 6. Edition, Leipzig 1902)

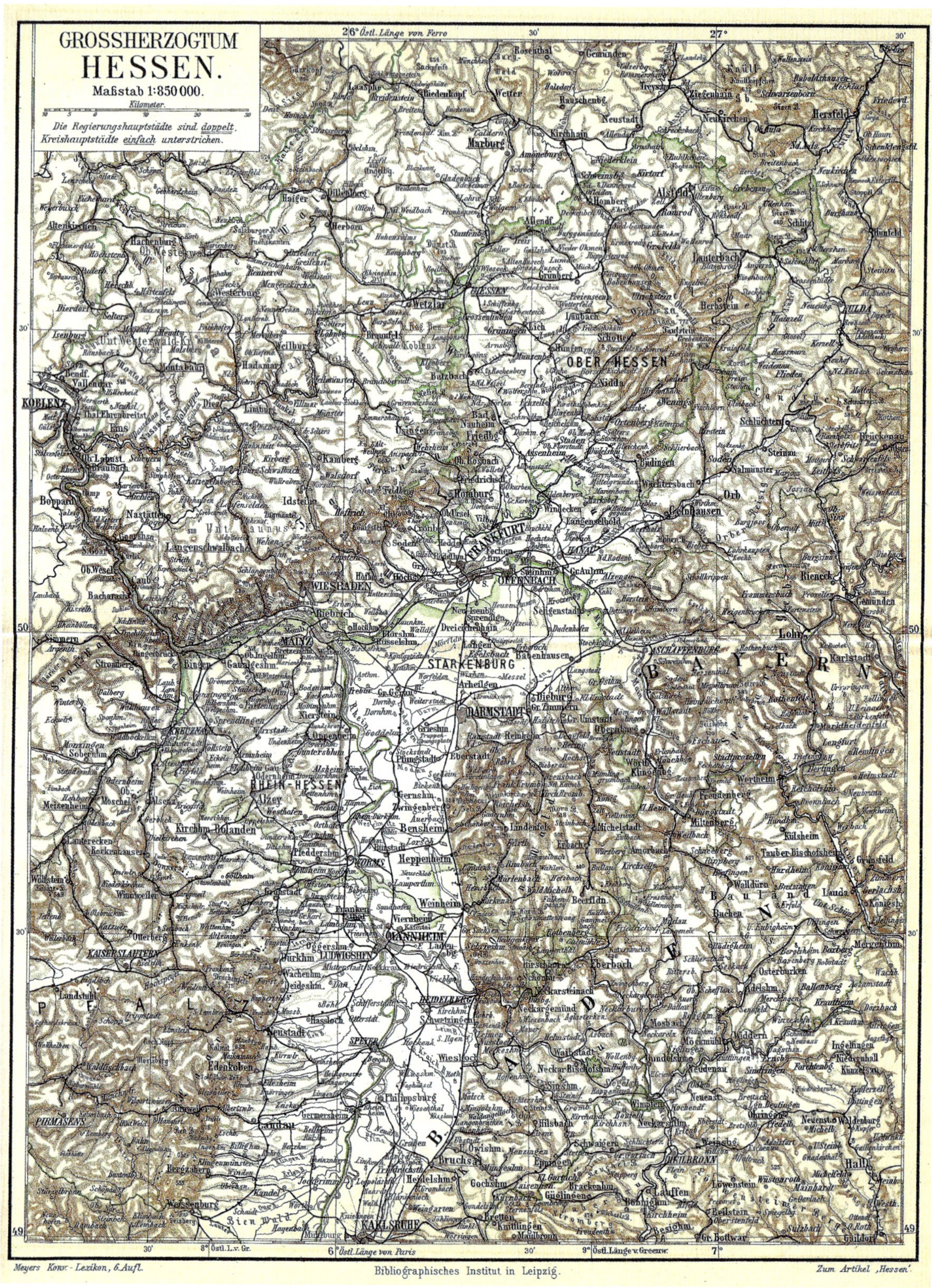

Map of Hesse-Darmstadt. (Source: Meyers Konversations-Lexikon, 6. Edition, Leipzig 1902)

Grand-Duke Ernst Ludwig of Hesse.

Friedrich Wilhelm, the Elector of Hesse.

Hairdresser.

Urban factory worker.

Agricultural workers.

Middle class Gasthaus.

Domestic servants.

Miners.

Language Distribution. Note the immense Polish speaking territories on the Eastern border with Russia. Please also note that Dutch is simply subsumed as Niederdeutsch language. (Source: Putzgers Historischer Schul-Atlas 1903)

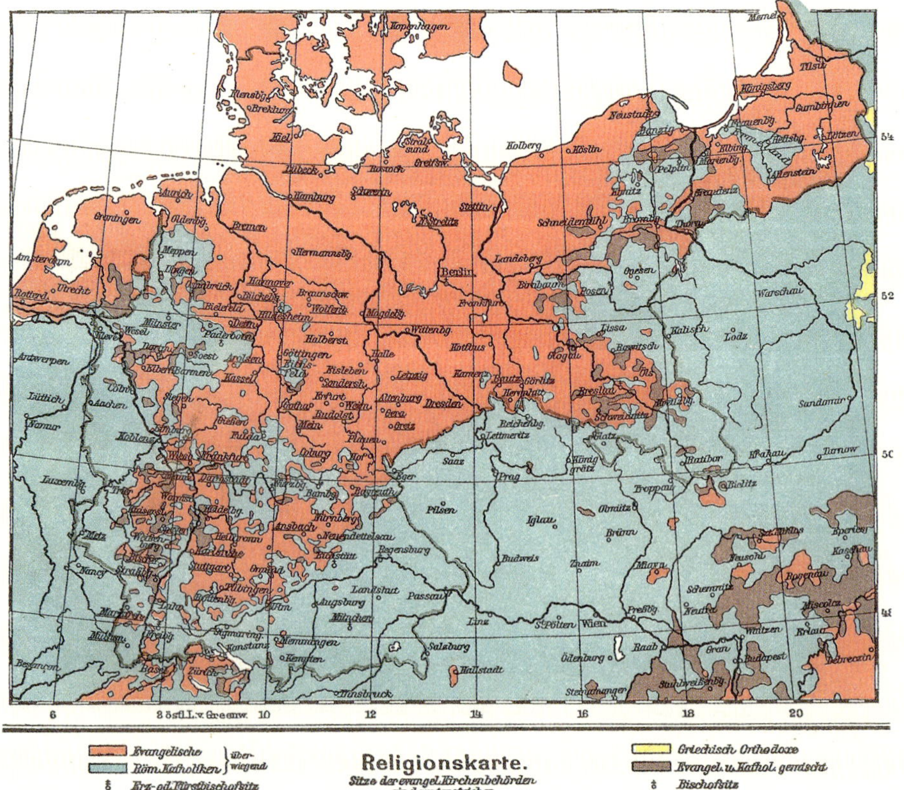

The Religious Divide. Note that the Polish speaking population in the East was also Roman Catholic; whereas, the Prussian territories where Protestant. (Source: Putzgers Historischer Schul-Atlas 1903)

Student society members—schlagende Verbindung.

Bragging scars.

After the Mensur. (Courtesy of Sam Wouters collection.)

The War Minister, Chief of General Staff and Chief of the Military Cabinet with the Kaiser. Note that the Younger Moltke is mistaken as "Graf (Count) Moltke." While his uncle was elevated to "Graf" in 1870 the Younger Moltke still belonged to the lower nobility.

The Kaiser and his Commanders. Includes the Reichskanzler v. Bethmann-Hollweg. Montage created during the early days of the war.

War Minister v. Roon

War Minister v. Einem.

War Minister v. Heeringen.

War Minister v. Falkenhayn.

Chief of General Staff v. Waldersee, depicted here as the Commander in Chief of the Eastern Asian Intervention Force.

The Younger Moltke as Chief of General Staff.

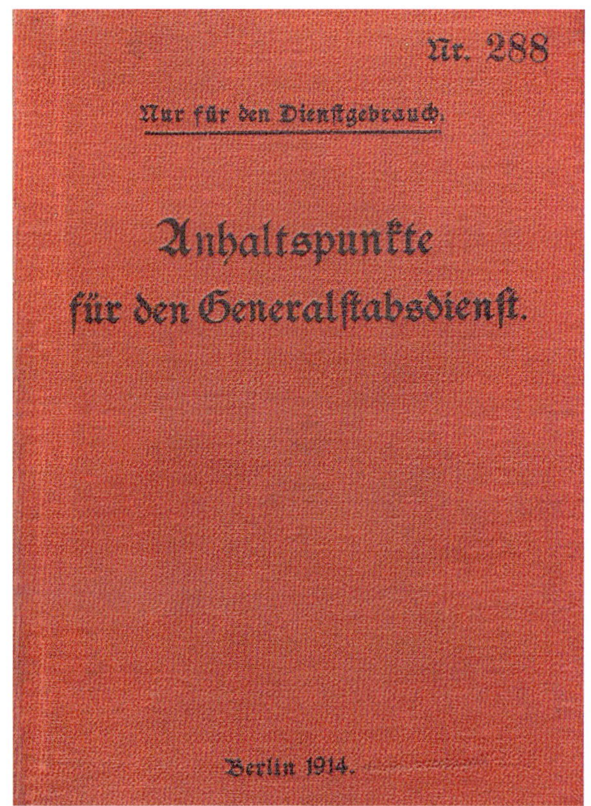

Nr. 288

Nur für den Dienstgebrauch.

Anhaltspunkte für den Generalstabsdienst.

Berlin 1914.

Cover of the General Staff Officer's Manual. Due to the red color it was nicknamed "roter Esel"—"red donkey" in German.

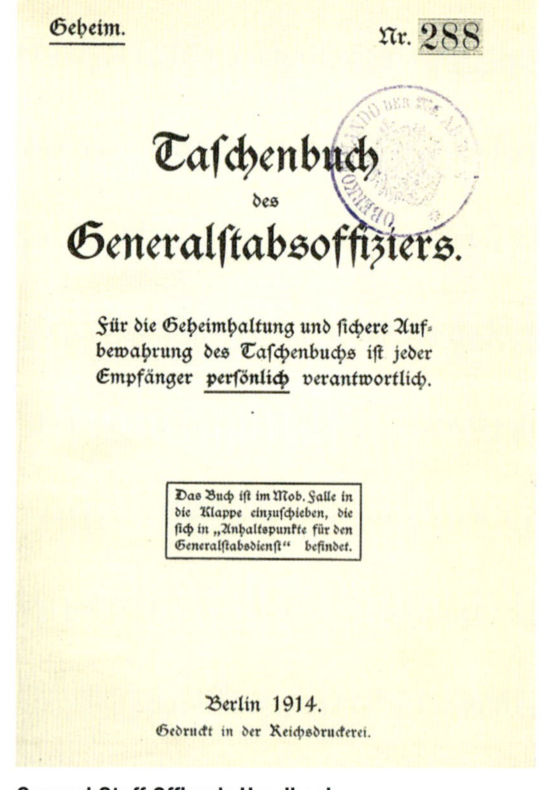

Geheim.

Nr. 288

Taschenbuch des Generalstabsoffiziers.

Für die Geheimhaltung und sichere Aufbewahrung des Taschenbuchs ist jeder Empfänger persönlich verantwortlich.

Das Buch ist im Mob. Falle in die Klappe einzuschieben, die sich in „Anhaltspunkte für den Generalstabsdienst" befindet.

Berlin 1914.

Gedruckt in der Reichsdruckerei.

General Staff Officer's Handbook.

Generaloberst v. Kluck (First Army).

Generaloberst v. Bülow (Second Army, here depicted as a Feldmarschall).

Generaloberst v. Hausen (Third Army).

Generaloberst Albrecht Duke of Württemberg (Fourth Army).

Generaloberst Crown Prince Wilhelm of Prussia (seated, Fifth Army) and his Chief of General Staff Generalleutnant v. Kuhl at Heeresgruppe Kronprinz. Picture taken in 1917. Kuhl was Chief of General Staff First Army in 1914.

Generaloberst Crown Prince Rupprecht of Bavaria (Sixth Army).

Generaloberst v. Heeringen (Seventh Army).

Generaloberst v. Prittwitz und Gaffron (Eighth Army).

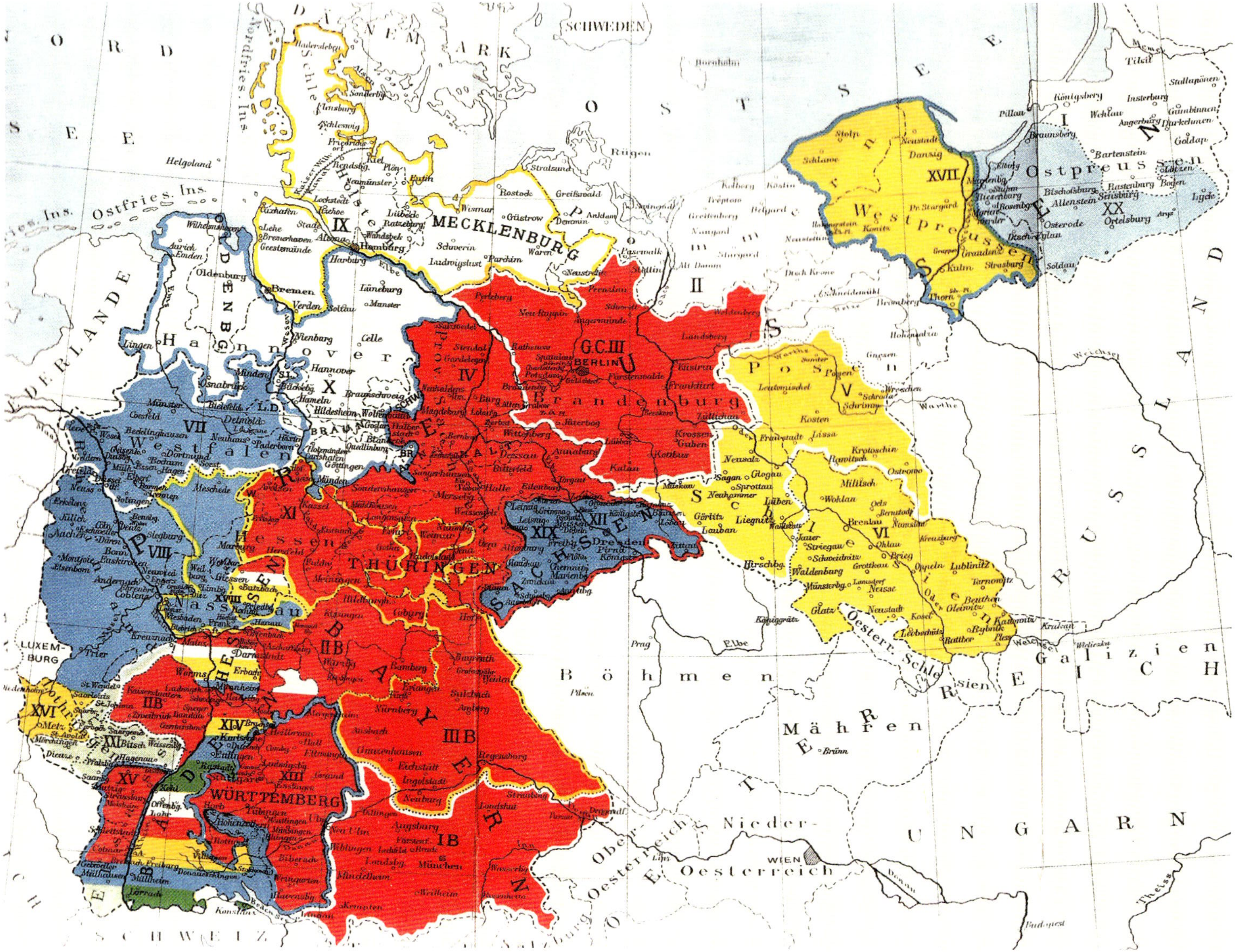

Corps Areas 1914.
(Courtesy of Andreas
Bauer collection.)

Soldiers from 1. Royal Saxon Leib-Grenadier-Regiment Nr. 100 during mobilization.

Machinegun of a MG detachment firing from limber.

Uhlans leaving their barracks during mobilization.

Dragoons fighting dismounted with their carbines 98A.

Horse artillery "riding battery"—all men are horse-mounted, no one riding on limbers.

Field artillery "driving battery"—note the men riding on guns and limbers.

Der Kronprinz beim Geschütz Exercieren
beim 1. Garde Feld Artillerie Regiment

Crown Prince Wilhelm in a field artillery firing position.

Crown Prince Wilhelm with scissor scope.

Railroad soldiers early in the war.

Feldgendarmen, nicknamed "Kettenhunde" in German.

Regimental switchboard early in the war.

Rumpler Taube aircraft.

Landwehr soldiers in 1914, armed with rifles model 1888 and bayonets model 1871.

Hauptmann der Landwehr Maximilian Emil Hugo Fehringer.

Picture of 4 company—Reserve Regiment XIV Army Corps, assembled in Bitche 1912.

Aristocratic Guard Officer from the Kaiser Alexander Garde-Grenadier-Regiment Nr. 1. Note the headgear reflecting the tradition of the army of Frederick the Great.

Very young cadets from a Voranstalt.

Pages from the Hauptkadettenanstalt.

King's Birthday (Judging from the uniforms and helmets it must be in Bavaria.): "The reserve officers are supposed to show up all at the divine services. Service for the Catholic gentlemen will be in the cathedral, for the Protestant gentlemen at the Lukaskirche and for the gentleman from the train it will be in the synagogue." (Source: Thöny: Kadetten)

Kaserne of Kürassier Regiment 6.

Stube of a Saxon regiment-early war picture.

Soldiers' canteen 3. Garde-Regiment zu Fuß.

Soldiers' store—early war picture.

Georg Balthasar Mohr: Königlicher Rechnungsrat und Garnisons-Verwaltungs–Direktor. Note the small silver eagle sitting on the Prussian eagle on his helmet and identifying him as Beamter.

The Letter J.

First day of service (Einstellungstag)—1,085 days to go.

Rifle Inspection.

Rifle range: Soldier recording results and signaling to the firing assistants operating the targets from covered positions. Rifle ranges were always embedded into the earthen walls to avoid uncontrolled ricochetting bullets from leaving the range.

Marksmanship training during the early war.

Maneuver—entraining troops.

Bavarian infantry battalion commander and his staff during war games with a field grade officer present wearing war games referee's white cover for the spike helmet and arm band.

Kaisermanöver, situational analysis.

Different types of units during maneuvers. Please note the band around the helmet covers indicating the "enemy" party always marked in red; whereas the other side was marked in blue on maps and had no special bands on their helmet covers.

Maneuvers 1907—the Commanding General of XVI Army Corps General v. Prittwitz und Gaffron (later commander Eighth Army) with his staff. Note the officer in the middle and the soldier lying in the foreground left wearing a band around their helmet covers marking them as members of the "enemy" party.

The Maneuvers of XI Army Corps in 1900. In 1901 umpires at maneuvers were authorized white armbands and helmet covers in an AKO. Clearly the white armbands were used in this instance prior to the AKO.

The Invincibles—Commander: "At the end we got the enemy successfully trapped." Adjutant: "Sir, may I please draw your attention to the fact that the enemy is led by the Prince." Commander: "What? Damned! Yes, all true—let the men turn around and hurry back." (Source: Thöny, Militaer)

Feldmarschall Graf v. Moltke (the Elder).

Typical maneuver picture: too dense firing lines.

Misapplication of the idea of firing lines.

Machineguns in firing position during early war training—note the range finder.

Machinegun company of a Hesse infantry regiment—typical peace-time training.

Kaisermanöver 1912—Bavarian cavalry division ready for attack.

Husaren werden über die
Gefechtslage unterrichtet.

Hussar patrol being briefed.

Hussar firing line 1912 shoulder to shoulder.

Uhlan firing line 1912—note the lances.

Telegraph formation on parade 1912.

Field Artillery in covered position by the books. (Source: field artillery manual D.V.E. Nr. 414a of 15 May 1913)

Flugzeug geht zur Beobachtung vor.

...and how it really looked.

French field guns model 1897.

Observation post for German battery commanders designed after the French model. (Source: field artillery manual D.V.E. Nr. 414a of 15 May 1913)

Austrian 30.5cm Skoda Mortar in firing position.

Brüssel.
Österreichische Kanonen in der „Caserne d' Artillerie".
(Mit diesen Kanonen wurden Namur und Maubeuge bombardirt.)
3393

Austrian 30.5 cm Skoda Mortar in travelling position with Austrian gunners in Brussels August 1914.

Super-heavy 42 cm Mortar Battery with γ—Gerät bedding guns. There were two mortars per battery, the second mortar can be seen in the background.

Original-Aufnahme vom Kriegsschauplatz.
Die durch ein einziges 42 cm Geschoss zerstörten Betondecken eines Panzerturmes des Forts Loucin.
Kr. 86.
VERLAG VON
GUSTAV LIERSCH & C
BERLIN, S.W.

Fort de Loncin (note the misspelling: "Loucin" on the postcard), northwest of Liège, destroyed by a 42 cm shell.

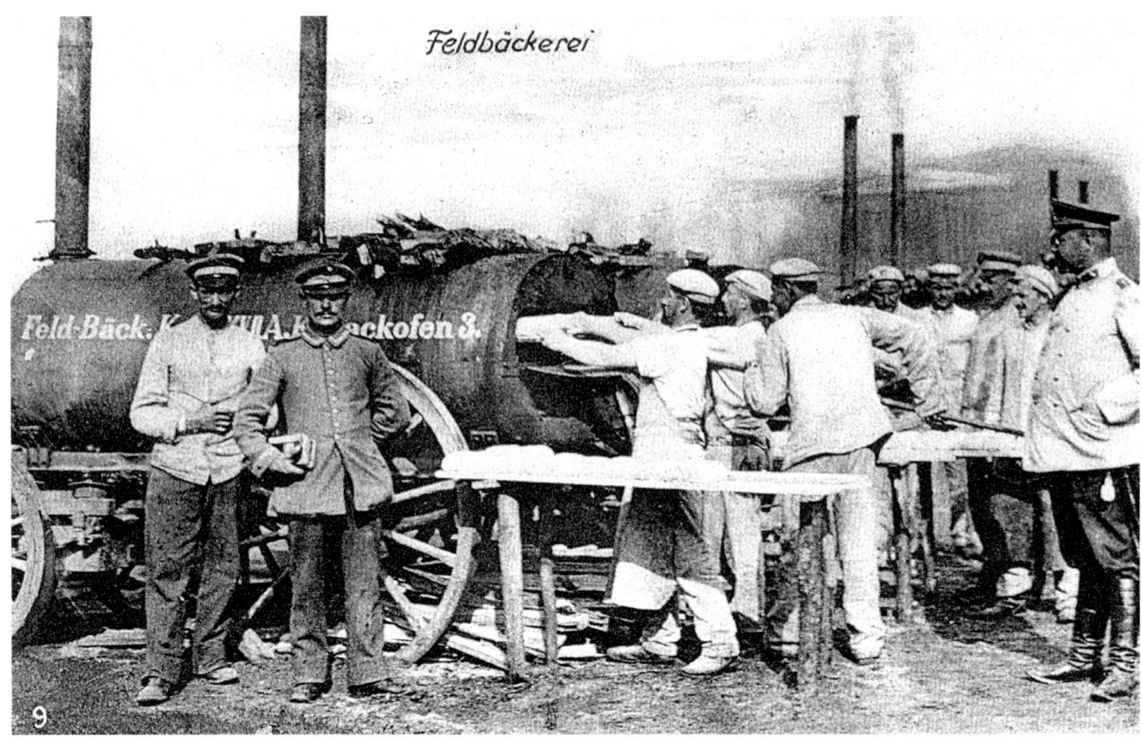

Field bakery.

Rolling field kitchen.

Horse-drawn subsistence supply column.

Cavalry motor transport column with light army trucks.

Chief of the Great General Staff: Generaloberst Graf v. Schlieffen.

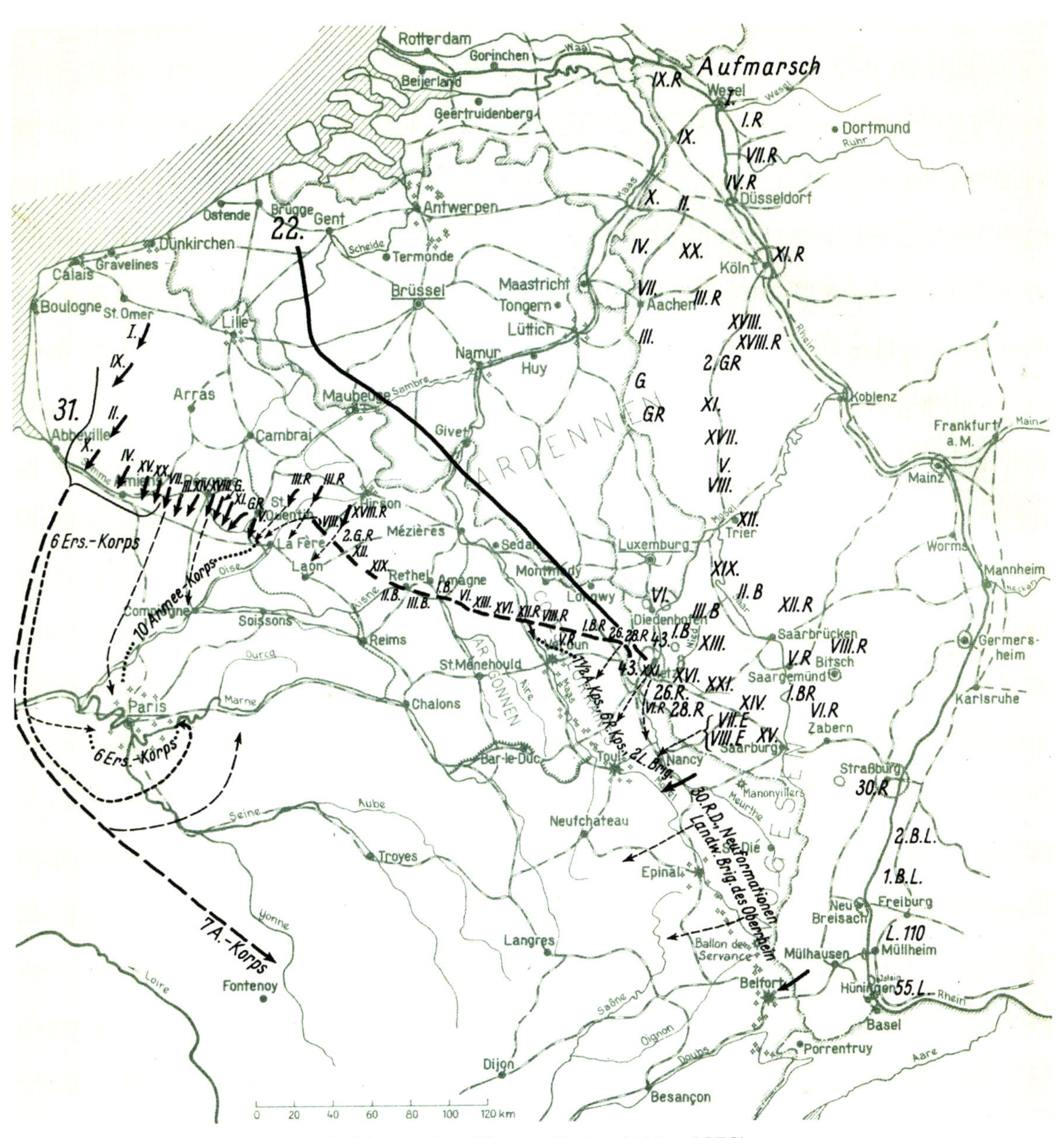

Schlieffen Plan. (Source: Gerhard Ritter 1956)

Decorated soldier ready to be deployed.

Catholic field service of a Bavarian formation before leaving for France.

Kriegsbilder aus den Vogesen Auf dem Marsche zur Stellung.

Deployment of an infantry unit in the Vosges mountains.

Infantry taking cover behind a wall.

Eisb. Nr. 1 Berlin, den 31. Juli 1914.

An

die Eisenbahn-Abteilung des großen Generalstabs, Sekt. II c

2 Pferde, { 1. M.T., 9^{10} abds, ab 9^{18} } Hamb. Güterbahnhof, 9^{10} abds. ab

Begleiter: Husar Stiller, Hus. R. 4.

Bestimmungsort: Hannover an 2. Tag 5^{30}

Marquard

Oberst u. Chef des Generalstabes X. Res. Korps.

Mobilization schedule of Oberst Marquard, Great General Staff, acting as Chief of General Staff X Reserve Corps after mobilization. The colonel sent two horses on first mobilization day (2 August) from Hamburg railroad station in Berlin to Hanover, where the X Reserve Corps was mobilized. Please note that Oberst Marquard was already signing as Chef des Generalstabes X. Res. Korps although mobilization was not yet officially announced on 31 July 1914. Both mobilization schedules found together with others in a Rangliste 1914 when bought from an antique book dealer.

Eisb. Nr. 6.

Anzahl der Pferde mit Zielpunkt	Mit welchen Sonderzug	vom Bahnhof	Abfahrt St.	Min.
1 Pferd nach Hannover	Zug Nr. 1 Fahrtnum. 13401	Hamburger Güterbahnhof	9	18

Baron de la Motte-Fouqué

Hauptmann.

Mobilization schedule of Hauptmann Baron de la Motte-Fouqué, Great General Staff, acting as Ib officer of the Second Army after mobilization. The captain sent his horse on the first mobilization day (2 August) from Hamburg railroad station in Berlin to Hanover, where the Second Army HQ was mobilized based upon the existing peacetime staff of the 3rd Army Inspection plus additional general staff officers.

An incredible picture of a group from Reserve Infanterie Regiment 219 on 4 October 1914 just before their deployment. What is most interesting is that these soldiers are equipped with police helmets not military helmets! The musician uniforms are "enhanced" artificially. What did they go to Flanders with? Picture taken at Lager Heuberg. (Courtesy of B. Butterworth collection.)

Station .... Abteilung ....

angenommen am ....../...... 19...... Uhr ...... Min. ...... mittags, durch ......

befördert am ....../...... 19...... Uhr ...... Min. ...... mittags, durch ......

aufgenommen am ....../...... 19...... Uhr ...... Min. ...... mittags, durch ......

Fern- Licht- Funk- **Spruch** von ....

Dienstliche Zusätze:

Absender:	Meldg.	Ort	Dat.	Zeit
	Abgegangen			
	Angekommen			

An

Kommandostelle	Station	Rufzeichen
1. Armee (A.O.K.)	Schw. Stat.	va
2. Armee (A.O.K.)	Schwere Stat.	cn
Höherer Kavallerie-Kommandeur 2: 2. Kav. Div.	Schwere Stat.	sa
	Leichte Stationen	sb, sc
4. Kav. Div.	Schwere Stationen	sd
	Leichte Stationen	sg, sl
9. Kav. Div.	Schwere Stationen	sm
	Leichte Stationen	sn, so
3. Armee (A.O.K.)	Schwere Stationen	km
4. Armee (A.O.K.)	Schwere Stationen	rn
Höherer Kavallerie-Kommandeur 1: Garde Kav. Div.	Schwere Stationen	ga
	Leichte Stationen	gb, gc
5. Kav. Div.	Schwere Stationen	gd
	Leichte Stationen	gf, gh

Radio call signs of the armies and HKKs on the Western front in 1914—handwritten note of a General Staff Officer of the Second Army, found in the General Staff Officer's Handbook of 1914. As can be seen, only the cavalry divisions carried their own radio stations, while the HKKs had none.

Gerhard Tappen—here with the rank of a Generalmajor.

Richard Hentsch.

Erich Friedrich Wilhelm Ludendorff, picture made in 1918.

French Generals Joffre, Castelnau and Pau.

Fieldmarshal French.

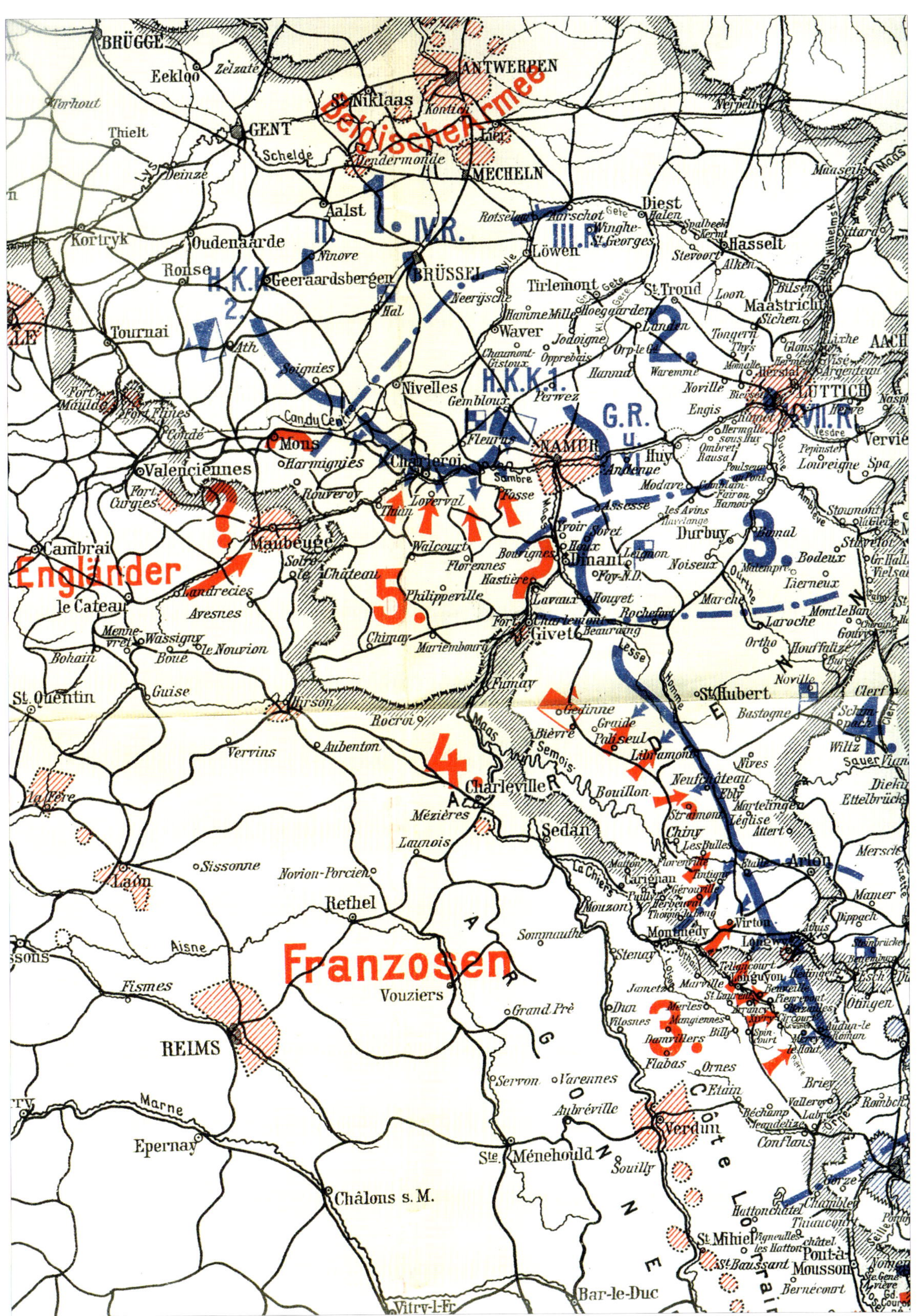

Tactical map of 22 August. (Source: Reichsarchiv vol 1, 1925, map 5)

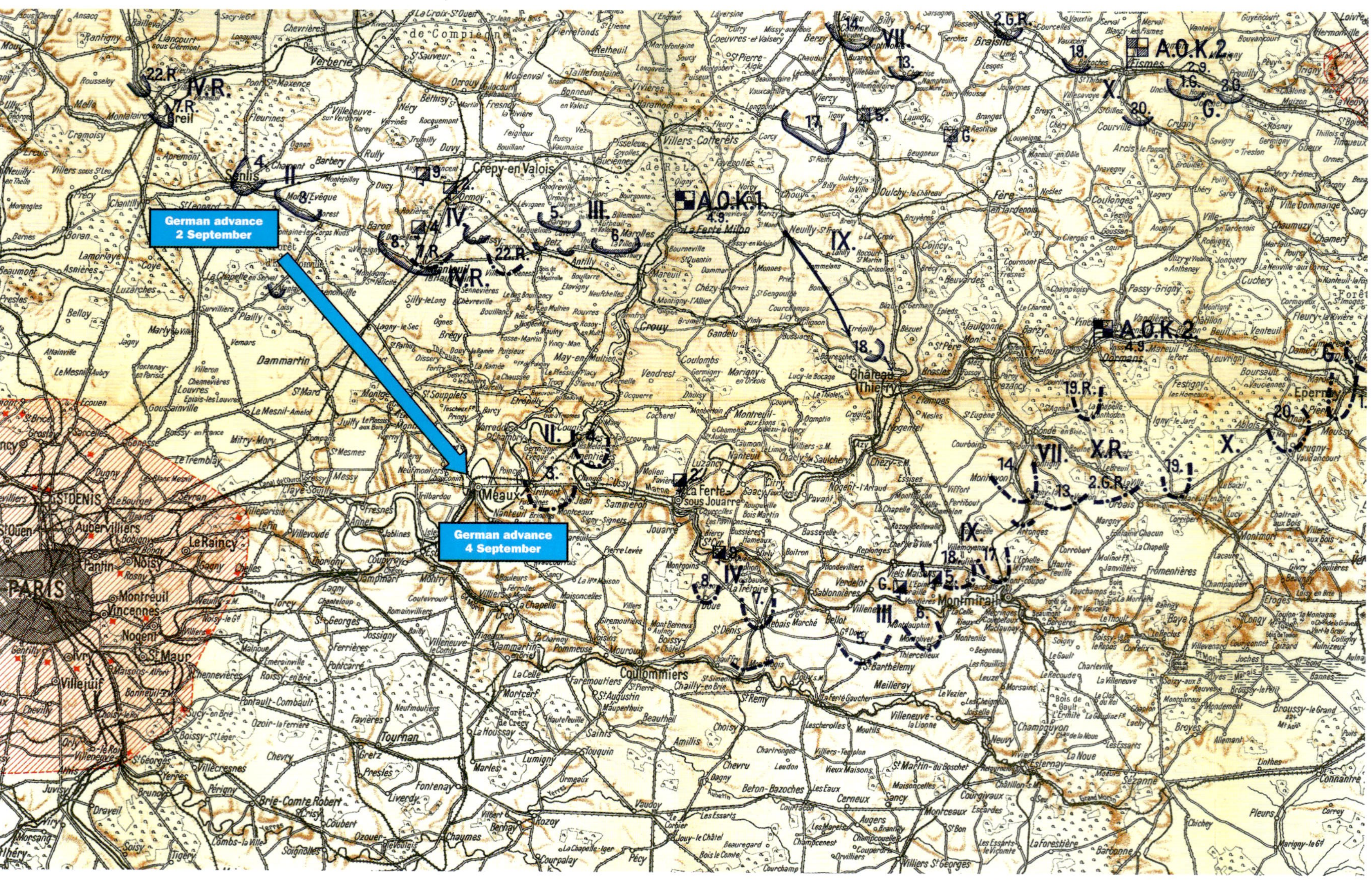

Tactical map of 2 and 4 September. (Source: Reichsarchiv vol 3, 1926)

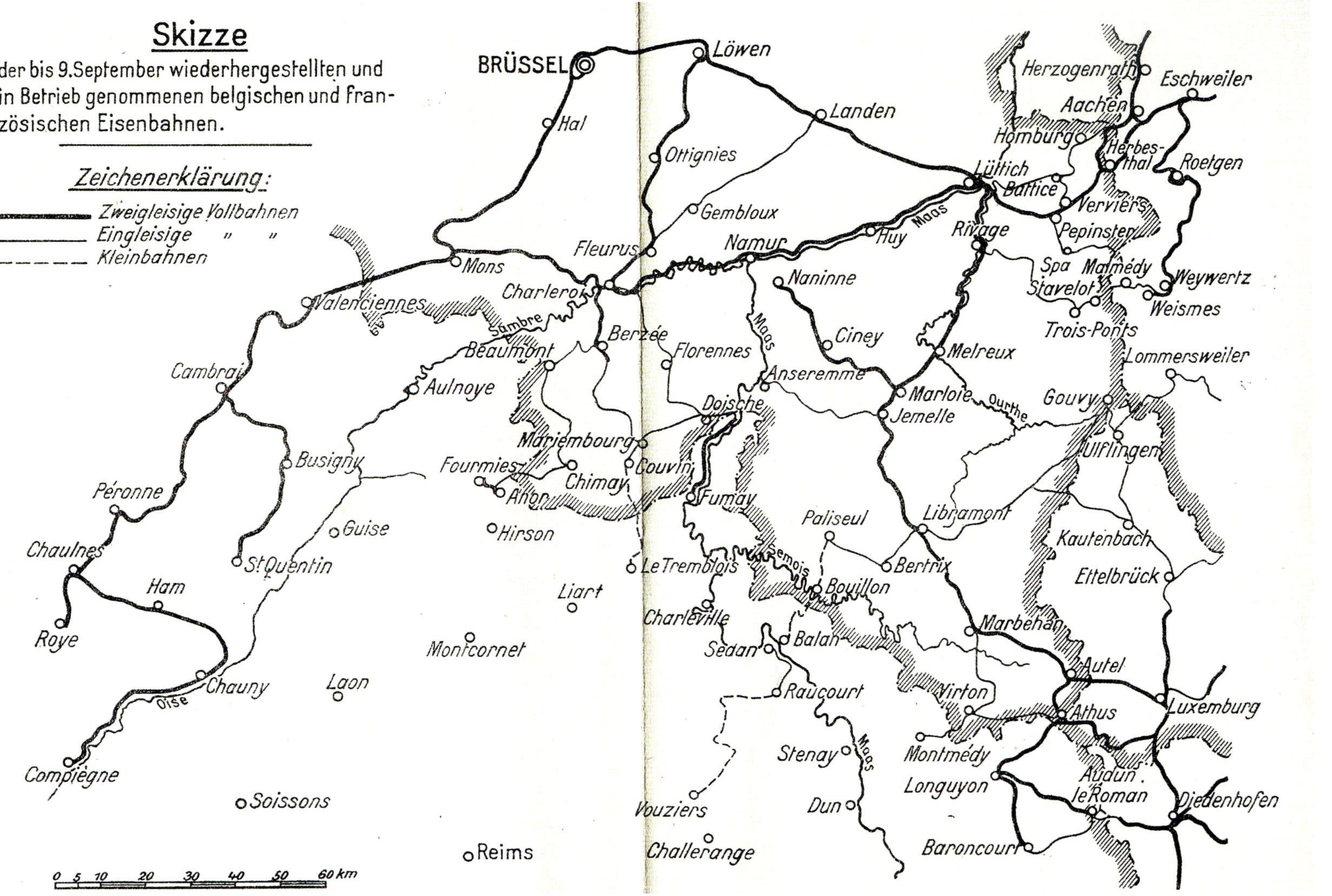

German operated railroad lines in Belgium and France 9 September. (zweigleisige Vollbahnen = double-track railways, eingleisige Vollbahnen = single-track railways, Kleinbahnen = narrow-gauge railways). (Source: Reichsarchiv vol 3, 1926, sketch 7)

REPUBLIQUE FRANCAISE
10c
POSTES
154e Régiment Infanterie, 10e Compagnie, à la frontière
Photo Leroy. - Lérouvil

10ᵉ Compagnie, 154ᵉ Régiment d'Infanterie at the French-German border. Picture taken west of Metz before the war—please note the German boundary post on the right.

French soldiers of several regiments in 1914.

Guerre Franco-Allemande 1914
Tambours et Clairons du 53e Territorial.

Horns and drum of the French 53ᵉ Régiment d'Infanterie Territoriale in 1914.

to successfully pass the Fähnrich[36] examination, which was taken in front of a special examination committee (*Oberexaminationskommission*) in Berlin. The commander would not give final approval until the candidate passed this Fähnrich exam. Cramming with a tutor for the exam was a standard practice.[37]

Those who were not cadets attempted to be selected as Fahnenjunker. This rank went through several iterations in an attempt to make it more professional. Prior to 1900, the regimental commander promoted the candidates after six months to the rank of Fähnrich. After 1900, more stringent criteria were enacted in an endeavor to end nepotism. The criteria required the candidate for Fahnenjunker to have a one-year certificate but not the Abitur. Then prior to selection, the candidate had to pass a specific written test of general knowledge. If the individual passed, he enrolled as a Fahnenjunker and was allowed to take the Fähnrich examination. In infantry and dragoon regiments, he was known as a Fahnenjunker; in other cavalry regiments, a Fahnenjunker was referred to as a *Kornett* or a *Standartenjunker*. In artillery regiments, the individual was called a *Stückjunker*. The amount of time spent as a Fahnenjunker varied a great deal.

Step 3—Pass the Fähnrich Examination

In theory, each candidate was supposed to have a Prima certificate (*Primareiferzeugnis*) or special dispensation to take the Fähnrich examination.[38] Ninety percent had a Prima certificate and 75 percent passed the Fähnrich exam the first time. A man could take it again; few failed the second time. If indeed there was a second failure, candidates were transferred into the ranks as an enlisted soldier or *Unteroffizier*. In 1890, the Kaiser demanded grading leniency for this examination. If leniency still did not work, he used dispensations that totaled over 1,000 between 1901 and 1912.[39] There still were failures. In 1878, eight cadets failed the exam. All eight eventually were made Fähnrich, and six of them earned their commission. Manfred von Richthofen, the Red Baron, failed the examination and was sent to the Ulanen-Regiment Kaiser Alexander III. von Rußland (Westpreußisches) Nr. 1 as an Unteroffizier. Eight months later, he was made a Fähnrich and eventually was commissioned. This promotion put his date of rank behind his classmates of 1911.[40]

Step 4—Spend Time in the Regimental Ranks

A patent or *charakterisierter* Fähnrich was a graduate of a *Kadettenschule*, who served with a regiment before gaining his commission. A Fahnenjunker was an officer candidate who held a certificate from a Gymnasium and who had passed the required examination in military subjects and served with a regiment before obtaining his commission. The non-cadet individuals who passed the Fähnrich exam joined the cadet Fähnriche and moved into the regiment as a *Gemeiner* (private) but were referred to as an *Avantageur*. Officially, the title was *Offizieraspirant*—that title was officially changed in 1899 to Fahnenjunker. He lived in the barracks for a period that varied by regiment from one to six weeks. He started as a *Gemeiner* and when he moved out of the barracks became a *Gefreiter*. A Patent Fähnrich was never a private but a Gefreiter. He bore all costs associated

[36] *Fahne* means flag in the German language. Going back to Frederick the Great, *Fahnenjunker* and Fähnrich carried the battalion flags. Similarly *Standarte* is the German language expression for the flag of a cavalry squadron, whereas *Stück*—piece in English language—is the traditional word for an artillery piece.

[37] (Pflugk-Hartung, 1896), pp. 110–111.

[38] For details about the Fähnrich examination, please check (Kriegsministerium, 1905), pp. 4–5 and pp. 39–48.

[39] (Clemente, 1992), p. 43.

[40] (Moncure, 1993), pp. 239–241.

with his service in the same way as a one-year volunteer. At this point, he could also have a civilian batman (personal servant).[41]

When promoted to Unteroffizier, he was permitted to dine in the officers' mess. At this point, he was called a Fähnrich. A *Fähnrichsvater* was appointed to be his mentor. The Fähnrichsvater was responsible for the practical military education of his officer candidates, although long drinking bouts were commonplace.[42] While the Fähnrich was encouraged to spend freely, indebtedness was a major embarrassment for the entire mess. The amount of time spent in Step Four decreased dramatically. At first, it was five to six months and then, by the turn of the century, it was three months (two if the individual came from a cadet school).[43] Eventually, the time in the ranks was so short that men had insufficient time to absorb the necessary understanding of the system. Only the reserve officers who went through the year as an OYV understood the difficulties of the lower enlisted ranks.[44] A major effort during the time in the ranks was an assessment of the Fähnrich. All officers dealing with the Fähnrich contributed to the appraisal that was then passed to the responsible battalion commander and from there to the regimental commander.[45]

Step 5—Be Promoted to Fähnrich if "All Went Well"

The aspirant applied to the colonel that he was "qualified" and deserved a military qualification certificate (*Dienstzeugnis*) that was issued by the regimental commander based upon the Fähnrich's appraisal. If approved by the colonel, the applicant was officially promoted to Fähnrich and paid a salary. He was also eligible to wear the silver sword knot (*Portepee*). Initially called *Portepeefähnrich,* that title was eliminated in 1899. For example, between 1892 and 1894, 59 percent of the cadets became Brevet Fähnrich, 10 percent Patent Fähnrich and about 33 percent were "Selekta."[46]

Step 6—A Course at the *Kriegsschule*

Cadet Abitur holders, Selekta cadets, and civilian Abitur holders who had been university students for a year were exempted from this requirement from the Kriegsschule. The ages of the attending students showed that longer civilian education took time and money; whereas, a man could skip the education and go into the commissioning system and start making money and seniority.[47] The course at the Kriegsschule took nine months and prepared the officer candidate for the officer examination. During these nine months, the Fähnriche were taught tactics of the different arms, weaponry, fortification and field fortification, sketching and drawing, army organization (*Truppenkunde*) and military administration.[48] The length of this course shortened as the need for officers became more pressing and cadets sought their commissions in a year. At the end of the course, the candidate took the officer's exam. This course was eventually reduced from 12 to seven months in length.[49]

---

41 (Clemente, 1992), p. 72.
42 (Pflugk-Hartung, 1896), pp. 112–113.
43 (Clemente, 1992), pp. 73–74.
44 (Clemente, 1992), pp. 150–151
45 (Kriegsministerium, 1905), pp. 5–6.
46 (Clemente, 1992), pp. 73–74.
47 (Kriegsministerium, 1905), pp. 7–9.
48 (Pflugk-Hartung, 1896), pp. 112–113.
49 (Clemente, 1992), p. 150.

Step 7—Pass Officer Examination and Return to Regiment

Selekta cadets went straight to Step 10 if they passed the officer exam. Passing was not a problem (98 percent passed with the re-take option).[50] If indeed a candidate did fail, he entered the army as a Fähnrich.[51] Some Fähnriche quit the service after failing examination. If a Fähnrich passed with very good marks, his officer's patent was subsequently backdated to the date he officially left the Kriegsschule and was transferred back to the regiment.[52] Obedience and attitude came before grades. The officers' examination was considered far easier than the Fähnrich exam.[53] At the regiment, the Fähnrich waited (briefly) for a vacancy and to complete the next steps.

Step 8—Regimental Officers Balloted to See if They Agreed to Accept the Candidate

Balloting made sure that only candidates with a desired social or family background were commissioned.[54] Selekta cadets did not have to undergo this process. Majority vetoes were final and were sent to the Kaiser for decision. If a candidate failed, he was either sent to another regiment for another try or to the reserves with a major stigma due to the veto. Few candidates failed, because it amounted to going against the colonel's wishes. Some were rejected because of a lack of personal wealth, in which case the candidate was sent to another regiment without stigma. [55]

Step 9—Colonel Recommends to the Kaiser Promotion to Second Lieutenant

The regimental commander reported the ballot to the *Militärkabinett* that prepared commissions and decided about the patent date. Newly commissioned officers received their patent, and that patent constituted their personal relationship to the King.[56] The Fähnrich became a second lieutenant and a member of the social élite, except those in the artillery or engineers. These two branches considered the newly commissioned as supernumeraries until they had served one (artillery) or two (pioneer) years, attended technical school, and passed a qualifying exam.[57] The nobility viewed technical schools as "schools for plumbers."[58] It is not surprising, therefore, that the nobles eschewed these branches.

Step 10—Promotion is Officially "Gazetted"[59]

There were numerous rules for seniority and backdating dates of rank. It is important to look at the different methods of commissioning and understand the pluses and minuses. Generally, the 10 steps took approximately 18 months after the Obersekunda year. Therefore a Fahnenjunker, or a cadet entering as a charakterisierter Fähnrich at the age of 17, could gain a commission at the approximate age of 18 ½ years. Selekta cadets stayed in the academy for an additional 12 months, but would be commissioned directly without a vote of officers—a full six months faster than a Fahnenjunker or other early graduating cadet. The

---

50 (Kriegsministerium, 1905), pp. 9–12, 15–17, and 19–21 about Selekta candidates.

51 (Moncure, 1993), p. 242.

52 (Pflugk-Hartung, 1896), p. 114.

53 (Clemente, 1992), p. 150–157.

54 (Pflugk-Hartung, 1896), p. 115. Although mentioned in the contemporary literature, the balloting is not written down in the respective manual about officer selection.

55 (Clemente, 1992), pp. 158–159.

56 (Kriegsministerium, 1905), p. 21.

57 (Clemente, 1992), p. 160.

58 (Clemente, 1992), p. 210.

59 (Martin, 1936), p. 16.

Prima cadets seeking the Abitur stayed in the Academy for two additional years, but still faced the vote in step eight. Originally, date of rank was 24 months after the Obersekunda year. In February 1900, royal order eliminated this penalty when the date of rank of Prima cadets was backdated to equal the same date as of the Selekta cadets. A Prima cadet now had the Abitur necessary to continue studies at the university and the same early date of rank as a Selekta.[60]

THE OFFICER CORPS: ITS SPIRIT AND SOCIAL LIFE

As a member of the élite of military officers, a man found himself in another world. The sovereigns of the four kingdoms governed promotions. Inspections, not examinations, determined suitability. With the exception of the General Staff, promotion through major took place within the regiment. Above the rank of major, there were centralized promotion lists. While there were no precise rules, promotion tended to be slow on average. A normal progression was eight years to first lieutenant, 14 years to captain, 25 to major, and 30 to lieutenant colonel. General Staff officers were usually promoted six years earlier than normal regimental officers.[61] Seniority and noble connections both mattered. Officers were held to the highest standards, both inside and outside the confines of the post. An officer wore his uniform at all times. There were streets in Berlin where an officer was not allowed to smoke during the day. In fact, there were entire areas that were off-limits. Much of this policy was to keep officers away from the influence of socialists.

An officer relying on his military salary alone simply could not live in an appropriate style, because the salary was only one-fifth of that of his American counterpart.[62] The uniform for an infantry lieutenant cost between 900 and 1,100 marks.[63] The low salary caused shocking problems for most officers. While most guard and cavalry officers had to prove that they had a sufficient outside income prior to acceptance in the regiment, other officers tended to just do without. It was not unusual for an officer to be short of food or warmth, and they often failed to wear their coats in an effort to avoid wearing them out. Many regiments had a small fund to bail out officers who became short of funds. Most officers had to balance debt and the stigma attached to poor financial management. Aristocratic families usually had the money to grant pay supplements to their sons in officers' careers. From commissioning, even infantry officers had to pay for two horses, uniforms, their side arms, etc. Becoming a cavalry officer was more expensive than it was for an infantry or artillery officer. The most expensive, when considering individual costs, certainly were the *Garde Kürassier* and the *Gardes-du-Corps*. Erich Ludendorff gives a very interesting account of his years as both an infantry lieutenant and captain—largely without any pay supplement by the family.[64]

Through the rank of captain, army pay was hardly sufficient to support the officer, let alone adequate to support a family; therefore, promotion to the rank of major was usually called *Majorsecke*, which means that financially, "going around that corner," would make his life much easier. Since most officers had to borrow money from their families, it was a com-

[60] (Moncure, 1993), pp. 168–170.
[61] (The General Staff, 1918), pp. 20–22.
[62] (Clemente, 1992), pp. 161–162.
[63] (Moncure, 1993), p. 244.
[64] (Ludendorff, 1933), p. 9.

mon saying that after successfully passing the meager years, officers had "*Schulden wie ein Stabsoffizier*" (debts like a field-grade officer).

The Kaiser was personally aware of the burden of extra expenses required of officers. As he attempted to enlarge the officer corps in 1890, he gave an order that officers in infantry, foot artillery, and engineer regiments should be required to have no less than 45 marks per month of additional private income. He expected field artillery officers to have 70 marks per month, and those of the cavalry 150 marks per month.[65] Bearing in mind that a newly commissioned lieutenant earned only 125 marks per month, there was no conceivable way to make ends meet on a salary alone.

Low pay with high status meant that marriage had to be a business deal in which the woman brought the "bacon" to the table. It was not unusual to use a marriage agency. A normal practice was for the bride's father to assume the officer's existing debts. The regimental commander had to approve the marriage to ensure the woman had at least an equal social background, enough money, and an unblemished record.[66]

The courting process was an interesting one. In the upper middle classes, attendance at a party or ball depended on the regiment that was garrisoned nearby. The host was responsible for ensuring that officers attended, or it reflected poorly on him. The most desirable dancing partners were lieutenants. Guard officers were particularly sought-after, while socially those of the "lesser" branches like artillery and engineers, were decidedly also-rans.[67]

Class distinction also entered the equation. A Württemberg officer who was non-noble but had a very rich, non-noble wife, i.e., the daughter of a Berlin publisher, could not take his wife to any formal events because of her background.[68] Perhaps this exclusion contributed to the rarity of smiles on German brides in their wedding pictures. Or, it could have been cultural, but it might also have been a function of dental care or the lack thereof. There were also restrictions on interfaith marriages. Prussian officers were required to raise their children as Protestants. This policy conflicted directly with the guidance of the Catholic Church.[69]

There was huge social status associated with wearing the uniform. Civilians were expected to step aside, allowing officers to pass on the street. Even Landwehr officers wore their uniforms on Sunday, a habit that continued throughout retirement for officers. A very famous example was the "Captain of Köpenick." In this 1906 incident, a 54-year-old career criminal (Wilhelm Voigt) went to the city of Köpenick looking for a passport to establish residency. He encountered problems because he could not find work in the cobbler trade he had learned in prison. Without a passport, he could not gain residency, and he discovered that the city did not process passport requests. After making a thorough reconnaissance, he went to several secondhand shops and pieced together a secondhand captain's uniform. He commandeered 10 soldiers on the street, led them to the town hall, arrested the mayor, and demanded that the city treasury be turned over to him. Everyone complied immediately because he was a captain, and he stole 4,000 *Marks*. This farce eventually became a stage play.[70] As a side note, Voigt became wildly popular. After a two-year prison term, he became a media personality, amassed significant personal wealth, but lost it during German hyperinflation. He died in Luxemburg in 1922.

[65] (Perris, 1912), p. 388.
[66] (Clemente, 1992), pp. 163–164.
[67] (Frevert, 2004), pp. 158.
[68] (Kitchen, 1968), p. 30.
[69] (Koenig, 2010)
[70] (Chickering, *Militarism and Radical Nationalism*, 2008), p. 196.

The military was the nation's highest source of pride, but this underestimated the position of the military in politics as well as in society. Militarism led to a series of constitutional struggles and attempts by the military to circumvent the civilian government. Militarism was inherent in all parts of German society; for example, schoolchildren were taught that the German victory over the French army in 1870 was the ultimate measure of success. Even the alphabet primer introduced in 1910 to the primary schools associated letters with lists of military objects such as P is for pistol.[71] The Germans also believed that God directed their success over the French (beginning with the liberation from Napoleon in 1813 and continuing in the 1870–71 war). The Prussian soldiers (NCOs and enlisted men) had the motto "*Gott mit uns*" (May the Lord be with us) on their belt buckles. On their helmets, Prussian soldiers had the motto "*Mit Gott für Koenig und Vaterland.*"[72] The other states relied on God a little less. The Bavarians had "*In Treue fest*" (Be firm in faith) on their helmets and buckles; Württemberg soldiers had "*Furchtlos und trew*"[73] (Fearless and faithful—with "trew" being an old-fashioned spelling of the word *treu*) on their buckles and helmets; and the Saxons used the motto "*Providentiae memor*" (Latin: Remember providence).

THE CODE OF HONOR

There was a constitutional and legal question about who disciplined the army. In the opinion of the War Minister, only strict adherence to the code of honor could maintain the reliability of the officer corps. The question really revolved around whether legal jurisdiction of the army fell under the command of the Kaiser alone or under the jurisprudence of the Reichstag.[74]

There were two separate court systems: the civil courts (controlled by the Minister of Justice who was responsive to the Reichstag) and the honor court (influenced by the Minister of War and made up of officers of the regiment). Military officers, according to the army, were supposed to take their grievances to an honor court where the two antagonists were of honorable status. The decision of the honor court made up of other officers was binding and took precedence over any decision in a civil court. The regiment annually elected the honor court, which consisted of a captain and two lower ranking officers. The constitutional underpinning was that military officers were not liable to the Minister of Justice and the civil courts, but rather would work out their issues in an honor court. Officers were duty bound to shake hands and try to solve the disagreement. If that did not work, the honor court would try to settle the dispute non-violently.

The final option to restore an officer's honor was a duel, whereby he could prove his worth.[75] Officers subject to the code of honor were expected to duel, but the issue was convoluted, because duels were not only illegal, but also were officially quasi-discouraged by a cabinet ordinance the Kaiser issued 1 January 1897.[76] Nevertheless, unwillingness to duel showed unreliability, and anyone refusing to duel would be drummed out of the army. The disgraced officer was not simply removed from the officer corps but excluded from the offi-

---

71 (Chickering, *Militarism and Radical Nationalism, 2008*), pp. 197–206.
72 For traditional reasons the word *König* was spelled *Koenig* on the helmets.
73 Correct spelling would be *Furchtlos und treu* but again for traditional reasons the old spelling *trew* was used.
74 (Perris, 1912), p. 385.
75 (Frevert, 2004), p. 168.
76 (Krüger, 1915), p. 90.

cer caste (*Offizierstand*). The individual became a non-person, forfeiting his pension and the right to wear a uniform. He could not use his old title or rank. Redemption was practically impossible until the actual casualties of the Great War began mounting and officials could look the other way. Decisions by the honor court were final, subject to the approval of the Kaiser.[77] History shows that regular officers wounded in duels received pensions. Reserve officers dueled much more commonly than regular officers in an attempt to mimic their respected active brothers. Some officers viewed one-year volunteers as not worthy of a duel. Preference for dueling was given to those who were members of dueling fraternities.

The constitutional question of who disciplined the army never came to a head. The Army won one major test case.[78] This revolved around a military commentator who was a retired officer. Was a retired officer subject to civil court or the honor court? The officer in question was *Oberst* Gädke, a retired colonel a.D., and a popular columnist, who had commanded a field artillery regiment. Gädke used his title of Oberst and wrote some things that irked the Kaiser. The objective in the honor court case was to deny the defendant the use of the title Oberst and the right to wear the uniform. The military's claim was that Gädke was still under their jurisdiction and would be for his lifetime. The War Minister's opinion was that the Kaiser alone granted the title, and the Kaiser had the right to withdraw it. An honor court so decided in February 1904. Things dragged on in different courts for another year. In 1905, the civil jury court decided that he was not guilty of using a title without authority. The Supreme Royal Court of Justice decided in 1906 that courts of honor had no jurisdiction over retired officers since the subjects were no longer constitutionally in the army. The fact Gädke had accepted the right to wear the uniform and the honors that go with the apparel when he left the army could under no circumstances imply that he agreed to the regulations governing courts of honor.

The War Minister argued that retired officers were part of the army. His justification included the fact that regular soldiers saluted retired officers; therefore, they had to accept the officer's code of honor and the decisions of the court of honor. This affair finally ended in 1908 with Oberst Gädke having lost his title.

ONE-YEAR VOLUNTEERS

A one-year volunteer (OYV) had to equip himself with rations, quarters, uniforms, and equipment). He had to pay also for a horse (if needed) or had to pay into the remount fund. The cost was generally equal to the cost of one year at university and depended on the kind of unit a one-year volunteer decided to join. He could choose his regiment; however, infantry, *Jäger*, engineers, and foot artillery were expected to pay between 1,750 and 2,200 Mark for their year. Field artillery and train units increased the cost to around 2,300–2,700 Mark. But for cavalry and mounted field artillery, the costs soared to 3,400 to 3,600 Mark a year.[79] There is a misconception that one-year volunteers purchased most of the uniforms and equipment from commercial sources. In reality, most of the uniforms and equipment were either purchased or rented from the regiment.[80]

---

[77] (Perris, 1912), p. 385.
[78] (Kitchen, 1968), p. 63.
[79] (Exner, 1897), pp. 102–104.
[80] *(Wehrordnung des Deutschen Reiches,* 1888) and *(Heerodnung des Deutsches Reiches*, 1904).

The payback was as follows:

- The OYV only had to do one-year of active service before transferring to the reserve. This service was in place of the two- to three-year active requirement.
- The OYV could start military training at age 17 at the earliest. The normal soldier started at age 20.
- If the OYV passed the prerequisite examinations, he could enter as an officer aspirant or NCO in the reserves. A reserve commission was an open door for a successful civilian life. Taking the test to become an officer was voluntary, conducted at the end of the active-duty year, and the active company commander had to sponsor the volunteer.[81]

Medical OYVs were different with a six-month active enlisted requirement before the candidate received a full commission in the Medical Department for the last six months as an assistant doctor, *einjährig freiwillger Arzt*.[82]

OYVs could join the service with a class on 1 October each year. They volunteered to join the regiment of their choice but had to be accepted as an OYV. They were grouped together with the other one-year volunteers and their training was separate. Often their training consisted of only a few hours work per day.[83] After three months, they could attend a special course, and after six months, if all went well, they could be promoted to supernumerary private first class (Gefreiter). After nine months, the best of the class could be promoted to supernumerary corporal (Unteroffizier). The reference to supernumeraries is merely a reinforcement of the understanding that these OYVs were extra or supernumeraries to the establishment. One-year volunteers were sometimes allowed to dine in the officer's mess, not with the officers of the regiment but in a separate room.[84]

The OYV could become an officer aspirant in the reserves if his active company commander recommended him and he passed the requisite tests at the end of his year of service. If the one-year volunteer did not meet all these criteria, he could be passed into the reserves as a normal enlisted man or as an aspirant NCO. If all of the criteria were met, he would become an officer aspirant in the reserves and promoted to supernumerary Unteroffizier if he were not already at that rank. Of those completing their one-year, the company commander recommended every second recruit as a potential officer. One-third of those who entered military service went on to become reserve NCOs, and 13 percent were discharged without any promotion.[85] A Bavarian army example in 1906 showed that 43 percent of the one-year volunteers left service with the recommendation of the company commander. Of that group only another 43 percent or a total of about 18 percent of the 1906 one-year volunteer intake, actually received a reserve officer commission.[86]

After completing his year of service, the OYV was granted leave from his service as a Gefreiter with the obligation of completing two reserve exercises of eight weeks each (exercises A and B) during the two following years; i.e., one session per year for two years after he took the reserve officer candidate test (*Reserveoffizier-Aspirantenprüfung*) and left active duty. During this first session, he learned how to be a platoon commander and took a test at the end of this eight-week session. After successful completion of exercise A, the reserve officer

---

81 (Exner, 1897), p. 40.
82 (Stubbs, 2004), p. 32.
83 (Frevert, 2004), p. 171.
84 (Frevert, 2004), p. 168.
85 (Frevert, 2004), pp. 159–160
86 (Frevert, 2004), p. 225.

candidate had to pass the reserve officer's examination and was promoted to the rank of *Vizefeldwebel*. In the event that he failed, but had showed good performance during his one year, he was retained as a reserve NCO with the rank of Gefreiter. During the following exercise B, he wore the rank of staff sergeant (*Vizefeldwebel*) but had to fulfill officer's tasks. During both exercises A and B, the deputy regimental commander (usually a lieutenant colonel) had to train the reserve officer candidates for their later role as officers.[87]

The reserve officers' candidate test focused upon the following topics:

- Weapons handling of the respective arm,
- Formal drill,
- Leading a platoon,
- Successfully mastering a given tactical task with his platoon,
- Drawing tactical sketches,
- Good theoretical knowledge about battalion tactics in cooperation with other arms,
- Good knowledge of the tactical manual (*Exerzier-Reglement*) of his arm,
- Good knowledge of the general field service regulations (*Feld-Dienstvorschrift*).[88]

After successfully completing exercise B, the regimental commander had to issue a certificate recommending the respective officer candidates for promotion to reserve officers of the respective regiment. Since the reserve officer candidates belonged to their regiment on the one hand, but also to the Landwehr-Bezirkskommando of their residence,[89] the reserve officer corps of the respective Landwehr area voted as to whether or not they would become reserve officers. In preparation for this vote, the commanding officer of the Landwehr area had to examine whether the candidate's civilian life-style and standard of living was up to the level the army expected of their officers. If all was in order, the commanding officer recommended the candidate for the vote. As a further prerequisite, the candidate had to commit himself for at least three further years of service as a reserve officer of his regiment—including extended reserve exercises that could interfere with his civilian job. After acceptance, the king promoted the candidate after a further recommendation by the military cabinet. He could remain with his regiment until the age of 27 and then was transferred by request to the second contingent of his Landwehr area.

Reserve officers formed the pool to produce military leaders for reserve formations and even active formations in case of mobilization. Their training had to be good enough to not only enable them to lead reserve or Landwehr platoons or companies, but also to also replace officers in active units after mobilization. Most reserve officers were first or second lieutenants; only few of them were captains. The rank of captain usually represented the limit to which reserve and Landwehr officers could be promoted. A very limited number of Landwehr officers had the chance to reach the rank of a major.[90]

Reserve officer training usually focused upon practical aspects of military life. The cadets had to learn military history and fortification. Staff work and languages, which active officer

---

[87] (Exner, 1897)

[88] For further details about the content of the examination, please check Spohn's "*Prüfungs-Aufgaben für Einjährig Freiwillige und Reserveoffizier-Aspiranten der Armee*," *Verlag* von Friedrich Engelmann, (Leipzig 1908).

[89] In the Rangliste, reserve officers were listed with their regiments as well as the first contingent of their Landwehr area and were allowed to wear the regimental uniform of their last active unit.

[90] For the following comments about reserve and Landwehr officers please see Dr. J. v. Pflugk-Hartung, *Die Heere und Flotten der Gegenwart*, Vol I, *Deutschland* (The part about the army in Vol I was written by General Lieutenant z. *D.* v. Boguslawski.), Verlag: Schall & Grund, (Berlin 1896).

candidates had to learn, were skipped for good reasons. The training of reserve officers had to focus upon topics necessary for a platoon and company commanders in case of war.[91]

There was a conscious class distinction between the one-year volunteers and the "common soldiers." The only way the "common soldiers" got revenge was to require the one-year volunteers to buy a round of drinks. For many of the one-year volunteers, military life was the first time they had come in contact with the lower levels of German society. One of the most common ways to differentiate these classes was that the one-year volunteers referred to each other using the formal *Sie*. Lower-class soldiers also use this form of address for one-year volunteers. "Common soldiers" used the more familiar *du* when addressing each other.[92]

Religion played an important part in the acceptance process. It is instructive that in 1913, almost 46 percent of all Jewish soldiers were one-year volunteers. Compare this number to two percent of the Protestants and one and one-half percent of the Catholics. Because the Jewish soldiers were of higher social standing than many of the common soldiers, a certain jealous resentment ensued.[93]Although there was basically no religious discrimination, the Prussian Army was essentially Protestant, and the Bavarian Army was mostly Catholic. Kaiser Wilhelm II was the protector of the Protestant order of St. John in Brandenburg (*Protektor der Balley Brandenburg des Johanniterordens*) and considered himself a dedicated Protestant monarch.

Jews were basically accepted as being equal in imperial Germany; there was no real anti-Jewish discrimination. But it was quite obvious that Jews played a minor role in the Army. Jews generally belonged to well-educated bourgeoisie families but were basically excluded from officer's positions in noble cavalry and guard regiments. Like other well-educated members of bourgeois families, they focused more upon technical branches such as engineers and artillery or the train. At a higher level of German society, acceptance was more elusive. A reserve commission was seen as a route to social mobility. The Jews often had the money to pay and were willing to do so to improve their own life chances. Traditionally, being tradesmen of higher social status, many Jews became reserve officers, preferably in train and medical formation, which in fact lead to some discriminative jokes.

An officer would remain in reserve status until he requested transfer into the Landwehr. This request was routinely approved. Likewise, officers moved between the first and second contingent of the Landwehr upon request. Many reserve officers preferred to stay in a func-

---

91 For reserve officers' training, several handbooks have been published, explaining the content of the one-year of training. For infantry, these books were *Bindewalds Anhalt für den Unterricht der Einjährig-Freiwilligen und Resereveoffiziers-Aspiranten der Infanteri,* Verlag: Richard Schröder, (Berlin 1902) or *Dilthey's Militärischer Dienstunterricht für Einjährig Freiwillige bei der Ausbildung zu Reserveoffizier-Aspiranten sowie für Offiziere des Beurlaubtenstandes der deutschen Infanterie*, E. S. Mittler & Sohn, (Berlin 1902). For the cavalry, read Frhr. v. Maltzahn's, *Handbuch für den Einjährig-Freiwilligen, sowie für den Reserve und Landwehr-Offizier der Kavallerie,* E. S. Mittler & Sohn, (Berlin 1909). For the field artillery, consult Wernigk's *Handbuch für die Einjährig-Freiwilligen Offizier-Aspiranten und die Offiziere des Beurlaubtenstandes der Feldartillerie,* E. S. Mittler & Sohn, (Berlin 1908) or its revised edition–Sommerbrodt's *Wernigks Handbuch für die Einjährig-Freiwilligen Offizier-Aspiranten und die Offiziere des Beurlaubtenstandes der Feldartillerie*, E. S. Mittler & Sohn, (Berlin 1913). For the train, see Eiswaldt's *Handbuch für Einjährig-Freiwillige, Reserve-Offizieraspiranten und Offiziere des Beurlaubtenstandes des Trains*, E. S. Mittler & Sohn, (Berlin 1901). Some interesting and very particular Bavarian aspects can be seen in Carl Theodor Müller, and Theodor v. Zwehl's, *Handbuch für den Einjährig-Freiwilligen, den Unteroffizier, Offiziersaspiranten und Offizier des Beurlaubtenstandes der kgl. Bayerischen Infanterie*, R. Oldenbourg Verlag, (Munich 1886). General knowledge is given in Gen. Hörnig M. v. Süßmilch's *Katechismus für den Einjährig-Freiwilligen*, Verlag: J.J. Weber, (Leipzig 1877). Interestingly, the last book refers to a pseudo-religious message in its title–obviously reserve officers had to learn this book by heart like a catechism.

92 (Frevert, 2004), p. 169.

93 (Frevert, 2004), p. 229.

tional organization where there was at least some training requirement. Officers who quit or were cashiered from the active army were enrolled into the reserve component appropriate to their age.[94] Reserve officers were often identified by the presence of a Landwehr cross on their headgear. By 1914, there were 120,000 reserve officers.[95]

Landwehr officers were trained similarly to reserve officers. The commander of the Landwehr area had to certify qualification to become a reserve officer. After successfully passing examinations, exercises, and election by the reserve officer corps of the Landwehr area, they were promoted to the rank of *Leutnant der Landwehr* and belonged to the first contingent of their Landwehr area. After reaching the age of 27, they were transferred to second contingent, together with the reserve officers.[96]

A field grade officer who was semi-retired (z.D.), commanded each Landwehrbezirk. Berlin was an exception and had four (in 1914, six) Landwehrbezirke commanded by active officers. The adjutant of a Landwehrbezirk was a regular Oberleutnant or Leutnant. Assisting the commander were several officers, known as Bezirksoffiziere and responsible for all aspects of personnel replacement. The Bezirksfeldwebel was the main point of contact for reservists and Landwehr men within his company district.

RESERVE AND LANDWEHR OFFICERS

The active-duty officers described above differed significantly from reserve officers. Active officers received their commissions and with that honor went a certain respect and admiration. Reserve officers followed a different route to commissioning. Once commissioned, they tended to try very hard to mimic the regular officers. The reserve commission was considered the "open door" to many advantages in private life. For the most part they had served as OYVs and were recommended by their company commander as potential reserve officers. Preparation and training amounted to two periods of annual training, each lasting eight weeks. The reserve officer corps of the corps district would then vote on them. If accepted, they would gain a commission and serve as a lieutenant of the reserve.[97]

The career of Friedrich Wolfgang Schmitt–Scharf illustrates the point and assists in the understanding of the following section. Born in October 1869, he became a one-year volunteer in the Kgl. Bayr. 2. Feldartillerie- Regiment Horn in October 1888 at the age of 19. As a one-year volunteer, he was promoted to the rank of Gefreiter in January 1889. He was further promoted to Unteroffizier in July of that year and after his year was over in October, he was released into the reserves. Two years later in August 1891, he was promoted to staff sergeant in a mounted unit (*Vizewachtmeister*) and was promoted to second lieutenant of the reserves in November 1891, after finishing his two annual training and preparation periods. Nine years later in March of 1900, he was promoted to Oberleutnant. Five years after that in February of 1905, he was made a captain. That same year, at the age of 36, he was transferred into the 1st contingent of the Landwehr. When the war broke out in 1914, he was made commander of a Landwehr company, and in 1915 promoted to characteristic (temporary) major and held various posts until his release from the Army in 1919.[98]

94 (The General Staff, 1918), pp. 22–25.
95 (Blackbourn, 2003), p. 286.
96 (Pflugk-Hartung, 1896), pp. 135–136.
97 (U.S. Army War College, 1917), p. 32.
98 (Brennfleck, 1939), pp. 753–754.

WARTIME OFFICERS

The wartime shortage of second lieutenants was meant to be filled by promoting retired Vizefeldwebel or Feldwebel to the rank of sergeant major lieutenant (*Feldwebelleutnant*). If the candidate had 12 years of service in the reserves or eight years of service in the Landsturm, he could be appointed to officer deputy (*Offizier-Stellvertreter*). Such officer deputies were never intended to command more than a platoon.[99] While they were treated as officers in the field, they were not permitted the privileges of permanent commissioned rank. Immediately upon demobilization or discharge, they reverted at once to their former rank. These ranks were not used extensively until 1914, which begged the question as to why not.[100] The Kaiser issued no fewer than two cabinet orders (AKOs) in late 1914 clarifying the rank of Offizier-Stellvertreter. There continues to be controversy over whether a person holding the rank of Offizier-Stellvertreter was considered an officer or a noncommissioned officer. It was possible for an Offizier-Stellvertreter to be promoted to the rank of Feldwebelleutnant.[101] Additionally, because of a mistake in an English language publication, *German Military Terms and Abbreviations* issued by GHQ in France in April 1917, there are notes as well as references that Feldwebelleutnant was "only appointed in war for depot and garrison troops." Feldwebelleutnants were indeed appointed only in wartime but certainly not only for depot and garrison troops. A cursory glance at any wartime regimental history or the published *Verlustlisten* will show their appointment and deployment in first line units. This promotion was an appointment, not a rank. It entitled them to nothing other than increased responsibility. This appointment was a very poor deal after they reverted to their previous rank.

RETIREMENT

Military service was not over quickly. Most officers were "promoted" upon retirement. Often the phrase *charakterisiert* (brevet promotion) is attached to a specific rank. If a person served a certain number of years, this "promotion" was granted upon retirement. It did not affect his pension because that was based on his permanent rank. The abbreviation *z.D.* after a name, *Oberleutnant z.D.* Müller for example, stands for *zur Disposition* (on disposition). An officer in this status was in effect a retired officer who had agreed to be available for further service or assignment as required. It was normal for an officer *z.D.* to be employed in peacetime in uniformed positions such as Landwehr District Commanders or Landwehr District Officers. They were also given front-line assignments on mobilization.[102]

Another abbreviation frequently seen in connection with retired officers is *außer Dienst* (a.D.) or out of service.[103] They, too, were often recalled or volunteered their services upon mobilization. It is confusing in that a man could be promoted in that status as well as use the abbreviation *a.D.* even when serving in a recalled status. There was another group of officers

---

99 Later in the war, they were used widely.

100 An email from Glenn Jewison pointed out that there was a provision for Feldwebelleutenant in some small way according to the AKO of 15 November 1877, and that uniform details for this rank are available in some older references in the 1880s and early 1890s.

101 (The General Staff, 1918), p. 24.

102 (The General Staff, 1918), p. 25. They were also paid a stipend if not "employed."

103 (The General Staff, 1918), p. 25.

known as *nichtregimentierte Offiziere*. This term refers to those officers serving extra-regimentally in special corps or appointments such as the following:

- General Staff;
- Adjutants of formations from brigade upwards;
- Adjutants to Royal Princes;
- Permanent staff of military establishments such as the War Academy, War Schools, Artillery and Engineer School, Cadet Corps, NCO schools, etc.;
- Fortress governments;
- Train Depots, etc.

For the most part these were officers serving outside their original arm of service or regiment in a special staff or instructors' appointment.

All members of the army officer corps were entitled to receive a pension if they could not continue their military career after at least 10 years of active service. Officers leaving the army after less than 10 years due to a disability or other health reasons received during active service were also entitled to receive a pension. In these cases, the pension would be granted only during the disability or invalidity that kept these officers from joining active service. Officers leaving the army before completing 10 years of service without a pension entitlement could receive a pension as an act of grace if they were in need due to poverty. This rule was only applied if those officers were officially declared to be unfit for service. In these cases, the pension did not exceed 20/60 (20 × the sixtieth part) of their last pensionable annual salary (*pensionsfähiges Diensteinkommen*). Only salaries, allowances, or bonuses received for longer than one year were counted as pensionable. The pension amount was calculated based upon position, rank and years of service. After 10 years of service, it was about 20/60 of the last pensionable salary and rose with each full year of service by one further sixtieth part. After 30 years of service and from the position of a regimental commander, this increase was reduced to 1/120 of the last pensionable annual salary. Usually, the "target pension" for retirement after a full life of service was about 2/3 (average)–3/4 (maximum) of the last pensionable annual salary.

CHAPTER 10

MILITARY LIFE AND TRAINING

MILITARY LIFE

Military life was harsh. Recruits were isolated from four to six weeks before they were allowed to mingle with civilians. Discipline was relentless. This was characterized by high conscript suicide. The yearly suicide rate was 220 to 240 recruits. That was 14 times higher than the civilian population. However, the barracks provided many recruits with more space, better lighting, and cleaner facilities than they had had in civilian life.[1]

The barracks were divided into squad rooms called *Stuben*. The number of recruits in a room varied from 10 to 20, but each man had a wall locker and a bunk bed. Latrine and sanitary facilities in the barracks were limited. Each battalion had its own barracks building in a *Kaserne*. In addition, there were multiple buildings for latrines and mess halls. Usually the mess hall included the tailor shop, barbershop, shoemaker, and armorer. A high brick or stone fence with the intent of keeping the public out surrounded the entire Kaserne. The battalion had cooks who had learned to cook in civilian life. Breakfast was normally coffee and bread. Lunch was generally stew prepared in large quantities. The evening meal consisted of tea, coffee, and bread. Soup was occasionally served. Fruits and desserts were not available.[2] The soldier was expected to supplement the meager rations or get care packages from home.

One of the members of the barracks guard awakened the NCO of the day (*Unteroffizier vom Dienst*, abbreviated "*UvD*") at approximately 04:45 a.m. The soldiers were then awakened and had approximately one hour for personal and barracks hygiene and breakfast before they paraded for squad inspection. Ten minutes later, there was a company formation led by the First Sergeant (*Feldwebel)*. The company's lieutenants would arrive at 06:00 a.m., and the senior lieutenant received the report from the Feldwebel. After the lieutenants inspected their platoons, the company commander would receive the report and the company was marched to the drill field. Training was conducted until 11:15 a.m., after which the soldiers were marched back for lunch. In the afternoon, the soldiers returned for afternoon training that could include physical exercise. When the afternoon training was completed, soldiers would have their evening meal and free time. It was possible to go to the battalion canteen where beer could be purchased for five *Pfennige* or a pipe full of tobacco for one Pfennig.[3]

---

1 (Blackbourn, 2003), p. 288.
2 (Bartsch, *Deutsches Soldatenleben*, 1907), pp. 1–46.
3 (Bartsch, *Deutsches Soldatenleben*, 1907), pp. 41–57.

Live-fire range training started in December, and the first regimental inspection was in February. After the inspection, the company started six weeks of intensive unit training followed by another regimental inspection. This training was followed by two weeks of battalion level training, its completion marked by an inspection by the regimental commander and perhaps a general officer. Summer training began in May and consisted of field exercises to prepare for another regimental inspection in August. Division exercises followed, and in September the annual fall maneuvers took place at army corps level.

Service souvenirs were important and are often seen in pictures and today's surviving relics. They took many different forms, from the traditional beer stein to schnapps flasks, walking sticks, pipes, individual pictures, and mother's cups. These souvenirs were not provided by the unit and were purchased by the individual soldier to celebrate the end of active service time.

One of the symbols frequently seen in group pictures is §11, often painted on the bottom of the barrel. There is controversy about what this symbol means, though there are basically two different interpretations. The first one is fairly straightforward. It suggests that it refers to the paragraph in the *Wehrordnung* governing *Reservepflicht* and refers either to the end of the active commitment or the required service in the reserves. Soldiers counted down the amount of time they still had to serve before they finished active service and entered the reserves.[4] The second explanation seems to be the more popular one, as it refers to an interpretation of one of the student beer laws. The concept is that the first 10 sections were blank and the eleventh encouraged a person to drink more. There are no real citations to validate either interpretation.

Another common picture is one of a soldier riding a ram (male sheep). There are several versions of this tradition, but the most often told is that the ram had a strong odor and was placed in the stables to keep the young recruit guards from leaving their post and trying to take a nap inside the stables or attempting to have an illegal rendezvous inside with a female companion. As offensive as the ram was, some soldiers would go to any lengths to see a local girl. In the pictures, these girls are often depicted as holding onto the ram's tail representing an undaunted girl.

Another version has the word *Hammel* (the word for an idiot) used as an insult, "*Blöder Hammel!*" (Stupid ram!) A new recruit was called a *Bock* (ram), just as older recruits close to being discharged were called *alte Knochen* (old bones). Moreover, whenever a young recruit entered a barracks room with older recruits, he had to recite the verse: "*Gott grüß euch, alte Knochen. Ein Hammel kommt gekrochen.*" (Good day, old bones, an idiot is crawling closer) or "*Ein Hammel ruft ins Ofenloch: Reserve hat (number) Tage noch*" (An idiot is calling into the open stove door; Reserves only have (number) days left).[5]

Soldiers were also notoriously poor and made far less than men in the civilian world. Soldiers pay also had to cover their personal needs. They had a hot lunch, coffee twice a day and 750 g. of bread. Anything more than that, including laundry, had to come from the approximate 2.2 *Mark* they were paid every 10 days. Girlfriends and parents frequently supplemented the income of soldiers.[6]

---

4 (*Wehrordnung des Deutschen Reiches*, 1888), pp. 22–23.

5 (Kim, 2009), p. 93. Others were, e.g., "*Es klingt wie eine Sage—noch (number) Tage.*" (It sounds like a fairy tale—just (number) days left.)

6 (Frevert, 2004), p. 178.

THE NON-COMMISSIONED OFFICER

Non-commissioned Officers (NCOs) came from two sources. They were either promoted from within the ranks or were graduates of one of the NCO training schools. Students graduated from *Volksschulen* approximately at the age of 14. Military service would not begin until age 17 when young men could be inducted into the Landsturm. They had the option of either working or joining an NCO preparatory school (*Unteroffiziervorschule*) after finishing Volksschule. There were nine such schools scattered throughout the empire (Weilburg, Sigmaringen, Annaburg, Jülich, Wohlau, Bartenstein, Greifenberg i.P., Fürstenfeldbruck, and Marienberg). The preparatory school had a general curriculum with emphasis on physical development throughout the two-year course. Upon graduation from the Unteroffiziervorschulen, students could go to an NCO school (*Unteroffizierschule*). There were nine of these (Potsdam, Jülich, Biebrich (in 1914 Wetzlar), Weissenfels, Ettlingen, Marienwerder, Treptow a.R. (on the Rhine), Fürstenfeldbruck, and Marienberg). The course lasted two years for preparatory school graduates or three years for those who joined the NCO school directly, without having gone through the preparatory school. This institution's graduates were either 19 or 20 years old. Upon graduation, they had a compulsory period of service of four years in the active army. Graduates were posted to the regiments with emerging as sergeants and others as *Gefreiter*. These schools accounted for about 25 percent of all NCOs.[7]

The NCOs who were promoted from the ranks were generally those who had re-enlisted (*Kapitulanten*). While there was no specific time in grade requirements for promotion, it was seldom less than two years. Annually, the members of the new class were scrutinized and those expected to re-enlist and be suitable as an NCO received special instruction within the regiment.[8]

There were three NCO ranks that were considered *Unteroffizier mit Portepee* or NCOs with officer sword knot. These were the top NCOs who had certain uniform and prestige differences. They were the Feldwebel, the *Vizefeldwebel,* and the *Fähnrich.*[9] The Feldwebel can best be equated to a company First Sergeant in the U.S. system. Each infantry battalion normally had four Feldwebel, one for each company. The name changed to *Wachtmeister* for mounted units. There was no rank or position of Sergeant Major, Command Sergeant Major, or Regimental Sergeant Major in the imperial Army, and the most senior line NCO on the staff of a regiment or battalion would have been the chief clerk usually in the rank of Vizefeldwebel or Sergeant. The Bandmaster held the same rank but was considered senior to the line Feldwebel. The Feldwebel was also known as the *Etatmäßiger* Feldwebel—also known as *Spieß* (one per company). And just to confuse the situation, there was a position/rank known as *Bezirksfeldwebel* in each home district recruiting/administrative area. The person holding this position could have been any non-commissioned officer, not just a Feldwebel. In the reserve and Landwehr, some selected soldiers were provided special training as potential NCOs—*Aspirant Unteroffizier*. Promotions to the rank of sergeant and above were not made until mobilization. However, Vizefeldwebel could be bestowed on older trainees and those whose social position was in accordance with a higher rank.[10] The Fähnrich was an NCO but never really treated as one. He was an officer in training.

---

7 (Stubbs, 2004), p. 33.

8 (Stubbs, 2004), p. 34.

9 In fact, "Fähnrich" although formally a non-commissioned officer was never was considered as an NCO.

10 (Stubbs, 2004), p. 34.

One substantial advantage in being a non-commissioned officer was that it was a requirement for employment for many positions as civilian clerks or shopkeepers. Typically, non-commissioned officers had low levels of education. Since NCOs were primarily responsible for recruit training, it was more important that they be reliable rather than well educated. There was a definite attempt to recruit small town peasants and the petty bourgeoisie, who had been traditionally loyal to the crown. The authorities insisted on recruiting poorly educated NCOs, who were then paid well and guaranteed positions in the civilian administration after their military service.[11] Non-commissioned officers represented 18.8 percent of the German army, but only 7.8 percent of those coming from the *Reichslande* (Alsace and Lorraine) ever achieved that rank.[12]

MILITARY OFFICIALS

There were many men who wore uniforms inside imperial Germany—customs officers, postal workers, railway men, and foresters—a breed known as *Beamten* or officials. Former soldiers received preferential hiring into these professions. These German bureaucrats quickly adopted the non-commissioned officer tone. The type of tone was known as *barsch*. This harsh or brusque tone was common among the police forces.[13]

Military officials (*Militär Beamten*) in imperial Germany had quasi-dual status; they were both civil servants (Reich or State) as well as members of the military. These Beamten were permanently counted against the personnel strength of the individual contingents. While they wore uniforms, they were not considered soldiers in the chain of command. They had the equivalent rank of officers or NCOs but not the command authority. They were given the courtesy and respect afforded to military personnel of their equivalent rank.

There were two categories of Beamte: military officials and civil officials of the military administration (*Civil Beamte der Militär-Verwaltung*), each divided into three classes:

- *Höhere* or upper (those university or academically trained officials), for example the *Vortragende Räte* in the War Ministry, the Intendants and *Intendanturräte, Kriegsgerichtsräte,* etc.
- *Mittlere* or Subalternbeamte—*Zahlmeister, Garnison-Verwaltungs, Lazarett-Verwaltungs, Bekleidungsamts*, War Ministry Clerical officials, etc.
- *Unter* or Lower; to include doormen at the Ministry, storemen, etc. at the Bekleidungsämter, Barracks wardens (Civil-Beamte), etc.

Upper officials ranked with the officers and the lower officials with the NCOs.[14] In addition to their title, they often had a further title such as *Wirklicher Geheimer Kriegsgerichtsrat* or *Geheimer Kriegsgerichtsrat* (Legal officer with the rank of a major).[15]

---

[11] (Förster, 2006), p. 465.
[12] (Silverman, 1972), p. 73.
[13] (Blackbourn, 2003), p. 289.
[14] (The General Staff, 1918), p. 20.
[15] Those titles were not always courtesy titles. They represented different ranks: a *Geheimer Kriegsgerichtsrat* was a kind of *Ober Kriegsgerichtsrat* and a *Wirklicher Geheimer Kriegsgerichtsrat* was another more senior rank. The actual rank was the Rat or Councilor. The Austrians still have the same system today. In Germany, those titles mainly applied to civil servants at military courts (like the *Kriegsgerichtsrat*). In Austria, they extended this system of ranks to other branches like the *Hofrat* (same as *Regierungsrat* in Germany), the *Geheimer Hofrat* and the *Wirklicher Geheimer Hofrat*.

TRAINING

The superiority of German training has been discussed in many books without providing an understanding of the cyclical nature of training in these units. There was a general expectation from a calendar perspective of how the soldier would train. Taking a look at the two-year service cycle, we have to overlay it on the annual calendar. In calendar year one, the new inductee would undergo somewhat different training than the second year "old soldiers." In the middle of October after harvest, those selected to begin their military service would report into their units. The starting date was known as the *Einstellungstag*. These brand-new soldiers were treated as recruits for 15 weeks in a period of basic training known as *Rekrutenschule*. Instruction included drill, hygiene, physical training, and dry fire marksmanship.

There were weekly training exercises in the countryside where the weight of the pack was increased gradually until it reached approximately 60 pounds. During this time, second-year soldiers also underwent a period of individual training and weapons drill. This training was known as *Exerzierausbildung*. The junior lieutenant in the company was responsible for the individual training that was conducted by the NCOs. The 15 weeks was interrupted by a week of Christmas holidays for all. Officers and senior NCOs went through their own winter training cycle (*Winterausbildung*) that included more advanced training such as staff rides, training rides, evaluation rides on the regimental and brigade levels (*Erkundungsritten, Geländebesprechungen*), wargames, and sand table exercises (*Sandkastenübungen*). Winter studies (*Winterarbeiten*) for the officers and senior NCOs also included research questions that were provided by the War Ministry (*Kriegsministerium*) or the War Academy (*Kriegsakademie*), as well as lectures and sports. Individual training ended in the first half of February with the evaluation of basic training success (*Rekrutenbesichtigung*) conducted by the battalion commander.

After individual training, seven to eight weeks of advanced training (*Kompanieschule*) began in February with emphasis on weapons' drill, live firing exercises, and tactical drill on the regimental training ground (*Standortübungsplatz*). This advanced individual training also included an additional week of vacation for Easter holidays and was usually completed by mid-April with an inspection and evaluation of company training success by the regimental commander (*Kompaniebesichtigung*). This focused on outdoor skills (*Aussendienst*) and technical skills.

Battalion level training then commenced for three to four weeks (*Bataillionschule*). Again using the regimental training ground, there would be battalion level technical training and live-fire exercises at the local rifle range (*Standortschiessanlage*). The commanding general of the army corps conducted the battalion training inspection (*Batallionbesichtigung)* in mid-May. It was executed whenever possible at the army corps training center (*Truppenübungsplatz*). The battalion inspection centered upon field skills and tactical training including night exercises (*Felddienst- und Gefechtsausbildung, Nachtausbildung*) as well as tactical marches and sports that were an important part of the training regimen.

Summer training started after the mid-May inspection and lasted until the end of July. This training concentrated on tactical drill at both the company and battalion levels to improve the deficiencies identified during the company and battalion inspections. Live firing was conducted on local firing ranges and resulted in the *Kaiserpreis* and marksmanship awards (*Schützenschnur*). Tactical marches increased in length and level of difficulty. During this time, soldiers both old and new (especially those coming from rural families), were sent home and exempted from service in the early summer to help out on the farms.

Once they returned, at the end of July, the units were moved by rail to the army corps training area. Here in the first week of August, live firing (*Gefechtsschießen*) took place on the company level, sometimes on a local firing range (*Standortschießanlage*). During the second week of August, the units experienced advanced tactical training on a regimental level (*Regimentsschule*) by doing regimental exercises. This training included one day of rest. The schedule during the third week of August was advanced tactical training on the brigade level (*Brigadeschule*) and included brigade exercises that were either two regiments fighting each other or the tactical use of the brigade as a whole, aided by artillery and/or cavalry reinforcements. This brigade training also included one day of rest. Around 20 August, the unit took railroad transport back to their garrison where they conducted tactical drill, weapons drill, and formal drill.[16]

Around 10 September, railroad transport was taken to the maneuver area in preparation of autumn maneuvers. The maneuver area was part of the countryside and included towns and villages. There were three or four days of brigade maneuvers followed by a day of rest. This training was followed by five days of division level maneuvers and then a day of rest. Three days of corps maneuver training followed, or if the unit was selected, it could become part of the *Kaisermanöver*. As the name implied, the Kaiser was present and participated in these maneuvers. Foreign dignitaries—officials and observers, who attended these maneuvers, included both Theodore Roosevelt and Winston Churchill.

This large exercise regularly consisted of three or four army corps. It was considered by some the most important training in the Army.[17] During Schlieffen's time, the Kaisermanöver became a joke. The maneuver was always decided by a massive cavalry charge, often ordered by the Kaiser, and he was not allowed to lose. It was part of Moltke the Younger's intended reforms to fix these maneuvers and make them militarily useful again.

When the maneuvers were over, units returned to the Kaserne and those soldiers due for discharge turned in all of their equipment except for one uniform to wear home and their field cutlery (forks and knives) that were usually "buried" in an informal ceremony on the last night in the field. Once they left, the unit prepared for the receipt of the new recruits in early October.

Marksmanship

Marksmanship training took a major role in military training. First, soldiers had to be drilled in weapons handling followed by theoretical lessons about ballistics, bullet trajectory, and the impact of fire on different distances. During their first drills on local training grounds (*Standortübungsplätze*), soldiers were trained to correctly judge distances by estimation methods. Soldiers who could deliver precise estimation results were assigned to their platoon commanders to act as range estimators. This skill would enable their commanders to gauge the effective range as accurately and as quickly as possible.

Prior to the war, German infantrymen were trained to maximize the impact of massed rifle fire, both at squad and platoon level. Aimed fire was of limited value against individual soldiers at distances beyond 400 meters. Squads and platoons were taught to lay down a beaten zone (*Garbe*) upon enemy formations. Using the beaten zone, soldiers shot at an area rather than individual targets.

16 (von Bartsch, 1907), pp. 1–250.
17 (Harrell, 1983), p. 71.

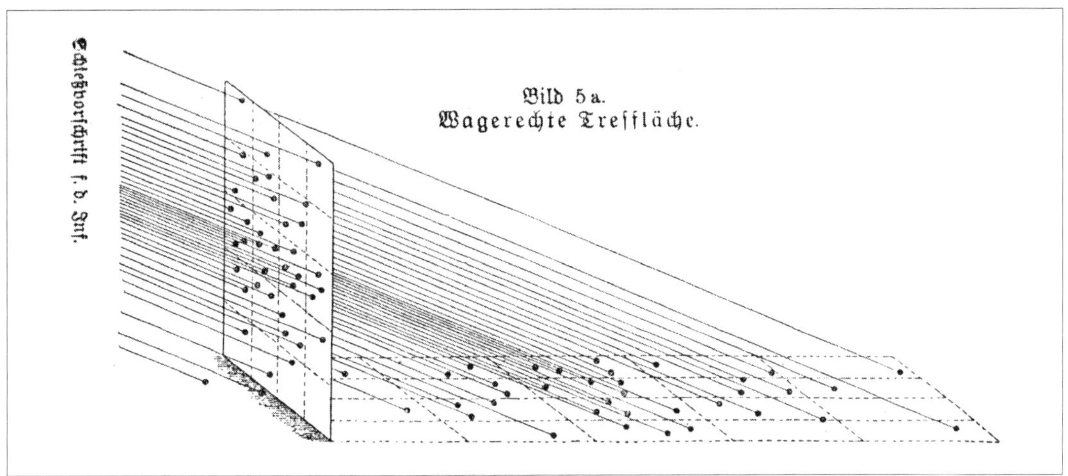

Beaten Zone of a Volley According to Infantry Marksmanship Manual.

Then marksmanship training was divided into two major sections: marksmanship training drill (*Schulschießen*) and actual firing at ranges (*Standortschießanlagen*). Marksmanship training drill was carried out by going through a sequence of marksmanship exercises at the local rifle or firing ranges (*Standortschießanlagen*). This Schulschießen prepared soldiers for the live firing exercises (*Gefechtsschießen*). This live fire was done either in the open terrain of local training centers (*Standortübungsplätze*) or corps training centers (*Truppenübungsplätze*).

Schulschießen drilled soldiers to fire their weapons precisely and accurately in all three major aiming positions—lying, kneeling, and standing. This training would prepare them for later live firing. The marksmanship training year started on 1 October and ended on 30 September. In addition to the enlisted men, all NCOs and lieutenants had to participate in marksmanship training.

The Schulschießen consisted of two different classes. The second class was the beginners' class for all new soldiers in their first year of training and theoretically started 1 October. But, in fact, Schulschießen would only begin after a minimum of weapons drill was successfully completed. After that the soldiers had to first go through a sequence of preparatory firing exercises (*Vorübungen*) and marksmanship exercises (*Hauptübungen*). After successfully completing these exercises, soldiers were promoted into the first training class for their second year of service. Soldiers showing poor marksmanship had to go through the second class again. In general, soldiers completed their exercises by using their personal weapons in order to learn about individual aiming errors of their weapons. To successfully complete the second class, six Vorübungen targets between 150 to 200 meters distance were engaged in each of the three firing positions.[18] In each position, three rounds had to be fired. These exercises were all different from each other by changing distance, aiming position, targets, and scoring requirements.

Eight Hauptübungen, again in all three aiming positions on targets 200 to 400 meters distant, followed these exercises. Each of the exercises required five rounds each. The Hauptübungen also differed: distance, aiming position, kind of targets, and minimum scores

[18] Lying (some free-handed, some with rifle resting on a sandbag), kneeling, and standing positions.

all changed. So during their first training year, soldiers fired at least 58 rounds—not a large quantity, bearing in mind the need for good rifle marksmanship. Since at least some exercises could be repeated, it can be estimated that soldiers fired about 60 to a maximum of 100 rounds during their first year.[19]

After promotion to the first class, they again had to fire four preparatory exercises at 150 to 200 meters with three rounds each and six main exercises at 300 and 400 meters with a budget of five rounds each. This training totaled 42 rounds during the entire second year of service. If they were lucky, soldiers of both classes joined an extended live firing exercise (*Gefechtsschießen*) allowing them to fire their rifles under war-like conditions with a higher allocation of rounds. Live firing exercises could be designed more freely to meet realistic battle conditions. Gefechtsschießen was not individual fire but rather volley fire, to be carried out on platoon or even company level. However, there was almost no nighttime firing in the German Army prior to 1914, which was a decided weakness.[20] Leaders went through the course twice. Lieutenants, first lieutenants, NCOs, and *Kapitulanten* (who had twice successfully met the conditions of the first class) were promoted into a special class of marksmanship (*besondere Schießklasse*) in which exercises comparable to the first class were conducted but with higher requirements.

German infantrymen were trained to adjust the rate of fire according to circumstances; otherwise, a prolonged firefight would rapidly consume ammunition. Slow fire (1.5 to 3 rounds per minute) was indicated for distant targets in poor light and for targets that were difficult to see. A high rate of fire (3–7 rounds per minute) was indicated for engaging advancing enemy march columns. High rate was also used to attain fire superiority and to support friendly troops that were bounding forward. Maximum rates of fire (7–12 rounds per minute) were used just before an assault was launched, against an enemy assault and in sudden close-range combat.

It was expected of officers and NCOs to deliver better marksmanship results than their enlisted men. To encourage better results, numerous prizes were offered by the regional nobility and commanders. For example, the first prize for a regimental officer's marksmanship's contest could be an honor sword. Awarded in 10 classes, the shooting lanyard became a very popular marksmanship award particularly for NCOs. Kaiser Wilhelm II introduced a special marksmanship award exclusively for NCOs and enlisted men—the Schützenschnur (shooting lanyard). On 27 January 1894, the Kaiser's birthday, this award was authorized by supreme cabinet order (*Allerhöchste Kabinettsorder* or *AKO*), an imperial order issued through the military cabinet.

Another highly sought after marksmanship award was the *Kaiserabzeichen*, a special award created for the first time by the Kaiser in 1895. It was awarded to only one infantry company per army corps, the best performing *Jäger* company of all Jäger and Schützen in the entire army, and the best performing battery of field- or foot artillery. Starting in 1903, the best performing machinegun formation also had an award. This award was worn with pride on the right arm of the uniform. EM kept their Kaiserabzeichen until they were dismissed

[19] (Kriegsministerium, 1909) pp. 30–35. Cavalry had a similar training system to improve marksmanship with their carbines (Kriegsministerium, 1909). In the respective manual for the field artillery the firing rules and exercises for field guns and field-howitzers were laid down (Kriegsministerium, 1914). For marksmanship with their carbines the field artillery made use of the cavalry manual. This was similar for the foot-artillery (Kriegsministerium, 1908).

[20] In fact, the infantry marksmanship manual offered some hints for nighttime firing, but they were rarely used, except by a few Army Corps in their training centers. Night training was not a particular strength of the German army prior to 1914.

from service; NCOs kept it as long as they served with the awarded company.[21] In Bavaria, Saxony, and Württemberg, similar awards named *Königspreis* were given for the best performing infantry company of their army corps.

In Spandau-Ruhleben northwest of Berlin, the Prussians maintained a marksmanship school (*Infanterie-Schießschule*). The school instructed special marksmanship training courses to NCOs and officers. In addition they cooperated with the armory in Spandau and with the Infantry Rifle Testing Commission (*Gewehr-Prüfungskommission*) in testing new kinds of infantry ammunition.

Army Corps Training Centers (Truppenübungsplätze) and Firing Ranges

Many, but not all, corps had a field-training center maintained by the corps. Of the 25 army corps, all but four of them had major training areas that were assigned to army corps. The size of the training areas is listed in hectares (1 ha = 2.47 acres). The average corps training area was about 4–5,000 hectares in size, but some like Friedrichsfelde, Darmstadt and Orb were far smaller.

Prussian Army[22]

Guard Corps: Döberitz (4,172 ha), Zossen (5,427 ha)
I Army Corps: none
II Army Corps: none
III Army Corps: Jüterbog (4,788 ha)
IV Army Corps: Alten-Grabow (4,802 ha)
V Army Corps: Posen (Warthelager)[23] (today in Poland, spelled Posznan) (5,197 ha)
VI Army Corps: Neuhammer am Queis (today in Poland, spelled Swietoszow) (5,492 ha)
VII Army Corps: Friedrichsfeld bei Wesel (969 ha), Senne (lager) (3,989 ha)
VIII Army Corps: Elsenborn bei Aachen (today in Belgium, Eupen-Malmedy area) (2,755 ha)
IX Army Corps: Lockstedt (today spelled Lokstedt) (4,467 ha)
X Army Corps: Munster (*lager*) (4,805 ha)
XI Army Corps: Ohrdruf (4,669 ha)
XIV Army Corps: Heuberg (*Lager* Stetten) (4,077 ha)[24]
XV Army Corps: Bitsch, Elsaß (today in France, spelled Bitche) (3,450 ha), Oberhofen, Elsaß (today in France, spelled Oberhoffen) (958 ha)
XVI Army Corps: none
XVII Army Corps: Gruppe (Tucheler Heide) (partly changed to Poland already in 1919, spelled Grupa) (1,252 ha), Hammerstein (today in Poland, spelled, Czarne) (1,343 ha)
XVIII Army Corps: Darmstadt (382 ha) (quite small), Orb (today Bad Orb) (692 ha)
XX Army Corps: Arys (today in Poland, spelled Orsysz)
XXI Army Corps: none

---

21 (Alten G. v., 1913), p. 224.
22 (Friedag, 1914), p. 52.
23 Names given in parentheses such as "Lager Stetten" or Munster ("lager") are common colloquial names frequently encountered together or even instead of the official names. *Lager* means "camp."
24 Also known as Sigmaringen.

Bavarian Army[25]

I.KB: (*Lager*) Lechfeld (2,379 ha)
II. KB: Hammelburg (2,381 ha)
III. KB: Grafenwöhr (~9,000 ha)

Saxon Army[26]

XII Army Corps (I. KS): Königsbrück[27] (4,709 ha)
XIX Army Corps (II. KS): Zeithain (3,919 ha)

Württemberg Army[28]

XIII Army Corps: Münsingen (3,672 ha)

Each training area had its own *Kommandantur*, usually headed by a major general or a colonel. It did not belong to the army corps but reported directly to the respective War Ministry.

The Kommandantur of such a Truppenübungsplatz did not belong to the organization of the respective army corps, so the Kommandant did not report to the commanding general of "his" army corps. In the Rangliste, they are not listed with the army corps organizations. On the other hand, it is not believed that they formally reported into the War Ministry since the responsible department (5. *Übungsplatz-Abteilung*) was headed by a lieutenant colonel (*Oberstlt*. v. Oven), and the commandants were usually colonels or major generals.[29] This department was basically responsible for the layout and administration of the training areas. Probably the Kommandanturen reported directly to the *Armee-Verwaltungs-Department* (BD) of the War Ministry that was headed by Major General v. Schöler (*Direktor*) in 1914.[30] This department was also superior to the 5. Department. At the end of the Rangliste, the Truppenübungsplätze are listed in the garrison list (*Verzeichnis der Standorte)* including the number of the army corps they belonged to—without specifying what "belonged to" exactly meant. It is the same in pages 137–139 of the Rangliste 1914 in which the Truppenübungsplätze are listed with the names of their commandants and adjutants and again the army corps they belonged to without specifying what that means.

Munster, for example, was a large training area that was certainly not used exclusively by the X Army Corps. The Guards Corps had two training areas assigned, while many corps in the East had no assigned training area at all. Some training areas like Friedrichsfelde in Wesel (VII Army Corps) were actually not big enough to accommodate an entire corps for field training and inspection purposes. The army corps were basically free to use other training areas as well; they just had to book the facilities in advance. The War Ministry had to coordinate the scheduled autumn maneuvers and to make sure that budgetary restrictions (railroad transportation) were observed so that all training facilities would be equally used. Most commanding generals insisted upon frequently changing the training areas to prevent their officers from getting too familiar with the local situation.[31]

---

25 (Friedag, 1914), p. 69.
26 (Friedag, 1914), p. 73.
27 Not in use today and closed to the public due to chemical contamination caused by Soviet troops before 1990.
28 (Friedag, 1914), p. 76.
29 (Kriegsministerium, 1914), p. 13, and (Friedag, 1914), p. 44.
30 (Kriegsministerium, 1914), p. 12.
31 All *Kommandanturen* were called *Königliche Kommandantur*, except Bitsch and Oberhofen in Alsace that were *Kaiserliche Kommandanturen*—another hint that those *Kommandanturen* were assigned to army corps but were not incorporated.

For the autumn inspections the training area that generally was used belonged to one of the army corps that was hosting the autumn maneuvers. Particularly in the East (Eastern Prussia and Pomerania), a kind of makeshift or improvised training grounds could be used in open land since there was enough sparsely populated land available. Except for artillery live firing, all other forms of training could be conducted there. Infantry live firing could be carried out at local rifle ranges (*Standortschießanlagen*) or at local training areas (*Standortübungsplätze*). Scheduling of exercises, maneuvers and inspections was based upon the regulations given by the *Bestimmungen für die größeren Truppenübungen (Manöver-Ordnung)*—D.V.E. Nr. 270 in Prussia, D.V. Nr. 80 in Bavaria. This manual laid out detailed schedules for the autumn maneuvers (except the Kaisermanöver) and inspections within an army corps. The War Ministry in cooperation with the Great General Staff scheduled the Kaisermanöver years ahead.

As most garrisons were in urban areas, these facilities or training grounds offered a lot more open area. They were called Trüppenubungsplätze and were mainly developed during the period when Waldersee and Schlieffen were Chiefs of the General Staff. Since the Kaisermanöver had been turned into a kind of military performance led by the Kaiser, there was a need for the exercise to be performed under "war-like" conditions. These Truppenübungsplätze were also used as forming up places for new divisions during the war. In addition, there were wartime training centers at Beverloo in Belgium and in Warsaw, on the Eastern front. In the summer and autumn of 1917, the training center at Warsaw as well as a field recruit depot on the Russian front, was sent westward as replacements due to the collapse of the Russian Army.[32] In addition to these corps training centers, many regiments usually had smaller local training grounds (*Standort-Übungsplatz*) for company and battalion drill. In fact, the most realistic drill and training were often carried out at these training centers, which really blossomed during the 1890s, rather than during maneuvers.

[32] (The General Staff, 1918), pp. 18–19.

CHAPTER 11

DOCTRINE IN GENERAL

Combat is about morale; the human factor is paramount. It is not simply about the infliction of casualties. Two recent books by Terence Zuber detail the awakening of doctrinal study from the German view in the early period of the war.[1] These books show German training and drills to be more efficient than Allied ones at inflicting casualties. That is only one leg of a three-legged stool. Shock action, mobility, and firepower create the environment. All of those elements need to be combined to have an effect on the enemy. The desired end is that the enemy runs away. It is most important to the reader to understand that the essence of combat is less about killing the enemy than it is about making him run away and **then** killing him. It is far easier to kill the opponent when his back is turned. The failure of morale in one soldier can easily lead to a failure of morale in the entire unit and is extremely contagious. Therefore, the essence of war revolves around the morale of the opponent. There is a famous tenet by Napoleon—the morale is to the physical as three is to one.[2] One author goes so far as to say that battles are fought with rifles and other materials; however, they are won in the morale dimension when one side or the other breaks and runs away.[3]

Training forces to prevent their morale from breaking is vital, but there is a significant difference between the practice of training and doctrine and its actual execution on the battlefield. Carl v. Clausewitz calls this difference a leap from war on paper to real war, though his phraseology has an old-fashioned ring to it.[4] He actually called the aim of warfare "disarming the enemy." Consequently, if you are to force the enemy to do your bidding by making war on him, you must either make him actually defenseless or at least put him in a position that makes this danger probable.[5]

Realistically, we are talking about August 1914, a time of untried armies that were maneuvering about the battlefield using the doctrine that they had been trained to perform during peacetime. This maneuvering was not the work of experienced armies or proven leadership. There had indeed been smaller wars but they were simply not on this scale. Zuber did a great service by introducing this concept and creating a dialogue about training,

1 (Zuber, *The Mons Myth: A Reassessment of the Battle*, 2010) and (Zuber, *Ardennes 1914: The Battle of the Frontiers*, 2007)

2 (Showalter D. E., *The Wars of German Unification*, 2004), p. 175.

3 (Echevarria II, 2000), p. 125.

4 (Clausewitz, 1989), p. 119.

5 (Clausewitz, 1989), p. 77.

doctrine, and execution. However, his conclusions revolve around training in the German army. He gives the impression that training and doctrine followed written regulations. This view is much too simplistic and ignores the independent training power of the army corps commanders.

These differences were based upon varying interpretations of how to harness modern technology to the martial spirit fostered by institutional bias and history. Each of the major weapons' branches had their traditional example of martial spirit that occurred during the Franco-Prussian War. For the infantry, the greatest example was the attack of the Guard at St. Privat; for the cavalry, the desperate charge of general v. Bredow's cavalry brigade at Mars-la-Tour; and for the artillery, the successful shelling at Sedan. Zuber says: "This chapter will concentrate on the final German tactical doctrine that was implemented in 1906 and used as a basis for subsequent training."[6] He also says that this 1906 document is his baseline for studying German tactics and training and shows what tactical doctrine was actually taught in the German army.[7] This doctrine changed dramatically depending upon interpretation by the army corps and the officers in charge. The 1906 document applied only to the infantry, and things changed a great deal in those 43 years of peace, during which there was no firm consensus on the application of the doctrine. Doctrine had not kept pace with technology, as Col. Charles Repington, the military correspondent for the *London Times* concluded after observing the 1911 maneuvers: "No other modern army displays such a profound contempt for the effect of modern fire."[8]

Ludendorff summarized the offensive dogma in a memorandum addressed to the Reichskanzler and the War Minister when he demanded a further build-up of force. He had worked together with Moltke the Younger and on 21 December 1913 said:

> The superiority of our artillery equipment is currently based on our primary focus on the development of steep angle fire (field howitzers) and on our heavy artillery. Besides this superiority, we are also ahead of the French concerning the equipment of our army with field kitchens and tents and by having better infantry weapons. But catching up to us in these fields will only be a matter of money and investments for the French. They will certainly catch up in these fields and certainly even overtake us. But where they will never be able to overtake us is in the number of men suitable for military service if we only completely employ all the men who are available to us.[9]

Pitching men against fire by pushing forward an offensive at all costs still was the leading doctrine of the more traditional German military leaders until the bitter experiences of trench warfare taught them differently.[10]

---

6 (Zuber, *The Mons Myth: A Reassessment of the Battle*, 2010), p. 13.

7 (Zuber, *The Mons Myth: A Reassessment of the Battle*, 2010), p. 11.

8 (Herwig H. , 2009), p. 47.

9 Translated by the author. Complete memorandum in two different versions is given in (Reichsarchiv, 1930), pp. 158–173; quotation from p. 166.

10 This doctrine of offensive at all cost was not exclusively German; it was also the leading doctrine in Austria, France, and Russia. (Howard M., 1984), p. 510–526.

LEADERSHIP DOCTRINE

To understand the operational decisions of higher German leaders in 1914, we have to discuss two basic axioms of the German leadership doctrine: *Auftragstaktik* and *Vernichtungsschlacht.*

Auftragstaktik is a relatively modern phrase used in the German Army, but the concept is of great antiquity, dating back at least as far as the time of the Prussian reformers, Scharnhost and Gneisenau. The elder Moltke once wrote:

> A favorable situation will never be exploited if commanders wait for orders. The highest commander and the youngest soldier must always be conscious of the fact that omission and inactivity are worse than resorting to the wrong expedient.[11]

This same thinking governed command and control during the Great War. In 1914, it was called *Führen durch Weisungen*—leadership by directions. Briefly, Führen durch Weisungen implies that the superior commander will not issue a detailed order that was absolutely binding for the subordinate commander. Rather the superior will issue a directive defining a mission and a briefing about his intent—why he would set such goals. This frees the superior leader from issuing too detailed orders; on the other hand, it gives freedom to the subordinate leader to accomplish the set goal in a flexible way. The subordinate could adjust to changes in the situation the superior leader could not have foreseen when setting the goal. To enable accomplishment of the goal, the superior commander had to assign the necessary forces and logistical support and to set a timeframe in which the mission could be accomplished. The subordinate leader was then given the planning initiative and enjoyed, to a certain extent, a freedom in execution, which allowed a high degree of flexibility on the operational and tactical levels of command. We will further use the term Auftragstaktik since it is shorter, more concise, and better known today. *Auftragstaktik*, which is translated as "mission-type command" in the English language, is certainly still a central component and a core element of the German leadership doctrine on each level today.

Moltke purposefully refused to call it "leading by orders." German military thinking also assumed that military leadership could only be learned to a certain extent—that military leadership could not be put into manuals and regulations to be stubbornly executed word-by-word and by-the-book. Freiherr v. Hammerstein-Equord, *Chef der Heeresleitung,* wrapped this idea up in his introduction to the manual on military leadership *H.Dv. 300/1* issued in 1933: "Leadership in war is a matter of artistry, a free and creative activity based upon scientific principles. It implies the highest personal requirements for the military leader practicing it."[12]

Auftragstaktik developed as a command and control principle after the end of the Fredrick the Great-style army at Jena and Auerstedt in 1806. The word Auftragstaktik is a modern word introduced during the Second World War and still widely used today. As mentioned above, prior to 1914, Auftragstaktik was named Führen durch Weisungen that changed into *Führen durch Aufträge* (meaning "to lead by assigning tasks") during the 1920s and 1930s. Auftragstaktik combined the intent that was expressed previously by other phrases. The reader should bear in mind that the wording was indeed different prior to 1914. The strict

[11] (Dupuy, *A Genius for War*, 1977), p. 116

[12] (Chef der Heeresleitung, 1933), p. 1.

and unconditional obedience Frederick the Great had demanded from his soldiers—who were frequently paid substitutes pressed into army service—had led to total disaster against the differently trained and organized revolutionary French armies. During the liberation wars against Napoleon 1812 to 1815, the citizen soldier served more or less voluntarily—it was no longer unconditional obedience.[13]

Auftragstaktik was not introduced into the German military doctrine by decree or order. Its adoption was a difficult, long-running process. After the disastrous defeat of the old Prussian Army in 1806, which still saw itself in the tradition of Frederick the Great, it became obvious that a thorough modernization of tactics, ordnance, and, finally, also of leadership doctrine, was needed to win the war against Napoleon. As discussed in Chapter 12 on infantry doctrine, Napoleon's entirely new style of military doctrine, executed with highly motivated soldiers instead of conscripts (often forced into military service against their will) led to very successful attacks in solid columns with *tirailleurs* ahead against the thin firing lines of the Prussian infantry and this style consequently exposed all deficiencies of the old Prussian Army. The first step towards a change in leadership doctrine was brought about by the *Exerzir-Reglement für die Infanterie der Königlich Preussischen Armee* from 1812, in which the formal orchestration of combat was abolished at least for the higher levels of leadership; independent situational assessment and decision-making became important factors.[14] For the lower levels, the change from line to columns tactics with its massive bodies of troops made things easier, but continued to impose severe limits on the conduct of battle.

In the Unification Wars between 1864 and 1871, the size of armies had definitely outgrown the ability of the supreme commander to exercise direct command of his deployed forces. To keep some form of control, it now became important to develop a new concept that, on one hand, would enable some independence of action while, on the other hand, would preclude misguided action by lower-level leaders. Avoiding such misguidance would require uniformly trained and thinking military leaders on all levels—the need for general staff officers. The elder Moltke addressed the problem by developing a leadership doctrine, going beyond tactical drill manuals like the aforementioned Exerzier-Reglement for the first time. Moltke became the creator of the operational-level command—a command level between the tactical leadership in the firing line and the strategic leadership of the headquarters with its multiple political implications. He also became the spiritual father of operational doctrines and principles, which then served as the basis for general officers' training. Moltke played a decisive role in the development of Auftragstaktik.[15]

The German Army put such a high emphasis on general staff officers training to make sure there were uniform ways of thinking and uniform understandings of the doctrine. Confronted with a certain tactical or operational problem, each general staff officer—and since the higher commanders usually were also recruited from the pool of general staff officers also each higher commander—should come to the same assessment of the situation and finally to the same decision. Given this uniformity in operative analysis and thinking, which was also pursued on the lower levels of company grade officers and even of NCOs, detailed orders became obsolete. A very brief communication of mission, goals, and leaders intention would be a sufficient guidance to make sure the goals would be accomplished as intended.

---

13 (Widder, 2002), pp. 3–9.

14 (Kriegsministerium, 1812). Please also check the tactical regulations for the cavalry and for the infantry, both issued in Berlin 1812.

15 (Widder, 2002), pp. 3–4

The elder Moltke used to lead his armies during the campaigns in 1866 and in 1870–71 by telegraphing quite short daily missions, usually only a few words per army. Before Moltke's communication style during the Unification Wars is taken as role model, it should be born in mind that Moltke's command style was tailored to the available communication channels. Whenever possible, Moltke preferred face-to-face meetings with the King and with his subordinate commanders.

Particularly with poor communication lines, Auftragstaktik allows the subordinate leader to pursue the given goals following the intent of his commander even if things develop differently under enemy fire. A core piece of Auftragstaktik is a clear understanding of the goals and of the intent of the assigned mission. Only if there has been clear guidance during the issue of the order will the subordinate leader be able to accomplish his mission given unexpected friction. When acting under mission-type command, there should never be any kind of "waiting for further advice," but independent attempts at trouble-shooting and problem solving instead. Such independent action is clearly taking the risk of violating other previously expressed constraints as a routine step to accomplishing the mission. Therefore, Auftragstaktik is seen as a leadership doctrine sustaining a particular type of innovative and independent leadership culture. Still today, this results in a leadership doctrine that teaches junior German army officers that when under fire, making a wrong decision is always better than making no decision and waiting for further direction.[16]

On the other hand, Auftragstaktik requires military leaders on all levels who have been trained to be able to command one or two levels higher than their current rank. The platoon commander should be trained how to lead a company and should understand how things are working on battalion level. The regimental commander should be able to lead a brigade. Even NCOs were trained in carrying out command assignments one level above. Therefore sergeants and *Vize-Feldwebel* were able to take temporary command of platoons and even of companies. Company grade officers frequently took temporary command of battalions; then, once another regular commander was made available, such temporary leaders stepped back into their former position. To distinguish such temporary commanders from regular commanders, they were called *Führer* in German.

Moltke the Elder did not call this doctrine Auftragstaktik; he called it "leading by direction and guidance." Based on his idea that leading big formations such as armies could not be learned in peace-time and that morale would be one of the overwhelming factors in combat, Moltke emphasized the absolute requirement for commanders to act independently in order to succeed in combat. These independent commanders and officers could not be led by orders regulating everything down to the least detail but only by directions and guidance, explaining the intentions of the higher level leader and then leaving the execution to the discretion of the subordinate commander.[17] From Moltke the Elder's *Advice to Higher Military Commanders (Verordnung für die höheren Truppenführer vom 24 Juni 1869)*, this doctrine found its way into the infantry manuals from 1889 and 1906 and into the *Directions to Higher Military Commanders (Grundzüge der Höheren Truppenführung vom 1 Januar 1910)*.[18] Interest-

[16] Bundesminister der Verteidigung (Ed.), *HDv 100/100 Truppenführung (TF)*, Bonn 1987, numbers 601–611 and 711–716. Similar in the updated 1998 edition.

[17] (Großer Generalstab, *Abtheilung für Kriegsgeschichte I*, 1900), pp. 171–174, *Verordnung für die höheren Truppenführer vom 24 June 1869*.

[18] (Kriegsministerium, 1889), pp. 108–109, (Kriegsministerium, 1906), pp. 78–79 and (Kriegsministerium, 1910), pp. 20–21. All three sources convey the essential message that military leaders on all levels should be trained to analyze the situation by themselves and to make their independent decisions based upon the task they were assigned by their superiors.

ingly, Auftragstaktik was not mentioned in the General Staff Officer's Handbook, but it was one of the essential doctrines upon which general staff officer's training was based.

Auftragstaktik was a perfect tool at lower levels of command. In the turmoil of battle, junior commanders were usually not able to refer to their superiors for further advice or orders; they had to be able to act independently within the framework of intention of their commanders. Auftragstaktik became difficult to apply at more senior command levels. Many generals tended to pursue their own ideas and these were not always in harmony with the intentions of their superiors. Among army corps and army commanders, there were many strong-willed personalities who would over-interpret their freedom of decision given by Auftragstaktik. In such a case, it required a strong and charismatic senior commander to keep all the strong-willed personalities in line with the intentions of the OHL. As long as personalities like Moltke the Elder or Schlieffen were in charge, there was no issue in transmitting the intent. With a softer or weaker commander like Moltke the Younger, the higher headquarter intent seemed negotiable. The younger Moltke certainly was a brilliant and highly intellectual analyst, but he did not have the charisma to ensure that his subordinate leaders would follow his intentions during critical situations such as the battle at the Ourcq. There he failed to impose his will upon the commander of the First Army in person, instead he sent a lieutenant colonel to the headquarters.

If Auftragstaktik was the first axiom of leadership, *Vernichtungsschlacht*—the battle of annihilation was the second axiom. For the German army around 1900, a dogma of the offensive became more and more central. Clausewitz considered the defensive as the stronger form of combat. Schlieffen turned that around into a dogma of the offensive—not only offensive but also annihilation, because for him, a victory achieved over the enemy by frontal attack was only an "ordinary victory." Rather, he considered that only total annihilation of the enemy force by envelopment was acceptable. At that time, all European armies focused more on the offensive than on the defensive. However, before 1914, the German doctrine of the offensive had been transposed into a dogma of annihilating the enemy in one huge battle, usually by enveloping the enemy force from the flanks.[19] Clausewitz contradicted this concept. His maxim that defense was a stronger form of fighting than attack was certainly not easy to explain when looking at offense at all cost.[20] To Moltke the Elder, both kinds of victory were of equal value. The elder Moltke urged his leaders to always push the tired troops forward after a victorious fight to make sure the beaten enemy was not able to settle down and prepare for further defense. Pursuit even became a major issue in the outline of higher-level military leadership that Moltke issued to his commanders in 1869.[21]

In his series of "Cannae" writings, Schlieffen declared Hannibal's victory over the vastly superior Roman army under the command of Consul Aemilius Paulus on 2 August 216 B.C. as the role model for the operational leadership of the German Army.[22] Schlieffen, who was a particular student of military history, went so far as to slightly bend historical truth to fit into his Cannae theories. In those writings, the wars of Frederick the Great and Napoleon and the Unification Wars were all re-interpreted under the focus of the Cannae-style battle.[23] Possibly

19 (Geyer, 1984), p. 532 and (Wallach, 1967). Jehuda Wallach was born in 1921 in Haigerloch in Germany, emigrated from Germany to Palestine in 1936 and made a military career up to the level of a division commander in the Israeli Defense Force.

20 (Clausewitz, 1989), p. 84.

21 (Großer Generalstab, *Abtheilung für Kriegsgeschichte I, 1900*), pp. 206–215.

22 (Freytag-Loringhoven G., 1913), pp. 27–30.

23 (Freytag-Loringhoven G., 1913), pp. 30–259.

the most famous quote from his works is: "the enemy's front is not the objective. The essential thing is to crush the enemy's flanks . . . and complete the extermination by attack upon his rear."[24] By doing so, he vastly influenced the operative thinking of an entire generation of military leaders who undertook general staff training. These leaders distinguished themselves from the old-school traditionalists, but still kept to traditional forms of tactical and operational doctrines. To them, too, a frontally won victory was no longer a real victory but just an "ordinary victory." The real victory had to be won through envelopment and by total annihilation of the enemy. It is probable that this doctrine (that can be found in Schlieffen's final study of 1905) is the real Schlieffen Plan that he imparted to the generation of military leaders who led the German armies in the field in 1914.

In the handbook on tactical training at officers' schools, a frontal breakthrough was considered to be dangerous, because the attacking forces breaking through could easily come under concentric fire from both flanks of the breakthrough or even be cut-off. Envelopment from the flanks was taught as the best and most efficient way of beating the enemy.[25] German tactical doctrine considered this Cannae dogma as superior to that of the traditionalists among their own officers and superior to the French doctrine. The French were still seen as operating in the Napoleonic tradition—seeking frontal breakthrough through columnar attack on the operational level. This doctrine led to German leaders focusing (perhaps obsessively) on trying to conduct outflanking operations and envelopments. Only Cannae-style attacks could lead to success; ordinary victories could only damage enemy forces, but not completely annihilate them. In a diary entry for 22 August 1914, about the British Expeditionary Force (BEF), General Wilhelm Groener wrote: "Just let them come! Our most ardent wish is to achieve no 'ordinary' victory against these scoundrels but rather one à la Schlieffen."[26]

THE COMBINED ARMS BATTLE

There was no one general manual that combined the doctrine of all of the different arms. While the modern American army is used to one overarching operations manual, a combined manual was unknown in Germany. As a result, doctrinal synchronization at all the various command levels was lacking. The primary policy was to attack. This concept worked well with the operational plan at the start of the war. Now the question was how to focus all of the different arms at one place and one time to have the desired effect? There were indeed initial thoughts about the "Combined Arms Battle" (*Kampf der verbundenen Waffen* as it is called in German language). But these first drafts were restricted to general staff officers and high-level commanders; the ideas being written only in the classified handbook for general staff officers[27] and in a manual having the concealing title *Grundzüge der höheren Truppenführung* (outline of high-level military leadership).[28] Basically, the German army had to gather experience in these issues on the battlegrounds of the Great War.

---

[24] (Shafritz, 1990), p. 120.

[25] (*General-Inspektion des Militär-Erziehungs- und Bildungswesen* , 1912), pp. 139–143.

[26] (Stoneman, 2006), p. 187.

[27] (Generalstab, *Anahltspunkte für den Generalstabsdienst*, 1914) Here particularly in the small amendment *Taschenbuch des Generalstabsoffiziers* (General Staff Officer's Pocket Book) that had to be amended to the *Anhaltspunkte* upon mobilization.

[28] (Großer Generalstab, *Abtheilung für Kriegsgeschichte I, 1900*), pp. 171–215.

After the war, Colonel Friedrich v. Cochenhausen published a handbook entitled *Truppenführung* about these experiences of military leadership in the field.[29] The term became one of the keywords in the tactical developments of the 1920s. Finally, Hans v. Seeckt introduced this issue into the *Reichswehr*. In 1923, a manual about leadership in the battle of combined weapons was issued.[30] In 1933, Generaloberst v. Hammerstein-Equord put all these thoughts together into the two-volume manual on military leadership, bearing the short title Truppenführung.[31] The phrase Truppenführung now became the standard German phrase for higher military leadership including the combined arms battle. Even today in the Federal Armed German Forces, the pivotal manual on leadership is called *H.Dv 100/100 Truppenführung*. Truppenführung is abbreviated "*TF*" among generations of general staff officers and nicknamed *Tante Frieda* (Aunt Frieda). Aunt Frieda became the mother of all doctrinal discussions in the German army.

ATTACK

In tactical terms, attacks were to be conducted almost entirely by dismounted troops. There were three recognized phases in the dismounted attack: the forming up or assembly (*Aufmarsch*), the deployment (*Entfaltung*), and the extension (*Entwicklung*). Deployment consisted of changing from marching formations to formations with broader fronts, but still close, such as battalions in columns or lines of companies in columns. Deployment was dependent on hostile fire and varied accordingly, but generally speaking, may be said to have taken place 2,000 to 1,500 yards from the enemy's position. This advance took the form of successive lines; firing line, support line, and reserves, with roughly 300 yards between each. The usual plan was to keep reserves in echelon on one or both flanks. Extension was the distribution of troops in fighting formations in the form of skirmishing lines and took place at 1,500–800 yards from the enemy. Then the soldiers would further disperse into smaller assault groups at somewhere between 600 and 800 yards. During maneuvers the original extension varied from four to six paces between men, and was sometimes as much as 10 paces, though the regulations lay down two paces as standard. Given the decentralization of Auftragstaktik, the distance had to be determined as low as the section level. This variation is followed in the regulation with an admonition to use terrain whenever possible to regroup and restore order and cohesion.[32]

The last 300–160 yards became the area of the final assault or *Sturm*. Between zero and 400 yards, soldiers could aim their fire at individual soldiers causing casualties and inflicting psychological effects on the enemy. Beyond 400 yards, riflemen would have to fire at area targets. This plan of attack inflicted fewer casualties, had a reduced psychological effect, and was a consistent drain on ammunition. During the final attack, supporting artillery and other fires would have to be lifted to avoid causing casualties among the attacking infantry.[33]

---

29 (Cochenhausen, 1928)
30 (Reichswehrministerium, 1923)
31 (Hammerstein-Equord, 1936)
32 (Echevarria II, 2000), p. 124.
33 (Echevarria II, 2000), p. 21.

COMMUNICATIONS

When trying to orchestrate the actions of the different arms or branches, there is nothing more important than communication. Armies throughout history have used different signaling methods to try to communicate with far-off subunits. Communicating the intentions of the infantry to the artillery would obviously increase effectiveness and reduce fratricide. Historically, artillery commanders had always been responsible for coordinating their own observed fire with the requirements of the infantry that they were supporting. The Great War offered the possibility for the first time of exploiting electronic means of communications on a large scale. However, the pre-war German army had seriously neglected this area. The primary means of communication during maneuvers and staff rides was to hand out written plans nightly. This plan would give subordinate units instructions for the next day. However, by 1914, each army corps had a company of wireless operators and telephone specialists. Some 21,000 carrier pigeons compensated for a shortage of telephones.[34]

Doctrinally, allowances had been made for the lack of electronic communications equipment. There was actually a chapter in the different manuals on bugle signals. In the infantry manual, there were 23 different bugle signals that were mainly used during tactical exercises or during live fire exercises. These signals could only be applied during peacetime exercises; they were forbidden in combat except for the following three:

- Fix bayonets! *(Seitengewehr pflanzt auf!)* To be used if a bayonet attack was ordered by the commander;
- Move fast forward! *(rasch vorwärts!);*
- Attention! *(Achtung!)* (An unexpected enemy attack).[35]

Several written sources indicate that signals such as "alarm," "open fire," and "withdrawal" were still in fact used during the first weeks of the war. Because there was no radio, a company or battalion commander had to lead by the power of his voice or of his whistle. He could point his sword into the intended direction or lead by his own example. Runners also forwarded orders. Obviously, there were inevitable differences between what could be used in peacetime practice or wartime execution.

Despite the lack of a governing doctrine, the infantry and artillery shared one common enemy, and that was time. To maintain momentum of the offensive, there was a need for both branches to close with the enemy and bring the battle to a successful conclusion. Artillery doctrine taught that dispersal and covered positions were essential for survival of the guns. The infantry was capable of moving without making these defensive preparations. It took time for the artillery to dig in. If the infantry did not wait for the artillery to do so before advancing, they ran the danger of advancing without proper artillery support. If on the other hand they delayed, it would give more time for the enemy forces to solidify their defense. Therefore, there was a natural dichotomy, and it was the job of the commander to have patience and use both branches wisely, finding just the right time to launch the infantry forward. Clausewitz talked about the passage of time helping the defender: "It is the fact that time that is allowed to pass unused accumulates to the credit of the defenders."[36] If the infantry got too far forward, their own artillery gunners could mistake them for the enemy. This mistake could be compounded further by poor communication between the infantry

---

[34] (Herwig H., 2009), pp. 47–48.
[35] (Kriegsministerium, 1906), p. 161.
[36] (Clausewitz, 1989), p. 357.

and the artillery, especially because non-electronic means were used. As a result, the coordination of the two was fraught with difficulty.

The artillery relied upon their forward observers to watch the enemy either with binoculars or range finders. After observation, they needed to signal back the results to the battery position by means of either a kind of heliotrope or by signal lamps or—if there was time enough to get them installed—by field telephone. Indirect fire would be directed either by an observer standing on the observation ladder or by the forward observer using the same methods. Infantry commanders were in an even worse situation as far as reconnaissance was concerned. If they were lucky, they had cavalry patrols assigned from the divisional cavalry squadron. Otherwise they could only make use of foot patrols making observations and taking prisoners.

RESERVE FORCES LIMITATIONS

The Chief of Staff lamented that annually only two or three army corps participated in the big *Kaisermanöver*. There were no maneuvers that prepared anyone for moving 16 Army Corps, as they would have to do by 1914. In addition, 35 percent of the invading troops in 1914 consisted of 24 reserve divisions. While these divisions were spread out among seven armies, the reserve officers represented relatively inexperienced commanders moving with very little artillery, machinegun support, or other equipment.[37] Think back to the organization of units. Remember that pre-mobilization active units were at about half strength. Upon mobilization, these units were augmented with 46 percent reservists. In the case of reserve units, they were supplemented with about 99 percent reservists and Landwehr soldiers. Looking at the start of the war, the active-duty soldiers were those who had turned 20 in 1912 and 1913 (those who were born in 1892 and 1893). The reservists were the next five classes: 1891, 1890, 1889, 1888, and 1887. There were more reservists than there were positions in the active regiments. Surplus reservists formed or filled out other units.

The reservists who filled out one-half of each active unit may have had their active duty training in 1907–1911. Compare those years to the timing of doctrine in those branches: infantry doctrine–1906, cavalry doctrine–1909, and artillery doctrine–1907. Many of those soldiers never received any training under the new manuals, and their officers' training completely predated their teaching. In the reserve units with their Landwehr soldiers, the situation was much worse. The classes represented in reserve units significantly predated the doctrine. There were significant variances in the performance of those units compared with active units based on knowledge of doctrine alone. There was also an issue of retention of knowledge. Generally speaking, it is a far better deal to have soldiers who trained together go into combat together. In the case of the German army, the training of each unit had to be melded with the 46 percent of soldiers that had just joined the unit.

[37] (Brose, 2001), p. 158.

RECONNAISSANCE

Reconnaissance orders were issued in writing by the Ia officer and delivered to the cavalry staffs or to the aircraft, in the case of active corps, by runner—or if distances were longer by horse-mounted dispatch rider. Usually the *Höherer Kavallerie-Kommandeur* (HKKs) kept liaison officers with the army HQs in order to receive such orders quickly. Observations and reconnaissance results were noted by pencil on response forms (*Meldeblock*) by the cavalry patrol leaders. These reports were combined reconnaissance reports by the Ia of the HKK or the cavalry division and delivered—again by runner—to the army HQ. The Ia and Ic analyzed the reports and condensed them into a picture about the enemy situation for briefings to the commander and/or the chief of staff. Reconnaissance results delivered that way were usually between six and eight hours old, sometimes even 12 hours old. This was certainly not real-time delivery. In cases when the HKKs made deep patrols into enemy territory, they might take their radio stations with them. Each cavalry division had one light and one heavy station to facilitate communication the heavy stations of the army HQs. That made reporting reconnaissance results a lot faster but less secure. Although reports had to be encrypted before sending, they were very often sent openly, and the enemy was eager and able to read them.

With aircraft reconnaissance, the flow was quite similar. Airplanes were used for the first time during the German Army maneuvers of September 1911. The field aircraft battalions were usually based close to the rear echelon of the army corps HQs. Therefore, reconnaissance orders were issued in writing, and because aircraft in these early days did not carry radio equipment, the reports had to be brought back in writing—written notes the pilot penciled on a sheet of paper on his lap while steering his aircraft and sometimes while being shot at by the enemy. Information sharing took place at army HQs. Reconnaissance reports from cavalry or aircraft were delivered there, processed, then disseminated back down to the corps, normally together with orders for next day's operations. Enemy information herein was at least 12 hours old.

FRANCS-TIREURS

One semi-doctrinal issue that the Germans faced was what to do with irregulars and civilians known as *francs-tireurs*. Who exactly were francs-tireurs? One army corps deputy commander tried to define them as any citizen of a combatant nation not in a uniform, who in any way disrupted German operations communications or supply. They had been a major concern to the Germans in the Franco-Prussian War. The French considered them partisans and the Germans regarded them as terrorists. If caught by German troops, the franc-tireurs could be shot out of hand if in the act or provided a one-officer court-martial that had the power of handing out death sentences. Residents of Alsace-Lorraine found with weapons could be shot and those suspected of being a franc-tireurs would be handed over to a formal court-martial.[38]

This "francs-tireurs doctrine" really dealt with the application of the rules of war and has been the food for atrocity discussions for decades. There certainly were atrocities and standing orders to shoot civilians who were resisting. In the wake of the Franco-Prussian War, there were many stories of francs-tireurs. For four decades, stories abounded and were

[38] (Herwig H. , 2009), p. 79.

embellished about how francs-tireurs had ambushed, mutilated, and poisoned German forces during that war. The advancing armies in 1914 expected to encounter francs-tireurs whether they were there or not. As early as 3 August, shots fired from the small Belgian town of Battice at a cavalry patrol scouting the way into Liège were interpreted as franc-tireurs. This event led to the execution of three civilians and the burning of the town.[39]

A view of the inevitability of civilian involvement in combat and an "appropriate" military response permeated the German military. There was an anti-French feeling against the "people's war" or "*levée en masse,*" which was seen as legal, but reprehensible. Julius v. Hartmann, a noted theorist, said: "where the people's war breaks out, terrorism becomes a principle of military necessity."[40] Senior commanders in their 60s and 70s during the invasion of 1914 had been young officers during the Franco-Prussian War and had distinct views based on their experiences with francs-tireurs. In the Hague conventions of 1899 and 1907, there was an international endeavor to more tightly define the laws of war. The intent was to make things more civilized and less barbarous. As a result of the first convention, the German General Staff developed a "war book" to offer some guidance. It required that prisoners of war be conditionally identified, if there was some proof that they were operating as enemy soldiers. The negotiations involved a seesaw battle between smaller countries that wanted the ability to have a mass "people's war" and imperial Germany that did not. In 1908, the German Army issued the *Felddienstordnung,*[41] which provided guidance that preventive security measures were justified when there were possible attacks by enemy civilians. This guidance included threatening the inhabitants with penalties, taking hostages, and burning streets. This rule was in direct conflict to the previous endorsment of the Hague Convention, which was actually published as an appendix to the Felddienstordnung in 1911.[42]

Despite this conflict, there was no change to the language of the Felddienstordnung. Imperial German officers were trained to expect civilian resistance and to treat it as a criminal act. Specifically, the *Kriegs-Akademie* taught that Article 2 of the convention did not comply with the German viewpoint. The noted theorist and writer v. d. Goltz dismissed the 1907 Hague Convention as hypocrisy because none of the signatories had any intention of sticking to it.[43]

In the long run, the franc-tireurs situation did not turn out well for imperial Germany. Not only did Germany sustain a propaganda defeat, but also a tremendous amount of energy was used chasing reported sightings in 1914. Some of them may have been true, others of them false. There certainly were atrocities that in the German literature may have been justified, but they did not stand up in the court of international opinion. The actions could not be justified with the extant Hague Convention. It seems as though inexperienced soldiers, in total fear—sometimes fueled with alcohol—and a lifetime of stories, overreacted in many cases shooting at the "bogeyman" and taking revenge on entire cities for the actions of a real or imagined few.

---

39 (Herwig H. , 2009), pp. 108–109.

40 (Horne & Kramer, 2001), pp. 142–143.

41 (Kriegsministerium, 1908). The Bavarian Army adopted this issue in the field manual in 1914.

42 (Horne & Kramer, 2001), pp. 143–149.

43 (Horne & Kramer, 2001), pp. 149–151.

CHAPTER 12

INFANTRY DOCTRINE

Sometime during mid-August in 1914, a young French cavalry lieutenant, René Chambe, met the exhausted remains of the routed French 18 Infantry Regiment. During the battle in Lorraine, within minutes the regiment had lost almost half of its men and all but two of its officers. They were still shocked from the terrible experience that had taken their friends and could not believe what had happened: "And even without seeing the enemy! I tell you, we haven't even seen a single German!"[1]

The heavy losses had a deep impact upon those who survived. Like their imperial German counterparts, they went to war having a specific idea in mind about how that war should look. Their idea of an open battle with skirmish lines advancing with flags flying and bugles sounding came from the battles of 1870 and 1871. Now disaster had struck like a bolt out of the blue. Why was there such a gap between the prevailing doctrinal idea of war and the truth of actual war in 1914?

The development of imperial German infantry doctrine goes back to the days of Napoleon. The doctrine of that time used basically three formations for foot troops: column, line, and square. The Napoleonic Army of France was equipped with a smooth bore musket that was dreadfully inaccurate even at 150 yards. A soldier could be trained to shoot the inaccurate musket or endeavor to stab their opponent with a bayonet.[2]

Column formation was primarily used for the offense. The formation was intended to strike fear into the hearts of the opponent. Deep narrow columns of soldiers tightly packed together would move quickly and with ease of direction. The concept was to close upon the enemy's position and stab him with a bayonet. This shock action and mobility were intended to strike fear into the defense and cause the defense morale to fail. The defense would run away—routed. In addition to shock action, column formation offered ease of maneuverability. It did not however provide firepower. Massive battalion columns on a narrow front really limited any firepower coming from the column.

The line formation was used for firepower. To get the most soldiers involved, the soldiers had to stand in line three deep so that each musket could be pointed at the enemy. This line formation was another form of shocking the enemy. The maximum number of weapons would be stretched out linearly with the intent to fire on the enemy and destroy him with firepower. The primary purpose of firing at the enemy was intended to shatter

1 (Storz, 1992), p. 11.

2 The length of bayonet was about 50 cm, giving those rifles a total length of approximately 2 meters; for soldiers, who were about 1.50 meters tall on average, handling such a weapon implied quite some challenge.

the defender's morale and cause him to run away—routed and maybe inflict a few casualties along the way. As the musket was dreadfully inaccurate, it was most effective when fired as a large volley thereby increasing the odds of something hitting the target. Soldiers stood shoulder-to-shoulder several ranks deep, pointed their weapons at the enemy, and fired a volley.

The musket was a single shot weapon that required reloading after every round. Consequently, the soldier had to remain standing while reloading and was protected only by the cloud of smoke and the inaccuracies of the opponent's weapon. This formation was effective, squeezing the most out of the existing weaponry and technology. Lines would often be brought close to an enemy line, and the soldiers could trade volleys using similar technology. Lines were awkward to maintain. They were very slow to move and turning consisted of a wheel-like motion. Leaders behind the line regularly maintained control. In general, since soldiers could not be sure to hit what they were aiming at, very colorful uniforms became the norm. It was a certain way to identify troop units. It also became a matter of heritage and pride for the soldiers wearing the uniform. Our minds quickly go to visions of French soldiers in August 1914 wearing red pants as part of their heritage, despite the obvious tactical problems.

The square formation was defensive in nature; in it, the foot soldiers formed a four-sided rectangle with the bayonets sticking out. Such a formation was supposed to be a major deterrent to cavalry; however, it had the disadvantage of presenting a tightly packed target to artillery and troops in line formation who could hit two sides of the square with one fired round. Squares could move, but they were extremely slow. They were not intended to be a shock to enemy infantry, but rather a rock in a sea of attacking cavalry that would lessen the cavalry's morale if the infantry were unshaken. The German armies of the time, like all the other armies in the world, were equipped with primitive smoothbore, flintlock rifles. After the wars of Napoleon, the percussion lock rifle was officially introduced in Prussia in 1839 and made firing rifles safer and more reliable. This safety and reliability was particularly true in wet and rainy weather, but the percussion lock rifle did not affect range and precision so did not really change infantry tactics. Infantry fire was commanded in volleys in which drill had to increase the speed of reloading those long and unhandy muzzleloaders. Victory was often accomplished through bayonet attacks upon an enemy who was shaken by previous volleys of fire.

Only a very few elite Prussian units, such as light infantry battalions (the Jäger), were equipped with the more precise rifled muzzleloaders. Staffed with NCOs and men having a hunting (Jäger) or forester background, Jäger formations did not operate in the rigidly drilled formations of the line infantry formations. This rigid infantry drill with its lines, columns, and square formations was very suitable during the age of black powder rifles. A few volleys of fire covered the entire battlefield with a screen of white smoke so even the massive columns of infantry did not provide clearly visible targets to the enemy. Officers on horseback could still easily oversee and lead their platoons, companies, and battalions. In Prussia the breakthrough came in 1841 when, under the cover of extreme secrecy, the Dreyse needle-lock rifle was introduced. This rifle was breech-loaded and did not require the operator to stand while reloading. Introduction of these new breech-loaded rifles was kept so secret that during the battles of 1848 and 1849, only the first *Jäger* and guard formations were equipped with Dreyse rifles.

Prussian regulations did not reflect the opportunities this new rifle provided. The *Exerzir-Reglement für die Infanterie* from 1847 was based on the percussion lock muzzleloader model 1839.[3] Therefore, during the wars of 1864 and 1866, the Dreyse breechloaders provided an unpleasant surprise for the enemy. The written doctrine did not cover the existing technology even though the writing postdated the technology by six years. Particularly, the battle of *Königgrätz* turned out to be a bloody massacre. The Austrians, while standing, firing, and reloading their muzzleloaders, were exposed to the Prussian Dreyse rifle fire that came from infantrymen who were kneeling or lying on the ground. The Austrians were still convinced during that war that column formation and the charge with the cold steel of a bayonet would be the deciding factor. The Austrian commander devoted a lot of time to exercises in closed formations. The general thought remained that the best way to deal with the Dreyse rifle, should it be encountered, was to provide a moving target. The Austrians believed that frontal attacks would succeed because the Prussians believed such an attack was impossible and would not know how to react.[4]

While there was some evidence of success on the Austrian side such as at Custozza against the Italians, the losses to the attacking columns were appalling. Even so, no one analyzed the effect of the massive casualties on the loser's morale. Further, the professional European armies disregarded lessons that could have been learned from the American Civil War because armies of the Western Hemisphere were considered amateurish and staffed with volunteers. Professional European armies were thought to provide a completely separate example.[5]

Moltke the Elder, the Chief of the Prussian Great General Staff, evaluated the 1864 and 1866 wars and issued an "Advice to Higher Military Commanders" (*Verordnung für die höheren Truppenführer vom 24. Juni 1869*) concluding that the destructive power of rapid infantry fire from modern breechloaders could no longer be successfully dodged by traditionally conducted frontal bayonet attacks.[6] Instead, infantry should attack by moving forward in thinner skirmish lines of soldiers firing and taking cover independently. Since the French had also introduced a newly designed needle-fire rifle with increased precision and about twice the range in 1868 (the Chassepot Rifle), a change in infantry tactics seemed to be inevitable to prepare for the next war.[7] Traditionally, the German military had always distinguished between *geleitetem Feuer* and *Schützenfeuer*.

Geleitetes Feuer or directed fire was where officers controlled distance, target, and direction. Schützenfeuer, on the other hand, was used mostly by Jäger units that had better-trained, independent marksmen, who were beyond the direct control of their officers. Schützenfeuer made the more traditional officers feel uncomfortable due to the perceived loss of control. Unfortunately the war against France came too quickly after this 1869 guidance, and the required doctrinal change in tactics did not happen. These shortfalls led to several very bloody lessons for the Germans. The German armies won that war starting with a series of swift victories over the imperial French Army. Those victories were accomplished through significant numerical superiority and were often bought at the cost of very high losses.

---

3 (Kriegsministerium, 1847)

4 (Showalter D. E., *The Wars of German Unification*, 2004), p. 163.

5 (Showalter D. E., *The Wars of German Unification*, 2004), pp. 165–166.

6 (Militärgeschichtliche Abteilung, 1900), pp. 171–215.

7 The Chassepot rifle was far superior to the German Dreyse rifle due to the smaller caliber and gas-tight chamber, leading to a higher muzzle velocity (11mm).

In particular, the bloody assault of the Guard Corps on the strong French position at St. Privat created the myth of the brave guard infantry dodging fire and facing death to earn victory for their king. Guard units performed intricate maneuvers in their prescribed battle order, and then they marched up the steep slope where the French Chassepot rifle started taking its toll at 1,200 m. On that slope, 30,000 Germans attacked for three hours sustaining 8,000 casualties, more than Pickett's charge during the battle of Gettysburg.[8]

At the same time, the consequences of St. Privat started a fierce discussion about infantry tactics and the optimum way to attack such strongly defended positions. Fritz Hoenig, a well-known German military author at the time, even called the assault of St. Privat a pointless slaughterhouse achieving little more than emptying the ammo pouches of the defending French regiments.[9] Nevertheless, this tactic became the standard of martial behavior. Objectives could be seized and accomplished if the unit had the correct attitude and discipline. This standard was repeated constantly in countless books and reports as the vision of what drove German victory.

But even after the experience of 1870 and 1871, the 1847 manual was neither changed nor replaced. Instead the myth was perpetuated. St. Privat-style attacks across more than 1,000 meters of open ground and ascending glacis against a well-defended position were considered brave and were systematically incorporated into training. The company column continued as the regular attack formation of the German infantry during the Franco-Prussian War. Regiments heading into attack first broke up into their battalions, one next to another, and then again into company columns. A company forming an attack column had its first and second platoons three lines deep, each following one another. The third platoon was put in front, usually half of the platoon forming a skirmish line advancing about 100 meters ahead of the battalion.

Traditionally in Prussian regiments, there were three traditional groups. The 1st and 2nd battalions were named "musketeer" battalions and the 3rd battalion was the "fusilier" battalion. The musketeers practiced more bayonet drill; whereas the fusiliers enjoyed a more intense rifle and firing drill. Even in 1918, recruits in the 1st and 2nd battalions were still called *Musketier* and recruits in the 3rd battalion were called *Füsilier*. The same structure was also kept among the three platoons of a company. The third traditional group was the "grenadiers," usually drawing their tradition from the grenadier regiments of the Old Prussian Army under Frederick the Great. Musketeers, fusiliers and grenadiers were considered as line infantry and armed, equipped, and trained alike (except the slightly higher emphasis on rifle training for the fusiliers). Besides this uniform line infantry (*Einheitsinfanterie*), only the light infantry of the Jäger battalions enjoyed different drill, more live firing, and different weapons. With the Dreyse rifles, the Jäger used the model 1865 *Jäger-Büchse* with a shorter but octagonal barrel, higher precision and a hair-trigger. Even with the rifle model 1871, the Jäger received a special Jäger-Büchse.

About 50–100 meters behind the skirmish line followed the second half of the platoon as *soutiens* (French word for reinforcements) to fill losses and to "swarm in" in case the firing line needed reinforcements. There were contentious experiments in dispersed formations in 1872; however, by March 1873, there was a royal decree codifying the company as the normal offensive formation. Lines would be permitted but not in a dispersed formation.[10] Each battalion had two companies advancing next to each other in the formation described above.

8 (Brose, 2001), pp. 18–19.
9 (Hoenig, 1890), p. 196.
10 (Brose, 2001), p. 20.

The third company followed in pure column formation (without a skirmish line) about 150 meters behind the first two companies and also flew the battalion flag. In the case of an unexpected cavalry attack, the companies formed squares with four firing lines one behind another on each of the four sides repelling the cavalry by volley fire. During the Franco-Prussian War, there was a strong tendency to break up the company columns into skirmish lines earlier in order to avoid heavy losses caused by Chassepot fire.[11] The establishment resisted this change as the army reprinted the official regulations in 1876. The army corps commanders continued to influence training and doctrine, and the company commanders continued to drill in column formations. This formation was repeated during the maneuvers in which thin skirmish lines were followed very closely by the attacking columns of the second wave from which a decision was expected. Maneuvers were often conducted on open terrain to allow for easy movement.[12]

Shortly after the Franco-Prussian War, an improved infantry rifle, the model 1871 designed by Paul Mauser, was introduced. This rifle replaced the outdated and difficult-to-handle Dreyse rifle with its fragile firing needle. The Mauser had an improved bolt-operated lock and fired stable brass cartridges instead of the quite fragile Dreyse paper cartridges. In short order, the model 1871/84 improved repeating rifle replaced the1871 rifle; it used the same lock as the model 1871 guns but had an eight-round tube magazine under the barrel. Although the model 1871/84 still fired black powder cartridges, it was a repeating rifle allowing a murderous rate of infantry fire at distances up to 1,600 meters. Starting with the rifle model 1871/84, they had to subscribe to the standard infantry rifle—again leading to long discussions trying to justify the need of a special Jäger rifle. Still the French were faster in taking the lead in the arms race by introducing their model 1886 Lebel rifle that fired 8 mm smokeless powder (cordite powder) cartridges. Those "small" caliber rounds had not only a much higher range and higher muzzle velocity, but they were also much lighter compared to the old black powder rounds; thus, they enabled the infantryman to carry more rounds in his ammo pouches.

The Prussians tried to compete against the Lebel rifle with the model 1888 "commission" rifle that was hastily designed by the Royal Prussian Rifle Commission (*Königlich Preußische Gewehr-Prüfungskommission*) that also fired smokeless 8 mm rounds. The initial technical design of the rifle revealed severe teething problems and required numerous redesigns before it was really operational by the mid 1890s.[13] The technical requirements of the new 8 mm caliber were widely unknown and were often discovered only after numerous accidents with bursting barrels. There was also an issue of cracking ammunition shells that led to explosive gases blasting into the shooter's face. The French seemed to face basically the same problems with their Lebel rifle since they also had to go through numerous redesigns until the final Lebel rifle M. 1886/93 was used until the end of the Great War.[14]

Bavaria was equipped with Werder rifles and all other contingents with Dreyse rifles. The model 71 single-loading rifle was introduced in the 1870s and replaced by the improved model 1871/84 during the second half of the 1880s. When the last 71/84 rifle was produced in 1888, the introduction of the model 1888 had already been decided. In 1898, the *Gewehr 98*—again designed by Mauser—followed and was redesigned for the 8 mm "S" cartridge in 1903. Although the model 98 rifle was the standard gun of the German army in

---

[11] (Schwarz, 1962), p. 164.
[12] (Brose, 2001), p. 21.
[13] (Scarlata, 2008)
[14] (Storz D., 2012), p. 100–117.

1914, many reserve and Landwehr formations were fielded with model 88 rifles, carbines, or model 91 rifles (a short and carbine-like version of the model 88 used by the foot artillery). It took until 1916 for almost all German formations to be equipped with model 98 guns.

The most important changes provided by both the Lebel and the commission rifle were range and the use of smokeless powder. Almost instantly, this change made many of the traditional infantry drill and tactics obsolete. Many of the densely manned line and column formations that still could be successfully employed on the smoke-covered battle fields of the black powder era would lead to disastrous losses under the conditions of rapid infantry fire by magazine-fed rifles firing smokeless rounds. With the introduction of the model 1888 rifle, a change in infantry tactics became inevitable, leading to an ongoing discussion between reform and traditional German officers. Triggered by Moltke's *Verordnung* from 1869 and fueled by the evaluation of the bloody experience of 1870 and 1871, as well as reports from the American Civil War, the discussion ran between these two parties.

General-Major Wilhelm v. Scherff and Oberst Albert v. Boguslawski represented the traditionalists. They helped to create the St. Privat myth that only dense formations and so-called "closed" (*geschlossene*) firing lines could really be under the full control of their officers, as opposed to loosely populated skirmish lines. Under the conditions of modern rifles, only these lines could develop enough firepower to win fire superiority over the enemy. They still believed that only the bayonet attack against an enemy shaken by the impact of fire superiority could achieve final victory. Scherff concluded that soldiers had to be supervised and closely led in combat. Only then would they overcome their fear and expose themselves to enemy fire. Even in the era of breechloaders, a soldier taking cover against fire and digging himself in appeared somehow contradictory to the "spirit of assault and heroism" that would be necessary to accomplish victory.

The reformers, represented by General Lieutenant Sisigmund v. Schlichting, saw the impact of technological development on combat. The Dreyse rifle had set off a development that would make it impossible now to just put men against fire. The increased range, rate, and precision of fire from magazine-fed repeating rifles would make it necessary to change the traditional formations. He championed ever-thinner skirmish lines of more independently acting riflemen who took cover by employing the terrain around them and by engaging their respective enemies at will. That would require an entirely different training of the individual soldier.

The reformers seemed to have better arguments, and Schlichting was asked to prepare the core second part of the new infantry manual. Although the 1889 infantry manual still listed company columns as a regular combat formation, there was a clear tendency towards a broader use of line formations and skirmish lines. Now an entire company of the battalion formed the skirmish line followed by the other two companies as *soutiens*. The traditionalists were pleased by the fact that company and even battalion columns could still be drilled in the 1889 manual. The reformers saw themselves justified by the core chapter about "infantry in combat" that Schlichting had written by himself. In it, emphasis was clearly put on more open line formations.[15]

Tactically, the reformers were envisioning company columns that would deploy into lines at 1,500 to 2,000 meters. Then the formation would further disperse into random assault groups somewhere between 600 and 800 meters. This movement was a slow process, envisioned as taking two or three days to close within a distance of a couple of hundred meters.

---

[15] (*Kriegsministerium*, 1889), pp. 58 and 89.

Only after those dispersed groups had established fire superiority would they perform a final charge. The decision to make this charge and how it was to be conducted was known as "delegated tactics." This lack of centralized control was one of the main points of the 1889 regulation. It also became the center of controversy between traditionalists who wanted control and the reformists who wanted to delegate it.[16] Knowing that the manual was open to interpretations, the Kaiser stated in the foreword that any acts against the first part (describing the formal drill from company up to brigade level) and third part (about parades) would be seriously reprimanded, whereas misunderstandings concerning the second part would be corrected during training.[17]

The second part of the manual also introduced a general change in leadership. Fighting in skirmish lines spelled the end of any direct control by commanding officers. NCOs as well as the individual musketeers and fusiliers would have to take a stronger role. As a result, army training introduced the previously explained Auftragstaktik as a leadership philosophy. Auftragstaktik meant that officers would no longer issue precise orders but instead would assign tasks and objectives to their men. The men, in turn, would exercise their own judgment to accomplish the task. This concept was also formally known as "delegated tactics." Scherff and Boguslawski continued to argue against Auftragstaktik, as they believed this leadership style would undermine the authority of commanding officers.[18] The reformers prevailed, and the 1889 manual not only improved the tactical set-up of infantry attacks but also significantly changed the leadership philosophy within the Prussian army. In addition to the infantry manual, Schlichting's writings[19] acted as kind of comment and higher explanation of the spirit of the manual.[20] Controversy did not end there as the execution of the new manual during maneuvers in 1891, 1895, 1896, and 1897 saw a stronger tendency for infantry units—often division sized—attacking en masse.

The Boer War revealed the next dilemma when it became obvious that the firepower of modern rifles led to a superiority of fire over movement. Translated into German military thinking, it seemed questionable whether attacks were the superior tactical approach. An anonymous contributor in the *Military Weekly* (*Militär-Wochenblatt*) in 1901 triggered the next round of discussions about a suitable infantry tactic. The Boers had limited formal military training, but they were equipped with superior Mauser rifles and they made use of the terrain. As a result, the Boers scored numerous successes over the formally approaching British infantry.[21] In March 1902, Lt Col v. Lindenau, a department lead in the Great General Staff, presented lessons from the infantry attacks of the Boer War at the *Militärische Gesellschaft* in Berlin.[22] Lindenau demanded that the infantry tactics included in the 1889 manual be improved. He maintained that the skirmish lines of attacking and defending infantry alike had to be made even thinner. This change meant more men following in subsequent lines under cover and swarming in if reinforcements were required.

Lindenau suggested that the British army had attacked in "thick," dense formations without proper preparation by fire. He pointed out that these British attack formations would have been in perfect compliance with the German manuals and were practiced during most

[16] (Brose, 2001), pp. 58–59.
[17] (*Kriegsministerium*, 1889), Foreword.
[18] Even with the influence of the Boer War, this discussion lingered on. (Boguslawski, 1903), p. 5 and (Scherff, 1904), pp. 56, 90 and 147.
[19] (Schlichting, 1897–1899)
[20] (Einem, 1933), p 61.
[21] (Frobel G. z., 1901)
[22] (Lindenau, 1902), pp. 1–174.

German maneuvers. Without openly raising a critique of the *Kaisermanöver*, it was crystal clear what Lindenau was referring to when mentioning that German infantry still could be seen advancing in dense lines regardless of any exposure to possible enemy fire. The photograph from the newspaper *Wochenschau* in September 1913 (discussed in the Introduction) that depicts German infantry lines advancing during the autumn maneuvers of 1913 shows that not all units were using the 1889 manual.[23]

Now called "the 1902-style infantry attack," the reformers and traditionalists discussed this Boer-style infantry attack and a further split between the factions ensued; Scherff and Boguslawski maintained their traditionalist side. But again the reformers prevailed. The Boer War and later the Russo-Japanese War showed the superiority of firepower over human attacks. Before completing the attack upon any well-defended position, there had to be an extended fight for fire superiority. The ever-thinner skirmish lines of advancing infantry had to be permanently supported and reinforced by soutiens swarming in and slowly moving closer to the defense lines while maintaining a well-targeted rifle fire.[24] Additionally, it was discovered that a final bayonet charge was required to dig out the defenders who were hesitant to leave their trenches and expose themselves to fire.[25]

The Japanese Army that defeated the Russians in 1905 was tactically trained according to the standards of the German 1889 infantry manual. The Japanese praised this manual as the right mixture between suitable and modern tactical standards combined with a high level of freedom for the military leaders, but Moltke the Elder felt that the room for tactical interpretation was too wide and needed to be filled by further explanatory guidelines. [26]

The Bavarian general, Ludwig Ritter v. Gebsattel, maintained that only some 20 percent of German officers would be intellectually above average, 50 percent would be around average, and 30 percent below average. He also believed that allowing 80 percent of the army officers the freedom of decision provided by the 1889 manual was to too wide and needed to be narrowed further.[27] So work on a new infantry manual began. This time General v. Bülow,[28] the Commanding General of III Army Corps and a widely respected drillmaster, designed the core part about the tactical application of the manual in combat—the part Schlichting had designed in 1889.

General v. Bülow headed up the rewrite of the infantry regulation but fearful of the dangers of spreading forces too thin, he still favored a frontal assault in skirmish attack formation. This rendition did not resonate with many of the division and corps commanders. These leaders' tactical freedom in the application of these principles is often overlooked in books about the Imperial German Army. It was well known that all Prussian officers knew that each army corps had its own set of rules. This freedom was obvious during the maneuvers of 1903 and 1904. The Kaiser and his Guard Corps were even involved when they attacked en masse with battalion and company columns without artillery support. The old Chief of Staff, Count Waldersee praised the spirit of the attack to the Kaiser.[29] In the fall of 1905, the Kai-

---

23 Although the picture taken from Wochenschau issue September 1913 obviously reveals another myth, the truth behind it was particularly evident during the battles of Mons and Le Cateau in August 1914. The British Expeditionary Corps encountered German infantry advancing exactly in such formations and therefore suffering extremely heavy losses. Please check our comment on page XXIV and the first picture given in our picture block.

24 (Großer Generalstab, *Krieggeschichtliche Abteilung* I, 1903), p. 16.

25 (Echevarria II, 2000), p. 123.

26 (Storz, 1992), p. 167.

27 (Storz, 1992), p. 167.

28 This same individual would command 2nd Army in 1914.

29 (Brose, 2001), pp. 90–91.

ser observed the II Army Corps maneuvers in Pomerania. His comment to the War Minister was that different corps were not uniformly applying the reforms of 1889: "When I'm in East Prussia I find one tactic, when in Metz another—and when I go to Hanover, I find something else entirely—which is itself different from Silesia."[30]

The Kaiser's discomfort alone compelled the Minister of War to direct a commission be formed in January 1906 to develop a new infantry regulation. Hans von Plessen, who espoused attacking without thought of personal danger, led the traditionalists. This tactic was considered true Prussian discipline. Maj. Gen. Karl v. Fasbender of Bavaria led the reformers. He incorporated lessons from the modern wars and sang the praises of delegated tactics. Von Bülow espoused the middle ground position in this argument and he agreed with dispersed formations but not with delegated tactics—Auftragstaktik.[31]

Their work resulted in a new infantry manual on 29 May 1906. In a nutshell, the 1906 manual was an iteration of the 1889 manual rather than something entirely new. It built on lessons from the Boer war; the Japanese experience in Manchuria and it rooted Auftragstaktik in the entire German military system.[32] It emphasized the necessity for fire superiority and the need for cover more clearly than the previous manual had. Now even the attacker had to seek cover and to dig in during phases of exchanging rifle fire.[33] Every man should carry a spade and sandbags were considered useful protective tools. The individual soldier had to be trained and drilled in detail to make sure he would be able to live up to the requirements of Auftragstaktik. He needed to be able to carry out his task even if not closely supervised by an officer or NCO.

A Model Infantry Attack (according to the 1906 manual that was used in 1914)

30 (Brose, 2001), pp. 152–153.

31 (Brose, 2001), pp. 153.

32 (*Kriegsministerium*, 1906) and (*Königlich Bayerisches Kriegsministerium*, 1906)

33 (Freytag-Loringhoven, O., 1907). Freytag-Loringhoven builds upon the St. Privat myth to explain the need for better individual training that, in fact, was already common sense within the army. (Byern, 1905)

When viewing the picture above, obviously the firing line in front was covering the firing line in the back, which was "jumping" forward. The infantry moved forward by running stretches of about 50 meters before taking cover again. This tactic is called *sprungweises Vorgehen* (jumping forward) in German today and called "bounding overwatch" in English. Another core change was to end the traditional doctrinal separation between the artillery and infantry battle. Both branches had to be coordinated and led together as combined arms. This coordination was difficult to achieve and caused a lot of headaches during the Kaisermanöver 1906 and 1907.[34] What worked well was the drill towards employing the terrain for cover and using the spade to dig in even during attacks. In Löbell's 1907 annual report, he maintained that infantry made a good and extensive use of the spade to create cover. He claimed that infantry units managed to keep "spade-work" (*Spatenarbeit*) in good balance with advancing during an attack.[35]

Theoretically, the German manuals after 1900 used all the experience of contemporary wars and also kept pace with technical developments such as the introduction of magazine-fed repeating rifles and machineguns, but many traditional officers tried to keep infantry tactics at the level of the Franco-Prussian war. Starting in the fall of 1906, the commanders of III and V Army Corps demonstrated the use of the new manual in their autumn maneuvers. However, the commander of VI Army Corps did just the opposite using massed infantry assaults and cavalry attacks without artillery support. In 1907, both VII and X Army Corps showed similar techniques.[36] The Chief of the General Staff critiqued the 1911 maneuvers as having skirmish lines too tightly packed. By 1912, infantry was once again advancing shoulder to shoulder in maneuvers.

Not only in Germany, but also elsewhere, there was the deeply engrained notion that war had to look like a poster of advancing dense lines of infantry flying their flags to the sound of the bugles, interrupted only by light artillery fire and surprising cavalry assaults. After 1914, an entire generation paid the price for this outdated picture of war. For those who think that the old 1870 way of attacking was outdated, we only have to take a look at the order of XV Army Corps on 3 November 1914: "I direct therefore that the attacks are to be pressed home with bugle calls and with the regimental bands playing. Regimental musicians who play during assaults will be awarded Iron Crosses."—v. Deimling.[37]

The heavy sled-mounted German machinegun 08 developed at the government armory at Spandau was a water-cooled Maxim system. It could fire hundreds of rounds in a row (*Reihenfeuer*), not the short bursts of fire like modern machineguns do (called *Feuerstoß* in German).[38] Chambered for the standard German service cartridge caliber 8mm (like the *Gewehr 98*), the ammunition was supplied in 250-round belts and fired at a rate of 500 rounds per minute. Later in the war, the light machinegun 08/15 was equipped with the lock model 1916 that allowed an increased rate of 600 rounds per minute.[39] Machinegun formations increased infantry firepower. Terrain cover that was much too small to accommodate an infantry platoon could easily accommodate an entire machinegun battalion. If mass fire delivered in volleys and at great distance were already an integral part of infantry marksman-

---

34 (Storz, 1992), p. 172.

35 (Pelet-Narbonne G. z., 1908), p. 258. The 1907 annual reports also stated that cooperation between artillery and infantry had become much smoother than during previous years.

36 (Brose, 2001), p. 154.

37 (Sheldon, *The German Army at Ypres 1914*, 2010), p. 256.

38 Modern machineguns have a far higher rate of fire. The German MG 42 could fire up to 2,000 rounds per minute that explains that short bursts of fire could be useful.

39 (Chinn, 1951), pp. 144–149.

ship, this concept applied far more to machinegun formations. Since the guns were equipped with a four power optical scope, they could be far more precise at long distance compared to rifle fire. In general, either machinegun battalions or machinegun companies were not broken up into platoons when used tactically. The tactical leader, usually the regimental commander, was supposed to utilize machineguns to define a center of gravity for his infantry fire. Ideally applied from a flanking position, these highly mobile machineguns could be used in offensive as well as in defensive missions.[40]

If infantry attacks were still carried out in such dense lines, the devastating effect of *Reihenfeuer* can easily be imagined. While comparatively small machineguns formations could provide huge firepower, the traditional doctrine still applied to infantry attacks.[41] Even with the massive build-up in 1912 and 1913 and the mobilization of the Falkenhayn corps in autumn 1914, the focus was on a better employment of the available manpower than on better use of firepower that machineguns offered.[42]

---

[40] (Kriegsministerium, 1904), pp 92–95 and (Kriegsministerium, *D.V.E. Nr. 130b IV. Teil des Exerzier-Reglements für die Infanterie* 1911).

[41] [41] (Geyer, 1984), pp. 527–533.

[42] (Storz, *Kriegsbild und Rüstung vor 1914*, 1992), pp. 295–299.

CHAPTER 13

CAVALRY DOCTRINE

When considering the German army, as well as most other European armies, prior to 1914, the imagination is caught by the colorful cavalry regiments and their long, gallant traditions. The highest form of romanticized combat was cavalry against cavalry with saber and lances only—no firearms. This kind of fight between brave and courageous noble gentlemen on horseback was considered a continuation of the aristocratic medieval tradition of knights. The truly classic examples of cavalry charges from the times of Frederick the Great were more than 100 years old. The battles of Roßbach, Leuthen, and Zorndorf took place back in 1757 and 1758. This style of cavalry employment was characterized by charges of three equal waves. During the Napoleonic wars, this tactical approach did not change much even after the battles of Leipzig and Waterloo, which showed that the cavalry did not have a realistic chance against a well-led infantry forming squares against cavalry assaults.[1]

For young officers, service with the cavalry continued to be more prestigious than service with the infantry or the technical arms such as artillery and engineers. Under Frederick the Great, the roles of infantry and cavalry were quite distinct. The infantry regiments were drilled to become "firing machines," firing up to three volleys per minute with their flintlock muzzle loaders. The cavalry enjoyed a higher level of freedom to exploit the impact of infantry fire upon the enemy by means of surprise assaults. The Prussian cavalry traditionally had five different arms, divided into light and heavy cavalry. Hussars (*Husaren*), dragoons (*Dragoner)* and *Jäger zu Pferde* belonged to the light cavalry; Uhlans (*Ulanen*) and cuirassiers (*Kürassiere*) made up the heavy cavalry. Traditionally, Hussars traced their tradition back to Hungarian light cavalry, a fact reflected in their uniforms. Dragoons were closest to the mounted infantry; Jäger zu Pferde were the latest arm of the cavalry created only around 1910. That uhlans followed the tradition of Polish lancers is reflected in the style of their shapkas (*Tschapkas*). Cuirassiers were the traditional heavy cavalry and they continued to wear their breast armor until 1888.

In Bavaria, the system was more simplistic: Bavarian cavalry consisted only of uhlans, *schwere Reiter* (Bavarian cuirassiers), and *Chevaulegers*, the light cavalry (chevaux legers meant light horses in French). Aristocratic Guard regiments such as the *Regiment Gardes-du-Corps,* the *Garde-Kürassier Regiment* in Prussia, the *Carabiniers* and the *Regiment schwere Reiter* in Saxony, and the *Hartschiere* in Bavaria were also found. Although all

1 (Brose, 2001), p. 9.

those different types had distinct traditions and wore different uniforms in the mid 19th century, the tactical differences were already obsolete and gone. The cavalry manuals only spoke about THE cavalry and focused on uniform cavalry (*Einheitskavallerie*); all armed and equipped alike with a sword or saber, a carbine and, after 1895, with the steel lance Model 1895.

The cavalry had several functions. The primary historical function was that of battle cavalry—charging in with mobility and shock action to cause a failure in morale of the enemy forces. Technology had proven to be a serious challenge to the viability of this role, because artillery and rifle fire could now cause unbearable casualties to the cavalry. This was shown all too clearly on 1 September 1870 with the vain efforts of General de Gallifet's French cavalry to break through the Prussian lines at Floing during the Battle of Sedan. In the same way that change was forced on the infantry, the introduction of breech-loading rifles entirely changed the face of battle for the cavalry. Infantry fire increased in both range and accuracy and became so rapid that infantry did not need to form squares any more to repel cavalry attacks.

The second function was as a support arm carrying out reconnaissance. This was an effort to observe the enemy and then report back what had been seen. The defensive side of reconnaissance is called screening. This is an endeavor to keep the enemy from closing with friendly forces and often results in clashes between the reconnaissance patrols of the opposing sides. The staff that received these reports was required to interpret them and to disseminate the intelligence to those who required it. This two-step process was fraught with problems and the risk of failure. The reconnaissance troops might not be able to obtain a comprehensive picture of the situation. Reports could be inadequate or intercepted. The staff's interpretation could be in error or the result wrongly distributed. The author's experience at the divisional level was that "the first report is 50 percent wrong."

A further supporting function was that supplied by the mounted infantry, which was capable of moving large distances and delivering limited firepower at a precise point—this implied dismounted operations. Interesting to note, the cavalry was given no major role during the wars between Denmark and Austria in the 1860s. It was often employed in rear areas. During the Franco-Prussian war a couple of very bloody cavalry attacks showed the inferiority of cavalry against well-trained infantry equipped with breech loading rifles.

Two classic examples of this infantry capability occurred at Morsbronn and during the attack of General Bonnemains' cuirassiers at Fröschweiler. The attack of a French cuirassier brigade on the village of Morsbronn during the battle of Wörth on 4 August 1870 was a complete disaster; the Prussian infantry fired from behind barricades and out of houses, which resulted in the brigade being annihilated in the streets. Later that day, the French cuirassier division of General Bonnemains tried to buy time for the already beaten army of Marshal Patrice de Mac Mahon to withdraw from encirclement by attacking the advancing Prussian infantry between Fröschweiler and Elsasshausen. This time the attacking cuirassiers met three regiments of Prussian infantry with attached artillery advancing in dense lines. The Prussian infantry remained in their firing lines and cut down the assaulting cuirassiers with murderous Dreyse rifle fire. Thanks to the thick black-powder smoke of these rifles many of the French cuirassiers escaped with their lives.

However, this technological problem was completely forgotten once attention shifted to the successful attack of the Prussian 11 Cavalry Brigade, commanded by Generalmajor Adelbert v. Bredow against French infantry on 16 August 1870 in the battle of Vionville and Mars la Tour. With the Army outnumbered and in a very difficult position, the brigade made a single wave charge, unsupported, with about 800 riders overrunning several enemy positions and penetrating 3,000 m. Although 379 men and 400 horses became casualties, the heroic charge gained valuable time to save the army. Participation in this "death charge" became the core of a legend. Dreams of a return to the glory of Frederick the Great enveloped the German cavalry. The draft regulation of 1873 emphasized significant maneuvers on the battlefield by cavalry groups to put them in positions to charge. Returning to the tactics of Frederick, the emphasis was placed on drilling formations and extending the attack from 800 to 1500 m. It became absolutely essential to the cavalry leadership that the branch maintain its position of a decisive combat arm and never again become an auxiliary force. This tradition was reinforced by the Konitz maneuvers of 1881.[2]

To most European armies, the cavalry was considered a decisive tool of the supreme commander to achieve victory by surprise mass attacks against already shaken infantry. European armies tended to look down upon the role cavalry played during the American Civil War.[3] To European cavalry leaders, it was simply not in line with their idea of bravery and gallantry to see cavalry roles reduced to a kind of mounted infantry carrying out long-distance raids. Comments on J.E.B. Stuart's Chambersburg raid acknowledged the bravery of the troops, and the seizure of horses was considered a success. However, it was thought that it would not be possible under European conditions with a better-drilled and equipped enemy. According to the analysis, Stuart would not have been successful under conditions of the Franco-Prussian war.[4] Similarly George Stoneman's raid in 1863 was considered noble but yielding small results at a very high cost. The analysis considered it an unsuitable use of cavalry.[5] In general, raids got a very low mark. A major on the Great Gen. Staff, Freytag-Loringhoven, carried out a significant analysis coming to the conclusion that raids would only work in an environment of amateurish militia type armies like in the Civil War. In a European War Theater with its professionally drilled infantry and tight leadership, such raids could not expect to enjoy success. He stressed cooperation with infantry forces to the exclusion of cavalry-only raids. He heavily criticized Philip Sheridan's Richmond raid in May 1864 for not cooperating with the infantry.[6] He also seemed to indicate that war against infrastructure such as William Tecumseh Sherman's Savannah Campaign was somewhat barbaric. He emphasized that when the Germans had used a scorched-earth policy during the Franco-Prussian war, (the German Second Army between Metz and the river Loire in 1871), the Germans allegedly paid the French people for the subsistence and supply goods they took from the country.[7]

To European cavalry officers, the decisive assaults of the battle cavalry were not just a suitable tactical maneuver but also "a whole way of life."[8] The bloody experience of August 1870 came as a complete shock. In contrast to their infantry comrades, rapid fire from breech-loaders did not just force them to reconsider their tactical doctrine; it questioned the need of such a traditionally oriented cavalry as a whole. In a time when infantry had begun to exploit the slightest cover the terrain offered, to fire their rifles while lying flat on the

---

2 (Brose, 2001), pp. 9–13.
3 (Freytag-Loringhoven M. F., 1903), p. 12.
4 (Freytag-Loringhoven H. F., 1901), pp. 26–27.
5 (Freytag-Loringhoven H. F., 1901), pp. 59–60.
6 (Freytag-Loringhoven M. F., 1903), pp. 52–53.
7 (Freytag-Loringhoven M. F., 1903), pp. 137–140.
8 (Bond, 1965), pp. 95–128.

ground did not seem viable. Furthermore, the thought of mounted assaults with riders offering clearly visible targets at long range seemed to be more than questionable.[9]

While the infantry's experience at St. Privat had triggered a serious discussion about tactical doctrine, the cavalry seemed to be completely dominated by traditionalists. The doctrinal discussions and disagreements revolved around whether charges should be made in three equal or unequal waves, and the use of complicated battlefield maneuvers. The 1886 regulation favored the use of unequal waves with, e.g., a thin first wave followed by massed squadrons against artillery. The cavalry manuals from 1876 and 1895 still described the assault in three echelons as the main combat role of the cavalry regiments and brigades.[10] The 1895 manual put more emphasis upon reconnaissance and screening the advance of the army, thereby accepting a secondary role for the cavalry. To accomplish the primary mission of battle cavalry on the one hand and as a reconnaissance arm on the other hand, the cavalry was organized in wartime into divisions and cavalry corps (Höherer Kavallerie-Kommandeur: HKK). Every infantry division received its own divisional cavalry (between a half and a full regiment, usually some two to three squadrons) as the reconnaissance arm of their division. The HKK was the reconnaissance arm of its respective army and could also act simultaneously as battle cavalry.

Cavalry divisions and HKKs were wartime-only organizations formed during mobilization. In the peacetime organization, each division had a cavalry brigade normally with two cavalry regiments.[11] The division also had two infantry brigades with two infantry regiments each and an artillery brigade with two field artillery regiments. During mobilization, the infantry and artillery brigades were retained, but the cavalry brigade headquarters were taken out of the divisions to provide the necessary staffs for the cavalry divisions and the HKKs. The divisions usually kept half of one cavalry regiment as divisional cavalry (the other half going to the second division of the army corps); the second cavalry regiment was used to form the cavalry divisions. The cavalry did form reserve regiments that were weaker than the active regiments. While active regiments usually had five squadrons (*Eskadrons*), sometimes even six, reserve regiments usually only had three. They also had *Ersatz* squadrons in their home garrisons to take in new recruits (and new horses) to replace losses in the field.

This employment of the cavalry created a bridge between the traditionalists and the reformers. In 1887, the Chief of the Great General Staff, Alfred v. Waldersee, convinced the War Ministry to issue "field service orders" for the cavalry. The direction was to use one cavalry regiment per infantry division for reconnaissance, screening, and flank security. This was met with massive complaints about diluting the cavalry strength by about half for internal infantry requirements. The traditionalists fought back. In the maneuvers of 1893, 12 cavalry regiments were amassed for one glorious charge. In 1894, a cavalry division covered more than 1,000 m of open ground in a frontal charge against fresh infantry. One corps commander consistently advocated for charges of up to 25 regiments! The draft cavalry regulation of 1893 was finished in 1895 after including the three unequal wave attacks as well as an entire section on the use of battle cavalry.[12]

---

9 (Wenninger, 1913), pp. 178–193

10 (*Kriegsministerium*, 1876), (*Kriegsministerium*, 1895), (Frobel G. z., 1909) The 1895 manual was considered later as a kind of a transitional manual between the old style drill manual from 1876 and the later more realistic training of the cavalry.

11 Prior to 1914, there were only divisions; the need to distinguish between infantry, cavalry, reserve, and *Ersatz* divisions came only after mobilization.

12 (Brose, 2001), pp. 54–55.

The Boer War led to the development of infantry tactics and also had a huge impact on cavalry doctrine. Similar to cavalry use during the American Civil War, the Boers employed cavalry very successfully as flexible mounted infantry, reinforcing weak points or carrying out raids. The Boer infantry, even in skirmish lines, easily repelled British cavalry attacks with their Mauser rifle fire. But in Germany, the cavalry was under the influence of General d. Kavallerie Ernst Edler v. d. Planitz, who became *Inspekteur* of the cavalry in 1898. Planitz was a very traditional cavalryman, an old-style drillmaster of the battle cavalry with its echeloned assaults. Kaiser Wilhelm II loved Planitz for his orchestration of the autumn maneuvers into great cavalry ballets, wherein the cavalry always conducted the last and decisive attack. Planitz was certainly not the reformer the cavalry needed to develop a new role. Discussing dismounted operations during reconnaissance, Planitz issued the memorable quote: "God and the German Kaiser forbid that this role will ever be expected of the German cavalry."[13]

Nevertheless, the days of colorful cavalry assaults were numbered. As soon as Moltke the Younger took over as Chief of General Staff, he significantly changed the style of the *Kaisermanöver* and of cavalry tactics at the same time. Yet the Kaisermanöver of 1906 still ended with a mass cavalry attack carried out by two divisions with just saber and lance. Moltke made it clear that such an attack would not meet his expectation of a realistic maneuver.

In 1907, Generalleutnant Paul v. Kleist became *Inspekteur* of the cavalry and paved the way for tactical reforms. Although Kleist certainly was no radical reformer, he endorsed numerous changes in tactical doctrine, which fed into the 1909 cavalry manual, where the use of cavalry as mounted infantry became more important, particularly during reconnaissance missions.[14]

But fighting as mounted infantry meant dismounted operations, which was an undesired tactical role for the cavalry. First, dismounted cavalry appeared weak. Since one-third of the personnel of a squadron had to handle the horses only about 90 to 100 troopers could build a skirmish line and fight with their carbines. A dismounted cavalry regiment developed less firepower than even a weak infantry battalion.[15]

Furthermore, German cavalry carbines were quite poor. The Model 1857 Dreyse carbine was completely inferior to the French Chassepot carbine; many troopers just picked up a Chassepot rifle or carbine on the battlefield to replace their inferior weapon. The next generation version of the Carbine 71 was so inferior to the infantry rifle in terms of range and accuracy that the cavalry felt completely unarmed. The next carbine Model 88 suffered from the same faults as the Commission Rifle. After fixing those problems the caliber of both the rifle and the carbine was changed to the "S" cartridge. This produced higher muzzle velocity and range but negatively impacted muzzle energy, recoil, and sound. Since the increased firepower of smokeless ammunition also easily penetrated the thin metal plates that the German cuirassiers wore as armor, their breast armor became obsolete and was taken away in 1888, except the Guards' regiments for parade purpose. Due to its short barrel the carbine 88 had such bad recoil, flash, and sound that firing it was almost unbearable.[16] Compared with the rifle, the carbine had shorter range and reduced accuracy.

---

13 (Brose, 2001). p. 155.

14 (*Kriegsministerium*, 1909)

15 This factor later was amplified because the size of a cavalry squadron was smaller than an infantry company. The ranks of cavalry commanders was much higher than that of comparably sized infantry units.

16 One of the authors had the pleasure to test the recoil of a carbine 88 with a piece of his own collection finding his right shoulder bruised after firing 40 rounds. Even compared to the carbine 98 and the Springfield 1903 both "kicking" pretty hard, the recoil and sharp sound of the carbine 88 is really almost unbearable.

Only with the introduction of the Carbine 98 derived from the Rifle 98 in 1909, did the cavalry receive a firearm with a performance near the same level of the rifle, allowing the cavalry for the first time to undertake dismounted fights against infantry, but they still lacked bayonets.[17] Armed with all those earlier poor quality carbines, one can certainly imagine that cavalrymen did not really feel encouraged to practice dismounted drill with their rifles. Saber and lance still seemed to be the more reliable and useful weapons to them. As a result, General d. Kavallerie z.D. Friedrich v. Bernhardi worked on the new tactical doctrine for the cavalry, further stressing reconnaissance and dismounted operations. This also supported the changes of the 1909 cavalry manual.[18]

The 1909 cavalry drill regulation still stated that the primary mode of fighting for the cavalry was mounted, albeit in conjunction with machineguns and horse artillery. Dismounted fighting was to take place with the support of the same machineguns and artillery. There was an increase in the manual in the number of paragraphs that covered dismounted operations. It soared from 11 paragraphs in the 1895 manual to 46 in the new 1909 manual. The cavalry was to rely on subordinate initiative—*Auftragstaktik*—and a sense that success on the battlefield would be accompanied by large losses. The future of the formerly premier regiments was not so bright.[19]

Gone was the doctrine of Mars-la-Tour. There was still a place for charges and swinging swords; however, this was intended for use against enemy scouts and advanced guards. The size of operations changed with the emphasis on squadrons and what were called "light formations." There was an endeavor to employ machinegun detachments, horse artillery, and bicycle mounted Jäger units. Large cavalry formations could best be used in pursuit of routed enemy units, to reinforce a trouble spot quickly and bulk up the infantry, or to conduct deep raids against the enemy line of communications. Most of the old parade ground drills were discarded.[20]

Oberst Richard Gädke, the noted military correspondent, who was discussed in the section on honor courts, applauded the maneuvers of 1909, where cavalry was used in a reconnaissance role. He basked in the end of shock troop cavalry and welcomed their role as an auxiliary support force. Comments supporting the use of modern techniques came out of maneuvers up to 1911. Unfortunately, there was no unanimity. Many officers doubted the new techniques and in some cases, offered their own methods. The Chief of Staff critiqued the 1911 maneuvers rather harshly, stating that both infantry and cavalry formations were advancing too quickly in tightly packed formations. The conservatives raised their heads again in 1912 and maintained a constant attack in the pages of a journal called the *Cavalry Monthly*. This journal emphasized that losses were no reason to shrink from the battlefield task. There was also ill-informed contempt for aerial reconnaissance

During the years that followed, the more conservative cavalrymen tried to roll back this technological development and attempted to revive the tradition of large-scale assaults. During the Balkan wars, a Turkish cavalry division managed to break through Bulgarian infantry

---

17 (Storz, 1992), pp. 273–274.

18 (Bernhardi, *Organisation und Ausbildung der Kavallerie für den nächsten Krieg*, 1907) p. 38 and (Bernhardi, *Denkwürdigkeiten aus meinem Leben nach gleichzeitigen Aufzeichnungen und im Lichte der Erinnerungen*, 1927) p. 281. For details of the cavalry tactical doctrine during the last years before the war, see (Bernhardi, *Reiterdienst. Kritische Betrachtungen über Kriegstätigkeit, Taktik, Ausbildung und Organisation unserer Kavallerie*, 1910).

19 (Echevarria II, 2000), pp. 132–133.

20 (Brose, 2001), p. 155.

lines at Lüle Burgas at full tilt on 1 November 1912.[21] Only the machinegun fire of reserve units stopped them.

That created an argument for the traditionalists to keep the myth of the successfully echeloned assault alive during the last years before the war. In addition to the doctrinal changes, cavalry had been greatly reduced in size since the Franco-Prussian War. During that war there were 56,800 cavalrymen in a force of 462,000. By the start of World War I, the two million marching troops had 90,000 cavalry.[22] There certainly was a desire to use traditional methods. General Maximillian v. Poseck, the Inspector of Cavalry, in his postwar book lamented the fact that neither the Belgians, French, nor the English ever "accepted the cavalry fight of closed divisions offered by us often enough."[23] He glorified the actions of mounted officers and even had the temerity to pass off mounted cavalry charges as a form of reconnaissance! "While the mounted attack near Haelen produced no immediate victory, the reconnaissance mission of determining the position of the left wing of the Gette sector was attained."[24]

> Moreover the cavalry is today only a diminishing part of an army, whereas the extent of operations and of Army fronts has grown wildly out of all proportion to the size of the cavalry masses. This renders very difficult the activities of reconnaissance and screening. The cavalry at the beginning of the war, with small potential fighting power, came in contact with a stronger and better-armed opponent. Successes of the cavalry brought about a minute part of the enemy forces within the range of the effects of that success, in comparison with former wars.[25]

Study of the organizations employed provides a clue to the understanding of cavalry doctrine. There were two main types of cavalry employment as shown by the organization of the corps cavalry (HKK) and the divisional cavalry. The main role of the HKK was to provide a protective screen tens of miles in front of the main infantry forces. This screen would prevent the enemy from closing with the main body of the friendly forces and so deceive them as to the whereabouts and intentions of their own forces. In addition, the screen would prevent the main body from being surprised. This required the corps cavalry to destroy the enemy cavalry whenever possible and then to observe the movement of the enemy main force. Once this was achieved the screen was then to be maintained by the division concerned, while the main body of the cavalry moved to one or both flanks in an effort to get around the enemy flank and stop him from doing the same.

There was also a concept similar to one used in the American Civil War; namely, the deep raid. Moltke the Elder, as far back as 1866, had advocated a scheme such as this, and others demanded unified command of large masses of cavalry. This was to ensure unified reconnaissance and the correct employment of cavalry resources. Conversely, combining the cavalry divisions would put a restraint upon the freedom of movement of the division and an additional layer of reporting. While a loss of time was admitted at the corps headquarters, it was argued that the reconnaissance would be more correctly interpreted.[26]

21 (Voß, 1913), p. 253.
22 (Herwig H., 2009), p. 47.
23 (Poseck M. v., 1921), p. 1.
24 (Poseck M. v., 1921), p. 28.
25 (Poseck M. v., 1921), pp. 223.
26 (Poseck M. v., 1921), pp. 225–226.

On the offensive, these bigger cavalry bodies also carried out reconnaissance operations in front of the advancing main body of the army. Enemy forces and their position, strength, and direction of movement had to be reconnoitered and reported to the commanders of army corps and armies to enable them to prepare for the coming encounter. According to the cavalry reconnaissance manual, a cavalry division consisting of three brigades with six regiments could cover a reconnaissance sector about 40–50 km wide in front of the advancing infantry. Within this sector, the divisions had reconnaissance squadrons, each (*Aufklärungseskadrons*) patrolling a strip 15–20 km wide. In the sector of a cavalry division, two to three reconnaissance squadrons took the role of driving their patrols forward against the enemy.[27] In fact, these sectors per reconnaissance squadron could be much wider, increasing to 35–70 km per squadron if the tactical situation required it. This was drawn from the evaluation of the big reconnaissance exercise in eastern Prussia in 1905.[28] After only a couple of days these reconnaissance squadrons had to be withdrawn and replaced by other squadrons to give the men and horses a rest.

Usually the reconnaissance squadrons came from different cavalry regiments, their regiments marching behind them in case they needed reinforcements to negotiate stronger enemy forces or to tear a hole in the enemy cavalry screen. On a different scale, this is a similar concept to the skirmish lines of advancing infantry with the support of the infantry formations following behind. These reconnaissance squadron main bodies operated as backup for their patrols in case they needed to replenish ammunition, exchange horses, etc.

In general, three different kinds of patrols were used:

1. Close distance patrols, reconnoitering the ground immediately in front of the reconnaissance squadrons. These patrols operated within the reach of the reconnaissance squadrons, so they could be reinforced easily. Close distance patrols were the usual method of cavalry reconnaissance.[29]

2. Long distance patrols were driven forward up to 40 or 50 km deep into enemy territory, sometimes even deeper. These patrols had to be of considerable strength so as to be able to operate independently deep into enemy territory. Usually, they were of platoon strength and were led by an officer. Long distance patrols were also trained to raid and destroy enemy infrastructure such as railroads, bridges, telegraph lines, baggage columns, etc.

   A problem addressed by the reconnaissance manual was the way to keep in touch with long distance patrols. To bridge long distance, they often had to leave behind single troopers operating as relay posts to convey messages back to the reconnaissance squadron main bodies and finally to the cavalry divisions. On the one hand, it was certainly dangerous to operate as a single relay rider deep within enemy territory. On the other hand, it is clear how time consuming it could be to deliver written reports from the patrol leader to the cavalry division staff. That staff could, however, transmit them by radio to the army command if they were able to operate their heavy radio station. Long-range patrols on reconnaissance missions of high importance could also take a light radio station with them. Patrol commanders tended to be against this, because these radio stations slowed

27 (*Generalinspektion der Kavallerie, 1914*), pp. 10–13.

28 (*Kriegsministerium*, 1907), p. 255. For the detailed reconnaissance reports of the reconnaissance squadrons of cavalry division D (this division was only mobilized for this exercise) during the 1905 reconnaissance exercise, please see pp. 227–232.

29 (*Generalinspektion der Kavallerie, 1914*), pp. 52–56.

down their speed of movement and reduced their ability to react when meeting an unexpected enemy. Due to all these difficulties, the manual stated that long distance patrols had to be an exception, reserved only for reconnaissance missions of high operational importance.

3. Two to three lieutenants or first lieutenants together with a couple of NCOs and distinguished troopers formed officers' patrols. These officer patrols were sent out to accomplish special missions. They were mainly used to clearly identify strength and probable intention of an enemy believed to be in a certain location.[30]

One of the major Achilles' heels of this cavalry force was its logistics. The units were extremely maintenance intensive. Horses had to be fed, watered, unsaddled, combed, and rested. This took time and the expectation was for a secure area to perform these functions. As a result, cavalry would normally withdraw behind a protective formation. They had to withdraw from contact to bivouac! This required not only time-consuming and energy-wasting marches on a daily basis but also led to cavalry being surprised by the enemy at some bivouacs.

Transmitting reconnaissance reports was a problem in itself. Each cavalry regiment had a telegraph troop, consisting of one officer and 10 NCOs and EM with a small horse-drawn wagon with 80 km of telephone line. The cavalry divisions were usually equipped with two light and two heavy radio stations, which they could use to either communicate with their army commands or with their patrols. Heavy stations could communicate with each other across a maximum distance of 150 km, whereas light stations had a range of up to 40 km. Heavy and light stations could communicate in a mixed network across up to 80 km distance.

These were theoretical distances. Very often in practical operations distances were much shorter due to weather conditions, terrain difficulties, and other problems. Because of the need for time-consuming encryption and the risk of enemy listening stations within range, radio traffic was only allowed if other communications tools, such as messengers, relay riders etc., were not available. In other words, the use of radio had to be reduced to the absolute minimum required to meet tactical requirements.[31] According to the manual, the use of both heavy stations was to be an exception as well. It was intended that one station would be employed to communicate with the army command, with the other one kept as a backup, which casts a harsh light upon the technical reliability of such radio equipment.

Divisional cavalry, on the other hand, was under the direct control of the division commander and used primarily for security. The divisional cavalry would take over control of the screen directly in front of the infantry force after the corps cavalry had established contact. This would usually happen as soon as the main body of the infantry was less than 50 km away from the enemy.[32] The divisional cavalry was reckoned to be too weak to be used as a flank protection force.

---

[30] *(Generalinspektion der Kavallerie, 1914)*, pp. 16–20 and *(Kriegsministerium, 1907)*, pp. 232–235. Based upon the report on the 1905 reconnaissance exercise, it can be assumed that officer patrols were not a really efficient tool since they found it difficult to get their reports home in time.

[31] *(Generalinspektion der Kavallerie, 1914)*, pp. 49–51. About the practical use of radio stations, please also check *(Kriegsministerium, 1907)*, pp. 207–209.

[32] (Kriegsministerium, 1907), p. 249.

CHAPTER 14

ARTILLERY DOCTRINE

Compared with the review of infantry and cavalry tactics, the development of artillery doctrine was driven more by the development of new weapons and ammunition than tactics. Artillery was divided into the light horse-driven field artillery and the heavy foot artillery. There was always professional rivalry between the field artillery that endeavored to be more cavalry-like and the foot artillery that had been a stepchild of the technical branch. The battle of Sedan from the Franco-Prussian War provided the classic example of direct-fire artillery vanquishing the enemy.

The change from bronze barrels to cast steel barrels was made with the introduction of the C61[1] and the Krupp-made 8 cm C64 field guns. These improved guns permitted the use of greater breech pressures and heavier charges that increased ranges. Until the 1870–71 war, the infantry and artillery had developed evenly side by side. With the introduction of steel barrels and breech loaded artillery, the effective range of artillery increased, albeit slowly. The Dreyse rifle quadrupled the effective range of infantry fire from about 100–150 meters to 400–500 meters. The effective range of field artillery during the 1870–71 war was still little more than 2,000 meters.[2] Given the longer rifle range, the field artillery had to expose itself to infantry fire more often than they traditionally had done. Fighting against French infantry with their Chassepot rifles meant exposing artillery crews to effective infantry volley fire at 800–900 meters.

Based upon the experience in the war against France, the Prussian artillery was organized into field and fortress artillery in 1872, establishing the artillery as an arm in its own right alongside the infantry and cavalry. Starting with the maneuvers of 1874, there was a major push to focus on the mobility of field artillery. Batteries were placed in open firing positions on slopes right in front of the infantry lines in order to start the artillery battle. The first phase of this artillery battle was the fight for fire superiority against opposing enemy artillery in direct counter-battery duels. After (hopefully) defeating the enemy artillery, the bulk of the German artillery could then begin the bombardment of the enemy infantry in order to weaken their lines. If this artillery fire was seen to have been effective against the enemy infantry, the emphasis shifted to the infantry battle, the attacking infantry exploiting the earlier work of the artillery. The concept of advancing to positions a mere 700 m in front of

1 While infantry guns are usually named with model and the respective year of official introduction, artillery pieces were named with a capital "C" for "Construction" (also spelled with "c" in Germany before 1901) and the last two figures of the respective year.

2 (Heydenreich, 1906), p. 64.

the enemy lines, unlimbering and firing became part of the glory of the attack. Field artillery batteries practiced taking up open firing positions and engaging over open sights. It was considered particularly brave, if a battery galloped into firing position and unlimbered its guns under enemy fire to support the infantry. Only foot artillery used indirect firing procedures against enemy fortifications and entrenchments.

Field artillery was a direct-fire weapon system. Ranges may have increased, but gunners still had to see the target to be effective. Artillery chauvinism became the focus of doctrinal discussions among the different branches, with the artillery trying to show that they deserved to be in the thick of the fight. Some traditionalists such as Albert v. Boguslawski and Wilhelm v. Scherff refused to view artillery as anything other than an auxiliary branch. In July of 1881, however, the army corps commanders were directed by the Chief of the General Staff to permit a few batteries to expose themselves forward. The bulk of the artillery was to fire from ranges of at least 2000 m.[3]

Three types of ammunition were available to the artillery enabling it to tailor its fire to each individual target. During counter-battery fire, high-explosive (HE) shells with impact fuzes were used in combination with shrapnel shells equipped with time fuzes (*Brennzünder*). The intent was to force opposing artillery crews to run for cover and silence enemy batteries. Against infantry, shrapnel was used with time fuzes to scatter fire in full depth across infantry columns. The main ammunition of the field artillery was the shrapnel round that could be used against infantry in open terrain with good results, but it was of limited value against entrenched positions. In 1911, the introduction of an HE round with a time fuze began to provide field artillery-guns a limited capacity against trenches and covered targets. For close defense, the guns carried some canister rounds. Against covered or entrenched targets, either field howitzers or heavy howitzers firing HE at steep angles, provided better results.[4]

For close defense against sudden infantry or cavalry assaults, artillery used canister shots that could be used like a huge shotgun.[5] An English language anomaly is that word use has changed over time. High explosive shells splintered apart upon detonation, and those pieces would fly through the air at great speed causing damage to both living creatures and equipment. At the time, these pieces of metal were called splinters. Shrapnel shells were packed with many marble-sized lead or steel balls that were thrown forward in a cone at high speed by a timed, secondary bursting charge. Those balls were known as shrapnel. Today in popular parlance the two types have been conflated and "shrapnel" is now used to describe any sort of metal fragment caused by exploding munitions of any kind.

Field guns (field artillery) as well as heavy guns (foot artillery) were fired over open sights. Due to the heavy recoil, the guns used to jump up and roll backwards so they had to be pushed back into firing position after each shot and laid once more on the target. This process was time-consuming, slowing down the rate of fire to such an extent that a contemporary field gun was not much faster in action (even after the introduction of breech loaders) than in the days of Frederick the Great and Napoleon.

Shortly after the Franco-Prussian War, the German army introduced its new C73 artillery system in succession to the successful C64 guns.[6] During the next 20 years, development focused upon improving fuzes and technical details. The C73 gun, the backbone of the field artillery, was now available in two versions: a light 8 cm (7.85 cm) gun for the riding batteries

3 (Brose, 2001), pp. 31–35.
4 (Mattuschka, 1979), p. 173.
5 (Ortenburg, *Waffe und Waffengebrauch im Zeitalter der Einigungskriege*, 1990), p. 86
6 Development of the C73 had already begun in 1870 but had to be delayed due to the start of the war.

and a heavy 9 cm (8.8 cm) version for the driving batteries of the field artillery regiments.[7] In the riding batteries, six horses towed the gun. There were four extra horses; thus, the entire crew of five gunners plus the NCO in command was on horseback. In addition, an ammunition wagon accompanied each gun, with another four soldiers running the supply chain between the ammunition train and the gun. Driving batteries did not have the four extra horses per gun. Their three gunners sat on the limber and two gunners on the gun carriage riding with the gun; only the commanding NCO was on horseback. Each horse assigned to the heavier (985 kg) 9 cm gun had to pull approximately 370 kg (share of gun, limber, ammunition, and crew), while in riding batteries with their lighter (895 kg) guns, each horse had to pull only about 275 kg. Therefore, the riding batteries—usually one battalion per regiment—were much faster and could operate with the cavalry. Please check Chapter 7 for details. Most artillery regiments still had two battalions, both equipped with three batteries of six guns each (*fahrende Abteilung*). Some regiments received a riding battalion (*reitende Abteilung*) with three batteries of four guns each.

A great increase in range was the main improvement of the C73 over the C64. The 8 cm version had a maximum range of 6,800 meters and the 9 cm version of 7,600 meters. For Krupp, the C73 turned out to be a great economic success since many of the world's armies ordered this field gun or one of its derivatives. With the C73 system in place, the German Army felt superior to its potential enemies, particularly the French, who seemed to be technically far behind, because they still depended primarily on the muzzle loaded Lahitte guns during the 1870–71 war.

There was an underlying problem in using artillery to destroy or even neutralize enemy infantry protected by trenches and fortifications. This came into sharp focus on 11 September 1877, at the battle of Plevna during the Russo-Turkish war. The Russians fired their field artillery at the entrenched defenders for three and one-half days. Following the low trajectory field artillery preparation, 60,000 Russian and Romanian soldiers advanced in dense columns against 25,000 entrenched Turks. Unfortunately, the bombardment had been almost totally ineffective and the attackers suffered a staggering 18,000 casualties. Field artillery has been described by at least one historian as lined up "flinging handfuls of dried peas against the wall." A heavier kind of gun with larger caliber ammunition and a high angle trajectory was needed to dislodge the defenders.[8]

In the 1880s, the much-derided lowly foot artillery developed the 150 mm heavy howitzer that supported infantry attacks at ranges of 1,200 to 2,000 m. Up to and including the Great War, the German army referred to these weapons as "mortars." When combined with the older 210 mm howitzer, these bourgeois technical experts simply destroyed earthworks and redoubts. Reinforced concrete, thickly added to defensive fortifications, kept the defense in front of the developments for a while. There were two different schools of thought. The traditional field artillery supporters, pointing to the battle of Sedan, praised the warlike attributes of German officers, while the technologically advanced foot artillery preferred to draw on the lessons of the battle of Plevna. The more traditional field artillery supporters aligned with the aristocratic tendencies of the infantry and cavalry and secured a majority of the resources allotted to artillery. The artillery regulations were revised in 1892, favoring open field positions over hidden positions. The use of shrapnel rounds at ranges closer than 1,500 m was an important part of this revision. Foreign observers and their military journals joined the

[7] (Ortenburg, *Waffe und Waffengebrauch im Zeitalter der Millionenheere*, 1992), p. 88.

[8] (Brose, 2001), pp. 35–38.

theoretician von der Goltz in believing that the lessons of St. Privat had been forgotten in Germany, in favor of glorious myth.[9]

When trials for a new German artillery system began, two companies were in competition for the contract. The first company, Ehrhardt (later renamed as the better known *Rheinmetall*), offered a very modern system equipped with an improved carriage, that featured a sliding mechanism to absorb the recoil of the barrel after each shot. The Ehrhardt field gun basically remained still during firing. Krupp, the second company, only offered an improvement of the C73 system they had sold so successfully. Compared with the Ehrhardt gun, the Krupp model still featured a traditional carriage that jumped up and rolled backwards due to the recoil after each shot. After intensive trials, the Prussian War Ministry chose the Krupp model in 1896 and introduced their 7.7 cm field gun as *Feldkanone* 96. They were proud to maintain continuity in their artillery systems. Ehrhardt then started selling their system to the British Army and others.

But this time, the Prussian War Ministry had overestimated its technological and tactical advantage. Just as had been the case earlier for rifles, the French gained a significant lead over the German artillery by introducing their revolutionary new 75 mm field gun Model 1897. The French gun had two major features, which gave it superiority over German field guns: a steel shield providing at least some protection for the crew against shrapnel and infantry fire and an improved carriage with a hydro-pneumatic mechanism which absorbed the recoil of the barrel, thereby rendering the carriage as stable as the Ehrhardt gun during firing. Since it was no longer necessary to push the gun back into firing position after each shot and to relocate the target, the new French 75 mm gun could develop a rate of fire more than twice as fast as the German field guns. It was believed that one French battery (with only four guns) would have the same firepower as two to three German batteries each with six guns. Furthermore, French Model 1897 guns carried about 2.5 times the load of ammunition in their limbers as the German Feldkanonen 96

The new French gun came as a shock to the German army; it had excellent accuracy, superior range, and rapid-fire capability. The French soon introduced a new doctrine with their November 1901 artillery manual—indirect rapid-fire assaults called *rafale* in French. This early kind of indirect fire was a very simple system. Gun lines were established on reverse slopes and the batteries then fired to clear the crest line, while being directed by the battery commander from an observation post within sight of the battery.[10]

The new French 75 mm field gun (like the German Feldkanone 96) fired smokeless rounds. It now became very difficult to identify battery positions and to engage them through counter-battery fire if the muzzle flash could not be seen. In addition, the new procedures meant that French field artillery could now hit their enemy from concealed positions with well-directed rapid fire, and the result was clear superiority over German field artillery. Like a bolt out of the blue, a French battery could silence or even completely wipe out an opposing battery without risking direct counter fire.[11] A side effect of indirect artillery fire with modern guns and recoil mechanisms carriages was a huge increase in the consumption of ammunition. The industrialized warfare of the Russo-Japanese War was already casting a shadow![12]

---

9 (Brose, 2001), pp. 40–42.

10 Later, one limber was equipped with a steel-clad observation ladder for the battery commander to peep over the hilltop. With their four guns, French batteries were also more flexible and easier to lead than German batteries with their six guns.

11 (Ortenburg, *Waffe und Waffengebrauch im Zeitalter der Millionenheere*, 1992), p. 200.

12 (Linnenkohl, 1996), pp. 137–149.

Due to this "French revolution" in artillery technology and tactical doctrine, an intense German effort began to completely overhaul (if not re-invent) German field artillery to keep up with the French.[13] This discussion fed into the introduction of the *Feldkanone 96 neuer Art* (field gun 96 new model) in 1905. Doctrinally, the argument between open positions using direct fire and concealed positions really became an argument between the offensive and defensive use of forces.

This model included all the features of the French system. Using the barrel and the breechblock of the Model 96, the field guns were also equipped with shields and improved carriages with a recoil mechanism. Ironically, Krupp also carried out this modification and so managed to earn money with the Model 96 guns twice over—even though it was already obsolete at the time of its introduction. The affair of the field gun Model 96 made it clear how powerful Friedrich Krupp was. Although the Ehrhardt system was more modern than the Krupp system, Krupp persuaded the War Ministry to buy his guns. When the French 75 mm gun proved to be better than the Krupp guns, Krupp was not penalized, but simply asked to improve the Model 96 guns to meet French standard.

Although field guns had significantly increased their range, they could not hit dug-in infantry from concealed positions behind hills due to the low trajectory of their guns. The answer was to equip the field artillery with howitzers able to exploit high angle fire capable of taking on targets in dead ground. Germany took the lead in this by introducing the 10.5 cm Model 98 light field howitzer. Once more Krupp earned money twice by first producing the guns and later in 1909 modifying them with shields and recoil mechanisms into *leichte Feldhaubitzen* 98/09.

Most German field artillery regiments now received a third battalion equipped with field howitzers. This gave the German field artillery a competitive edge over the French.[14] A basic field artillery regiment still had two battalions (*Abteilungen*) with three batteries of six field guns Model 96 (new model) each. A few regiments had an extra riding battalion; others had a third battalion equipped with field howitzer Model 98/09. During mobilization, the riding battalions were usually taken out of the field artillery regiments and assigned to the cavalry divisions.

German artillery doctrine had to keep up with that of the French, and indirect fire procedure was introduced into the field artillery. In the 1899 field artillery manual, indirect fire was exclusively described for the (then still very few) field howitzers, while the bulk of the field artillery was still drilled according to classical methods.[15] During maneuvers, the artillery was expected to feature batteries galloping into open firing positions and then unlimbering gallantly in front of the enemy. Galloping horses, dust clouds, and very fast opening of fire were considered the most important features of artillery tactics. That way the field artillerymen could also feel themselves the equal to the cavalry in dash and spirit.

Meanwhile the artillery manual began to emphasize that indirect fire from covered positions was of increasing importance. The 1907 field artillery manual was based upon the experience of the Russo-Japanese War of 1904–05 in Manchuria. However, use of indirect fire was time-consuming and demanding as did the preparation of observation posts, range finders, scissor scopes, and firing positions. In addition, the various locations positions had to be connected by field telephone. Although the manual listed the tactical advantages of

---

[13] (Reichenau, 1902), p. 15 and (Alten, 1903), p. 9.

[14] (Ortenburg, *Waffe und Waffengebrauch im Zeitalter der Millionenheere*, 1992), p. 110. In 1914, the German army had 5,068 field guns and 1,260 field howitzers; the French had 4,780 field guns and only 84 field howitzers.

[15] (*Kriegsministerium*, 1899)

indirect fire from covered positions, it did contain one paragraph that could be exploited by the traditionalists:

"To push for decision by bolstering the fighting infantry, the field artillery will often be forced to abandon the advantages of indirect fire to support the infantry with direct fire delivered from open positions."[16]

Because this sentence was highlighted in print, it delivered the perfect excuse to continue with the traditional methods. As a nod in the direction of the manual, usually some improvised cover was hastily dug out around the guns. As a result, the artillery practiced unrealistic maneuvers until the war taught, with bloody lessons, that well-prepared indirect fire from covered positions was infinitely preferable.

The field artillery adopted a lofty attitude to the less mobile foot artillery, shaking their heads at the sluggish siege trains. In 1891, under the decisive influence of Schlieffen, the heavy artillery developed from fortress and siege artillery into field usable foot artillery. At first the foot artillery received a new long 15 cm howitzer to replace the old and immobile 15 cm ring-cannon. Soon after, a heavy 15 cm howitzer developed by Krupp entered service. This howitzer was the real turning point in the development of the foot artillery into heavy artillery deployable in the field. This gun was comparatively lightweight, could easily be moved by the crew and was capable of firing more than 6,000 meters. Soon after it was fielded, Krupp began the construction of a new 21 cm howitzer.

Between the years 1893 and 1902, the foot artillery developed four strong foot artillery detachments intended to smash French frontier fortresses. The 21 cm C/82 round filled with smokeless cordite explosives (*Schießbaumwolle*) delivered such an increase in explosive power that the French had to reinforce their fortresses. In 1888, 1896, and 1904, more modern HE rounds with even greater explosive power were developed for use against fortifications. However, by 1900, many of the foot artillery commanders felt that the forts represented impregnable structures. As a result, the Chief of Staff focused on using the light howitzers of the field artillery in the counter-battery role. The foot artillery continued to argue that, given enough horses, they could reinforce the field artillery during the counter-battery battle and then turn on the enemy infantry. A shooting competition in 1900 demonstrated that heavy howitzers were far more effective in countering dug-in enemy batteries than the light howitzers. By 1904, the Great General Staff provided guidance to the corps commanders to use 150 mm heavy howitzers at every opportunity. While there were only 10 horse-drawn heavy foot artillery regiments in 1904, almost every army corps had at least one by the start of the war.[17]

A new edition of the German artillery drill regulations appeared in 1907. It emphasized rates of concentrated fire for effect rather than the mere massing of guns. There was a discussion concerning the balance of advantage between open and covered firing positions. Open ones offered rapid engagement times, and the latter afforded protection. The regulations emphasized the need to continually suppress the enemy artillery during the infantry attack. This compromise brokered a middle course between the arguments of the traditionalists, who favored open positions and rapid engagement, and the reformers, who sought the use of covered positions based on the lessons of the 1905 Russo-Japanese War. The middle ground was that both schools of thought shared a common goal to support the infantry attack "in the most effective manner possible." All doctrinal writers emphasized the requirement to work

[16] (Kriegsministerium, 1907), p. 167. Translated by the author.
[17] (Brose, 2001), pp. 165–166.

closely and inseparably with the infantry. While the principle of infantry/artillery combination was accepted, discussed, and practiced, there were numerous communication problems to overcome and these were made much worse by the chronic shortage of telephones and wire right up until the early months of the Great War.[18]

The influence of Moltke the Younger led to more realistic and "war-like" (*kriegsnahe*) doctrine and training. With the appearance of the 1907 field artillery manual, indirect fire became the main tactical approach and was equally applied to field guns and field howitzers.[19] During the years before the war, indirect fire was intensively trained through live firing in the corps training centers. During maneuvers, this new tactical doctrine led to complaints that artillery was no longer visible except during marches. Certainly following the changes in infantry doctrine, artillery developments contributed to the creation of what was called later the "void of the battlefield." Right up to 1914, the German field artillery made good progress with the development of doctrine. It absorbed developments made by other armies, as well as the experience of contemporary wars, although some traditionalists still favored the traditional role and the heroic pictures of galloping horses and guns firing from open positions.[20] But what was really striking with the German artillery prior to 1914 was the emphasis upon heavy artillery. Here the German army of 1914 was far superior to all of her Western enemies. Schlieffen paved the way for the heavy artillery's fast and diverse development. One of Schlieffen's major concerns had been the fortresses along the French eastern border and in Belgium. Reinforced and equipped with good quality artillery, those fortresses threatened to pose major problems to the German Army and its doctrine of fast pre-emptive attacks into enemy territory.

In 1914, the heavy German artillery was equipped with mortars (heavy howitzers), field howitzers, and heavy field guns. To smash forts and fortresses, the foot artillery had the 15 cm *schwere Feldhaubitze* 02 (heavy field howitzer Model 02), an outdated gun without a recoil mechanism, but with a range of more than 7,450 k meters and the very modern 21 cm mortar. For long-range tasks, the foot artillery had numerous pieces including the modern 10 cm "*Kanone 04*" and some of the older heavy 12, 13, and 15 cm guns. Usually the 12, 13, and 15 cm guns belonged to siege forces and were not fielded with the regular foot artillery regiments.[21] In 1914, the backbone of the German heavy artillery was the 21 cm mortar introduced in 1910 that possessed good mobility and a range of 9,400 meters.[22] In addition, there were 10 cm cannons. In all a total of 630 pieces could be fielded, compared with the 372 heavy artillery pieces of the French and British armies. Imperial Germany had only 256 of the 21 cm mortars, of which 112 were fielded with foot artillery formations, 32 belonged to fortresses, and 112 were held back as a reserve.

Within the foot artillery, there was a theoretical division concerning their employment. One side focused on mobility and a need to keep the calibers smaller. The other side concentrated on fortress reduction and a need to increase the size of the calibers. The dividing line seemed to come around the 210 mm level. Max Bauer conducted a one-man campaign within the general staff to get approval for a monster gun. The product was a 42 cm

18 (Echevarria II, 2000), pp. 140–146.

19 (Kriegsministerium, 1907) Imitating the French, the German army introduced an ironclad observation ladder. (Kriegsministerium, 1913), pp. 21.

20 (Hoehn, 1913)

21 (*Kriegsministerium*, 1911), and (Mummenhoff, 1907).

22 The 21 cm mortars fired an HE round model 1896 that had a weight of 120 kg and which showed a devastating result when used against any kind of field fortifications. Even against concrete structures, multiple hits showed satisfying results. These mortar battalions had only two batteries with four guns each. (Mattuschka, 1979), p. 177.

super heavy howitzer—the so called *γ-Gerät* model 1912—capable of hurling a 2000 pound shell over 14,200 meters. Since the γ-Gerät had to be fired from a concrete bedding and moved by railroad, it was virtually immobile. The general staff and the Artillerie-Prüfungs-kommission therefore asked Krupp for a more mobile version that resulted in the 42 cm mortar M-Gerät model 1914 that had a shorter barrel than the γ-Gerät and a shorter range of 12,500 meters. In 1914, five M-Geräte and two γ-Geräte were available and could be mobilized in batteries of two guns each; the fifth γ-Gerät was mobilized a little later as a half-battery.

This new development came as a complete surprise to the allies. The 42 cm super heavy howitzers appeared on the battlefields around the fortresses of Liège, Namur, Fort Manonviller, and Antwerp in August and September 1914.[23] Developed under perfect secrecy and based upon specifications from the General Staff—most probably from Ludendorff and Bauer—these Krupp mortars were fielded under the camouflage of being Navy-owned, "short-cannon batteries" (*kurze Marine-Kanonen Batterien*).[24] They were operated by Krupp personnel and men of the Artillerie-Prüfungskommission in navy and, later, army uniforms.[25] Initially, the 2nd (γ -Gerät) and 3rd (M-Gerät) 42cm batteries were deployed under control of the OHL; whereas, the 3rd (γ –Gerät) battery was subordinated to Sixth Army. The super-heavies smashed the forts at Liège and paved the way for the infantry to take the city. On 12 August, the bombardment of Fort de Pontisse started and soon after Fort de Loncin exploded after a direct hit into its ammunition magazine.

At Liège, the Germans also employed super-heavy 30.5 cm howitzers type β-Gerät as well as Austrian made model 1911 30.5 cm mortars manufactured at the Skoda plant in Bohemia and borrowed at mobilization from their Austrian ally. The German army had its own 30.5 cm mortars introduced in 1898 and reworked in 1909 to extend their range from 8,700 to 11,900 meters. The β-Gerät mortars also operated under the camouflage of being Navy operated "heavy coastal mortars" (*schwere Küstenmörser*). In 1914, twelve of these mortars were available, but since most of them could only be operated on a railroad, the more mobile Austrian models were preferred. Crews in Austrian uniforms operated the Austrian mortars openly.[26] Based upon the mobilization plan, the 3rd and 4th (β-Gerät) batteries were under direct control of OHL, to be used against fortresses in the main thrust. Deployment against Liége was not intended since the General Staff believed that that place would be taken by a coup de main. The 2nd (β-Gerät) battery was with the Sixth Army in Lorraine. As soon as the advance was checked at Liége, the 3rd and 4th batteries were employed to join the 42cm mortars in smashing the fortifications at the Eastern end of the fortress. The 2nd battery followed on 16 and 17 August.

These 30.5 and 42 cm mortars were handled with such secrecy that no hints concerning their existence could be found in the top-secret *Manual for General Staff Officers* (*Taschenbuch des Generalstabsoffiziers*). The 30.5 cm Skoda mortar could fire an 800-pound shell over 12,300 meters. Also a super-heavy gun, it was more mobile than the 42cm Krupp mortar and could change firing positions faster.

Starting in 1911, the idea of breaking through France's fortress wall re-emerged. Ludendorff in the General Staff championed attacking the fortresses on the Belgian frontier instead

---

23 (Solf, 1920), pp. 7–16, (Deuringer, 1929), pp. 506–513, and (Balck, 1921), pp. 100–117

24 Nicknamed "*dicke Bertha*" after Friedrich Krupp's wife—in English known as the "Big Bertha."

25 (Generalstab des Heeres 7 Ab., 1939), (Kybitz, 1939) and (Henningsen, none given)

26 (Mattuschka, 1979), pp. 177–178. The Austrian guns do not show up in the *ordre de bataille* given in the appendix.

of bypassing them. While reawakening the heavy artillery fortress-smashing concept, the Army ran into budgetary reluctance on the part of the War Ministry. Not only were fewer guns provided than requested, but also the amount of ammunition provided was significantly less than that which was desirable. The 21 cm howitzers deployed with fewer than 600 shells per weapon as opposed to usage estimates of 800 to 1,000. Technical capabilities were starting once again to affect operational planning. Shortages of heavy guns and munitions would mean that the German armies could not take on both the French fortresses and the Belgian fortresses at the same time.[27]

In short, of the three arms described, the artillery can be considered the best prepared and trained for the coming war. The technical and doctrinal development of the field and foot artillery prior to 1914 hinted already at the industrialized battles of attrition along the Western Front in the years after 1914.[28] If the infantry was considered the Queen of Battle before 1914, the artillery became the King once the war stalled in the trenches of France and Flanders.

---

[27] (Brose, 2001), pp 166–172.

[28] *Materialschlacht* (material battle) showed that operational genius no longer sufficed but that industrial potential would determine the outcome of the war.

CHAPTER 15

LOGISTICS

The German Army considered logistics and supply as areas of secondary importance when compared with infantry, cavalry, and artillery doctrine. Operational leadership was an attractive task to general staff officers while logistics was considered a bothersome responsibility. Iron Crosses and the Pour le Merité medals were won by bravery in battle or through successful leadership of troops. Responsibility for supply was considered mundane at best. The most prestigious regiments for officers' careers were cavalry and guards regiments, followed by infantry. A distant third was the artillery and other technical arms. Train formations came at the end of the list. To traditionalist officers, modern technical arms and the necessary logistics to keep them running were a burden rather than a vital requirement needed for increased firepower and fighting capacity.

The army corps had ever-growing logistical formations trailing behind them like a comet tail, thus reducing flexibility and mobility. The increased firepower of modern weapons, such as super-heavy artillery, was essential for destroying the Belgian fortress of Liège and the fortresses along the French eastern border. The price for having these weapons available was a growing logistical tail that reduced operational mobility. However, logistical problems could no longer be treated as purely theoretical issues. While officers made regular staff rides to analyze given tactical or operational problems, logistical specialists, quartermasters, and intendants began such staff rides only around 1900. These logistical staff rides were disparagingly called "flour rides" (*Mehlreisen*).[1] Nevertheless, they became the subject of regular war games, which were based upon an assumed military operation, planned and led by General Staff officers and in the course of which, intendancy officials had to simulate the entire supply and logistics processes supporting the combat operations. Although General Staff officers used to look down upon these flour rides because they were not dealing with combat, these war games succeeded in revealing certain logistical deficiencies prior to1914.[2]

When considering logistics, it is imperative to understand that the battlefield extended from the front lines all the way back to the source of sustenance in the homeland. This battlefield structure was divided into three primary zones: the combat zone, the communications zone, and the homeland rear zone. In German, these were known as *Operationsgebiet, Etappengebiet,* and *Heimatgebiet*. In theory, the combat zone stretched from the front lines to the depth of enemy artillery range. The communications zone would then start and could extend as far

1 Officially they were called *Intendantur-Reisen* and after 1908, *Verwaltungs-Generalstabsreisen* (administrative general staff rides). (Alten, 1903), p. 48.

2 (François, 1910), pp. 7–11.

back as the political border with the homeland. In some cases, the communication zone ended at a political border of occupied or allied territory. There would then be some sort of rear area transportation zone. The homeland zone in imperial Germany was centered on the army corps area described earlier. A view of the zone map should make this placement fairly clear.

These columns and trains were the backbone of the supply system, which bridged the gap between the combat zone and the railheads where the supply railroad-trains were unloaded. They were part of the supply process that was, in theory, organized down to the last detail during peacetime preparations for mobilization. However, the basic assumptions governing these processes did not meet the realities of 1914. As in the case of all belligerents, the ammunition consumption estimates were much too low, leading to shortages and improvised actions to fill the gap. The word *Ersatzstoffe* (meaning "low quality replacement materials"), started its cynical career in the summer of 1914. The supply chain was almost exclusively based upon horse-drawn transportation, which meant low speed of movement and serious load capacity limitations.

ORGANIZATION OF LOGISTICS AND SUPPLY AT THE BEGINNING OF THE WAR

Top Ranks of the Logistical Organization[3]

During mobilization, the top ranks of the German armies were reshuffled and formally merged as the *Deutsches Feldheer* under the command of the Kaiser. The carefully maintained differences between Prussian, Bavarian, Saxon, and Württemberg armies that were so important in peacetime, became blurred on mobilization. Generaloberst v. Moltke would no longer simply be the Chief of the General Staff but *Chef des Generalstabes des Feldheeres*. That new role formally gave him command authority over all contingents, including Bavaria. The core organization of the headquarters was the *Großes Hauptquartier*, Great Headquarters or Supreme Command (*Oberste Heeresleitung*—abbreviated OHL).

The OHL was structured into two divisions: the first reported to the Chief of General Staff and was responsible for operations; the other reported to the Quartermaster General (*Generalquartiermeister*) about logistics. The Quartermaster General was in charge of the entire supply system between the armies operating in the field and the zone of the homeland.

In 1914, the operational division comprised the following departments:

- Central Department (*Zentral-Abteilung*) under Obstlt. v. Fabeck,
- Operations Department (*Operations-Abteilung*) under Obstlt. Tappen,
- Intelligence Department (*Nachrichten-Abteilung*) under Oberstlt. Hentsch,
- Political Department (*Politische Abteilung*) under Obstlt. v. Dommes.

The following Logistical Division departmental heads reported in 1914 to the Quartermaster General Lieutenant General v. Stein:

- General Responsible for Supplies (*Generalintendant*): Gen. Maj. v. Schöler, head of the administration department in the War Ministry (*Armee-Verwaltungs-Departement BD*) before mobilization;

[3] Please refer to attachment 1.

- Chief Railroad (*Chef des Feldeisenbahnwesens*): Obstlt. Gröner, head of the railroad department (*Eisenbahn-Abteilung*) in the Great General Staff before mobilization;
- Chief, Field Munitions Service (*Chef des Feldmunitionswesens*): Gen. Lt. Sieger, previously President of the Artillery Testing Commission (*Artillerie-Prüfungskommission*);
- Chief, Medical Service (Chef des Feld-Sanitätswesens): General Stabs Arzt d. Armee, Prof. Dr. v. Schjerning, previously the head of the medical department in the War Ministry (*Medizinal-Abteilung MA*).

Management of Supply on Army and Army Corps Level

In a corps staff, the commanding general was responsible for the logistical operations, and on his behalf, the chief of staff. In practice the Ib, the second general staff officer (usually a captain) ran them. He was responsible for orders addressed to the heavy baggage, the ammunition columns, and the train formations. He had to create all logistical inserts to the corps orders worked out by the Ia. Since the two echelons of train formations and ammunition columns were not formally established and had no commanders, the Ib acted as a kind of a commanding officer over all these formations. He was also responsible for any kind of war booty or prisoners and had to arrange the clearance of battlefields after action. The Ib reported to the Chief of Staff and the Ic represented him during his absences. This responsibility exposed the Ib to such an immense workload that he and his very small department of just a handful of NCOs and men could barely cope.

In corps staffs, the IVa was the Corps Intendant (*Korps-Intendant*) and headed Department IV, the intendancy. He was responsible for managing all financial and administrative issues of the army corps and for overseeing all supply issues, food supply columns, field bakeries, etc. He had to set up warehouses and depots to make sure there was a working logistical and supply chain between the army and the *Etappe* (communications zone) warehouses and the combat formations of the army corps. Close cooperation with Ib was required to implement the logistical orders of the Ib.

While the Ib was usually a General Staff captain, the corps intendant was a *Beamte* or military official. The corps intendant reported directly to the commanding general of the corps but also had a kind of dotted reporting line into the administration department of the War Ministry (*Armee-Verwaltungs-Departement BD*) before mobilization.[4] On the other hand, the corps intendant was superior in "rank" with disciplinary authority over all military personnel within the corps staff. He also had to oversee the small intendancies of the divisions, as well as all military installations led by military officials within the corps area.[5]

Like the corps staff, the army had an intendancy headed by the army intendant (*Armee-Intendant*), who also had to closely cooperate with the Ib of the army staff. Because armies were only created upon mobilization from the cadres of the existing army inspections, army staffs had to be built from scratch and the roles were similar to those positions in an army corps; the commander and chief of staff carried the final responsibility, and the senior quartermaster of the army (a captain) oversaw the logistical operations. The Ib did the day-to-day work.

So the second general staff officers (Ib's), together with the corps and the army intendants (IVa's), provided the link in the supply chain between the combat formations and the rear communications zone. As soon as the combat formations had consumed their unit loads of

---

4 The head of the Armee-Verwaltungs-Department, Major General v. Schöler, became the General Responsible for Supplies (Generalintendant) in the OHL upon mobilization.

5 (Alten, 1913), p. 48.

ammunition, food, horse rations, or any other item of supply, the army corps' trains and columns, which had to be refilled from supplies stocked up in the communications zone, resupplied them.

Mobile Supply Formations of the Communications Zone

As previously mentioned, the communications zone was the area between the combat formations fighting their way deeper into enemy territory and the German border. The German name for this communications zone was *Etappe* or *Etappengebiet* and was viewed negatively during the war, because the combat formations witnessed the constant expansion of the supply formations and noted how they performed their tasks almost under peacetime conditions.[6] This became particularly true after the start of the positional warfare. It was said that the Etappe became a kind of pool, gathering soldiers who tried to avoid the hardships and dangers of the war, and who lived comparatively luxurious lives at a safe distance from the dangerous combat zones.[7] In fact, the reputation of the Etappe was so bad that Lieutenant Colonel Karl Schroeder started his paragraph on the Etappe in the volume of Lieutenant General Schwarte's book series on the Great War with four pages of excuses, trying to explain and to justify the great work that had been performed by the staffs, formations, and organizations of the Etappe right from the start of the war.[8]

Later in the war, the basic rule was that the Etappengebiet had to be out of the reach of enemy artillery. Each army had its own Etappengebiet led by an *Etappen-Inspektion,* the section headquarters of the respective Etappengebiet. An Etappeninspekteur, usually a General Leutnant z.D, headed the Etappen-Inspektion with the power of a commanding general of an army corps, assisted by an adjutant. The Etappen-Inspektion had a staff comparable to a corps staff. The staff was headed by a Chief of General Staff, usually a colonel, sometimes a general-major z.D. There were two General Staff officers (Ia and Ib), usually a major and a captain, supporting the Chief of Staff. The Ia was mainly responsible for operational tasks and acted as commander of the mixed *Landwehr* brigades and *Landsturm* formations assigned as occupation and security forces to the Etappen-Inspektion. The Ib acted as a liaison officer between the Ib of the army and the Department of the Chief of the Field Ammunitions Services in the OHL.

An adjutant dealt with personnel issues and a *BBa* (*Beauftragter des Chefs des Feldeisenbahnwesens*), an authorized representative of the Chief Railroad, oversaw the railroad operations in the communications zone; in August and September 1914 that meant the reconstruction of damaged railroad junctions. Upon mobilization the different BBa's belonged to the army staffs but were transferred to the staffs of the Etappen-Inspektion soon after operations began. A communications zone medical officer (*Etappenarzt*) oversaw the entire medical organization within a communications zone. A veterinarian officer (*Etappenveterinär*) did the same for the veterinarian organization.

The intendant of the communication zone (*Etappenintendant*) was responsible for the organization of all subsistence supplies and horse rations within the communications zone. The communications zone even had its own legal official (*Etappen-Kriegsgerichtsrat*) to handle all military jurisdiction issues and to act as a legal advisor to the Etappeninspekteur. A postal director (*Armee-Postdirektor*), a communications director (*Etappen-Telegraphendirektor*),

---

6 Etappengebiet means Etappe area, if translated literally.

7 (Wandt, 1921)

8 (Schroeder, 1923). Lieutenant Colonel Schroeder was the Ia of the 4th Etappen-Inspektion and was responsible for the same Etappe Gent Heinrich Wandt had written about in his book mentioned above.

and a construction director (*Baudirektion*) completed the technical functions of an Etappen-Inspektion. In addition, there was a captain of the artillery, supporting the Ib and responsible for all artillery, ordnance, ammunition, and horse replacement issues. There was another captain of the engineer corps in charge of technical and transportation issues. There was also a military police commander (*Kommandeur der Feldgendarmerie*) and a paymaster.[9]

The commander of the field ammunition services (*Kommandeur des Etappenmunitionswesens*) was responsible for arranging the supply of ammunition of all kinds and replacement material for machinegun and artillery formations. He headed the following two organizations:

- The field ammunition administration (*Etappen-Munitionsverwaltung*) was in charge of ammunition supply trains arriving by railroad from the interior zone. It staffed, organized, and ran ammunition depots and distribution points (*Ausgabestellen*) to ensure that the ammunition columns of the army corps were resupplied.
- The ammunition columns battalion (*Etappenmunitionskolonnen-Abteilung*) had its own battalion commander. These columns had to transport ammunition across the communications zone from the railheads to the respective depots and distribution points. In urgent cases, these columns delivered the ammunition supply directly to the combat units. Depending upon the size of the army, the Etappen-Inspektion had to supply the combat zone with about six to 12 columns, most of them motor transport columns.

These motor transport columns (*Etappen-Kraftwagenkolonnen*) usually were comprised of 17 standard army trucks (*Armee-Lastzüge*) with trailers. The trucks had a load capacity of four metric tons and the trailers two tons; this combination gave the motor transport columns a total load capacity of 102 tons—almost twice the capacity of heavy horse-drawn columns with their 62 wagons. Nine trucks could carry 54 tons and had almost the same load capacity as one heavy horse-drawn column.[10] The motor transport columns could move at an average speed of about 30 kilometers per hour and had an average range of 100 kilometers before they needed to refill with gasoline.[11] Some Etappen-Inspektionen mobilized light motor transport columns (*leichte Etappen-Kraftwagenkolonnen*). These light columns comprised 15 trucks with three metric tons load capacity and no trailers, 45 tons in total. These columns were identical to the motor transport columns of cavalry divisions.

These figures alone demonstrate how efficient such motor transport columns were compared with horse-drawn columns. They were particularly useful if an army advanced into enemy territory whose railway system had been destroyed—an eventuality that was anticipated in Belgium and northern France during the logistic planning for a campaign in the west.

In 1914, only 9,639 trucks were registered in Germany and, of these, few were standard army trucks. As mentioned earlier, the government subsidized these trucks if private owners purchased the exact specifications and held them ready for mobilization.[12] Besides these standard trucks, civilian trucks were requisitioned soon after the mobilization. To avoid severe transportation shortages within Germany, only a certain percentage of the available trucks could be taken up in this way. Based upon the number of all mobilized motor

---

9 (Schroeder, 1923), p. 204. Also check (Kuhl, 1929), pp. 199–201.

10 (Rabenau, 1914), pp. 113–118 and (Kuhl, 1929), p. 71. Besides the Etappen-Inspektionen only the cavalry was equipped with motor transport formations. Each cavalry division was given a cavalry motor transport column (*Kavallerie-Kraftwagenkolonne*) with 15 light trucks, carrying a load of about three tons.

11 (Kuhl, 1929), p. 195.

12 (Stoneman, 2006), p. 116.

transport formations, it can be estimated that about 2,000 trucks were requisitioned upon mobilization.

In all, about 4,000 motor vehicles were mobilized together with 8,000 drivers and mechanics, who operated and maintained these vehicles. This number includes all passenger cars mobilized for higher staffs and for communications purposes.[13] As we shall see later, the German Volunteer Automobile Corps (*Deutsches Freiwilliges Automobil-Corps*) that was founded in 1904 under the lead of Prinz Heinrich v. Preußen (the brother of the Kaiser) played a vital role in supporting the mobilization of automobiles in numbers far larger than had been planned for before the war.

The other important authority of an Etappen-Inspektion was the commander of the field trains of the communications zone (*Kommandeur des Etappentrains*). He oversaw all other columns of the communications zone that were mobilized from requisitioned horses and wagons. They were manned with mobilized reservists from train formations, who were primarily responsible for subsistence supply. The logistical role of these columns was similar to that of the ammunition transport columns. They had to deliver rations and supplies from the railheads to depots and distribution points where the stocks of the combat formations were replenished.

In addition to this procedure, in 1914, depot service trains (*Magazinfuhrparkkolonnen*) were mobilized by requisitioning horses and wagons in the assembly area of the army or elsewhere on enemy territory. Although these types of columns had a confusing variety of horse wagons and were even less efficient than a communications zone column, they had to meet the important task of refilling depots and stocking up distribution points as well. These depot service trains usually had to be twice the size of the communications zone columns if they were to lift an adequate load. Thus, the fact that they numbered some 100 to 120 wagons made them difficult to control. In contrast to motor transport columns and communications zone columns, the depot service trains were not used, even in emergencies to advance into the combat zone. The number of these columns assigned to an Etappen-Inspektion depended upon the size of the army they had to support. On average the armies of 1914 were fielded with about 12 communications zone columns and two depot service trains each. Later in the war, these depot service trains were suspended, equipped with standard field service wagons, and uniformly organized as communications zone columns.[14]

In addition to these trains and columns, the Etappen-Inspektion had usually one, sometimes two, field bakery columns (*Etappen-Bäckereikolonne*) to facilitate bread supply. In contrast to the field bakeries of the army corps, those bakeries were not mobile and were exclusively designed for stationary use. There also was a train column for the medical equipment depot of the communications zone (*Trainkolonne des Etappen-Sanitätsdepots*) that was used to carry medical supplies from the medical depots to the field hospitals.

To safeguard all these military installations of the communications zone, plus railroads and main supply roads, the mixed Landwehr brigades of the army were assigned to the Etappen-Inspektion. By the end of August, the combat forces of the army corps absorbed these Landwehr brigades. Landsturm battalions started replacing the Landwehr and soon were performing occupation tasks in Belgium and Northern France.[15]

---

13 (Sußdorf, 1921), p. 342.
14 (Schroeder, 1923), pp. 204–205.
15 (Schroeder, 1923), pp. 214–215.

Logistical Installations of the Communications Zone[16]

As already described, the communications zone provided an essential link in the supply chain between the Heimatgebiet and the combat formations advancing deep into enemy territory. Because each Army had its own communications zone, what follows is a description of the logistical infrastructure of this zone and the supply chains between the Heimatgebiet and the combat zone.

The Quartermaster General attached to OHL was in charge of the organization of the communication zones of all the armies. He headed all the logistical and organizational concerns of this area (*Etappenwesen*) and of the military railroad service (*Feldeisenbahnwesen*) in the entire theater of operations. The Chief Railroad commanded the field railroad services in accordance with the general directives (*Weisungen*) of the Quartermaster General.[17]

Upon mobilization, the mobilized army corps and the reserve corps were entrained in their home garrisons and mobilization bases and were shipped into their assembly areas from there. Back home a wartime organization was formed to replace their roles. Therefore, each infantry brigade command was replaced by a *stellvertretende Infanterie-Brigade* that translates best as "being in place of." This replacement brigade took on the role of the active brigade commands in respect of personnel replacements and the training of reservists and new recruits in the Ersatz formations. In the same way, there were *stellvertretende Generalkommandos* in the active army corps; a replacement General Staff (*stellvertretender Generalstab)* was created in Berlin after the OHL moved to Koblenz. These replacement organizations were usually led by generals z.D. Officers on those staffs were mostly elder reserve or Landwehr officers.

One major role of the stellvertretende Generalkommando was to control the artillery depots, repair workshops, and garment depots. Garment Repair Workshops (*Bekleidungs-Instandsetzungs-Ämter (BJA)*) were created at the end of 1914 when clothes and uniforms were so worn out that they had to be mended and repaired before being reissued.

When war began, the War Ministry's field equipment and ordnance department (*Feldzeugmeisterei*) had one of the most important roles within the German army organization. The Feldzeugmeisterei controlled the manufacturing of ordnance and ammunition in the *Militärtechnische Institute.* These factories could be either privately- or state-owned. Examples of private factories were Mauser in Oberndorf, Württemberg; the Deutsche Waffen- und Munitionsfabriken (DWM) in Berlin; the Krupp factories in Essen; and Rheinmetall in Düsseldorf. Examples of state facilities included the Prussian rifle factories (*Gewehrfabriken*)—where all types of handguns and rifles were manufactured—in Spandau, Erfurt, Danzig, and the Bavarian armory in Amberg. Other facilities included "powder factories" (*Pulverfabriken*) or other kinds of ammunition and field equipment factories.

The Feldzeugmeisterei controlled the distribution of the factory output of all these ordnance and ammunition factories into the artillery depots of the army corps controlled by their stellvertretendes Generalkommando in the home district (*Korpsbezirk*). From the artillery depots, this ordnance and ammunition was shipped to the field by railroad and was then handed over to the Chief Field Munitions Service in the OHL, who passed these supplies on to the control of the Ib officers of the individual armies.

The process for distributing subsistence goods and horses was similar, but followed a different supply channel. Here the General Responsible for Supplies in the OHL (*Gener-*

---

16 Please refer to attachment 2.

17 (Kuhl, 1929), p. 6.

alintendant) handled the supply chain from the subsistence depots and reserve depots (*Ersatzmagazine*) of the army corps to the combat formations in cooperation with the IVa officials, the army, army corps, and division intendants. Prior to the war there was no such central organization as the Feldzeugmeisterei with the responsibility for distributing subsistence supplies.

The link between the army corps in the field and their stellvertretende Generalkommandos back in Germany was essential to keep the supply chain going. Because reserve corps did not have stellvertretende Generalkommandos to control the depot infrastructure of the corps area, they had to rely upon cooperation with the active army corps that had supported the territorial structure of the *Bezirkskommandos* during the mobilization of these reserve formations.

Each army corps had one of its depots designed as a corps base (*Etappenanfangsort*) that acted as the entry point of the supply channel into the communications zone.[18] Supplies coming by rail from these corps bases were often gathered in an army base (*Sammelstation*) to be assembled and forwarded to the Etappe. From the corps base or army base, the supplies ran by rail—organized by the Chief Railroad in the OHL—to transfer stations (*Übergangsstationen*), that later were then located along the German border where the control over these railways and trains changed from the German railroad authorities (*Eisenbahndirektionen*) to the communications zone's military control.

Usually, each army was assigned only one line of communication across the communications zone. The principal means of transport was by railroad. These standard-gauge lines (*Vollbahnen*) could be used both by standard peacetime locomotives and railcars requisitioned for military service. These lines were ideally double-tracked to allow two-way traffic between the zone of the interior and the railheads (*Eisenbahnendpunkte*). Returning trains came back empty or were used to evacuate wounded and sick soldiers from the combat zone.

As a rule these railheads usually contained the main depot of the respective communications zone, as well as the staff of the respective Etappen-Inspektion. It was known as *Etappenhauptort* in German, which is roughly translated as the main base of the communications zone. In addition to the Etappenhauptort, there was often also an *Etappenort* for one or for several army corps. To the normal soldier, the Etappenhauptort and Etappenort were more familiar than were the headquarters of his army or army corps.[19]

In and around the Etappenhauptort, the following logistical installations had to be set up:

- Etappe field hospital (*Etappen-Lazarett*);
- Field bakery (*Etappen-Bäckereikolonne im Betrieb*);
- Main ammunition depot (*Haupt-Munitionsdepot*);
- Etappe subsistence depot (*Etappenmagazin*);
- Remount depot (*Etappen-Pferdedepot*);
- Cattle livestock depot (*Viehdepot*), including a slaughtering section;
- Medical equipment depot (*Etappen-Sanitätsdepot*);
- Motor transport repair workshop (*Etappen-Kraftwagenpark*);
- Gasoline filling station (*Tankstelle*);
- Engineer equipment depot (*Gerätedepot*);

18 Direct translation of the German language word would be "Starting point of the Etappe."

19 (Kuhl, 1929), pp. 4–6.

- Aircraft spare parts depot (*Etappen-Flugzeugdepot*) to hold in readiness aircraft personnel, airplanes, and a full range of spare parts for the repair organization;
- Telegraph and telephone equipment depot (*Etappen-Fernsprechdepot*) containing the necessary replacements of telegraph and radio station equipment and materials for the telegraph and radio stations and for the telephone units of the combat formations.

In an Etappenort, the following logistical installations had to be set up:
- Field hospital (*Kriegs-Lazarett*),
- Etappe subsistence depot (Etappenmagazin),
- Ammunition depot (*Munitionsdepot*),
- Gasoline filling station (Tankstelle).[20]

As a rule, the Etappenhauptort would be not more than 100 km away from the combat zone—ideally only 85 km as proven by peacetime maneuvers. If this distance was exceeded, it was impossible to maintain the supply chain that depended on slow-moving, horse-drawn transportation. At an average speed of about 10 kilometers per hour, these columns would take about 10 hours to cover those 100 km, and 10 more hours to return and to reload. This method would require about 20 hours per day plus extra time for loading and unloading the wagons. This task was further complicated because the soldiers were in unknown enemy country and a lack of signposts, particularly at night, increased the challenge. In addition, everyone needed time for rest and for the care of the horses. Unlike a poorly maintained truck, an overtired horse would simply refuse to go on.

This plan looked very much like the Five-Marches-System of Frederick the Great who had set up numerous subsistence depots. Under that plan, the infantry could only move five marches (about 150 kilometers) away from such a depot before they had to be resupplied again. This plan was so rigid that Napoleon gave up the depot systems and let his entire army live off the country. This policy led to marauding and looting in and around the theater of operations.[21] But compared with the armies of 1914, the Grand Armée of Napoleon was small. A German cavalry division in 1914 had 5,000–6,000 men operating together in a small zone of operations. With an HKK comprising three cavalry divisions (plus four of five *Jäger* battalions), this number could easily amount to 23,000 men who had to live off the country.

In theory, the logistical installations of the Etappenorte were meant to be outside the range of enemy artillery.[22] Later in 1914, the railroad formations built small-gauge railways (*Feldbahnen* or *Schmalspurbahnen*) to connect the Etappenhauptort with the Etappenorte or with distribution points in the combat zone.[23]

Railway Infrastructure in the Communications Zone

Railroads played a major role in the supply chain. During the Franco-Prussian War of 1870–71, railroads had been essential to keep supplies running. It had been a major problem to get the French railways running under German control after the retreating French destroyed the

---

20 (Großer Generalstab (Hrsg.), 1914), Attachment 2. Please also check (Kuhl, 1929), pp. 147–158.

21 (Alten G. v.), p. 889.

22 Later in the war, the Etappe came in reach of long-range artillery and of air raids that indeed showed significant impact upon of the flow of supplies in 1918.

23 Standard-gauge railroad tracks were 100 cm wide and used by civilian railroads before the war. Small-gauge railroad tracks were 60 cm wide and used to build makeshift field-railroad lines. Small-gauge lines and trains were of significantly lower efficiency compared to standard-gauge railways.

railway tracks.[24] Until the end of the war, the transport capacity of the French railway system was never really sufficient to deliver the full quantity of supplies needed. Only late in the war were the railheads close enough to the front lines to deliver supplies efficiently. In addition, Prussia was unable to fully protect the railway system against attacks of regular French troops or of *franc-tireurs*. Consequentially, many railways were destroyed.[25] The major lesson was that all railroad affairs—operations, construction, and repairs—had to be put under one uniform control, ideally the railroad department of the General Staff.

Upon mobilization, the Chief Railroad assigned to the OHL (who had previously been head of the railroad department of the Great General Staff), assumed responsibility over all military railroad affairs within Germany. The mobilization transports were mainly controlled and directed by the 26 line commanders (*Linienkommandanturen*) who closely cooperated with the civilian railroad directorates (*Eisenbahndirektionen*) within Germany.

Each army command had assigned one BBa (*Beauftragter des Chefs des Feldeisenbahnwesens*), an authorized representative of the Chief Railroad. This person was usually a General Staff Officer mobilized by the Railroad Department. Similarly, the Etappeninspektionen received representatives from the Chief Railroad. The railroad department in Berlin would be relieved by the replacement railroad unit (*stellvertretende Eisenbahn-Abteilung*). In the west, two military railroad directorates (*Militär-Eisenbahndirektionen*) were mobilized to take over railroad operations behind the advancing armies. These railroad directorates were comparable with the line commanders plus railroad directorates. In addition, they controlled railroad units, which repaired or rebuilt railway lines and Landwehr or Landsturm formations, which secured those lines. By November 1914, six military railroad directorates existed in northern France and Belgium: the directorate *Lüttich* in Liège, *Brüssel* in Bruxelles, *Luxemburg* in Luxembourg, *Militär-Eisenbahndirektion* 1 in Gent, *Militär-Eisenbahndirektion* 2 in Sedan, and *Militär-Eisenbahndirektion* 3 in Charleroi.[26]

Each army or each Etappeninspektion was given its own railway line (*Eisenbahn-Etappenline*) reaching from the respective army base (*Sammelstation der Armee)* to the railhead in the Etappengebiet behind the combat zone.[27] To operate these railway lines, four railroad regiments (*Eisenbahn-Regimenter*) were fielded. They mobilized six military railway-operations departments (*Militär-Eisenbahnbetriebsabteilungen*)—staffs to control railway formation put under them—and two fortress military railway-operations departments (*Festungs-Militäreisenbahnbetriebsabteilungen*). So 21 railway operations companies (*Eisenbahn-Betriebskompagnien*) and one fortress railway operations company (*Festungs-Eisenbahnbetriebskompagnie*) had to keep the railways running just as civilian railway personnel would have done before mobilization. The 125 mobile railway station commandants' offices (*Mobile Bahnhofskommandanturen*) stood ready to take over railway stations on enemy territory; 15 railroad depot workers companies (*Magazinarbeiter-Kompagnien*) had to run the railway depots in the Etappe and the army bases from where the railway supply lines for the armies started. The Bahnhofskommandanturen were responsible for dispatching trains at their stations, for guarding the stations, and for maintaining military discipline among the troops during temporary halts at their stations.

To repair interrupted or destroyed lines, 30 railway construction companies (*Eisenbahnbau-Kompagnien*), 26 reserve railway construction companies (*Reserve*

24 (Budde, 1904), pp. 64–137.
25 (Budde, 1904), p. 422 and map I.
26 (Reichsarchiv, 1928), map 5.
27 (Reichsarchiv, 1928), sketches 16–21.

Eisenbahnbau-Kompagnien), and 11 fortress railway construction companies (*Festungs-Eisenbahnbaukompagnien*) were mobilized. In addition, seven static Landwehr railway construction companies and four railway construction worker battalions (*Eisenbahn-Arbeiterbataillone*) were created.[28]

Except the static Landwehr railway formations, all active, reserve, and fortress railway formations were organized and equipped alike. These battalions had 26 officers and 1,148 NCOs and EM, mainly mobilized from civilian railroad personnel. The railroad construction companies and the construction worker battalions proved to be very experienced and efficient technical formations. In August 1914, the railway construction formations in the west had about 18,000 men.

The railway construction formations had prefabricated bridging material to quickly replace destroyed railway bridges and to build standard-gauge or small-gauge tracks. Each railway construction company had a construction train (*Bauzug*) of 10 wagons with spare tracks and prefabricated bridges. These were both the older bridges of the *Schultz* model or the more modern and flexible bridges of the *Lübbecke* model, both capable of bridging up to 60 meters. For smaller requirements a light standard bridge (*Gelenkbrücke*) could bridge gaps up to 40 meters length. To increase mobility, these bridges could also be transported by horse-driven wagons.[29]

Mobile Supply Formations of the Army Corps and the Combat Formations

There were two different preparation modes for units. They were considered either immobile or mobile formations. Different sources use the word static in place of immobile; in this book we use the word static. Formations were called static before they went through all the restructuring and reinforcement procedures of the mobilization. Mobile formations were filled up and ready to be fielded after mobilization. Usually the German Army refrained from fielding static formations. One of the very few exceptions was the use of six static infantry brigades for the coup de main on Liège immediately after the mobilization was announced.

Combat formations were reinforced by calling up reservists and by mobilizing reserve and Landwehr formations in moderate numbers, but train and supply formations virtually exploded in strength. The train battalions of the army corps were disbanded and the trains increased from their peacetime strength of five companies to 30 companies and company-like columns. This number included the two remount depots, two field bakery columns, and the corps bridge train. Altogether a mobile corps had 12 field hospitals (these could be merged into bigger hospitals), six subsistence columns (*Proviant-Kolonnen*), seven heavy supply columns (*Fuhrpark-Kolonnen*), two remount (horse replacement) depots (*Remonte-Depots*), two field bakery companies (Feldbäckerei-Kolonnen), and a corps bridging train (*Korps-Brückentrain*).

More than any other arm or service, the mobile supply formations of all types had to rely upon reservists and formations only assembled upon mobilization. Only a few trains and columns were mobilized and practiced during peacetime exercises. This demonstrates once more the low appreciation the army had for its logistical system. It was seen as a necessary evil rather than an essential component for success. The following describes the train and column formations of a mobile army corps. These columns were usually divided more or less

[28] (Velsen, 1921), pp. 292–294.
[29] (Reichsarchiv, 1928), pp. 54–56.

in half into two echelons (*I* and *II Staffel der Kolonnen*) to allow a more flexible use adapted to quickly changing tactical situations.

Mobile field hospitals had a total strength of six medical officers (one *Oberstabsarzt*, one *Stabsarzt*, four *Assistenzärzte*), three administrative officials, 51 NCOs and EM from medical formations, 29 horses, and nine wagons. Each company could set up and run a field hospital with about 200 beds. They had to provide hospital treatment, including surgery, to the wounded, who were unable to walk or had to be further transported. These patients were given first aid at the dressing stations (*Verbandplätze*) of the battalions and regiments (*Sanitätskompanien der Divisionen*). The evacuation of all transportable wounded to the rear—either to the communications zone or to reserve hospitals in Germany—after applying medical treatment was an operational requirement. The field hospitals were to be emptied at the earliest possible moment.[30]

The subsistence companies had a total strength of three officers (one captain or Rittmeister, two lieutenants or second lieutenants), 125 NCOs and EM, 183 horses, and 38 wagons. The carrying capacity of a standard four-horse field wagon model 1895 (*Feldwagen 95*) was 750 kilograms; that of the entire company amounted to 27 metric tons.[31] There were also heavy subsistence columns of the old type (*schwere Proviantkolonnen*) that had only 27 wagons, carrying about one metric ton each. These heavy subsistence columns were usually assigned to reserve corps. Comparison of these figures with the load capacity of 102 metric tons of the motor transport columns of the communications zone reveals how inefficient those slow, horse-drawn columns really were. One motor transport column could replace four of the six army corps subsistence columns. This imbalance was even worse if the train and columns formations were forced to use a variety of different wagons resulting from the different sources of mobilization. It is true that this difference gave them the advantage of greater flexibility (and sometimes greater efficiency), but it also had drawbacks as far as the replacement of complete vehicles or supply of spare parts was concerned. Requisitioned wagons of the old-type heavy-subsistence columns could carry more weight but proved too heavy for use on dirt and gravel roads and insufficiently durable for military use. For this reason efforts were made later to equip all these columns uniformly with Feldwagen 95.[32]

Heavy supply columns had a total strength of three officers, 109 NCOs and EM, 163 horses, and 62 wagons. The carrying capacity of the (usually requisitioned) heavy supply company wagons averaged about 1.2 metric tons. The load that the entire column could carry was about 57–58 tons. The average load of rations and grain carried by the column was approximately sufficient to support an infantry division for one day.[33]

A mobile horse-replacement or remount depot had a total strength of one officer, 63 NCOs and EM, 107 horses, and two forage (horse ration) wagons. Remount depots were responsible for the replacement of horses in all non-mounted formations such as staffs, foot troops, and technical formations. Mounted formations, such as field artillery and cavalry, drew their

---

[30] (Kuhl, 1929), p. 140 and (Altgelt, 1921), pp. 413–414. Please refer also to attachment 5.

[31] Slight differences between the figures given here and the figures given in Chapter 7 on army organization result in the plans for these mobile supply formations as described by Rabenau, 1914, pp. 68–74 and 120–125 and the after-war treatises compiled by the Generals v. Kuhl and v. Bergmann, (Kuhl, 1929), pp. 138–142.

[32] (Kuhl, 1929), p. 143.

[33] (Kuhl, 1929), p. 139. For details about the transport capacity of columns and trains please see (Großer Generalstab, 1914), pp. 64–65.

horse replacements from trained horses sent forward from their garrisons or mobilization base by rail transport.[34]

A field bakery column had a total strength of two officers (one train *Rittmeister*, one lieutenant or second lieutenant), one paymaster, 184 NCOs and EM, including 162 bakers by trade, one master baker (*Bäckermeister* or *Feldbackmeister*), seven mechanics, 99 horses, and 25 wagons. Each column was able to operate 12 mobile ovens (divided into sections of two ovens each) and to bake—under favorable conditions—23,000 bread rations per 24 hours. Thus, a company could furnish one day's supply of bread to an infantry division with a few other units attached. So both field bakery columns combined could meet the demand of their own army corps. Due to the technical restrictions of the baking process, the field bakery columns rarely marched with the combined train formations.[35] This lack of mobility resulted in a poor supply of bread, particularly on the advancing right wing (First and Second Armies) in August 1914.

The corps bridging train carried mobile bridge-building equipment and could construct pontoon bridges, up to 130 meters in length and strong enough to permit the passage of units of all arms by one-way traffic. Or, it could build a 75-meter bridge of a heavier type, which could handle two-way traffic. In addition, the bridging train of each division could build a simple one-way pontoon bridge of 35 meters length. The combined bridging trains of an army corps, i.e., one corps bridging train and two divisional bridging trains, were able to construct an ordinary pontoon bridge of 200 meters in length or a heavier two-lane bridge of 120 meters long. The corps bridging train column had a total personnel strength of three officers, 131 NCOs and EM, 224 horses, and 35 wagons.

Just like the columns, the corps train formations were also divided into two echelons (*I* and *II Staffel der Trains*) marching behind the army corps. These echelons were tactical organizations and not formalized and structured military units. One of these echelons during an advance into action was usually brought up closer to the combat formations of the army corps and was then referred to as a combat echelon (*Gefechtsstaffel*).[36] It was not until 1 May 1915, that a commander of the columns and the train (*Kommandeur der Munitionskolonnen und Trains*, abbreviated *Komut*) was assigned to each army corps staff and the two echelons were organized as two separate train battalions (*Munitionskonnen-Abteilungen*).[37] After the experience of 1916, when the battles at the Western Front had turned into *Materialschlachten,* the entire supply infrastructure was reorganized. The columns and trains were taken away from the army corps and concentrated under the control of the army commands.[38]

Mobile divisions had their own bridging trains (*Divisions-Brückentrain*) and one or two medical companies. Each medical company could run two field hospitals.

Ammunition supply was separated from the trains that mainly dealt with food, horse rations, medical care, spare parts, and material replacements. First there was the first line ammunition stock the combat formations carried themselves. This so-called unit load (*Grundbeladung*) was broken down into two parts. The combat load (*Gefechtsbeladung*) was the stock carried by the infantrymen (150 rounds per man) plus the other 14,400 rounds

---

34 (Kuhl, 1929), p. 139.

35 (Kuhl, 1929), p. 141. Also check (Großer Generalstab, 1914), p. 97.

36 (Kuhl, 1929), p. 2.

37 (Cron, 1937), pp. 250–256.

38 There was no commonly used corresponding term for "battle of attrition" in the German language—which would read *Abnutzungsschlacht* in direct translation; the imperial German Army called these battles *Materialschlachten*—battles of material.

and the company's entrenching tools in the infantry company ammunition wagons. The other part was the basic load (*Truppenbeladung*) carried by the ammunition wagons of the infantry battalions and the light ammunition columns (*leichte Munitionskolonnen*) of the artillery battalions.[39] The heavy artillery battalion attached to the army corps upon mobilization had its own light ammunition column.

The army corps ammunition columns (*Munitions-Kolonnen*) carried additional ammunition stocks. These were four columns for infantry ammunition, three columns for field howitzer ammunition, and seven columns for field gun ammunition. The ammunition columns were each divided into two echelons (I and II Staffel der Munitionskolonnen) that could detach a combat echelon when a major combat action was imminent. The heavy artillery had its own ammunition columns (up to eight) depending upon the type of guns and the number of batteries assigned to the army corps

Naturally, the artillery ammunition loads were much bigger than the infantry loads that would fit on one wagon per company and an extra wagon per battalion. Artillery batteries (field guns) carried a combat load of 756 rounds of shrapnel plus 36 rounds of HE. Field howitzer batteries carried less. Since the shrapnel soon proved to be largely unsuitable, the ratio was changed towards more HE rounds. The combat load of a field gun battery could sustain seven hours of fire during a major combat action; the combat load of a field howitzer battery would last for four and one-half hours. The combat load of a heavy field howitzer battery would last only for three and one-half hours.

The basic load of the light ammunition columns would last for another six hours for field gun battalions, four hours for light field howitzer battalions, and two and three-quarter hours for heavy field howitzers. The ammunition stocks carried by the ammunition columns of the army corps would allow another seven hours of fire for gun batteries, five hours for light field howitzers, and 15 ¼ hours for heavy field howitzers. If the entire ammunition stock carried by an army corps was used up, the field gun batteries of this corps could keep on firing for 20 hours, the light field howitzers for 13 ½ hours, and the heavy field howitzers for 21 ½ hours.[40]

In 1914, the light ammunition trains and ammunition trains of the army corps used limbers (*Protzen*) and trailers (*Hinterwagen*) and could only carry that type of ammunition that fitted the special construction of these vehicles. Field gun ammunition columns could only carry ammunition for field guns, field howitzer columns only for field howitzer batteries, and heavy howitzer columns ammunition for heavy howitzer batteries. Since these columns could not be used for other types of ammunition, the light ammunition columns had only a limited flexibility to respond to changing tactical situations. For instance, if more rounds of howitzer ammunition were needed, the ammunition train might only have rounds of gun ammunition. Early in 1915, these companies were equipped with Feldwagen 95 to create uniform light ammunition columns that had a higher level of flexibility than the previous model.

All the formations listed above were horse-drawn and did not include any motor transport. The heavy baggage of an infantry division required three kilometers of road; the heavy baggage of an army corps, seven km. The first echelon of the trains and columns of an Army Corps required 10 km of road; the second echelon about 11 km. The fighting baggage of the infantry and artillery units is not included in the length measurements of these columns. All these trains, and columns made up a huge "tail" that the combat units dragged behind them.

39 (Pflugk-Hartung, 1896), pp. 45–46 and (Rabenau, 1914), p. 48.
40 (Großer Generalstab, 1914), pp. 58–59 and pp. 62–63.

Moving slowly, equipped with heavy horse-drawn vehicles, the columns congested roads and villages, required protection against enemy cavalry raids and were immensely inflexible when quick operational reactions to changing tactical situations were required.

While the combat troops of an infantry division required "only" 15 km of road, the combat troops of an army corps would cover 31 km if marching in a single column on one road. If artillery was included, the columns would be even longer.[41] In 1914, a mobile infantry division comprised 17,000 men and 4,000 horses.[42] If an army corps marched on a single road, it would cover about 60 km, if all combat units, artillery, staff, baggage, columns, and trains are included. Keeping these figures in mind assists in understanding the immense logistical and organizational challenges of just keeping such an army corps or army marching. Reaction to sudden changes in the operational situation further complicated matters. The figures as mentioned above only relate to supply formations in the combat zone. If all supply formations of the communications zone are also taken into consideration, it becomes clear how difficult it was to control and schedule all these mostly slow and inflexible columns.

Reserve Corps were not only weaker in artillery and heavy artillery compared with army corps—they had only four battalions of field guns, no field howitzers, and usually no heavy artillery—they were also considerably handicapped by their supply system. Although the unit loads were comparable with those of active formations, each artillery battalion, for example, had its own light ammunition column, but the equipment with columns and trains was much reduced. Just as for active corps, there were four infantry ammunition columns, but only five artillery ammunition columns and—because there was no heavy artillery—no heavy artillery ammunition columns. In the same way as the trains and columns of the active army corps, the supply formations of the reserve corps were also divided into two echelons, which lacked designated commanders.

Even though the equipment with artillery columns reflects the actual amount of artillery available to a reserve corps, overall the equipment with trains was far less than was available to an active corps. Reserve corps had only seven field hospitals, two subsistence columns—which were larger but fewer than the columns of active formations—six heavy supply columns, and two field bakery companies. There was no corps bridging train; only the divisions had bridging trains like the active divisions. The train formations were divided into two echelons as in active corps.

In approximating the ammunition consumption, the War Ministry had directed that the ammunition stocks carried by an army corps were to be sufficient to last for a day of battle (*Schlachttag*), a full day of major combat activity. For field gun battalions this supply meant an average consumption of 273 rounds of shrapnel or HE per gun per day of battle. For field howitzer battalions, the War Ministry had laid down 126 rounds per gun per day.[43] The Great General Staff was less optimistic, calculating that the first line ammunition stocks of an army corps would not last for a full day of battle.

The "battle day" was an approximation or rule of thumb for estimated ammunition consumption during a major action based upon historical experience. These estimated amounts were much too low. During the Franco-Prussian War, each German artillery piece fired only 199 rounds on average during the entire war. By contrast, the Japanese artillery expended an average of 174.5 rounds per gun just on a single day during the battle at Nanshan on 26 May

[41] (Großer Generalstab, 1914), pp. 86–87, please see also (Kuhl, 1929), p. 11–12

[42] (Stachelbeck, 2012), p. 35.

[43] (Rabenau, 1914), pp. 68–74

1904.[44] The Russian army fired an average of 87,000 rounds per month during the Russo-Japanese War. In the First Balkan War of 1912, the Bulgarian army almost tripled this rate to 254,000 rounds per month—an amount soon dwarfed during the Great War.[45]

Quick firing weapons of infantry and artillery, particularly artillery pieces with advanced recoil mechanisms, increased ammunition consumption dramatically. These guns did not jump back after each shot, and no re-aiming was needed before the next round could be fired. The German calculations for combat load and basic load were already below the figures of the Balkan Wars. The War Ministry and General Staff used the experience of the Russo-Japanese War to re-calculate the estimated ammunition consumption figures in 1912. The experience of the Balkan Wars was not included into these calculations. The huge extra demand of stocked artillery ammunition resulting from the 1912 recalculations was only partially met by 1914, so the German Army went to war in 1914 with ammunition stocks much too low to even sustain a short war of movement.[46]

Supplies for the Cavalry

As explained in Chapter 7, there was no provision in the peacetime Army for any type of division or corps structure for the cavalry. There was only one peacetime cavalry division. The concept of forming divisions was practiced during the maneuvers of 1905. Many lessons were learned from this practice, but the study did not lead to a workable logistical structure for these formations, which had a great many horses. Plans and structures did exist at squadron and regimental level for cavalry, but nothing had been worked out in detail for division and corps.

When the General Staff Officer's handbook is checked for mention of the sustainment of cavalry formations, it becomes clear that regular supply was not foreseen. Although the subsistence of army corps, reserve corps, and other formations was estimated in considerable detail, no estimates can be found for the cavalry.[47] Rather, it was directed that cavalry divisions had to live off the country.[48] Living off the country meant requisitioning food and horse rations from the farmers in the field of operations. Such requisitions were often made without handing a requisition note to the farmer, making it impossible for him to be paid for the food later. In practice, this system led to a form of tolerated pillaging that also jeopardized the military discipline in cavalry units.

Operational orders of cavalry divisions did not only list operational targets for the regiments and detailed logistical specifications for the supply formations, they also specified requisition areas (*Beitreibungsbezirke*) per brigade where the necessary food and horse rations had to be sourced. In order to determine the necessary size of such requisitioning areas, calculation was based upon peacetime experience that approximately six inhabitants could sustain one trooper and one horse. So subsistence patrols were sent out by the squadrons and regiments to requisition the necessary supplies. During peacetime exercises this supply was quite easy to obtain because the officers and intendancy officials charged with these tasks would purchase food from a friendly rural population and would pay cash. But would this plan work in enemy territory with a hostile population? How would this system work if the rural population or the inhabitants of towns and villages had fled the advancing

44 (Tettau, 1910), pp. 181–213.
45 (Stoneman, 2006), pp. 114–115.
46 (Wurtzbacher, 1921), pp. 70–71.
47 (Großer Generalstab, 1914), pp. 53 and 94.
48 (Großer Generalstab, 1914), p. 100, marginal no. 243.

German troops and had taken most of their food stocks and cattle with them? What if operations started before the harvest was finished, so most of the grain was still in the field and not ready in the barn? It was certainly not easy to supply highly mobile cavalry formations by means of slow and clumsy horse-driven trains and columns, so it might have been feasible to let single squadrons or even regiments of the divisional cavalry live off the country. For bigger cavalry formations such as divisions with 5,000–6,000 men or even entire HKK with their 20,000–23,000 men, this plan was likely to lead straight to a logistical disaster.

According to the cavalry manual of 1909, the dismounted fight was as important as the mounted use of cavalry.[49] Although the cavalry doctrine had already ended the role of the battle cavalry by mainly focusing upon use of the cavalry as a reconnaissance body, cavalry regiments were not properly equipped to take on extended dismounted fights. For example, they did not carry any entrenchment tools, not even in their fighting or heavy baggage.

The cavalry also lacked almost all the entire mobile logistical infrastructure of columns and trains that the active and the reserve corps enjoyed. The cavalry squadrons had only their combat load of infantry ammunition for the carbines. Each trooper carried 36 rounds in his ammunition pouches (the cavalry ammunition pouches were smaller than the infantry ones) plus four wagons per regiment, partly loaded with infantry ammunition. The machinegun battalion had an extra ammunition wagon carrying more than 14,000 rounds in addition to the ammunition carried on the machinegun limbers. In case of emergency, machinegun ammunition was interchangeable with the carbine ammunition of the same caliber. The horse-riding field artillery battalions carried their combat load on the gun limbers of their four field guns Model 96. The driving batteries of the field artillery did the same with their six guns. A modest stock of basic load was carried in the light ammunition column assigned to each field artillery battalion. The light ammunition columns of these horse-riding field artillery formations were smaller than these of the regular driving battalions. Altogether the basic load of this artillery battalion was intended last for 12–13 hours of heavy combat—about half of an estimated standard battle day. To increase mobility, the only equipment cavalry formations had with them was limited to their fighting baggage and the heavy baggage.

Cavalry regiments had a fighting baggage of the following: 58 replacement horses, two medical aid horses, two bridging wagons with two steel pontoons and four bridge elements, each four meters long and one meter wide) each. This equipment could build either a small footbridge of one meter width and 20 meters length, a small bridge two meters wide and 12 meters long, a wide bridge of three meters and eight meters length or a pontoon ferry of about 16 sq.m. Each bridge wagon carried 32 explosive cartridges. The fighting baggage also had one telephone wagon carrying up to 15 km of field telephone line, plus 350 meters of waterproof telephone line. Two communications detachments were also assigned.

Cavalry heavy baggage amounted to the following: one baggage wagon for the regimental staff, four wagons for the squadrons—basically to carry infantry ammunition and other light equipment, five food wagons for subsistence, and five forage wagons with horse rations.[50]

The wagons of the heavy baggage were designed to carry either 1,100 kilograms of food (subsistence wagons) or 1,250 kilograms of horse rations each. But these load capacities were rather theoretical; during long marches with little or no sleep, these capacities had to be cut almost by half because the horses were underfed and became exhausted. Bad road conditions would further reduce these capacities.[51] During peacetime exercises it became

49 (Kriegsministerium, 1909), p. 134.
50 (Rabenau, 1914), pp. 64–66.
51 (Urach, 1905), p. 7.

evident that larger cavalry formations could not possibly be supported adequately by the existing logistical infrastructure and attempts were made to assign some motor transport capacity to the cavalry.

Although cavalry formations had fewer men than comparable infantry formations, they had to feed all their horses. A squadron (*Eskadron*) was about 170 officers, NCOs, and EM strong and had 180 horses. A mobile cavalry regiment of four squadrons counted 710 heads with 750 horses. The horse artillery battalion usually attached to a mobile cavalry division had another 320 men and 420 horses. Last, the light ammunition column of the horse artillery had 110 men with 150 horses. [52]

The subsistence rations for the cavalry were calculated as for the infantry and were estimated per man per day:

- 750 grams of bread (one portion),
- 375 grams of raw meat,
- 1,500 grams of potatoes,
- 25 grams of salt,
- 25 grams of ground coffee.

Unlike the infantry where this food could be cooked and prepared by the mobile field kitchens on the march, the troopers of the cavalry had to cook food themselves in their field dinner sets, usually over an open fire. Furthermore, unlike the army corps, the cavalry did not have any field bakeries. For a mobile cavalry regiment of 710 officers, NCOs, and EM, the demand was about 532.5 kg of bread, 266.25 kg of raw meat, 1,065 kg of potatoes, 17.75 kg of salt and 17.75 kg of coffee per day. But these supplies were only for the men; in addition, the 750 horses would need 6,000 grams of oats, 2,500 grams of hay and 1,500 grams of straw each and per day, summing up to 4,500 kg of oats, 1,875 kg of hay and 1,125 kg of straw every day.[53] If oats were not available, they could be replaced by barley. Since the horses would need oats and roughage (hay and straw), an important component of the horse rations was already missing.

Because the cavalry divisions did not have a logistical infrastructure of trains and columns like an army corps, it would always be very difficult to replenish the stocks of this basic load when they were used up. Since the usually overstretched supply lines of the cavalry were normally much too long for any kind of horse-driven supply, subsistence and horse rations really had to be taken from the country in which the cavalry operated. Concerning ammunition, the cavalry was well advised to avoid major combat actions, not just because they had considerably less firepower compared with infantry formations, but also because they simply would lack the necessary ammunition supply to endure through an extended fight. The only advantage the cavalry had over the infantry was the light motor transport columns that were attached to each cavalry division during mobilization. These columns comprised 15 light trucks (not the standard army trucks) with three metric tons load capacity and no trailers—45 tons lift in total. On these columns, the cavalry divisions carried about a day's stocks of horse rations, basically of oats.

Cavalry divisions were comparatively small, so it was assumed that any army corps would be able to supply them along the way with whatever was needed, and the rest had to be taken

---

[52] (Urach, 1905), attachment 2.
[53] (Urach, 1905), pp. 16–17.

from the country. During an intendancy General Staff ride in 1909, it became clear that such an unplanned supply of larger cavalry formations by army corps would lead to difficulties. For example, a cavalry division was assigned to the VI Army Corps. After a day of heavy fighting the cavalry division had lost the bulk of its heavy baggage. Soldiers and horses received no food the entire day. In the evening the cavalry division was pulled back from enemy contact and rested close to a distribution point of the VI Army Corps. This distribution point was filled with subsistence and horse rations for the army corps. However, the head of the distribution point, a first lieutenant, refused to distribute his supplies to the cavalry, as the distribution point belonged to the VI Army Corps not the IV Army Corps. So the cavalry division commander, a major general, stepped in and overruled the first lieutenant. The general ordered his troopers to confiscate the supplies. In order to replace the heavy baggage the division had lost he also ordered the confiscation of the train wagons of the VI Army Corps that were waiting at the distribution point.[54] Watched in retrospect from a 1914 perspective, this scene must have appeared prophetic.

THE SUPPLY PROCESS

The following section describes the supply process for ammunition and for food and rations. These two processes should be seen as exemplary, because many other supply processes were much the same. However, these different processes are not going to be analyzed in detail because they had only a minor impact upon the operations in 1914.

Ammunition Supply[55]

The reordering and supply process with ammunition followed six rules:

1. The combat formations ordered their ammunition through the division staffs to the Ib of the army corps. Usually the Ib consolidated these orders, forwarded them to the Ib of the Etappen-Inspektion and reported the demand to the Ib of the army command. Normal supply amounts would be replenished by the ammunition stocks available in the communications zone; extraordinary amounts and supplies had to be ordered through the Chief Field Munitions Service (*Chef des Feldmunitionswesens*) attached to the OHL, who had to meet this extra demand through stocks available in the zone of the interior.
2. It was the responsibility of the Etappen-Inspektion to use the ammunition stocks loaded on supply trains and parked on sidings or railway yards (*abgestellte Eisenbahnzüge*) somewhere between the Etappenhauptort and army base. These stocks were called First Demand of Ammunition Supply (*Erster Bedarf des Munitionsnachschubes*). Only if there were no ammunition trains of this first demand available could the stocks of ammunition depots in the communications zone be employed.

   Beyond army level, the standard supplies were usually ordered and distributed by trains. Although the word is the same, these trains had nothing to do with the trains and columns on lower levels but were railroad trains. These trains were standard military supply trains pulled by a standard G3/53, or comparable steam engine. These trains had about 250–300 metric tons of load capacity and travelled at an average speed of 30 km per hour. There were six different kinds of standard ammunition trains:

54 (François, 1910), pp. 185–186.
55 Please refer to attachment 3.

- Infantry ammunition trains, carrying 2,738,400 rounds of rifle or machinegun ammunition.
- Field gun ammunition trains, carrying 26,880 rounds for the light field gun.
- Field howitzer ammunition trains with 12,000 rounds.
- Ammunition trains for 10 cm cannons with 10,000 rounds.
- Heavy field howitzer ammunition trains with 6,000 rounds.
- 21 cm mortar ammunition trains, carrying 2,000 rounds.[56]

Other types of ammunition, e.g., 30.5 cm or 42 cm, were transported on extra trains.

These parked trains had to be directed as close to the front line as possible so as to allow the replenishment of ammunition columns of the communications zone or, ideally, of ammunition columns of the combat formations already there and to keep ammunition stocks mobile. In 1914, this procedure was widely possible on the left wing, where Sixth and Seventh Armies fought on former German territory in Alsace and Lorraine and in eastern Prussia. On the right wing, the process was hampered by the railway demolitions in Belgium.

3. The combat formations replenished their ammunition columns either from these parked trains or from the depots in the communications zone. If necessary and in exceptional situations—if a decisive battle were imminent, for example—the columns of the communications zone that had a higher load capacity compared with the columns of the combat formations could be employed to deliver the needed ammunition directly to the front line. In such cases, even the motor transport columns could be employed to deliver ammunition directly into the combat zone. Whenever it could be foreseen with some degree of accuracy when and where an increased expenditure of ammunition would occur, the Etappeninspektion would establish a number of distribution points as close to the combat troops as possible and keep them filled.[57]
4. The Ib of the Etappen-Inspektion was responsible for maintaining the depots in the communications zone fully stocked and to re-order stocks through the Chief Field Munitions Service as required. The Ib had to frequently report the exact stocks of his depots to the Chief Field Munitions Service, in order to allow balancing of ammunition stocks between the armies.
5. The Chief Field Munitions Service was enjoined to primarily use fully packed ammunition trains parked somewhere on sidings within the zone of the interior to resupply the armies in the field. Only if there were no ready trains available on short notice could the supplies be directly taken from artillery depots.
6. The War Ministry arranged in cooperation with the stellvertretende Generalkommando that ammunition stocks were permanently loaded on trains in the artillery depots, and that the depots were refilled again by deliveries from the respective factories.[58]

Subsistence and Rations[59]

The re-ordering and supply process with subsistence and horse rations followed five rules:

1. The combat formations ordered their daily requirements from the IVa of the division (Divisions-Intendant) and replenished their trains at the divisional distribution points (Ausgabestellen). The trains of the army corps usually operated these distribution points.

---

[56] (Kuhl, 1929), p. 164 and (Wurtzbacher, 1921), p. 92.
[57] (Kuhl, 1929), p. 155.
[58] (Großer Generalstab, 1914), Attachement 3
[59] Please refer to attachment 3.

Cavalry divisions had to live off the country in their operations area, which simply meant they had to requisition in the countryside—though pillaging might be the more precise description of their methods. The cavalry carried a one-day supply of horse rations, especially oats, within their cavalry motor transport columns.

2. The Korps-Intendant (IVa of the corps staff) consolidated the orders of the divisions and other formations and forwarded them to the Etappen-Intendant (IVa of the Etappen-Inspektion), copying the demand to the Armee-Intendant (IVa of the Army Command). All formations also reported their daily ration strength—known in German as the *Verpflegungsstärke*. Based upon this Verpflegungsstärke, the entire requirement for bread and provisions was calculated. The corps trains and columns would be replenished with the ordered subsistence and rations at distribution points of the communications zone or, in exceptional cases, in depots of the communications zone.
3. The Etappen-Intendant reported the subsistence and rations stocks of the Etappe to the Armee-Intendant in a daily standard report. In urgent cases, the Etappen-Inspektion could order food and rations directly from the respective depots in the zone of the interior.

   The Etappen-Inspektion controlled the number and types of subsistence and ration trains parked on sidings. There were three different types of trains:
   - General subsistence trains carrying food. These were so called *Verpflegungs-Züge*, abbreviated *V-Züge* (subsistence trains) carrying food and horse rations to supply an army corps for about two days;
   - Trains carrying the flour and further ingredients for baking bread. These were so-called *Mehl-Züge*, abbreviated *M-Züge* (flour trains), which carried the necessary baking materials to support an army corps for about 10 days with bread;
   - Trains loaded with horse rations, so called *Hafer-Züge*, abbreviated *H-Züge* (oats trains), with oats rations for an army corps (not for cavalry divisions or an HKK!) for about three days.[60]

   Transport between these trains and the distribution points in the combat area would be performed by depot service trains, motor transport columns, and other transport columns of the Etappe. At the distribution points, the trains of the combat formations would pick up the supplies.
4. The Armee-Intendant coordinated the entire flow of food and rations supplies from the zone of the interior to the communications zone and to the army. He dealt directly with the respective depots and the stellvertretende Generalkommando. The Armee-Intendant reported daily to the General-Intendant (General Responsible for Supplies) attached to the OHL about the subsistence situation and the Verpflegungsstärke of his army.
5. The General-Intendant was in supreme charge of the entire food and rations supply of the German Army in the field. He had to balance food stocks between the armies and managed the stocking of all respective depots back in Germany. To achieve a higher level of flexibility, he also controlled the food and rations reserve, namely a number of subsistence trains unassigned to individual armies.[61]

---

[60] (Lau, 1921) , p. 6.
[61] (Großer Generalstab, 1914), Attachment 4.

CHAPTER 16

WAR AND MOBILIZATION

STATE OF WAR

Imperial Germany as a whole did not decide to go to war in 1914. A small group of officials appointed personally by the Kaiser made that decision. Nonetheless, the Great War has been cast as a people's war, one in which the common citizen viewed as a defensive war.[1] There were three distinct steps in the process that escalated to war.

1. The announcement of the imminent danger of war (*Zustand drohender Kriegsgefahr*).
2. The announcement of the State of Siege (*Belagerungszustand*).
3. The announcement of the State of War (*Kriegszustand*).

There was a declaration of "threatening state of danger of war" on 31 July 1914. The Chief of Operations executed the most recent deployment plan. The telegraph section instructed 200,000 telegraph employees and 100,000 telephone operators at the post offices across Germany to send out news of the declaration to the 106 infantry brigades scattered throughout the empire. The railroad section requisitioned 30,000 locomotives, 65,000 passenger coaches, and 800,000 freight cars. The empty mobilization transports started moving immediately.[2]

The first day of mobilization was 2 August.[3] Upon mobilization, the entire German territory automatically became subject to a State of Siege. This meant that the army corps commanders took over much of the executive power of the civilian authorities. The State of Siege was authorized in Art. 68 of the Imperial Constitution:

> Should the public safety of the federal territory be threatened, the Kaiser may declare any part of the same under martial law. Up to the publication of an imperial law regulating the occasions, the form of announcement, and the effects of such a declaration, the provisions of the Prussian law of 4 June 1851 (Gesetzes-Sammlung für 1851, p. 451), shall be valid in such case.[4]

---

1 (Verhey, War and Revolution, 2008), p. 243.
2 Please check the personal mobilization schedules by Hauptmann Baron de la Motte-Fouqué and Oberst Marquard from 31 July in this chapter.
3 (Herwig H., 2009), p. 48.
4 (Howard B. E., 1906), p. 431. See Appendix A.

In fact an imperial law was never enacted; therefore, the Prussian law of 1851 continued in force. The 1851 law did not specify in detail how this State of Siege was to be executed. This lack of specificity gave considerable leeway to the army corps commanders on how to implement it. Some commanders only introduced a dusk-to-dawn curfew and restrictive police regulations. Some included press censorship, prohibition of political assemblies, and control of the price of foodstuffs. Others used or abused this State of Siege to systematically act against socialist politicians, union leaders, and the press—even beyond the requirements of military censorship. The net effect was to make the military legally dominant over the rest of the government. This law was primarily used against the liberal elements on the left wing of the Reich. Interesting to note, one of the major demands of the mutiny in Kiel in 1918 that helped end the Great War was the elimination of this power.[5]

The declaration of war against Russia came on 1 August. Prussian law regulated how the proclamation would be made, the suspension of certain rights, and any other effects of the State of War. When the Kaiser announced the proclamation of State of War, military courts were established, numerous fundamental rights were put in abeyance, most of the checks and balances upon government action were suspended, and there was a transfer of executive powers from the civil government to military authorities.

Upon mobilization, the army corps and their divisions and brigades were assembled and deployed forward. Back home, a wartime organization had to replace their roles, so each infantry brigade command was replaced by a *stellvertretende Infanterie-Brigade*, which is translated best as "being in place of." The stellvertretende *Brigadekommando* took the role of the active brigade commands in regards to personnel replacements. In the same way there were stellvertretende *Generalkommandos* in place in the active army corps, a stellvertretende *Generalstab* was created in Berlin after OHL departed for Koblenz. When Falkenhayn replaced Moltke the Younger after the Marne disaster, Moltke took the position of the *Chef des stellvertretende Generalstabes*—probably the biggest humiliation he had to endure.

The stellvertretende brigade and corps staffs were usually commanded by generals z.D. Officers on those staffs were mostly elder reserve or Landwehr officers, and they took over a very special role. Although the War Ministry issued orders during the war to achieve a uniform handling of the state of siege, the over-restrictive handling, particularly by the stellvertretende Generalkommandos II, VI and VII,[6] led to political unrest and triggered several strikes later in the war.[7]

The working-class Social Democratic Party (SPD) had never voted for military appropriations in the Reichstag, and, in fact, had always shown a policy of complete opposition to the military. In the last week of July 1914, the SPD staged massive antiwar demonstrations throughout the empire. Yet, on 4 August 1914, it voted in favor of military appropriations. This historic event led the Kaiser to say: "I no longer acknowledge any parties; I recognize only Germans."[8] The social classes and political parties allegedly came together and stopped fighting under a concept dating back to medieval times—*Burgfrieden,* an informal understanding of peace among rivals or political parties for the purpose of conducting a war. Burgfrieden originally represented peace within a fortress when it came under attack. Theoretically, it applied to all parties. Peace between the social classes of the population lay at the heart of the concept, but it had little practical application, as the classes did not mix.

---

5 (Rossiter, 2002), p. 36–37.
6 VII was responsible for the Ruhr area; therefore, for the most important weapons' factories of the Reich.
7 (Mattuschka 1979), pp. 127–131.
8 (Verhey, *War and Revolution*, 2008), pp. 244–245.

The real difference provided by the Burgfrieden on this occasion was that the socialists united with other parties in the *Reichstag* to support the war. The Reichstag delegated its legislative powers to the *Bundesrat*. In other words, the democratically elected house delegated its authority to the appointed house of the nobility. Any emergency legislation under this agreement would be binding on all civil authorities. In theory, the Reichstag could still review all laws; however, of the 800 orders issued during the war, none were vetoed.[9]

The decisive flaw in this procedure was that the Bundesrat responded to the Ministers of War of the four different contingents to oversee mobilization and production. Neither the Ministers of War nor the Bundesrat had control over the deputy commanding generals of the military corps districts. There was no civilian primacy within the military districts, unless the Kaiser willed it.[10]

THE TOTAL REQUIREMENT

The dispute about the size of the army between the War Minister and the Chief of the General Staff is well documented. Schlieffen always argued vehemently for a larger army. A series of War Ministers rejected his call, stating that the army was already large enough. In 1899, War Minister Heinrich von Goßler first crossed swords with Schlieffen, the Chief of the General Staff. His argument centered on quality over quantity. Schlieffen's argument was the army had to be bigger than the French army or at least big enough to take on the French and the Russian armies simultaneously. The arguments intensified when Karl von Einem became the War Minister. Von Einem indicated to the Reichstag and to the budget committee that the army was large enough and that the argument should end.[11] He had entirely the opposite view from Schlieffen though. Surprising to note, von Einem had no insight into the operational war plan at all until Schlieffen was replaced in 1906.[12]

Some have claimed that Germany lost the war because the Reichstag would not provide the funding to increase the size of the army. This does not hold up to critical examination as both liberals and conservatives in the Reichstag continued to vote for the "estimates" or army budget in the years leading up to 1914. In reality, the size of the army revolved around the size of the officer corps. The War Minister insisted that the officer corps remain aristocratic and responsive to the Kaiser; the Chief of the General Staff looked at the required number of units to fight France.[13] The younger Moltke, when he followed Schlieffen as Chief of the General Staff, continued to insist on an increase in the size of the army, but as late as 1909, he and von Einem were still at odds. Moltke believed that an increase of 6,500 to 7,000 soldiers net, spread out over five years, was the maximum that he could achieve.[14] In 1911, Moltke, spurred on by Ludendorff, wrote another memo based on an updated assessment, saying that an increase of 300,000 men was needed to defeat France and for the "right to survive," but both the Kaiser and the War Minister were against such an increase.[15]

---

9 (Chickering, *Imperial Germany and the Great War, 1914–1918*, 2004), p. 34.
10 (Chickering, *Imperial Germany and the Great War, 1914–1918*, 2004), pp. 34–35.
11 (Groß, 2008), p. 414. Schlieffen allegedly silently acquiesced to this idea.
12 (Groß, 2008), p. 414.
13 (Kitchen, 1968), pp. 31–33.
14 (Kitchen, 1968), p. 34.
15 (Kitchen, 1968), p. 34.

Difficulties in the system continued to show and finally, in March 1912, von Einem agreed that in time of war the infantry was short 81 staff officers and 557 captains; the artillery lacked 60 staff officers and 134 captains. There was an overall shortage of 1,200 lieutenants. Yet when von Heeringen replaced von Einem as War Minister, the new War Minister argued that an increase would mean acceptance of less suitable elements in the officer corps, which could lead to a dangerous democratization of the army. He placed the increases into a percentage and was very cautious, fearing that an increase of only 17 percent in the size of the Prussian army would dilute the officer corps and NCOs. Moltke argued that suitable officers could be found and von Heeringen answered with a testy, "how?"[16]

A compromise led to an overall increase of 136,000 men between 1912 and 1914.[17] Ludendorff, who had argued so vehemently in favor of increasing the army, was posted to a regiment. This was a far larger increase than the War Minister had sought. The new War Minister, Erich von Falkenhayn, lamented to the Chancellor that any further increase would have a negative effect on the officer corps and would lead to a deterioration of the army. Moltke countered that the increase was required at all costs.[18] When the Chief of Staff repeatedly laid out the requirement, and the War Minister admitted he had a shortfall of officers, a potential disaster loomed. The Germans were faced with a two-front war. In general, the Germans had two plans: *Aufmarsch* I targeted France with 55 to 65 divisions and only 10 to 15 divisions deployed against Russia, and Aufmarsch II targeted Russia, with some 40 divisions going east and 30 deployed to the west. In 1914, Plan I was used.

The forces involved in 1914 were massive. There were 880,000 active soldiers; 794,000 of them from the regular Army, 79,000 from the Navy, 7,000 colonial forces and, with the addition of both contingents of the Landwehr, the total reached 2.1 million men in almost 88 divisions with 55 cavalry brigades. Additionally, there was a pool of almost 1,000,000 Ersatz reserves. Seventy of those infantry divisions were earmarked for the West.[19] They initially marched out to the front under the command of one of the armies. Upon mobilization, that number grew to three million. By January 1915, the German army comprised 4,357,000 men of whom 2,618,000 were in the field. Those astounding numbers were achieved despite the enormous losses of 1914. Not only did the army numbers increase, but also their departure created a significant hole in the economy. During the first six months of the war, four million men were removed from the civil economy and processed into the military. In late 1914, the problem was not a shortage of manpower, but rather a lack of trained officers and modern equipment.[20]

Depending on where they were deployed, the strength of each army varied.[21] First Army had 320,000 men; Second Army–260,000; Third Army–180,000; Fourth Army–180,000; Fifth Army–200,000; Sixth Army–220,000; Seventh Army–127,000; and Eighth Army–150,000.[22] The total of the eight field armies: 1,637,000.

Additionally, there were other groups as follows:

- Ersatz formations in Lorraine (six Divisions, one Brigade) 120,000 men;

16 (Kitchen, 1968), pp. 34–35.
17 (Strachan, *The First World War*, 2003), pp. 45–46.
18 (Kitchen, 1968), p. 36.
19 (Herwig H., 2009), p. 46.
20 (Bessel, 2006), p. 438.
21 (Cron, *Imperial German Army 1914–1918*, 2002), pp. 299–329, (Herwig H. , 2009), p. 51.
22 This is an often-quoted figure that we could not verify independently. It seems way too high.

- Army of the North (IX Reserve Corps and 1 *Landwehr* Division used as a covering force for Schleswig-Holstein against British landings and assault operations), 60,000 men;
- Border Fortress Commands (roughly equivalent to six divisions), 120,000 men;
- 1–4 Landwehr Divisions 16,000 each; one Landwehr Division assigned to Army of the North, transported to Eastern Prussia at the end of August; 2 Landwehr Division assigned to Fifth Army around Metz; 3 and 4 Landwehr Divisions constituted the Landwehr Korps Woyrsch (as a covering force for Silesia.)

Adding the eight armies and the other groups together yields 2,097,000 Field Army requirements in total.

There is some skepticism with these figures. In particular, the strength of the First Army at 320,000 is a prime example. While this is clearly quoted in several sources it can be traced back to an original estimate by Edmonds in the *British Official History*. Finding support for this number in a German language document seems elusive. It is less important to understand the exactness of the figure than to wonder if this is another example of a British history "truth" handed down uncritically for a century.

PLANNING

The war plan was amended and issued by the Chief of the General Staff on a biannual basis. For example, planning for 1904–1905 took effect from 1 April 1904 to 31 March 1905. Broad guidance was issued to the Army commanders in a document known as the *Aufmarschanweisung*. This was an initial direction with no real stipulations about what to do after enemy contact. The General Inspectors (*General-Inspekteure*) of the army inspections had wartime roles as commanders of field armies (*Armee-Oberbefehlshaber*). Upon mobilization they and their chiefs of general staff received sealed envelopes containing secret deployment orders. These orders would include the order of battle of their armies, deployment areas, reporting lines, some general directives about railroad deployment and logistics, together with a concept of operations covering the first days of hostilities. During the first days of mobilization Chief of the General Staff called the newly appointed Army Commanders together with their Chiefs of General Staffs army by army to his office to explain and discuss further details of the deployment order and of the goals of the coming operations. For example, the Commander of the First Army together with his Chief of General Staff had their appointment with Moltke on 2 August.[23] Based on these briefings, the commanders and their chiefs went back to their staff quarters to draw up initial operations plans, while their troops were mobilized and transported to the deployment areas.

Planning for mobilization was done in annual cycles known as mobilization years. The mobilization year (*Mobilmachungsjahr*) commenced 1 April and lasted until 31 March. The General Staff prepared their mobilization orders for the army corps, army inspections, and railroad line commanders (among others) for the mobilization year 1914–15 in March 1914. Based on these orders, the chiefs of staff and the Ia officers had to implement the changes into their own mobilization calendar (*Mobilmachungskalender*). Because of the large expansion of the Army in the mobilization years 1913–14 and 1914–15, this meant a huge amount

[23] (Kuhl D. H., 1921), pp. 8–14; (Kluck, 1926); (Krafft v. Dellmensingen, 1931), pp. 13–17; (Xylander, 1935), pp. 7–14; (Kayser, 1942), pp. 7–17

of work. All of the new reserve formations and reservists of active formations had to be staffed with reserve personnel in cooperation with the *Bezirkskommandos*. They had to be fed, accommodated, armed, fitted out with uniforms, and finally, moved by train to their assembly areas.

The assembly areas had to be prepared. There had to be sufficient accommodation—usually one family house or small farmhouse was assumed sufficient per *Gruppe*. This meant about three to four houses per platoon were required, about 10 per company, etc. Medical officers had to check the hygiene standards of the villages, farmhouses, water wells, etc., in the assembly areas.[24] Hundreds of thousands of men in an often very remote countryside along the western border had to be fed. If assembly areas were changed, railroad connections had to be changed, and, if necessary, new railroad head stations had to be built. This would explain why small Eifel villages had such extensive track layouts and unloading ramps.

Train transportation had to be arranged. There was a mobilization railroad timetable that overruled the civilian timetable during the two weeks of mobilization. The planners had to take into account the capacity and speed of the mobilization trains. Because the trains were moved at slow speeds, food, water, and coffee had to be prepared at many railroad stations to feed the soldiers coming through. The sheer quantity of planning is mind-boggling. To cover the 20 days of initial mobilization, 20,800 trains of 50 cars each were planned down to the minute; they transported 2.07 million men, 118,000 horses, and 400,000 tons of assorted supplies.[25] All of these preparations meant a lot of detailed planning work, particularly for the Ia officers. Because the mobilization calendar was top secret, there were strict limitations on its handling. In practice this meant that the Ia had to do all the work by itself; it could not delegate it to NCOs or men.

THE SCHLIEFFEN PLAN

This German plan is so well-known as to be dogma. Called the Schlieffen Plan, it is taught in every school and repeated in virtually every book on German plans in World War I. Even Holger Herwig, one of the leading historians on imperial Germany, retells the story of the Schlieffen Plan and adds that the Germans had 40 days to complete the plan.[26] At the end of 40 days, the Russians would enter the Eastern Front and Germany would be trapped in a two-front war. Therefore, dogmatic historical accounts tell us that Schlieffen sent seven-eighths of the army against the French, in what has been described by Herwig as "one throw of the dice."[27]

The maps are widely known and show Schlieffen's plan encircling Paris and enveloping the French army. Schlieffen considered this to be "pinning the French against Switzerland."[28] Schlieffen had sought in his planning to tackle the deficiencies in his force structure. He thought, for example that each corps could create maneuver brigades from its four Ersatz battalions. The problem with this idea, of course, was that although the brigades would have the requisite number of men and rifles, they would lack both support equipment and sufficient officers.[29]

---

24 When the author grew up there was still a joke passed around in the Rhine area saying that the high hygienic standard of the small villages in the Eifel forests could only be achieved with the help of the Prussian army.
25 (Herwig H., 2009), p. 36.
26 (Herwig, 1997), pp. 46–49.
27 (Herwig, 1997), p. 47.
28 (Department). Printed with the written permission of United States Military Academy.
29 (Zuber, Inventing the Schlieffen Plan, 2002), p. 272.

Recently, historians have questioned the Schlieffen Plan. Did the staff realize there was no chance to win and so committed "suicide from fear of death?"[30] The Schlieffen Plan was supposedly based on Schlieffen's written 1905 *Denkschrift*, which in fact was completed in early 1906, but many of the key documents were supposedly destroyed during World War II. Terence Zuber, in his 2002 book, *Inventing the Schlieffen Plan*, asserts that there never was a Schlieffen Plan.[31] What is clear is that the 1905 Denkschrift, written by Schlieffen, envisioned a one-front war where almost all of the German forces would be launched in a hammer blow to pin the French army against Switzerland. There was a timetable of about 40 days and certain unit placements associated with it. Additionally, there were also 16 make-believe Ersatz Divisions that strengthened the right wing of the German army. Schlieffen envisioned 82 divisions going into the right wing alone out of the existing total army strength of 79 divisions.

It was clear that the total requirements of the Schlieffen Plan could not be met. Schlieffen himself drew up his operational study by employing imaginary *Ersatz-Korps* to complete the encirclement of the French left wing by wheeling around Paris between the 31st and 40th day after mobilization.[32] Obviously, these *Ersatz-Korps* were meant to be created by fielding the Ersatz-battalions of active and reserve regiments, which would lead to formations with basically untrained men and without any kind of support equipment and supply infrastructure. Looking at these Ersatz-Korps, we have to come to the conclusion that Schlieffen was obviously aware of the gap between his total requirements and the active, reserve, and Landwehr formations that were really available to him to conduct operations in the West. They were essentially wishful thinking, intended somehow to fill the gap between his requirements and the limits of reality the War Minister put on these plans.

In contrast to other European nations, imperial Germany found itself trapped by the two-front dilemma of being surrounded by the *Entente Cordiale* with the British and the French armies on the one side and the Russians on the other. The Russian Army (or "the Russian steamroller," as it was called) seemed to be the less dangerous threat. The Russo-Japanese War made it clear that the Russian Army—although vastly superior in numbers—would be a beatable slow-moving giant with uninspired leadership. The French were different; as attack-obsessed as the imperial German Army was, the French were quick moving, equipped with modern arms, a superior field gun, good railway infrastructure, and they were entrenched behind a fortress system that was widely considered to be impenetrable. Under Schlieffen, the strategy outline became clear: first defeat the French by applying quick and decisive strikes that would annihilate the French Army, and then quickly shift the entire army to the East to take on the slowly deploying and advancing Russians. Because the French fortress front that protected their Eastern border (from Verdun along the rivers Meuse and Moselle down to Belfort) was considered impenetrable, the attack had to swing around and bypass the fortress line through Belgium—the Schlieffen doctrine was born and with it the associated risk of violating the Belgian neutrality and thus providing the United Kingdom with a *casus belli*.

This doctrine posed a dilemma to the German army—on the one hand the Germans had to move fast to be successful in the West. Ideally, the first strikes had to be landed before the French Army had completed deployment after mobilization. Then the Germans had to pursue the French forces and outflank them by pushing forward at an unprecedented speed, while

[30] (Showalter D. , 2000), p. 679.

[31] (Zuber, *Inventing the Schlieffen Plan*, 2002).

[32] (Ritter, 1956), Appendix 3–map showing the further advance after 31st mobilization day. Please also see (Groß, 2006), pp. 117–160.

not allowing the French Army to recover. Either outflanking operations or pursuit until final exhaustion would be necessary to complete the task. This required very efficient and highly mobile military formations that would have superior firepower. Infantry, cavalry, and artillery had to function as a combined force based upon their experience in combined peacetime exercises. To outflank the French fortresses, the Belgian neutrality would need to be violated. But, if the Dutch neutrality was not to be violated as well, the Germans had to occupy the bottleneck at Liège swiftly. In short the Belgian forts around Liège had to be captured in a coup de main before the Belgian Army had been completely mobilized and the trenches between the forts could be manned for defense. The German army broke an iron rule here and assigned static brigades for this task for the sake of speed. If they failed to take the fortress before the defenses were completed, the coup de main might become a bloody disaster.

Schlieffen, and later Moltke, had repeatedly asked for heavy and super-heavy artillery, strong enough to smash such forts in case the surprise attacks had failed. This created the dilemma between the need for ultimate speed and mobility and the growing complexity of operational formations if they were equipped with heavy artillery and siege trains. As can be seen in the chapter on army organization, the formation of ever more logistical units, let the size of the army corps grow rapidly in the years before the war. Upon mobilization, the number of train and other logistical formations expanded explosively. It was not just a matter of attaching one battalion of heavy artillery per army corps; it was also about making sure that a sufficient supply with ammunition could be guaranteed.

In the few years prior to 1914, technical developments within the European armies advanced rapidly. The German army introduced numerous formations of heavy artillery. All armies increased their telegraph and communications formations, built-up air force and motor transport formations, and increased infantry firepower by introducing machinegun formations. These developments led to rapidly increasing demands on the logistical system. Additional artillery required more ammunition columns to keep them firing; machineguns not only increased firepower, but also caused consumption of infantry ammunition to skyrocket. Telegraph and radio formations, technical formations such as airplane battalions, army motor parks, engineer parks, and siege trains required a rapidly growing number of mainly horse-drawn wagons trailing behind the army corps, which made them slower and less flexible. Finally, the German army never resolved the dilemma between essential operational mobility and the necessary firepower. The build-up of heavy artillery firepower was designed to smash numerous French forts simultaneously. Air force capabilities were too small and the planes were too fragile and too vulnerable to be used as an air reconnaissance arm deep into enemy territory. The trains and columns were not sufficient to deliver the needed supplies to the rapidly advancing armies. Available motor transportation was insufficient to fill the logistical gap.

MOBILIZATION OF RESERVE UNITS IN 1914

Infantry reserve regiments (*Reserve Infanterie Regimenter–RIR*) were mobilized from reserve personnel who had completed their training and service with the active army—men 22–26 years old and of first contingent Landwehr personnel—men 27–31 years old.[33] Depending on the availability of manpower from these two sources, the composition of reserve formations

[33] For details please see the section on Landwehr and reserve formations between 1888 and 1914.

varied for different RIRs. On average 36–60 percent were reservists. After completing their service within their regiments, they were usually drafted to a reserve exercise within the same formation the following year. During the first year they were administered by the *Bezirkskommando*, but assigned to their regiments. *Reservistenbilder* were mostly taken at the end of this first reserve exercise. After 1900, their photographs were taken at the end of active service and not at the end of the first reserve exercise, which would seem to indicate that reservists were no longer assigned to their "old" regiments, not even during the first exercise.

The reservists were then administered by the Landwehr-Bezirkskommando of their hometowns or home regions and were assigned to different reserve formations. The reserve and Landwehr formations that mobilized in 1914 were usually made up of men who had neither trained nor exercised together. Although the reservists were called up every year to reserve exercises by their Landwehr-Bezirkskommando, they were usually not called to their "old" regiments, but to other formations—usually these were improvised reserve regiments just assembled for those exercises and maneuvers.[34]

The Landwehr-Bezirkskommando assigned 39–62 percent from first contingent Landwehr to their respective reserve formation. About one to one and one half percent of each reserve unit were active soldiers who came from active formations mobilized at the same time as the reserve formations.[35] Upon mobilization, the active regiments were brought up to war strength by mobilizing reservists, i.e., infantry companies, for example, were increased from 150 to 250 men. This meant that after mobilization, 50 percent of the active regiments were made up of reserve soldiers. Additionally, many officers and NCOs of active regiments were sent to reserve formations during mobilization to provide a stable and experienced framework; their ranks in the active regiments were filled with reserve officers and reserve NCOs. Half of the company and platoon commanders in reserve formations were active duty officers; all battalion commanders and regimental commanders were active officers. Most NCOs were active duty NCOs.

In short, the active line formations contained more than 50 percent reservists after mobilization. Reserve formations comprised a smaller proportion of reservists and a larger share of first contingent Landwehr reservists. Landwehr formations were only allocated second contingent Landwehr reservists.[36] The War Ministry feared that the number of reserve formations was too high and the share of first and second contingent Landwehr reservists too great to create units with a high level of combat effectiveness. In 1899, War Minister v. Goßler wrote an aide memoire to Schlieffen complaining about the loss of quality in active and reserve formations upon mobilization.[37] War Minister v. Einem continued this position after 1903, and frequently opposed demands of the General Staff to build up further active and reserve formations.

In 1914, after the war started, 113 reserve regiments were mobilized. These were already assigned to their corps in the mobilization calendar (*Mobilmachungsplan*).[38] For administrative purposes, the reserve regiments were usually allocated the same regimental numbers as

---

[34] "Every year" was indeed "every second year"—while belonging to the army reserve, reservists had to complete at least two reserve exercises. (Storz, 1992), p. 323.

[35] (Kraus, 2012), p. 1.

[36] (Storz, *Kriegsbild und Rüstung vor 1914*, 1992), p. 323.

[37] (Reichsarchiv, 1930), pp. 57–59.

[38] Regrettably, the German mobilization details were lost during a bombing raid on Potsdam on 14 April 1945, destroying the historical center of Potsdam together with the *Garnisonskirche*, the *Stadtschloß* and the military archives (*Heeresarchive*). Many details of the 1914 mobilization plan have to be assumed from secondary sources rather than surviving documents.

the respective active regiments (e.g., Infantry Regiment 118 and Reserve Infantry Regiment 118). This was not usually a case of active parent regiments and reserve dependent regiments. This numbering was purely for administrative purposes. Active regiments within the Landwehr-Bezirk provided the cadre personnel. The active regiments also provided arms and clothing. Artillery depots—depots storing weapons were generally called *Artilleriedepots*, even if storing only small arms—and garment depots could also provide arms and clothing. The active formation only supported the mobilization with administrative personnel. Within the Guard Corps, in addition to the Guard reserve formations, two line (non-Guard) reserve formations (Reserve Infantry Regiment 64 and Reserve Infantry Regiment 93) were mobilized and then assigned to the III and IV Reserve Corps.

Just like active regiments, the reserve regiments were mobilized on the first mobilization day (2 August 1914). Two reserve regiments were assembled in a reserve brigade area and then grouped, first into reserve divisions and then reserve corps. Reserve corps mobilized in August 1914 usually had the following structure after mobilization (see table below).[39]

The most significant difference between active formations and reserve formations lay in the quality of equipment in the active corps: artillery, particularly heavy artillery, train units, and supply columns. Active corps were usually equipped with four artillery regiments, totaling 18 batteries of field-guns Model 96, and six batteries of field-howitzers Model 98, while reserve corps usually had only two reserve artillery regiments with a total of 12 batteries of field-guns Model 96. There were no field howitzers to use against entrenchments. Active corps usually had one battalion (four batteries) of heavy artillery attached from their army corps. Very few active and reserve artillery regiments contained three battalions in 1914. With less than half the artillery firepower of an active corps, a reserve corps had a significant tactical deficit that would be keenly felt when fighting against entrenched positions during the 1914 campaigns.

Another significant difference was the lack of the corps bridging equipment (*Korps-Brückentrain*) allocated to each active army corps.[40] Cavalry divisions assembled only upon mobilization and merged into cavalry corps (*Höherer Kavallerie-Kommandeur* (HKK)).

Mobilization of Reserve Regiments

Army Corps	Reserve Infantry Regiment	Mobilizing Formation	Infantry Brigade	Reserve Infantry Brigade
Guard	1 Guard Reserve Regt	1 Foot Guards	1 Guard Inf. Brig.	1 Guard Res. Inf. Brig.
	2 Guards Res. Regt.	3 Foot Guards	1 Guard Inf. Brig.	
I	RIR 1	IR 4, IR 45	3 and 4 Inf. Brig.	1 Res. Inf. Brig.
	RIR 3	Bez. Kdo.	2 Inf Brig	
II	RIR 2	IR 2, IR 42	5 and 6 Inf. Brig	5 Res. Inf. Brig.
	RIR 9	GR 9	5 Inf. Brig	
	RIR 34	IR 149 and Bez. Kdo.	7 Inf. Brig	6 Res. Inf. Brig.
	RIR 49	IR 49, IR 140	7 and 8 Inf. Brig	

39 (Großer Generalstab, 1914), pp. 6–7.
40 (Pflugk-Hartung, 1896), pp. 93–98.

I. R. 25—6—12.

2. R.

4. R.

R. 7.

R. 8.

3. R.

R. 5.

R. 6.

1. R.

2. R.

R. 3.

R. 4.

R. J. 1.

1. R.

R. 1.

R. 2.

R. U. 1.

R. D. 1.

R. 2.

II. l. R. M. K.

I. l. R. M. K.

R. 1.

II. l. R. M. K.

I. l. R. M. K.

R. S. K. 2. R. D. Br. 2. 2. R. Pi 1.

R. S. K. 1. R. D. Br. 1. 1. R. Pi. 1. 4. Pi. 1.

R. Fernsp. A. 1.

(Einführung 1915 beendet).

Munitions-Kolonnen.

R. II.

R. 5. R. 4. A.

R. 4. R. 3. J.

R. I.

R. 3. R. 2. R. 1. A.

R. 2. R. 1. J.

Trains.

R. 2. R. 1. B. K.

R. II.

R. 7. R. 6. R. 5. F. L.

R. 6. R. 5. R. 4. Fp. K.

R. I.

R. 4. R. 3. R. 2. R. 1. F. L.

R. 2. R. 1. Pr. K. *)

R. 3. R. 2. R. 1. Fp. K.

Organizational chart of a Reserve Corps from the General Staff Officer's Handbook

Army Corps	Reserve Infantry Regiment	Mobilizing Formation	Infantry Brigade	Reserve Infantry Brigade
III	RIR 8	IR 8	9 Inf. Brig.	–
	RIR 12	Bez. Kdo.	10 and 12 Inf. Brig.	–
	RIR 20	Bez. Kdo.	11. Inf. Brig.	–
	RIR 24	IR 24, IR 64	12 Inf. Brig.	–
	RIR 35	IR 35, Bez. Kdo.	11 Inf. Brig.	–
	RIR 48	IR 48, IR 64	9 and 12 Inf. Brig.	–
	RIR 52	IR 52, Bez. Kdo.	10 Inf. Brig.	–
	RIR 64	2 Foot Guards	2 Guards Inf.Brig.	–
IV	RIR 26	IR 26, Bez. Kdo.	13 Inf. Brig.	12 Res. Inf. Brig.
	RIR 27	Bez. Kdo.	14 Inf. Brig.	13 Res. Inf. Brig.
	RIR 36	FR 36	15 Inf. Brig.	
	RIR 66	Bez. Kdo.	16 Inf. Brig.	14 Res. Inf. Brig.
	RIR 72	IR 72, Bez. Kdo.		
	RIR 93	4 Foot Guards	2 Guards Inf. Brig.	15 Res. Inf. Brig.
V	RIR 6	IR 19, IR 58	17 Inf. Brig.	17 Res Inf Brig
	RIR 7	IR 7, Bez. Kdo.	17 und 18 Inf. Brig.	
	RIR 19	IR 19, Bez. Kdo.	17 und 18 Inf. Brig.	19 Res. Inf. Brig.
	RIR 37	IR 47, Bez. Kdo.	20 Inf. Brig.	18 Res Inf. Brig.
	RIR 46	Bez. Kdo.	19 und 20 Inf. Brig.	
VI	RIR 10	GR 11, Bez. Kdo.	22 Inf. Brig.	21 Res. Inf. Brig.
	RIR 11	GR 10, FR 38, Bez. Kdo.	21 Inf. Brig.	
	RIR 22	IR 62, Bez. Kdo.	24 Inf. Brig.	23 Res. Inf. Brig.
	RIR 23	IR 63, Bez. Kdo.	78 Inf. Brig.	22 Res. Inf. Brig.
	RIR 38	Bez. Kdo.	22 Inf. Brig.	
	RIR 51	IR 22, IR 23	23 and 24 Inf. Brig.	23 Res. Inf. Brig.
VII	RIR 13	Bez. Kdo.	25 and 79 Inf. Brig.	25 Res. Inf. Brig.
	RIR 15	IR 15, IR 55	26 Inf. Brig.	26 Res. Inf. Brig.
	RIR 16	Bez. Kdo.	Ldw. Insp.	27 Res. Inf. Brig.
	RIR 39	FR 39, Bez. Kdo.	28 Inf. Brig.	28 Res. Inf. Brig.
	RIR 53	Bez. Kdo.	Ldw. Insp.	27 Res. Inf. Brig.
	RIR 55	Bez. Kdo.	Ldw. Insp.	26 Res. Inf. Brig.
	RIR 56	IR 56, IR 57	79 Inf. Brig.	25 Res. Inf. Brig.
	RIR 57	Bez. Kdo.	28 Inf. Brig.	28 Res. Inf. Brig.

Army Corps	Reserve Infantry Regiment	Mobilizing Formation	Infantry Brigade	Reserve Infantry Brigade
VIII	RIR 25	Bez. Kdo.	30 and 80 Inf. Brig.	30 Res. Inf. Brig.
	RIR 28	Bez. Kdo.	Ldw. Insp.	31 Res. Inf. Brig.
	RIR 29	IR 25, IR 160	29 and 80 Inf. Brig.	29 Res. Inf. Brig.
	RIR 65	Bez. Kdo.	80 Inf. Brig.	
	RIR 68	Bez. Kdo.	Ldw. Insp.	31 Res. Inf. Brig.
	RIR 69	IR 29, IR 69	31 Inf. Brig.	30 Res. Inf. Brig.
IX	RIR 31	IR 31, Bez. Kdo.	33 Inf. Brig.	34 Res. Inf. Brig.
	RIR 75	IR 75	33 and 36 Inf. Brig.	33 Res. Inf. Brig.
	RIR 76	IR 76	Ldw. Insp.	
	RIR 84	IR 85, Bez. Kdo.	34 and 36 Inf. Brig.	35 Res. Inf. Brig.
	RIR 86	IR 84, IR 86	35 Inf. Brig.	
	RIR 90	GR 89, FR 90	34 Inf. Brig.	34 Res Inf. Brig.
X	RIR 73	IR 73, IR 77, IR 92	40 Inf. Brig.	37 Res Inf. Brig.
	RIR 74	IR 74, IR 91	37 Inf. Brig.	39 Res Inf. Brig.
	RIR 77	Bez. Kdo.	39. Inf. Brig.	38 Res Inf. Brig.
	RIR 78	IR 92, Bez. Kdo.	38 und 40 Inf. Brig.	37 Res Inf. Brig.
	RIR 79	Bez. Kdo.	37 Inf. Brig.	-
	RIR 91	IR 82, IR 164	39 Inf. Brig.	38 Res Inf. Brig.
	RIR 92	IR 78, Bez. Kdo.	37 Inf. Brig.	39 Res Inf. Brig.
XI	RIR 32	IR 96	83 Inf. Brig.	44 Res Inf. Brig.
	RIR 71	IR 32, IR 167	44 Inf. Brig.	43 Res Inf. Brig.
	RIR 82	IR 71, IR 95	76 Inf. Brig.	44 Res Inf. Brig.
	RIR 83	IR 83, Bez. Kdo.	43 and 44 Inf. Brig.	50 Res Inf. Brig.
	RIR 94	IR 94	83 Inf. Brig.	43 Res Inf. Brig.
XII	RIR 100	Leib-GR 100	45 Inf. Brig.	45 Res Inf. Brig.
	RIR 101	IR 102, IR 182	45 and 46 Inf. Brig.	
	RIR 102	Bez. Kdo.	46 and 64 Inf. Brig.	46 Res Inf. Brig.
	RIR 103	GR 101, IR 103	45 and 63 Inf. Brig.	
XIII	RIR 119	Bez. Kdo.	51 Inf. Brig.	52 Res Inf. Brig.
	RIR 120	Bez. Kdo.	51 and 52 Inf. Brig.	
	RIR 121	Bez. Kdo.	52 Inf. Brig.	51 Res Inf. Brig.

Army Corps	Reserve Infantry Regiment	Mobilizing Formation	Infantry Brigade	Reserve Infantry Brigade
XIV	RIR 40	GR 110, Bez. Kdo.	55 Inf. Brig.	55 Res Inf. Brig.
	RIR 109	Leib-GR 109, Bez. Kdo.	55 Inf. Brig.	
	RIR 110	FR 40, Leib-GR 109, GR 110, IR 111	55. and 56 Inf. Brig.	56 Res Inf. Brig.
	RIR 111	IR 114, Bez. Kdo.	57 and 84 Inf. Brig.	
XV	RIR 99	IR 99, 132, 136, 143	60, 82 and 85 Inf. Brig.	60 Res Inf. Brig.
XVI	RIR 30	IR 30	86 Inf. Brig.	32 Res Inf. Brig.
	RIR 67	IR 67, IR 145, IR 173	86 Inf. Brig.	66 Res Inf. Brig.
	RIR 98	IR 135	67 Inf. Brig.	–
	RIR 130	IR 98, IR 130, IR 144	66 Inf. Brig.	66 Res Inf. Brig.
XVII	RIR 5	Bez. Kdo.	71 Inf. Brig.	70 Res Inf. Brig.
	RIR 21	IR 21, Bez. Kdo.	70 and 87 Inf. Brig.	69 Res Inf. Brig.
	RIR 61	Bez. Kdo.	71 Inf. Brig.	
XVIII	RIR 80	FR 80, Bez. Kdo.	41 Inf. Brig.	41 Res Inf. Brig.
	RIR 81	Bez. Kdo.	41 and 42 Inf. Brig.	42 Res Inf. Brig.
	RIR 87	IR 81, IR 87	41 and 42 Inf. Brig.	41 Res Inf. Brig.
	RIR 88	IR 88, IR 118	42 and 50 Inf. Brig.	42 Res Inf. Brig.
	RIR 116	IR 115, 116, 168	49 Inf. Brig.	49 Res Inf. Brig.
	RIR 118	IR 115, IR 117	50 Inf. Brig.	
XIX	RIR 104	IR 104, Bez. Kdo.	88 Inf. Brig.	47 Res Inf. Brig.
	RIR 106	IR 179, IR 181	47 and 88 Inf. Brig.	
	RIR 107	IR 107	48 Inf. Brig.	48 Res Inf. Brig.
	RIR 133	IR 133, IR 134	89 Inf. Brig.	
XX	RIR 18	IR 18, IR 59, IR 148	72 and 74 Inf. Brig.	72 Res Inf. Brig.
	RIR 59	IR 147, IR 150, IR 151	73 and 75 Inf. Brig.	
XXI	RIR 17	Bez. Kdo.	Ldw. Insp.	32 Res Inf. Brig.
	RIR 60	IR 60, IR 137	62 Inf. Brig.	60 Res Inf. Brig.
	RIR 70	IR 166, Bez. Kdo.	62. Inf. Brig.	–
I KB*	bayer.** RIR 1	IR 1	1 bayer Inf. Brig.	1 bayer. Res. Inf. Brig.
	bayer. RIR 2	2 IR, 16 IR	2 bayer Inf. Brig.	
	bayer. RIR 3	3 IR, 20 IR	3 bayer Inf. Brig.	2 bayer. Res. Inf. Brig.
	bayer. RIR 12	12 IR	4 bayer Inf. Brig.	
	bayer. RIR 15	15 IR	4 bayer Inf. Brig.	3 bayer. Res. Inf. Brig.
II KB	bayer. RIR 4	5 IR, 9 IR	7 bayer Inf. Brig.	3 bayer. Res. Inf. Brig.
	bayer. RIR 5	17 IR, 18 IR	6 bayer Inf. Brig.	5 bayer. Res. Inf. Brig.
	bayer. RIR 8	9 IR, Bez. Kdo.	5 and 7 bayer Inf. Brig.	

Army Corps	Reserve Infantry Regiment	Mobilizing Formation	Infantry Brigade	Reserve Infantry Brigade
III KB	bayer. RIR 6	IR 14, IR 21	9 bayer Inf. Brig.	9 bayer. Res. Inf. Brig.
	bayer. RIR 7	IR 7, IR 19	10 bayer Inf. Brig.	
	bayer. RIR 10	IR 10	11 bayer Inf. Brig.	11 bayer. Res. Inf. Brig.
	bayer. RIR 11	IR 11	12 bayer Inf. Brig.	10 bayer. Res. Inf. Brig.
	bayer. RIR 13	IR 13	11 bayer Inf. Brig.	11 bayer. Res. Inf. Brig.
	bayer. RIR 14	IR 6	12 bayer Inf. Brig.	10 bayer. Res. Inf. Brig.

* KB abbreviates the German word *Königlich Bayerisch*–Royal Bavarian.
** Bayer. abbreviates the German word *bayerisch*–Bavarian.

(Kraus, 2012), pp. 2–6.

Although detailed information is missing, it can be assumed that mobilization of artillery and cavalry reserve formations was conducted in a similar way. As mentioned above, the more densely populated regions of the empire tended to have more trained reservists on the rolls of their Bezirkskommandos than the less populated regions. To balance the numbers of available reservists, the army corps of these more densely populated regions assigned a certain number of men to other army corps.

Exchange of Reservists between Army Corps

Army Corps	Number of reservists (infantry) sent to another Army Corps
III	3,700 to the Guard Corps 21,260 to I Army Corps 10,340 to XX Army Corps
IV	500 to V Army Corps
VI	2,000 to V Army Corps
VII	4,500 to Guard Corps 6,300 to II Army Corps 500 to IV Army Corps 24,890 to V Army Corps 3,050 to VI Army Corps 2,270 to X Army Corps 670 to XI Army Corps 1,100 to XIV Army Corps 11,400 to XV Army Corps 20,700 to XVI Army Corps 13,450 to XVII Army Corps 2,090 to XVIII Army Corps 5,430 to XX Army Corps 10,140 to XXI Army Corps

Army Corps	Number of reservists (infantry) sent to another Army Corps
VIII	4,340 to XVI Army Corps
IX	4,400 to II Army Corps 3,820 to XX Army Corps
X	3,400 to I Army Corps
XI	1,000 to XIV Army Corps
XIV	160 to XV Army Corps 2,000 to XIII Army Corps

(Kraus, 2012), pp. 7., (Reichsarchiv, 1928), p. 12.

The Reichsarchiv goes even beyond these figures. In the first volume about field railroads during mobilization, it states that 148,000 reservists were transported from Berlin and the Rhineland to Eastern Prussia during the first six mobilization days. It is most probable that these 148,000 men included not only army reservists, but also men manning the fortresses along the eastern borders. The figures given for reserve personnel mobilized for the Guard Corps are much higher. According to the Reichsarchiv, 68,000 men, mostly from Westphalia, were mobilized for the Guard Corps and were transported to Berlin.[41]

An analysis of the chart above shows that upon mobilization, 54,300 infantry reservists (probably many more—mainly from Berlin and the Ruhr) were assigned in Eastern Prussia to I, XVII, and XX Army Corps. It becomes obvious that a significant share of the soldiers of the Eighth Army came not from Eastern Prussia, but from elsewhere in the empire. Reservists from the Ruhr area therefore were sent to Berlin or Pomerania upon mobilization, only to return to the West a couple of days later on the way to the deployment areas of their formations. This demonstrates the fallacy of the propaganda in the Reichsarchiv, *Schlachten des Weltkrieges* Volumes of the 1920s that the soldiers fighting at Tannenberg were morally superior to the attacking Russians because they were defending their homesteads. These books intended for the popular market differed from the official history produced by the Reichsarchiv. The work of the *Kriegsgeschichtliche Forschungsanstalt des Heeres* was completed by the Federal German Bundesarchiv in 1956, when the final 14th volume of *Der Weltkrieg 1914 bis 1918* (the so-called Reichsarchiv red series) appeared. The *Schlachten des Weltkrieges* series was a popular narrative history, usually written by eyewitnesses. These books gave more space to propaganda than the red books did, tending to emphasize the heroism of the individual fighting against huge odds of manpower and material.[42]

After the start of the 1914 campaign, it became clear that Germany had too few troops to meet all its operational plans. As the National Service chapter points out, almost half of the candidates at the Musterung were excused from active service and sent to the *Landsturm*. They received a formal paper excuse pass called a *Landsturmschein*. Because many drafted conscripts had these passes, there were plenty of untrained recruits. Thousands of volunteers had reported to the different garrisons without needing to be called up. For the time being, the army had far more men knocking at its door than were needed.

41 (Kraus, 2012), pp. 7., (Reichsarchiv, 1928), p. 12.
42 (Schäfer, 1927), p. 15.

MOBILIZATION OF LOGISTIC UNITS

Supply formations such as trains and columns were the branch of the army by far the most dependent on mobilization. Completely new formations were assembled during the 1914 mobilization. Many rear echelon columns and train formation were almost 100 percent reservists, many of them lacking any peacetime military training. Upon mobilization the following were created: about 480 ammunition columns, approximately 150 subsistence columns, 300 service trains and columns of the communications zone, 60 remount depots, about 120 field bakeries and bakeries for the communication zone, 110 medical companies, and 400 field hospitals. While in 1870, 2,500–3,000 train wagons were necessary to supply an army of about 100,000 men; this number increased to 7,000 in 1914. Not mentioned here are the motor transport columns that were mobilized by the motor transport battalion, not by the train battalions. Soon after the start of the operations it became evident that even these vast numbers were insufficient, and in September 1914 numerous new formations were formed.[43]

Columns and trains were mobilized from reservists who had served either in train battalions or in the cavalry. In contrast to the reserve formations of the combat troops, these supply units usually had never trained before mobilization. Therefore, they had less cohesion, less discipline, lower demonstrated performance, and were prone to panic if they encountered any unexpected setbacks. The column grapevines (*Kolonnengerüchte*) or rumor mills were noted for inflating uncertain or even untrue news into disaster stories. At times panic even affected nearby combat formations when the negative impact of such rumors spread.

RAILROADS DURING MOBILIZATION

During the wars of 1866 and 1870–71, railroads played a major role, carrying both men and supplies forward.[44] Based upon this experience, Article 41 of the Imperial Constitution reserved rights to the army, when new railroad construction was planned, even by single states.[45] A central railroad administration (*Reichseisenbahnamt*) made sure that railroad planning was carried out according to central goals. For example, during the late 1840s, the General Staff influenced the construction of the Minden-Cologne railroad (*Cöln-Mindener Eisenbahn*) to ensure fast mobilization in case of war with France.

After the Franco-Prussian War, it was comparatively easy for the General Staff to budget money for the further strategic build-up of the railroad network. With a changing strategic focus between the East and West and the rising threat of a two-front war, railroads became a force multiplier for the fast and easy transportation of huge military formations between both war theaters. Especially during the Schlieffen era, a rapid switching of forces across Germany was essential to fight the Russian enemy after achieving a victory in the West. To Clausewitz, the defensive is superior to the offensive and gives multiple advantages to the defender. One of them is the defense along so-called "interior lines," (*innere Linien*) which means that a defender is able to shift and concentrate his forces faster and more efficiently than the attacker could do given his "exterior lines." To Schlieffen, interior lines aided strate-

[43] (Cron, *Die Entwicklung des deutschen Heeres von seinen Anfängen bis auf unsere Tage,* part I, 1935), pp. 248–262.

[44] (Lehmann, 1905) and (Budde, 1904).

[45] Article 41. See Appendix A.

gic planning in a two-front scenario. To finally succeed, the defender has to push for decision by fast and sudden counterattacks—the "flashing sword of revenge" (*das blitzende Schwert der Vergeltung*) as Clausewitz called it.[46] Well-planned railroads provided essential support to such an operational doctrine.

Due to the booming German economy in the 1880s, a massive railroad build-up was needed to support the economy. In parallel, many mergers and acquisitions occurred, bringing together small and privately operated railroad companies with a few large state-owned companies. This centralization made it easier for the General Staff to plan new lines in close cooperation with the railroad companies and to introduce new processes and standards for military railroad operations. The railroad department of the General Staff, military railroad formations, and the civilian railroad administration liaised closely to ensure centralized planning. Before the war, the German railroad infrastructure comprised 57,000 km of full-gauge track (*Vollbahn*) and 11,000 km of narrow gauge and light rail track (*Schmalspurbahn*).[47]

Eisenbahndirektionen made sure that these uniform processes and standards were followed throughout the Empire. In addition to the Eisenbahndirektionen, 26 military line commanders (*Linienkommandanturen*) were installed to make sure that railroad plans made by the General Staff were correctly implemented. A field grade officer with a railroad background—ideally a General Staff officer, who previously had served in the railroad department—commanded the Linienkommandantur. The second in charge was a senior civilian executive from the regional railroad authorities—ideally from the regional *Eisenbahndirektion*.[48] The line commanders played a pivotal role in coordinating the mobilization preparations between the General Staff and the railroad authorities. A cornerstone of the plan was to annually review the military timetable (*Militärfahrplan*) that was to be used upon mobilization.

The Militärfahrplan was based on the standard military train with 110 axles and 600 tons capacity, made up of passenger cars and freight cars.[49] The freight cars were used for the ordinary men or horses with up to 40 men or eight horses in one car. A certain number of freight cars were turned into flat bed cars by taking away the sidewalls and roofs for the transport of wagons. Standard military trains were usually pulled by a G3/BR 53 steam engine or one comparable. The trains traveled at a comparatively slow average speed of 30 kilometers per hour on major lines or 25 kilometers per hours on narrow gauge lines. This slow speed was chosen to create enough slack in case of technical problems or other delays. In the autumn of 1913, the railroad department started calculating a new Militärfahrplan, based upon an average speed of 40 kilometers an hour to speed up mobilization, but this was not ready for use during the mobilization in 1914.

On dual-tracked lines trains could be dispatched every 20 minutes, while on single-tracked lines, in order to allow for return journeys, the frequency was halved to one train every 40 minutes. Beginning in 1912, the Militärfahrplan also scheduled local trains for civilian traffic and to supply essential goods to civilians in urban areas during the mobilization and the initial deployment of the army (*Militärlokalzüge*).[50] The Militärfahrplan distinguished between mobilization transports (*Mobilmachungstransporte*) and war transports (*Kriegstransporte*).

---

[46] (Clausewitz G. v., 1832), p. 125–127 and p. 143. Please also see (Schmid, 2011), pp. 78–87 and (Schössler, 2009) pp. 218 and 250.

[47] (Stoneman, 2006), p. 172

[48] (Reichsarchiv, 1928), pp. 2–8.

[49] After the start of the war, it was decided that a significant reduction in the length of the standard military train would achieve a higher level of flexibility. (Reichsarchiv, 1928), p. 26.

[50] (Stoneman, 2006), p. 173

The purpose of the mobilization transports was to bring all military formations and the fortresses up to war strength. The purpose of the war transports was the deployment of the operationally ready formations into their assembly areas as per the operations plan. To that end, hundreds of trains were dispatched down designated transportation lines into clearly defined assembly areas along the eastern and western borders. Mobilization transports, on the other hand, undertook many different roles with various loads and to different locations, sometimes crossing the transportation lines of the war transports.

Some of these transports formed the massive coal and tanker trains travelling from the Ruhr area and Upper Silesia to the ports of Kiel or Wilhelmshaven to supply coal and fuel oil to the Navy. Others were huge transports of reservists from populated areas of the empire, who were sent to Eastern Prussia; other trains were used to evacuate the civilian population from the border areas together with their cattle.[51] They were also involved in the evacuation of precious horses from horse-breeding farms and military horse-breeding depots (e.g. *Trakehnen*) in Eastern Prussia, where they were in danger of being captured by Russian cavalry.

As mentioned at the start of this chapter, the mobilization transports started moving when imminent danger of war was announced on 31 July. Upon mobilization, a number of high priority early mobilization trains had to be scheduled to ship the 48, 50, 53, 64, and 3 Bavarian, 7 Bavarian, and 11 Bavarian Infantry Brigades into their assembly areas in the *Reichslande*. These brigades had the task of guarding the border against early French strikes. The 16th Infantry Division also had to be sent to the Luxembourg border, so as to be in position to occupy it and its train lines. A second wave of early mobilization transports shipped six reinforced infantry brigades (11, 14, 27, 34, 38, and 43 Brigades) to their assembly area west of Aachen for the planned coup-de-main against the fortress of Liège.[52] This assault force was under the command of General Otto v. Emmich. All these formations were still at peacetime strength when shipped to their assembly areas. Mobilization had to be carried out during their border guard or during the assault on Liège.

During the first days, the army's railroad personnel and the railroad formations had to carry out their own mobilization operation. During the first and second mobilization day the mobilization transports started carrying reservists to the railroad units or to the places where they received their equipment and their weapons. These transports then had to carry them back to their active or reserve formations where they were to be integrated. During the first and second mobilization day the Militärfahrplan and the pre-war civilian timetable still widely ran in parallel. Civilian traffic was fully stopped on the third mobilization day. The mobilization transports reached their peak between the third and the fifth mobilization day. Altogether 20,800 mobilization transports were scheduled in the Militärfahrplan.

Starting on the evening of the fifth mobilization day, the war transports began to deploy the mobilized active and reserve formations into their assembly areas. This huge wave of transports required 165,000 closed freight cars and 60,000 open platform cars that carried the bulk of the army between the fifth and the 14th mobilization day. On 16 August, Liège was taken in a bloody assault. Meanwhile, the advance in the west commenced; 2,070,000 men,

[51] Ninety-eight trains with 4,900 cars were required to evacuate the civilian population of 23,000 people living close to the French border in the Reichslande. (Reichsarchiv, 1928), pp. 28 and 33.

[52] These high priority war transports required 1,440 standard military trains of which 340 had to be integrated into the civilian timetable on the first mobilization day. (Reichsarchiv, 1928), p. 34.

118,000 horses, and 400,000 tons of material had already been brought forward.[53] In the west, there were 13 double-laned transport lines available for the 660 trains per day that were planned to run along each line. Trains crossed the river Rhine over 15 railroad bridges at the rate of 563 trains of 54 cars each per day at an average speed of 30 km an hour. At the Hohenzollern bridge alone, 2,150 trains crossed between 2 and 8 August; one every 10 minutes.[54]

The deployment of troops (including all columns and trains) required the following railroad car capacities:

	Passenger cars for officers	Freight cars for personnel	Freight cars for horses	Platform freight cars	Total
Army corps	170	965	2,960	1,915	**6,010**
Reserve corps	110	755	1,440	920	**3,225**
Cavalry Division	30	85	920	140	**1,175**

On average, an army corps required about 140 standard military trains (two trains required by the corps staff); a reserve corps needed significantly less with only 85 trains. A cavalry division managed with about 31 standard military trains. Army commands (*Armee-Oberkommando*) required seven trains.[55] Usually, an army corps was allocated 20 trains per day, which meant that it took seven days on average to have an army corps with all its columns and supply trains operationally ready in its assembly area. Some corps were transported with higher priority and used 30 or 40 trains per day. Formations of the II, V, and VI Army Corps spent up to four days sitting on their trains before arrival at their railroad head stations. This was due to the long distances from Pomerania and Silesia in the east to their western border assembly areas and the slow average speed of the military trains. After detraining, the troops often had to march another 50 or more kilometers before arriving in their scheduled assembly areas.

The railroad deployment was the most important piece of the entire mobilization plan. Mobilized active and reserve formations needed to arrive to their assembly areas in time, and they had to be operationally ready for the start of the offensive. This was the most essential task in the transformation process from a peacetime army to a fully mobilized war machine. This railroad deployment seemed to work with clockwork precision and exactly as scheduled in the mobilization plan. But this clockwork precision had one major and unintended side effect: it created inflexibility. During the first 15 mobilization days, the army was busy carrying out the scheduled mobilization and deployment plans. Because the General Staff had decided in 1913 to focus exclusively upon the Western Theater and to skip the alternative deployment plans to both east and west, things slipped out of political control. The 16th Infantry Division had to conquer Luxembourg before dawn of the first mobilization day to make use of the scheduled Luxembourg train connections. The coup de main on Liége had to suc-

53 The logistical problems of deploying the huge 1st and 2nd Army west of the river Rhine in the area between Aachen, Cologne and Krefeld and channeling them with all their battalions, batteries, and train columns through the bottleneck of Liége are not discussed here.

54 (Herwig H., 2009), p. 48.

55 (Reichsarchiv, 1928), p. 19 and (Großer Generalstab, 1914), pp. 70–76.

ceed by the fourth mobilization day to allow the First and Second Army to advance through the Liège bottleneck, which unfortunately was closed and barred by a Belgian fortress.

But the political side suffered the most from this inflexibility, because the clockwork mobilization schedule took away any control from the Kaiser and the *Reichskanzler* once it was set in motion. Moltke the Younger ruled out any attempt to limit the war to the Eastern Theater (today we know that it would have been impossible to limit the war to the east due to the alliances among Russia, France and England). The Chief of General Staff stated very clearly that it was impossible to change the current deployment with focus in the west into a new deployment with the trains moving eastwards. Moltke told the Kaiser on 1 August that doing so would create an "unorganized mass of armed men being concentrated in the East without having proper food and supplies available."[56] The Reichskanzler was only informed on 1 August that the mobilization plan, deployment schedule, and early operations would limit the diplomatic leeway to either localize the war in the east or to avoid the outbreak of hostilities at all. The assault on Liège required the violation of Belgian neutrality, which—bearing in mind that the political decision-makers were not informed in advance—was probably the climax of German militarism before 1914. The Versailles Treaty later labeled Germany as the aggressor and stated that Germany alone was responsible for beginning the war. This limitation was caused exclusively by a military-focused mobilization and deployment plan that lacked any consideration of possible political repercussions. This limitation is the real tragedy of Schlieffen's idea of shifting the operational focus exclusively to the west.

WAR VOLUNTEERS

During the war, a great many young men between the ages of 17 and 20 volunteered for active service before their class was called up. In 1914, there were large numbers of these volunteers, including some men over the age of 20, who were in the untrained Landsturm. These men had been released from their peacetime obligation but volunteered anyway. There was a significant decrease in this number by 1915 and estimates were that approximately only five percent of the later classes were volunteers.[57]

The exact number of these volunteers is somewhat controversial. The number 1,300,000 was repeated in several newspapers including the government's unofficial voice *Norddeutsche Allgemeine Zeitung*. This number has been repeated and copied from book to book for years. More than likely the numbers were exaggerated. Prussia reported that 260,000 had attempted to volunteer, but only 144,000 were accepted. There were 32,000 from Bavaria; Württemberg had 8,600; and there were about 10,000 from Saxony. That is a total of about 185,000. The numbers were a classic example of the press building enthusiasm for the war. The newspapers claimed that these came from all social classes, but the evidence surviving from two regiments shows the proletariat represented 33 of 413 volunteers in an artillery regiment and 64 of 450 volunteers in an infantry regiment. Students and the bourgeoisie were heavily represented.[58]

---

[56] (Reichsarchiv, 1925), p. 22 and (Reichsarchiv, 1928), p. 31. (Bethmann-Hollweg, 1919), pp. 156–157. (Haffner, 1982), pp. 22–27. (Moltke, 1922), pp. 430–432.

[57] (The General Staff, 1918), pp. 13–14.

[58] (Verhey, *The Spirit of 1914*, 2000), pp, 97–100.

FALKENHAYN MOBILIZATIONS

Mobilization had only been prepared for the predicted number of reserve, Ersatz, Landwehr, and Landsturm units. For additional formations, there were neither arms (except the totally outdated rifles Model 1871 and 71/84) nor uniforms, helmets, and other equipment. There were neither train formations nor supply columns. There was no artillery; there were no reserve or Landwehr officers or NCOs to be mobilized as potential leaders. It soon became clear that this mass of unarmed, non-uniformed, and disorganized men had to be structured into field formations if the operational plan in the west was to have any chance of success.

On 16 August 1914, the War Minister, General v. Falkenhayn ordered the mobilization of six further reserve corps[59] and a Bavarian reserve division, which were supposed to be operationally ready on 10 October 1914.[60] The mobilization of these formations was ordered only two weeks after the war broke out; it was driven by a kind of desperation that can be seen from their structure, their skimped training, and the unrealistic rush in which they had to be fielded.[61] Unlike other active, reserve, or even Landwehr formations, no infantry brigades had been formed. Thus, there were initially no brigade commanders in the division. The division staff had to attempt to command all four reserve infantry regiments and the artillery. Controlling the inexperienced, cursorily trained men and officers, who generally had no field experience, was an almost impossible task.

Thus, in September 1914, the XXII–XXVII Reserve Corps were mobilized. These formations were made up of the 43rd–54th Reserve Divisions and the 6th Bavarian Reserve Division. Reserve Infantry Regiments 201–248 and Bavarian Reserve Infantry Regiments 16, 17, 20, and 21 belonged to those corps. Bavarian Reserve Infantry Regiment 16, known as Regiment "List" after the regimental commander, was dispatched to Flanders with the Kriegsfreiwilliger, Adolf Hitler marching in its ranks. A battalion of these regiments consisted of 21 officers (the commander, adjutant, four company commanders, 12 platoon commanders, one *Stabsarzt*, and two medical officers) and 947 NCOs and enlisted men. Original reserve regiments mobilized in August 1914 had 26 officers and 1,038 NCOs and EM. There was a real shortage of junior leadership. Older men from the Landwehr or the Landsturm replaced the junior NCOs and lieutenants, who were normally found at the company level. These men were not only older, but senior in rank and had to be trained before they could train others. The doctrinal training of the retired officers was overwhelmingly out of date and not up to modern standards. They had neither a good understanding of weaponry, nor were there any trained staffs. The equipment was desperately short in every category, especially footwear. Some of the uniforms were as much as 40 years old. Much of the equipment was not delivered to the units until just prior to deployment, eliminating the chance for the troops to train and familiarize themselves with the equipment.[62]

---

59 Initially Falkenhayn ordered mobilization of five new reserve corps (XXII–XXVI). Number seven (XXVII reserve corps) was built up in cooperation with the Saxon War Ministry, and its mobilization was ordered a little later than the initial five reserve corps. The 6 Bavarian Reserve Division was mobilized in cooperation with the Bavarian War Ministry.

60 *Bundesarchiv / Militärarchiv "Aufstellungsweisung des Kriegsministers v. Falkenhayn für die Aufstellung 5 Reservekorps vom 16.8.1914" Akten des Militärkabinetts* PH 1/3, is the organizational chart of the XXII reserve corps; other corps were similar. Mobilization of the XXVII with mobilization base was ordered a few days later in cooperation with the Saxon war ministry.

61 For further details about mobilization, military drill, and first operational use during the first battle of Ypres and at Langemarck during the first half of November 1914, please see the book by (Unruh, 1986), which is regretfully only available in German. In English, see the explanation in (Sheldon, *The German Army at Ypres 1914*, 2010).

62 (Sheldon, *The German Army at Ypres 1914*, 2010), p. 4.

There was also a shortage of training pamphlets and live ammunition. In Reserve Infantry Regiment 239, 48 men had only civilian clothes as late as 25 September.[63] This quote from Reserve Infantry Regiment 236 sums up the situation clearly:

> On the other hand, nothing at all was ready for the unplanned formations called into life during mobilization in 1914. To clothe the flood of Kriegsfreiwilligen who came into the Army, there were peacetime uniforms but no wartime field gray clothing. In addition there were no rifles or machineguns and no personal equipment such as knapsacks or ammunition pouches, etc. There were also no vehicles, no field kitchens, or other mobilization stores necessary to equip troops. All the necessary instruction manuals were also lacking.[64]

There was also a lack of artillery in the reserve divisions. There was only one reserve field artillery regiment (the first and second battalions were equipped with field guns, the third battalion with field-howitzers) in the division; consequently, there was no brigade organization. The artillery brigade commander and the artillery officer, normally the primary consultant to the division commander in artillery matters, were not present. The recruits had no experience or training in dealing with the horses or horse teams. Not only could the recruits not drive the horse-wagons, but also, given the terrain and the weather, they had no concept of caring for the horses. Many horses died or fell ill. The state of gunnery training was equally bad. Their training was cut short, and live training with ammunition had been reduced to 40 shrapnel and 10 high explosive shells per battery. This resulted in badly misfiring batteries that were not trained to direct their fire in cooperation with the infantry.[65]

Despite these problems, after an inspection, these formations were deemed ready for war by the end of September 1914. One of the inspectors, General Alfred von Loewenfeld was quite downhearted about the new units.

> Everything in the way of training that could be done, was done. The infantry, which is still rather cautious in its movements, may be regarded as trained. Within the field artillery, the lack of officers is painfully evident . . . The tactical ability of the commanders, especially at company and battery level, is not good. These appointments have, for the most part, been filled with non-active officers of advanced age. In general they have found it difficult to meet the demands of modern warfare. Furthermore, their physical robustness and horsemanship, mounted as they are on mostly untrained and barely broken horses, is in many cases deficient. One particular fault is their lack of awareness of the risk posed by enemy artillery, even at long-range. This manifests itself in a willingness to maneuver ineffectually in massed formations only a short distance from the enemy. In addition there is a lack of awareness of cooperation between the arms in the context of the all-arms battle. This applies not only to the artillery but also to the infantry.[66]

---

[63] (Sheldon, *The German Army at Ypres 1914*, 2010), pp. 2–6.
[64] (Sheldon, *The German Army at Ypres 1914*, 2010), pp. 2–4.
[65] (Sheldon, *The German Army at Ypres 1914*, 2010), pp. 6–7.
[66] (Sheldon, *The German Army at Ypres 1914*, 2010), p. 8.

Based on perceived requirements, these formations received an extremely short period of training as little as eight weeks. Again, despite these problems the decision was made to press these formations into service in the so-called "Race to the Sea." By 8 October, four of the new army corps were headed for Flanders.

Because these reserve corps had almost no time for systematic battalion, regimental, or divisional training, the mobilization of these reserve corps directly fed into the disaster of the first battle of Ypres and Langemarck. There is an overwhelming belief that the majority of these troops were volunteers—students or Kriegfreiwillige. This led to an enduring myth about the singing attacks by young student troops. The Nazis later used this "Spirit of Langemarck" in their public relations campaigns. While singing attacks are recorded in almost every German regimental history that was even remotely connected to the area, many of those were published in the late 1930s under Nazi supervision. The majority of men in the reserve regiments were not even students. Research indicates that only 18 percent were Kriegsfreiwillige and that included teachers, not quite the band of students of later legend.

DECEMBER 1914 MOBILIZATIONS

In December 1914, a third wave of reserve formations was mobilized, making up XXXVIII–XXXXI Reserve Corps with 75th–82nd Reserve Divisions and the Bavarian 8th Reserve Division. These corps were made up of Reserve Infantry Regiments 249–272 and Bavarian Reserve Infantry Regiments 18, 19, 22, and 23. These formations were organized in the same improvized way as the reserve formations mobilized in September. Upon mobilization in August, all reserve regiments had a regimental staff with four officers and 12 men, which was already smaller than the regimental staff of active regiments. The next two waves of reserve formations which mobilized in September and December had regimental staffs—only four officers and nine men strong.[67] Based upon the devastating experience at Langemarck, the December 1914 Reserve Infantry Regiments 249–272 were reinforced by the War Ministry, which on 20 December 1914, directed the assignment of 10 NCOs and 300 men from active regiments to each newly mobilized reserve regiment as a stabilizing cadre. All these differences between active regiments and reserve regiments disappeared the more those reserve formations were used side-by-side with active formations. In 1915, reserve regiments were equipped with machinegun companies and, at the beginning of 1916, reserve regiments also received trench mortars. By War Ministry order of 7 May 1916, all reserve regiments were brought to the same strength and the same organization as active regiments.[68]

Mobilization of Landwehr Units in 1914

Landwehr regiments (*Landwehr Infanterie Regimenter–Landw. IR* or *LIR*) were mobilized from the first and second contingent Landwehr reservists. They comprised men who had completed their military training many years ago, and who were between 27 and 39 years old. In August 1914, mobile Landwehr regiments contained up to 62 percent first contingent reservists (up to 31 years old); whereas, static regiments (most of them garrisoning for-

[67] (Kraus, 2012), p. 8.
[68] (Kraus, 2012), p. 9.

tresses) had between 78 and 100 percent second contingent reservists (between 32 and 39 years old). That meant that the enlisted men were usually more than 30 years old, and their military training had taken place about 10 years previously.

That meant they had frequently trained with weapons no longer in service, and the soldiers were in a physical condition that made it hard for them to stand the rough conditions and the challenges of war. Cadres were reserve or Landwehr officers and NCOs. Most officers came from the local or regional Bezirkskommando, but almost all regimental commanders and about 50 percent of the battalion commanders were active officers.

This structure changed during the war. During the first half of 1915, younger but untrained *Ersatzreservisten* and *Landsturmpflichtige* were drafted into the Landwehr and were trained there. During 1916, these younger soldiers had to be assigned to active and reserve regiments, and older untrained men started filling the ranks of the Landwehr. In the second half of the war, the average age of Landwehr soldiers significantly increased compared with the mobilization of 1914. Upon mobilization, 96 Landwehr regiments were formed. This task was accomplished by the local infantry regiments—personnel being drawn from the local Bezirkskommando. Arms and equipment were stored in artillery and garment depots.

Landwehr regiments were traditionally numbered according to the active regiments mobilizing them; therefore, the numbers ranged up to 133, although only a total of 96 regiments was mobilized. On the other hand, the numbering was often purely traditional or had a regional background, if the active regiment mobilizing a particular Landwehr regiment had changed. In the same way as reserve personnel, Landwehr reservists were exchanged between densely and less populated corps areas.[69] Landwehr regiments were mobilized a little later than active and reserve regiments. Staffs and cadres started working on the third mobilization day (4 August) and the Landwehr reservists arrived between 5 and 7 August, by which time the active formations had already entrained and departed. Mobile Landwehr regiments were intended to be operationally ready between 10 and 13 August.

Mobilization of Landwehr Regiments

Army Corps	Landwehr Regiment	Mobilizing Formation	Infantry Brigade	Comments
I	LIR 1	IR 4	3 Inf. Brig.	2 battalions
	LIR 3	IR 43	2 Inf. Brig.	static, 2 battalions
	LIR 4	IR 41	1 Inf. Brig.	4 battalions
	LIR 33	IR 45	4 Inf. Brig.	–
II	LIR 2	IR 2, IR 42	5 and 6 Inf. Brig.	–
	LIR 9	IR 9, IR 54	5 Inf. Brig.	–
	LIR 34	IR 14	7 Inf. Brig.	–
	LIR 49	IR 49, IR 140	8 Inf. Brig.	–

69 (Kraus, 2012), p. 269.

Army Corps	Landwehr Regiment	Mobilizing Formation	Infantry Brigade	Comments
III	LIR 8	Leib-GR 8	9 Inf. Brig.	static, 2 battalions
	LIR 12	GR 12, IR 24	10 and 12 Inf. Brig.	–
	LIR 20	IR 20	11 Inf. Brig.	–
	LIR 24	IR 24, IR 64	12 Inf. Brig.	static
	LIR 35	IR 35	11 Inf. Brig.	–
	LIR 48	IR 48, IR 64	9 and 12 Inf. Brig.	static
	LIR 52	IR 52	10 Inf. Brig.	–
IV	LIR 26	IR 26, IR 66	13 Inf. Brig.	–
	LIR 27	IR 27	14 Inf. Brig.	–
	LIR 36	IR 36, IR 153	15 and 16 Inf. Brig.	–
	LIR 66	IR 93	15 Inf. Brig.	–
	LIR 72	IR 72	16 Inf. Brig.	2 battalions
	LIR 93	–	13 Inf. Brig.	mobilized 1915
V	LIR 6	IR 58	17 Inf. Brig.	–
	LIR 7	GR 7	18 Inf. Brig.	–
	LIR 19	GR 7, IR 58	17 and 18 Inf. Brig.	–
	LIR 37	GR 6, IR 46	19 Inf. Brig.	–
	LIR 46	IR 47	20 Inf. Brig.	–
	LIR 47	FR 37, IR 50	20 and 77 Inf. Brig.	static, 2 battalions
VI	LIR 10	GR 11, IR 51	22 Inf. Brig.	static
	LIR 11	IR 63	78 Inf. Brig.	–
	LIR 22	IR 22, IR 62	23 and 24 Inf. Brig.	–
	LIR 23	IR 22, IR 156	23 Inf. Brig.	–
	LIR 38	GR 10, FR 38	21 Inf. Brig.	static
	LIR 51	IR 157	78 Inf. Brig.	–
VII	LIR 13	IR 13, IR 158	25 Inf. Brig.	–
	LIR 15	IR 55	26 Inf. Brig.	static
	LIR 16	IR 16 (?)	27 Inf. Brig.	–
	LIR 39	FR 39, IR 159	28 Inf. Brig.	static, 4 battalions
	LIR 53	IR 57 (?)	79 Inf. Brig.	–
	LIR 55	IR 56		–
	LIR 56	assembled from *Landsturm* infantry	79 Inf. Brig.	mobilized December 1914
	LIR 57	Assembled Landwehr battalions	28 Inf. Brig.	mobilized 1915

Army Corps	Landwehr Regiment	Mobilizing Formation	Infantry Brigade	Comments
VIII	LIR 25	IR 28, IR 68	30 Inf. Brig.	–
	LIR 28	IR 25	29 Inf. Brig.	–
	LIR 29	IR 65	80 Inf. Brig.	–
	LIR 65	IR 68, IR 160	30 and 80 Inf. Brig.	–
	LIR 68	IR 29	31 Inf. Brig.	–
IX	LIR 31	IR 31, IR 85	36 Inf. Brig.	–
	LIR 75	IR 75, IR 76	33 Inf. Brig.	4 battalions
	LIR 76	IR 75, GR 89, FR 90	33 and 34 Inf. Brig.	5 battalions
	LIR 84	IR 84, 85, 86	35 and 36 Inf. Brig.	–
	LIR 85	IR 84, IR 86	35 Inf. Brig.	–
	LIR 86	–	35 Inf. Brig.	mobilized 1917
X	LIR 73	IR 74	38 Inf. Brig.	–
	LIR 74	IR 79, IR 92, IR 164	39 and 40 Inf. Brig.	–
	LIR 77	IR 78, IR 91	37 Inf. Brig.	–
	LIR 78	IR 77, IR 92	40 Inf. Brig.	–
XI	LIR 32	IR 32, IR 94	44 and 83 Inf. Brig.	–
	LIR 71	IR 71, IR 96	76 and 83 Inf. Brig.	–
	LIR 82	IR 95	76 Inf. Brig.	2 battalions
	LIR 83	IR 83, IR 94, IR 167	43, 44 and 83 Inf. Brig.	–
	LIR 94	–	76 Inf. Brig.	mobilized 1917
XII	LIR 100	LKeib-GR 100	45 Inf. Brig.	–
	LIR 101	IR 102, 103	63 Inf. Brig.	static, 4 battalions
	LIR 102	–	*Ldw. Insp.*	–
	LIR 103	–	64 Inf. Brig.	mobilized 1915
XIII	LIR 119	IR 119, IR 125, IR 180	51 and 54 Inf. Brig.	static, 4 battalions
	LIR 120	IR 121	52 Inf. Brig.	static
	LIR 121	IR 122, IR 125	51 and 52 Inf. Brig.	static, 4 battalions
	LIR 122	IR 120, 123	53 and 54 Inf. Brig.	static
	LIR 123	IR 120, IR 124	53 and 54 Inf. Brig.	static
	LIR 124	IR 120	54 Inf. Brig.	–
	LIR 125	IR 120	54 Inf. Brig.	–
	LIR 126	–	51 Inf. Brig.	mobilized 1915

Army Corps	Landwehr Regiment	Mobilizing Formation	Infantry Brigade	Comments
XIV	LIR 40	IR 110	55 Inf. Brig.	–
	LIR 109	–	*Ldw. Insp.*	–
	LIR 110	IR 113, IR 142	57 and 58 Inf. Brig.	4 battalions
	LIR 111	–	56 Inf. Brig.	mobilized 1916
XV	LIR 99	IR 99, IR 136, IR 177	60, 82 and 85 Inf. Brig.	4 battalions
XVI	LIR 30	IR 98	66 and 86 Inf. Brig.	–
XVII	LIR 5	?	70 Inf. Brig. (?)	–
	LIR 21	IR 128	71 Inf. Brig.	static
	LIR 61	IR 61	70 Inf. Brig.	static, 2 battalions
XVIII	LIR 80	FR 80, IR 88	41 and 42 Inf. Brig.	–
	LIR 81	IR 81	42 Inf. Brig.	–
	LIR 87	IR 87, IR 118	41 and 50 Inf. Brig.	static, 4 battalions
	LIR 116	IR 115, 116	49 Inf. Brig.	–
	LIR 118	IR 117, 118	50 Inf. Brig.	–
XIX	LIR 104	IR 104, 181	88 Inf. Brig.	–
	LIR 105	–	47 Inf. Brig.	mobilized 1917
	LIR 106	IR 106, IR 134	48 and 89 Inf. Brig.	–
	LIR 107	IR 133	89 Inf. Brig.	–
	LIR 133	IR 106, IR 139, IR 179	47 and 48 Inf. Brig.	static
XX	LIR 18	IR 18, 59, 147, 152	72, 73 and 74 Inf. Brig.	4 battalions
XXI	LIR 17	IR 70 (?), IR 174	32 Inf. Brig.	2 battalions
	LIR 60	IR 60	62 Inf. Brig.	2 battalions
I KB	bayer. LIR 1	IR 1	1 bayer. Inf. Brig.	4 battalions
	bayer. LIR 2	IR 2, IR 16	2 bayer. Inf. Brig.	4 battalions
	bayer. LIR 3	IR 3, IR 20	3 bayer. Inf. Brig.	–
	bayer. LIR 12	IR 12, IR 15	4 bayer. Inf. Brig.	–
	bayer. LIR 15	–	3 bayer. Inf. Brig.	mobilized December 1914
II KB	bayer. LIR 4	IR 5, IR 9	7 bayer. Inf. Brig.	–
	bayer. LIR 5	IR 9, IR 18, IR 23	5, 6 and 7 bayer. Inf. Brig.	–
	bayer. LIR 8	IR 17	6 bayer. Inf. Brig.	static, 2 battalions

Army Corps	Landwehr Regiment	Mobilizing Formation	Infantry Brigade	Comments
III KB	bayer. LIR 6	IR 7, IR 19	10 bayer. Inf. Brig.	–
	bayer. LIR 7	IR 13, IR 14	9 and 11 bayer. Inf. Brig.	–
	bayer. LIR10	IR 6, IR 10, IR 11, IR 13	11 and 12 bayer Inf. Brig.	static, 4 battalions

(Kraus, 2012), pp. 270–274.

During the war, only a few further Landwehr regiments were mobilized. Those regiments were assembled from extra Landwehr or Landsturm battalions and were merged together into regiments. Later mobilizations were numbered outside the regular numbering system and received their own numbers—usually in the 300 or 400 range. In addition to the regiments listed here, numerous temporary or surplus formations existed, sometimes named after cities, sometimes after their leaders. It seems as if the line between Landwehr and Landsturm was not always clear.

Landwehr regiments mobilized after August 1914

Year	Newly mobilized Landwehr regiments
1914	LIR 56, bayer. LIR 15
1915	LIR 57, 93, 103, 126, 349, 350, 379, 382
1916	LIR 111, 383, 384, 385, 386, 387, 388, 429, 430, 435, 436
1917	LIR 86, 94, 105, 153, 327, 328, Landwehr infantry battalion 89

(Kraus, 2012) p. 274.

Including the listed regiments, there were 127 Landwehr regiments. At the outset of the war, 56 mobile Landwehr regiments were assigned to 28 Landwehr brigades, which were operating in the rear army areas as "Mixed Landwehr Brigades" (*gemischte Landwehr Brigaden*), securing communications lines and garrisoning occupied cities and fortresses. Some Landwehr brigades were even merged together into Landwehr divisions; in the east, there was the Landwehr Corps Woyrsch. This created particular difficulties, because these improvised divisions lacked almost everything at the beginning of the war. They had no machineguns, only a few artillery pieces, no field kitchens, very few supply and train formations, and very poor medical support.

Twenty-one Landwehr regiments were static and garrisoned fortresses, mainly in the east; even these static regiments were soon used as operational formations. Landwehr regiments had small staffs compared with active or reserve regiments. They only had four officers and seven men—even fewer than the hastily mobilized September and December 1914 reserve regiments. Landwehr infantry battalions had 25 officers and 1,016 NCOs and EM and were only slightly smaller than active infantry battalions. Some Landwehr battalions, particularly static formations, were on a low budget with only 25 officers and 816 men. These static regiments also had smaller staffs, only three officers and two NCOs. In contrast to the mobile regiments, static regiments had no train soldiers, nor any supply and transport wagons. Operational use of such static battalions outside their fortresses or garrisons was virtually impossible unless they received some improvised wagons as transportation means.

Upon mobilization the following types of active, reserve and Landwehr infantry battalions existed:

Battalion type	Officers	NCO and EM
Active infantry battalion	26	1,054
Reserve infantry battalion	26	1,038
Reserve infantry battalion, mobilized in September or December 1914	21	947
Landwehr infantry battalion	25	1,016
Landwehr infantry battalion low budget	25	816
Immobile Landwehr infantry battalion	25	1,006
Immobile Landwehr infantry battalion low budget	25	806

(Kraus, 2012), p. 276.

Because no Landwehr regiments had machineguns, a field kitchen, and fewer baggage supply and transport wagons, they had far less firepower and operational mobility than active regiments. Slowly Landwehr regiments were equipped with machinegun platoons, very often equipped with captured machineguns of various French, British, and Russian models; this resulted in firing ammunition that was difficult to replace, though over time, many of these weapons were rechambered to take standard German ammunition. These platoons were merged together into machinegun companies during 1915 and uniformly equipped with MG 08/15. By the end of 1916, Landwehr regiments usually had three machinegun companies, the same as an active or reserve regiment.

RECRUIT CLASSES

The large bulk of the reserve and Landwehr soldiers were absorbed in the initial expansion of the Army that took place in July and August 1914. By September 1914, the Ersatz-Reserve filled out the newly formed reserve divisions. The class of 1914 was called up more or less on time at the end of September 1914. They were inducted into the military, along with the *Restanten* of the 1914 muster and mixed in with certain Kriegsfreiwillige. Their induction took more than three months as they filled the depots after the Ersatz-Reserve. This resulted in approximately one million recruits. They had three or four months of training and refilled the existing units, as well as creating reserve divisions that were numbered 75 to 82 and the Bavarian 8th Infantry Division.[70] When mobilization came, not every soldier was jumping for joy. Specifically, those that were in the second year of their mandatory

[70] (The General Staff, 1918), p. 14.

training and were due to leave the Army in six weeks. Many of those soldiers reported a feeling of great depression. The songs the soldiers sang tended not to be patriotic, but rather dreams of leaving.[71]

After the losses of the winter 1914–1915, the Landsturm made up for the losses. Landsturm classes were called up in successive batches and continued to provide replacements until the second contingent was exhausted late in 1915. Between April and June 1915, the class of 1915 was called up early and was followed very quickly by the class of 1916 between August and November. The permanently unfit soldiers from the musters, as well as those previously excused, were re-examined for possible inclusion in the ranks.[72]

THE SPIRIT OF 1914

Conventional wisdom has it that all of imperial Germany rejoiced at the war and rushed to the colors. A study by Jeffrey Verhey exposed the dichotomies of this spirit. The notion of the "Spirit of 1914" was primarily used later in the war as a propaganda tool. There certainly was a thread of truth in it, but the primary enthusiasm was found mostly in the larger cities and among members of the bourgeoisie. It was also true in student societies where students held large demonstrations supporting the war with both singing and drinking.[73] It is true that in August of 1914, national flags were spotted in the working-class suburbs of Berlin. On the other hand, there was a meeting in Düsseldorf where the government tried to decide how to get the working class in the Ruhr to fly the national flag.[74]

Social Democrats were absent from these demonstrations. In some locations, the socialists held rallies in favor of peace. This often led to confrontations with student groups late in July 1914. Sometimes these became violent and the police sided with the patriotic student groups. These scenes between the student groups and the Social Democrats indicated a real lack of patriotic unanimity.[75] In early August, the population was tense but, when the newspaper reports of late August reported victory, patriotism swelled. A type of social panic was present in the background of these demonstrations. Banks stopped making loans after thousands of depositors removed their savings. Some banks actually restricted withdrawals. Some merchants stopped taking paper money. Food stores witnessed panic that emptied the shelves. Visitors and foreigners fled. Newspapers were the primary form of information distribution but this information flow was augmented in taverns that provided meeting places where news could be shared.[76]

There are many *Aufmarschphotos* of young soldiers heading out to the front. As was the tradition of the time, their uniforms were adorned with flowers, and they were given so much candy that the Red Cross actually had to ask for people to hold back their generosity as the soldiers were getting sick.[77] The national outpouring of support for soldiers was said to have led to a propensity for German Red Cross nurses to become romantically involved with French prisoners. But, by 1916 the enthusiasm of crowds had disappeared.

---

71 (Neiberg, 2011), p. 142.
72 (The General Staff, 1918), p. 14.
73 (Verhey, *The Spirit of 1914*, 2000)
74 (Verhey, *The Spirit of 1914*, 2000), pp. 110–111.
75 (Chickering, *The Great War and Urban Life in Germany*, 2007), p. 60–63.
76 (Chickering, *The Great War and Urban Life in Germany*, 2007), pp. 64–65.
77 (Verhey, *The Spirit of 1914*, 2000), p. 2.

Given the law of unintended consequences, the civilian countryside certainly became emptier. Huge numbers of gainfully employed, working age individuals went off to military service. Most of these soldiers' families had been living on the edge of poverty anyway. The Federal Government on 4 August implemented a law that provided separation allowances to the families of soldiers. The departure of the workers led hundreds of firms to close their doors, creating unemployment for other workers.[78]

[78] (Chickering, *The Great War and Urban Life in Germany*, 2007), pp. 69–70.

CHAPTER 17

EXECUTION ISSUES

Imperial Germany lost the war. The German army failed to win the initial battle at the Marne River. There are manifold reasons for that, not just societal norms, army structure, and doctrine. The problem of operational execution is the first reason for defeat that comes to mind. None of the units had fought or even trained together. The German armies were untried, built on tradition and lore that had been embellished by 40 years of peace. The army was made up of inexperienced soldiers and inexperienced leaders placed in positions of unnatural stress with weapons. There were three major organizational deficiencies, discussed in previous chapters that could have been corrected by the German staff before the start of the war. Although there were many problems, the focus of this discussion is on the following three major areas: leadership issues, logistics, and the cavalry; and, there are significant overlaps within these issues. There was no doubt that there would have been problems specific to men with no battlefield experience. On 8 August 1914, for example, General v. Einem complained that many soldiers had fired on friendly forces.[1] But, putting aside the problems born of inexperience, what is left are systematic problems.

LEADERSHIP CRACKS

The Auftragstaktik Problem

As discussed in Chapter 12 on infantry doctrine, the years after 1871 were characterized by an intense discussion about two conflicting trends. The conventional tacticians or *Normaltaktiker* (spearheaded by General-Major v. Scherff and Colonel v. Boguslawski) were supporters of tight control, who wanted to specify battle actions down to the last detail. These conventional tacticians argued that detailed orders would counteract the dispersal effect brought about by the devastating impact of enemy fire and the supposed unrestrained independence at lower command levels. On the other side were the mission-type command supporters of *Auftragstaktik* (spearheaded by Lieutenant General v. Schlichting), who urged the independence of small units. Schlichting stated that mission-type command was the necessary consequence of modern combat. The resulting ever-thinner firing lines made it difficult for company grade officers to tightly control their platoons and

1 (Herwig H., 2009), p. 115.

companies. The mission-command supporters did not want to issue detailed orders limiting the freedom of action of the lower leadership levels. Rather mission-type command supporters assigned each unit a clearly defined task—the mission. Although Auftragstaktik was incorporated into German military doctrine in the 1888 infantry manual, it still met resistance.[2] Prior to the war in 1914, Auftragstaktik formed a permanent part of officer and General Staff training.

On lower command levels, Auftragstaktik proved to be an excellent tool that increased the combat the effectiveness of German formations during the war. Auftragstaktik helped by increasing flexibility and reactivity. Flexibility was of particular importance in combat situations in which higher command levels were frequently only partially informed about tactical developments and the enemy situation. Acting immediately to accomplish a mission usually proved to be more effective than waiting for further orders or information. On higher command levels, Auftragstaktik was also a perfect tool to increase combat effectiveness. In 1914, higher level command and control connections were poor and slow. The headquarters connecting the seven armies in the west had only a single Morse-type telegraph transmitter. Its range was limited to just 300 km under ideal weather conditions, and it required relay stations. As a result, transmission delays of up to 24 hours happened frequently. In addition, the radio signals coming from the Eiffel Tower usually drowned out the German messages, so that they were interrupted and required retransmission. Wire connections had only gone as far as the Luxembourg border by as late as 3 September. The two most important armies on the right wing had unreliable radio communications with each other; communication was only possible by making use of messengers and liaison officers. Their subordinate corps had no communication with the army headquarters. After the battle of Mons, First Army established communications with the subordinate corps by wire. Second Army established wire communication only after the battle of St. Quentin. Cavalry divisions were equipped with two light and two heavy radio stations each, which were of very limited range. The radio stations were also quite unpopular among the cavalry commanders.

Schlieffen described the Supreme Commander as a kind of a modern Alexander (referring to the ancient Greek King, Alexander the Great) sitting in a comfortable chair in his headquarters, bent over a map following the operations of his armies and sending encouraging messages by telephone to his army commanders.[3] The younger Moltke saw himself as the intellectual mastermind behind the beginning of operations, in that he had overhauled the Schlieffen doctrine during his term as a Chief of General Staff and adapted it to current operational and technical developments. Moltke was certainly personally brave, as he had shown as a young *Fähnrich* during the battle of Weissenburg on 4 August 1870, but he did not want to play the role of the heroic military leader. He wanted to convince by his sparkling intelligence rather than by determined military behavior. Groener, who was a confirmed Schlieffen follower, was heavily biased about Moltke as the responsible leader, who had, in his opinion, gambled away the sure recipe of victory by watering down the Schlieffen plan. Groener called Moltke a reluctant commander in his book written in 1931 and accused Moltke of softness, weakness, and the lack of guts to guide his army commanders and to keep them on the track of victory.[4]

In peacetime, Moltke had the reputation of being a highly intellectual analyst with a very courteous, friendly attitude towards his fellow commanders and other officers. In the

---

2 (Widder, 2002), pp. 4–5.
3 (Schlieffen, 1909), pp. 15–16.
4 (Groener, 1931), pp. XI-XVI.

1920s and 1930s, there were additional criticisms raised about Moltke, saying he was under the influence of his wife Eliza *Gräfin* v. Moltke-Huitfeld and of the anthroposophist Rudolf Steiner. He was denounced for spiritualism and occultism. The head of the Military Cabinet, Graf v. Hülsen-Haeseler, had called him a religious dreamer. "Luckily" Moltke died from a stroke in June 1916 and because he could no longer defend himself, he became the ideal scapegoat for the 1914 disaster. Due to the way he was appointed as Schlieffen's successor in 1905, Moltke always felt that he was a kind of a compromise between all involved stakeholders, a less-than-ideal solution. This was a view shared by many among the top ranks of the army.[5]

An in-depth analysis of the 1914 Battle of the Marne is beyond the scope of this book, so no more will be said about the younger Moltke's military career. It is, however, important to understand that Moltke tried to avoid direct personal confrontation. He was not a tough and resolute military leader who rolled over any kind of resistance and countervailing opinions like a steamroller—a leader who would sell his soldiers' lives by the millions to achieve final victory. If Moltke wanted to be successful in 1914, he needed one of two things: either a permanently available direct communication channel with his army commanders to discuss changes in the operational situation and to pass on his ideas and directives, or Army Groups (*Heeresgruppen*) and army group commanders positioned between him and his army commanders to translate the directives of the OHL into orders and clear, explicit guidance. Army groups could have been geographically closer to the army commands. These group HQs should have been located halfway between OHL in Koblenz or Luxembourg and the army commands. The shortened distance would have helped bridge the communications gaps exposed by poor radio or telegraph communications. The distances between headquarters was certainly a problem that had never occurred during peacetime maneuvers. During maneuvers the civilian telephone network had always been available for military communication. Furthermore, vigorous army group commanders could have provided robust leadership, influencing the actions of the army commanders in ways that Moltke was reluctant to pursue. Unfortunately, neither of these two options was available in 1914.

The Reverse Side of Auftragstaktik

The German army that was fielded in 1914 has been described in detail in earlier chapters The composition of its units and formations—be they active, reserve, or *Landwehr*—has been analyzed. Focus was brought to supply problems and logistical processes. The doctrines of the different arms have been described, as has the way in which they were translated into daily training and maneuvers. Finally, a detailed examination of officers' and of General Staff officers' recruitment and training has been provided. A picture has been developed of an army taking pride in its leading military role. This army was proud to have been a role model for many other armies including Japan, Russia, Sweden, and numerous other countries in Europe and South America. This was an army that boasted the best General Staff in the world that had the sure recipe for victory in the coming Great War. The German army was known as a center of military excellence. Then, suddenly, because of major professional and systemic failures, this army found itself in an adverse situation only six weeks after the start of the war; this was a situation that was regarded by several members of the military elite as tantamount to losing the war, or at least having forfeited sure victory.

---

5 (Mombauer, 2003), pp. 46–59.

How could this failure happen to an army that considered itself superior to all other armies in the world? In the following paragraphs on leadership problems and the misapplication of Auftragstaktik, there will be no comment on operational decisions. There will be no analysis concerning when and how the Germans lost the Battle at the Marne, nor will there be any discussion of the failed coup de main on Liège or of the bloody battles fought in August and September 1914. Instead, the focus will be on the leadership and decision-making processes on the German side. In order to analyze these failures, we will explore several significant situations.

In contrast to many officers on lower command levels, army commanders had extremely strong-willed personalities and needed to be directed by an equally strong-willed Supreme Commander or Chief of General Staff. Army commanders were used to having their own way on operational and strategic problems. These individuals had participated in the debate about the development of tactical doctrine during the past decades and had their own positions. Bülow, the Commander of the Second Army, was known as a systematic and formalistic drill-master. Kluck, the commander of the First Army, was willing to take risks, to move quickly, and to pursue success—if necessary at all costs. Kuhl, who was Kluck's Chief of Staff, was a comparatively aggressive, fast moving, and belligerent personality bent on success. Putting Kluck and Kuhl under Bülow's control led to difficulties and friction right from the beginning of the operation. A similar situation was found on the left wing, where the Bavarian Crown Prince was Commander of the Sixth Army and Heeringen was Commander of the Seventh Army. Heeringen had a significant and well-known dislike for the Bavarians as a result of his term as War Minister between 1909 and 1913. Because the Seventh Army was under the control of the Sixth Army, it soon became obvious that Heeringen tried to slip out of this arrangement, leading to severe friction in the cooperation between both armies. This was made worse by Moltke's ambiguity about the strategic and operational goals set for Sixth and Seventh Army. Originally, the left wing armies were designed to shield the left flank of the huge attack wing wheeling around Paris. However, Moltke was also influenced by the idea of breaking through the French fortress belt along the river Moselle in the course of a massive pursuit operation once French Second Army was defeated in a major battle in Lorraine. This would permit the creation of a huge double-pincer movement, annihilating the entire French army.

In both cases, it was Moltke's task to keep these armies on track and within the missions he gave them. With the poor communication lines between the OHL and the army commands, this turned out to be very difficult to achieve. The younger Moltke attempted to follow the leadership style of the elder Moltke, wishing to command his armies by means of short directives like his uncle did during the Unification Wars. The Younger probably misinterpreted the Elder's loose leadership style as a kind of Auftragstaktik leadership doctrine. In reality, much of the elder Moltke's leadership style was forced on him due to the very poor communication lines that allowed only short directives transmitted by Morse telegraph. The leadership of the younger Moltke was in direct contrast to the leadership Schlieffen had executed and described as the role model in an article in the *Deutsche Revue* printed in 1909. Schlieffen was also an advocate of Auftragstaktik but had a different understanding of its execution.[6]

The first situation for analysis is the advance of the right wing through Belgium and France with the First and Second Army as the spearheads. After the capture of Liège, the

[6] (Müller-Loebnitz, 1939), pp. 15–16.

First and Second Army had to deploy forward and then advance in a coordinated way in accordance with the guidance provided by the OHL. This advance demanded clear leadership, either by establishing a stable communication channel through telephone, radio, or telegraph, or by having an army group headquarters set up to control the operations of the right wing on behalf of OHL. Instead, OHL tried to somehow muddle through with the available resources and existing poor communications channels. As long as the army HQs were still based in Germany, communication by telephone was straightforward. However, in the operations departments of OHL, only a handful of officers reporting directly to the Chief of General Staff were available to carry out the necessary operational analysis and planning or to handle contact with the armies in the west and in the east.[7]

Staffing of OHL Departments Controlling Tactical Operations

Department	Number of field grade officers	Number of company grade officers
Central Department	1	1
Operations Department	4	8
Intelligence Department	2	11
Political Department	1	0

This staffing had been sufficient to command armies of the same size and in the same way as occurred in 1866 or 1870. For the complex operations of eight armies in two different theaters, the operational departments of the OHL were certainly understaffed to actually manage the necessary command and control functions.

Kluck opposed Bülow's control from the start of the operations, seeing himself in competition with Bülow, and developing his own interpretation of the mission assigned to him. For his part, Bülow did not execute control over the First Army too tightly. Bülow never ordered Kluck to obey him, he never entered into a head-on confrontation with Kluck; Bülow always just asked for support and tried to align the operations of First and Second Army in accordance with the directives set by the OHL. The OHL only discovered where operational objectives were in conflict when it received the separate evening reports of the armies. When the Battle of Mons started, Kluck officially asked for the first time to be released from Bülow's control. The Battle of Mons of the First Army against the British Expeditionary Forces (BEF) and the parallel Battle of Namur of the Second Army against the French Fifth Army revealed for the first time that Kluck and Bülow were aiming at competing targets. Bülow wanted the First Army acting as a flank guard, while he enveloped the French Fifth Army from the West. This plan would complete the envelopment started by Second and Third Army. Kluck instead intended to attack the BEF with all available power.

Kluck's plan was not a refusal to obey orders, but it was certainly an over-interpretation of the freedom of decision given to him. Mission-type leadership could only work if the superior commander organized logical command structures and reporting lines, together with clear missions and goals. The subordinate leader could then act clearly and without ambiguity within the given intentions of the superior leader. The result of the diverging operations

7 Please check out detailed staffing of these positions in the Ordre de Bataille, given in Appendix F. In addition to these officers, there were only a couple of NCOs to handle legwork.

of First and Second Army led to suboptimal results: although the BEF and the French Fifth Army had been beaten, both formations managed to escape without being caught in envelopment and without being pursued. Moltke should have drawn the correct conclusion from this, and he should have taken steps to make sure that Kluck accomplished the missions assigned to him.

This is not an attempt to picture Kluck as a kind of pariah in the west. When starting an offensive, a determined and resolute commander like Kluck was certainly important to push forward the offensive with the necessary aggression. We should never forget that the First Army between Mons and the Marne produced a marching performance that was beyond anything seen previously in military history. Only the mechanized operations of the Second World War led to faster movements covering longer distances. A commander like Kluck required a strong hand to channel his energy to the correct target. Certainly Kluck was one of the best German army commanders in 1914. His Chief of Staff, Kuhl, was one of the masterminds among the higher general staff officers. However, Moltke gave Kluck too much leeway and let him and the First Army slip out of control.

The next incident to be examined came on 2 September. The OHL issued a directive imposing a clear directional change for the armies of the right wing. Instead of marching on in a southwesterly direction and wheeling around west of Paris, Moltke now directed the armies south, passing to the east of Paris. Consequently, the OHL assigned to the First Army the task of guarding the right flank of the advancing right wing and following the Second Army in echelon. This directive was a reaction by the OHL to the assembly of French forces in and around Paris. OHL also reinforced the directive issued on 27 August.

This directive of 2 September found Kluck in a difficult situation: he was already about one day's march ahead of the Second Army and pushing into the flank of the enemy in front of the Second Army. The directive required him to halt his army for two days—one day to allow Bülow to catch up and another day to be overtaken by Bülow. For an aggressive commander like Kluck, a two-day pause was out of the question, particularly because it meant that his rival Bülow would then be in advance of his army. Even more problematic for him, however, was the mission to regroup the First Army to act as a flank guard oriented toward Paris.

Kluck and Kuhl decided to make use of the ambiguity of the directive and to deceive the OHL. Kluck decided that the First Army would only leave the comparatively weak IV Reserve Corps as flank guard to protect against the French Sixth Army assembling east of Paris. As far as the rest of the directive was concerned, Kluck decided to focus upon the mission to squeeze off the Allied forces in front of First and Second Armies. According to his interpretation, only the First Army could accomplish this mission because it was already clearly ahead of the Second Army and in the flank of the enemy forces.[8] This interpretation was not only sophism, but also came close to rank disobedience. Kluck did not discuss his decision with the OHL; he only informed Moltke by transmitting his orders and goals for First Army on 4 September and not until then could Moltke see that he was not following his directive.

This reaction of the First Army led to a dispute between the department heads of the OHL and Moltke. Tappen called Kluck's response to the directive of the OHL an act of disobedience and urged Moltke to consider a dismissal. Moltke refused, referring to the doctrine of Auftragstaktik. Instead, the OHL would make the operational goals for the continuation of

---

[8] (Haffner, 1982), pp. 48–50.

the advance so crystal clear that Kluck would be left no room for maneuver; he would be forced to follow Moltke's intentions.[9]

On 4 September, the OHL issued a new directive by radio message to all armies in the west that implied an even more radical change in strategic direction.[10] This directive clearly laid down that the First Army was to remain between the rivers Oise and Marne (i.e, north of the river Marne); the Marne bridges around Château Thierry were to be captured and held for future crossings. Second Army between the rivers Marne and Seine was to occupy the Marne bridges between Nogent and Méry sur Seine. HKK 2 remained with First Army but deployed one cavalry division to HKK 1. HKK 1 remained with Second Army and was to deploy one cavalry division to the Third Army.

At a glance, this directive ordered an extremely difficult move, aimed at diverting both First and Second Army from their advance across the Marne to form a shield against Paris instead. This would be a difficult and complex move, especially when the train and supply formations trailing behind the armies were taken into consideration. In addition, this directive was based on a completely different operational approach compared with the advance thus far. If ever the OHL under Moltke had followed any kind of Schlieffen plan or Schlieffen doctrine, its goals were abandoned from the moment of issue of this directive. In short, the directive amounted to a complete strategic turn around and put an end to the *Blitzkrieg*-style advance in the west.[11] Moltke and the OHL had obviously realized that the initial goal of enveloping the entire French and British forces had failed; they realized that the French forces around Paris would impose a massive threat on the right flank of the advancing armies—particularly to the flank of the First Army. They had accepted the consequence and ordered two armies to face against Paris and the other armies to slowly and carefully continue their advance with much more limited objectives. Finally, the OHL had admitted that the German opening moves in the west had bogged down; the initial operational attempt had failed, and that the German forces had to regroup for a second attempt.

In contrast to the OHL, the army commanders in the west, at least the army commanders of the First through the Fifth Armies, still thought they were on the final stage of the road to victory. The army commanders thought it would simply require a last huge effort to beat the already routed and weakened Allied forces. However, the latest directive implied such a radical change for the continuation of the operations that it had been necessary for the Chief of General Staff to explain in person his situational analysis, his reasons, and his intentions to the army commanders so that they would act according to his plan and his intentions. This meant that Moltke ought to have either called the army commanders to Luxembourg for a joint briefing or to have toured the army HQs to explain the changes to the army commanders individually. Instead Moltke sent General Staff officers to the army HQs to brief the directive. Lieutenant Colonel Hentsch was sent to First Army Headquarters. It is easy to imagine what a difference there would have been had Chief of General Staff personally explained his intentions. As it was, a messenger delivered the explanation. Although he had the prestige of the General Staff to underpin his presence, his rank dictated that Hentsch could only meet the Chief of General Staff, General-Major v. Kuhl; the Commander, Generaloberst v. Kluck made himself unavailable. The reception of the liaison officers by the other

9 (Haffner, 1982), pp. 50–52.

10 Since the order was issued on 4 September but arrived at the army headquarters only on 5 September in the morning due to delays caused by the time consuming forwarding through radio relay stations, it is referred to as directive from 5 September in several sources.

11 (Reichsarchiv, 1926), pp. 128–133.

army commands was slightly better; at least they were able to deliver their message to the army commanders in person. Unfortunately, supplementary information that the OHL later sent in writing to the Army HQs sowed confusion instead of creating clarity.

Since the communication channels between the OHL and the army HQs were poor and time consuming, and because no intermediate command level such as an army group was available, there should have been no other choice for the Chief of General Staff than to convey such important changes in person. Morse telegraph and messengers were unequal to the task. If Moltke wanted to command in mission-type or Auftragstaktik style, he ought to have invested the necessary time and effort to lay his intentions out to the army commanders. Otherwise he could not expect them to understand and follow these intentions. Again it should be emphasized this is not a judgment or comment on the content of the decision made; the aim is simply to analyze how the decisions were made and how they were given to the army commanders and to pose the question: was this action appropriate if following the Auftragstaktik doctrine?

The analysis of the 4 September shows a defining moment during which the operations of the right wing finally slipped out of control of the OHL. Two days later, the Allied offensive on the Marne revealed the dangerous and exposed situation of the German right wing. When the climax of the battles at Marne and Ourcq was reached on 8 September, the OHL had only fragmentary information about the situation and even these bits and pieces of information were delayed due to the poor communications. Had the army commanders been sufficiently briefed about Moltke's intention on 4 September, they could have been expected to command their troops during this climax accordingly. But since the basic rules of Auftragstaktik had been already violated on 4 September, the situation spiraled increasingly out of control under the blows of the Allied attacks. The situation was exacerbated by the unresolved rivalry between Kluck and Bülow. Coming under immense pressure at the Ourcq, Kluck did not hesitate to open Bülow's right flank to enemy attacks by throwing two army corps from Montmirail to the Ourcq. This attack created the 50 km wide gap between First and Second Army that the BEF was able to exploit in its operations against the German right wing.

The climax of the battle had been reached, but instead of taking control of the situation by driving to the army HQs, the Chief of Staff remained in his headquarters in Luxembourg.[12] The OHL again sent Hentsch as a messenger to the armies to coordinate further operations. Again Hentsch did not receive a clear written order to pass on, just an ambiguous verbal directive. Even today it is unclear whether or not Hentsch was authorized to order a retreat. So Hentsch became the scapegoat for the disaster at the Marne, "luckily" he also passed away later in the war and could not defend himself during the fierce debates during the 1920s.

Moltke's counterpart, Joffre, reacted differently to a similar situation. The French *grand quartier général* (GQG) was quite a small organization built around a handful of field grade general staff officers just like the German OHL.[13] But one of the major differences was in the structure at the top. While in the German Army, the Kaiser was still the Supreme Commander and Moltke acted formally on his behalf, in the French Army the Chief of General

---

[12] On 9 September, the distance between the OHL in Luxembourg and the First Army headquarters in Mareuil was about 331 kilometers. Considering that Hentsch visited the Army HQs of Fifth to Second Army before, he certainly covered about 500–600 kilometers before he finally visited the First Army headquarters. This movement is quite a distance if one considers the poor conditions of the roads (which were congested by supply columns and trains) and the technical fragility of the cars.

[13] The French GQG had the following departments:—1er Bureau (Personnel),—2ème Bureau (Military intelligence),—3ème Bureau (Operations),—Direction de l'Arrière (Supply and logistics),—Direction des chemins de fer (DCF) (Military railroad).

Staff became Supreme Commander of the Army upon mobilization reporting to War Minister and President. Unlike Moltke, Joffre had a second in command: Général Henri Mathias Berthelot, the Chief of Staff of the GQG, who freed Joffre up to personally visit the army commands and the BEF.[14] On the French side, the commander of the Fifth Army, Général Lanrezac, was an equally aggressive and determined commander like Kluck. He was regarded as the best French army commander and, like Kluck, tended to develop his own interpretation of orders and directions issued by the Supreme Commander. Unlike Kluck, however, Lanrezac could appear personally rude and impolite in communication.

Lanrezac's personality first came into focus on 17 August, when Field Marshal French, the Commander of the BEF, paid his inaugural visit to Général Lanrezac at his headquarters in Rethel. French tried to create a relaxed atmosphere by starting with some casual conversation. In response, Lanrezac verbally attacked him for being late. French again tried to save the situation by asking Lanrezac in French for his opinion about the intended operations of the German Third Army: "What do you think the Germans are going to do at Huy [small fortress town at the bank of the river Meuse]?" Lanrezac turned to the interpreter and said: "Tell the [Field] Marshal, that in my opinion the Germans have merely gone to the Meuse to fish."[15] From that moment on, French would never be willing to pardon this insulting behavior. From their first encounter, the working relationship between both commanders was poor. Some days later the BEF was engaged at Mons, and Lanrezac barely saved his army from envelopment by a retreat—the lost Battle of Namur. Lanrezac blamed the British for exposing his left flank to the German attacks.

A few days later, on 28 August, Joffre ordered the French Fifth Army to launch a counterattack at Guise and St. Quentin against the advancing Second German Army under Bülow, who had already beaten him at Namur. Lanrezac felt himself threatened by far superior German forces moving against him—the Second Army in front of him, the First Army on his left flank, and the Third Army on his right flank. Because he believed that the British were already too far behind and would not be available to cover his left flank, Lanrezac refused to carry out this order. Joffre reacted very similarly to Moltke in comparable situations: he sent a messenger, Colonel Alexandre from the GQG, to Lanrezac to explain his intentions. Again Lanrezac clearly refused to follow this order.

On 29 August, Joffre personally drove to the headquarters of the Fifth French Army, accompanied by Major Maurice Gustave Gamelin (who would become Allied Supreme Commander 25 years later in the autumn of 1939) to drive his order home. The distance between the French GQG in Vitry le François and the Fifth Army headquarters was about 189 km—significantly less than the distance between Luxembourg and the HQs of the German right wing armies. Joffre was determined to dismiss Lanrezac on the spot if he still refused to obey. The following Battle of St. Quentin ended with another tactical defeat for the already beaten Fifth Army. But Joffre successfully interrupted the German advance and won time to assemble the French Sixth Army in the German flank. A couple of days later, right before the decisive offensive of the Marne, Joffre finally dismissed Lanrezac and replaced him by Franchet d'Esperey; Joffre had still not forgotten Lanrezac's disobedience at St. Quentin.

---

14 The French Army had only two different generals ranks: général de brigade and général de division. All corps commanders and all army commanders were général de division.

15 (Spears E., 2000), p. 75. In the renowned BBC TV series (in cooperation with the Imperial War Museum), "The Great War" from 1964, Lieutenant Edward Spears is interviewed in Episode 3 ("We must hack our way through."), Part 4 ("War flows westward.") personally describing this key scene.

A comparison of the command styles of Moltke and Joffre reveals two entirely different patterns. While Moltke remained in his headquarters and restricted himself to issuing directives and sending messengers, Joffre took personal action when necessary and personally visited the army commands to bring order and insist on obedience. Joffre felt it more important to maintain his command authority than to retain in place intelligent, but insubordinate leaders. This comparison casts a harsh light on Auftragstaktik. Certainly this doctrine, (which could today be described as Management by Exceptions) required a strong—ideally charismatic—leader with a good deal of natural authority. After issuing his directive and explaining his intentions (ideally face-to-face with the army commanders), the leader had to be visible, had to ask for intermediate reports, had to encourage and motivate to follow his directions, and had to offer support if exceptional or unexpected situations jeopardized his goals. A commander, who remained in his headquarters without any personal contact with the army commanders between 2 August and 11 September, was running serious risks.

The second misapplication of Auftragstaktik occurred during the battles on the southern wing of the German Western Front. There were two different occasions, the first was when the Seventh Army was placed under the control of the Sixth, but tried to fight its own battles. The second instance involved the discussions between OHL and Sixth Army during the Battle in Lorraine. The first incident took place during the Battle of Mulhouse, the counterattack of the Seventh Army with XIV and XV Army Corps on 9 and 10 August 1914. In the same way that the First Army was under the control of the Second Army, Heeringen was subordinated to the Bavarian Crown Prince, but he found this command relationship irksome. By counterattacking Mulhouse, he created a highly political issue. The German operations plan envisaged the loss of territory in the *Reichslande* in case of a French offensive. It could occur on the southern stretch of Alsace, because this area was considered less important, provided that the German forces could fall back on the upper Rhine and on the fortified Breusch line west of Straßburg. The Kaiser, however, opposed any loss of German territory, even if it were in the Reichslande. Aware of this, Heeringen acted against the plans of the Sixth Army, and he also opposed Moltke's plans.

Moltke intended to draw the French Second Army deeper into Lorraine and to annihilate it in an envelopment carried out by the Sixth and Seventh Armies. When Heeringen asked for the endorsement of his counterattack from the OHL, he knew that Moltke could not turn him down without running into conflict with the Kaiser. Although Heeringen gained an initial success, it was at the cost of a delay of the German operations in the Reichslande. At the end of the Battle of Mulhouse, the XIV and XV Army Corps found themselves around Mulhouse. They were exhausted from the marches, combat, and losses; they had used up their artillery ammunition and needed to be transported back northward. Altogether the counterattack constituted a loss of three to four days for the commencement of the major operations in Lorraine. In view of the fact that the French offensive into Lorraine started on 14 August, this sidestep at Mulhouse could have caused severe problems at the joint between Sixth and Seventh Armies. Luckily, the Mulhouse operation did not lead to negative consequences, but it must have appeared to Moltke as if his operational objectives were already compromised.

Even worse for the further course of operations in the Reichslande were the ever-changing goals set by the OHL. Auftragstaktik required a clear goal and explanations of the intentions of the Supreme Commander. The first goal for the armies in the Reichslande was kept quite vague since Moltke was unclear about the French operations plan. So initial guidance amounted simply to a "wait and see" strategy. The Sixth Army's Chief of General Staff, General-Major Krafft v. Dellmensingen, documented this strategy in his aide mémoire that had received Moltke's endorsement.

After the slowing of the French offensive in Lorraine, dissent between OHL and the Sixth Army was fully exposed. The OHL wanted the Sixth Army to continue with delaying operations and to pull French forces deeper into Lorraine to be beaten by envelopment, the Sixth Army did not want to continue with the fighting retreat towards the river Saar. Dellmensingen and the Bavarian Crown Prince instead wished to take the battle to the advancing French forces in Lorraine with the help of the Seventh Army. Since he moved to Koblenz on 16–17 August, Moltke failed to visit the Sixth Army headquarters to explain his intentions personally. Instead, he sent Lieutenant Colonel v. Dommes to the Sixth Army headquarters to explain why Sixth Army was to carry out a fighting retreat and pull the French Second Army behind it. Only then, after the French Second Army exposed its flanks, were the Germans to attack. They would then launch an enveloping attack carried out by Sixth and Seventh Army in which the French could be either annihilated or beaten so seriously that the subsequent pursuit could be carried forward across the river Moselle. Once more this is not a discussion or evaluation of the operational decisions made. So it matters not whether Moltke's idea of a battle of annihilation against the French Second Army, and a subsequent counter offensive carried across the river Moselle and through the French fortress belt in pursuit of the French Second Army, would have been successful or not. But certainly this option would have been worth discussing in detail among Moltke, Dellmensingen, and the Bavarian Crown Prince in a face-to-face meeting either in Koblenz or in St. Avold.

Instead Lieutenant Colonel v. Dommes went to St. Avold lacking a clear, written directive. He did not have any maps or further details with him. Dommes completed his mission as well as he could by explaining Moltke's intention to the Bavarian Crown Prince and to Dellmensingen. But, the Crown Prince came to the conclusion that a further fighting retreat and delay would mean the risk of ending up with a "passive" defense deep in the Reichslande. It is probable that this "defense" referred to the Nied position that had been prepared for exactly that purpose. Together with his chief of staff, the Crown Prince came to the decision that an immediate decision against the already shaken French Second Army would offer a lower risk than further withdrawal.[16] So, on 17 August, the Sixth Army ordered Seventh Army to join the offensive in Lorraine that was planned to start on 19 August. Lieutenant Colonel v. Dommes had done his best but could not dissuade the Bavarian Crown Prince from a premature attack. Crown Prince Rupprecht, on the other hand, clearly acted within the limits of Auftragstaktik by deciding to do what he did. Without Moltke convincing him, or ordering him, to act differently, the operations had to take their course.

As Moltke anticipated, the attack of the Sixth Army resulted in a frontal victory (Schlieffen had called it an "ordinary victory") over the French. The French Second Army was beaten again, but it was not annihilated and could still conduct a systematic retreat behind the French fortress line. This situation was obviously exaggerated by the upbeat victory reports of the Sixth Army. Communication connections between OHL and Sixth Army were through the German homeland telephone network. Still the OHL had only fragmentary knowledge of the situation in Lorraine. As a consequence, Moltke ordered vigorous pursuit of the beaten French forces to prevent them from shifting troops to Northern France where they would encounter the German right wing advancing towards Paris. Knowing about the real situation, however, the Sixth Army carried out only a very cautious and half-hearted pursuit.

[16] (Xylander, 1935), p. 80.

On 25 August, Moltke sent another messenger, Major v. Redern, to Sixth Army headquarters. Redern verbally delivered a directive from Moltke setting the breakthrough of the French fortress belt between Toul and Épinal as a new operational objective for the Sixth Army.[17] The pursuit of the beaten French Second Army was to be driven forward across the river Moselle. Sixth Army immediately had to start pounding French positions around Nancy with heavy artillery. Again the liaison officer arrived empty-handed so, once more, he could not hand over a written directive or a map explaining the operational objectives. In addition, reality had started to overtake the operations plans of the OHL. The French Second Army had begun a fierce counterattack against the German Sixth Army, bringing any pursuit operations to a standstill. The fragmentary information about the real situation had created a significant gap between reality and the mission Moltke had assigned to the Sixth Army. After an intervention by the Bavarian Crown Prince, the Sixth Army was released from the mission to immediately attack the French positions at Nancy.

Just one day later the OHL issued a new directive to all armies in the west containing new missions for the Sixth and Seventh Army, which were to break through the French fortress belt between Toul and Épinal **if the French continued to withdraw**. The Seventh Army was promised independence from Sixth Army as soon as the Sixth Army had managed to cross the river Moselle.[18] This directive with its constraint "if the French continued to withdraw" was so vague that it kept open all opportunities for the Sixth Army to come up with its own interpretations without violating the doctrine of Auftragstaktik. When on 27 August, Moltke decided that he could lead a huge double-pincer envelopment of the French and British forces with both of his wings, this plan implied such a radical change from anything directed or discussed before, that he should have communicated his reasons for this strategic direction change to his army commanders face to face.[19]

Instead, the OHL once more sent a liaison officer to the Sixth Army headquarters. On 30 August Major Bauer, the artillery specialist, arrived in Dieuze to discuss plans for the destruction of the French fortifications around Nancy using heavy and super-heavy artillery. Just two days previously, the French Fort Manonviller surrendered after being pounded by heavy artillery. This coincidence convinced the Sixth Army command that the OHL was obviously serious about its breakthrough plans. The Sixth Army therefore sent its Ib officer, Major v. Xylander, to the OHL in Luxembourg to confirm the operations plan of a breakthrough. Xylander went to Luxembourg and received disturbing news. To his astonishment, Xylander was informed that the breakthrough was no longer of such a priority to the OHL as explained by Major Bauer just a day before! Dellmensingen was baffled about the continuing ambiguity of the operational directives and goals received from the OHL through Major v. Xylander, so he did his own estimate of the situation together with the Crown Prince and decided to pursue the operational objective of taking the French positions around Nancy.

There is an old proverb within the French army that is said to originate from Napoleon: *Orde—contreordre—disordre* (in English: order—counter-order—disorder). In other words, keep goals and missions clear and straightforward. Too many changes inevitably lead to misunderstandings and disorder. Disorder was the consequence of these ambiguous directives issued by the OHL. Obviously the OHL had come to the conclusion that the original Schlieffen-style Blitzkrieg approach was about to fail in the west, and it was seeking alternatives.

[17] (Xylander, 1935), pp. 136–139

[18] Please check content of the directive issued on 27 August in the time line below.

[19] Again we have to state that it is not the authors' intention to discuss here, whether such an operation was realistic or not.

But, to repeat, such fundamental strategic direction changes should have been explained to the army commanders. If the situational analysis of the OHL and Moltke's decisions were not clear to the commanders, the armies would be unable to understand and follow any order.

General Krafft v. Dellmensingen drove to Luxembourg on 2 September to receive personal guidance and to obtain clarity. Luckily, the distance between the Sixth Army headquarters in Dieuze and the OHL in Luxembourg was only about 125 kilometers, so Dellmensingen could afford to make the trip without losing a full day. In Luxembourg, Moltke convinced him to delay the attack on Nancy for a couple of days and to focus instead on the goal of pinning down as many French troops as possible in the Reichslande. Obviously Moltke was pursuing two different objectives as far as the German forces in the Reichslande were concerned. These were:[20]

1. Prevent further French forces from being deployed to the new French left wing built up around Paris.
2. Break through the French fortress belt along the river Moselle, so as to catch the bulk of the French army in a huge double pincer operation.

The sequence of these goals also reflected their priority: first prevent the French from pulling further troops out of the Reichslande, then break through across the Moselle. It is likely that the decision-making process about how to continue the offensive in the west was still going on in the OHL. Dellmensingen's visit to Luxembourg casts a sharp light on Moltke's leadership style. Dellmensingen came on his own initiative; whereas Moltke ought to have summoned the army commanders with their chiefs of staff to Luxembourg to share his situational analysis and to personally explain his directives.

On 2 September, the OHL issued the directive to the right wing armies to push the French forces away from Paris in a southeasterly direction. On 4 September (arriving at most army HQs on 5 September), the next directive followed, bringing with it the complete change of strategic direction for the right wing armies. For the Sixth and Seventh Army, the existing older directives still remained valid.

There are lessons to be learned from these events:

1. Auftragstaktik or mission-type leadership is a perfect tool of delegating a high degree of decision-making to a subordinate command level if the Supreme Commander is clear about his goals and if he can share his situation analysis with his subordinate commanders to help them understand his intentions.
2. If there are changes in strategic direction, they must be the result of a decision-making process based upon a changed situational analysis. In such cases the superior commander has to share his new insights and his new analysis to his subordinates to make them understand why the goals now are changing.
3. Such changes in strategic direction should not happen too often; otherwise the consequences of ordre—contreordre—disordre will certainly come true.

Moltke preferred to issue his directives in writing and have them transmitted by radio or Morse telegraph than convey them in person, and thereby risk conflicting questions. Moltke was a highly analytical leader, who certainly was one of the first higher German leaders to understand that the Schlieffen-style western offensive would fail. Somewhere

[20] (Xylander, 1935), pp. 135–136.

between 30 August (Battle of St. Quentin) and 4 September, he decided that he could not continue carrying on the offensive as the Germans had done during the last four weeks. Radical change was required. Communicating the directive of 4 September by radio left the army commanders confused, since they did not know about Moltke's situational analysis and therefore they did not understand what lay behind it. We can only guess that Moltke discussed his situational analysis and his ideas with his general staff officers working with him at the OHL, but obviously he did not share his intentions with anyone outside his own headquarters.

The German army did not lose the Battle of the Marne because of the performance of its soldiers. They delivered an unprecedented marching performance and were still able to enter combat successfully. Rather, the Battle of the Marne was lost by the OHL and by the German generals, army commanders, and General Staff officers. It was this military élite, who considered themselves the best in the world before 1914 that performed so poorly in August and September 1914. Finally, this poor performance was linked to the misapplication of Auftragstaktik on the higher levels. Succinctly, Moltke confused delegating some freedom of decision to his army commanders—what Auftragstaktik was all about—with conflict averse, laissez-faire behavior. Issuing written directives instead of personal contact might have worked out fairly well during peacetime war games and maneuvers, but it was just not enough to keep such a big military force on track in real war.

Timeline

The following timeline is not a comprehensive listing of all the events during the opening campaign of 1914, nor during the Battle at the Marne. Instead it lists those events that contributed to command deficiencies and the misapplication of Auftragstaktik.

2 August—First day of mobilization. Army Commanders received their deployment orders and were called to the Chief of the Great General Staff in Berlin to discuss their missions and initial operational objectives together with the strategic and operational intention of the OHL. First Army (v. Kluck) was put under the control of the Second Army (v. Bülow). Seventh Army (v. Heeringen) was put under the control of the Sixth Army (Bavarian Crown Prince Rupprecht).

2 August—The mission for the First Army given in the deployment order was as follows:

The German deployment against France is based upon the following intention: The bulk of the German armies shall move through Belgium and Luxembourg into France. If the information about French deployment is correct, the advance has to be carried out by swinging the entire right wing around the pivot point Metz-Thionville. The movement of the army shall be led and determined by the right wing. The movements of the inner armies shall be directed to always keep in touch with the pivot point Metz-Thionville. The commencement of the advance of the bulk of the army shall be ordered by OHL as soon as the right wing armies (First and Second) have completed their deployment around Liège.[21]

3 August—Oberste Heeresleitung (OHL) formed in Berlin.

[21] (Kuhl, 1921), p. 8. Please see also (Kluck, 1926), pp. 11–14.

4 August—Start of the coup de main on Liége. Although the Germans took the city of Liège on 7 August, the coup de main on the fortification belt (Liége had 12 forts) failed at the first attempt.[22]

6 August—General Krafft von Dellmensingen, Chief of General Staff Sixth Army, explained his interpretation of the deployment order and the briefing given by Moltke in an aide mémoire reflecting the operational plan of the Sixth Army for the opening moves of the Battle in the Reichslande. Moltke endorsed the aide mémoire. The general outline of this aide mémoire was as follows:[23]

- An offensive by the bulk of the French army was expected in Lorraine.
- Sixth and Seventh Armies—called group in the Reichslande (*Gruppe in den Reichslanden*) by Dellmensingen—delay the French offensive and shield the left flank of the German forces in the west until the goal of French operations finally becomes clear.
- Surprise breakthrough of French forces at the link between the Sixth and Seventh Armies must be prevented at all costs.
- Counterattack as soon as all troops of the Sixth and Seventh Armies are deployed and operationally ready.

7 August—Landing of the BEF starts in complete secrecy. The Germans receive first vague information about the BEF on 20 August.

8 August—Ft. Barchon was the first fort at Liége to surrender after being pounded by 21 cm heavy howitzers (mortars).

7–8 August—Beginning of the Battle of Mulhouse: in Southern Alsace, the French VII Corps took Mulhouse in a surprising attack on 8 August. Seventh Army asked OHL to endorse a counterattack with two army corps. After endorsement by OHL, Seventh Army informed Sixth Army that XIV and XV Army Corps would counter-attack Mulhouse. Sixth Army command was displeased about this bypassing of its control function. In the Sixth Army staff, the operation was called the Mulhouse "sidestep."[24]

9–10 August—Counterattack of Seventh Army on Mulhouse using XIV and XV Army Corps. Although Mulhouse was successfully taken back, and the first victory over French forces could be announced, the price was high: XV Army Corps was more than 100 km south of its original deployment area around Straßburg, jeopardizing the connection between the Sixth and Seventh Armies. XIV and XV Army Corps had fought their first battle day and had completely used up their stocks of artillery ammunition. The battle of Mulhouse jeopardized the entire operations plan of the Sixth and Seventh Armies for the coming battle in Lorraine.

10 August—OHL tried to bring operations back in line with the following directive: "His Majesty has ordered: Sixth and Seventh Armies, together with HKK 3 are to operate from now on under the command of the Sixth Army." This directive reinforces the directive given in the deployment order in which the Seventh Army was put under the control of the Sixth Army.

---

22 (Generalstab des Heeres 7 Ab., 1939)

23 Gackenholz, Hermann, *Entscheidung in Lothringen*, Junker und Dünnhaupt, Berlin 1935, Attachment 1.

24 (Xylander, 1935), p. 29 and (Kayser, 1942), p. 18.

11 August—Sixth Army sent the Ib officer, Major v. Xylander, to Seventh Army headquarters in Straßburg to again convey Dellmensingen's aide mémoire and to outline future cooperation. Dellmensingen expected Seventh Army to join the operations in Lorraine by 15 or 16 August at the latest. Seventh Army requested a couple of days more to rearrange its formations after the Battle of Mulhouse.

11 August—Ft. Evegnée (Liége) was taken after being pounded by heavy artillery.

12 August—The remaining forts of Liège were pounded with super heavy artillery (30.5 and 42 cm) to force them to surrender. First the forts north of Liège had to be taken to allow First and Second Army to deploy their troops forward through the Liége bottleneck before the advance on the right wing began. The forces assigned to carry out the attack on Liège, which had been fielded in peacetime strength (static) had to complete their mobilization and the absorption of reserve personnel during the fights around Liège.[25]

14 August—Start of the offensive of the French First and Second Army in Lorraine towards Saarburg and Saarbrücken.

14 August—After a surprise French attack west of Straßburg, Seventh Army cooperated only reluctantly with Sixth Army. Sixth Army informed OHL about the difficulties of obtaining compliance from Seventh Army.

16 August—The last two forts of Liège, Hollogne and Flemalle, surrendered. Due to heavy losses, the French offensive in Lorraine slowed down. Dissent between Sixth Army and OHL began to have repercussions. OHL wanted Sixth Army to continue with delay operations and to lure French forces deeper into Lorraine. Sixth Army was disinclined to continue the fighting withdrawal towards the river Saar. Dellmensingen and the Bavarian Crown Prince wanted to attack the advancing French forces in Lorraine with the help of the Seventh Army.

16–17 August—OHL moved from Berlin to Koblenz and took quarters in the palace of the former Electors of Trier (*Kurfürsten von Trier*) after the final capture of Liège and before the launch of the advance on the right wing. The OHL left Berlin by train at 07:55 a.m. on 16 August and arrived in Koblenz on 17 August in the early morning.

17 August—First and Second Armies completed deployment in Belgium along the following line: Hasselt–St Trond–positions west of Liège–Huy–Durbuy and were ready to advance. OHL informed the other armies in the west that the advance of the right wing would begin on 18 August and OHL then subordinated First Army to Second Army.

17 August—Commander Sixth Army (now called Supreme Commander in the Reichslande–*Oberbefehlshaber in den Reichslanden*) ordered Seventh Army to join a combined offensive against the French forces in Lorraine on 19 August. This order was conveyed again by messenger; Major v. Xylander acting as a kind of liaison officer from Sixth Army to Seventh Army.

---

[25] (Generalstab des Heeres 7 Ab., 1939), pp. 42–62.

17 August—OHL sent Lieutenant Colonel v. Dommes, the head of the political department, to the headquarters of the Sixth Army in St. Avold. He was there to convey and explain the intent of the OHL for the operations in the Reichslande. Moltke intended that the Sixth and Seventh Army continue delaying actions and conduct a fighting withdrawal behind the river Saar. This action would expose the French to a flanking offensive and threaten to trap them in a pocket in Lorraine. Dommes discussed these issues directly with the Bavarian Crown Prince, but, since he had neither a written directive by Moltke nor a map showing this operational plan, the Bavarian Crown Prince sent him back with the message: "The OHL might either give me the necessary freedom or direct me step-by-step." Dommes' recollection of the meeting was different; he believed that Sixth Army would do its best to continue delaying actions.

18 August—Start of the advance of First and Second Armies on the right wing.

19 August—Start of the Battle in Lorraine.

19 August—Belgian forces started to withdraw towards Antwerp. First Army headquarters moved from Grevenbroich in Germany to Louvain in Belgium. Second Army headquarters moved from Monschau in Germany to Jodoigne (about 20 kilometers southeast of Louvain) in Belgium. Second and Third Armies prepared for an attack on the fortress of Namur.

20 August—Information arrived at OHL based on articles in *The Times* that the BEF had already landed in French ports (true) and were deploying around Lille (false). Start of the combined offensive of Sixth and Seventh Army in Lorraine. After losing the Battle of Gumbinnen, Generaloberst v. Prittwitz ordered withdrawal of the Eight Army behind the river Vistula and was ready to sacrifice East Prussia to the Russians. Moltke ordered HKK 1 to move to the right of Second Army changing his original plan significantly.

20–25 August—Siege and conquest of Namur. After the bad experience at Liège, Namur was systematically pounded by heavy and super-heavy artillery from the beginning.

21 August—Information received by OHL that the BEF was about to land in Northern France but that significant landing of troops had not happened yet. In fact this was incorrect. The British I and II Corps were in their concentration areas, east of Bohain and Landrecies respectively, by 20 August. Despite any uncertainty, First Army expected to meet British forces within the next several days. Second Army changed operational goals for the First Army from a western direction to a southbound direction.

21 August—French forces in Lorraine started a withdrawal behind their fortification line.

22 August—Prittwitz was dismissed from command of the Eighth Army in Eastern Prussia. Instead Generaloberst v. Hindenburg was appointed to act as new commander together with General-Major Ludendorff as Chief of General Staff.

22 August—Between 11:00 a.m. and 12:00 p.m., cavalry patrols encountered British cavalry around Mons. In the afternoon, the IX Army Corps also reported British troops in Mons and along the *Canal du Centre* between Nimy and Ville sur Haine. "All of a sudden the British

appeared in front of us."[26] Bülow was more concerned about the French Fifth Army south of the river Sambre than of the BEF and wanted to employ the First Army as his flank guard around Maubeuge. Kluck cared more about attacking the BEF and questioned whether he was still under the control of Second Army. After all, the initial directives and the deployment orders had put First Army under the control of Bülow only for the operations around Liège. In a telephone call with Lieutenant Colonel Tappen, Kluck received the confirmation that he was still under the control of Bülow. This telephone call had been technically very difficult.

22 August—Sixth Army reported victory and "overwhelming success" to the OHL—obviously to conceal the fact that the premature attack did not achieve the expected success. OHL assigned Sixth Army the objective to pursue the beaten enemy with the intention of breaking through the French fortress belt between Toul and Épinal. The situational analysis of the OHL differed from that of the Sixth Army. Based upon the success reports of the Sixth Army the OHL seemed to believe that the French forces in Lorraine were routed, disorganized, and trying to escape. The situation analysis of the OHL was based upon a telephone call between Lieutenant Colonel Tappen and Krafft von Dellmensingen.[27] This situation analysis underpinned Moltke's decision to direct pursuit and further attacks in Lorraine, instead of shifting forces to the North to reinforce the advancing right wing.

22–24 August—Battle of Namur: Second and Third Armies attacked the French Fifth Army in the triangle between Maubeuge, Namur, and Dinant across the rivers Sambre and Meuse. The French Fifth Army managed to escape the encirclement on 24 August.

23–24 August—Battle of Mons: First Army defeats BEF and the BEF withdraws from the Canal du Centre in a southwesterly direction.

23–24 August—Battles at Neufchâteau and Longwy. French Third and Fourth Armies launched a huge offensive in the Ardennes and were beaten by German Third, Fourth, and Fifth Armies. After the Battles of Mons, Namur, Neufchâteau, and Longwy (the Frontier Battles—*die Grenzschlachten*), the withdrawal of the Allied left wing started giving way to the advancing German right wing and created the impression with the OHL that the campaign in the west was more or less won.

25 August—A fierce counteroffensive by the French Second Army in Lorraine brought the half-hearted pursuit by the Sixth Army to a standstill. At 09:00 p.m., the Ia of the Operations Department of the OHL, Major v. Redern, arrived at Headquarters Sixth Army in Dieuze bringing a message from Moltke, containing the breakthrough of the French fortress lines between Toul and Épinal as the new operational goal for the Sixth Army. The Sixth Army immediately was directed to start pounding the French positions with heavy artillery. Like Lieutenant Colonel v. Dommes on 17 August, Major v. Redern did not have any written directive from Moltke; he just explained the intention of the OHL.

---

[26] (Kuhl, 1921), p. 45 and p. 77. Kuhl complains that the First Army didn't have any detailed information about the BEF before the battle of Mons and called this a major malfunction of the HKK 2. Please check our chapter on cavalry cracks.

[27] (Xylander, 1935,) p. 108.

25 August—Second Army made Guard Reserve Corps and Third Army made XI Army Corps available to the OHL. OHL believed that a breakthrough victory was already achieved on the right wing, but the situation was still unclear in Lorraine. Therefore, the OHL that same day ordered the transport of both corps to East Prussia.

26 August—Attacks of Eighth Army started the Battle of Tannenberg in Eastern Prussia.

26 August—Battle of Le Cateau. German First Army defeats British II Corps. As at Mons, British forces managed to escape.

26 August—After intervention of the Bavarian Crown Prince, the Sixth Army was released from the mission to immediately attack the French position at Nancy.

27 August—OHL issued a directive to all armies in the West about continuation of the operations to achieve final victory following the successful Frontier Battles (General directive to First through Seventh Armies for the continuation of the operations—*Allgemeine Anweisung an die 1. bis 7. Armee für den Fortgang der Operationen*):

- The advance was to be continued at high speed to pursue the defeated enemy and to prevent them from setting up further resistance. The next leg of the advance was now to aim for Paris.
- First Army and HKK 2—still under the control of the Second Army—was to move sharply south towards the river Seine from its current position around Péronne.
- First Army was also to protect the right flank of the advancing German armies against attacks of newly formed allied troops.
- Second Army with HKK 1 was to turn southbound towards Laon and was to take La Fère and Maubeuge.[28]
- The Fourth and Fifth Armies with HKK 4 were to be directed towards a line Epernay—Châlons sur Marne—Vitry le François.
- The combined forces of the Sixth and Seventh Armies with HKK 3 again was given the task to break through the French fortress belt between Toul and Épinal if the French continued to withdraw. The Seventh Army was promised independence from Sixth Army as soon as Sixth Army had managed to cross the river Moselle.

28 August—Due to communication problems with radio and telegraph, the directive from 27 August did not arrive at most army HQs until the early morning of 28 August.

28 August—French Fort Manonviller about 35 kilometers southeast of Nancy surrendered after being pounded with heavy artillery for 54 hours.

28–30 August—Battle of St. Quentin (the French called it Battle of Guise). Counter-attack of the French Fifth Army against the German Second Army. Although this battle ended with a tactical defeat of the French Fifth Army and Lanrezac again only just managed to escape from encirclement. This battle, nevertheless, slowed the German advance and bought time for the French to build up a new Sixth Army on the right flank of the German First Army. This new French army consisted almost entirely of reserve and territorial formations.

---

[28] (Kuhl, 1921), pp. 87 and 90–91.

30 August—Major Bauer, the specialist on super-heavy artillery in the OHL, was sent to the headquarters of the Sixth Army in Dieuze to discuss plans for a capture of the French fortifications around Nancy. Bauer left the impression that the strategic victory of the advancing right wing was almost complete and that breakthrough of the French fortress belt was necessary to accomplish a final victory.

30 August—OHL relocated to Luxembourg and took up quarters in a small and completely undersized, inappropriate school building. Koblenz and Luxembourg were compromise solutions to be close to the decisive Western Front, while avoiding loss of contact with the Eastern Front. There were discussions as to whether or not it was too dangerous to relocate the Kaiser into former enemy territory—Luxembourg was still somehow seen as a part of the Reich.

31 August—German victory at Tannenberg in East Prussia. The Russian Second Army was almost completely annihilated. During the climax of the battle, Guard Reserve Corps and XI Army Corps were still on railroad transport and arrived only after the end of the battle.

31 August—Major v. Xylander was sent as messenger from Sixth Army to the OHL and received word that the capture of Nancy was not as urgent or important as Major Bauer had explained just one day before. OHL gave direction to pin down as many French forces in the Reichslande as possible and to prevent the French Army from deploying significant numbers of troops to other areas. Upon Xylander's return, Dellmensingen was baffled about the ambiguity, if not contradiction, of the operational directives and goals received from the OHL and decided to continue the operational goal of taking the French positions around Nancy.

1 September—After repeated interventions of Generaloberst v. Kluck, the First Army was no longer under the control of the Second Army.

2 September—Austrian offensive in Galicia failed at the cost of heavy losses. On 2 September, the Russians took Lemberg.

2 September—General-Major Krafft v. Dellmensingen drove to the GHQ in Luxembourg to discuss personally the situation with Moltke and to get an endorsement for the attack on Nancy. Moltke convinced him to delay this attack for a couple of days and to focus instead upon the goal of pinning down as many French troops as possible in the Reichslande. Obviously, Moltke was following two different goals for the German forces in the Reichslande:

1. Prevent further French forces from being deployed to the new French left wing built up around Paris;
2. Break through the French fortress belt along the river Moselle to catch the bulk of the French army in a giant double pincer movement.

2 September—OHL issued a new directive to all armies of the advancing right wing about continuation of the operations. Due to slow communications by radio and telegraph, this directive only arrived at the army HQs during the night 2–3 September: "It is a major intention of the OHL to push the French forces away from Paris in a southeasterly direction. First Army is to follow Second Army in echelons and resume with the guarding of the right flank

of the advancing army."[29] This directive implied a complete change of direction if compared with that of 27 August: it was no longer the goal to catch all French forces in a giant pincer movement reaching through or around Paris, but to trap them in front of the Second Army and further south. Against the newly formed French forces around Paris, the First Army was intended to act as a flank guard. A follow-on radio message from OHL asked the armies to send strong cavalry forces into the surrounding areas of Paris to destroy all French railroads leading into Paris.

3 September—Commander First Army, Generaloberst v. Kluck, came to his own interpretation of the OHL directive and directed only the IV Reserve Corps as a flank guard oriented towards Paris. He then swung around the bulk of his army southeast to carry the flank of the French Fifth Army in front of Bülow's Second Army. Kluck was therefore no longer echeloned behind the Second Army but stumbled into the advance of the Second Army.

3 September—Joffre dismissed general Lanrezac from command of the Fifth Army and appointed General Franchet d'Esperey (the British called him "the desperate Frenchy") as the new commander.

4 September—Radio message by OHL with new directives for the armies in the west. Due to poor radio connections and numerous relay stations this directive did not arrive at most army HQs until the morning of 5 September:

- The enemy escaped the combined attack of the First and Second Army and has managed to keep Paris within its defense line. French army is deploying troops from the area Toul-Belfort; they are also pulling out troops from Third to Fifth Army. Pushing the French army southeastwards and squeezing it against the Swiss border is no longer possible. Instead, the enemy is assembling troops and newly created formations in and around Paris to jeopardize our right flank.
- First and Second Armies are to remain opposite of the eastern front of Paris. It is their mission to oppose any hostile operations out of Paris by counter-attack and to support each other by accomplishing this mission.
- Fourth and Fifth Armies are to push the enemy in front of them into southeastern direction, thus opening the crossing over the river Moselle between Toul and Épinal for the Sixth Army. Whether it will be possible to push significant enemy forces against the Swiss border cannot yet be forecasted.
- Third Army is heading towards Troyes-Vendeuvre. Depending upon the situation, Third Army is either support to First and Second Armies by advancing in a westerly direction across the river Seine or Third Army is to support the left wing by operating in southern or southeastern direction.
- First mission of Sixth and Seventh Armies is to pin down the enemy ahead of them. Then they are to advance against the river Moselle between Toul and Épinal.
- Following these missions, "the Kaiser" ordered:
  First and Second Armies are to remain opposite the eastern front of Paris to meet any enemy action by counter-attack. First Army is to remain between the Oise and the Marne; the Marne bridges around Château Thierry are to be held for future crossings. Second Army between the Marne and Seine is to occupy the Marne bridges between Nogent and

[29] (Kuhl, 1921), p. 118

Méry sur Seine. HKK 2 is to stay with First Army but is to deploy one cavalry division to HKK 1. HKK 1 is to remain with Second Army and to deploy one cavalry division to Third Army. HKK 1 is to reconnoiter and observe the southern front of Paris between Marne and Seine and push forward reconnaissance towards Caen, Alencon, Le Mans, Tours, and Bourges. Mission aircraft support will be needed. Both HKKs are to destroy all railroads leading into Paris.

Third Army is to advance towards Troyes-Vendeuvre and push forward cavalry reconnaissance towards Nevers-Le Creuzot.

Fourth and Fifth Armies are to push in a southeasterly direction to open the Moselle bridges for Sixth and Seventh Armies. Right wing of Fourth Army is to advance towards Vitry le François and Montierender. Right wing Fifth Army is to advance towards Revigny-Stainville-Morley. Left wing of Fifth Army is to guard the flank against the French fortifications at the river Meuse. Forts Troyon, Les Paroches, and Camp des Romains are to be captured. HKK 4 is to reconnoiter towards Dijon, Besancon and Belfort.

Orders for Sixth and Seventh Army remain unchanged.[30]

4 September—Evening report of the First Army reported successful advance in a southeasterly direction towards Coulommiers and Montmirail and announced a further advance in that direction on 5 September. This report together with the goals for 5 September showed how far that army had deviated from the directive given by the OHL.

4 September—OHL sent officers to all army commands to explain the directive radioed the same day and to discuss details of the massive strategic and operational implications. Lieutenant Colonel Hentsch was sent to First Army with the mission to bring First Army back in line with the directives of the OHL.[31]

5 September—Since the directive dating from 4 September created an entirely new mission for the armies advancing on the right wing, the OHL sent further written details to the army HQs.

6 September—The Marne Battle opened with a combined offensive by the BEF, the French Fifth and the newly formed French Sixth and Ninth Armies.

6 September—Start of the Battle on the river Ourcq between the German IV Reserve Corps and the French Sixth Army. First Army informed OHL in a radio message about the intended redeployment of troops to successfully fight at the Battle at the Ourcq. OHL realized that operations were slipping out of control.

6 September—OHL ordered headquarters Seventh Army together with 7th Cavalry Division and two army corps, one each from Sixth and Seventh Armies, to deploy by train towards Brussels.

6–14 September—First Battle of the Masurian Lakes. After the victory at Tannenberg, Hindenburg swung the Eighth Army into a northeasterly direction and attacked the Russian First Army.

---

30 (Reichsarchiv, 1926), pp. 3–5 and (Kuhl, 1921), pp. 130–131.

31 (Kuhl, 1921), p. 129 and (Haffner, 1982), pp. 48–59.

7 September—First Army withdrew III and IX Army Corps to the Ourcq and exposed the right flank of the Second Army at Montmirail.

8 September—Lieutenant Colonel Hentsch was sent as a messenger of the OHL to the army commands in the west to establish the detailed situation and to coordinate operations between the armies. Hentsch did not have any written directive with him. It remains unclear whether he was empowered to order a retreat on behalf of Moltke. Hentsch left the GHQ together with captain Koeppen (Lieutenant Colonel Hentsch was the Head of the Intelligence Department and Captain Koeppen was responsible for radio, telegraph and communications in the Operations Department) at 11:00 a.m. and visited the HQs of Fifth, Fourth, Third, and Second Armies. They did not arrived at Second Army until 07:45 a.m. and spent the night at the headquarters in Château Montmort before they continued to the First Army headquarters in Mareuil the following morning.[32]

9 September—Retreat of the German right wing from the rivers Marne and Ourcq to the Aisne—the so-called "Miracle of the Marne." Kluck decided to disengage from the Battle at the Ourcq and retreat based upon Hentsch's reports from the Second Army and from the OHL.

11 September—Moltke toured the army HQs of from the Fifth to the First Armies with the intent of obtaining a personal impression about the situation and to coordinate further operations. Lieutenant Colonel Tappen and Lieutenant Colonel v. Dommes accompanied Moltke.[33] After the tour Moltke decided that not only First and Second Armies had to withdraw into positions behind the river Aisne and to Reims, but also that Third, Fourth, and Fifth Army were to withdraw into rear positions. Moltke returned to the GHQ in the morning of 12 September seriously psychologically depressed.

11–18 September—Austrian withdrawal in Galicia; Austrian army routed.

14 September—Hindenburg defeated the Russian First Army in the First Battle of the Masurian Lakes. In contrast to Tannenberg, Hindenburg did not manage to completely annihilate the Russian First Army but drove them out of East Prussia with devastating losses. Despite that setback, the Russians still imposed a threat to the northern flank of the Eastern Front.

14 September—Dismissal of Moltke after the retreat to the river Aisne. Official reason for the dismissal was Moltke's illness. Moltke was replaced by Falkenhayn but had to remain at OHL to conceal his dismissal from the public.[34] The strategic situation of Germany turned out to be very difficult only six weeks after the beginning of the Great War:

- Schlieffen-style offensive in the west failed at the Marne. German armies retreated to the Aisne;
- Bloody deadlock in Lorraine; breakthrough of French fortress belt impossible;
- Shortages of artillery ammunition already seriously felt;
- German Navy locked in the German Bight; British blockade cut Germany efficiently off from supplies of strategic raw materials;

[32] Please refer to the tactical situation map of 8 September (attachment 6).
[33] (Reichsarchiv, 1926), pp. 448–452.
[34] (Reichsarchiv, 1926), pp. 481–485.

- New offensive in Northern France intended for autumn 1914; strategic goal unclear;
- Victories in East Prussia (Tannenberg and Masurian Lakes);
- Austrian offensive in Galicia failed after devastating losses; Austrian army retreated in desperate condition. German support needed to avoid collapse;
- Austrian offensive against Serbia failed.

25 September—GHQ relocated to Charleville-Mézières (located in France at the river Meuse, north of Sedan) to be closer to the Western Front.

LOGISTICAL PROBLEMS

Based on the outline of the supply system in Chapter 15, there now follows an analysis of the logistical issues that caused the *Generalquartiermeister* major problems that led to a general under-supply as well as critical shortages of food and artillery ammunition the deeper the German armies marched into enemy territory. In general, the German supply system appeared well planned and effective, but in fact it was one of the primary weak points, particularly during the war of movement.

Compared with previous wars, the First World War saw armies millions strong going to war for the first time. In 1870, the German forces going to war against France amounted to approximately 300,000 men; during the entire Franco-Prussian War, the German armies mobilized about 1.4 million men. In August 1914, the German army mobilized more than 2 million men; the First Army of v. Kluck alone had 320,000 men; Bülow's Second Army had 260,000 men.[35]

This number of soldiers could no longer be fed "out of the country" as was possible in 1870–71, when subsistence was short and trains and columns did not get through to the combat zone. These armies of unparalleled size advanced at an unprecedented pace through enemy territory. Kluck's First Army out marched any logistical calculation that had been made before the war.

The following logistical problems had a significant impact upon the combat effectiveness of the German army in France in 1914:

1. The railhead problem, in other words the growing distance between railheads and combat forces, particularly during the advance of the First Army;
2. The motor transportation problem; that is to say, the inability of the standard supply formations to bridge the growing gap between railheads and advancing combat formations;
3. The artillery ammunition problem, which added an extra level of complexity since the pre-war calculated amounts of artillery ammunition needed were much too low.

Due to the fast advance of the right wing, the railroad destruction in Belgium and Northern France was comparatively easy to repair. In Belgium, 17 crashed locomotives blocked the tunnel at Nasproué—but the explosive charges failed to explode; two other tunnels at Hombourg and Trois-Ponts (all close to Liège) and the railway bridges over the river Ourthe at Melreux were blown up. These places had to be bypassed or repaired. The repair of these bridges proved to be difficult and took until mid-October. Except around Antwerp, where the

[35] Please refer to the discussion of these strength numbers in chapter 16.

Belgian forces had time to prepare more thoroughly, the demolitions that occurred in Belgium and Northern France were all comparatively minor and easily repairable. In the central sector, where French forces opposed the German Third and Fourth Armies, the destruction between the rivers Sambre and Meuse was more thorough; in all, 14 bridges across the river Meuse were destroyed.

After the capture of Liège, the railroad was quickly pushed forward to support the advancing right wing armies. On 21 August, the railhead for the First Army was in Hasselt, on 22 August in Landen, on 24 August in Louvain, and on 26 August in Brussels. Supply trains could reach Mons on 29 August, Cambrai on 30 August, Péronne on 3 September, and St. Quentin on 4 September. On 5 September, the railhead was in Chauny, on 8 September in Noyon, and on 9 September in Compiègne; starting from 10 September, Laon could be used.[36]

From a railroad perspective, the repair works in Northern France and Belgium went quickly because the damage was mostly minor. But what would have happened if it had been more serious and the railroad situation less ideal than it actually was?

The Railhead Problem

As mentioned in Chapters 15 and 16, the railheads should have been a maximum of 100 kilometers away from the combat zone to allow proper supply. Ideally the distance would have been much less than 100 kilometers. Otherwise, the slow horse-drawn columns would not be able to bridge the distance to ensure the needed steady flow of supplies.

At the start of operations, the main problem was the bottleneck around Liège. With the fortress still not completely taken, the entire supply of the First Army deploying northwest and the Second Army deploying west of Liège had to be channeled around the city. As mentioned above, it turned out that the railroad destruction in Belgium was not really very serious. So the railroad formations found it easier than expected to get the railroad operable again and to push the railheads forward behind the advancing armies station by station. Even after crossing the French border, where the railroad demolitions carried out by the French Army were more serious, the railroad formations were still easily able to keep up a fast rate of repair.

The railheads could be moved forward almost daily. Nevertheless the advancing infantry out marched the pace of the logistics, resulting in an ever-growing distance between railheads and the combat zone.

In the table below, the advancing railhead locations are derived from information provided by the Reichsarchiv in the volume of the official history dealing with field railroads. In the combat zone, a central point was selected as a distribution point behind the advancing army. Usually in the First Army, the corps marching on the right wing were involved in the most serious fighting. During the battle of the Marne, the authors used Crouy, located fairly centrally behind the First Army, as a distribution point. The distance given is that between the railheads and these distribution points where the trains and columns of the army corps assumed responsibility for the movement of subsistence and ammunition from the columns of the communication zones. Distances are calculated based on the available road network in 1914 and represent measurements taken from original maps of 1:80,000 scale; the ones used by German supply formations in 1914—as far as maps were available to the train at all.

[36] (Reichsarchiv, 1928), pp. 59- 65.

Table showing the distance between railhead and combat zone of First Army:

Date	Railhead First Army (Etappe)	Combat zone First Army (right wing)	Distance	Events
21.8.	Hasselt	Drogenbos	85 km	
22.8.	Landen	Ath (HKK2, IV Army Corps)	117 km	
23.8.	Landen	Ath	117 km	Battle of Namur / Battle of Mons
24.8.	Louvain	Condé	114 km	
25.8.	Louvain	Denain	134 km	
26.8.	Brussels	Cambrai Le Cateau	131 km 122 km	Battle of Le Cateau
27.8.	Brussels	Gouzeaucourt (IVR) Moislains (II)	148 km 163 km	
28.8.	Brussels	Bray (II) Péronne (IV)	187 km 174 km	Battle of St. Quentin
29.8.	Mons	Villers-Bretonneux	141 km	
30.8.	Cambrai	Villers-Bretonneux	77 km	
31.8.	Cambrai	Montdidier	85 km	
1.9.	Cambrai	St. Just	108 km	
2.9.	Cambrai	Senlis	128 km	
3.9.	Péronne	Crouy (II)	118 km	
4.9.	St. Quentin	Viels Maisons (III, IV)	123 km	
5.9.	Chauny	Coulommiers	112 km	Marne Battle
6.9.	Chauny	La Ferté sous Jouarre	96 km	
7.9.	Chauny	Vendrest Crouy	80 km 74 km	
8.9.	Noyon	Vendrest Crouy	75 km 68 km	
9.9.	Compiègne	Mareuil	45 km	
10.9.	Laon	Crouy	78 km	

Table is based upon information from the following sources: (Reichsarchiv, 1925), map 2. (Reichsarchiv, 1926), map 2. (Reichsarchiv, 1926), maps 2, 3, and 4. (Reichsarchiv, 1928), pp. 59–65.

Obviously, the distance grew during the advance exceeding 100 km during the Battles of Mons (First Army) and Namur (Second Army). After that the distance grew further day-by-day until it reached a distance between 148 and 187 km on 27 and 28 August between the battles of Le Cateau and St. Quentin. Even on 29 August, when the railroad formations were able to push forward their railhead from Brussels to Mons, the distance was still 141 km. During the following two days, the distance shrank below 100 km, only to increase once more up to 128 km during the days immediately before the battle at the Marne. It is easy to see that covering such distances would easily require several days for horse-drawn columns, thus making logistics inflexible and inefficient.

The horse-drawn ammunition columns and the trains of the communications zone encountered great difficulties during the rapid advance of the First Army, despite the fact that it attempted to overcome the excessive distances separating its formations from the corps transportation companies a few days after the beginning of the forward movement. Until the time marked by the withdrawal behind the Aisne, about 12 September, the horse-drawn ammunition columns were so far in the rear that they could not be fully used.[37]

Between 23 and 27 August, another difficulty was added by transporting the IX Reserve Corps, the "Army of the North," previously protecting Schleswig-Holstein against an assumed British landing operation, to the First Army. The IX Reserve Corps was transported on 112 trains and was detrained in Landen, Neerwinden, Esmael, Tirlemont, and Louvain, putting an extra burden upon the railroad line between the First Army base (Sammelstation) in Düsseldorf and the railhead of the communications zone in Belgium. As the table illustrates, this extra bottleneck was created during the critical days after the battle of Mons, when the supply chain between the railhead and the combat formations of the First Army was already stretched. The railroad priorities were clear: troop transports first, then the transport of ammunition; the last priority was transport of subsistence and horse rations.[38]

Beginning on 30 August, the Guard Reserve Corps (142 trains), the XI Army Corps (134 trains) and the 8th Cavalry Division (40 trains) had to be transported from the Western Front to East Prussia. Only limited use could be made of empty trains that had already delivered ammunition or supplies to the railheads. The bulk of these trains had to be driven empty to the railheads, there to entrain the troops—again an extra burden for the bottleneck of the very few repaired railroads through enemy territory during the critical days (from a logistical point of view) between the battles of St. Quentin and at the Marne.[39]

During the battle at the Marne, the distance decreased again to a manageable number of kilometers to be covered by the already exhausted trains and columns. But then another logistical problem appeared. Due to the French attacks at the river Ourcq, the First Army was in grave danger, so Kluck decided to turn around his southbound forces in forced night-marches into a westbound direction for a counter-attack at the Ourcq. This change created a logistical nightmare because the communication zone columns found themselves roaming around between both wings of the First Army, without finding their intended (and often changed) distribution points.

To support the advance as efficiently as possible, the quartermaster general had made sure to keep as many supply trains as possible close to the railheads, so as to have enough supplies immediately available. The result was that many trains blocked available sidings and some of them were only partially unloaded and sometimes left without locomotives

---

[37] (Kuhl, 1929), p. 189

[38] (Lau, 1921), p. 14 and (Reichsarchiv, 1928), pp. 106–107

[39] (Reichsarchiv, 1928), pp. 107–110 and (Reichsarchiv, 1925), pp. 439–440

(because the availability of locomotives constituted another serious bottleneck) before the railhead was moved on to the next station.

When the First Army railhead moved along the 300 kilometers of railways from Liège to Brussels and Cambrai to Chauny on 5 September, 34 V-trains (V-train: *Verpflegungszug*–subsistence train), 2 M-trains (M-train: *Munitionszug*–ammunition train), and 7 H-trains (H-train: *Haferzug*–oats train, train with horse rations) were parked somewhere along the railroad line. Furthermore, 15 V-trains, 1 M-train and 2 H-trains were halted along the railroad between Liège and the army base in Düsseldorf. All these trains contained subsistence and horse rations that were desperately needed by the combat formations.[40]

It might seem that the German forces had maintained their fighting capacity during the winter of 1870–71 even though the supply situation was far worse compared with August and September 1914. In 1870–71 the infantry often had to live off the land and for longer periods of time. Ammunition supply, particularly for the artillery, came only at rare intervals. But, through improvisation and a high capacity for suffering, things somehow worked out.

Assuming that the capacity for suffering was equally high in August and September 1914, the main difference was that the armies of 1914 were so much larger than the armies of 1871. As a result in 1914, subsistence based upon the resources of the country to supply the troops advancing through it was virtually impossible. The other major difference lay in the increased firepower of the field artillery and the heavy artillery. As analyzed in Chapter 15, the average ammunition consumption rate of the artillery during a major combat action had increased approximately 20-fold between the Franco-Prussian War and the Balkan Wars. This rate was soon dwarfed by the ammunition consumption in the First World War. In 1870, artillery batteries could fight an entire battle only using the ammunition stored in the gun limbers. This feat was not possible in 1914. The increased demand on artillery ammunition could no longer be met by improvised measures; it required a supply system tailored to the demand.

The Motor Transportation Problem

Motor transport formations became the preferred method of movement because of the slow speed and the limited load capacities of the horse-drawn communications zone supply columns. Unfortunately, motor transports were only available in very limited numbers. This shortage became an important factor in the army supply service.[41] Since the First Army was the westernmost right wing army advancing at the fastest pace, it is worth having a more detailed look at the supply formations of this army.

The following motor transport formations had been assigned to the First Army upon mobilization:

- Commander of motor transport formations (*Kommandeur der Kraftfahrtruppen*) had his own staff. This command was an anomaly. Usually it was called ammunition columns battalion (*Etappenmunitionskolonnen-Abteilung*) only responsible for supplying ammunition. With the First Army this responsibility was extended to the entire range of supplies. The commander was Captain Petter, who originally came from the motor transport battalion (*Kraftfahr-Bataillon*) and acted as an instructor at the Military-Technical Academy before mobilization. The commander acted as the technical advisor on motor transport issues to the army commander and to the *Etappeninspektion*.[42]

---

[40] (Lau, 1921), p. 13.
[41] (Kuhl, 1929), p. 189.
[42] (Sußdorf, 1921) pp. 337–341 and (Kuhl, 1929), p. 189

- Communications zone motor transport park (*Etappen-Kraftwagenpark*), included an initial supply of gasoline and oil for one week. It was originally intended to always have a week's supply of gas and oil available. This required one full railroad train of 300 tons load capacity. To send the prescribed new supply each week created great difficulties and, as a rule, was not possible. The stereotypical phrase "ammunition will be given priority" could not be eliminated from orders. The realization that trucks were required to haul ammunition from the railheads to the combat zone, and that, in return, the trucks could only move if supplied with gasoline, was a lesson learned only slowly.
- Eight mobile gas stations—tanker trucks (*bewegliche Kraftwagen-Tankstellen*).
- Twelve communications zone motor transportation columns (*Etappen-Kraftwagenkolonnen*). By having 12 motor transportation columns assigned, the First Army was equipped better than all other German armies in 1914.

In the army base in Düsseldorf, a static motor transport depot was established to requisition further civilian trucks into the service of the First Army.[43]

In its pre-war estimate of the supply situation, the General Staff had assumed that the destruction of the Belgian railways would be complete and thorough, and would create serious difficulties for the supply of the advancing right wing. For this reason, the First and Second Armies were given a considerably larger number of motor transport columns attached than were made available to other armies.

The events of the first few days of advance, with the quickly increasing distance between railheads and combat troops, convinced the Commander of the First Army that his 12 Etappen-Kraftwagenkolonnen were insufficient to meet the needs of his army, particularly since the extent of the Belgian railway destruction and the repair capabilities of the railroad formations were still unclear. He asked the OHL for more motor transport capacity and received six additional light motor transport columns.[44]

But even with 18 motor transport columns at their disposal, First Army and Etappeninspektion 1 doubted their ability to meet the demands of the troops. That being the case, the commander of the motor transport formations was ordered to mobilize further motor transport columns. Since all available standard military trucks (standard army trucks of six tons load capacity—four tons on the truck and two on the trailer, and light trucks of three tons load capacity of the light and cavalry motor transport columns) were already requisitioned to mobilize the existing motor transport columns, Captain Petter had to source civilian trucks and delivery vehicles of one, one and a half, and two ton load capacity into military service in order to set up a further 12 improvised motor transport columns.

These light civilian trucks brought several problems with them. Compared with the standard military truck and the light military truck, both equipped with solid rubber tires, these civilian trucks had pneumatic tires. Such pneumatic tires were very comfortable for delivery use in cities with clean and well-maintained streets, but would tend often to puncture when used on land roads. They also multiplied the problem of maintenance and supply of spare parts. The standard and the light army trucks were designed to make maintenance easier by having as many identical parts as possible. The civilian trucks came from several different manufacturers and did not have interchangeable parts. This created a large problem for the maintenance teams.

43 (Kuhl, 1929), pp. 189–190 and 196.
44 (Kuhl, 1929), p. 190.

The motor transport commander had to obtain special permission, not only to purchase the vehicles for these 12 extra motor transport columns, but also to recruit the required personnel (drivers and mechanics). It required considerable effort to mobilize these extra columns and to set-up the necessary maintenance organization. The OHL authorized the First Army to set-up a volunteer automobile park (*freiwilliger Automobilpark*) in Aachen, in cooperation with the German Volunteer Automobile Corps (*Deutsches Freiwilliges Automobil-Corps*). The volunteer automobile park in Aachen not only maintained these improvised extra 12 motor transport columns; it soon maintained some 100 or more small trucks and passenger cars of all sizes. Although the load capacity of this park was small, it rendered valuable service because the vehicles were small and fast. When the new motor transport formations of the First Army were deployed and proved operable, the volunteer automobile park was permitted to continue with its special status and was attached to the Etappeninspektion of the First Army. They were only used on special missions, such as forwarding demolition equipment, supplying single batteries with urgently needed ammunition, or evacuating wounded soldiers, etc.[45]

When the advance began, the regular motor transport park of the communications zone had to be moved forward to remain close enough to the motor transport columns to guarantee proper repair and maintenance of the vehicles. This forward deployment was to be effected by railroad in accordance with existing plans. However, owing to the general state of railroad transportation facilities, rail transportation was never granted. The railroads were reserved for troop movements and supply trains. The result was that the commander of the motor transport troops of the First Army split the motor transport of the communications zone into two echelons. The first echelon including a repair workshop, replacement personnel, and spare parts stores, and was ordered to proceed to the *Etappenhauptort* at the railhead as soon as possible. The second echelon, comprising the tow trucks of the salvage section and the section handling captured and confiscated enemy motor vehicles, followed behind.[46]

The motor transport commander reported both to the Etappeninspektion and to the commander of the First Army. This double hatting caused a lot of friction because tasking was sometimes duplicated. The motor transport columns of the communications zone were employed in accordance with the requirements of the various corps and the daily information that the chief of staff of the Etappeninspektion received from the representative of the Chief Railroad (Bba) assigned to the First Army. This information contained the actual location of the railhead and the whereabouts of the railroad trains en route between the army base and railhead. It also contained the locations of the distribution points, where the columns and trains of the corps would take responsibility for supply. Based on this information, the chief of staff of the Etappeninspektion had to calculate the load capacity needed, the time of loading, the march objectives, and the time of unloading supplies at the distribution points. The various corps usually obtained their supplies by direct reload from the trucks of the motor transport columns.

Motor transportation had to fill the widening gap between the railheads and the advancing combat formations, which were beyond the capacity of the horse-drawn transport columns. As a result, the horse-drawn columns of the communications zone and depot service trains soon became more or less redundant as far as the supply of the First Army during the advance to the Marne was concerned. They simply had to be replaced by regular and improvised

45 (Kuhl, 1929), pp. 191–192.
46 (Kuhl, 1929), p. 196

motor transport columns. This change created several problems since originally the motor transport columns were designed to be merely an adjunct to the horse-drawn columns.

The trucks of 1914 were not as reliable as modern trucks and needed frequent and intensive maintenance. Motor transport columns could average about 100 km a day over favorable terrain and well-maintained land-roads. There was meant to be one day each week set aside for repairs, but this provision was consistently ignored until after the withdrawal from the Marne. Motor transport columns had only two to three hours of rest daily. As a result, drivers often fell asleep from over-exertion, and the trucks ran into a ditches or trees, leading to immense wear and tear on these columns within only a few weeks. If the need for frequent repair and maintenance was substantial for the standard army trucks, the problem was even worse for passenger cars and light civilian trucks.

After only four weeks of campaigning, the motor transport columns were in an increasingly poor condition. The trailers turned out to be too heavy and unwieldy and were frequently either abandoned or left behind in the railheads or in field depots. This reduced the load capacity of the motor transport columns from 102 tons to 68 tons. In addition, the breakdown of the trucks led to further loss of carrying capacity. By 12 September about 60 percent of the trucks at the disposal of First Army had become unserviceable; and, to make things worse, no reserve vehicles were available.[47]

The next difficulty was communication with the motor transport columns. Since they were covering immense distances, they were often roaming around in hostile territory at night covering 150 or more kilometers. The withdrawing French forces frequently removed the signposts along the roads. They were without maps, often only equipped with hand-made sketches and, in part, commanded by reserve NCOs unable to speak, read, or understand the French language. Information about distribution points in the combat zone and liaison points with trains and columns of the combat troops were often more than a day old. The motor transport columns frequently arrived at these places after the distribution points had moved on. Therefore, march orders could only be issued by giving vague targets, e.g., III Army Corps headquarters was yesterday in the village of A; the second section of the corps ammunition columns will be found in that vicinity today.[48]

The telegraph formations of the communications zone were required to establish connections with the signal lines in the rear of the communications zone and to extend these lines forward to the army headquarters. However, the available equipment proved insufficient for the rapid advance. The building of telephone and telegraph lines could not keep pace with the forward movements of the troops and their headquarters. Since the communications zone did not have any radio communications equipment, communications with the motor transport columns proved to be very difficult.

The Etappeninspektion was not able to communicate with any formation of the advancing troops. The Etappeninspektion could only communicate with the army staff by wire, if there was a proper wire connection, and then had to ask the army staff to convey their messages to other third parties. They could neither agree upon meeting points or distribution points with trains and columns of the combat forces, nor could they ask for protection if the motor transport columns had to operate in or close by to enemy territory when supplying the cavalry.[49] The available communications tool proved completely insufficient to support the rapid advance of the right wing. Wire connections were too slow to follow the advancing troops.

47 (Kuhl, 1929), p. 196
48 (Kuhl, 1929), p. 194
49 (Kuhl, 1929), p. 193.

Radio connections that were only available to army headquarters and to cavalry divisions, were too few in number, too short of a range, and were technically unreliable.

Finally, motor transport columns attempting to supply formations of the HKK 2 were often operating on the exposed right flank of the First Army. That position frequently placed the motor transport columns in jeopardy from the attacks of French cavalry. It also became necessary to send numerous liaison officers in passenger cars back and forth to convey information and orders. Often these information and orders were received too late, and when finally received, the need for them had passed.

When an anticipated battle did not take place and if the corps ammunition column was a motor transport column, it often had to wait at the distribution point fully loaded and unable to deliver the ammunition. In such cases the commander of the corps ammunition column frequently refused to accept the load and instead demanded that the motor transport columns follow his slow horse-drawn columns, thus wasting valuable lift capacity. Once the motor transport columns were emptied, they had to return to the railhead intermediate ammunition depots, which were usually set up without proper guards. As a result, and especially during the retreat from the Marne, they were threatened by the advancing allied forces. During the Battle of the Marne, motor transport columns were sometimes sent directly to the combat forces to refill the ammunition vehicles of the infantry battalions and artillery batteries. This action occurred more than 30 times during the battle of the Marne.[50]

Although motor transport was of crucial importance to supply the rapidly advancing First Army with all necessary supplies, motor transportation was not given sufficient priority. Neglected during peacetime, the mobilization of motor transport formations was widely improvised when the war began. Worse, the military commanders did not allow the motor transport formations to properly maintain their vehicles, thus creating additional shortfalls when vehicles became unserviceable.

The Artillery Ammunition Problem

No German unit actually ran out of ammunition on a large scale during the opening stages of World War I. The artillery ammunition problem did not relate to a function of an interruption of the flow of ammunition. Rather it was a problem with consumption estimations and the ability to produce ammunition in the homeland factories. While the number of rounds carried in 1914 significantly dwarfed the number carried in the Franco-Prussian war, it was just not enough. During the Franco-Prussian War, the average German gun use was 199 rounds. In 1914, the Prussian War Ministry stocked 1000 rounds per barrel. This ammunition was almost entirely gone in the first month and a half.[51]

The supply system of the German army in August 1914 was designed for a short mobile war, in which quick and decisive operational strikes were more important than extended battles of attrition.[52] Such illusions had led to severe problems in the winter of 1870–71 and would again create major difficulties after mobile warfare came to an end in the autumn of 1914. Before 1914, artillery ammunition supplies were estimated to sustain four days of heavy fighting called "battle days" (*Schlachttage*), but soon after the start of the operations in 1914, it became clear that the use of ammunition was far greater than the pre-war study had suggested.[53] Naturally not every day was a battle day, nevertheless, the optimistic

50 (Kuhl, 1929), pp. 194–195.

51 (Creveld, 1994), p. 110 and (François, 1910), p. 9.

52 (Kuhl, 1929), p. 1.

53 The reasons for this faulty estimation were discussed in Chapter 15 in some detail.

estimates of ammunition consumption led to shortages in artillery ammunition beginning in September 1914. Then the campaign in the west changed from mobile warfare with a comparatively low ammunition consumption to positional warfare with a skyrocketing consumption. The Battle of the Aisne was a defining moment in the development of increasing consumption of artillery ammunition. The shortage of artillery shells was absolutely acute. The ability to coordinate different branches was totally limited by the lack of ammunition. On 8 October 1914, the Kaiser asked General Schubert, the Inspector General of Artillery, "and who is to blame for the fact that we have so little ammunition? What were you doing all of those years as my Inspector General of Artillery?"[54] Gen. von Muller, the commander of the First Army Communications Zone stated: "I personally had apprehensions right along with regard to the supply of ammunition. It was evident that the enormous expenditure of ammunition at the front far exceeded our peacetime estimates."[55]

Although the 1914 mobilization was mirrored by an economic mobilization, the production of artillery ammunition did not significantly increase. Before the war, the War Ministry had anticipated that the major constraints would be the shortages of fuzes and shells. In fact, the main shortages were of powder and explosives, the exact reverse of what the War Ministry had previously assumed.[56]

There were two different reasons for these shortages. During mobilization, many industrial workers were drafted into the forces and had to be replaced by new workers, who were usually inexperienced and had to be trained. Many of them were female, a situation that was unusual in German industrial firms of the time. The second issue was that strategic raw materials were in short supply. Copper, brass, and bronze were desperately needed for the manufacturing of infantry ammunition, artillery shells, cartridge cases and fuzes. This was entirely due to lack of foresight and incompetence. The German military had been in charge of all preparations for war and was obsessed with secrecy. As a result, the civilian bureaucracy had almost no role to play. One consequence was that although German vulnerability to blockade in time of war should have been obvious, absolutely no effort had been made to build up stocks of critical strategic imports. Even when war broke out nothing was done officially. It took the combined initiatives of Walther Rathenau, head of the massive AEG electronic concern, and Albert Ballin, who was a major figure in German shipping, to persuade the authorities to set up a War Materials Department in the War Ministry to allocate scarce materials strategically and to create a Central Purchasing Organization.

There were also shortages of saltpeter and nitric acid that were essential to manufacture gunpowder and explosive agents. The British blockade had almost completely cut off the supply. Germany purchased the bulk of its saltpeter from Chile and most of its copper from the Belgian Congo before the war. They still continued to receive some imported copper from Norway, Sweden, and Bulgaria. A couple of hundred tons of copper could be produced by the copper mines around the German town of Mansfeld. Later in the war, historical monuments and church bells were gathered and melted to produce copper, bronze and brass. Particularly in Belgium, this led to a systematic looting of all available stocks of strategic raw materials. In addition to large monuments and church bells, pots and pans were collected from the civilian population.[57]

54 (Brose, 2001), p. 225.
55 (Kuhl G. v., 1929), p. 124.
56 (Strachan, 2001), p. 1027.
57 (Strachan, 2001), pp 1027–1028.

The War Ministry planned to produce 200,000 field artillery shells within 12 to 16 weeks of mobilization. The Krupp firm alone already manufactured 150,000 shells monthly. Imperial Germany produced 170,000 rounds in the first month of mobilization.[58]

The manufacturing of ammunition required per month:
- 150,000 tons of steel,
- 2,000 tons of copper (for jackets of infantry bullets and obturation rings of artillery shells),
- 4,000 tons of lead (basically for shrapnel shells and infantry rounds).

The monthly manufacturing of cartridge cases for infantry and artillery ammunition required:
- 42,000 tons of brass,
- 1,600 tons of zinc,
- 2,100 tons of sheet steel.

For fuzes, the following raw materials were needed per month:
- 1,000 tons of aluminum (to replace brass),
- 2,100 tons of copper,
- 2,900 tons of zinc.[59]

These figures indicate clearly why copper was regarded as a strategic raw material of immense importance. Eventually, but not until the Ministry had been persuaded of the need, the Raw Materials Management and Rationing Department (Kriegsrohstoffabteilung) was created in the Ministry of War. This agency oversaw available raw materials and confiscated available stocks for military use.

Saltpeter and nitric acids were soon replaced by a procedure invented and patented in 1910 by Fritz Haber and Carl Bosch from BASF, Inc. This procedure was based upon synthesizing ammonia from nitrogen and hydrogen. The Haber-Bosch process not only supported the manufacture of explosives without strategic materials, but it also helped the agricultural industry by producing a very efficient fertilizer. All sorts of substitutes were found very quickly to replace missing chemicals and compounds. This experimentation led to the creation of an explosive substance known as ammonal instead of the prewar more explosively powerful TNT. Germany produced 1,240 tons of propellant in the first month of 1914. The War Minister calculated that 6,000 tons were required. Though the goal was reduced to 4,500 tons by December 1914, production had only reached 2,170 tons.[60] In 1915, the monthly demand for explosives had grown to 23,000 tons. To produce all these explosives, about 6,000 tons of saltpeter and 34,000 tons of nitric acid were needed.[61]

One at a time the mechanical parts of fuzes were made of aluminum instead of brass. Zinc also replaced brass.[62] This change of metals led to a deteriorating quality and an increased rate of duds. It turned out to be very difficult to replace brass with aluminum. Fuzes work in a similar fashion to clocks and brass has more flexibility than the more brittle aluminum. Artillery shell cases were made of brass before the war. By the end of 1914, most of the cases were replaced by steel or iron. This change in itself was a problem because of a shortage of

58 (Strachan, 2001), pp. 1031–1032.
59 (Wurtzbacher, 1921), p. 86.
60 (Strachan, 2001), p. 1036.
61 (Wurtzbacher, 1921), pp. 85–86.
62 (Strachan, 2001), p. 1027.

high quality compressed steel that depended on manganese from Hungary. The high-speed production of artillery shells led to wildly different standards. Artillery gunners did not trust the new shells and considered them good only for training. Quality was sacrificed for speed and scale of production. The initial deliveries of the auxiliary ammunition arrived in the third week of September.[63] Cartridge cases for small arms still had to be made of brass; iron cases led to malfunctions and jamming weapons, particularly with automatic weapons. Also, the explosives made by replacement raw materials based upon the Haber-Bosch process turned out to be less efficient compared to traditional explosives manufactured before 1914.[64]

Initially the supply of small arms ammunition did not cause much of a problem in the field since an Army Corps carried about nine and a half million rounds of infantry ammunition—a reserve corps carried about seven and a half million rounds and a cavalry division about half a million rounds. This stock was intended to last for a number of battle days and could be resupplied easily. But lack of artillery ammunition swiftly became critical. Battle days were calculated for artillery on an average ammunition consumption of 20 rounds per gun per hour (real consumption turned out to be far higher in 1914). With gun batteries it was estimated that fire based upon battery stocks could last for seven hours; the light ammunition columns could supply ammunition for another six hours. As a last resort, the ammunition columns of the Army Corps could supply ammunition for another seven hours. So the artillery ammunition stock of an Army Corps could sustain 20 hours of heavy combat—less than one battle day! For light field howitzers it was only about 13 ½ hours, for heavy field howitzers about 21 ½ hours.[65]

When the Army Corps ran out of stock they had to be replenished by ammunition railroad trains. This resupply required proper railroad connections and railhead stations very close to the firing positions of the artillery. For an army advancing through Belgium, railroad demolitions caused real problems. The longer the distance between railheads and fighting positions, the harder it was for horse-drawn columns to bridge the gap. Another problem was that there had been insufficient nighttime prewar training. Some units adopted white armbands or advanced with unloaded weapons to avoid accidental firing. The endeavor to overcome adversity through courage and daring led only to staggering casualty rates, particularly among infantry officers.[66]

In October 1914, the Chief of Staff of the Sixth Army, Krafft von Dellmensingen, gave the following guidance to the "well-oiled machine" that was his army:

> In recent days, several promising opportunities have been wasted because entire corps have allowed themselves to be held up by vastly inferior forces. This situation can be traced to the fact that attacks are not being pressed home with the utter disregard for danger that each attack which aims at a decisive result demands. Naturally it must be recognized that the high officer losses have seriously damaged the offensive power of the Army. However, if as a consequence we frequently conduct halfhearted attacks, the enemy will soon lose respect for us. We shall spare the blood of our infantry if we contain ourselves to attacks which are essential and make sure that they are strongly supported by all available artillery and other technical resources. If, however,

63 (Strachan, 2001), p. 1028.
64 (Wurtzbacher, 1921), p. 89–92.
65 (Großer Generalstab, 1914), pp. 57–62.
66 (Herwig H., 2009), p. 112.

a decisive attack is ordered, then every commander, including those in high levels, is personally to ensure, including by example that he is so engaged that the attack will be conducted with the utmost power. Superior officers are also to appear at the front sufficiently frequently to bring their personalities to bear on the troops.

Valuable advantages are often not being exploited properly because, in the case of formations advancing alongside one another, instead of driving forward ruthlessly within their boundaries, troops are pausing to allow their neighbors to catch up, or halting as soon as they come under enfilade fire from neighboring sectors. From receipt of this directive there is an explicit ban on delaying or halting if the planned advance is delayed or disrupted on neighboring fronts, or to see what effect the outflanking maneuver might have. Even if neighboring attacks are held up, there is no excuse for failing to act.

It is a fundamental principle of the French artillery to bring down flanking fire and it cannot be avoided when adjacent formations are advancing simultaneously. The troops must arrange for their own protective measures. It must also be the unvarying case that the neighbors may never be left in trouble. Individual units and formations have often suffered heavy casualties because neighbors delayed far too long before coming to their assistance, or believed wrongly, after reports from other troops, that they were occupying places, which were actually in enemy hands. It is essential, therefore, that reports and information concerning the lines reached for points captured are absolutely reliable. If a formation is unable to reach a particular piece of terrain, or cannot do so in time if it believes that the situation has changed, or that it cannot reach the designated place for reasons unknown to superior level of command, it is to make the fact known to all relevant places, without fail.

An extremely threatening squandering of artillery ammunition, far beyond even the most pessimistic estimates, has occurred. This has been caused because many units and formations have constantly engaged inadequately reconnoitered enemy positions with a wide ranging, harassing fire; either that or attempts have been made by bombarding enemy positions for days or hours at a time to eliminate them in that manner, instead of the infantry, through during direct action, forcing a weaker enemy to occupy and attempt to defend their positions. For the future it is essential that troops draw the lesson that careful husbandry of artillery ammunition is of decisive importance; that simply bringing fire down will never have an effect and, furthermore, that fire may only be directed against clearly identified targets and only for strictly limited tactical purposes. As a result, the artillery may not meet every request by the infantry for fire support and may only respond to the senior commander. The infantry must always cooperate with the artillery in the attack; the artillery must never try to attack alone.

It is very regrettable to note that up to now there has been a constant lack of liaison between neighboring formations. This is another reason for the undesirable situations described earlier. The dispatch of live liaison officers is only useful when they are furnished with ample means to pass on information. In the future, commanders will be held personally responsible for failures of this type. Every effort is to be made by all commanders to designate reserves or make them available once again after redeployment. Every individual might is to be pressed into service to this end.

Troops not involved in attacks must spend their time thoroughly reinforcing their positions and developing them with all means available, so that they are strong enough to enable a minimal garrison to beat off all enemy attacks. Reserves are to be used

> constantly to reinforce. Even when battles are drawn out, it is essential to arrange for troops in the frontline to be relieved, so that they can rest and regain their ability to strike. The men are never to be left with nothing to do. Every opportunity is to be taken to re-impose discipline through the use of drill.
>
> Commanders at all levels who fail to meet the requirements outlined above will be summarily dismissed. No special consideration will be given to any individual, not even if previously he has been thoroughly worthy. The names of all individuals who are not completely fit for their posts are to be passed immediately to Supreme Army Headquarters through official channels. Belief in a favorable outcome must always be maintained at a high level. Every individual must be made to realize what is at stake. Patience will certainly be required. It will be a long time before a final decision is achieved but, if every single individual is absolutely determined to see it through to the end, then all enemy efforts will be for nothing and final victory will be assured.[67]

"How keenly must this sudden contrast have been felt by all concerned when, after the army had made a new stand behind the Aisne, the ammunition deliveries from the factories in the sum of the interior began to lag and fail!"[68] After the experience of the Franco-Prussian War, in which a successful summer campaign was followed by a long and bloody winter, it is amazing that the German army again planned for an optimistic scenario of a short war. Numerous military analysts had warned before 1914 that a coming war would be most probably very bloody and last longer than expected. It should have been expected that the British Navy would efficiently block almost all supplies of strategic raw materials. But, despite this, strategic preparations for anything other than a short war were totally lacking.

CAVALRY CRACKS

The Command Problem

While considering cavalry operations, it is necessary to define the scope of the subject clearly. In a previous chapter, distinct cracks were identified in the organizational structure of the cavalry. This section aims to expand on those points. The highest pure cavalry organization was called the HKK. This abbreviation stands for *Höherer Kavallerie-Kommandeur*. The HKK was a corps-sized unit but it was not an army corps. Many inaccurate or mistaken works refer to these as cavalry corps. That is an easy but inexact English translation. Some works used the word *Heereskavalleriekorps.*[69] That is not correct and gives the wrong impression. Heeereskavalleriekorps is what they became in 1915, after the organization received a staff and a logistical function. They were renamed then and became much more like normal corps. It is not what they were in 1914. Interestingly, the editors of the 1940 book attributed to the commander of HKK 2, General von der Marwitz, frequently called the organization Kavallerie-Korps in their commentary designed around his letters.[70] The first impression might be, "Who cares? What is in a name?" But that belies the issue. At the very top was the Kaiser. The individual below him, who was in charge of executing his war plan, was the Chief

[67] (Sheldon, *The German Army at Ypres 1914*, 2010), pp. 228–230.
[68] (Kuhl, 1929), p. 124.
[69] (Zuber, *The Mons Myth: A Reassessment of the Battle*, 2010), p. 76.
[70] (Tschischwitz, 1940), p. 17.

of the General Staff, Moltke the Younger. He was trying to control eight separately numbered armies. In peacetime, the individuals who were destined to become army commanders were the commanders of the eight army inspections. Each one of the inspections oversaw about three army corps. Each army corps, with the exception of the Guards, had a geographical responsibility over an entire corps area. These were extremely powerful men. The army corps commanders, the so-called commanding generals, and the inspectors each had the right of immediate access (*Immediatvortragsrecht*) to the Kaiser.[71] They could exercise this right without anyone else being present.

When mobilization occurred, these inspectors were mobilized as numbered army commanders.[72] In addition, many reserve corps were mobilized and these reserve corps did not have a geographic responsibility. They also did not have Immediatvortragsrecht. Neither did the commanders of the HKKs. In contrast to the infantry in peacetime, the cavalry had four cavalry inspections. The cavalry inspectors had the rank of division commanders. The Prussian cavalry inspections reported into a general inspection (*Generalinspekteur*) of the cavalry. The General Inspector of the cavalry became one of the *Höhere Kavallerie-Kommandeure* commanders, and each of the four cavalry inspectors took over a cavalry division. The General Inspector alone had the same immediate access to the Kaiser as the commanding general of an army corps. So by this right alone, the commander of the HKK was not on the same level as the commanding general of an active army corps or the commanding general of an army.

Armies were composed of a group of corps, some active and some reserve. Corps were composed of a series of divisions and, as explained in Chapter 6, these formations were caught in a tug of war between the War Ministry and the General Staff concerning who would control the assets. The War Ministry wanted only division-sized cavalry organizations that were integral to the army and worked for the army commander. The General Staff wanted a corps-sized cavalry organization that worked directly for OHL bypassing the army commander. The compromise was the HKK.

Confusion also arises because of the nomenclature used in 1914 to distinguish between *Divisionskavallerie*—the cavalry formations assigned to the infantry corps upon mobilization—and *Heereskavallerie*—the cavalry formations mobilized in cavalry divisions within the HKKs. All cavalry reserve formations were mobilized as Divisionskavallerie. There were four HKKs created upon mobilization, but they were not all of equal size. HKKs 2 & 3 each had three divisions, while HKKs 1 & 4 each had two divisions.

H.K.K. 1
Kdr. Gen.: Gen. Lt. Frhr. v. Richthofen
Chef: Obstlt. v. Raumer
Ib: Hptm. Simon

Jg. Btl. 11, Jg. Btl. 12 (1. sächs.), Jg. Btl. 13 (sächs.)

G.K.D.
Kdr.: Gen. Maj. v. Storch
Ia: Hptm. Niemann

---

71 See Chapter 6.
72 There were some changes made to the players in accordance with the mobilization plan.

Ib: Hptm. Graf Wolfskehl v. Reichenberg
1. G. Kav. Brig. (Oberst v. Baerensprung): Rgt. Gardes du Corps, G. K. R.
2. G. Kav. Brig. (Gen. Maj. Graf v. Rothkirch u. Trach): 1. G. U. R., 3. G. U. R.
3. G. Kav. Brig. (Oberst Frhr. v. Senden): 1. G. D. R., 2. G. D. R.
reit. Abt. 1. G. Feld-Art. Rgt.
1. G. MG-Abt., G. Jg. Btl., G. Schtz. Btl.

5. K.D.
Kdr.: Gen. Maj. v. Ilsemann
Ia: Maj. Buchfink
Ib: Hptm. Henning
9. Kav. Brig. (Gen. Maj. Rusche): D. R. 4, U. R. 10
11. Kav. Brig. (Oberst v. Wentzky u. Petersberg): Leib-Kür. Rgt. 1, D. R. 8
12. Kav. Brig. (Gen. Maj. Graf v. Pfeil u. Klein-Ellguth): H. R. 4, H. R. 6
reit. Abt. Feld-Art. Rgt. 5
MG-Abt. 1

H.K.K. 2
Kdr. Gen.: Gen. Lt. v. d. Marwitz
Chef: Maj. Hoffmann v. Waldau
Ib: Hptm. v. Bülow

Jg. Btl. 3, Jg. Btl. 4, Jg. Btl. 7, Jg. Btl. 9, Jg. Btl. 10.

2. K.D.
Kdr.: Gen. Maj. Frhr. v. Krane
Ia: Hptm. Frhr. v. d. Osten gen. Sacken
Ib: Hptm. Janssen
5. Kav. Brig. (Oberst v. Arnim): D. R. 2, U. R. 3
8. Kav. Brig. (Gen. Maj. Frhr. Thumb v. Neuburg): K. R. 7, H. R. 12
Leib-Hus. Brig.: Leib-Hus. R. 1, Leib-Hus. R. 2
MG-Abt. 4
reit. Abt. / Feld-Art. Rgt. 35

4. K.D.
Kdr.: Gen. Lt. v. Garnier
Ia: Hptm. Brüggemann-Ferno
Ib: Hptm. Blankenhorn
3. Kav. Brig. (Oberst Graf v. der Goltz): K. R. 2, U. R. 9
17. Kav. Brig.: (Gen. Maj. Graf v. Schimmelmann) D. R. 17, D. R. 18
18. Kav. Brig. (Oberst v. Printz): H. R. 15, H. R. 16
G. MG-Abt. 2
reit. Abt. / Feld-Art. Rgt. 3

9. K.D.
Kdr.: Gen. Maj. Graf v. Schmettow (Eberhard)
Ia: Maj. Herwarth v. Bittenfeld

Ib: Hptm. Braemer
13. Kav. Brig. (Oberst Seiffert): K. R. 4, H. R. 8
14. Kav. Brig. (Oberst v. Heuduck): H. R. 11, U. R. 5
19. Kav. Brig. (Oberst Frhr. v. Zedlitz u. Leipe): D. R. 19, U. R. 13
MG-Abt. 7
reit. Abt. / Feld-Art. Rgt. 10

H.K.K. 3
Kdr.: Gen. d. Kav. Ritter v. Frommel
Chef: Maj. v. Meiß
Ia: Maj. Graf v. Podewils-Dürniz

1. bayer. Jg. Btl., 2. bayer. Jg. Btl.

Bayer. K.D.
Kdr.: Gen. Lt. v. Stetten
Ia: Maj. Graf v. Tattenbach
Ib: Hptm. Jahreiß
1. bayer. Kav. Brig. (Gen. Maj. v. Staudt): bayer. 1. schw. Reiter Rgt., bayer. 2. schw. Reiter Rgt.
4. bayer. Kav. Brig. (Oberst Frhr. v. Crailsheim): bayer. U. R. 1, bayer. U. R. 2
5. bayer. Kav. Brig. (Gen. Maj. v. Hößlein): 1. Ch. R., 6. Ch. R.
reit. Abt. bayer. Feld-Art. R. 5
bayer. MG-Abt. 1

7. K.D.
Kdr.: Gen. Lt. v. Heydebreck
Ia: Maj. Frhr. v. Rotberg
Ib: Hptm. Prausnitzer
26. Kav. Brig. (Gen. Maj. Herzog Norbert v. Württemberg): D. R. 25, D. R. 26
30. Kav. Brig. (Oberst v. Graevenitz): D. R. 15, H. R. 9
42. Kav. Brig. (Gen. Maj. v. Koscielski): U. R. 11, U. R. 15
reit. Abt. Feld-Art. R. 5
MG-Abt. 3

8. K.D.
Kdr.: Gen. Lt. Graf v. d. Schulenburg
Ia: Maj. Tillmanns
Ib: Hptm. v. Schwerdtner
23. Kav. Brig. (Gen. Maj. v. der Decken): sächs. Garde Reiter Rgt., U. R. 17
38. Kav. Brig. (Gen. Maj. Weinschenk): Jg. Rgt. z. Pf. 2, Jg. Rgt. z. Pf. 6
40. Kav. Brig. (Gen. Maj. Frhr. v. Luttitz): sächs. Carabiniers Rgt., U. R. 21
reit. Abt. Feld-Art. R. 12
MG-Abt. 8

H.K.K. 4
Kdr. Gen.: Gen. Lt. Frhr. v. Hollen

Chef: Obstlt. Frhr. v. Brandenstein
Ib: Hptm. Frhr. v. Willisen

Jg. Btl. 5, Jg. Btl. 6

3. K.D.
Kdr.: Gen. Lt. v. Unger
Ia: Hptm. Lamotte
Ib: Hptm. Graf v. Brandenstein-Zeppelin
16. Kav. Brig. (Oberst Kleemann): Jg. Rgt. z. Pf. 7, . Rgt. z. Pf. 8
22. Kav. Brig. (Oberst v. Wurmb): D. R. 5, H. R. 14
25. Kav. Brig. (Oberst v. Glasenapp): hess. Garde-Drag. Rgt. Nr. 23, hess. Leib-Drag. Rgt. Nr. 24
reit. Abt. Feld-Art. Rgt. 11
MG-Abt. 2

6. K.D.
Kdr.: Gen. Lt. Graf v. Schmettow
Ia: Hptm. v. Werner
Ib: Hptm. Klewitz
28. Kav. Brig. (Oberst v. Selchow): Leib-Drag. R. 20, D. R. 21
33. Kav. Brig. (Gen. Maj. v. Etzel): D. R. 9, D. R. 13
45. Kav. Brig. (Gen. Maj. v. Hofacker): H. R. 13, . Rgt. z. Pf. 13
reit. Abt. Feld-Art. Rgt. 8
MG-Abt. 6

Another related problem is the failure by many analysts to understand the size of the organization under discussion. As has been mentioned, the meaning of HKK is often misunderstood. There is a further language anomaly that causes even more problems. It is with the translation of the word *Abteilung* that many dictionaries translate as "detachment" or even as "section." In both cases the impression is given that the Abteilung is a subset of a unit and is relatively small. This inference is incorrect. The word Abteilung has several meanings and is a multi-purpose word in the German language. In a staff, Abteilung translates into "department." In a field artillery regiment, the meaning of Abteilung is "battalion" and a machinegun Abteilung had approximately company strength. For clarification, here is an example of a cavalry division taken from the relevant appendix.

9. K.D.
Kdr.: Gen. Maj. Graf v. Schmettow (Eberhard)
Ia: Maj. Herwarth v. Bittenfeld
Ib: Hptm. Braemer
13. Kav. Brig. (Oberst Seiffert): K. R. 4, H. R. 8
14. Kav. Brig. (Oberst v. Heuduck): H. R. 11, U. R. 5
19. Kav. Brig. (Oberst Frhr. v. Zedlitz u. Leipe): D. R. 19, U. R. 13
MG-Abt. 7
reit. Abt. / Feld-Art. Rgt. 10

In this example "reitende Abteilung" means the "mounted battalion of the 10th field artillery regiment" that went to the 9th cavalry division upon mobilization. Such a "riding battalion" (reitende Abteilung) was comprised of three batteries of four field guns. The reduced strength of four guns per battery was (together with the higher number of horses to have the entire crews horse-mounted) the major difference compared to a regular six-gun field artillery battery. In the given example, there is also the "MG-Abteilung 7," which equates almost exactly to a machinegun (MG) company. A mobilized MG-Abteilung was comprised of a gun detachment (*Gefechtsabteilung*) with six mounted guns and three ammunition wagons, a fighting baggage of one big four-horse ammunition wagon, one material wagon and 11 surplus horses and a heavy baggage of one two-horse baggage wagon, one food wagon, and one wagon with horse rations.[73] The word "section" is misleading in this context.[74]

The commander of the Second Army was given operational control of the right wing to include First Army and HKK 2; Second Army was given control of HKK 2 as an integral element. HKK 2 operated on the right flank and in front of First Army. At the time of the advance, HKK 2 was to revert to the operational control of OHL. They were supposed to send intelligence reports to the First Army.[75] Therefore, geographically First Army was between HKK2 and Second Army. So an army headquarters that was not contiguous to the area of operations had a command relationship with the cavalry forces. Kluck called that an "unfortunate decision."

To clarify, bear in mind, as mentioned in Chapter 7, the HKKs had no radio. There was no way to communicate electronically between Second Army and HKK 2. The divisions had radio equipment, but the headquarters that controlled them did not. Messages between the Second Army and HKK 2 had to traverse the area of First Army. The only way to communicate electronically was if, by chance, the commander of the HKK was co-located with the radio equipment of one of the divisions. HKK 2 (2nd, 4th, and 9th Cavalry Divisions) was initially placed under the command of the Second Army. When the advance began, this command line changed to the OHL. HKK 2 was then tasked to advance north of Namur against Antwerp-Brussels and Charleroi to reconnoiter the remains of the Belgian Army, to find out about possible landings of British forces, and to reconnoiter whether French forces were operating in northern Belgium. HKK 2 had to copy its reports to Headquarters First Army as well.[76]

The Staff Problem

In an army corps, the chief of staff was normally a full colonel. In an HKK, the chief of staff was either a major or a lieutenant colonel. In addition, a normal corps had a full staff with four sections, four General Staff officers, three adjutants, and a host of other officers and *Beamten*. The HKK had only two officers: the chief of staff and one other, the Ib. There were no intendants or Iva's in the HKK staffs. This hierarchy meant that the chief had to do many jobs. It seems as though the chief also had to be the Ia. The cavalry division staffs also had only one Ia and a Ib officer. Examination of Appendix F in which those officers are identified reveals an anomaly in the assignment of the Ib officers at both the HKK and the division level. These individuals are captains. They are not the traditional cavalry rank of *captain-Rittmeister*. So the officer running the logistics function of the cavalry was not a cavalry

73 (Rabenau, 1914), p. 54.
74 (Zuber, *The Mons Myth: A Reassessment of the Battle*, 2010), p. 77.
75 (Kuhl, 1929), p. 86.
76 (Kluck, 1926), p. 17.

officer but rather someone with General Staff training. He would not have had the background of having served in a mounted unit for his entire career. Although the HKKs were often referred to as cavalry corps, and obviously treated as such by higher commanders, they could at best assume a coordination role, but they could not replicate all the functions of corps staffs, leading and supplying their troops. While the cavalry divisions had their own IVa intendancy branch, this was completely missing at the HKK level. So the entire logistics of the cavalry formations had to be overseen by the Ib officers, in cooperation with the IVa intendancy officials of the division with very few subordinates. The division intendant (IVa) had an assistant secretary (*Intendantur-Sekretariats-Assistant*), three intendance secretaries (*Intendantur-Sekretäre*)—usually one attached per cavalry brigade—and a handful of lower ranking intendance officials with NCO ranks.[77] The entire staff of a cavalry division was about 80 officers, NCOs, and EM, and had about 70 horses.

The Logistics Problem

Even greater than the supply problems of the army corps, were those of the HKK. Within the HKKs, the conflicting issues of high operational mobility vs. sufficient supply for ammunition and rations became obvious from the first days of the campaign. Because planning the mobilization of the HKKs only began in 1913, there was absolutely no experience in operating such big cavalry formations in the field. Before 1914, only cavalry divisions had been mobilized for maneuvers. The HKKs did not have a sufficient command and control infrastructure. They did not even own a radio station.

The cavalry divisions had only very small supply units trailing behind them. The attached horse artillery battalions (the "mounted" battalions) had their unit loads of ammunition—the combat load carried in the gun limbers and the basic load carried by the light ammunition columns. The artillery and the combat formations had their heavy baggage and their fighting baggage, and that was all. With the exception of the attached Jäger battalions, none of the artillery or cavalry units had mobile field kitchens like the infantry. Nor was any supply infrastructure mobilized. The entire trains and columns organizations integral to the army corps were missing in these improvised cavalry corps. The only supply formation that cavalry divisions had were the light motor transportation columns—one per division, created upon mobilization.

On the one hand, this structure kept the cavalry divisions really small and mobile; on the other hand, it deprived them of the logistical assets necessary to ensure a systematic supply of food, horse rations, and ammunition. The cavalry divisions had to live off the land.[78] Since the motor transportation columns were much too small to secure the supplies of the highly mobile cavalry divisions, soldiers had either to live off the countryside or make use of the so-called iron rations.

The HKKs were usually attached to army staffs for tactical lead and for supply. Because the HKK had no real staff, logistical issues were usually handled between the cavalry divisions and the army commands. In practice, that meant that the cavalry divisions had to rely upon the service of the nearest army corps with which they were operating. Since the supply situation of army corps was already quite limited, this additional and unpredictable demand had serious implications for the army corps' supply situation and resulted in severe food and

[77] (Urach, 1905), p. 7.
[78] (Großer Generalstab, 1914), p. 94.

ammunition shortages. The cavalry was reduced to begging the nearest army corps for help with food, horse rations, and even artillery ammunition.

Living off the country without having a reliable supply chain behind led to further problems for mobility. Lt. Col. Ludloff of II Army Corps also complained about the HKK:

> The transportation of the cavalry divisions caused a good deal of trouble, on more than one occasion. The mobility of the cavalry trains, in particular, is greatly impaired by requisitioning from the inhabitants' vehicles of every description. The commanders of the train seem to think that this practice was necessary, in order to meet the difficulties of supplying ammunition and subsistence and of transporting men without mounts. As a rule, the cavalry ammunition companies and trains were required to make long marches in order to keep up with the advance by bounds of the cavalry divisions . . . The final outcome was that the cavalry divisions were, to a greater or lesser extent, always short of ammunition, probably because the hauling of supplies could not keep pace with the march performances of the cavalry. For this reason, the cavalry divisions eventually were an actual burden on the II Army Corps.[79]

The transportation personnel of the cavalry divisions rode on these wagons to a far greater extent than is ordinarily the custom, resulting in discipline that deteriorated more rapidly among them than in other units. The additional soldiers contributed to the congestion of roads planned for other columns of the army corps cooperating with the respective cavalry divisions. Gen. von Hammerstein commented on the cavalry around III Army Corps living off the land by saying:

> On a few occasions we were embarrassed in our supply by the cavalry . . . Up to September 1 the HKK on account of deliveries in its own supply, occasionally came into our assigned area and requisitioned supplies from the inhabitants, to the detriment of our own requisitions. Furthermore, on 26 August near Cambrai, the HKK made an urgent request for ammunition thereby upsetting all our own dispositions and reducing seriously our stocks that on account of the numerous daytime encounters had been greatly depleted. But those requests had to be put up with. The independent cavalry had to rely for its supplies on the nearest Army Corps since it could not be encumbered with the trains.[80]

The hauling of supplies could not keep pace with the march pace of the cavalry. For this reason the cavalry divisions were an actual burden upon the army corps with whom they had to cooperate. Interestingly, the independent cavalry became less burdensome to the supply service when, because of exhaustion, they had to maintain closer contact with the army corps. This contact put an end to the sudden and unpredictable requests of the cavalry that, for that very reason, were so hard to satisfy.[81]

The 2nd Cavalry Division was already suffering from severe shortages of subsistence and horse rations on 13 August when located south of Liége—still on the eastern bank of the river Meuse. This occurred during the closing phase of the assault on Liége, but five days before the actual advance of the right wing started. The formation was south of the Fort de

79 (Kuhl, 1929), p. 122.
80 (Kuhl, 1929), pp. 120–121.
81 (Kuhl, 1929), p. 121.

Chaudefontaine and only between 35 and 40 kilometers from the German border. Although the 2nd Cavalry Division was affected most, these shortages applied to all formations of HKK 2 around Liége at the same time.[82] This did not bode well for prospects as the cavalry advanced deeper into enemy territory. This shortage soon pushed the motor transport commander of First Army to mobilize a further 12 improvised motor transport columns equipped with light civilian vehicles, thus fixing one problem by creating another one, because these civilian vehicles were not built to withstand heavy-duty military use and quickly broke down.

The most compelling problem was not just confined to the cavalry. Without question it was most acute for that arm, but it extended to all units equipped with horses. The issue was horse food. The ratio of men to horses was approximately four to one during the Franco-Prussian war, but it had decreased to three to one by the 1914 campaign. The warning signs raised about Franco-Prussian War fodder issues went unheeded.[83] The total fodder requirement for the German army in 1914 was so huge that trying to bring it up through the communication zone would have rendered the campaign impossible. As a result, **the Army entered into the campaign with little or no arrangements to feed any horses**. First Army alone had 84,000 horses, which consumed at least 2,000,000 pounds of food per day. That would fill up over 900 fodder wagons.[84]

Frequently horses were fed locally with green corn that caused sickness in the horse population. There are reports of the horses from artillery teams dying even before they crossed the border into Belgium. The logistics for this effort was completely ignored when it came to the HKKs. There was no logistical function at the HKK level. None. Normally one would expect a corps level unit to be logistically tied into its respective army headquarters. By these means, reordering of supplies, ammunition, and food for the horses could be made relatively routinely. Instead, in the case of the cavalry, the plan was for each division to create ad hoc links directly with the army individually.

Given that the right wing was the main effort, no one would alternate the logistical function of cavalry divisions from one army to the next. Yet, unbelievably, that is exactly what was done. This élite force that was incredibly high maintenance in the care of the horses was neglected. The staff had planned down to the level of cups of coffee at train stops, but apparently not for the care of their horses. The logistical shortfalls were a clear crack in the system that could not easily be repaired. Was there enough mechanization available to transport tons of supplies quickly? Perhaps a short war had been the primary planning assumption, so the need for logistical replenishment was limited. However, such an assumption, if it existed, does not appear to have been stated explicitly.

When it came to food, the HKK was at a distinct disadvantage. Unlike infantry troops, there were no mobile kitchens that in infantry units were part of the combat trains. The cavalry units had to wait for the arrival of their field trains to receive food. This arrival normally happened late in the day or at night. This timing led to a method of feeding that had an operational effect. In order to "meet the field trains," cavalry units generally had to bivouac at a location that was somewhat behind the front. This placement was sort of a withdrawal out of contact into a more secure bivouac location. Their food would be issued and prepared at the squad level. Food for the horses would also be issued if available. The alternative was to fall back on the idea of living off the land. That meant that time was lost from reconnaissance in order to search for food. There was also the issue of requisition-

82 (Kluck, 1926), p. 23.
83 (Großer Generalstab, *Kriegsgeschichtliche Abteilung I,* 1911), pp. 287–289.
84 (Creveld, 1994), pp. 124–125.

ing and all of the dangers surrounding a breakdown in discipline and potential looting.[85] Another point about living off the land is that it was believed that, except on rare occasions, only meat "on the hoof" could be procured in sufficient quantities. Bread, the major staple of the soldiers' diet, probably never would be obtainable. Rations that could not be found locally, such as bread, were supposed to be drawn from the subsistence companies of the army corps. The HKK did not have such a company. It was assumed that cavalry divisions would be able to live entirely off the land.

Each division carried in its motor transport company sufficient grain and oats to last one day. After that day's supplies were used, the divisions were supposed to draw replenishment from an army corps that had been specially designated by the Army, or directly from the communications zone. This arrangement was inherently weak. The corps designated would have to belong to the army that controlled the HKK. In the case of HKK 2, this was Second Army. However, HKK 2 was integral to, but not geographically contiguous to Second Army. Furthermore, the communication zone was so distant that the divisional truck organization was not likely to visit it. In case of emergency, each cavalry soldier was issued three reserve rations, the so-called iron rations; they also carried two or three grain rations for their animals.[86]

Ammunition and weaponry created a unique problem for the cavalry. Captured Belgian stores could not replace the precision-made ammunition and spare parts required by the cavalry units. The horse-drawn ammunition columns could not keep up with the pace of movement and have been referred to as "rolling magazines." Therefore, motor transport was required once again. There was a strange anomaly due to the prioritization of ammunition. Because the movement of ammunition took precedence over all other classes of supply, the drivers could frequently not find fuel for their vehicles that were intended to haul the ammunition.[87]

Consider this simple change of command relationship. Operationally it is not important. One day a soldier might be assigned to one unit and a different one the following day. But when logistics is considered, a huge problem arises. The soldier is supposed to draw his supplies through the communications zone of the Army to which he is attached. As long as the cavalry divisions operated with one particular army it was possible to establish a working relationship with the supply line. However, in the event of a change of army, the logistical relationship had to change as well. As the HKK had no logistical function, the entire logistics burden fell upon the divisions, which would be attached to an infantry corps for the purpose of drawing supplies. That would generally be an ad hoc function as the cavalry divisions were not organic. They were considered "a constant burden on the army corps so unfortunate as to be responsible for them." It is easy to visualize a supply sergeant with an empty cup begging for supplies from a strange and different army corps, only to be told when he got to the front of the line that his numbered army affiliation had changed and he was no longer permitted to draw supplies from there. Add in the time involved for horse-drawn convoys to make it to the supply source and the lack of efficient communication, and it is clear that resupply would have been a highly precarious matter that was worsened by changing army affiliations.[88]

---

[85] (Kuhl, 1929), p. 8.
[86] (Kuhl, 1929), pp. 9–10.
[87] (Creveld, 1994), pp. 125–127.
[88] (Creveld, 1994), p. 127.

The Culture/Doctrine Problem

Having failed to locate opposing elements of the Belgian Army, a division of cavalry tried to force its way through the village of Haelen. German accounts of the battle of Haelen show that this 12 August cavalry action was conducted in historically romantic three mounted waves. Specifically, the charge of the Dragoon Regiment 18 is instructive. This charge happened after the Dragoon-Regiment 17 was mauled by Belgian dismounted cavalry fire: "During the attack by the Dragoon-Regiment 18, the 4th and 1st squadrons in echelons made a frontal attack, and the 3d squadron, echeloned in depth, on the left, assaulted in a northwesterly direction."[89] This action was followed by the attack of 3 Cavalry Brigade: "Here, however, the squadron received murderous infantry and machinegun fire. Horses, struck by enemy bullets, dragged others with them to the ground as they fell."[90] A survivor reportedly said: "The brigade is destroyed. Rode in against infantry, artillery, and machineguns—hung up in the wire, fell into a sunken road—all shot down."[91] The era of mounted cavalry charges had not quite ended. It was part of the social structure and despite more recent doctrine, the units fell back upon mounted charges very quickly.

> Our brave troopers had shown that they were eager to encounter the enemy with their lances and that they were not afraid to ride into the enemy as long as possible under the strongest opposing fire. On the other hand, this day taught that these modern fire positions could not be successfully attacked by mounted troops and that in such case, only a fire and maneuver action would be successful.[92]

Surely this is precisely what the development of prewar doctrine and all of the maneuvers was about. It appears, however, that the lessons the doctrine had been intended to drive home had to be relearned under fire. This battle produced a 16 percent casualty rate for the division, and it lost 28 percent of its horses.[93]

Another problem of culture and doctrine was reconnaissance. There was no successful endeavor to screen forces from enemy aircraft reconnaissance. Reconnaissance in general seems to have been a dismal failure. On 21 August, the Second Army was unable confirm whether an entire French army was south of the Sambre River through either cavalry scouts or aerial reconnaissance[94] The success rate of getting reports from the aviation section to the Army commanders was only about 50 percent.[95]

After that battle, the reconnaissance improved. Each Army Corps had six single-winged Taube or comparable aircrafts that were spread out ahead of the advancing infantry. While successful, a lack of understanding the technical capability limited the range to a 50 km radius. However, longer-range reconnaissance by Zeppelin failed miserably in August due to the weather. Nine BEF brigades disembarked at Le Havre and made their way across northern France undetected. The right wing remained poorly informed with Generaloberst v. Kluck expecting the BEF to land in the vicinity of Dunkirk. As a result, most of the cavalry and aviation assets were scattered in the northwesterly direction. Many of First Army movements can be explained by the lack of reconnaissance on the right flank and the unknown

89 (Poseck M. v., 1921), p. 24.
90 (Poseck M. v., 1921), p. 25.
91 (Brose, 2001), p. 190.
92 (Poseck M. v., 1921), p. 28.
93 (Brose, 2001), p. 190.
94 (Herwig H., 2009), p. 143.
95 (Herwig H., 2009), p. 246.

whereabouts of the BEF.[96] There was no mechanism in place to share information between the aviation assets of the different Army Corps. There were no aviation assets available to IV Reserve Corps that was operating on the extreme right, as it was a reserve army corps. It was also argued that the subordination of HKKs to different army headquarters was the primary reason for the misuse of reconnaissance assets by HKK 2 and therefore, they missed the BEF. Many lamented that HKK 3 had been wasted and would have been better utilized in the open spaces of the right wing in Belgium.[97]

While the aviation assets complemented the cavalry, this quotation from a British source provides an assessment of German reconnaissance efficiencies:

> . . . As to the fog of war, . . . the Germans had no idea of our whereabouts or our strength. In his orders for the 23rd, so our Official History tells us, all the German Commander, General v. Kluck, could tell his troops was that he knew of a British Squadron of Cavalry near Mons, and that a British aeroplane had been shot down. The Germans do not appear to have known where we had landed, or that we were actually in the line of battle . . . Von Kluck's failure to pursue was again due, as at Mons, to faulty intelligence. He had been assured by his intelligence service that as the British army was based on Calais their lines of communication must run through Lille and Cambrai . . . He maneuvered accordingly, that is, he extended his right the more surely to prevent the British from connecting up with their supposed lines of communication farther north. Von Kluck, misled by his intelligence, went on a wild goose chase and meanwhile the British army escaped.[98]

Neither Kluck, Bülow, nor OHL had any clear idea of the location of the BEF and therefore they could not agree on how to sweep around it.[99]

Dismounted operations presented another set of issues not adequately practiced pre-war. "The fighting on foot of large units alone has not sufficiently been taken care of [trained]." "It need only be mentioned that the great numbers of led horses immediately following the regiments into battle often interfered with operations." "Despite the improvements made in fighting dismounted, there was nevertheless a lack of schooling in fire practice in larger units."[100] The planning, structure and training of the HKK was such an obvious flaw as to be almost unbelievable. No planning was done until 1913! The Chief of Staff would not share the plans with a potential commander who was general inspector of the cavalry at that time! No wonder reconnaissance was poorly conducted.

While the terrain to be fought over had not changed since the time of the establishment of doctrine, there was a significant adaptation to the formations used in simple march column. The brigade column gave way to the brigade in regimental column. This change meant that instead of a 215 paces front, it was replaced by a 100 pace front. Eventually, these frontages were replaced by double columns and platoon columns, a 13-pace front. This change was significant from the close order formations practiced in maneuvers. Narrow longer formations indicated more speed and far less security, with the concomitant risk of surprise attacks.[101] Not only did marching change, but also patrolling. It was found that the dispatch

96 (Brose, 2001), pp. 191–192.
97 (Poseck M. v., 1921), pp. 225–226.
98 (Spears, 2000)
99 (Brose, 2001), p. 202.
100 (Poseck M. v., 1921), pp. 222–232.
101 (Poseck M. v., 1921), pp. 228–229.

of mixed arms patrols supplied with guns, machineguns, and cyclists did far better than a cavalry pure reconnaissance squadron. Also, officer patrols were eliminated due to the high losses of leaders.[102]

Timeline

1 August—Imperial Germany declared war on Russia.

2 August—First day of mobilization. The Army Commanders were given their orders and began meetings with Moltke in Berlin to get further guidance. HKK 2 put under operational control of Second Army.

3 August—Shots fired from the small Belgian town of Battice at a cavalry patrol scouting the way into Liège were interpreted as *franc-tireurs*. This event led to the execution of three civilians and the burning of the town.[103] Imperial Germany declares war on France. OHL began operations in Berlin.

4 August—Imperial Germany declared war on Belgium. 9th Cavalry Division attached to the X Army Corps for operations against Liège. 4th Cavalry Division crossed the Belgian frontier. They were not able to cross the Meuse River.[104]

5 August—2nd and 4th Cavalry Divisions sent long-range patrols across the river. Two reconnaissance squadrons followed these from each division. One of the squadrons from the 4th Cavalry Division did not cross until the sixth. On the night of the fifth and sixth, the original assault on Liège took place.[105]

6 August—The reconnaissance squadrons were able to complete their crossing and Poseck noted specifically "a shortage of oats was already being felt."[106]

7 August—HKK 1 put under the command of OHL and proceeded to the same objective as of the Third Army. HKK 4 was to precede the Fifth Army. HKK 3 was placed under the command of Sixth Army. The Guard Cavalry Division moved from Bitburg to Diekirch as part of HKK 1. Here the divisional war diary is instructive:

> The roads were very muddy on account of the heavy rain. Consequently, both the weakened regiments, especially the Guard Cuirassiers, were very much exhausted. The artillery was especially handicapped. The horses it had received for its light ammunition column were a cold-blooded inferior lot, which were unaccustomed to move rapidly. As a result of overexertion four of them died and the remainder were almost useless. In addition to this, the horses delivered were so late that about one third of them were improperly hitched up and as a result, many of them ran away.[107]

The first fort of Liége surrendered.

---

[102] (Poseck M. v., 1921), p. 230.
[103] (Herwig H., 2009), pp. 108–109.
[104] (Poseck M. v., 1921), p. 10.
[105] (Creveld, 1994), p. 125.
[106] (Poseck M. v., 1921), p. 13.
[107] (Poseck M. v., 1921), pp. 5–6, 41.

8 August—2nd and 4th Cavalry Divisions sent their main bodies across the Meuse River. The supply trains of the two divisions could not cross the improvised bridges, which made the shortage of oats even more acute.[108] The Battle of Mulhouse began in Southern Alsace.

9 August—2nd and 4th Cavalry Divisions continued their reconnaissance to the west. The 2nd Division relieved its reconnaissance squadrons and took the light radio station with the new squadron.

10 August—9th Cavalry Division was directed to cross the Meuse. It is important to note that the other divisions both had dismounted engagements, stayed in contact with the enemy, and then broke contact, as was their norm in order to bivouac. Contact with the enemy was suspended for the night. HKK 1 crossed the Luxembourg-Belgian frontier and continued onto Bastogne.[109] Directive from OHL reinforce HKK 3 under control of Sixth Army.

11 August—2nd Cavalry Division had to be taken out of the line due to starving and exhausted horses. The commander of HKK 2 lamented that his troops had had very little rest and were suffering from the shortage of food and forage. "Advance by these weakened troops seems impossible and their further employment should not be considered." Second Army directed that IX Army Corps bring up forage for the horses, directed HKK 2 to slow down if necessary, and told the cavalry to "requisition and live off the land." Interestingly, this direction was sent by wireless. So it is not entirely clear whom they expected to receive it. The Guard Cavalry Division noted that from this time until the end of the war they could no longer move in the peacetime column of fours. Such a column was too wide to permit motorcars to pass. They adopted a two-wide column formation for marching.[110]

12 August—The Battle of Haelen, also known as the "Battle of the Silver Helmets." The battle produced a 16 percent casualty rate for the division, and it lost 28 percent of its horses.[111] Essentially two of the three brigades of the 4th Cavalry Division were wrecked taking mounted action against dismounted infantry. It is instructive again that the battle was called off at dark, and the divisions moved out of contact into a bivouac area. HKK 1 used 12 and 13 August to rest its horses.[112] The BEF started to disembark.

13 August—Ft. Pontisse in Liège fell, clearing the way for First Army to cross the Meuse. The cavalry's task was to remain where it was and cover the advance of the enemy until the arrival of the First and Second Armies. They were also to "ease the shortage of forage and to assist in the bringing up of ammunition, which was rapidly failing."[113] The commander of the First Army put the situation a little bit more critically.

All cavalry proceeding. First and Second Armies had to halt and rest for four days. "First Army made a request to Second Army to move 9th Cavalry Division, still standing southwest of Liége on the eastern bank of the river Meuse to be united with the rest of HKK 2. Second Army granted this request. All divisions of HKK 2 were suffering from shortages of horse

108 (Poseck M. v., 1921), p. 14.
109 (Poseck M. v., 1921), pp. 17–21, 42.
110 (Poseck M. v., 1921), pp. 20–21, 41–42.
111 (Brose, 2001), p. 190.
112 (Poseck M. v., 1921), 21–28, 43.
113 (Poseck M. v., 1921), p. 28.

rations and ammunition so First Army had to mobilize further motor transport columns to deliver the needed supplies."[114] At this point wireless communication was established between 9th Cavalry Division and Guard Cavalry Division. Therefore subordinate commands of HKK 1 and HKK 2 could talk to each other on the radio. However their parent headquarters had no such radio sets.[115]

15 August—9th Cavalry Division joined up with the rest of HKK 2. The crossing of the river was transmitted to the HKK commander by radio. So he must have been co-located with a divisional radio set. There was a reallocation of Jäger battalions by Second Army. The intent was to increase the number of motor transport trucks to help alleviate the condition of supplies and forage of the cavalry. Second Army sent another radio message: "Whether supplies will arrive is questionable. Live off of land, regardless."[116] HKK 1 contributed to the battle of Dinant.

16 August—OHL directed that 4th and 9th Cavalry Division march towards Perwez while the 2nd Cavalry Division screened the advance of the First Army. An entire brigade of the Guard Cavalry Division was committed to a reprisal attack on the inhabitants of Houx.[117] OHL moved from Berlin to Koblenz.

17 August—"04:30 p.m. the OHL gave the order that First and Second Army together with HKK 2 (Marwitz) is to operate under the command of Second Army when advancing north of the river Meuse. Advance is to commence on 18 August. It was essential to push the enemy forces in the position Diest-Tirlemont-Wavre away from Antwerp. Further objectives for both armies would be transmitted as soon as the position Brussels-Namur was reached and flank-guard against Antwerp was installed."[118] Kluck then argued against being put under the command of Second Army and stated that it would have been more suitable if HKK 2 had been put under the command of First Army. He also wanted First Army to be made independent of the Second Army. In his view, Second Army would be free to pursue tactical targets and First Army could follow a strategic approach.[119] The end result was that the 2nd Cavalry Division was removed from HKK 2 and was attached directly to Second Army.[120] Although Kluck did not mention this change, he must have intervened at the OHL on 18 August to get HKK 2 under his control and most probably to be released from control by Second Army. Obviously Moltke decided for some compromise. BEF main body finished disembarkation.

18 August—2nd Cavalry Division received an order to cross the river Veerle in order to cut off enemy forces.[121] At 10:00 p.m., Second Army ordered 2nd Cavalry Division to advance ahead of the right wing of Second Army in the early morning. The advance was to go from Aerschot towards Brussels and then towards Antwerp, bypassing Brussels.[122] HKK 2 skirmished with

---

[114] (Kluck, 1926), p. 23.
[115] (Poseck M. v., 1921), p. 43.
[116] (Poseck M. v., 1921), pp. 29, 45–46.
[117] (Poseck M. v., 1921), p. 47.
[118] (Kluck, 1926), p. 26.
[119] (Kluck, 1926), pp. 26–27.
[120] (Poseck, 1921), p. 31.
[121] (Kluck, 1926), p. 28.
[122] (Kluck, 1926), pp. 31–32.

the French Cavalry Corps of Sordet and was once again placed under command of the Second Army.[123]

19 August—2nd Cavalry Division was brought to a standstill due to supply difficulties.[124] HKK 1 held the high ground to the east of Dinant and used the day focused on horseshoe repair as well as sharpening lance points.[125]

20 August—Order issued by Second Army directed 2nd Cavalry Division to remain ahead of right wing of First Army and coordinate with II Army Corps about how the available roads were to be used. 2nd Cavalry Division began operations around the village of Wolverthem. 2nd Cavalry Division pursued the most important task to reconnoiter for approaching British forces between Brussels and Antwerp.[126] HKK 2 skirmished with the French Cavalry Corps of Sordet. Long-range patrols were sent out to the south. It is instructive to note that when the 4th Cavalry Division withdrew into bivouac they went all the way behind the Second Army's infantry.[127] Moltke directed that a "strong cavalry force west of the Meuse is desirable. Therefore, HKK 1 will clear away from the front of the Third and Forth Armies and begin moving around the northern side of Namur. Once it has arrived on the right bank of Meuse it will pass under orders of Second Army."[128] This directive from OHL was remarkably significant. Two days after the general advance started on the right wing, Moltke realized his entire deployment was wrong and ordered HKK 1 to move to the right of Second Army–changing armies. Operationally this redirection is huge.

Although it was easily stated, in fact what Moltke was ordering, was a cavalry force of two divisions to break contact, move back, and conduct a major river crossing under the control of Third Army. Then after crossing the river, they would change operational subordination and move to the operational control of Second Army. HKK 1 was to move at a 90° angle across the communications zone of Second Army without disrupting the flow of units and goods, always avoiding entrapment in the siege of Namur. It was to travel entirely around the communications zone of Second Army, establish these units on the right flank of Second Army, and make contact with the enemy. Poseck says: "In this manner much time was lost and the HKK was able to work its way only slowly towards the front of the Army. With the result that the HKK was again, up to 28 August, making its way to the front of the Army advance." It took eight days to complete this maneuver![129]

21 August—2nd Cavalry Division sent out two reconnaissance squadrons to locate the British advancing from the coast. The Belgians had withdrawn to the fortress of Antwerp. HKK 2 was given a change of mission directive that it was to march west to take a position in front of the right wing of the First Army. The reconnaissance patrols previously sent out by the 4th Cavalry Division could not be contacted or recalled. They did not rejoin the division until the next day or later.

123 (Poseck, 1921), p. 33.
124 (Creveld, 1994), p. 125.
125 (Poseck M. v., 1921), p. 47.
126 (Kluck, 1926), p. 34–35.
127 (Poseck, 1921), p. 36.
128 (Senior, 2012), p. 72 and (Poseck M. v., 1921), pp. 47–48.
129 (Poseck M. v., 1921), pp. 48–49.

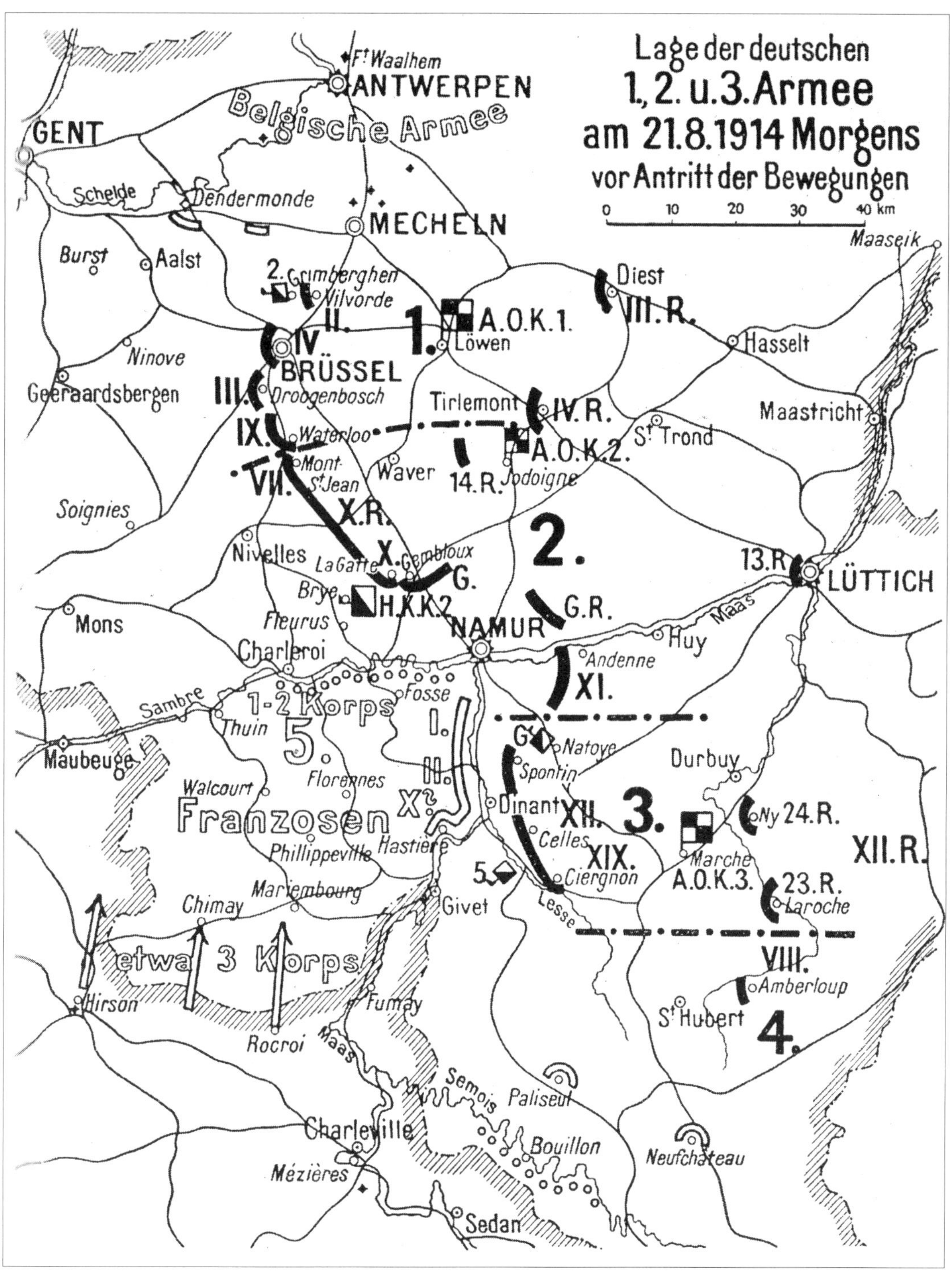

Tactical map, situation August 21, cavalry. (Source: Reichsarchiv vol 1, 1925)

22 August—The 2nd Cavalry Division was again attached to HKK 2. Western movement continued and its reconnaissance assignments were to cover the ground between Thourout-Lille-Condé. HKK 1 was to reconnoiter Condé-Maubeuge-Philippeville. The Guard Cavalry Division after diverting around Namur arrived at Gembloux with the Fifth Cavalry Division far behind. Due to severe road congestion around Namur and behind the Second Army, HKK 1 did not believe it had completed the move to the right of the Second Army until 28 August.[130] There was no clear intelligence picture about the location of the BEF. Cavalry patrols encountered British cavalry around Mons, and Spears reported the downing of a British aircraft.[131] First Army considered HKK 2 reconnaissance to be poor.[132] The commander of the Eighth Army in Eastern Prussia was relieved.

23 August—HKK 2 was given another change of mission. It was relieved of the requirement to remain in front of the right wing and was placed directly under the command of Second Army. It was ordered to take a position in front of Courtrai oriented northwest. It was not observing the BEF.[133]

24 August—In yet another change in the command relationship, HKK 2 was given to First Army and directed southward to march on Denain via Tournai. This change was an endeavor to get behind the flank of the British army. It advanced along the Schelde River. In the lead on the west side of the river was the 9th Cavalry Division, which engaged a brigade of French infantry at Lamain, pushed them aside, then continued on to Marchiennes. That meant a march of between 65 and 70 km that day, which included a battle with French infantry. Fourth Cavalry Division also covered 65 km that day and ended up in a bivouac near Orchies.[134] While reconnaissance squadrons made contact with the right wing of the BEF, the intent of the commander of HKK 1 was to join in the battle with IX Army Corps. Therefore, he would continue to move west behind the infantry of Second Army and closer to HKK 2.[135]

25 August—HKK 2 pursued the British army and unsuccessfully tried to cut the line of retreat. The pursuit was not conducted vigorously and was in fact dismissed as impossible, since the men and horses were completely exhausted.[136] Two Army Corps transferred to the Eastern Front from Second Army.

26 August—HKK 2 continued its pursuit of the British and engaged heavily in dismounted combat with the intent of fixing the British in position at Le Cateau. Many units ran out of small arms ammunition and some dismounted soldiers had pursued four kilometers ahead of their led horses and reserve ammunition supply. Failure to outflank and annihilate the enemy was blamed squarely on the time lost on 23 August when the cavalry moved towards Courtrai.[137] The Battle of Tannenberg started in Eastern Prussia.

---

130 (Poseck, 1921), pp. 33–37, 48–49.
131 (Spears, 2000)
132 (Kuhl D. H., 1921), p. 77.
133 (Poseck, 1921), p. 37.
134 (Tschischwitz, 1940), p. 25.
135 (Poseck M. v., 1921), pp. 38–40, 48–49.
136 (Poseck M. v., 1921), p. 56.
137 (Poseck M. v., 1921), pp. 53–66.

27 August—With HKK 2 around Cambrai, the pursuit was broken off and the decision was made by First Army to cross the Somme River Valley with the II Army Corps in front of HKK 2. An OHL directive was dispatched giving guidance to aim at Paris. The First Army and HKK 2 (still under the control of the Second Army) were to move sharply south and First Army was to protect the right flank. Second Army with HKK 1 was turned southbound, oriented on Laon. The left wing was ordered to break through the French fortress line creating a huge double-pincer envelopment of the French and British forces using both wings

28 August—HKK 2 started moving behind II Army Corps toward the Somme. 2nd Cavalry Division was surprised by French forces in its bivouac area in Moslains. These French forces were able to go through the positions of II Army Corps.[138] According to Bergmann:

> The cavalry . . . had drifted to the left flank of the First Army. It was subsequently put in line in support of IX Army Corps, which was preparing to attack south of Roye. Such an employment was, in my opinion, not quite in accordance with the nature of the cavalry arm in its proper mission. Nevertheless, the cavalry should not have neglected reconnaissance along the unprotected flank of the Army in the region of Amiens-Bapaume.[139]

29 August—HKK 2 was given a change of mission to stay west of the Oise River, to be prepared to assist Second Army, and guard the flank of the First Army. HKK 1 along with the Second Army was to advance on Paris by the La Fère.[140] This position was the left flank of the First Army. This meant that it was intended that HKK 2 and HKK 1 would combine forces to fill the gap between First Army and Second Army. This flank change led to a near miss between an ammunition column and French forces on the right flank. The 1b of II Army Corps attributed this near disaster entirely to the lack of cavalry reconnaissance on the right flank by HKK 2.[141]

30 August—HKK 1 and HKK 2 make direct contact. OHL relocated to Luxembourg.

31 August—While the advance continued, HKK 2 lost contact with the 4th Cavalry Division.[142]

1 September—Fourth Cavalry Division engages the British Army at Néry. The division allegedly covered 120 km in 24 hours. HKK 1 successfully pursued enemy forces but lost contact in the darkness. First Army was made independent of Second Army.

2 September—Generaloberst Frhr. v. Hausen, Commander of Third Army, lamented in his memoirs about exhausted cavalry with underfed horses having a negative impact upon the combat strength (number of combat ready troopers per squadron). Third Army was not able to pursue withdrawing French forces due to the lack of a cavalry division. The commander of the Third Army merged the divisional cavalry of the XII and XIX Army Corps into a kind of

[138] (Poseck M. v., 1921), pp. 67–69.
[139] (Kuhl, 1929), pp. 111–112.
[140] (Poseck M. v., 1921), p. 70.
[141] (Kuhl, 1929), p. 112.
[142] (Poseck M. v., 1921), p. 79–80.

improvised cavalry division.[143] OHL issued a new directive changing the concept of the entire operation. No longer was the major goal envelopment:

> It is the major intention of the OHL to push the French forces away from Paris in a southeasterly direction. First Army follows Second Army in echelons and resumes guarding the right flank of the advancing army.

A radio message followed this directive that requested the armies to send: "strong cavalry forces" into the area around Paris with the intention of destroying French railroads. This request sounds strikingly similar to an American Civil War cavalry raid so long disparaged by the German cavalry. Unfortunately, the cavalry was now completely out of position to act on any such request. [144]

The Dawn of the Great War was over for the cavalry by 30 August. "The vital element of the cavalry is mobility in a large space, a free path for an advance, and elbow room laterally. Once deprived of this vital necessity, the cavalry is condemned to quiescence and its role as a mounted arm has been played out."[145] The flank was still there. The entire "race to the sea" was an endeavor by both sides to outflank each other. The open space was still there somewhere off to the right or west of the First Army. But there was no HKK with any kind of elbow room. This area had been given up when HKK 1 and HKK 2 were joined in an interior position. When discussing the changes of command subordination between 21 August and 24 August, Poseck lamented: "Had it not been for this loss of time, it would have been possible for HKK 2 . . . to have gotten in the rear of the British Army and materialized the Schlieffen idea of the Cannae battle by surrounding it."[146]

The Force Distribution Problem

A quote from the diary of British General Haig: "This looks as if a great effort is to be made to turn the French left, which rests on Namur fortress, by an advance through Belgium. In fact, the solution of the problem which was given as the most likely one when I was at Camberley Staff College in 1897."[147]

When the author (Joe Robinson) was a young lieutenant, he was given the opportunity to watch some senior US officers compare solutions to a problem with some old German generals from World War II. The occasion was a type of war game where US forces drew in Soviet forces and then launched a counterattack onto the flank of those Soviet forces. The Soviets would be allowed to advance and the "nose" of the penetration would stretch like a rubber band allowing the Soviets to advance but not break through the resistance. At the appropriate time, a counterattack was to be launched destroying the Soviet force from the flank. The American generals were concerned that the rubber band was a bit too weak. They were quite afraid that the Soviet forces would be able to break through this thin veneer of covering forces. Being young, sitting in the bleachers, and listening to this briefing was a little bit above the pay grade of a lieutenant in a reconnaissance squadron. After the American generals finished their explanation, the retired German generals got together in a corner and discussed the situation in private. I had been somewhat bored up until then. What transpired

[143] (Hausen, 1920), pp. 171–172
[144] (Kuhl, 1921), p. 118
[145] (Poseck M. v., 1921), p. 221.
[146] (Poseck M. v., 1921), p. 226.
[147] (Stein, 1921)

next had a deep impact not only on the war game, but also on how I learned to structure troop distributions throughout my career.

Surprisingly, when the old German generals returned, they took even more forces away from the rubber band and added them to the counterattacking force. There was no disagreement. There was no hesitation. And in their minds, the only question was the positioning of supporting artillery. That was it. Making the attack as strong as possible was the underlying lesson. If we apply this scenario to the early stages of World War I it is easy to come to conclusions. Looking at a map we can easily identify the Schlieffen Plan.

The 1914 deployment looks to be a very similar scenario. The Sixth and Seventh Armies formed the rubber band. The First, Second, and Third Armies were the counterattack forces that were going to sweep around the flank of the French Army. The story might be apocryphal, but many of us grew up hearing that Schlieffen's last words were: "to keep the right wing strong." If indeed there was such a plan, it certainly fits nicely into this scenario. Like the generals from World War II, the German generals of World War I intended to put everything into the attack on the right wing.[148] Of course there were significant modifications to the 1905 plan, so what was actually enacted was a modified Schlieffen plan with similar goals. In 1912, Moltke the Younger informed both the Chancellor and the War Minster in writing that imperial Germany needed a thin screen against one enemy in order to hurl of its primary forces against the other. "That side always can only be France." Furthermore he wrote that the neutrality of Belgium was going to be violated.[149] General v. Stein explained it simply: "It could not be Russia, for the Russians would have had no hesitation about retreating further and further into their vast country and so avoid a decisive issue until their allies were able to make themselves felt. The only course that remained open, then, was an attack on France and the march through Belgium."[150]

It seems that the true plan would have required adequate forces on the right flank and a rubber band that had just enough strength to hold the French back long enough. If this stratagem is so intuitively obvious to any planner, if this were the intent of Moltke, why did he not do that? It is obvious that Moltke had problems with the seven to one ratio of troops in the right wing to the left wing that Schlieffen had envisioned in his 1905 document. Over time during his tenure as Chief of Staff, he reduced that ratio down to three to one. The ratio change alone should make it clear that Moltke had a completely different concept than had Schlieffen. There were similarities—a right-wing attack, but not nearly the objectives—or strength of the 1905 memorandum. It was easy to find fault with Moltke in the late 1920s. He was dead and could not fight back. General Groener and others joined the denigrators giving the impression that Schlieffen had handed Moltke a perfect plan. The Schlieffen school said Moltke watered down the plan, failed to give enough guidance to the right-wing armies, and sent messengers rather than personally enforcing his will.[151] "[OHL] . . . distributed its forces disadvantageously, owing to their wrong estimate of the situation, not only at the beginning, but also during the further course of operations."[152]

As Moltke ruled over the force requirements, it is amazing that he did not either create the forces equal to the 1905 requirements or intensify his investment into modern war material such as communications and aircraft. While there was a significant increase in forces, it

148 (Kuhl, 1929), p. 228.
149 (Herwig H., 2009), pp. 42–43.
150 (Stein, 1921), pp. 62–63.
151 (Kuhl, 1929), pp. vii-viii.
152 (Kuhl, 1929), pp. 228–233.

primarily went to the major arms and not to communication and reconnaissance technology. Much larger than the ratio issue was the distribution of cavalry forces.[153]

If indeed the intent were to keep the right wing strong and outflank the French Army, the single most important element of the force structure would have been reconnaissance forces. In this case, he should have massed cavalry on the right flank to find the enemy's flank, screened the movements of the main body, exploited, and pursued. Schlieffen, in his writings about the Battle of Cannae, talked about the weak infantry center while cavalry and light infantry moved around the flanks and into the Roman rear.[154] Hans Delbrück, who also wrote about the battle of Cannae, said that the decisive factor was the attack on the rear of the formation by the Carthaginian cavalry.[155] There would be no better use of cavalry troops except on the far right flank. There were four cavalry corps available to the German army. Only one of the four was employed on the right flank. It is almost as though the other three were assigned to armies on a fair share basis as opposed to the basic tenant of troops applied to task. Why? Why did he put large numbers of cavalry in front of troops that were not involved in the turning movement?

If blocks of troops are being moved around and the intent is to get around the enemy's left flank and into his rear by making the main effort on his own right flank, what proportion of the cavalry should be used in support? In the example of 1914, there would seem to be a clear case for the use of three of the HKKs on the right flank. Which ones they should have been, or what number of divisions should have been assigned to each HKK in the main effort, is a matter of debate. However, it is not likely that any planner would leave this right wing shorthanded in cavalry forces. Instead, the deployment actually amounted to three cavalry divisions in front of First and Second armies. There were four cavalry divisions in front of the Third and Fourth Armies and three cavalry divisions on the left flank. The cavalry situation was even more unbalanced if we take into account the prewar plans that included the Italian Third Army. In theory and according to prewar plans, this force of three infantry corps and two cavalry divisions was supposed to be added to the left wing and to be able to storm Belfort on the 17th day of mobilization. When Italy declared neutrality on August 2, these forces disappeared.[156]

If indeed the Great General Staff was one of the perfect organizations of its time, how could it make such an error? This mistake is compounded by the identified shortcoming that showed that these higher cavalry organizations were at best ad hoc. The commanders were not on the same level as commanders of the infantry corps. Logistics was a disaster. The training of the collective group was seriously lacking. But even with all of these shortcomings, it seems as though the HKKs were mainly assigned to the wrong place. Why? General Bergman in his review of the operation was very clear in stating that the cavalry divisions could have been readily spared at other points of the front. ". . . It would have been possible to withdraw from the southern wing and from the remainder of the line at least four army corps and several cavalry divisions for transfer to the northern wing where the decision was sought."[157] Poseck is similarly damning. He points out that Schlieffen had placed eight of 11 divisions of cavalry on the right wing in his one front scenario. Moltke put 10 of those cavalry divisions on the Western Front but only the three divisions of

---

[153] (Herwig H. , 2009), pp. 44–45.
[154] (Herwig H. , 2009), p. 35.
[155] (Delbrück, 1975), p. 319.
[156] (Herwig H. , 2009), pp. 80–82.
[157] (Kuhl, 1929), p. 230.

HKK 2 could truly be considered on the right flank. The two divisions of HKK 1 were only marginally on the right flank. "This would have left, besides the divisions of HKK 1 and HKK 2, another HKK of three divisions for the extreme swinging army wing where the decisive battle was to be expected."[158]

The directive on 20 August, moving the location of HKK 1, really demonstrates that there was a total initial planning failure. With the help of 20–20 hindsight, senior leaders were able to explain and to lament that HKK 3, as a minimum, should initially have been allocated to the right flank. But then to move HKK 1 into a more advantageous position only two days after the advance started makes it clear that it should have been deployed differently to begin with. This major force was out of full commitment for eight critical days, simply to accomplish this repositioning. Was this force allocation mistake the result of cultural issues? Was it the result of leadership issues? Did Auftragstaktik play a role? Did someone determine that the divisions could not feed more than one HKK on the right wing? In other words, was this misplacement a decision made because of a logistical problem?

There would seem to be only two likely reasons why the cavalry force distribution was not heavily weighted on the right. Possible reason number one is that cavalry were distributed on a fair share basis. An army commander needs a balanced all-arms force so, if his order of battle does not contain enough cavalry, it is not an army. The second reason is whether it was the intent to get around the enemy's left flank. This opens up two possible paths—one being an attempt to punch through the French left without going around the flank—or two, the real concept was some sort of double envelopment in which the left wing would also be required to punch through. Of course there are no doubt other reasons, but from a purely force distribution analysis we always return to a heavily weighted right wing in cavalry forces.

CONCLUSION

This book has taken you on a significant ride through the past, during the course of which imperial German political, social, cultural and military structures have been examined in some depth. Understanding these structures helps to unravel the systemic issues that contributed to the disastrous beginnings of the Great War. The impact of imperial German weaponry and technology on the development of doctrine has been discussed. As chapter succeeded chapter the picture darkened. The peacetime cultural and military norms pointed the way to some of the anomalies that the German military should have taken into account. Technology was continually marching forward, but the way both society and the military embraced it had lasting effects. The doctrine that continually evolved during 40 years of peace was not a panacea. As with all military machines, the evolving doctrine experienced some unexpected setbacks. The traditionalists and reformers were continually at loggerheads.

But this was imperial Germany. Everything should have been perfect. The mighty juggernaut of the army was well known and respected. This is the vision that has been ingrained in American military historians whether they are professional or armchair students. However, there were cracks. How much impact did these failures have on the conduct of the start of the Great War? The focus of this book has been on three of these cracks: leadership, logistics, and the cavalry organization. Other areas could be studied as sources of potential

[158] (Poseck M. v., 1921), p. 227.

problems, but these three issues are perhaps the most significant problems; they are also ones that could have been identified and corrected before the start of the war.

If the OHL had created army groups, this would have gone a long way to ameliorate the command and control leadership issues. Further, it would have made the correct application of Auftragstaktik much more effective. This restructuring would have provided quicker and closer guidance to both the left and right wings. The idea of putting someone in charge who does not have a staff and then never sending someone of equal rank to check on him and reinforce mission orders is fraught with danger. It had the end result of the distant OHL making decisions with limited grasp of the current situation. A pre-war formed and exercised army group could have provided closer supervision that would have ensured compliance as well as making sure OHL did not make vacuous decisions from afar. Then the leadership could have implemented the simple fix of putting more resources into where they were needed. Electronic communications may have been in their infancy, but they existed and would have solved many issues. Command and control with easy and reliable communications among entities should have been addressed before the war. Exchanging a little troop strength for technology in the budget should have been a recurring theme in the months leading up to the war.

While logistics was problematic, it does not seem to have stopped the operation. No soldiers starved. Captured and looted foodstuffs allowed the Army to live off the land as envisioned by Schlieffen. However, there were still problems. The solution to supply distribution should have been obvious. While the railheads created a fixed-distance problem, more motor transports could have offered a reasonable solution. Simply analyzing the loads of motor transports compared to horse-drawn convoys would easily have shown the advantages of modernization. Once again, the use of existing technology should have been addressed. By 1914, it was clear that horse-drawn columns were too slow and had too low of a transport capacity to rapidly advance. Why were more automobile transport formations not planned for and mobilized?

Additionally, the artillery ammunition estimates were woefully inadequate even though the supply system was generally able to keep up in the short-term—largely by completely emptying the homeland zone factories. Once again, there was no backup plan. There was a significant shortfall—more like an ammunition disaster—right over the horizon.

Beginning in September 1914, the French and the British also started to suffer from logistical problems such as ammunition shortages. This was not unlike the problems in the German Army. But from an army that went to war following a kind of a Blitzkrieg doctrine, (at least in the west) a different logistical system should have been expected—a logistical system that would operate more smoothly and that would emphasize technical solutions to cope with classical problems.

The German military élite, before 1914, was generally averse to technology. Perhaps the disdain for the technical arms ensured the reliance on classical transportation means. Consider the disastrous results of the coup de main at Liège, where the classical attack failed, and the German army sustained high losses. If their super-heavy artillery had not succeeded in smashing the Liège forts, the results of the coup de main would have been even more devastating.

It was clear before the war began that putting "men against fire" would be no solution for further military success. Yet, the traditionalists insisted on following this classical doctrine. Ludendorff and a few other General Staff officers were the exception when they asked for technological solutions for increasing firepower and replacing men. From such a technologically advanced nation (as Germany was in 1914), one would have expected a better application of existing know-how. But, the entrenched ideology of the military élite disallowed any doctrinal modernization. The logistical issues alone did not lose the war. But, these logistical cracks, in combination with the leadership issues and the failure of the cavalry structure, led to the loss of the Marne campaign.

The third crack, the lack of a functioning higher cavalry organization, seems absolutely dumbfounding. The force structure of the army put a great deal of emphasis on cavalry. Socially and culturally, the cavalry was the epitome of military might. If anyone wanted to have a successful party, a cavalry officer was highly sought after. Yes, cavalry units were expensive, not only for the government, but also for the officers who had to supplement these significant expenses. Imperial German lore revered the cavalry. That was all well and good, but, when trying to include the lore in force structure planning, the issue came to a head. Why were there were no division-level exercises annually? How was that possible? Why was there was no cavalry corps organization? None. How was that possible? Furthermore, when the Kaiser was told that cavalry division commanders would fail without some sort of peacetime training, the Kaiser did nothing. And then you take into account that there were no logistical considerations for the cavalry at all; the problem is magnified.

To live off the land is an impossible directive when there were so many horses involved. How could this lack of foresight happen in imperial Germany? How is it possible that a noted historian could find that imperial Germany entered the war with no plan at all to feed the horses?[159] Culturally, the secrecy of the General Staff played a significant role in the failure when they in refused to share the deployment plan with those who would be in charge of a large cavalry formation. How could Auftragstaktik work in a situation in which subordinates could not see the organization that they were supposed to command? How could the OHL envision a corps-sized organization that did not have a staff or a logistical function?

When we put these three issues against a timeline, the dawning of the Great War did not last very long, but the effects of the cracks were felt almost immediately. By 30 August, the cavalry was doing nothing but plugging the line. By 4 September, OHL had given up on the entire idea of envelopment. The Great General Staff learned too late that even some planning effort into the cavalry higher organizations and more focus on technology (motor transports and communications among others) would have helped heal these cracks dramatically.

Over the years the belief has built up that the German army of 1914 was a perfectly-formed and led juggernaut that should have most certainly defeated France and Britain. It was only through the bravery, audacity, and skill of the British and French forces that the Allies were victorious. However, as this book shows, there were at least three systemic failures that contributed to the defeat of the imperial German army. If the book has provided food for thought and those thoughts lead to further study, its object will have been achieved.

---

[159] (Creveld, 1994), p. 124.

APPENDICES

APPENDIX A

THE IMPERIAL CONSTITUTION[1]

His Majesty the King of Prussia, in the name of the North German *Bund*, His Majesty the King of Bavaria, His Majesty the King of Württemberg, His Royal Highness the Grand Duke of Baden, and His Royal Highness the Grand Duke of Hesse and by Rhine for those parts of the Grand Duchy lying south of the Main, do conclude an everlasting *Bund* for the protection of the federal territory and of the rights valid within the same, as well as for the furtherance of the welfare of the German people. This *Bund* shall bear the name of the German Empire and shall have the following Constitution:—

I. Federal Territory

Article 1

The territory of the *Bund* shall consist of the States of Prussia with Lauenburg, Bavaria, Saxony, Württemberg, Baden, Hesse, Mecklenburg-Schwerin, Saxe-Weimar, Mecklenburg-Strelitz, Oldenburg, Brunswick, Saxe-Meiningen, Saxe-Altenburg, Saxe-Coburg Gotha, Anhalt, Schwarzburg-Rudolstadt, Schwarzburg-Sonderhausen, Waldeck, Reuß older Line, Reuß younger Line, Schaumburg-Lippe, Lippe, Lübeck, Bremen, and Hamburg.

II. Imperial Legislation

Article 2

Within this federal territory the Empire shall exercise the right of legislation in accordance with the content of this Constitution, and with the effect that imperial law shall take precedence of State law. The laws of the Empire shall receive their binding force through their publication by the Empire, which shall take place through the medium of an Imperial Gazette. So far as no other time is indicated in the published law for the going into effect of the same, it shall take effect on the 14th day following the expiration of the day on which it was published in the Imperial Gazette in Berlin.

Article 3

For all Germany there shall exist a common citizenship—*Indigenat*—with the effect that the members (subjects, citizens) of each State in the *Bund* shall be treated in every other State of the *Bund* as natives and shall accordingly be admitted to permanent domicile, to the

[1] (Howard, 1906), pp. 403–437. This entire appendix was copied as is from this book. As a result, the language is 100 years old.

pursuit of trade, to public office, to the acquiring of land, to the obtaining of citizenship, and to the enjoyment of all other civil rights, under the same conditions as the native born, and with reference to the prosecution of their rights and the protection of their rights they shall be treated like the native born. No German shall be limited in the exercise of these rights by the authority of his native State or by the authority of any other State of the *Bund*.

The regulations, which have reference to the care of the poor and their reception into the local communal associations will not be affected by the principle enunciated in the first paragraph. Likewise, until further action the treaties in force between the individual States with reference to the taking charge of persons to be exported, the care of the sick, and the burial of deceased citizens, shall stand.

With regard to the fulfillment of military duty in relation to the home State, the necessary steps will be ordered in the way of imperial legislation.

As against foreign lands, all Germans have an equal claim upon the protection of the Empire.

Article 4

The following matters shall be under the supervision of the Empire and subject to the legislation of the same:—

1) Regulations with respect to free migration; matters of domicile and settlement; citizenship, passports, and the police surveillance of strangers; the pursuit of trade, including insurance, so far as these matters are not already provided for in Art. 3 of this Constitution—in Bavaria, however, with the exclusion of matters of domicile and settlement—likewise, matters pertaining to colonization and emigration to foreign lands;
2) Legislation with respect to the tariff, commerce, and those taxes to be applied for imperial purposes;
3) The fixing of a system of weights, measures, and coinage; and the laying down of principles for the emission of funded and unfunded paper money;
4) General regulations with reference to banking matters;
5) Patents for inventions;
6) The protection of intellectual property;
7) The organization of a common protection for German trade in foreign lands, for German navigation and for the flag upon the high seas, and the arrangement of a common consular representation, which shall be maintained by the Empire;
8) Railway matters, subject to the reservations, so far as Bavaria is concerned in Art. 46, and the construction of roads and waterways in the interest of public defense and of the general traffic;
9) Rafting and navigation upon waterways common to several States and the condition of the same, as well as the river and other water dues; likewise the navigation marks—beacons, barrels, buoys, and other marks;
10) Postal and telegraph matters—in Bavaria and Württemberg, however, only in accordance with the provisions in Art. 52;
11) Regulations with respect to the reciprocal execution of judgments in civil matters and the fulfillment of requisitions in general;
12) Also with respect to the accrediting of public documents;
13) General legislation with respect to the whole domain of civil and criminal law and legal procedure;
14) The imperial military establishment and the navy;

15) The regulations governing the medical and veterinary police;
16) The laws relating to the press and the right of association.

Article 5
The legislative power of the Empire is exercised by the *Bundesrat* and the *Reichstag*. The consent of a majority vote of both assemblies is necessary and sufficient for the passage of a law.

In bills relating to military affairs, to the navy and to the imposts specified in Article 35, the vote of the Praesidium shall decide in case of a difference of opinion in the *Bundesrat*, if said vote is cast for the maintenance of the existing arrangements.

III. The Bundesrat

Article 6
The *Bundesrat* consists of representatives of the members of the *Bund*, among whom the votes shall be divided so that Prussia, with the former votes of Hannover, Jur-Hesse, Holstein, Nassau, and Frankfurt, shall have 17 votes; Bavaria, 6; Saxony, 4; Württemberg, 4; Baden, 3; Hesse, 3; Mecklenburg-Schwerin, 2; Saxe-Weimar, 1; Mecklenburg-Strelitz, 1; Oldenburg, 1; Brunswick, 2; Saxe-Meiningen, 1; Saxe-Altenburg, 1; Saxe-Coburg-Gotha, 1; Anhalt, 1; Schwarzburg-Rudolstadt, 1; Schwarzburg-Sonderhausen, 1; Waldeck, 1; Reuß older Line, 1; Reuß younger Line, 1; Schaumburg-Lippe, 1; Lippe,1; Lübeck, 1; Bremen, 1; Hamburg, 1,—total 58 votes.

Each member of the *Bund* may appoint as many pleni-potentiaries to the *Bundesrat* as it has votes, but the vote accredited to each State shall be given only as a unit.

Article 7
The *Bundesrat* shall take action upon:
1) Propositions to be made to the *Reichstag*, and the resolutions passed by the same;
2) The general administrative provisions and arrangements necessary for the carrying out of the imperial laws, so far as it is not otherwise provided for by law;
3) Defects which may come out in the execution of the imperial laws, or of the provisions and arrangements heretofore mentioned.

Every member of the *Bund* is empowered to make propositions and to speak to them, and the Praesidium is bound to submit them to deliberation.
Decisions shall be had by simple majority, with the exceptions provided for in Arts. 5, 37 and 78. Votes not represented or not instructed shall not be counted. In case of a tie the vote of the Praesidium shall decide.
When action is taken with reference to a matter, which, according to the provisions of this Constitution, is not common to the whole Empire, the votes of those States alone shall be counted which the matter jointly concerns.

Article 8
The *Bundesrat* shall appoint from its own members permanent Committees:—
1) On the Army and Fortifications.
2) On Marine Affairs
3) On Customs Duties and Taxes
4) On Commerce and Traffic.
5) On Railways, Post, and Telegraph.

6) On Judicial Affairs.
7) On Accounts.
In each of these Committees at least four States shall be represented, besides the Praesidium, and within the same each State shall have but one vote. In the Committee on the Army and Fortifications, Bavaria shall have a permanent seat; the remaining members of the Committee, as well as the members of the Committee on Marine Affairs, shall be appointed by the Kaiser; the members of the other Committees shall be elected by the *Bundesrat*. The composition of these Committees is to be renewed at each session of the *Bundesrat*, i.e., each year, whereupon the retiring members shall be re-eligible.

In addition, there shall be formed in the *Bundesrat*, out of the plenipotentiaries of the kingdoms of Bavaria, Saxony, and Württemberg, and two plenipotentiaries to be elected each year from the other States, a Committee on Foreign Affairs, in which Bavaria shall have the chair.

Article 9
Every member of the *Bundesrat* has the right to appear in the *Reichstag,* and must be heard there at any time upon his request, in order to represent the views of his Government, even when the same shall not have been adopted by a majority of the *Bundesrat*. No one shall be at the same time a member of the *Bundesrat* and of the *Reichstag*.

Article 10
It is incumbent upon the Kaiser to guarantee to the members of the *Bundesrat* the usual diplomatic protection.

IV. The Präsidium

Article 11
The *Präsidium* of the *Bund* belongs to the King of Prussia, who shall bear the title German Kaiser. It shall be the duty of the Kaiser to represent the Empire among the nations, to declare war and conclude peace in the name of the Empire, to enter into alliances and treaties with foreign States, to accredit and receive ambassadors.

For the declaration of war in the name of the Empire the consent of the *Bundesrat* is required, unless an attack is made upon the federal territory or its coasts.

So far as treaties with foreign States relate to matters which, according to Art. 4, belong to the sphere of imperial legislation, the consent of the *Bundesrat* is required for their conclusion and the approval of the *Reichstag* is necessary for their validity.

Article 12
It is the right of the Kaiser to convene, to open, to adjourn, and to close the *Bundesrat* and the *Reichstag*.

Article 13
The convening of the *Bundesrat* and of the *Reichstag* shall take place annually, and the *Bundesrat* may be summoned for the preparation of business without the *Reichstag;* but the latter shall not be convened without the *Bundesrat*.

Article 14
The *Bundesrat* must be convened whenever a meeting is demanded by one-third of the total number of votes.

Article 15
The chairmanship in the *Bundesrat* and the conduct of business belongs to the Imperial Chancellor, who is to be appointed by the Kaiser.

The Imperial Chancellor has the right to delegate the power to represent him to any other member of the *Bundesrat*. This delegation shall be made in writing.

Article 16
The necessary bills shall, in accordance with the resolutions of the *Bundesrat*, be laid by the Kaiser before the *Reichstag*, where they shall be represented by members of the *Bundesrat* or by special commissioners appointed by them.

Article 17
It is the business of the Kaiser to engross and publish the imperial laws and to supervise the carrying out of the same. The orders and decrees of the Kaiser shall be promulgated in the name of the Empire, and require for their validity the counter-signature of the Imperial Chancellor, who thereby assumes the responsibility.

Article 18
The Kaiser appoints the imperial officials, administers the oath for the Empire, and orders their dismissal should such case be necessary.

State officials called to an imperial office shall enjoy, so far as has not been otherwise determined by imperial legislation prior to their entry into the imperial service, the same rights in the Empire, which belonged to them in their own State by virtue of their official position.

Article 19
When members of the *Bund* do not fulfill their constitutional duties as members of the federation, they may be compelled to perform them through an "execution." This execution is to be determined upon by the *Bundesrat* and carried out by the Kaiser.

V. The Reichstag

Article 20
The *Reichstag* is the result of a general and direct ballot with secret vote.

Until the legal regulation, which is reserved in § 5, of the Election Law of 31 May 1869 (*Bund*esgesesetzblatt, 1869, p. 145), there shall be elected in Bavaria 48 delegates; in Württemberg, 17; in Baden, 14; and in Hesse south of the Main, 6; and the total number of votes shall accordingly amount to 382.[1] [*This number grew to 397, counting in the delegates from Alsace-Lorraine*]

Article 21
Officials shall not require a leave of absence in order to enter the *Reichstag*.

When a member of the *Reichstag* accepts a salaried office under the Empire, or in one of the States of the *Bund*, or enters the service of the Empire, or of a State, in an office with which a higher rank or higher salary is connected, he thereupon loses his seat and vote in the *Reichstag*, and can acquire his place in the same only through a new election.

Article 22
The transactions of the *Reichstag* are public.

Truthful reports of the proceedings of the *Reichstag* in the public sittings remain free from every responsibility.

Article 23
The *Reichstag* has the right to propose laws within the competence of the Empire, and to transmit to the *Bundesrat* or to the Imperial Chancellor petitions directed to it.

Article 24
The legislative period of the *Reichstag* lasts for five years. For the dissolution of the *Reichstag* during this period a resolution of the *Bundesrat* is required together with the consent of the Kaiser.

Article 25
In case of dissolution of the *Reichstag,* the voters shall be called together within a period of sixty days after the dissolution, and the *Reichstag* shall be assembled within ninety days after the dissolution.

Article 26
Without the consent of the *Reichstag*, an adjournment of that body shall not exceed a period of thirty days, and shall not be repeated during the same sessions.

Article 27
The *Reichstag* shall prove the legitimation of its own members and decide thereon. It regulates its own procedure and its discipline through its order of business, and elects its president, vice-presidents, and secretaries.

Article 28
The *Reichstag* shall decide questions by absolute majority. For the validity of any action the presence of a majority of the statutory number of members is required.

Article 29
The members of the *Reichstag* are representatives of the whole people, and are not bound by propositions and instructions.

Article 30
No member of the *Reichstag* shall be prosecuted, either legally or by way of discipline, at any time, because of his vote, or because of any utterance made in the exercise of his functions, or in any other manner be held responsible outside the assembly.

Article 31
Without the consent of the *Reichstag,* no member of it, during the session, shall be brought to trial or arrested, because of a penal offence, unless he is taken in the commission of the act or during the course of the following day.

Like consent is required in the case of arrest for debt.

At the request of the *Reichstag*, all criminal proceeding against one of its members, and all detentions for judicial inquiry or civil action, shall be suspended during the session.

Article 32
The members of the *Reichstag* as such, shall draw no salary or compensation.

VI. Customs and Commerce

Article 33
Germany forms one territory for customs and commerce, defined by a common tariff boundary. Those parts of the territory, which, by reason of their situation, cannot properly be embraced within the customs frontier, shall be excluded.

All Articles of free commerce in any State of the Union may be brought into any other State of the Union, and in the latter shall be subjected to an impost only in so far as similar domestic productions are subject to an internal tax there.

Article 34
The Hanse cities, Bremen and Hamburg, together with a part of their own or of the surrounding territory suitable for such purpose, shall remain free ports outside the common tariff borders, until such time as they shall request admission into the same.

Article 35
The Empire has the exclusive right of legislation as to all tariff matters; as to the taxation of salt and tobacco produced in the federal territory; as to prepared brandy and beer, and sugars and syrups produced from beets or other domestic sources; as to the mutual protection, against fraud, of the consumption taxes levied in the several States of the *Bund*, as well as to the regulations which may be required in the excluded districts for the security of the common customs boundaries.

In Bavaria, Württemberg, and Baden, the right to tax the domestic brandies and beers is reserved to the legislation of the State. The States will, however, use every effort to bring about uniform legislation with regard to the taxation of these Articles also.

Article 36
The collection and administration of the customs duties and of the taxes on Articles of consumption (Art. 35) is left to each State, within its own territory, so far as these functions have heretofore been exercised by each State.

The Kaiser supervises the observance of the legal conduct of affairs, by means of imperial officials, whom he appoints, with the consent of the Committee of the *Bundesrat* on Customs Duties and Taxes, to act in conjunction with the officials and Directive Boards of the several States.

Reports made by these officials as to defects in the carrying out of the joint legislation (Art. 35), shall be laid before the *Bundesrat* for action.

Article 37
In taking action with reference to the administrative provisions and arrangements for carrying out the joint legislation (Art. 35), the vote of the *Praesidium* decides when it is cast in favor of maintaining the existing provision or arrangement.

Article 38
The revenues from the customs and from the other taxes mentioned in Art. 35, so far as these latter are subject to imperial legislation, flow into the treasury of the Empire.

This amount consists of the total income from the customs and from the other taxes, after deducting there from: –

1) The tax allowances and reductions resting upon the laws or general administrative provisions.
2) Reimbursements for taxes unlawfully collected.
3) The costs of collection and of administration, viz.—
   a) In the department of customs, the costs required for the protection, and for the collecting, of the duties on the borders of a foreign country and in the district adjacent thereto.
   b) In the department of the salt tax the costs, which are applied toward the salaries of the officials, charged with the collection and control of this tax at the salt works.
   c) In the department of the beet-sugar tax and the tobacco tax, the compensation which, according to the regulations of the *Bundesrat* at the time, are to be guaranteed to the governments of the several States of the Union for the costs of administering these taxes.
   d) In the other tax departments, fifteen per cent of the total receipts.

The territories lying outside the common customs borders contribute to the expenses of the Empire by the payment of a lump sum (*Aversum*).

Bavaria, Württemberg, and Baden have no share in the revenues flowing into the imperial treasury from the taxes on brandy and beer nor in that part of the aforementioned *Aversum* corresponding to this amount.

Article 39
The quarterly abstracts to be made by the collection officials of the States at the end of each quarter, and the final statement, to be drawn up at the end of each year, and after the closing of the books, of the receipts which have fallen due during the quarter or during the fiscal year, as the case may be from customs and from the taxes on Articles of consumption which, according to Art. 38, flow into the imperial treasury, shall be grouped by the Directive Boards of the States, after a preliminary audit, into general summaries, in which each impost is to be separately indicated, and these summaries are to be sent in to the *Bundesrat's* Committee on Accounts.

The latter fixes provisionally, every three months, on the basis of these summaries, the amount due the imperial treasury from each State in the *Bund*, and informs the *Bundesrat*, and the States, of the amount fixed; it also lays its final determination of these amounts, with its remarks, annually before the *Bundesrat*. The *Bundesrat* takes action on the fixing of the amounts.

Article 40
The stipulations in the Customs Union Treaty of 8 July 1867 remain in force, so far as they have not been amended by the provisions of this Constitution, and so long as they shall not have been amended in the manner provided for in Arts. 7 and 78.

VII. Railway Matters

Article 41

Railways, which are considered necessary for the defense of Germany or in the interests of general traffic, may be constructed at the expense of the Empire, even against the opposition of that member of the *Bund* through whose territory the railway cuts, without prejudice to the sovereign rights of the State; or may be granted as a concession to private persons for construction and furnished with rights of expropriation.

Every existing railway is bound to grant connection with it of newly constructed lines, at the cost of the latter.

The legal regulations which grant to existing railway undertakings a right of injunction against the laying of parallel or competing lines, are hereby repealed for the whole Empire, without prejudice to the rights already acquired. Such a right of injunction cannot be further granted, even in concessions to be given in the future.

Article 42

The governments of the several States bind themselves to administer the German railways in the interest of the general traffic, as a single system, and to this end shall cause the railways newly to be constructed to be built and equipped according to a uniform standard.

Article 43

To this end there shall be made, as speedily as possible, uniform traffic regulations, and especially shall identical railway police rules be put in force. The Empire shall see to it that the railway administrations shall keep the roads always in a condition which shall guarantee the necessary safety, and shall furnish them with such equipment as the needs of traffic may demand.

Article 44

The railway administrations are bound to furnish passenger trains of suitable speed, necessary for through traffic and for the securing of connecting time tables; in the same way to provide trains necessary for the conduct of freight business, as well as to arrange for the direct forwarding of passengers and of freight, providing a system of transfer from one train to another for the usual remuneration.

Article 45

The control of the tariff charges shall be in the hands of the Empire. It shall work to this end:

1) That at the earliest possible moment uniform regulations governing the business shall be introduced on all German railways.
2) That the tariff charges be minimized and equalized as speedily as possible, especially that, in the long distance transportation of coal, coke, wood, ore stone, salt, pig-iron, manures, and similar Articles, a tariff shall be introduced suitably modified to the needs of farming and of industry, and indeed, at the first practicable moment, the one pfennig tariff.

Article 46

When conditions of distress shall arise, especially an unusual rise in the price of provisions, the railroads shall be bound to introduce temporarily a low special tariff, suited to the necessities of the case, and to be fixed by the Kaiser on motion of the competent Committee of the *Bundesrat*, for the transport of grain, flour, legumes, and potatoes, which price, however, shall not be less than the lowest existing rate for raw products over the said line.

The aforesaid provisions, as well as those found in Arts. 42 to 45 have no application to Bavaria.

The imperial government has the right, however, even as against Bavaria, to lay down by law uniform standards for the construction and equipment of railways which may be of importance in the defense of the country.

Article 47

All the administrative authorities of the railways shall yield implicit obedience to the demands of the imperial authorities, with respect to the use of the railways for the purpose of the defense of Germany. Especially shall troops and all materials of war be forwarded at uniform reduced rates.

VIII. Post and Telegraph

Article 48

The post and telegraph systems shall be arranged and administered throughout the entire German Empire as uniform institutions of public intercourse.

The legislation of the Empire in post and telegraph matters, as provided for in Art. 4, shall not extend to those matters whose regulation is left to governmental determination and administrative ordinance, in accordance with the principles which have been authoritative in the administration of the post and telegraph in the North German *Bund*.

Article 49

The revenues from the post and telegraph systems for the whole Empire shall belong to a common fund. The expenses shall be paid out of the joint income. The surplus shall flow into the imperial treasury (§ XII.).

Article 50

To the Kaiser shall belong the supreme control of the post and telegraph administration. It shall be the duty and the right of the authorities appointed by him to see to it that uniformity in the organization of the administration and in the conduct of the business, as well as in the qualification of the officials, is established and maintained.

The Kaiser shall have power to issue governmental decisions and general administrative ordinances, as well as the exclusive supervision of the relations with other post and telegraph administrations.

All officials of the post and telegraph administration are bound to obey the imperial orders. This obligation is assumed in the oath of office.

The appointment of such superior officers in the various districts as may be required by the administrative authorities of the post and telegraph, for instance, the directors, counselors, superintendents, and, further, the appointment of the officials of the post and telegraph who shall act in the capacity of organs of the aforesaid authorities in maintaining the supervisory and other service in the several districts, such as inspectors, controllers, shall be made throughout the Empire by the Kaiser, to whom these officials shall take the oath of office. Due notice shall be given to the several State governments, of the aforementioned appointments, so far as they may affect their territory, in order that they may be ratified and published by the ruler thereof.

The other officials required by the post and telegraph administrative authorities, as well as those destined for the local and technical work, including those officials acting at the stations proper, and so forth, shall be appointed by the State governments concerned.

Where an independent State post and telegraph administration does not exist, the provisions of special treaties shall be decisive.

Article 51

In consideration of the differences hitherto existent with respect to the net income received from the State postal administrations of the several districts, the following method of procedure shall be observed in assigning the surplus of the postal administration for general imperial purposes (Art. 49), to the end that a corresponding equalization may be had during the transition period fixed below.

From the postal surpluses, which have accumulated in the several postal districts during the five years, 1861–1865, a yearly average shall be computed, and the share which each individual postal district has had in the postal surpluses for the whole Empire resulting therefrom shall be fixed according to percentage.

On the basis of the ratio thus determined, the quota ascribed to the several States, out of the accumulated postal surpluses of the Empire, shall, for the eight years following their entry into the imperial postal administration, be credited to the contributions which they would otherwise make for imperial purposes.

At the end of eight years this distinction shall cease, and the postal surpluses shall flow into the imperial treasury, without division, in accordance with the principle laid down in Art. 49.

Of the quota of postal surpluses arising in favor of the Hanse cities during the aforesaid eight years, one-half shall be placed at the disposal of the Kaiser, at the beginning of each year, chiefly for the purpose of meeting the expense involved in providing regular postal arrangements in the Hanse cities.

Article 52

The provisions of the foregoing Arts. 48 to 51 do not apply to Bavaria and Württemberg. In place of them the following provisions shall be valid for both these federal States.

Legislation with respect to the privileges of the post and telegraph, the legal relations of both institutions to the public, the franking privileges and the post charges, as well as the fixing of the fees for telegraphic correspondence, shall belong exclusively to the Empire, with the exception, however, of the administrative regulations and the determination of tariffs for the internal communication within Bavaria and Württemberg.

Likewise the regulation of the postal and telegraphic communication with foreign lands shall belong to the Empire, with the exception of Bavaria's and Württemberg's own immediate traffic with neighboring States not belonging to the Empire, the regulation of which is governed by the provisions of Art. 49 of the Postal Treaty of 23 November 1867.

In the income from the post and telegraph flowing into the imperial treasury, Bavaria and Württemberg have no share.

IX. Marine and Navigation

The navy of the Empire is a unitary one under the supreme command of the Kaiser. The organization and composition of it shall be the duty of the Kaiser, who appoints the officers and officials of the navy, and to whom they, together with the crews, take an oath of obedience.

The harbor of Kiel and that of jade are imperial war ports.

The requisite expense for the establishment and maintenance of the fleet and the arrangements connected therewith shall be defrayed out of the imperial treasury.

All the seafaring male population of the Empire, including the machinists and ship laborers, is exempt from service in the army, but is liable to service in the imperial navy.[2]

Article 54

The merchantmen of all the federated States shall constitute a united commercial marine.

The Empire shall determine the process for ascertaining the tonnage of sea-going vessels, shall regulate the making out of certificates of measurement as well as of ship certificates, and shall fix the conditions on which permission to sail a sea-going ship shall be granted.

The merchantmen of all the federated States shall be granted like access to, and accorded similar treatment in, the seaports and all natural and artificial watercourses of the several States of the *Bund.* The taxes, which shall be levied upon the ships or their cargoes in the harbors, for the use of the institutions of navigation, shall not exceed the cost necessary for the maintenance and ordinary repairs of these establishments.

On all the natural watercourses, taxes may be levied only for the use of special establishments, which are designed for the facilitating of traffic. These taxes, as well as the taxes for the navigation of such artificial watercourse as may belong to the State, shall not exceed the cost necessary for the maintenance and the usual repairs of these institutions and establishments. These provisions apply to rafting, in so far as it is carried on upon navigable watercourses.

The power to lay other or higher taxes upon foreign ships, or their cargoes, than upon the ships of the federated States or their cargoes, belongs only to the Empire and not to any one of the States.

Article 55

The flag of the navy and of the merchant marine is black, white, and red.

X. Consular Affairs

Article 56

All consular affairs are under the supervision of the Kaiser, who appoints the consults, after hearing the Committee of the *Bundesrat* on Commerce and Traffic.

In the official districts of the German consuls, no new State consulates may be created. The German consuls exercise all the functions of a State consul for the federated States not represented in their districts. All the State consulates now existent shall be abolished as soon as the organization of the German consulates shall be completed in such manner that the representation of the particular interests of all federated States shall be recognized by those States as secured through the German consulate.

---

2 Article 53 contained another paragraph, which was omitted by the amendment of 26 May 1893. The paragraph read:—"Die Vertheilung des Ersatzbedarfes findet nach Massgabe der vorhandenen seemännischen Bevölkerung statt, und die hiernach von jedem Staate gestellte Quote kommt auf die Gestellung zum Landheere in Abrechnung."

XI. Military Affairs of the Empire

Article 57

Every German is liable to military duty and in the discharge of this duty no substitute can be accepted.

Article 58

The costs and burdens of the entire military system of the Empire are to be borne by all the federated States and their subjects equally, in such manner that neither preference nor special burden upon any individual State or class shall be in principle permissible. Where an equal distribution of the burdens cannot be brought about *in natural* without injury to the public welfare, the equalization is to be effected by legislation according to principles of fairness.

Article 59

Every German capable of bearing arms shall belong for seven years to the standing army, as a rule from the completion of his 20th to the beginning of his twenty-eighth year. During the next five years he shall belong to the "national Guard (*Landwehr)* of the first call," and then, up to the 31 March of that year in which he shall have completed his thirty-ninth year, to the national guard of the "second call."

During the period of service in the standing army the cavalrymen and the mounted artillerymen are bound to uninterrupted service with the colors the first three years, all others the first two years.[1] *[Amendment of 15 April 1905.]*

In those States of the *Bund* in which heretofore a longer term of total service than twelve years was required by law, the gradual reduction of the term of liability to service shall take place only so far as this is compatible with due regard for the readiness of the imperial army for war.

With reference to the emigration of men belonging to the reserves, simply those provisions shall be authoritative which control the emigration of members of the national guard. *(Landwehr).*

Article 60

The number of men in the German army in time of peace shall be fixed, up to 31 December 1871, at one per cent of the population of 1867, and shall be furnished by the several States of the *Bund* in proportion to their population. After that date the effective force of the army in time of peace shall be fixed by imperial law.

Article 61

After the publication of this Constitution, the entire Prussian military legislation shall be introduced without delay throughout the entire Empire—the laws themselves as well as the rules, instructions, and rescripts issued for their execution, explanation, or completion, to wit, the Military penal Code of 3 April 1845, the Military Code of Criminal Procedure of 3 April 1845, the Ordinance respecting Courts of Honor of 20 July 1843, the provisions for recruiting, time of service, matters of allowances and the commissariat, the quartering of troops, compensation for injury done to fields, for the mobilizing of troops etc., in peace and in war. The military ordinance with respect to religious observances is, however, excepted.

On the completion of a uniform military organization of the German army, a comprehensive imperial military law shall be laid before the *Reichstag* and the *Bundesrat* for their action, in conformity to the Constitution.

Article 62

For meeting the expenses of the entire German army and the arrangements incident thereto, there shall be placed annually at the disposal of the Kaiser, up to 31 December 1871, as many times 225 thalers—in words, two hundred and twenty-five thalers—as the numerical strength of the army on a peace footing according to Art. 60, amounts to. See § XII.

After 31 December, these contributions must be paid by the several States of the Bund into the imperial treasury. In computing the same, the peace footing of the army, temporarily fixed in Art. 60, shall be adhered to until it is altered by imperial law.

The expenditure of these sums for the entire imperial army and its arrangements shall be fixed by the budget.

In determining the budget of military expenditure, the organization of the imperial army legally fixed according to the principles of this Constitution shall be taken as a basis.

Article 63

The total land force of the Empire shall constitute a uniform army, which, in peace and in war is under the command of the Kaiser.

The regiments, etc., throughout the entire German army shall bear continuous numbers. As to the uniform, the ground-colors and the cut of the Prussian army shall be authoritative. The determination of the external marks of distinction (cockades, etc.) is left to the heads of the respective contingents.

The Kaiser has the right and the duty to see to it that all divisions of the troops are in full muster and fit for war, throughout the whole German army, and that uniformity in organization and formation, in equipment and command, in the training of the men, and in the qualification of the officers, shall be brought about and maintained. To this end, the Kaiser has the authority to satisfy himself at any time, by inspection, of the condition of the several contingents, and to order the abolishing of any defects thereby found.

The Kaiser determines the numerical strength, the organization, and the division of the contingents of the imperial army, as well as the organization of the national guard, and has the right to determine the garrisons within the federal territory, as well as to order the putting of any part of the imperial army in a state of readiness for war.

To the end that the indispensable uniformity in the administration, commissariat, arming, and equipment of divisions of the German army may be preserved, the orders issued to the Prussian army in the future with reference to such matters shall be communicated to the commanders of the other contingents by the Committee on the Army and Fortifications mentioned in Art. 8(1) for their proper observance.

Article 64

All German troops are bound to render unconditional obedience to the commands of the Kaiser. This obligation is to be included in the military oath.

The chief commanding officers of a contingent, as well as all officers who command troops of more than one contingent, and all commandants of fortresses, shall be appointed by the Kaiser. The officers appointed by him shall take the military oath to him. The appointment of generals and of officers performing the duties of generals, within a contingent, is made dependent in each case upon the consent of the Kaiser.

The Kaiser is authorized, with respect to the transfer of officers, with or without promotion, to positions to be filled by him in the imperial service, be it in the Prussian army of in other contingents, to make his choice from the officers of all contingents of the imperial army.

Article 65

The right of erecting fortifications within the federal territory shall belong to the Kaiser, who shall request the grant of the requisite means thereto, so far as the ordinary budget does not guarantee it, according to § XII.

Article 66

Where it is not otherwise provided for by special convention, the princes of the *Bund* and the Senates shall appoint the officers of their contingents, subject to the restriction of Art. 64. They are the heads of all the divisions of troops belonging to their territory and enjoy the honors connected therewith. They have particularly the right of inspection at any time, and receive, besides the regular reports and notices of changes about to take place, timely information of promotions and appointments touching their respective divisions of troops, in order that the necessary publication of them may be made by the State.

They also have the right to employ for purposes of police, not only their own troops, but also to requisition all other divisions of troops of the imperial army which may be stationed in their territories.

Article 67

Unexpended portions of the military budget shall fall, in no circumstances, to an individual government, but at all times to the imperial treasury.

Article 68

Should the public safety of the federal territory be threatened, the Kaiser may declare any part of the same under martial law. Up to the publication of an imperial law regulating the occasions, the form of announcement, and the effects of such a declaration, the provisions of the Prussian law of 4 June 1851 (*Gesetz-Samml. for 1851,* p. 451), shall be valid in such case.

Final Provision of Sec. XI

The provisions contained in this section are to be applied to Bavaria in conformity with the more detailed stipulations of the Treaty of alliance of 23 November 1870 (*Bundesgesetzbl.* 1871, p. 9) under III. § 5, and to Württemberg in conformity with the more detailed stipulations of the Military Convention of 21–25 November 1870 (*Bundesgesetzbl.* 1870, p. 658)

XII. Imperial Finance

Article 69

All receipts and expenditures of the Empire shall be estimated for each year, and included in the imperial budget. The latter shall be fixed by law before the beginning of each fiscal year according to the following principles:—

Article 70

For the defraying of all common expenses there shall be used first of all the joint receipts from the customs and common taxes, from the railway, post and telegraph systems, as well as from the remaining branches of administration. In so far as the expenditures are not covered by these receipts, they are to be met by contributions from the several States of the *Bund* according to the measure of their population, which contributions are to be charged to them by the Imperial Chancellor, to the extent of the amount fixed in the budget. In so far as these contributions are not covered by the amounts handed over to the several States, they shall be returned to the States of the Bund at the end of the year in the same measure as the remaining regular receipts of the Empire exceed its needs.

Any surpluses from the preceding years shall be used, so far as the imperial budget law does not provide otherwise, for defraying the joint extraordinary expenses.[1] [*Amendment of 14 May, 1904 (RGBl.* P. 169)]

Article 71

The general expenditures shall, as a rule, be granted for one-year, but may, in special cases, however, be granted for a longer period.

During the transition period laid down in Art. 60, the estimate of the expenditures of the army, arranged according to titles, shall be laid before the *Bundesrat* and the *Reichstag* for their information and as a memorandum.

Article 72

An annual report of the expenditure of all receipts of the Empire shall be laid by the Imperial Chancellor before the *Bundesrat* and the *Reichstag* for their discharge.

Article 73

In cases of extraordinary need, a loan may be contracted, or a guarantee assumed as a burden on the Empire, by way of imperial legislation.

Final Provision of Sec. XII

As to the expenditures for the Bavarian army, Arts. 69 and 71 find application only according to the provisions of the Treaty of 23 November 1870, mentioned in the Final Provision of § XI, and Art. 72 find application only to the extent that the transfer of the sum required for the Bavarian army is to be reported to the *Bundesrat* and *Reichstag*.

XIII. Settlement of Disputes and Penal Provisions

Article 74

Every attempt against the existence, the integrity, the security or the Constitution of the German Empire; finally, any affront offered to the *Bundesrat*, the *Reichstag,* a member of the Bundesrat or Reichstag, an authority or a public official of the Empire, while in the exercise of their calling, or in relation to their calling, by word, writing, print, drawing, pictorial or other representation, shall be adjudge and punished in the several States of the *Bund* according to the laws therein existing, or which shall hereafter go into effect, by which a similar act committed against the individual State of the *Bund,* its constitution, its chambers or estates, the members of its chambers or estates, its authorities, or its officials is adjudged.

Article 75
For those attempts against the German Empire, mentioned in Art. 74, which, if directed against the individual State, would be considered high treason or treason against the State, the common Superior Court of Appeals of the three free and Hanse cities in Lübeck is the competent deciding tribunal in first and last instance.

Detailed provisions with reference to the competence and the procedure of the Superior Court of Appeals shall follow in the way of imperial legislation. Until the passage of an imperial law, the competence of the courts in the individual States up to this time, and the provisions relating to the procedure of these courts, shall remain as at present.

Article 76
Disputes between different States of the *Bund,* so far as they do not partake of the nature of disputes at private law and accordingly are to be decided by the competent judicial authorities, shall be adjusted, on appeal of one of the parties, by the *Bundesrat.*

In disputes involving constitutional matters in those States of the *Bund* in whose constitution no authority is provided competent to settle such controversies, the *Bundesrat* shall, on appeal of one of the parties, effect an amicable settlement, or, if this does not succeed, shall bring about an adjustment in the way of imperial legislation.

Article 77
If, in any State of the *Bund*, a case of refusal of justice shall arise, and sufficient relief cannot be obtained by legal measures, then it shall be the duty of the *Bundesrat* to receive substantiated complaints respecting the denial or obstruction of justice, which shall be judged according to the constitution and existing law of the State concerned, and thereupon to effect judicial relief through the government of the State which shall have given occasion to the complaint.

Article 78
Amendments to the Constitution shall follow the regular course of legislation. They shall be considered rejected when they have against them fourteen votes in the *Bundesrat.*

Those provisions of the constitution, by which certain rights are secured to individual States of the *Bund* in their relation to the whole, may be amended only with the consent of the States affected.

APPENDIX B

THE GERMAN ARMY IN EARLY 1914[1]

RANGLISTEN, MILITÄRHANDBÜCHER

Glossary

The glossary shows which abbreviations are used in the lists.

Abt.	Abteilung
Adj.	Adjutant
a.D.	außer Dienst
A.H.Qu.	Armee-Hauptquartier
A.K.	Armeekorps
AOK or A.O.K.	Armee-Oberkommando
Art. Brig.	Artillerie-Brigade
bayer.	bayerisch
Bez. Kom.	(*Landwehr*) *Bezirkskommando*
Brig.	Brigade
Btl.	Bataillon
Bttr.	Batterie
Ch.R.	*Chevaulegers-Regiment* (sometimes also spelled in the more correct French way *Chevauxlegers-Regiment*)
Chef	either *Abteilungs-Chef* (department head) or *Chef des Stabes* (army corps or lower)
Chef d. St.	*Chef des Stabes* (army corps or higher)
Dr.	Doktor
D.R.	Dragoner-Regiment
E.	*Ersatz* (sometimes can also be *Eskadron*)

E.D.	Ersatz-Division
elsäss.	elsässisch
Ers.	Ersatz
Ers. K.R.	Ersatz Kavallerie Regiment
Esk.	Eskadron
F.R.	Füsilier-Regiment
Feld-Art.	Feldartillerie
Feld-Flieg. Abt.	*Feldflieger Abteilung* (field aircraft battalion)
Fernspr.	*Fernsprecher* (telephone)
Fest.	*Festung* (fortress)
Festungs-MG Abt.	*Festungs Maschinengewehr-Abteilung* (fortress machinegun detachment)
Frhr.	Freiherr
Fuß-Art.	Fußartillerie
G.	Garde
G.D.	Garde-Division
geh.	*geheim* (secret)
Geh. Kr. Rat	Geheimer Kriegs-Rat
G.K.D.	Garde Kavallerie-Division
G.R.D.	Garde Reserve Division
gem.	*gemischt* (mixed)
gen.	*genannt* ("named as": often used with aristocratic titles)

1 (Based upon the 1914 Prussian (incl. Württemberg), Bavarian and Saxon Ranglisten and Militärhandbücher.)

Gen. d. Art.	General der Artillerie
Gen. d. Inf.	General der Infanterie
Gen. d. Kav.	General der Kavallerie
Gen. Kdo.	*Generalkommando* (staff, army corps level)
Gen. Lt.	Generalleutnant
Gen. Maj.	Generalmajor
Gen. Oberst.	Generaloberst
Ghz.	großherzoglich
Gouv.	*Gouverneur* (fortress)
HKK or H.K.K.	Höherer Kavallerie-Kommandeur/ *Heeres Kavalleriekorps*
H.R.	Husaren-Regiment
Halb-Regt.	*Halb-Regiment* (half [cavalry] regiment)
hanseat.	hanseatisch(es)
hess.	hessisch(es)
Hptm.	Hauptmann
Hptm. d.L.	Hauptmann der Landwehr
Hptm. d.R.	Hauptmann der Reserve
I.	I. Bataillon or I. Abteilung
I.D.	Infanterie Division
I.R.	Infanterie-Regiment
II.	*II. Bataillon* or *II. Abteilung*
III.	*III. Bataillon* or *III. Abteilung*
Inf. Brig.	Infanterie-Brigade
Jg. Btl.	Jäger-Bataillon
Jg. Rgt. z. Pf.	Jäger-Regiment zu Pferde
K.B.	königlich bayerisch
K.D.	Kavallerie-Division
K.S.	königlich sächsisch
K.P.	königlich preußisch
K.W.	königlich württembergisch
Kapt. z.S.	*Kapitän zur See* (Commander, Navy)
Kav. Brig.	Kavallerie-Brigade
Kdr.	Kommandeur
Kdr. Gen.	*Kommandierender General* (Commander of an Army Corps)
Korv. Kapt.	*Korvettenkapitän* (Lieutenant commander, Navy)
kdt.	kommandiert
Kp.	Kompanie
Landst.	Landsturm
Landw.	Landwehr

Leib-Hus. Brig.	*Leibhusaren Brigade* (Life hussars brigade)
lothring.	lothringisch
Lt.	Leutnant
Lt. d.L.	Leutnant der Landwehr
Lt. d.R.	Leutnant der Reserve
Maj.	Major
Marine-D.	Marine-Division
Marine-Div.	Marine-Division
Meckl.	mecklenburgisch
MG-Abt.	Maschinengewehr-Abteilung
Mrs.	*Mörser* (heavy howitzer)
O.Qu.	Ober-Quartiermeister
Ob.Bef.	*Ober-Befehlshaber* (Commander of an Army)
Obit.	Oberleutnant
Oberstlt.	Oberleutnant
OLt.	Oberleutnant
OLt. d.L.	Oberleutnant der Landwehr
OLt. d.R.	Oberleutnant der Reserve
Pi.	Pionier(e)
Prof.	Professor
R.D.	Reserve-Division
reit. Abt.	Reitende Abteilung
Res.	Reserve
Res. Inf. Brig.	Reserve Infanterie-Brigade
Rgt.	Regiment
s.F.H.	schwere Feldhaubitze
sächs.	Sächsisch
Schtz. Btl.	Schützen-Bataillon
schw.	schwer
schw. Reiter Rgt.	schweres Reiter-Regiment
Seew.	*Seewehr* (similar to *Landwehr* but with Navy)
St.	Stab
Stabsoffz.	Stabsoffizier
U.R.	Ulanen-Regiment
v.	*von* (aristocratic title)
Wirkl. Geh. Kr. Rat	Wirklicher Geheimer Kriegs-Rat
württ. or württemb.	württembergisch
z.D.	zur Disposition
z.F.	zu Fuß

GENERAL REMARKS

- This lists all German formations in their last peace-time appearance as listed in the respective *Rangliste* 1914.
- Sources for this list were the *Rangliste* of the Prussian army from 1914 (as of May 6th 1914), which also covers the Württemberg XIIIth corps. Bavarian and Saxon formations were taken from the Bavarian Military Handbook 1914[2] and from the Saxon *Rangliste* 1914[3].
- Abbreviations are usually written in their German 1914 form. Please refer to the glossary given above.
- List only focuses upon military formations, e.g., adjutants of princes are not listed, neither are the lists of reserve officers nor officers à la suite.
- Top organizations (e.g. Ministry of War) are listed completely; formations are listed with their officers down to the brigade staffs. To keep the list short, officers in regiments are not listed.
- Numerous central organizations (e.g., medical inspections, general inspection of military training, officer schools, officer's examination committee, cadet institutes, military orphanage, veterinary inspection, veterinary academy, military correctional institutes, and many more) are left out in order to keep the list compact.
- In the peace-time organization, several fortresses were still listed although considered obsolete. These fortresses were not put on a war footing or armed during mobilization.
- Please also note the sequence of listings shows the hierarchy of the different formations and organizations.
- Within organizations and formations officers are sorted by function, by military rank, and within the same rank according to seniority.
- K.B., K.S., and K.W. is only used to indicate respective officers and formations outside the Bavarian, Saxon and Württemberg contingents.
- Indication of regional origin is only used within peace-time list and then only for formations coming from states still having independent status (*regierende Häuser*) within Germany or for formations coming from the *Reichslande*. Purely regional origin of formations such as "East Prussian" or "Rhineland" is not listed.

Headquarters of His Majesty the Emperor and King (aides-de-camp)

The following list only shows those aides-de-camp who were permanent members of the imperial entourage. Other high-ranking officers holding positions such as chief of general staff, commanding generals of army corps, or even regimental commanders or adjutants of a royal prince, very often also carried titles of an aide de camp. To avoid confusion and redundant listings those officers are not listed with the headquarters but with their original positions.

***Vortragender Generaladjutant Seiner Majestät des Kaisers und Königs*:**
Gen. d. Inf. Frhr. v. Lyncker (also head of the Military Cabinet)
Admiral v. Müller (Imperial Navy, also head of the Naval Cabinet)

---

[2] K.B. *Kriegsministerium, Abteilung für Persönliche Angelegenheiten* (Ed.) *"Militär-Handbuch für das Königreich Bayern nach dem Stande vom 16. Mai 1914 (47. Auflage)" Drucksachen-Verlag des Kriegsministerium, gedruckt im Kriegsministerium* (published and printed by the Bavarian Ministry of War,) Munich 1914.

[3] K.S. *Kriegsministerium, Abteilung für die persönlichen Angelegenheiten* (Ed.) *"Rangliste der Königlich Sächsischen Armee für das Jahr 1914 (nach dem Stande vom 20. Dezember 1913)" Druck von C. Heinrich, Dresden-Neustadt 1914*

***Diensttuender Generaladjutant Seiner Majestät des Kaisers und Königs*:**
Gen. Oberst (with the rank of a field-marshall) v. Plessen
Admiral v. Usedom (Imperial Navy)

***Diensttuender General à la suite Seiner Majestät des Kaisers und Königs*:**
Gen. Lt. v. Gontard

***Diensttuende Flügeladjutanten*:**
Oberst v. Mutius
Oberstlt. v. Estorff
Kapt.z.S. v. Trotha (Imperial Navy)
Kapt. z.S. v. Karpf (Imperial Navy)
Kapt. z.S. v. Bülow (Imperial Navy)
Oberstlt. v. Hahnke
Major v. Kleist
Major v. Caprivi
Korv. Kapt. Frhr. v. Paleske (Imperial Navy)
Major Graf v. Moltke
Major v. Hirschfeld

Military Cabinet (Berlin)

Chef: Gen. d. Inf. Frhr. v. Lyncker
Oberst Frhr. v. Marschall gen. Greiff
Oberst v. Langendorff
Oberst v. Wickede
Major v. Hake
Major v. Wehrs
Major v. Hoffmann
Rittm. v. Götz
K.W. Major Holland

Ministry of War (Berlin)

Minister of War: Gen. Lt. v. Falkenhayn
First adjutant: Major Milchling v. Schönstadt
Second adjutant: Hptm. v. Steuben
Oberst Rausch
Oberstlt. Kotze
Oberstlt. Berlin
Oberstlt. Eltester
Oberstlt. v. Wright
Major v. Recklinghausen

Central department (*Zentral Department ZD*)
Direktor: Oberst Schëuch
Adjutant: Hptm. Henrici
Hptm. v. Stosch

Minister's office (*1. Ministerial-Abteilung Z1*)
Abt. Chef: Oberstlt. Hoffmann
Major Lange
Major Deutelmoser
Major Lademann
Hptm. v. Rohrscheidt
Wirkl. Geh. Kriegsrat Lt. a.D. Lehmann

Archive *(Archiv-Verwaltung Av)*
Vorstand: Wirkl. Geh. Kriegsrat Lt. a.D. Lehmann
Library *(Bücherei-Verwaltung Bv)*
Vorstand: Major z.D. Frantz
Printed manuals and regulations *(Druckvorschriften Dv)*
Vorstand: Oberstlt. z.D. Lehmann
Major z.D. v. Spoenla
Major z.D. v. Schmeling-Diringshofen

Intendance department (*2. Intendantur-Abteilung Z2*)
Abt. Chef: Wirkl. Geh. Kriegsrat OLt. d.L.a.D. Dr. Meyer
Wirkl. Geh. Kriegsrat Lt. D.L.a.D. Neugebaur

General war department (*Allgemeines Kriegs-Departement AD*)
Direktor: Gen. Maj. Wild v. Hohenborn
Adjutant: Hptm. Baron v. Ardenne

Army department (*1. Armee-Abteilung A1*)
Abt. Chef: Oberstlt. v. Wrisberg
Major von den Bergh
Major Ritter
Major v. Hahnke
Major Frhr. v. Gall
Major Stiehler v. Heydekampf
Hptm. Schniewindt
Hptm. Barthold

Infantry department (*2. Infanterie-Abteilung A2*)
Abt. Chef: Oberstlt. v. Wodtke
Major Weller
Hptm. Schmidt
Hptm. Frhr. v. Hammerstein-Loxten

Cavalry department (*3. Kavallerie-Abteilung A3*)
Abt. Chef: Oberst v. Lenthe
Major Graf v. Klinckowstroem
Major Würtz
Stabs-Veterinär Grammlich
Stabs-Veterinär Rakette

Field-artillery department (*4. Feldartillerie-Abteilung A4*)
Abt. Chef.: Oberstlt. v. Schwerin
Major Stavenhagen
Major Koeth
Major Frhr. v. Weitershausen
Major Vogt
Hptm. Werneburg

Foot-artillery department (*5. Fußartillerie-Abteilung A5*)
Abt. Chef: Oberst Jung
Major Frahnert
Major Schacht
Hptm. Körner
Major Schoof
Hptm. v. Winning

Engineer department (*6. Ingenieur- und Pionie-Abteilung A6*)
Abt. Chef: Oberstlt. Gundelach
Major Langenstraß
Major Gronen
Major Schultze
Hptm. Delvendahl
Hptm. Hertzer

Mechanical traffic department (*Verkehrs-Abteilung A7V*)
Abt. Chef: Oberstlt. Meyer
Major Schott
Major Kopsch
Major Wentrup

Air force department (*Luftfahrt-Abteilung A7L*)
Abt. Chef: Oberstlt. Oschmann
Hptm. Bartsch

Factory department (*8. Fabriken-Abteilung A8*)
Abt. Chef: N.N.
Major Giebe
Geh. Baurat Klinkenberg

Personnel replacements department (*9. Ersatzwesen-Abteilung A9*)
Abt. Chef: Oberstlt. Ritter und Edler v. Braun
Major Lüder
Major Karwiese
Hptm. Düsterberg

Appendix B—The German Army in early 1914

Overseen by the general war department:

- Machinegun inspection (Inspector: Oberst Jancke, adjutant: Hptm. v. Brandenstein)
  Inspection of infantry schools (Inspector: Gen. Maj. Herhudt v. Rohden, adjutant: Hptm. Viebig, Hptm. Sattig)

- **Rifle commission:**
  President: Oberstltn. Thorbeck
  Adjutant: OLt. Frhr. v. Buol-Berenberg,
  Department heads: Major Müller, Major du Vignau,
  Members: K.W. Major Frhr. v. Gültlingen, Hptm. Borell du Vernay, Hptm. v. Knobelsdorff-Brenkenhoff, Hptm. Knauff, Hptm. Kleinhans, Hptm. Bensberg, Hptm. Siveke, Hptm. Erdmann, K.B. Hptm. Ruchti, K.B. Hptm. Köttnitz,
  Extra-ordinary members: Oberst Reinhardt, Oberst Brassart, Oberst Neuland, Oberst Sckeyde, Oberstltn. Weishaupt, Oberstltn. Kotze, Oberstltn. v. Wright, Major Doutrelepont, Major v. Recklinghausen, Major Straehler,
  Assistants: OLt. Schmidt, OLt. Müller, OLt. Messerschmidt, K.S. OLt. Birkholz, OLt. Gießer, K.W. OLt. Kopf, OLt. Schulze, OLt. Tannert, Lt. v. Wussow, K.B. OLt. Gränzer, K.S. Hptm. Maaß, K.B. OLt. Frhr. v. Großschedel zu Berghausen und Aigelsbach, K.B. OLt. Fuchs, Lt. Himstedt, Lt. Weber, Lt. Schmeißer

- **Artillery commission:**
  President: Gen.Lt. Sieger
  Adjutant: Hptm. Scharlach
  Department I (field artillery): Department head: Oberstltn. Isbert
  Members: Major Giese, K.W. Hptm. Jacobi, Hptm. Eylerts, Hptm. Hasse, Hptm. Stapelfeld, Hptm. Briegleb, Hptm. Hammer, K.B. Major Pracher, Hptm. Abel
  Assistants: Hptm. Kellner, Hptm. Frhr. v. Wolzogen und Neuhaus, Hptm. Blumenthal, Hptm. Schilling, Hptm. Plaskluda, OLt. Schulz, OLt. Riedel, OLt. Spieß, OLt. v. Hamm, OLt. Krüger, OLt. Kersten, K.W. OLt. Burk, K.S. OLt. OLt. Schmidt, K.B. OLt. Rüdel
  Department II (foot artillery): Department head: Oberstltn. Trenkmann
  Members: Major Arnold, Hptm. Scharf, Hptm. Grzybowski, K.S. Hptm. Michaux, K.B. Hptm. Apfelstedt
  Assistants: Hptm. Becker, OLt. v. Roth, OLt. Christ, OLt. Weidemann, OLt. Heims, OLt. Melms, OLt. Schaefer, OLt. Zimmer, OLt. Baur, OLt. Statz, OLt. Ahlers, OLt. Behrend, OLt. Zustrow, K.B. OLt. Sturm
  Extraordinary members: Oberst Reinhardt, Oberst Brassart, Oberst Neuland, Oberstltn. Muther, Oberstltn. Koepke, Oberstltn. Berlin, Oberstltn. Eltester, Major Doutrelepont, Major Bartolomaeus
  Test and trials department: Oberstlt. Trenkmann
  Test and trials battery: Hptm. Kunze, OLt. Heims, OLt. Ahlers, OLt. Motz, OLt. Justrow, OLt. Busch, OLt. Kupke, Lt. Lampel
  Depot administration: Oberstltn. z.D. Herold
  Samples collection: Major z.D. v. Baumbach

- **Mechanical traffic commission:**
  President: Oberst Friedrich
  Adjutant: OLt. Ludewig

Department heads: Major Hecker, Major Gonell, Major v. Bezold, Major Roethe, K.B. Major Krafft
Members: K.W. Major Hundert, Hptm. Koppen, K.S. Hptm. Heger, K.S. Hptm. John, Hptm. Ammon, Hptm. Sommer, Hptm. George, Hptm. Nellstab, Hptm. v. Bylburg, Hptm. v. Weiher, Hptm. Rinneberg, Hptm. Meier, OLt. Fries, Hptm. Schoof, OLt. Sommerfeldt, K.B. OLt. Schlee, OLt. Höpker, K.B. OLt. Ströbl, OLt. Keller
Extraordinary members: Oberst v. Barfuß, Oberst v. Eberhardt, Oberst Bock, Oberst v. der Chevallerie, Oberstltn. Meyer, Major Kuhlwein, Major Hille
Test and trials department: Major Roethe, OLt. V. Beaulieu
1st test and trials company: Hptm. Meier, OLt. Fries, Lt. Haase, Lt. Remy, Lt. Koreuber
2nd test and trials company: Hptm. Goebel, OLt. Kolbe, Lt. Siber, Lt. v. Buttlar, Lt. Fink

- **Veterinarian inspection:** (Oberst v. Kleist, Rittm. Hevelke)
  Berlin military warehouse administration (Zeughaus-Verwaltung)

- Military music inspector

Administered by the general war department:
- Military horse-riding institute
- Officers' horse-riding school in Paderborn
- Officers' horse-riding school in Soltau
- Field equipment inspection (Feldzeugmeisterei)

Administration department (*Armee-Verwaltungs-Departement BD*)
Direktor: Gen. Maj. v. Schöler
Adjutant: Hptm. v. Oertzen
Hptm. Hoefer

Treasury department (*1. Kassen-Abteilung B1*)
Abt. Chef: Wirkl. Geh. Kr. Rat, OLt. d.L.a.D. Dr. Wrubel
Wirkl. Geh. Kr. Rat, OLt. d.L.a.D. Guntelmann
Wirkl. Geh. Kr. Rat, Lt. d.L.a.D. Hilgers
Geh. Kr. Rat, Lt. d.L.a.D. Heller

Supply department (*2. Verpflegungs-Abteilung B2*)
Abt. Chef: Wirkl. Geh. Kr. Rat, OLt. d.L.a.D. Dr. Selle
Wirkl. Geh. Kr. Rat, Lt. d.L.a.D. Eyber
Wirkl. Geh. Kr. Rat, OLt. d.L.a.D. Lemmel
Wirkl. Geh. Kr. Rat, OLt. d.R.a.D. Dr. Domino
Intendantur Rat, OLt. d.L.a.D. Hamann
Intendantur Rat, OLt. d.L.a.D. Dr. Brill

Garment department (*3. Bekleidungs-Abteilung B3*)
Abt. Chef: Oberstltn. v. Feldmann
Major v. Flotow
Major Brendel

Ober-Ingenieur Müller
Ober-Intendantur Rat, OLt. d.L.a.D. Bartels

Barracks department (*4. Unterkunfts-Abteilung B4*)
Abt. Chef: Oberst Friedrich
Major Salzenberg
Major Dix
Major Langguth
Major v. Hoffmann
Major Bonhard
Geh. Kr. Rat, OLt. d.L.a.D. Kieser

Training Center Department (*5. Übungsplatz-Abteilung B5*)
Abt. Chef: Oberstlt. v. Oven
Hptm. Wrzodek
Geh. Kr. Rat, OLt. d.L.a.D. Spellerberg
Geh. Kr. Rat, Lt. d.L.a.D. Dr. Schultz
Ober-Intendantur RatHptm. d.L.a.D. Wollert

Construction department (*6. Bau-Abteilung B6*)
Abt. Chef: Geh. Ober-Baurat Andersen
Geh. Ober-Baurat Wutsdorff
Geh. Baurat OLt. d.R.a.D. Schild
Geh. Baurat Hptm. d.L. Schultze
Geh. Baurat Wellroff
Geh. Baurat Zeyß
Intendantur- und Baurat Wefels

Payment and Legal Department (*Versorgungs- und Justiz Departement CD*)
Direktor: Gen. Maj. Frhr. v. Langermann u. Erlencamp
Adjutant: Hptm. v. Freyhold

Pensions department (*1. Pensions-Abteilung C1*)
Abt. Chef: Oberstlt. v. Aschoff
Major Hartwich
Major v. Kornatzki
Major Rothenbücher
Major v. Westrell
Major Schimmelpfeng
Hptm. Meier

Payment department (*2. Versorgungs-Abteilung C2*)
Abt. Chef: Oberstltn. Fischer
Major van den Bergh
Major v. Buch
Major z.D. Weiß

Wirkl. Geh. Kr. Rat, OLt. d.L.a.D. Grall
Wirkl. Geh. Kr. Rat, OLt. d.L.a.D. Großcurth

Legal department (*3. Justiz-Abteilung C3*)
Abt. Chef: Wirkl. Geh. Kr. Rat Hptm. d.L.a.D. Müller
Wirkl. Geh. Kr. Rat, Hptm. d.L.a.D. Kleberger
Wirkl. Geh. Kr. Rat, Hptm. d.L.a.D. Dr. Mielcke
Geh. Kr. Rat, Hptm. d.L.a.D. Dr. Mörler
Geh. Kr. Rat, Hptm. d.L.a.D. Dr. Lehmann
Wirkl. Geh. Kr. Rat Dr. v. Schelling
Wirkl. Geh. Kr. Rat, OLt. d.L.a.D. Dr. Grünwald
Wirkl. Geh. Kr. Rat, Hptm. d.L.a.D. Stieme

Horse mobilization inspection (*Remonte-Inspektion RJ*)
Inspektor: Oberstltn. Haack
Adjutant: Rittm. Frhr. v. Rotenhan
Wirkl. Geh. Kr. Rat, Hptm. d.L.a.D. v. Tippelskirch

Medical department (*Medizinal-Abteilung MA*)
Chef: Generalstabs Arzt der Armee Prof. Dr. v. Schjerning
General-Arzt Dr. Paalzow
General Ober-Arzt Dr. Hamann
Ober-Stabs-Arzt Dr. Niehues
Ober-Stabs-Arzt Prof. Dr. Hoffmann
Ober-Stabs-Arzt Dr. Schmidt
Wirkl. Geh. Kr. Rat, OLt. d.L.a.D. Grützmacher
Stabsarzt Dr. Martineck
Stabsarzt Dr. Schulze
Stabsarzt Dr. Neumann
Stabsarzt Dr. Wirth
Ober-Stabs-Apotheker Dr. Devin

Overseen by the medical department:

- Medical inspection
- Kaiser Wilhelm Academy for military medicine
- Medical administration
- Medical recovery institutes for officers

General Staff of the Army (Berlin)

Großer Generalstab

Chief of the General Staff: Gen. Oberst v. Moltke
First adjutant: Major Tieschowitz v. Tieschowa
Second adjutant: Hptm. Köhler

In contrast to the War Ministry, the organizational structure of the general staff was considered to be secret. The Rangliste therefore does not list the individual departments.

Ober-Quartiermeister I: Gen. Lt. Schmidt v. Knobelsdorff
Adjutant: Hptm. Wahl

Ober-Quartiermeister II: Gen. Lt. v. Bertrab
Adjutant: Major v. Poncet

Ober-Quartiermeister III: Gen. Maj. Graf v. Waldersee (Georg)
Adjutant: Hptm. v. Hammerstein-Equord

Ober-Quartiermeister IV: Gen. Maj. v. Kuhl
Adjutant: Hptm. v. Rundstedt

Ober-Quartiermeister V: Gen. Maj. v. Redern
Adjutant: Hptm. Weyland

Oberst Graf v. Posadowsky-Wehner, Oberst Weidner, Oberst v. Griesheim, Oberst Buchholtz, Oberst v. Kemnitz, Oberst v. Barttenwerffer, Oberst Marquard, K.W. Oberstltn. Renner, K.W. Oberstltn. Gröner, Oberstlt. Tappen, Oberstlt. v. Fabeck, Oberstlt. v. d. Heyde, Oberstlt. Launhardt, Oberstlt. Scherenberg, Major Jany, Major v. Redern, Major Kersten, Major Herwarth v. Bittenfeld, Major v. Haeften, Major Bauer, Major Brüggemann, Major Keller, Major Starck, Major v. Klewitz, Major v. Barttenwerffer, Major v. Dücker, Major v. Natzmer, Major Nicolai, Major Jochim, Major Faupel, Major Garcke, Major v. Tschudi, Major v. Henning auf Schönhoff, Major Henoumont, Major Frantz, Major Thamm, K.W. Major Müller, Major v. Rauch, Major v. Knauer, Major v. Belsen
Hptm. Humser, Hptm. Looff, Hptm. Baron de la Motte-Fouqué, Hptm. v. Wendt, Hptm. Matthiaß, Hptm. v. Stockhausen, Hptm. Lamotte, Hptm. v. Keßler, Hptm. Neuhof, Hptm. Koeppen, Hptm. Stotten, Hptm. Brinckmann, Hptm. Solger, Hptm. v. Heeringen, Hptm. Halm, Hptm. v. dem Bussche-Ippenburg, Hptm. Dunst, Hptm. v. Roques, Hptm. Mooyer, Hptm. Thilo, Hptm. Brause, Hptm. Heller, Hptm. v. Dewitz gen. v. Krebs, Hptm. Osius, Hptm. v. Cochenhausen, Hptm. v. Kalckreuth, Hptm. Steinbömer, Hptm. Loeschebrand-Horn, Hptm. Kaupisch, Hptm. Zeitz, Hptm. Prausnitzer, Hptm. Stieler v. Heydekampf, Hptm. Landfried, Hptm. Frhr. v. Fritsch, Hptm. v. Tempelhoff, Hptm. Hellwig, Hptm. Tybusch, Hptm. Janssen, Hptm. Boehm, Hptm. Hemmerich, Hptm. Held, Hptm. Blankenhorn, Hptm. Franke, Hptm. v. Holleuffer, Hptm. Metz, Hptm. Hasse, Hptm. v. Bogen, Hptm. Henning, Hptm. Bührmann, Hptm. v. Bose, Hptm. Koch, Hptm. v. Schickfus u. Neudorff, Hptm. Hausser, Hptm. v. Harbou, Hptm. Müller, Hptm. v. Falkenhausen, Hptm. Scultetus, Hptm. Beck, Hptm. Frhr. v. Bothmer, Hptm. v. Hepke, Hptm. v. Roques (Karl), Hptm. Mierzinsky, Hptm. Frantz, Hptm. Baare, Hptm. Crantz, K.W. Hptm. Muff (Friedrich), Hptm. Schönheinz, K.W. Hptm. Muff (Wolfgang), Hptm. Albrecht, K.W. Hptm. Graf v. Brandenstein-Zeppelin, Hptm. v. Brauchitsch, Hptm. Braemer, Hptm. v. Stuckrad, Hptm. v. Arnim

Temporary members of the Great General Staff (*kommandiert zur Dienstleistung*):
Oberst Friedrich Wilhelm Viktor August Ernst Kronprinz des Deutschen Reiches und Kronprinz von Preußen K.u.K.H.

Major Frhr. v. Rössing

Hptm. Aust, Hptm. Scherlau, Hptm. Lierau, Hptm. Vogel, Hptm. Schreiber, Hptm. Schmolke, Hptm. Hessig, Hptm. Carlsen, Hptm. Rittm. v. Berghes, Hptm. Panitzki, Hptm. v. Oppeln-Bronikowski, Hptm. Klug, Hptm. Bock, Hptm. v. Weise, Hptm. Rittm. v. Rieben, Hptm. Hinze, Hptm. Edler Herr u. Frhr. v. Plotho, Hptm. v. Bose, Hptm. Frey, Hptm. Kühlenthal, Hptm.Kühlenthal, Hptm. Fellinger, Hptm. Feige, Hptm. v. Schleicher, Hptm. v. Waldow, Hptm. Friese, Hptm. Wagner, K.W. Hptm. Edelmann, Hptm. Krüger, Rittm. Hesse Edler v. Helffenthal

OLt. v. Rochow, OLt. Lund, OLt. Senftleben, OLt. Sander, Olt. Eilker, OLt. Mülter, OLt. Vollmar, OLt. Soldan, OLt. Fusban, OLt. Deutelmoser, OLt. Schaller, OLt. Kolaczek, OLt. Weste, OLt. Becké, K.W. OLt. Geyer, K.W. OLt. Bruckmann, OLt. Zurborn, K.W. OLt. Deifel, OLt. V. Winterfeld, OLt. Bulcke, OLt. König, OLt. Siefert, OLt. Wagner, OLt. v. Wedderkop, OLt. Lüdke, OLt. v. Perthes, OLt. Otto, OLt. v. Tippelskirch, OLt. Zipper, OLt. Schwantes, K.W. OLt. Nuber, OLt. Evers, OLt. v. Theobald, OLt. Treusch v. Buttlar-Brandenfels, OLt. v. Kluge, OLt. Frhr. v. Tettau, OLt. Oertel, K.W. OLt. Berrer, OLt. v. Küchler, OLt. Isenburg, OLt. v. Arnoldi, OLt. v. Poncet, OLt. v. Kuhlmann, OLt. Laenge, OLt. Ernst, OLt. Kühns, OLt. Crato, OLt. v. Santen, OLt. Schaefer, OLt. Mattner, OLt. Bahnstedt, OLt. Josupeit, OLt. v. Jagow, OLt. Groth, OLt. Schöne, OLt. Poppe, OLt. Mewes, OLt. v. Rothkirch u. Panthen, OLt. Kutzfeld, OLt. Lieber, K.W. OLt. Taute, K.W. OLt. Höring, OLt. Petersen, OLt. Mackensen, OLt. Dingelfinger, OLt. v. Nida, OLt. Poten, OLt. Wendorff, K.W. OLt. Oßwald, OLt. v. Wietersheim, OLt. Klevemann, OLt. v. Stephani, OLt. Kühne, OLt. v. Wedelstädt, OLt. Hesse, OLt. Liebisch, OLt. Hoffmann, OLt. Boehm, OLt. Maenß, OLt. Neugebauer, OLt. Ehrhardt, OLt. v. Hahnke, OLt. Potthoff, OLt. v. Borries, OLt. Erlenwein, OLt. Weiser, K.W. OLt. Nühling, OLt. Burggraf u. Graf Zu Dohna-Schlobitten, OLt. Kohrt, OLt. Stempel, OLt. Bertrams, OLt. v. Steuben, OLt. Graf v. Westarp, OLt. v. Schwedler, OLt. v. der Osten, OLt. Hoth, OLt. Karmann, OLt. v. Poser u. Groß-Raedlitz, OLt. Lindemann, OLt. Hansen, OLt. v. Wallenberg, OLt. Seiffert, OLt. v. Rosenberg Gruszczynski, OLt. v. Egan-Krieger

Assigned to the Great General Staff (*dem Großen Generalstabe zugeteilt*):

Gen. Maj. v. Friedrich

Gen. Maj. v. Zglinicki

Oberstlt. v. Schmerfeld, Oberstlt. Buddecke, Major Nethe, Major Graf v. der Recke v. Volmerstein, Major Schwertfeger, Major Frhr. v. Haverbeck, Major Wagler, Major Fingerhuth, Hptm. v. Tresckow, Hptm. Richter, Hptm. Witte, Hptm. Lüders, Hptm. Gudowius, Hptm. Gempp, Hptm. Buchenthaler, Hptm. Schiller, Hptm. Fischer, Hptm. Gabriel, Hptm. Janensch, Hptm. Geisler, K.W. Hptm. Odlé, Hptm. v. Langendorff, Hptm. Frhr. v. Canstein, Hptm. Lübcke, Hptm. Kroeger, Hptm. Weste, Hptm. Volkmann, Hptm. Starke, Oberst z.D. Troschel, Oberst z.D. Frhr. v. Wangenheim, Oberstlt. z.D. Roth, Oberstlt. z.D. Erich, Oberstlt. z.D. Klitzkowski, Oberstlt. z.D. Maurhoff, Oberstlt. z.D. Ehlert, Oberstlt. z.D. Funck, Oberstlt. z.D. v. Guinneau

Railroad department:

Department head: K.W. Oberstltn. Groener

Oberstlt. Rohdewald, Oberstlt. v. Tronchin, Oberstlt. Krause, Major Langemak, Major Otto, Major Schwerdtfeger, K.W. Major Majer, Hptm. Hoffmann, Hptm. Levin, Hptm. Heubes, Hptm. v. Kathen, Hptm. Blümchen, Hptm. Mertens, Rittm. v. Gontard, Hptm. Vollmar, Hptm. Fleck, Hptm. Böwing, Hptm. Kretzschmann

Appendix B—The German Army in early 1914

Railroad line commands:
Oberstltn. Frhr. v. Wrangel, Major Koenemann, Major Kawelmacher, Major v. Bothmer, Major Langemak, Major Krause, Major Voigt, Major Rogge, Major Ziemsen, Major Kuhl, Major v. Lutz, Major Bode, Major v. Ziegner, Major Böhme, Major Breitenbach, Major Lancelle, Major Graf v. Hardenberg, Major Knobel, Major Toelle, Major v. Strube, Hptm. Böttrich

War Academy (Berlin):
Direktor: Gen. Lt. v. Steuben
Adjutant: Hptm. v. Knoblauch

Directorate:
Oberstlt. Frhr. Schenck zu Schweinsberg
Major Springefeld
Major v. Bothmer
Major v. Gerlach

Studies committee:
President: Gen. Lt. v. Steuben
Members:
Gen. Lt. Schmidt v. Knobelsdorff (senior quartermaster I)
Gen. Maj. v. Kuhl (senior quartermaster IV)
Gen. Maj. v. Redern (senior quartermaster V)
Oberst Buchholtz (head 7th department)

Chiefs of staff of army corps and Ia officers of divisions were members of the "Truppengeneralstab" and were ranked and listed in the Rangliste of the General Staff. Here they are listed further down exclusively with their army corps or divisions.

Leibgendarmerie (Potsdam)
Kommandeur: Gen. Oberst v. Scholl
OLt. v. Platen, OLt. Walzer

Schloßgarde-Kompanie (Berlin, Potsdam and Cassel)
Kommandeur: Oberst v. Mutius
Hptm. v. Pfannenberg
OLt. Thiele, OLt. v. Linsingen, OLt. Turner, Lt. v. Lülsdorff, Lt. Hancke, Lt. Altwasser

ORGANIZATIONAL STRUCTURE OF THE ARMY (ARMEE-EINTEILUNG)

Army Inspections

Army inspections were not command and control organizations comparable with the armies after mobilization.

First Army Inspection (Danzig)

General-Inspekteur: Gen. Oberst v. Prittwitz u. Gaffron
General staff officer: Oberst v. Studnitz
Ist, XVIIth and XXth Army Corps

Second Army Inspection (Berlin)

General-Inspekteur: Gen. Oberst v. Heeringen
Adjutant: Major Buchfinck
Guards corps, XIIth (1st K.S.), XIXth (2nd K.S.) Army Corps

Third Army Inspection (Hannover)

General-Inspekteur: Gen. Oberst v. Bülow
General staff officer: Major Graf Schack v. Wittenau
VIIth, IXth and Xth Army Corps

Fourth Army Inspection (Munich)

General-Inspekteur: K.B. Gen. Oberst d. Inf. Rupprecht Maria Luitpold Ferdinand Kronprinz von Bayern k.H.
Adjutant: K.B. Rittm. Müller
General staff officer: Major Hassenstein
IIIrd Army Corps, Ist, IInd and IIrd Bavarian Army Corps

Fifth Army Inspection (Karlsruhe)

General-Inspekteur: Gen. Oberst (mit dem Range eines General-Feldmarschalls) Friedrich II. Großherzog von Baden K.H.
General staff officer: Major Frhr. v. Rotberg
VIIIth, XIVth and XVth Army Corps

Sixth Army Inspection (Stuttgart)

General-Inspekteur: K.W. Gen. Oberst Albrecht Maria Alexander Philipp Joseph Herzog von Württemberg K.H.
General staff officer: Major Bronsart v. Schellendorff
IVth, XIth and XIIIth (K.W.) Army Corps

Seventh Army Inspection (Saarbrücken)

General-Inspekteur: Gen. Oberst v. Eichhorn
General staff officer: Major Ehrhardt
XVIth, XVIIIth and XXIst Army Corps

Eighth Army Inspection (Berlin)

General-Inspekteur: Gen. Oberst v. Kluck
Adjutant: Hptm. v. Schenckendorff
General staff officer: Major v. dem Hagen
IInd, V[th] and VIth Army Corps

Oberkommando in den Marken (Berlin, incl. fortress Berlin)

Governor: Gen. Oberst v. Kessel
Chief of General Staff: Major v. Schwartzkoppen
Kommandant (Berlin fortress): Gen. Lt. v. Bonin
Adj.: Hptm. v. Rundstedt

Gardekorps (Berlin)

Kdr. Gen.: Gen. d. Inf. Frhr. v. Plettenberg
Chief of General Staff: Gen. Maj. v. Voigts-Rhetz
Ia: Maj. v. Thaer
Ic: Hptm. v. Bock
Adjutants: Major Frhr. v. Hadeln, Rittm. v. Kummer
Oberstlt. z.D. v. Frankenberg u. Ludwigsdorf
Major v. Gleißenberg

Vorstand des Kontrollbureaus der Garde: Oberstltn. z.D. Orlovius

1. G.D. (Potsdam)
Kdr.: Gen. Lt. v. Hutier
Ia: Major Frhr. v. der Goltz
Adj.: Hptm. v. Beerfelde
1. G. Inf. Brig. Potsdam (Gen. Maj. v. Kleist, Adj.: Hptm. v. Helldorff): 1. G.R.z.F., 3. G.R.z.F., G.Jg.Btl., Lehr-Inf. Btl
1. G. Landw.R (I. Btl. Königsberg, II. Btl. Graudenz), 3. G. Landw. R. (I. Btl. Hannover, II. Btl. Schleswig)
2. G. Inf. Brig., Berlin (Gen. Maj. Schach v. Wittenau, Adj.: Hptm. v. Bismarck): 2. G.R.z.F., G.Füs.R., 4. G.R.z.F.
2. G. Landw. R (I. Btl. Berlin, II. Btl. Stettin), 4. G. Landw. R. (I. Btl. Magdeburg, II. Btl. Cottbus), G. Füs. Landw. R. (I. Btl. Frankfurt a.M., II. Btl. Wiesbaden)
1. G. Feld-Art. Brig., Berlin (Gen. Maj. Frhr. v. Buddenbrock, Adj.: Hptm. v. Kessel): 1. G. Feld-Art.R., 3. G. Feld-Art.R.

2. G.D. (Berlin)
Kdr.: Gen. Lt. v. Winckler
Ia: Major v. dem Hagen
Adj.: Hptm. Frhr. v. Türckheim zu Altdorf
3. G. Inf. Brig., Berlin (Gen. Maj. Albrecht, Adj.: Hptm. v. Olberg):
Kaiser Alexander Garde-Gren. R. Nr. 1, Königin Elisabeth Garde-Gren. R. Nr. 3, G. Schtz. Btl
1. Garde-Gren. Landw.R. (I. Btl. Görlitz, II. Btl. Lissa), 3. Garde-Gren. Landw. R. (I. Btl. Breslau, II. Btl. Liegnitz)
4. G. Inf. Brig., Berlin (Gen. Maj. v. Gontard, Adj.: Hptm. Müldner v. Mülnheim):

Kaiser Franz Garde-Gren. R. Nr. 2, Königin Augusta Garde-Gren. R. Nr. 4
2. Garde-Gren. Landw. R. (I. Btl. Hamm, II. Btl. Cassel), 4. Garde-Gren. Landw. R. (I. Btl. Coblenz, II. Btl. Düsseldorf)
5. G. Inf. Brig., Spandau (Gen. Maj. v. Below, Adj.: Hptm. v. Kurnatowski):
5. G.R.z.F., Garde-Gren. R. Nr. 5
2. G. Feld-Art. Brig., Potsdam (Gen. Maj. Trimborn, Adj.: Hptm. v. Hymmen): 2. G. Feld-Art.R., 4. G. Feld-Art.R.

Garde-Kavallerie-Division (Berlin)
Kdr.: Gen. Lt. v. Pelet-Narbonne
Ia: Hptm.Niemann
Adj.: Rittm. v. Bredow
1. G. Kav. Brig., Berlin (Oberst v. Baerensprung, Adj.: Rittm. v. Zobeltitz):
Regt. D. Gardes du Corps, Garde-Kür. R.
2. G. Kav. Brig., Potsdam (Gen. Maj. Graf v. Rothkirch u. Trach, Adj.: Rittm. v. Livonius):
1. G. Ulanen R., 3. G. Ulanen R.
3. G. Kav. Brig., Berlin (Gen. Maj. v. Bülow, Adj.: Rittm. v. Lieres u. Wilkau):
1. G. Drag. R., 2. G. Drag. R.
4. G. Kav. Brig., Potsdam (Oberst Frhr. v. Senden, Adj.: Rittm. Graf v. Schmettow):
Leib-Garde-Hus. R., 2. G. Ulanen R.

G. MG Abt. Nr. 1
G. MG Abt. Nr. 2
G. Fuß-Art. R.
Telegr. Btl. Nr. 1
Telegr. Btl. Nr. 2
Zeppelin-Btl. Nr. 1
Zeppelin-Btl. Nr. 2
Aircraft-Btl. Nr. 1
Motor-Btl.
G. Train Abt.

Training Center (Truppen-Übungsplatz) Döberitz
Kommandant: Gen. Maj. z.D. v. Bonin
Adj.: OLt. v. Gerlach

Training Center (Truppen-Übungsplatz) Zossen
Kommandant: Gen. Maj. z.D. Schneider
Adj.: OLt. Frhr. Spiegel von und zu Peckelsheim

I. Armeekorps (Königsberg)

Kdr. Gen.: Gen. Lt. v. François
Chief of General Staff: Oberst Frhr. Schmidt v. Schmidtseck
Ia: Hptm. Jarosch
Ic: Hptm. Schubert
Adjutants: Major v. Schiller, Rittm. Frhr v. Brandenstein

Hptm. Gempp
Oberstlt. z.D. Hahn

1. I.D. (Königsberg)
Kdr.: Gen. Lt. v. Conta
Ia: Major v. Graberg
Adj.: Major Fürsen
1. Inf. Brig., Tilsit (Gen. Maj. v. Trotha, Adj.: Hptm. Saxer): Gren. R. Kronprinz Nr. 1, I.R. 41
2. Inf. Brig., Königsberg (Gen. Maj. Mühlenbruch, Adj.: Hptm. Feige): Gren. R. König Friedrich Wilhelm I. Nr. 3, I.R. 43, Bez. Kom. I + II Königsberg
1. Kav. Brig., Königsberg (Oberst v. Glasenapp, Adj.: Rittm. v. Goßler): K.R. 3, D.R. 1
1. Feld-Art. Brig., Königsberg (Gen. Maj. Moewes, Adj.: Hptm. v. Rodenberg): Feld-Art. R. 16, Feld-Art. R. 52

2. I.D. (Insterburg)
Kdr.: Gen. Lt. v. Below
Ia: Hptm. Goedel
Adj.: Hptm. Kettner
3. Inf. Brig., Rastenburg (Gen. Maj. Mengelbier, Adj.: Hptm. Jacobi): Gren. R. König Friedrich der Große Nr. 4, I.R. 44
4. Inf. Brig., Gumbinnen (Gen. Maj. v. Walther, Adj.: Hptm. Wollermann): F.R. 33, I.R. 45
2. Kav. Brig., Insterburg (Gen. Maj. Frhr. v. Kap-herr, Adj.: Rittm. v. Plehwe): U.R. 12, Jg. Rgt. z. Pf. 9
43. Kav. Brig., Gumbinnen (Oberst Frhr. v. Lupin, Adj.: Rittm. v. Hauenschild): U.R. 8, Jg. Rgt. z. Pf. 10
2. Feld-Art. Brig., Insterburg (Oberst Fouquet, Adj.: Hptm. Werner): Feld-Art. R. 1, Feld-Art. R. 37

Landwehr-Inspektion Insterburg (Insp. Gen. Maj. Barre, Adj.: Hptm. Steinmann): Bez. Kom. Bartenstein, Goldap, Gumbinnen, Insterburg, Rastenburg, Tilsit
MG-Abt. Nr. 5
Fest. MG-Abt. Nr. 1
Fußart. R. 1
Pion. Btl. 1
Pion. Btl. 18
Fest. Fernsprech-Kp. Nr. 5
Zeppelin-Btl. 5
Train-Abt. Nr. 1

Fortress (Festung) Königsberg
Kommandant: Gen. Lt. v. Pappritz
Chief of general staff: Oberstlt. Nehbel
Ia: Major Jahn
Hptm. Friedrichs
Adj.: Hptm. Hardt

Feste Boyen
Kommandant: Oberst Busse
Platzmajor: Hptm. Schlesinger

II. Armeekorps (Stettin)

Kdr. Gen.: Gen. D. Inf. v.Linsingen
Chief of general staff: Major Mengelbier
Ia: Hptm. Ludloff
Ic: Hptm. v. Bock u. Polach
Adjutants: Major v. Cranach, Rittm. Friedrich Graf zu Waldeck und Pyrmont
Oberstlt. z.D. v. Tiezelsky

3. I.D. (Stettin)
Kdr.: Gen. Lt. v. Trossel
Ia: Hptm. Gr. v. Poninski
Adj.: Major Fischer
5. Inf. Brig., Stettin (Gen. Maj. Frhr. Treusch v. Buttlar-Brandenfels, Adj.: Hptm. Schmidt): Gren. R. König Friedrich Wilhelm IV. Nr. 2 Colberg, Gren. R. Graf Gneisenau Nr. 9, I.R. 54, Bez. Kom. Belgard, Stargard
6. Inf. Brig., Stettin (Gen. Maj. Nieland, Adj.: Hptm. Fabian): F.R. 34, I.R. 42, Bez. Kom. Stettin
3. Kav. Brig., Stettin (Oberst Graf v. der Goltz, Adj.: Rittm. v. Prittwitz u. Gaffron): K.R. 2, U.R. 9, Bez. Kom. Anklam, Stralsund
3. Feld-Art. Brig., Stettin (Gen. Maj. Rhazen, Adj.: Hptm. Huppertz): Feld-Art. R. 2, Feld-Art. R. 38, Bez. Kom. Naugard, Swinemünde

4. I.D. (Bromberg)
Kdr.: Gen. Lt. v. Pannewitz
Ia: Major Klette
Adj.: Major Stoltz
7. Inf. Brig.; Bromberg (Gen. Maj. v. Runckel, Adj.: Hptm. Rohde): I.R. 14, I.R. 149
8. Inf. Brig., Gnesen (Gen. Maj. v. Schmettau, Adj.: Hptm. Weißermel): I.R. 49, I.R. 140
4. Kav. Brig.; Bromberg (Gen. Maj. v. Hoepner, Adj.: OLt. v. Stockhausen): D.R. 12, Gren. Rgt. z. Pf. 3
4. Feld-Art. Brig.; Bromberg (Gen. Maj. Krafft, Adj.: Hptm. Grosser): Feld-Art. R. 17, Feld-Art. R. 53

Landwehr-Inspektion Bromberg (Insp. Gen. Maj. Krause, Adj. Hptm. Menzel): Bez. Kom. Bromberg, Deutsch-Krone, Gnesen, Hohensalza, Neustettin, Schneidemühl
Jg. Btl. 2
Fußart. R. 2
Fußart. R. 15
Pion. Btl. 2
Train-Abt. Nr. 2

III. Armeekorps (Berlin)

Kdr. Gen.: Gen. d. Inf. v. Lochow
Chief of general staff: Oberstlt. v. Seeckt
Ia: Major Wetzell
Ic: Hptm. v. Lindequist
Hptm. v. Behr

Adjutants: Major v. Usedom, Major v. d. Hude, Major v. Schmelzing

Oberstlt. z.D. v. Steuben

5. I.D. (Frankfurt a. d. Oder)
Kdr.: Gen. Lt. Wichura
Ia: Major v. Westhoven
Adj.: Major Frhr. v. Müffling sonst Weiß gen.
9. Inf. Brig., Frankfurt a. d. Oder (Gen. Maj. v. Doemming, Adj.: Hptm. Mertens): Leib-Gren. R. König Friedrich Wilhelm III. Nr. 8, I.R. 48, Bez. Kom. Cüstrin, Frankfurt a.d.O.
10. Inf. Brig., Frankfurt a. d. Oder (Gen. Maj. Sontag, Adj.: Hptm. v. Zerboni di Sposetti): Gren. R. Prinz Carl v. Preußen Nr. 12, I.R. 52, Bez. Kom. Calau, Cottbus
5. Kav. Brig., Frankfurt a. d. Oder (Oberst v. Arnim, Adj.: Rittm. Sengenwald): D.R. 2, U.R. 3, Bez. Kom. Crossen, Guben
5. Feld-Art. Brig., Frankfurt a. d. Oder (K.W. Oberst v. Lotterer, Adj.: Hptm. Hoge): Feld-Art. R. 18, Feld-Art. R. 54, Bez. Kom. Landsberg a.d.W., Woldenberg

6. I.D. (Brandenburg a. d. Havel)
Kdr.: Gen. Lt. Frhr. v. Richthofen
Ia: Major v. Viereck
Adj.: Major Sandner
11. Inf. Brig., Brandenburg a. d. Havel (Gen. Maj. v. Wachter, Adj.: Hptm. v. Rundstedt): I.R. 20, F.R. 35, Bez. Kom. Jüterbog, Potsdam
12. Inf. Brig., Brandenburg a. d. Havel (Gen. Maj. v. Gabain, Adj.: OLt. Rust): I.R. 24, I.R. 64, Bez. Kom. Prenzlau, Ruppin
6. Kav. Brig., Brandenburg a. d. Havel (Gen. Maj. Graf v. Schmettow, Adj.: OLt. v. Jeinsen): K.R. 6, H.R. 3, Bez. Kom. Brandenburg a. d. H., Spandau
6. Feld-Art. Brig., Brandenburg a. d. Havel (Gen. Maj. v. Kleist, Adj.: Hptm. Kulau): Feld-Art. R. 3, Feld-Art. R. 39, Bez. Kom. Perleberg

Landwehr-Inspektion Berlin (Insp.: Gen. Lt. Frhr. v. Süßkind, Adj.: Hptm. v. Bülow, further: Oberstlt. z.D. Haushalter, Major z.D. Erhard): Bez. Kom. Berlin I, II, III, IV, V + VI
Jg. Btl. 3
Pion. Btl. 3
Pion. Btl. 28
Telegr. Btl. 2
Train-Abt. Nr. 3

Training Center (Truppen-Übungsplatz) Jüterbog
Kommandant: Gen. Maj. z.D. v. Müller
Adj.: Lt. Eichberg

IV. Armeekorps (Magdeburg)

Kdr. Gen.: Gen. d. Inf. Sixt v. Arnim
Chief of general staff: Gen. Maj. v. Stocken
Ia: Major v. Mantey

Ic: Hptm. Kriegsheim
Adjutants: Major v. Usedom, Major Gündell, Hptm. Vollerthun
Oberstlt. z.D. Wenzel

7. I.D. (Magdeburg)
Kdr.: Gen. Lt. Riedel
Ia: Major v. Aweyden
Adj.: Hptm. Bagge
13. Inf. Brig., Magdeburg (Gen. Maj. v. Schüßler, Adj.: Hptm. Jaenisch): I.R. 26, I.R. 66, Bez. Kom. Magdeburg
14. Inf. Brig., Halberstadt (Gen. Maj. v. Wussow, Adj.: Hptm. v. Frankenberg u. Ludwigsdorf): I.R. 27, I.R. 165, Bez. Kom. Aschersleben, Halberstadt
7. Kav. Brig., Magdeburg (Oberst Saenger, Adj.: Rittm. v. Hoffmann): H.R. 10, U.R. 16
7. Feld-Art. Brig., Magdeburg (Gen. Maj. v. Stumpff, Adj.: Hptm. v. Kamlah): Feld-Art. R. 4, Feld-Art. R. 40

8. I.D. (Halle a. d. Saale)
Kdr.: Gen. Lt. Hildebrandt
Ia: Major Lämmerhirt
Adj.: Hptm. Woltersdorf
15. Inf. Brig., Halle a. d. Saale (Gen. Maj. Reichenau, Adj.: Hptm. v. dem Knesebeck): F.R. 36, I.R. 93 (Anhalt), Bez. Kom. Bernburg, Dessau
16. Inf. Brig., Torgau (Gen. Maj. v. Jarotzky, Adj.: Hptm. Hoffmeister): I.R. 72 (1. Thüring.), I.R. 153 (4. Thüring.), Bez. Kom. Altenburg, Torgau
8. Kav. Brig., Halle a. d. Saale (Gen. Maj. Frhr. Thumb v. Neuburg, Adj.: Rittm. v. Westrem zum Gutacker): K.R. 7, Thüring. H.R. 12
8. Feld-Art. Brig., Halle a. d. Saale (Gen. Maj. Bothe, Adj.: Hptm. v. Seydlitz und Gohlau): Feld-Art. R. 74, Feld-Art. R. 75

Landwehr-Inspektion Halle a.d.S. (Insp.: Gen. Maj. v. Dehn-Rotfelser, Adj.: Hptm. Reuter): Bez. Kom. Bitterfeld, Burg, Eisleben, Halle a.d.S., Naumburg a.d.S., Neuhaldensleben, Sangerhausen, Stendal, Weißenfels
Jg. Btl. 4
Fußart. R. 4
Pion. Btl. 4
Train-Abt. Nr. 4

Training Center (Truppen-Übungsplatz) Alten-Grabow
Kommandant: Gen. Maj. z.D. v. der Decken
Adj.: OLt. Holfeld

V. Armeekorps (Posen)

Kdr. Gen.: Gen. d. Inf. v. Strantz
Chief of general staff: Oberst Meister
Ia: Major Dove
Ic: Hptm. Foerster
Hptm. Wachenfeld

Adjutants: Major Krebs, Rittm. v. Gagern
Oberstlt. z.D. Noel, Hptm. Lüders

9. I.D. (Glogau)
Kdr.: Gen. Lt. v. Below
Ia: Major Föhrenbach
Adj.: Major Bielitz
17. Inf. Brig., Glogau (Gen. Maj. Melms, Adj.: Hptm. v. Seebach): I.R. 19, I.R. 58, Bez. Kom. Görlitz, Glogau, Lauban
18. Inf. Brig., Liegnitz (Gen. Maj. Falckenheiner, Adj.: Hptm. v. Raven): Gren. R. König Wilhelm I. Nr. 7, I.R. 154, Bez. Kom. Hirschberg, Jauer, Liegnitz
9. Kav. Brig., Glogau (Gen. Maj. Rusche, Adj.: Rittm. v. Oertzen): D.R. 4, U.R. 10, Bez. Kom. Muskau, Neusalz a.d.O., Sprottau
9. Feld-Art. Brig., Glogau (Gen. Maj. Müller, Adj.: Hptm. Selle): Feld-Art. R. 5, Feld-Art. R. 41

10. I.D. (Posen)
Kdr.: Gen. Lt. Kosch
Ia: Major Aubert
Adj.: Major Bielefeld
19. Inf. Brig., Posen (Gen. Maj. Liebeskind, Adj.: OLt. v. der Marwitz): Gren. R. Graf Kleist v. Nollendorf Nr. 6, I.R. 46
20. Inf. Brig., Posen (Gen. Maj. Frhr. v. der Horst, Adj.: Hptm. Boldt): I.R. 47, I.R. 50
77. Inf. Brig., Ostrowo (Gen. Maj. v. Dewitz, Adj.: Hptm. Pfaff): F.R. 37, I.R. 155
10. Kav. Brig., Posen (Gen. Maj. Neven Du Mont, Adj.: OLt. v. der Schulenburg): U.R. 1, R. Königs-Jg. Z. Pf. Nr. 1
10. Feld-Art. Brig., Posen (K.W. Gen. Maj. Frhr. v. Watter, Adj.: Hptm. v. Cleve): Feld-Art. R. 20, Feld-Art. R. 56

Landwehr-Inspektion Posen (Insp.: Gen. Maj. Glahn, Adj.: Hptm. Lübbert): Bez. Kom. Kosten, Neutomischel, Ostrowo, Posen, Rawitsch, Samter, Schrimm, Schroda

Jg. Btl. 5
Fest. MG Abt. Nr. 6
Fußart. R. 5
Pion. Btl. 5
Pion. Btl. 29
Fest. Fernsprech-Komp. 8
Aircraft-Btl. 2
Train-Abt. Nr. 5

Fortress (Festung) Posen, Training Center (Truppen-Übungsplatz) Posen / Warthelager
Kommandant: Gen. Lt. v. Koch
Ia: Major Merkel
Hptm. Heller
Adj.: OLt. Frhr. v. Gablenz

VI. Armeekorps (Breslau)

Kdr. Gen.: Gen. d. Inf. v. Pritzelwitz
Chief of General Staff: Oberst v. Derschau
Ia: Major v. Pommer Esche
Ic: Hptm. v. Taysen
K.W. Hptm. Spemann
Adjutants: Major Cramer, Major Bollmann
Hptm. Gudowius
Oberstlt. z.D. Wahrendorff

11. I.D. (Breslau)
Kdr.: Gen. Lt. v. Webern
Ia: Major Graf Yorck v. Wartenburg
Adj.: Major v. Wolfersdorff
21. Inf. Brig., Schweidnitz (Gen. Maj. v. Drabisch-Waechter, Adj.: Hptm. Jacobs): Gren.R. König Friedrich Wilhelm II. Nr. 10, F.R. 38, Bez. Kom. Glatz, Schweidnitz
22. Inf. Brig., Breslau (Gen. Maj. Surén, Adj.: Hptm. v. Wulffen): Gren.R. König Friedrich III. Nr. 11, I.R. 51, Bez. Kom. II Breslau, Wohlau
11. Kav. Brig, Breslau. (Oberst v. Wentzky u. Petersheyde, Adj.: Rittm. Ritter u. Edler v. Rogister): Leib-Kür.R. Großer Kurfürst Nr. 1, D.R. 8
11. Feld-Art. Brig., Breslau (Gen. Maj. v. Bischoffshausen, Adj.: Hptm. v. Rundstedt): Feld-Art. R. 6, Feld-Art. R. 42

Landwehr-Inspektion Breslau (Insp.: Gen. Lt. V. Worgitzky, Adj.: Hptm. Menchen): Bez. Kom. Beuthen, I Breslau, Kattowitz, Kreuzburg, Oels, Striegau, Waldenburg

12. I.D. (Neiße)
Kdr.: Gen. Lt. Chales de Beaulieu
Ia: Hptm. v. Miaskowski
Adj.: Major Haun
23. Inf. Brig., Gleiwitz (Gen. Maj. Neff, Adj.: Hptm. Scultetus): I.R. 22, I.R. 156, Bez. Kom. Cosel, Gleiwitz
24. Inf. Brig., Neiße (Gen. Maj. Boeß, Adj.: Hptm. Bursy): I.R. 23, I.R. 62, Bez. Kom. Münsterberg, Neiße
78. Inf. Brig., Brieg (Gen. Maj. Vollbrecht, Adj.: Hptm. v. Schmiterlöw): I.R. 63, I.R. 157, Bez. Kom. Brieg, Oppeln
12. Kav. Brig., Neiße (Gen. Maj. Gr. v. Pfeil u. Klein-Ellguth, Adj.: Rittm. Frhr. v. Seherr-Thoß): H.R. 4, H.R. 6, Bez. Kom. Ratibor, Rybnik
44. Kav. Brig., Gleiwitz (Oberst v. Mutius, Adj.: Rittm. v. Sauerma): U.R. 2, Jg. Regt. z. Pf. Nr. 11
12. Feld-Art. Brig., Neiße (Gen. Maj. Zietlow, Adj.: Hptm. Sperl): Feld-Art. R. 21, Feld-Art. R. 57

Jg. Btl. 6
MG Abt. 1
Fußart. R. 6
Pion. Btl. 6
Train-Abt. Nr. 6

Fortress (Festung) Breslau
Kommandant: Gen. Lt. Schalscha v. Ehrenfeld
Platzmajor: Hptm. Busch
Adj.: Hptm. Hübner

Training Center (Truppen-Übungsplatz) Neuhammer a. Q.
Kommandant: Gen. Maj. z.D. Kretzschmer
Adj.: OLt. Geyer

Preliminary Training Center (Vorläufiger Truppen-Übungsplatz) Lamsdorf (Neiße)
Kommandant: Gen. Maj. z.D. Gabriel
Adj.: Lt. Eichberg

VII. Armeekorps (Münster)

Kdr. Gen.: Gen. d. Kav. v. Einem gen. v. Rothmaler
Chief of General Staff: Oberst v. Wolff
Ia: Major v. Caprivi
Ic: Hptm. Knuth
Hptm. Henke
Adjutants: Major v. der Gablentz, Rittm. Frhr. v. Richthofen

Hptm. Kroeger
Oberstlt. z.D. Springborn

13. I.D. (Münster)
Kdr.: Gen. Lt. v. dem Borne
Ia: Hptm. v. Platen
Adj.: Hptm. v. Quednow
25. Inf. Brig., Münster (Gen. Maj. Quade, Adj.: Hptm. v. Brömbsen): I.R. 13, I.R. 158 (7. Lothring.), Bez. Kom. Coesfeld, Münster
26. Inf. Brig., Minden (Gen. Maj. Rogalla v. Biederstein, Adj.: Hptm. Rohde): I.R. 15, I.R. 55, Bez. Kom. Detmold, Minden
13. Kav. Brig., Münster (Gen. Maj. Grünert, Adj.: Rittm. v. Pape) K.R. 4, H.R. 8
13. Feld-Art. Brig, Münster. (Oberst Klipfel, Adj.: Hptm. Peltzer): Feld-Art. R. 22, Feld-Art. R. 58

Landwehr-Inspektion Dortmund (Insp.: Gen. Lt. v. Harbou, Adj.: Hptm. Brenner): Bez. Kom. Bielefeld, Bochum I + II, Dortmund I + II, Paderborn, Soest

14. I.D. (Düsseldorf)
Kdr.: Gen. Lt. v. Lauenstein
Ia: Hptm. v. Bock
Adj.: Major v. Bosse
27. Inf. Brig., Cöln (Gen. Maj. Fleck, Adj.: OLt. Heine): I.R. 16, I.R. 53
28. Inf. Brig., Düsseldorf (Gen. Maj. Dieffenbach, Adj.: Hptm. Suffert): F.R. 39, I.R. 159 (8. Lothring.)

79. Inf. Brig., Wesel (Gen. Maj. Schwarte, Adj.: OLt. Hildebrandt): I.R. 56, I.R. 57, Bez. Kom. Geldern, Wesel
14. Kav. Brig., Düsseldorf (Oberst v. Heuduck, Adj.: Rittm. v. Felbert): H.R. 11, U.R. 5
14. Feld-Art. Brig., Wesel (Oberst Lang, Adj.: Hptm. Berndt): Feld-Art. R. 7, Feld-Art. R. 43

Landwehr-Inspektion Düsseldorf (Insp.: Gen. Maj. Neuhauß, Adj.: Hptm. Moers): Bez. Kom. Barmen, Crefeld, Düsseldorf I + II, Elberfeld, Hagen, Lennep, Solingen

Landwehr-Inspektion Essen (Insp.: Gen. Lt. Sunkel, Adj.: Hptm. Rietzsch): Bez. Kom. Duisburg, Essen I + II, Gelsenkirchen, Mülheim a.d. Ruhr, Recklinghausen

Jg. Btl. 7
MG Abt. 7
Fußart. R. 7
Pion. Btl. 7
Pion. Btl. 24
Train-Abt. Nr. 7

Fortress (Festung) Wesel, Training Center (Truppen-Übungsplatz) Friedrichsfeld
Kommandant: Gen. Maj. Knoch
Platzmajor: Hptm. Frhr. v. Wachtmeister
Adj.: OLt. Müller

Training Center (Truppen-Übungsplatz) Sennelager
Kommandant: Gen. Maj. z.D. v. Pawel
Adj.: Lt. Wiemann

VIII. Armeekorps (Coblenz)

Kdr. Gen.: Gen. Lt. Tülff v. Tschepe u. Weidenbach
Chief of General Staff: Oberst v. Cramon
Ia: Major van den Bergh
Ic: Hptm. Reuter
Hptm. Mackowsky
Adjutants: Major Frhr. v. Hammerstein-Gesmold, Major Zehr

Hptm. Witte
Oberstlt. z.D. Matthei

15. I.D. (Cologne)
Kdr.: Gen. Lt. Riemann
Ia: Hptm. Henz
Adj.: Hptm. Hülsmann
29. Inf. Brig., Aachen (Gen. Maj. v. Minckwitz, Adj.: Hptm. Rodatz): I.R. 25, I.R. 161, Bez. Kom. Aachen, Monschau (Montjoie)
80. Inf. Brig., Bonn (Gen. Maj. Frhr. Raitz v. Frentz, Adj.: Hptm. Spilling): I.R. 65, I.R. 160, Bez. Kom. Bonn, Neuwied

15. Kav. Brig., Cologne (Gen. Maj. v. Storch, Adj.: Rittm. Jänecke) K.R. 8, H.R. 7
15. Feld-Art. Brig., Cologne (Gen. Maj. v. Woyna, Adj.: Hptm. v. Trotha): Feld-Art. R. 59, Feld-Art. R. 83

Landwehr-Inspektion Cologne (Insp.: Gen. Lt. V. Ditfurth, Adj.: Hptm. Vielhaber): Bez. Kom. Cologne I+II, Deutz, Jülich, Neuß, Rheydt, Siegburg

16. I.D. (Trier)
Kdr.: Gen. Lt. v. Fuchs
Ia: Major v. Stülpnagel
Adj.: Major Heesemann
30. Inf. Brig., Coblenz (Gen. Maj. v. Pfuel, Adj.: Hptm. Lange): I.R. 28, I.R. 68, Bez. Kom. Andernach, Coblenz
31. Inf. Brig., Trier (Gen. Maj. Wellmann, Adj.: Hptm. v. Bönninghausen): I.R. 29, I.R. 69, Bez. Kom. Trier I+II
16. Kav. Brig., Trier (Oberst Kleemann, Adj.: Rittm. Boehmer): Jg. Regt. z. Pf. 7, Jg. Regt. z. Pf. 8
16. Feld-Art. Brig., Trier (Gen. Maj. Beckmann, Adj.: Hptm. v. Treskow): Feld-Art. R. 23, Feld-Art. R. 44

MG Abt. 2
Fest. MG Abt. 7
Fußart. R. 9
Pion. Btl. 8
Pion. Btl. 30
Train-Abt. Nr. 8
Telegr. Btl. Nr. 3
Fest. Fernspr.-Komp. Nr. 6
Aircraft-Btl. Nr. 3
Luftschiff.-Btl. Nr. 3

Fortress (*Festung*) Cologne
Kommandant: Gen. Lt. v. Wandel
Ia: Major Budde
Adj.: Hptm. v. Glan

Fortress (Festung) Ehrenbreitstein / Coblenz
Kommandant: Gen. Lt. v. Luckwald
Platzmajor: Hptm. Enneccerus

Fortress (Festung) Mainz
Kommandant: Gen. d. Inf. v. Kathen
Chief of general staff: MajornFüßlein
Ia: Hptm. v. Nolte
Adj.: Hptm. Tietz

Training Center (Truppen-Übungsplatz) Elsenborn / Aachen
Kommandant: Gen. Maj. z.D. Zechlin
Adj.: OLt. Siebe

Foot-Artillery Training Center (Fußartillerie-Schießplatz) Wahn / Cologne
Kommandant: Gen. Maj. z.D. v. Fichte
Adj.: Lt. Nütten

IX. Armeekorps (Altona)

Kdr. Gen.: Gen. Lt. v. Quast
Chief of General Staff: Oberstlt. Sydow
Ia: Major Auer v. Herrenkirchen
Ic: Hptm. Wende
Hptm. v. Platen
Adjutants: Major Wessig, Rittm. v. Behr

Oberstlt. z.D. Schütze

17. I.D. (Schwerin)
Kdr.: Gen. Lt. v. Bauer
Ia: Hptm. v. Voß
Adj.: Hptm. v. Coler
33. Inf. Brig., Altona (Gen. Maj. v. Lewinski, Adj.: Hptm. v. Sommerfeld): I.R. Bremen Nr. 75, I.R. Hamburg Nr. 76, Bez. Kom. I Bremen, Bremerhaven
34. Ghz. Meckl. Inf. Brig., Schwerin (Gen. Maj. v. Kraewel, Adj.: Hptm. Hesse): Ghz. Meckl. G.R. 89, Ghz. Meckl.F.R. 90, Bez. Kom. Rostock, Wismar
81. Inf. Brig., Lübeck (Gen. Maj. v. Morgen, Adj.: Hptm. v. Prittwitz u. Gaffron): I.R. Lübeck Nr. 162, I.R. 163, Bez. Kom. II Bremen, Lübeck
17. Ghz. Meckl. Kav. Brig., Schwerin (Gen. Maj. Gr. v. Schimmelmann, Adj.: Rittm. v. Bredow) Ghz. Meckl. D.R.17, Ghz. Meckl. D.R.18
17. Feld-Art. Brig., Schwerin (Gen. Maj. v. Ditfurth, Adj.: Hptm. v. Strzemieczny): Feld-Art. R. 24, Ghz. Meckl. Feld-Art. R. 60

18. I.D. (Flensburg)
Kdr.: Gen. Lt. v. Kluge
Ia: Major v. Gellhorn
Adj.: Major v. Fuchs
35. Inf. Brig., Flensburg (Gen. Maj. Hunaeus, Adj.: Hptm. Gemoll): I.R. 84, I.R. 86, Bez. Kom. Flensburg, Schleswig
36. Inf. Brig., Rendsburg (Gen. Maj. Frhr. v. Troschke, Adj.: Hptm. Schemmann): I.R. 31, I.R. 85, Bez. Kom. Rendsburg, Stade
18. Kav. Brig., Altona (Oberst v. Printz, Adj.: Rittm. v. Bonin): H.R. 15, H.R. 16
18. Feld-Art. Brig., Altona (Gen. Maj. Bloch v. Blottnitz, Adj.: Hptm. Neydecker): Feld-Art. R. 9, Feld-Art. R. 45

Landwehr-Inspektion Altona (Insp.: Gen. Lt. Dernen, Adj.: Hptm. Dreyer), Bez. Kom. I + II Altona, I, II + III Hamburg, Kiel, Neumünster

Jg. Btl. 9
Fußart. R. 20
Pion. Btl. 9
Train-Abt. Nr. 9

Training Center (Truppen-Übungsplatz) Lockstedt
Kommandant: Gen. Maj. z.D. v. Bonin
Adj.: OLt. Soltau

X. Armeekorps (Hannover)

Kdr. Gen.: Gen. d. Inf. v. Emmich
Chief of General Staff: Oberst Frhr. v. der Wenge
Ia: Major Kirch
Ic: Hptm. Krall
Hptm. v. Stülpnagel
Adjutants: Major v. Berg, Hptm. v. der Heyde

Oberstlt. z.D. Hoppe

19. I.D. (Hannover)
Kdr.: Gen. Lt. Hofmann
Ia: Major v. Dommes
Adj.: Hptm. Grußdorf
37. Inf. Brig., Oldenburg (Gen. Maj. v. Scheliha, Adj.: Hptm. v. Waldow): I.R. 78, Oldenburg. I.R. Nr. 91, Bez. Kom. Oldenburg I+II
38. Inf. Brig., Hannover (Gen. Maj. v. Oven, Adj.: Hptm. Hesse): F.R. 73, I.R. 74, Bez. Kom. Lüneburg
19. Kav. Brig., Hannover (Gen. Maj. Frhr. v. Zedlitz u. Leipe, Adj.: Rittm. v. Pelet-Narbonne) Oldenburg. D.R.19, Königs U.R. Nr. 13
19. Feld-Art. Brig., Oldenburg (Gen. Maj. Heygster, Adj.: Hptm. v. Düring): Feld-Art. R. 26, Feld-Art. R. 62

20. I.D. (Hannover)
Kdr.: Gen. Lt. Schmundt
Ia: Major v. Wiarda
Adj.: Hptm. Steinkopff
39. Inf. Brig., Hannover (Gen. Maj. Frhr. v. Lüttwitz, Adj.: Hptm. Sartorius): I.R. 79, I.R. 164, Bez. Kom. Göttingen, Hildesheim
40. Inf. Brig., Braunschweig (Gen. Maj. v. Lindequist, Adj.: Hptm. Niebelschütz) I.R. 77, Braunschweig. I.R. 92, Bez. Kom. Braunschweig I+II
20. Kav. Brig., Hannover (Gen. Maj. v. Unger, Adj.: OLt. Hans Prinz v. Ratibor und Corvey): D.R. 16, Braunschweig. H.R. 17

20. Feld-Art. Brig., Hannover (Gen. Maj. Wentscher, Adj.: Hptm. Frhr. v. Brackel): Feld-Art. R. 10, Feld-Art. R. 46

Landwehr-Inspektion Hannover (Insp.: Gen. Maj. Weese, Adj.: Hptm. Frhr. v. Rolshausen), Bez. Kom. Aurich, Celle, Hameln, Hannover I+II, Lingen, Nienburg a.d. Weser, Osnabrück

Jg. Btl. 10
Telegr. Btl. Nr. 6
Pion. Btl. 10
Train-Abt. Nr. 10

Training Center (Truppen-Übungsplatz) Munster
Kommandant: Oberst z.D. v. Grothe
Adj.: OLt. Sauer

XI. Armeekorps (Cassel)

Kdr. Gen.: Gen. Lt. v. Plüskow
Chief of General Staff: Oberst v. Sauberzweig
Ia: Major v. Brandenstein
Ic: Hptm. v. Bahlkampf
Hptm. Kaupisch
Adjutants: Major Heuser, Hptm. v. Bloedau

Major z.D. Rommel

22. I.D. (Cassel)
Kdr.: Gen. Lt. Frhr. v. Freytag-Loringhoven
Ia: Hptm. Caracciola
Adj.: Hptm. v. Stosch
43. Inf. Brig., Cassel (Gen. Maj. v. Leyser, Adj.: Hptm. v. Dobbeler): I.R. 82, I.R. 83, Bez. Kom. Arolsen, I Cassel
44. Inf. Brig., Cassel (Gen. Maj. Nordbeck, Adj.: Hptm. Geim): I.R. 32 (2. Thüring.), I.R. 167 (1. Ober-Elsäss.), Bez. Kom. II Cassel
22. Kav. Brig., Cassel (Oberst v. Wurmb, Adj.: Rittm. v. Wickede) D.R. 5, H.R. Nr. 14
22. Feld-Art. Brig., Cassel (Gen. Maj. Gronau, Adj.: Hptm. Hederich): Feld-Art. R. 11, Feld-Art. R. 47

38. I.D. (Erfurt)
Kdr.: Gen. Lt. Wagner
Ia: Major Sydow
Adj.: Rittm. v. Einem
76. Inf. Brig., Erfurt (Gen. Maj. v. Versen, Adj.: Hptm. v. Witzendorff): I.R. 71 (3. Thüring.), I.R. 95 (6. Thüring.), Bez. Kom. Gotha, Sondershausen
83. Inf. Brig., Erfurt (Gen. Maj. Frhr. v. Hanstein, Adj.: Hptm. v. Heineccius) I.R. 94 (3. Thüring.), I.R. 96 (7. Thüring.), Bez. Kom. Gera

38. Kav. Brig., Erfurt (Gen. Maj. Weinschenck, Adj.: OLt. v. Schwerin): Jg. Rgt. z. Pf. Nr. 2, Jg. Rgt. z. Pf. Nr. 6
38. Feld-Art. Brig., Erfurt (Gen. Maj. Krahmer, Adj.: Hptm. Mertens): Feld-Art. R. 19, Feld-Art. R. 55

Landwehr-Inspektion Erfurt (Insp.: Gen. Maj. v. Mühlenfels, Adj.: Hptm. Plewig), Bez. Kom. Eisenach, Erfurt, Hersfeld, Marburg, Meiningen, Mühlhausen i. Th., Weimar

Jg. Btl. 11
Fußart. R. 18
Pion. Btl. 11
Train-Abt. Nr. 11

Training Center (Truppen-Übungsplatz) Ohrdruf
Kommandant: Gen. Maj. z.D. Chelius
Adj.: OLt. Gristede

XIV. Armeekorps (Karlsruhe)

Kdr. Gen.: Gen. d. Inf. v. Hoiningen gen. Huene
Chief of General Staff: Oberstlt. v. Brauchitsch
Ia: Major v. Lettow-Vorbeck
Ic: Hptm. Thümmel
Hptm. v. Sydow
Adjutants: Major Heuser, Hptm. v. Bloedau

Oberstlt. z.D. Melchior, Hptm. Melchior

28. I.D. (Karlsruhe)
Kdr.: Gen. Lt. v. Kehler
Ia: Major Frhr. v. Coburg
Adj.: Major Tietze
55. Inf. Brig., Karlsruhe (Gen. Maj. Ritter u. Edler v. Oetinger, Adj.: Hptm. v. Bonin): 1. Bad. Leib-Gren R. Nr. 109, 2. Bad. Gren. Rgt. Kaiser Wilhelm I. Nr. 110, Bez. Kom. Mannheim
56. Inf. Brig., Rastatt (Gen. Maj. Freyer, Adj.: Hptm. Freytag): F.R. 40, I.R. 111 (1. Bad.), Bez. Kom. Rastatt
28. Kav. Brig., Karlsruhe (Oberst v. Selchow, Adj.: Rittm. v. Arnim): 1. Bad. Leib-D.R. Nr. 20, D.R. 21 (2. Bad.)
28. Feld-Art. Brig., Karlsruhe (Gen. Maj. Fabarius, Adj.: Hptm. Benary): Feld-Art. R. 14 (1. Bad.), Feld-Art. R. 50 (3. Bad.)

Landwehr-Inspektion Karlsruhe (Insp.: Gen. Maj. v. Sieg, Adj.: Hptm. Baader), Bez. Kom. Bruchsal, Donaueschingen, Freiburg, Heidelberg, Karlsruhe, Lörrach, Mosbach, Pforzheim

29. I.D. (Freiburg)
Kdr.: Gen. Lt. Isbert
Ia: Major Helfritz

Adj.: Hptm. Hofmann
57. Inf. Brig., Freiburg (Gen. Maj. v. Trotta gen. Treyden, Adj.: Hptm. John v. Freyend): I.R. 113 (5. Bad.), I.R. 114 (6. Bad.), Bez. Kom. Stockach
58. Inf. Brig., Mülhausen i.E. (Gen. Maj. Stenger, Adj.: Hptm. Frölich) I.R. 112 (4. Bad.), I.R. 142 (7. Bad.), Bez. Kom. Mühlhausen i. Elsaß I+II
84. Inf. Brig., Lahr (Gen. Maj. v. Koschembahr, Adj.: Hptm. v. Heineccius) I.R. 196 (8. Bad.), I.R. 170 (9. Bad.), Bez. Kom. Offenburg
29. Kav. Brig., Mülhausen i.E. (Oberst v. Graevenitz, Adj.: Rittm. Mezger): Jg. Rgt. z. Pf. Nr. 5, D.R. 22 (3. Bad.)
29. Feld-Art. Brig., Freiburg (Oberst Hamann, Adj.: Hptm. v. Hartwig): Feld-Art. R. 30 (2. Bad.), Feld-Art. R. 76 (5. Bad.)

Bad. Fußart. R. 14
Bad. Pion. Btl. 14
Telegr. Btl. Nr. 4
Zeppelin Btl. Nr. 4
Bad. Train-Abt. Nr. 14

***Oberrheinbefestigungen* (Upper Rhine fortifications) Freiburg**
Kommandant: Gen. Lt. v. Bodungen
Adj.: Hptm. Fischer

Training Center (Truppen-Übungsplatz) Heuberg / Lager Stetten
Kommandant: Gen. Maj. z.D. v. Hammerstein-Equord
Adj.: OLt. Mechlenburg

XV. Armeekorps (Straßburg i. Elsaß)

Kdr. Gen.: Gen. d. Inf. v. Deimling
Chief of General Staff: Oberst Graf v. Waldersee
Ia: Major Meister
Ic: K.W. Hptm. Fischer
Hptm. v. Kalm
Adjutants: Major Wasserfall, Major Reinecke

Oberstlt. z.D. v. Keserstein, Hptm. Starcke

30. I.D. (Straßburg i. Elsaß)
Kdr.: Gen. Lt. v. Eben
Ia: Major Frhr. v. Nettelbladt
Adj.: Major Bethcke
60. Inf. Brig., Straßburg i. Elsaß (Gen. Maj. v. Altrock, Adj.: Hptm. Petri): I.R. 99 (2. Oberrhein.), I.R. 143 (4. Unt-Elsäss.),
85. Inf. Brig., Straßburg i. Elsaß (Gen. Maj. Ludendorff, Adj.: Hptm. v. Guretzky-Cornitz): I.R. 136 (4. Lothring.), K.S. I.R. 105
30. Kav. Brig., Straßburg i. Elsaß (Gen. Maj. v. Zieten, Adj.: Rittm. Nolte): D.R. 15, H.R. 9

30. Feld-Art. Brig., Straßburg i. Elsaß (Gen. Maj. Kühne, Adj.: Hptm. Ulfert): Feld-Art. R. 51 (2. Ober-Elsäss.), Straßb. Feld-Art. R. 84

39. I.D. (Colmar i. Elsaß)
Kdr.: K.W. Gen. Lt. Frhr. v. Watter
Ia: Major v. Bernewitz
Adj.: Major Mannkopff
61. Inf. Brig., Straßburg i. Elsaß (Gen. Maj. v. Frankenberg u. Ludwigsdorf, Adj.: Hptm. Gottschalk): I.R. 132 (1. Unter-Elsäss.), K.W. I.R. Nr. 126,
82. Inf. Brig., Colmar i. Elsaß (Gen. Maj. Balck, Adj.: Hptm. Jebens): I.R. 171 (2. Ober-Elsäss.), I.R. 172 (3. Ober-Elsäss.)
39. Kav. Brig., Colmar i. Elsaß (Gen. Maj. Frhr. v. Krane, Adj.: Rittm. Frhr. v. Frydag): D.R. 14, Jg. Rgt. Z. Pf. Nr. 3
39. Feld-Art. Brig., Colmar i. Elsaß (Gen. Maj. Erythropel, Adj.: Hptm. Kleemann): Feld-Art. R. 66 (4. Bad.), Feld-Art. R. 80 (3. Ober-Elsäss.)

Jg. Btl. 8
Jg. Btl. 14
Fest. MG Abt. Nr. 9
Fest. MG Abt. Nr. 10
Fußart. R. 10
Fußart. R. 13
Pion. Btl. 15 (1. Elsäss.)
Pion. Btl. 19 (2. Elsäss.)
Fest. Fernsprech-Kp. Nr. 4
Train-Abt. Nr. 15 (Elsäss.)

Fortress (Festung) Straßburg, including *Feste* Kaiser Wilhelm II in Mutzig
Governor: Gen. Lt. v. Eberhardt
Kommandant: Gen. Lt. v. Vietinghoff gen. Scheel
Chief of General Staff: Oberstlt. v. Böckmann
Ia: K.W. Major Mohs
Hptm. Hosse
Adj.: Hptm. v. Glasenapp
Ing. Offz. v. Platz (K.W. II): Oberstlt. Karbe

Fortress (Festung) Neubreisach
Kommandant: Gen. Maj. v. Beck
Platzmajor: Major v. Voigt

Training Center (Truppen-Übungsplatz) Oberhofen
Kommandant: Gen. Maj. z.D. Stehr
Adj.: OLt. Heyser

XVI. Armeekorps (Metz)

Kdr. Gen.: Gen. d. Inf. v. Mudra
Chief of General Staff: Oberst v. Borries
Ia: Major Frhr. v. Esebeck
Ic: Hptm. v. Gößnitz
K.W. Hptm. Köthe
Adjutants: Major Schultz, Major Poetter

Oberst z.D. v. Mayet, Hptm. Lübcke

33. I.D. (Metz)
Kdr.: Gen. Lt. Reitzenstein
Ia: Major Ludwig
Adj.: Rittm. v. Löbbecke
66. Inf. Brig., Metz (Gen. Maj. Bausch, Adj.: Hptm. Roese): Metz I.R. 98, I.R. 130 (1. Lothring.),
67. Inf. Brig., Metz (Gen. Maj. Brosius, Adj.: Hptm. Schütte): I.R. 135 (3. Lothring.), I.R. 144 (5. Lothring.)
33. Kav. Brig., Metz (Gen. Maj. v. Etzel, Adj.: Rittm. Krug): D.R. 9, D.R. 13
33. Feld-Art. Brig., Metz (Gen. Maj. Kühne, Adj.: Hptm. Ulfert): Feld-Art. R. 33 (1. Lothring.), Feld-Art. R. 34 (2. Lothring.)

Landwehr-Inspektion Metz (Insp.: Gen. Maj. Rehbach, Adj.: Hptm. Brodersen): Bez. Kom. Diedenhofen, Metz, Saarlouis

34. I.D. (Metz)
Kdr.: K.W. Gen. Lt. v. Heinemann
Ia: K.W. Hptm. v. Greiff
Adj.: Major v. Below
68. Inf. Brig., Metz (Gen. Maj. v. Estorff, Adj.: Hptm. Charisius): I.R. 67, I.R. 145 (6. Lothring.)
86. Inf. Brig., Saarlouis (Gen. Maj. Miesitscheck v. Wischkau, Adj.: Hptm. Küpper): I.R. 30, I.R. 173 (9. Lothring.)
34. Kav. Brig., St. Avold (Gen. Maj. v. Ilsemann, Adj.: Rittm. Hesterberg): U.R. 14, Jg. Rgt. Z. Pf. Nr. 12
45. Kav. Brig., Saarlouis (K.W. Gen. Maj. v. Hofacker, Adj.: Rittm. v. Bitter): H.R. 13, Jg. Rgt. Z. Pf. Nr. 13
34. Feld-Art. Brig., St. Avold (Gen. Maj. v. Müller, Adj.: Hptm. v. Massow): Feld-Art. R. 69 (3. Lothring.), Feld-Art. R. 70 (4. Lothring.)

MG Abt. Nr. 6
Fest. MG Abt. Nr. 11
Fest. MG Abt. Nr. 12
Fest. MG Abt. Nr. 13
Fest. MG Abt. Nr. 14
Fest. MG Abt. Nr. 15
Fußart. R. 8
K.B. 2. Fußart. R.
K.S. Fußart. R. 12

Pion. Btl. 16 (1. Lothring.)
Pion. Btl. 20 (2. Lothring.)
Fest. Fernsprech-Kp. Nr. 3
Train-Abt. Nr. 16 (Lothring.)

Fortress (Festung) Metz
Governor: Gen. Lt. v. Winterfeld
Kommandant: Gen. Lt. v. Ingersleben
Chief of General Staff: Oberst Kabisch
Ia: K.W. Major Madlung
Hptm. v. Westernhagen
Adj.: Hptm. Richter

Fortress (Festung) Diedenhofen
Kommandant: Gen. Maj. v. Lochow
Ia: Hptm. Obkircher
Platzmajor: Hptm. Frowein

XVII. Armeekorps (Danzig)

Kdr. Gen.: Gen. d. Kav. v. Mackensen
Chief of General Staff: Oberstlt. v. Duncker
Ia: Major Gr. v. Schwerin
Ic: Hptm. Gr. v. Stillfried u. Rattonitz
Hptm. Bartenwerfer
Adjutants: Major v. Grothe, Major Graßhoff

Oberstlt. z.D. Müller, Hptm. Weste

35. I.D. (Thorn)
Kdr.: Gen. Lt. Hennig
Ia: Major Engelien
Adj.: Major v. Keiser
70. Inf. Brig., Thorn (Gen. Maj. Schmidt v. Knobelsdorf, Adj.: Hptm. Clemens): Metz I.R. 21, I.R. 61
87. Inf. Brig., Thorn (Gen. Maj. v. Hahn, Adj.: Hptm. Tiedemann): I.R. 141, I.R. 176
35. Kav. Brig., Graudenz (Gen. Maj. v. Unger, Adj.: Rittm. v. Kleist): H.R. 5, Jg. Rgt. Z. Pf. Nr. 4
35. Feld-Art. Brig., Graudenz (Gen. Maj. Uhden, Adj.: Hptm. Mantell): Feld-Art. R. 71, Feld-Art. R. 81

Landwehr-Inspektion Graudenz (Insp.: Gen. Maj. v. Homeyer, Adj.: Hptm. Kowalski): Bez. Kom. Danzig, Graudenz, Konitz, Neustadt, Preußisch-Stargard, Thorn

36. I.D. (Danzig)
Kdr.: Gen. Lt. v. Heineccius
Ia: Major v. Winning
Adj.: Major Steffen

69. Inf. Brig., Graudenz (Gen. Maj. v. Engelbrechten, Adj.: Hptm. Kurz): I.R.129, I.R. 175
71. Inf. Brig., Danzig (Gen. Maj. Kruge, Adj.: Hptm. Frhr. v. Grote): Gren. R. König Friedrich I. Nr. 5, I.R. 128, Bez. Kom. Schlawe, Stolp
Leib-Husaren-Brig., Danzig (Gen. Maj. Gr. v. Schmettow, Adj.: Rittm. v. Brünneck): 1. Leib-Hus. Rgt., 2. Leib-Hus. Rgt.
36. Feld-Art. Brig., Danzig (Gen. Maj. Hanhndorff, Adj.: Hptm. v. Bächer): Feld-Art. R. 36, Feld-Art. R. 72

Jäg. Btl. 2
MG Abt. Nr. 4
Fest. MG Abt. Nr. 3
Fest. MG Abt. Nr. 4
Fest. MG Abt. Nr. 5
Fußart. R. 11
Fußart. R. 17
Pion. Btl. 16
Pion. Btl. 20
Fest. Fernsprech-Kp. Nr. 1
Fest. Fernsprech-Kp. Nr. 2
Train-Abt. Nr. 17

Fortress (Festung) Graudenz
Governor: Gen. Lt. v. Zastrow
Kommandant: Oberst Gropp
Chief of General Staff: Oberstlt. Wilckens
Ia: Major Stapf
Hptm. Liebmann
Adj.: Hptm. Klawitter

Fortress (Festung) Thorn
Governor: Gen. Lt. v. Dickhuth-Harrach
Kommandant: Gen. Maj. v. der Lancken
Chief of General Staff: Oberstlt. Wachs
Ia: Major v. Thadden
K.W. Hptm. Schmidt
Adj.: Hptm. Beyer

Training Center (Truppen-Übungsplatz) Gruppe / Graudenz, Tucheler Heide
Kommandant: Gen. Maj. z.D. Heye
Adj.: OLt. Haase

Training Center (Truppen-Übungsplatz) Hammerstein
Kommandant: Gen. Maj. z.D. v. Reichenbach
Adj.: Lt. Afheldt

Foot Artillery Training Center (Fußartillerie-Schießplatz) Thorn (located in corps area XVII army corps but operated by 1st foot artillery inspection)

Kommandant: Gen. Maj. z.D. Schwierz
Ad.: OLt. Graßhoff

XVIII. Armeekorps (Frankfurt a. M.)

Kdr. Gen.: Gen. d. Inf. v. Schenck
Chief of General Staff: Oberstlt. v. Blücher
Ia: Major Major Frhr. v. Stoltzenberg
Ic: K.W. Hptm. Mayer
Hptm. v. Roques
Adjutants: Major Ritter v. Poschinger, Major Martens

Oberst z.D. Schulz

21. I.D. (Frankfurt a. M.)
Kdr.: Gen. Lt. Frhr. v. Hollen
Ia: Hptm. v. Müller
Adj.: Major v. Fabeck
41. Inf. Brig., Mainz (Gen. Maj. v. der Esch, Adj.: Hptm. Bornhausen): I.R. 87, I.R. 88, Bez. Kom.: Höchst, Oberlahnstein, Wiesbaden
42. Inf. Brig., Frankfurt a. M. (Gen. Maj. Elstermann v. Elster, Adj.: Hptm. Dieckmann): F.R. 80, I.R. 81, Bez. Kom.: Frankfurt a. M. I+II
21. Kav. Brig., Frankfurt a. M. (Oberst v. Glasenapp, Adj.: Rittm. Frhr. v. Wilmowski): D.R. 6, Thüring. U.R. 6
21. Feld-Art. Brig., Frankfurt a. M. (Gen. Maj. Scherbening, Adj.: Hptm. Holzapfel): Feld-Art. R. 27, Feld-Art. R. 63

Ghz. Hess. 25. I.D. (Darmstadt)
Kdr.: Gen. Lt. Frhr. v. Lüttwitz
Ia: Major Keim
Hptm. Frhr. Neubronn v. Eisenburg
Adj.: Major v. Klipstein
49. Inf. Brig. (1. Ghz. Hess.), Darmstadt (Gen. Maj. v. Uthmann, Adj.: Hptm. Gr. zu Lynar): Ghz. Hess. Leibgarde-Inf. R. Nr. 115, I.R. 116, I.R. (2. Ghz. Hess.), 168 (5. Ghz. Hess.), Bez. Kom.: Friedberg, Gießen
50. Inf. Brig. (2. Ghz. Hess.), Mainz (Gen. Maj. Frhr. v. Speßhardt, Adj.: Hptm. v. Rodewald): Ghz. Hess. Inf. Leib-R. Großherzogin Nr. 117, I.R. (3. Ghz. Hess.), I.R. 118 (4. Ghz. Hess.), Bez. Kom. Mainz, Worms
25. Kav. Brig. (Ghz. Hess.), Darmstadt (Oberst v. Bodelschwingh, Adj.: Rittm. Wätjen): Ghz. Hess. Garde-Drag. R. Nr. 23, Ghz. Hess. Leib-Drag. R. Nr. 24
25. Feld-Art. Brig. (Ghz. Hess.), Darmstadt (Gen. Maj. Freise, Adj.: Hptm. Hertel): Feld-Art. R. 25 (1. Ghz. Hess.), Feld-Art. R. 61 (2. Ghz. Hess.)

Fest. MG Abt. Nr. 8
Fußart. R. 3
Pion. Btl. 21
Pion. Btl. 25

Ghz. Hess, Train-Abt. Nr. 18
K.S. Fest. Fernsprech-Kp. Nr. 7
Railroad R. Nr. 2
Railroad R. Nr. 3
Depot of 2nd railroad brig.

Training Center (Truppen-Übungsplatz) Darmstadt
Kommandant: Gen. Maj. z.D. v. Randow
Adj.: OLt. Liman

Training Center (Truppen-Übungsplatz) Orb
Kommandant: Oberst z.D. Tscheuschner
Adj.: OLt. Muhl

XX. Armeekorps (Allenstein)

Kdr. Gen.: Gen. d. Art. v. Scholtz
Chief of General Staff: Oberst Hell
Ia: Major Kunhardt v. Schmidt
Ic: Hptm. Waenker v. Dankenschweil
Hptm. Erfurth
Adjutants: Major Notz, Major v. Krieß

Oberstlt. z.D. Bacmeister, Hptm. Volkmann

37. I.D. (Allenstein)
Kdr.: Gen. Lt. v. Staabs
Ia: Major v. Gazen gen. Gaza
Adj.: Hptm. v. Bünau
73. Inf. Brig., Lyck (Gen. Maj. Wilhelmi, Adj.: Hptm. Appuhn): I.R. 147, I.R. 151
75. Inf. Brig., Allenstein (Gen. Maj. v. Böckmann, Adj.: Hptm. Scharioth): I.R. 146, I.R. 150
37. Kav. Brig., Allenstein (Gen. Maj. Krahmer, Adj.: OLt. v. Kaufmann): D.R. 10, D.R. 11
37. Feld-Art. Brig., Allenstein (Gen. Maj. Buchholz, Adj.: Hptm. Selle): Feld-Art. R. 71, Feld-Art. R. 81

Landwehr-Inspektion Allenstein (Insp.: Gen. Maj. Licht, Adj.: Hptm. Hoefer): Bez. Kom.: Allenstein, Braunsberg, Deutsch-Eylau, Lötzen. Marienburg, Osterode

41. I.D. (Deutsch-Eylau)
Kdr.: Gen. Lt. v. Stein
Ia: Major Weniger
Adj.: Major Wilsdorff
72. Inf. Brig., Osterode (Gen. Maj. Schaer, Adj.: Hptm. v. Klöden): I.R.18, I.R. 59
74. Inf. Brig., Marienburg (Gen. Maj. Reiser, Adj.: Hptm. Trommer): I.R. 148, I.R. 152
41. Kav. Brig., Deutsch-Eylau (Gen. Maj. Gr. v. Hofmann, Adj.: Rittm. Frhr. v. Preuschen): K.R. 5, U.R. 4

41. Feld-Art. Brig., Deutsch-Eylau (Gen. Maj. Neugebauer, Adj.: Hptm. Graßmann): Feld-Art. R. 35, Feld-Art. R. 79

Jäg. Btl. 1
Fest. MG Abt. Nr. 2
Pion. Btl. 23
Pion. Btl. 26
Train-Abt. Nr. 20

Training Center (Truppen-Übungsplatz) Arys
Kommandant: Oberst z.D. Nusche
Adj.: OLt. Kleinau

XXI. Armeekorps (Saarbrücken)

Kdr. Gen.: Gen. d. Inf. v. Below
Chief of General Staff: Oberst v. Haxthausen
Ia: Major Völckers
Ic: Hptm. Massow
Hptm. Wäninger
Adjutants: Major v. le Fort, Major v. Hagen

Oberstlt. z.D. Schacht, Hptm. Richter

31. I.D. (Saarbrücken)
Kdr.: K.W. Gen. Lt. v. Berrer
Ia: Major Riedel
Adj.: Major Fischer
32. Inf. Brig., Saarbrücken (Gen. Maj. v. Behr, Adj.: Hptm. Heckert): I.R. 70, I.R. 174 (10. Lothring.)
62. Inf. Brig., Hagenau (Gen. Maj. Maschke, Adj.: Hptm. Schürmann): I.R. 137 (2. Unter-Elsäss.), I.R. 166
31. Kav. Brig., Saarbrücken (Gen. Maj. Heidborn, Adj.: OLt. Gädeke): D.R. 7, U.R. 7
31. Feld-Art. Brig., Hagenau (Gen. Maj. Glokke, Adj.: Hptm. v. Hake): Feld-Art. R. 31 (1. Unter-Elsäss.), Feld-Art. R. 67 (2. Unter-Elsäss.)

Landwehr-Inspektion Saarbrücken (Gen. Maj. Scholz, Adj.: Hptm. Ebinger): Bez. Kom.: Forbach, Hagenau, Kreuznach, Saarbrücken, Saargemünd, St. Wendel

42. I.D. (Saarburg)
Kdr.: Gen. Lt. v. Bredow
Ia: Major Bürkner
Adj.: Major Schorcht
59. Inf. Brig., Saarburg (Gen. Maj. v. Wurmb, Adj.: Hptm. Lotz): I.R.97 (1. Oberrhein.), I.R. 138 (3. Unt. Elsäss.)
65. Inf. Brig., Mörchingen (Gen. Maj. v. Kehler, Adj.: Hptm. Frhr. v. Rechenberg): I I.R.131 (2. Lothring.), I.R. 17

42. Kav. Brig., Saarburg (Gen. Maj. v. Koscielski, Adj.: Rittm. v. Reden): U.R. 11, U.R. 15
42. Feld-Art. Brig., Saarburg (Oberst Krahmer, Adj.: Hptm. v. Nippold): Feld-Art. R. 8, Feld-Art. R. 15 (1. Ober-Elsäss.)

MG Abt. Nr. 3
Pion. Btl. 27
Train-Abt. Nr. 21

Training Center (Truppen-Übungsplatz) Bitsch, including Fortress Bitsch
Kommandant: Gen. Maj. Woyde
Adj.: OLt. Scheringer

ROYAL BAVARIAN ARMY

His Majesty's Adjutants (aides-de-camp)

Vortragender Generaladjutant:
Gen. Lt. Walther v, Walderstötten
Generaladjutanten:
Oberst Gr. v. Horn
Gen. d. Kav. v. Könitz
Gen. d. Art. v. Wiedenmann
Gen d. Inf. Ritter v. Haag
Flügeladjutant:
Oberstlt. Gr. zu Castell-Castell
Ordonnanz-Offiziere:
Oberstlt. von und zu der Tann
Oberstlt. Frhr. v. Perfall
Kanzlei-Sekretär:
Geh. Kanzlei-Sekr. Rank

Ministry of War (Munich)

Minister of War: Gen. d. Kav. v. Kreß v. Kressenstein
Adjutant: Major Schuster
Central Department (Zentral-Abteilung)
Abt. Chef.: Gen. Maj. Huber-Liebenau
Geh. Kanzlei-Vorsteher Bauer
Geh. Registrar Böhm
Geh. Kanzlei-Sekr. Fischer
Geh. Kanzlei-Sekr. Schafnitzl
Geh. Kanzlei-Sekr. Guter
Geh. Kanzlei-Sekr. Frauenknecht
Geh. Kanzlei-Sekr. Eberl
Geh. Kanzlei-Sekr. Rödel
Kanzlei-Sekr. Meyer
Geh. Kanzlei-Sekr. Beyer

Kanzlist Leitmeier
Kanzlist Kuchler

Overseen by central department:
Registry for classified documents
Oberst z.D. Röger
Library
Oberstlt. z.D. Kollmann
Military publishing house
Printing shop
General administration

Personnel Department (Abteilung für persönliche Angelegenheiten)
Abt. Chef: Gen. Maj. Ritter v. Kneußl
Major Melchior
Major Schuster
OLt. Kieffer
Geh. Rechnungs-Rat Auers
Rechnungs-Rat Moritz
Rechnbungsrat Freyland
Geh. Kalkulator See
Geh. Kanzlei-Sekr. Gößl

First Army Department (Armee-Abteilung I)
Abt. Chef.: Oberst Köberle
Major Haack
Major Heiden
Major Roth
Major Pflügel
Hptm. Ruhwandl
Hptm. Preitner
Hptm. Bonn
Hptm. Fischer
Hptm. Madriley

Second Army Department (Armee-Abteilung II)
Abt. Chef.: Oberst Ebermayr
Hptm. Beckh
Hptm. Ertel
Hptm. Schweigart
OLt. Auer

Administration Department (Militär Verwaltungs-Abteilung)
Abt. Chef.: Gen. Maj. Hörnle
Geh. Kanzlei-Sekr. Horn
Geh. Kanzlei-Sekr. Tausendpfund

1st Section (Budget and finance)
Vorstand: Wirkl. Geh. Kriegsrat Strauß
Intendantur-Rat Rexroth
Rechnungs-Rat Gütt
Geh. exped. Sekr. Wopperer
Geh. exped. Sekr. Gackstatter

2nd Section (Horse replacements)
Vorstand: Wirkl. Geh. Ober-Kriegsrat Hptm. d.R. a.D. Hellmuth
Rechnungsrat Miller
Geh. exped. Sekr. Kannamüller

3rd Section (Clothing department, travelling administration)
Vorstand: Wirkl. Geh. Kriegsrat Hptm. d.L. a.D. Fischer
Intendantur-Rat OLt. d.L. a.D. Scherer
Rechnungsrat Schmitt
Geh. exped. Sekr. Helm
Geh. Kalkulator Ströbel

4th Section (Barracks)
Vorstand: Wirkl. Geh. Kriegsrat OLt. d.L. a.D. Nies
Intendantur-Rat OLt. d.R. a.D. Dames
Geh. Rechnungsrat Bömmels
Rechnungsrat Strauß
Rechnungsrat Ulsamer
Geh. exped. Sekr. Meyer
Geh. exped. Sekr. Ehras

5th Section (Construction department)
Vorstand: Wirkl. Geh. Oberbau-Rat Lt. d.L. a.D. Mellinger
Geheimer Baurat Hptm. d.L. a.D. Winter
Baurat Haase
Geh. Bau-Sekr. Barth
Geh. Bau-Sekr. Bergmann

General affairs (Haus-Verwaltung)
Garnbisons-Verwaltungs-Inspektor Cramer

Pension and Payment Department (Pensions- und Versorgungs-Abteilung)
Abt. Chef.: Gen. Lt. z.D. Kuchler
Geh. Kanzlei-Sekr. Thumann
Geh. Kanzlei-Sekr. Koch

1st Section (Pension and payment affairs of officers, NCOs and enlisted men)
Vorstand: Oberst z.D. Schierlinger
Oberst z.D. Baumüller
Oberst z.D. Rehm

Major Hoffmann
Geh. Kalkulator Heilmann

2nd Section (Pension and payments affairs of civil servants [*Militär-Beamte*], military widows and orphans)
Wirkl. Geh. Kriegsrat Lt. d.L. a.D. Rommelé
Geh. Rechnungsrat Schmauser
Rechnungsrat Bleifuß
Rechnungsrat Kellerhals
Geh. exped. Sekr. Schweiger

3rd Section (Financial support, administration of foundations)
Vorstand: Wirkl. Geh. Kriegsrat Tempel
Rechnungsrat Beck
Geh. exped. Sekr. Osterkorn
Geh. Kalkulator Güth
Geh. Kalkulatur Pesch
Geh. Kanzlei-Sekr. Wiebach

Medical Department (Medinzinal-Abteilung)
Abt. Chef: K.P. Gen. Ober-Arzt Dr. Mandel
Ober-Stabsarzt Dr. Ammon
Stabsarzt Meyer
Geh. Kanzlei-Sekr. Eberth
Gen. Ober-Arzt z.D. Dr. Zäch

Legal Department (Abteilung für Rechtsangelegenheiten)
Abt. Chef.: Wirkl. Geh. Ober-Kriegsrat Rittm. d.L. a.D. Ritter v. Nischler
Ober-Kriegs-Gerichtsrat Oppler
Kriegs-Gerichtsrat Dr. Erhard

Financial Audit Section (Rechnungs-Revisionsstelle im Kriegsministerium)
Vorstand: Intendantur-Rat Rexroth
Intendantur-Rat Dennert
Intendantur-Rat Dames
Intendantur-Rat Storch
Rechnungsrat Scheitel
Rechnungsrat Ebenböck
Geh. Kalkulator Winter
Geh. Kalkulator Eibecker
Geh. Kanzlei-Sekr. Mährlein

Leibgarde der Hartschiere (Munich)
General-Kapitän: Gen. d. Inf. Gr. v. Bothmer
Premier-Lieutenant: Gen. Lt. z.D. Ritter und Edler v. Rauscher auf Weeg
Second-Lieutenant: Gen. Maj. z.D. Reisner Frhr. v. Liechtenstern

Kornett: Oberstlt. z.D. Frhr. Besserer v. Thalfingen
Exempt: Oberstlt. Frhr, Freyschlag v. Freyenstein
Adjutant: Rittm. Weber
Premier-Brigadiers: Strauß, Hellwig, Schmirl, Höhne
Sous-Brigadiers: Gebhardt, Hegwein, Müller, Hugo
Medical officer: St. Arzt Dr. Ring

General Staff (Munich)

Chief of General Staff: Gen. Maj. Krafft v. Dellmensingen
Adj.: Major Ritter v. Xylander

Oberst Frhr. v. Nagel zu Aichberg
Oberst Zoellner
Oberstlt. Hierthes
Oberstlt. v. Lossow
Oberstlt. Brau
Major Stängl
Major Hemmer
Major Herrgott
Major Kreß v. Kressenstein
Major Ruith
Major Schmitt, Paul
Major Schraudenbach
Major Schmitt, Konstantin
Major Gr. v. Holnstein aus Bayern
Major Reichert
Major Luxburg
Major Tattenbach
Major Trautmann
Major riedel
Major Podewils-Dürnitz
Major Seißer
Major Kaspar

Hptm. Griesheim
Hptm. Baur, Hugo
Hptm. Voit
Hptm. Leeb
Hptm. Frhr. v. Berchem
Hptm. Verstl
Hptm. Giehrl
Hptm. Eberth
Hptm. Jareiß
Hptm. Kriebel
Hptm. Sperr
Hptm. Neusser

Hptm. Deuringer
Hptm. List

Assigned officers:
Hptm. Distel, Hptm. Kiesling auf Kieslingstein, Hptm. Roschmann, Hptm. Glöckle, Hptm. Hößlin, Hptm. Weichs, Hptm. Pirner, Hptm. Mittelberger,
Hptm. Baur, Friedrich

Line commanders:
Major Hofmann
Major Möslinger
Hptm. Kalbfus

I. bayer. Armeekorps (Munich)

Kdr. Gen.: Gen. d. Inf. Ritter v. Xylander
Chief of General Staff: Oberst Frhr. Nagel zu Aichberg
Ia: Major Hemmer
Ic: Hptmr Leeb
Hptm. Berchem
Adjutants: Major Peringer, Eugen, Major Koch, Major Loeffelholz v. Colberg, Friedrich
Oberstlt. z.D. Kleemann

bayer. 1. I.D. (Munich)
Kdr.: Gen. Lt. Ritter v. Schoch, Albert
Ia: Major Kasparr
Adj.: Major Hößlin
bayer. 1. Inf. Brig., Munich (Gen. Maj. Rauchenberger, Adj.: Hptm. Brößler): bayer. Inf.-Leib-Rgt., bayer. 1.I.R., Bez. Kom. Rosenheim
bayer. 2. Inf. Brig., Munich (Gen. Maj. Ritter v. Endres, Adj.: Hptm. Naegelsbach): bayer. 2. I.R., bayer. 16. I.R., bayer. 1. Jg. Btl., Bez. Kom. Passau, Wasserburg
bayer. 1. Kav. Brig., Munich (Gen. Maj. v. Staudt, Adj.: Rittm. Frhr. Kreß v. Kressenstein): bayer, 1. schw, Reiter-Rgt., bayer, 2. schw, Reiter-Rgt.
bayer. 1. Feld-Art. Brig., Munich (Gen. Maj. Frhr. v. Stein, Adj.: Hptm. Dollmann): bayer. 1. Feld-Art. R., bayer. 7. Feld-Art. R.

Landwehr-Inspektion München (Insp.: Gen. Maj. Müller, Adj.: Hptm. Hörl): Bez. Kom.: Munich I, II + III, Landshut, Weilheim

bayer. 2. I.D. (Augsburg)
Kdr.: Gen. Lt. Ritter v. Hetzel
Ia: Major Gr. v. Holnstein aus Bayern
Adj.: Major Maier
bayer. 3. Inf. Brig., Augsburg (Gen. Maj. Schoch, Emil, Adj.: Hptm. Dümlein): bayer. 3. I.R., bayer. 20. I.R., Bez. Kom. Augsburg, Kempten
bayer. 4. Inf. Brig., Neu-Ulm (Gen. Maj. Schoch, Karl, Adj.: Hptm. Frhr. v. Stengel): bayer. 3. I.R., bayer. 20. I.R., Bez. Kom. Augsburg, Kempten

bayer. 2. Kav. Brig., Augsburg (Gen. Maj. Schrott, Adj.: Rittm. Feßmann): bayer. 4. Ch. R., bayer. 8. Ch. R.
bayer. 2. Feld-Art. Brig., Augsburg (Gen. Maj. Uffelmann, Adj.: OLt. Deßloch): bayer. 4. Feld-Art. R., bayer. 9. Feld-Art. R.
bayer. 1. Fußart. R.
bayer. 1. Pion. Btl.
bayer. 1. Train-Abt.
bayer. 1. Telegr. Btl.
bayer. 2. Telegr. Btl.
bayer. aircraft Btl.
bayer. motor Btl.

Training Center (Truppenübungsplatz) Lechfeld
Kommandant: Gen. Maj. z.D. Slevogt
Adj.: Hptm. z.D. Frhr. v. Welser

II. bayer. Armeekorps (Würzburg)

Kdr. Gen.: Gen. d. Inf. Ritter v. Martini
Chief of General Staff: Oberstlt Stängl
Ia: Major Schraudenbach
Ic: Hptm. Griesheim
Hptm. Neusser
Adjutants: Major Werkmann, Major Zürn, Major Loeffelholz v. Colberg, Georg

Oberstlt. z.D. Becker

bayer. 3. I.D. (Landau)
Kdr.: Gen. Lt. Ritter v. Breitkopf
Ia: Major Trautmann
Adj.: Major Peringer, Julius
bayer. 5. Inf. Brig., Zweibrücken (Gen. Maj. Danner, Adj.: Hptm. Greß): bayer. 22. I.R., bayer. 23. I.R.,Bez. Kom. Zweibrücken
bayer. 6. Inf. Brig., Landau (Gen. MajClauß, Adj.: Hptm. Kühlmann): bayer. 17. I.R., bayer. 18. I.R., bayer. 1. Jg. Btl., Bez. Kom. Neustadt a/H
bayer. 3. Kav. Brig., Dieuze (Oberst Frhr. von und zu Egloffstein, Adj. OLt. Zeyß): bayer. 3. Ch. R., bayer. 5. Ch. R.
bayer. 4. Feld-Art. Brig., Landau (Oberst Held, Adj.: Hptm. Danzer): bayer. 5. Feld-Art. R., bayer. 12. Feld-Art. R.

Landwehr-Inspektion Landau (Insp.: Gen. Lt. Ipfelkofer, Adj.: Hptm. Biechele): Bez. Kom.: Kaiserslautern, Landau, Ludwigshafen

bayer. 4. I.D. (Würzburg)
Kdr.: Gen. Lt. Gr. v. Montgelas
Ia: Major Seißer
Adj.: Major Frhr. v. Ruffin

bayer. 7. Inf. Brig., Würzburg (Gen. Maj. Henigst, Adj.: Hptm. Claus): bayer. 5. I.R., bayer. 9. I.R., bayr. 2. Jg. Btl., Bez. Kom. Kitzingen, Würzburg
bayer. 8. Inf. Brig., Metz (Gen. Maj. Riedl, Adj.: Hptm. Hagen): bayer. 4. I.R., bayer. 8. I.R.
bayer. 4. Kav. Brig., Bamberg (Gen. Maj. Frhr. v. Redwitz, Adj.: Rittm. Schöninger): bayer, 1. U.R., bayer. 2. U.R,
bayer. 4. Feld-Art. Brig., Würzburg (Gen. Maj. Burkhardt, Adj.: Hptm. Frauenholz, Karl): bayer. 2. Feld-Art. R., bayer. 11. Feld-Art. R.

bayer. 2. Fußart. R.
bayer. 2. Pion. Btl.
bayer. 2. Train-Abt.

Fortress (Festung) Germersheim
Kommandant: Gen. Lt. Ritter v. Fischer
Ia: Hpt. Voit
Adj.: Hptm. Berthold

Training Center (Truppenübungsplatz) Hammelburg
Kommandant: Gen. Maj. z.D. Etzel
Adj.: Rittm. z.D. Niedbauer

III. bayer. Armeekorps (Nürnberg)

Kdr. Gen.: Gen. d. Kav. Frhr. v. Gebsattel
Chief of General Staff: Oberstlt. Braun
Ia: Major Frhr. Kreß v. Kressenstein, Gustav
Ic: Hptm. Eberth
Hptm. Kriebel
Adjutants: Major Buchner, Major Hemmer, Rittm. Frhr. Kreß v. Kressenstein

Oberstlt. z.D. Bartz

bayer. 5. I.D. (Nürnberg)
Kdr.: Gen. Lt. Ritter v. Schoch, Gustav
Ia: Major Ritter v. Reichert
Adj.: Major Edler v. Braunmühl
bayer. 9. Inf. Brig., Nürnberg (Gen. Maj. Jäger, Adj.: Hptm. Frhr. v. Berchem): bayer. 14. I.R., bayer. 21. I.R.,Bez. Kom. Amberg
bayer. 10. Inf. Brig., Bayreuth (Gen. Majv. Heydenaber, Adj.: Hptm. Lüst): bayer. 7. I.R., bayer. 19. I.R., Bez. Kom. Bayreuth, Hof
bayer. 5. Kav. Brig., Nürnberg (Gen. Maj. v. Hößlin, Adj. OLt. Zippelius): bayer. 1. Ch. R., bayer. 6. Ch. R.
bayer. 5. Feld-Art. Brig., Fürth (Gen. Maj. Paul, Adj.: Hptm. Riederer): bayer. 6. Feld-Art. R., bayer. 10. Feld-Art. R.

Landwehr-Inspektion Nürnberg (Insp.: Gen. Lt. Hurt, Adj.: Hptm. Groß): Bez. Kom.: Nürnberg, Erlangen, Ansbach, Weiden

bayer. 6. I.D. (Regensburg)
Kdr.: Gen. Lt. Ritter v. Höhn
Ia: Major Schmitt
Adj.: Major v. Baligand
bayer. 11. Inf. Brig., Ingolstadt (Gen. Maj. Lang, Adj.: Hptm. Frauenholz, Otto): bayer. 10. I.R., bayer. 13. I.R., Bez. Kom. Gunzenhausen, Ingolstadt
bayer. 12. Inf. Brig., Regensburg (Gen. Maj. Maunz, Adj.: Hptm. Geis): bayer. 6. I.R., bayer. 11. I.R., Bez. Kom. Deggendorf, Regensburg, Straubing
bayer. 6. Kav. Brig., Regensburg (Gen. Maj. v. Hellingrath, Adj.: OLt. Hörmann v. Hörbach): bayer. 2. Ch. R., bayer. 7. Ch. R.
bayer. 6. Feld-Art. Brig., Nürnberg (Gen. Maj. Ritter v. Gyßling, Adj.: OLt. Bitsch): bayer. 3. Feld-Art. R., bayer. 8. Feld-Art. R.

bayer. 3. Fußart. R.
bayer. 3. Pion. Btl.
bayer. 4. Pion. Btl.
bayer. 3. Train-Abt.

Fortress (Festung) Ingolstadt
Kommandant: Gen. Maj. Samhaber
Adj.: Hptm. Schuster

Training Center (Truppen-Übungsplatz) Grafenwöhr
Kommandant: Gen. Maj. z.D. Menzel
Adj.: Hptm. z.D. Lang

ROYAL SAXON ARMY

Military Entourage of His Majesty the King (aides-de-camp)

Diensttuender General à la suite Seiner Majestät des Königs:
Gen. Maj. v. Tettenborn
General à la suite Seiner Majestät des Königs:
Gen. Maj. Frhr. Leuckart v. Weißdorf
Generaladjutant Seiner Majestät des Königs:
Gen. Lt. v. Carlowitz
Diensttuende Flügeladjutanten Seiner Majestät des Königs:
Major Frhr. v. Koenneritz
Major v. Metzsch
Hptm. v. Schweinitz
Flügeladjutanten Seiner Majestät des Königs:
Oberst Meister
Oberstlt. Baron ô Byrn
Generaladjutant weiland Seiner Majestät des Königs Georg:
Gen. d. Inf. v. Treitschke

Generaladjutant weiland Seiner Majestät des Königs Albert:
Gen. d. Inf. v. Minckwitz

Ministry of War (Dresden)

Minister of War: Gen. Oberst Frhr. v. Hausen
Adjutant: Major Bramsch

General Army Department (I. Allgemeine Armee-Abteilung)
Abt. Chef.: Oberstlt. v. Koppenfels
Major Kell
Hptm. Klose
Reg.-Baumeister Hofmeister

Military Administration Department (II. Armee-Verwaltungs-Abteilung)
Abt. Chef: Oberstlt. Rohde
Major Schulz
Major Hoepner
Major Brückner
Geh. Oberbaurat OLt. d.L. a.D. Grimm
Geh. Kriegsrat OLt. d.L. a.D. Dr. Carl

Legal and Payment Department (III. Justiz- und Versorgungs-Abteilung)
Abt. Chef.: Wirkl. Geh. Kriegsrat Hptm. d.L. a.D. Sturm
Wirkl. Geh. Kriegsrat OLt. d.L. a.D. Dr. Höckner
Hptm. d.R. a.D. Walde
Legal counselor of the Minister of War:
Wirkl. Geh. Kriegsrat Major d.L. Feine

Personnel Department (IV. Abteilung für die persönlichen Angelegenheiten)
Abt. Chef: Major Moritz
Major v. Sichart
Hptm. v. Minckwitz
Retirement committee (Kollegium zur Entscheidung von Pensionierungsfragen):
Major Kell
Generaloberarzt Dr. Wagner
Wirkl. Geh. Kriegsrat OLt. d.L. a.D. Dr. Höckner

Medical Department (V. Medizinal-Abteilung)
Abt. Chef: Ober-Generalarzt Dr. Müller
Generaloberarzt Dr. Wagner
St. Arzt Tottmann

General Staff (Dresden)

Chief of General Staff: Gen. Maj. Leuthold
Oberst Fortmüller
Oberstlt. v. Eulitz
Major Hentsch (playing a major role during the Marne battle 1914, then Lt.Col. Hentsch)
Major Frhr. v. Oldershausen
Major v. Loeben
Major Hoffmann
Major Gysae
Major Kretzschmar
Major Tillmanns
Major Benzien
Major v. Hingst
Major v. Kirchbach
Hptm. Gr. Vitzthum v. Eckstädt
Hptm. v. Zanthier
Hptm. Thränhardt
Hptm. Bramsch
Hptm. Pramann
Hptm. v. Loeben
Hptm. Bahrdt
Hptm. Gr. Vitzthum v. Eckstädt

Central Department (Zentral-Abteilung des Generalstabes):
Gen. Maj. Leuthold
Major Benzien
Hptm. Bahrdt

Mapping Department (Abteilung für Landesaufnahme):
Vorst.: Major Ritter und Edler Herr v. Berger
Hptm. Zanthier

Assigned to the General Staff:
Major Böhmer
Major Petzhold

Military Archive (Kriegsarchiv):
Vorst.: Oberst z.D. Hottenroth

XII. (I. K.S.) Armeekorps (Dresden)

Kdr. Gen.: Gen. d. Inf. d'Elsa
Chief of General Staff: Oberstlt. v. Eulitz
Ia: Major Loeben
Ic: Hptm. Pramann

Adjutants: Major v. Zeschau
Major v. Funcke
Oberstlt. z.D. Lüddecke

23. I.D. (1. K.S.) (Dresden)
Kdr.: Gen. Lt. Frhr. v. Lindeman
Ia: Major v. Hingst
Adj.: Gericke
45. Inf. Brig. (1. K.S.), Dresden (Gen. Maj. Lucius, Adj.: Hptm. Biehl): 1. K.S. Leib-Gren R. Nr. 100, 2. K.S. G.R. 101
46. Inf. Brig. (2. K.S.), Dresden (Gen. Maj. v. Watzdorf, Adj.: Hptm. v. Wittern): K.S. Schützen-R. Nr. 10816. K.S. I.I. 182, 1. K.S. Jg. Btl. 12, Bez. Kom.: Meißen
23. Kav. Brig. (1. K.S.), Dresden (Oberst v. der Decken, Adj.: Rittm. v. der Decken): K.S. Garde-Reiter Rgt., 1. K.S. U.R. 17
23. Feld-Art. Brig. (1. K.S.), Dresden (Oberst Zincke, Adj.: Hptm. Neumann): 1. K.S. Feld-Art. R 12, 4. K.S. Feld-Art. R. 48

Landwehr-Inspektion Dresden (Insp.:Gen. Maj. Falcke, Adj.: OLt. Baßet): Bez. Kom.: Dresden I + II, Flöha, Freiberg, Pirna

32. I.D. (3. K.S.) (Bautzen)
Kdr.: Gen. Lt. Edler v. der Planitz
Ia: Hptm. Gr. Vitzthum v. Eckstädt
Adj.: Major v. Beulwitz
63. Inf. Brig. (5. K.S.), Bautzen (Gen. Maj. v. Gersdorff, Adj.: Hptm. v. Hartwig): 3. K.S. I.R. 102, 4. K.S. I.R. 103, Bez. Kom.: Bautzen, Löbau, Zittau
64. Inf. Brig. (6. K.S.), Dresden (Gen. Maj. Hempel, Adj.: Hptm. Koerner): 12. K.S. I.R. 177, 13. K.S. I.R. 178, 2. K.S. Jg. Btl. 13, Bez. Kom.: Großenhain
32. Kav. Brig. (2. K.S.), Dresden (Oberst Gr. Vitzthum v. Eckstädt, Adj.: Rittm. Kirsch): 1. K.S. H.R. 18, 3. K.S. H.R. 20
32. Feld-Art. Brig. (2. K.S.), Bautzen (Gen. Maj. Schramm, Adj.: Hptm. Michaelis): 2. K.S. Feld-Art. R. 28, 5. K.S. Feld-Art. R. 64

2. K.S. Fußart.-R. 19
1. K.S. Pion. Btl. 12
K.S. Telegr.-Btl. 7
1. K.S. Train-Abt. Nr. 12

7., and 8. K.S. coy. railroad regiment 1
K.S. Festungs-Fernspr. coy. Nr. 7
3. K.S. coy. Zeppelin-Btl. 2
3. K.S. coy aircraft-Btl. 1

Fortress (*Festung*) Königstein
Kommandant: N.N.

Training Center (*Truppen-Übungsplatz*) Königsbrück
Kommandant: Gen. Maj. z.D. Stark
Adj.: OLt. OLt. Görler

XIX. (II. K.S.) Armeekorps (Leipzig)

Kdr. Gen.: Gen. d. Inf. Laffert
Chief of General Staff: Oberst v. Fortmüller
Ia: Major Hentsch
Ic: Hptm. Thränhardt
Adjutants: Major v. Eschwege
Major Keyßerlitz

Oberstlt. z.D. Cramer v. Clausbruch

24. I.D. (2. K.S.) (Leipzig)
Kdr.: Gen. Lt. Krug v. Nidda
Ia: Major Kretzschmar
Adj.: Major v. Zeschau
47. Inf. Brig. (3. K.S.), Döbeln (Gen. Maj. Ullrich, Adj.: Hptm. Schulze): 11. K.S. I.R. 139, 14. K.S. I.R. 179, Bez. Kom.: Döbeln, Wurzen
48. Inf. Brig. (4. K.S.), Leipzig (Gen. Maj. Wilhelm, Adj.: Hptm. Kloeppel): 7. K.S. I.R. 106, 8. K.S. I.R. 107, Bez. Kom.: I Leipzig
24. Kav. Brig. (2. K.S.), Leipzig (Gen. Maj. Gr. v. der Schulenburg, Adj.: Rittm. Stengel): 2. K.S. H.R. 19, 2. K.S. U.R. 18
24. Feld-Art. Brig. (2. K.S.), Leipzig (Gen. Maj. v. Watzdorf, Adj.: Hptm. Ledig): 7. K.S. Feld-Art. R 77, 8. K.S. Feld-Art. R. 78

40. I.D. (4. K.S.) (Chemnitz)
Kdr.: Gen. Lt. Götz v. Olenhusen
Ia: Major Gysae
Adj.: Major Leonhardi
88. Inf. Brig. (7. K.S.), Chemnitz (Gen. Maj. Bärensprung, Adj.: Hptm. Hille): 5. K.S. I.R. 104, 15. K.S. I.R. 181, Bez. Kom.: Glauchau, Rochlitz
89. Inf. Brig. (6. K.S.), Zwickau (Gen. Maj. v. Seydewitz, Adj.: Hptm. Sickel): 9. K.S. I.R. 133, 10. K.S. I.R. 134, Bez. Kom.: Zwickau
40. Kav. Brig. (4. K.S.), Chemnitz (Oberst Frhr. v. Luttitz, Adj.: OLt. v. Globig): K.S. Carabinier-Regt., 3. K.S. U.R. 21
40. Feld-Art. Brig. (4. K.S.), Riesa (Oberst Devrient, Adj.: Hptm. Fiedler): 3. K.S. Feld-Art. R. 32, 6. K.S. Feld-Art. R. 68

Landwehr-Inspektion Chemnitz (Insp.: Gen. Maj. Gr. Vitzthum v. Eckstädt, Adj.: Hptm. Heitsch): Bez. Kom.: Annaberg, Auerbach, Chemnitz, Plauen, Schneeberg

K.S. MG-Abt. Nr. 8
2. K.S. Pion. Btl. 22
2. K.S. Train-Abt. Nr. 19

Training Center (*Truppen-Übungsplatz*) Zeithain
Kommandant: Gen. Maj. z.D. v. Schmieden
Adj.: OLt. OLt. Jungnickel

ROYAL WÜRTTEMBERG ARMY

Military Entourage of His Majesty the King (aides-de-camp)

Diensttuender Generaladjutant Seiner Majestät des Königs:
Gen. d. Kav. Frhr. v. Starkloff
Diensttuende Flügelladjutanten Seiner Majestät des Königs:
Oberstlt. v. Marval
Major Frhr. Capler v. Oedheim
Major v. Rom
Flügeladjutant Seiner Majestät des Königs:
Major Holland
Generaladjutanten Seiner Majestät Königs:
Gen. d. Inf. Frhr. v. Bilfinger
Gen. d. Inf. Frhr. v. Marchtaler
Generale à la suite Seiner Majestät des Königs:
Gen. Lt. v. Graevenitz
Gen. Maj. Mohn
Gen. Lt. Frhr. v. Reischach

Ministry of War (Stuttgart)

Minister of War: Gen. d. Inf. v. Marchtaler
Adjutant: Hptm. Frhr. v. Neurath

Central Department (Zentral-Abteilung Z)
Abt. Chef.: N.N.
Hptm. Ruoff
Hptm. Klewitz

Army and Personnel Department (Abteilung für allgemeine Armee- und für persönliche Angelegenheiten A)
Abt. Chef: Oberst v. Schroeder
Major Dreyer
Hptm. Melsheimer
Hptm. Graeter
Oberstlt. z.D. v. Bockshammer
Rittm. Griesinger

Hptm. Zimmermann
OLt. Schulze
OLt. Aichholz
OLt. Lammel
OLt. Wimmer
Lt. Leicht

Ordnance Department (Abteilung für Waffen und Feldgerät W)
Abt. Chef.: Oberst v. Haldenwang
Major Klotz
Oberstlt. z.D. Bauer
Oberstlt. z.D. Gr. v. Reischach

Administration Department (Verwaltungs-Abteilung B)
Abt. Chef.: Wirkl. Geh. Kr. Rat Hptm. d.L. a.D. v. Wunderlich
Wirkl. Geh. Kr. Rat Lt. D.L. a.D. v. Gerhardt
Geh. Kr. Rat K.B. OLt. D.L. a.D. Tafel
Geh. Ober-Baurat Lt. D.L. a.D. v. Glocker

Payment and Legal Department (Versorgungs- und Justiz Abteilung C)
Abt. Chef.: Oberst v. Haldenwang
Gen. Ober-Arzt Dr. Hopfengärtner
Geh. Kr. Rat Horn

Medical Department (Medizinal-Abteilung MA)
Abt. Chef: K.P. Gen Arzt Dr. Lasser

Retirement Committee (Kollegium zur Entscheidung von Pensionierungsfragen)
Major Breyer
Hptm. Graeter
Gen. Ober-Arzt Dr. Hopfengärtner

Schloßgarde-Kompanie (Stuttgart)
Kommandeur: Oberstlt. v. Marval
Lt. Kopf

General Staff (Stuttgart)
K.P. Oberstlt. v. Loßberg (General Staff XIII. A.K.)
Major Reinhardt (General Staff XIII. A.K.)
Major Wöllwarth
K.P. Major Frhr. v. Stotzingen
K.P. Hptm. v. Brandenstein (General Staff XIII. A.K.)
Hptm. Klewitz
Railroad line commander: Major Triebig

XIII. (K.W.) Armeekorps (Stuttgart)

Kdr. Gen.: K.P. Gen. d. Inf. v. Fabeck
Chief of General Staff: K.P. Oberstlt. v. Loßberg
Ia: Major Reinhardt
Ic: Hptm. v. Brandenstein
Adjutants: Rittm. Gleich, Hptm. Triebig
Oberstlt. z.D. v. Titschin

26. I.D. (1. K.W.) (Stuttgart)
Kdr.: Gen. Lt. Wilhelm Herzog v. Urach, Graf v. Württemberg
Ia: Major Wöllwarth
Adj.: Major Schwab
51. Inf. Brig. (1. K.W.), Stuttgart (Gen. Maj. v. Stein, Adj.: Hptm. Müller): 1. K.W. G.R. Königin Olga Nr. 119, 7. K.W. I.R. 125, Bez. Kom.: Calw, Horb
52. Inf. Brig. (2. K.W.), Ludwigsburg (Gen. Maj. v. Teichmann, Adj.: Hptm. Brandt): 3. K.W. I.R. 121, 4. K.W. F.R. 122, Bez. Kom.: Leonberg, Ludwigsburg
26. Kav. Brig. (1. K.W.), Stuttgart (Gen. Maj. Robert Maria Clemens Philipp Joseph Herzog v. Württemberg K.H., Adj.: OLt. Gädeke): 1. K.W. D.R. Königin Olga Nr. 25, 2. K.W. D.R. 26
26. Feld-Art. Brig. (1. K.W.), Ludwigsburg (Gen. Maj. v. Mohn, Adj.: Hptm. Deyle): 2. K.W. Feld-Art. R. 29, 4. K.W. Feld-Art. R. 65

Landwehr-Inspektion Stuttgart (Insp.:Gen. Maj. V. Steinhardt, Adj.: Hptm. Frhr. v. Weiler): Bez. Kom.: Ehingen, Eßlingen, Gmünd, Hall, Heilbronn, Reutlingen, Stuttgart I + II

27. I.D. (2. K.W.) (Ulm)
Kdr.: K.P. Gen. Lt. Gr. v. Pfeil u. Klein-Ellguth
Ia: K.P. Major Frhr. v. Stotzingen
Adj.: Major Ebner
53. Inf. Brig. (3. K.W.), Ulm (Gen. Maj. v. Moser, Adj.: OLt. Baeßler): 5. K.W. G.R.König Karl Nr. 123, 6. K.W. I.R. 124
54. Inf. Brig. (4. K.W.), Ulm (K.P. Gen. Maj. Langer, Adj.: Hptm. v. Mauch): 9. K.W. I.R.127, 10. K.W. I.R. 17, Bez. Kom.: Biberach, Ravensburg
27. Kav. Brig. (2. K.W.), Ludwigsburg (Gen. Maj. Frhr. Thumb v. Neuburg, Adj.: Rittm. Henke): 1. K.W. U.R. 19, 2.K.W. U.R. 20
27. Feld-Art. Brig. (2. K.W.), Ulm (Gen. Maj. v. Bernhard, Adj.: Hptm. Scherer): 1. K.W. Feld-Art. R. 13, 3. K.W. Feld-Art. R. 49

K.W. Pion. Btl. 13
K.W. Train-Abt. Nr. 13

Fortress (Festung) Ulm
Kommandant: Gen. Lt. v. Gerok
Ia: Hptm. Wittmer
Adj.: Hptm. v. Brietzke

Training Center (Truppen-Übungsplatz) Münsingen
Kommandant: Gen. Maj. z.D. v. Dinkelacker
Adj.: OLt. Wagner

APPENDIX C

THE RANK STRUCTURE

Prussian officers of the rank of *Generalleutnant* or higher were referred to as *Exzellenz*; *Generalmajor* was addressed as *"Herr General;"* Prussian officers from the rank of *Leutnant* to the rank of *Oberst* were referred to as *Hochwohlgeboren* when addressed by civilians or by lower ranking soldiers.

German Rank	British or American equivalent
Generalfeldmarschall	Field Marshal
Generaloberst	Colonel General
General der Infanterie	General of Infantry
General der Kavallerie	General of Cavalry
General der Artillerie	General of Artillery
Generalleutnant	Lieutenant General
Generalmajor	Major General
	Brigadier General
Oberst	Colonel
Oberstleutnant	Lieutenant Colonel
Major	Major
Hauptmann	Captain
Rittmeister	Captain from a mounted unit
Oberleutnant	Lieutenant
Leutnant	Second Lieutenant
Feldwebelleutnant	Sergeant Major Lieutenant
Offizierstellvertreter	Officer Deputy
Feldwebel	First Sergeant
Wachtmeister	First Sergeant (mounted unit)
Vizefeldwebel	Staff Sergeant / Sergeant First Class US.
Vizewachtmeiser	Staff Sergeant (mounted unit)
Sergeant	Sergeant Staff /Sergeant US
Unteroffizier	Corporal
Oberjäger	Corporal (*Jäger*)
Obergefreiter	Corporal (Foot Artillery)
Korporal (only before 1872)	Corporal (Bavarian Units)
Gefreiter	Lance Corporal/US Private First Class

Appendix C—The Rank Structure

The following ranks all equate to a soldier in the rank of private

Chevauleger	Private in Bavarian Chevauxleger regiment (also quite often spelled: Chevauleger)
Dragoner	Private in dragoon regiment-less No. 3
Ersatz-Reservist	Soldier normally a private belonging to the Ersatz-Reserve
Fahrender Artillerist	Mounted private in Bavarian field artillery
Fahrer	Driver in general or a private in Saxon mounted field artillery or draft-horse detachments of the foot artillery.
Füsilier	Private in any füsilier regiment or III battalion Guard Regiment zu Fuss 1–5 or Garde- Grenadier Regiment 1–5, IR115, students in Prussian or Württemberg Unteroffiziers- vorschule
Gardist	Private in Prussian Guard formation, in battalion I or II IR 115 or Saxon Guard Reiter Regiment
Gemeiner or *Traingemeiner*	Privates in train units with long (Saxon 3yr.) active requirements
Grenadier	Private in any grenadier regiment or battalion, I or II Guard Regiment zu Fuss 1–5 or Garde- Grenadier Regiment 1–5, or Grenadier Regiments 1–12, or Regiments 89, 100, 101, 109, 110, 119, 123.
Garde-Füsilier	Private in Guard-Füsilier Regiment
Grenadier zu Pferd	Private in Grenadier Regiment zu Pferd No.3
Hornist/Hoboist	Trumpeter
Husar	Private in hussar regiment
Infanterist	Private in a Bavarian infantry regiment
Jäger	Private in Jäger battalion
Jäger zu Pferd	Private in Jäger zu Pferd regiment-less No. 1
Kanonier	Private in foot artillery or Prussian field artillery or the dismounted members in Bavarian and Saxon field artillery units
Karabinier	Private in Saxon Karabinier regiment
Königsjäger	Private in Jäger zu Pferd regiment No. 1
Kriegsfreiwilliger	Wartime Volunteer
Kürassier	Private in Kürassier regiment
Landsturmmann[1]	Soldier normally a private belonging to the Landsturm
Musketier	Private in Prussian or Württemberg infantry Regiments
Pionier	Private in sapper/engineer battalion, technical troops
Reiter	Private in Bavarian Schwere Reiter Regiment

[1] (Sheldon, Email, 2009) *Landsturmrekrut; Landsturmpflichtiger; Armierungs-Soldat*. He knows these existed because he built his list from a walk round the massive German cemetery at Neuville St. Vaast near Vimy.

Reservist	Soldier, normally a private, belonging to the reserves
Schütze	IR 108, Garde-Schützen Bataillon, private in the machinegun and bicycle companies
Soldat	Private in Saxon infantry battalion
Tambour	Drummer
Trainsoldat	Private in train units from Prussia, Württemberg, and Saxony with short (1 yr.) active requirements, and all privates from Bavaria.
Ulan	Private in Ulan regiment
Unteroffiziersvorschüler	Private in Saxon or Bavarian *Unteroffiziersvorschulen*
Wehrmann	Soldier normally a private belonging to the Landwehr

Medical Personnel

Generalstabsarzt	Lieutenant General
Generalarzt	Major General
Oberfeldarzt	Lieutenant Colonel
Oberstabsarzt	Major
Stabsarzt	Captain
Oberarzt	Lieutenant
Assistenzarzt	Second Lieutenant

Bataillonsarzt or *Regimentsarzt* was no indicator of rank, just position.

Sanitäter	Medical Assistant
Krankenträger	Stretcherbearer

Frequently the prefix '*Sanitäts-*' appears in front of a normal NCO rank, such as *Gefreiter* or *Unteroffizier*. This simply indicates that a man of that particular seniority was part of the medical services.[2]

Certain rank names changed officially in 1899. The earlier names had a decidedly French sounding slant. These were replaced by German sounding names
Sekondelieutenant became *Leutnant*
Premierlieutenant became *Oberleutnant*
Oberstlieutenant became *Oberstleutnant*
Portepee-Fähnrich or *Degen-Fähnrich* all became just *Fähnrich*
Offiziers-Aspirant or *Avantageure* became *Fahnenjunker*
Generallieutenant became *Generalleutnant*

[2] (Sheldon, The German Army on Vimy Ridge, 2008), pp. 345–346. Much of this chart was copied verbatim from the Sheldon book.

APPENDIX D

MILITÄR BEAMTE

GRADES OF OFFICIALS

There were two general types: military officials and civil officials of the military administration.

Military
The following list shows the class of appointments held by military officials, higher being marked (A), subaltern (B), and lower (C):

Zahlmeister (B)	Paymaster (also responsible for many of the duties of a Quartermaster
Waffenmeister, formerly *Büchsenmacher* (C)	Armorer, gunsmith
Sattler (C)	Saddler
Intendantur-Beamter	Intendance official
Korps-Intendant (A)	Corps Intendant
Intendantur-Rat (A)	Intendance councilor (a *Rat* is equal to the military rank of a major, The Räte or Councilors were rank ranged from the 1st to 5th Class, with the highest holding the equivalence to a Generalmajor, the lowest or 5th that of a Hauptmann. Subalternbeamte could after long service receive the character of a Rechnungsrat/Kanzleirat and in the War Ministry even Geheimer Rechnungsrat/Kanzleirat (Major))
Intendantur-Assessor (A)	Intendance assessor (The lowest rung of the higher grade intendance career—equivalalent to a captain)
Intendantur-Sekretär (B)	Intendance secretary (a *Sekretär* was a Subalternbeamte with sergeants' rank.)
Intendantur- Sekretariats-Assistent (B)	Assistant secretary
Intendantur-Registrator (B)	Intendance registrar
Intendantur-Registratur-Assistent	Assistant intendance registrar
Auditoriat	Judge-advocate's officials

General-Auditeur[1] (A)	Judge-advocate-general
Ober- or Korps Auditeur (A)	Chief or corps judge-advocate (The A.K.O. of 31 March 1900 introduced new titles for Justice Officials with effect from 1 October 1900. Hence forward the previous Auditeur ranks were replaced by those of Kriegsgerichtsräte, etc.)
Divisions- or Garnisons-Auditeur (B)	Division/garrison judge advocate
Militär-Gerichts-Aktuar (B)	Military actuary
Militär-Geistlicher (A)	Military chaplain(s)
Militär-Küster (C)	Military sacristans
Armee-Musik-Meister (B)	Inspector of military bands
Waffenmeister der Feldartillerie (C)	Armorer in charge of field artillery material
Fortifikations-Beamte	Engineer officials
Festungsoberbauwart (B)	Chief superintendant of fortifications
Festungsbauwart (B)	Superintendant of fortifications
Ingenieur- Sekretariats-Assistent (B)	Assistant engineer secretary

The civil officials of the military administration were not divided like the military officials; they merely had grades in their own service.

Feld-Kriegs-Kassen-Verwaltung	Field treasury officials
Feld-Zahlmeister	Field paymaster
Kassierer	Cashier
Buchhalter	Bookkeeper
Montierungs-Depot-Verwaltung	Clothing depot officials (Retitled as Bekleidungsämter WEF 1 April 1888. Henceforward officials titled Bekleidungamts. . .)
Montierungs- Depot-Rendant	Clothing depot accountant
Montierungs[2]*- Depot-Kontrolleur*	Clothing depot controller
Montierungs- Depot-Assistent	Clothing depot assistant
Magazin-Verwaltung (Later Proviantämter)	Magazine officials
Proviant-Meister	Supply master
Proviant-Amts-Rendant	Supply office accountant

1 The name changed from *Auditeur* to *Auditor* at an unknown date.

2 Before 1899, *Montirung* was spelled just with an "i;" with the language reform this turned into "ie." Same thing happened to *Exerzir-Reglements*, which changed to *Exerzier-Reglements* and *Pharmaceuten* became *Pharmazeuten*).

Proviant-Amts-Kontrolleur	Supply officer controller
Proviant-Amts-Assistent	Supply office assistant
Garnison-Verwaltung[3]	Garrison Administrative officials
Garnison-Verwaltungs-Direktor	garrison administration (*Direktor* was a Subaltern-beamte equivalent to a captain. Could receive the character of a Rechnungsrat.)
Garnisons-Verwaltung	
Ober-Inspektor	Inspector of garrison administration (*Inspektor* equaled the military rank of lieutenant)
Inspektor	
Kasernen-Inspektor	Inspector of barracks
Militär-Bau-Verwaltung	Military works administration
Militär-Bau-Rat	Architect of military works
Lazarrett-Oekonomie-Verwaltung	Hospital administration officials
Lazarrett-Ober-Inspektor	Chief inspector of hospitals
Lazarrett-Inspektor	Inspector of hospitals
Miltär-Pharmazeeutisches Personal	Apothecaries
Ober-Stabs-Apotheker	Chief apothecary
Korps-Apotheker	Corps apothecary [4]

3 According to German grammar it should be *Garnisons-Verwaltung*, but for whatever reasons they kept the traditional name *Garnison-Verwaltung* like in the *Garnison-Verwaltungsordnung* dated 1911.

4 (Stubbs, 2004). Appendix I. Much of this listing has been adjusted from the source with the aide of Glenn Jewison. Spelling errors are my own.

APPENDIX E

PAY CHARTS

While soldiers and their titles changed, for many the important thing was what they could be expected to be paid. Officers were notoriously indebted. To give you a feel for how much money a soldier earned, we have included the pay scale for the year 1914 in German marks. As a rule of thumb 4.2 Mark=1 US Dollar. Payday was held on the 1st, 11th, and 21st of each month. As an aside, the accumulated mail since the last payday was delivered to the soldier on that day.

Monthly Base Pay—salaries in 1914:

Gemeine	9.00–10.50 Mark
Gefreite	10.50–12.00
Kapitulanten Gefr.	15.00–16.50
Fahrer wie für	15.60
Berittene, für Hoboisten, Tamboure usw.	
Fähnriche and Unteroffizier with less than 5 ½ of service	25.20
Sergeanten and Unteroffiziere with more than 5 ½ years of service	39.60
Vizefeldwebel, Sergeanten and NCOs after nine years of service	47.10
Feldwebel, Wachtmeister	62.10

For a General-Feldmarschall, General der Infanterie., Gen. Lt.	
a) with the salary of a Commanding General	1,165
b) with the salary of a Division Commander	1,129

For a Generalmajor or an Obergeneralarzt	855.00

For a field grade officer	
a) as Brigade Commander	755.00
b) as Regimental Commander or similar	731.00
with similar pay level[1], Generalarzt	
c) as patented Oberstlt. with extra-pay,	641.75
Generaloberarzt with extra-pay	
d) with the pay-level of a Battalion Commander,	546.00
Oberstabsarzt, Korpsveterinär	

[1] *Gebührnisse* can be roughly translated as salary

For a Hauptmann, Rittmeister, Stabarzt, Oberstabs- or Stabsveterinär	
a) from 1–4 years	283.33
b) from 5–8 years	383.33
c) after 9 years	425.00
For a Leutnant or Oberleutnant	
a) from 1–3 years	125.00
b) from 4–6 years	141.66
c) from 7–9 years	158.33
d) from 10–12 years	175.00
e) after 13 years	200.00
For an Assistenzarzt, Oberarzt, Veterinär, Oberveterinär	
a) from 1–3 years	141.66
b) from 4–6 years	175.00
c) after 7 years	200.00
For a Zeug-, Feuerwerks- Festungsbau-Leutnant or Oberleutnant	
a) from 1–3 years	166.66
b) from 4–6 years	191.66
c) from 7–9 years	216.66
d) from 10–12 years	241.66
e) after 13 years	258.33[2]

[2] (Rabenau, 1914), pp. 20–21.

APPENDIX F

THE GERMAN ARMY AFTER MOBILIZATION

GENERAL REMARKS:

- This lists all German formations that were mobilized and fielded through the mobilization order of 1 August 1914, which were operationally ready for the advance in the west and the Russian attack in the east.
- Also appearing on the list are all formations that were ordered into existence by mobilization but were available only later, such as the "Marine Division," the six new reserve corps, and the extra Bavarian reserve division that was created in August 1914 by absorbing many war volunteers, which was ready for operations in October.
- Non-active formations such as *Stellvertretende Generalkommandos* left behind in Germany (*Heimatkriegsgebiet*) are not listed.[1]
- In order to keep the list short, detailed staffing is only shown down to division staffs. For the brigades only the brigade commanders are shown. Regimental and battalion commanders have been omitted.
- Usually only regiments and independent battalions (*Jäger*, machinegun battalions. . .) represent the lowest given level of detail. Only for heavy and super-heavy artillery are smaller units shown.
- As far as fortress garrisons are concerned, detailed and reliable information is generally lacking. Usually only the mobilized formations of the *Hauptreserve* and the fortress machinegun units are listed. Those fortresses usually had a great number of additional *Landwehr* and *Landsturm* formations, as well as artillery and engineer personnel.
- For the sake of brevity, only combat troops (infantry, cavalry, artillery, engineers) are listed. All the numerous train columns, engineer, and artillery parks and supply units have been left out. This also applies to all the *Etappen-Inspektionen* together with their *Landwehr* and *Landsturm* formations.

---

1 Each army corps fielded its army corps command and also formed a stellvertretende Generalkommando (replacing general command) in its home base concerned with personnel replacement, supplies, equipment, and taking over command functions in the corps area. The general staff was also broken up into the field headquarters (*Großes Hauptquartier*) and the *stellvertretende Generalstab* (replacing general staff) left behind in Berlin. Moltke took over the function of Chief of Replacing General Staff following his dismissal after the Marne disaster in 1914.

- Fielded *Landwehr*, *Landsturm* and *Ersatz* formations are listed with the armies under whose tactical control they operated.
- For reasons of clarity, the IX Reserve Corps, the 1st Landwehr Division, and the Landwehr Corps Woyrsch are listed as Strategic Reserve, which is formally wrong since there was no such reserve. The six Falkenhayn reserve corps and the extra Bavarian reserve division are also listed there.
- Abbreviations are those used by the Germans in 1914.

GROSSES HAUPTQUARTIER *(KOBLENZ)*

Chef des Generalstabes des Feldheeres: Gen. Oberst. v. Moltke
1. Adj.: Maj. Tieschowitz v. Tieschowa
2. Adj.: Hptm. Köhler

Zentral-Abteilung (Central Department)
Abt. Chef: Obstlt. v. Fabeck
Adj.: Hptm. v. Wedderkop
Büro-Vorsteher: Geheimer Rechnungs Rat Schliewe (+21 civil servants)

Operations-Abteilung (Operations Department)
Chef: Obstlt. Tappen
Büro-Offz.: Hptm. Mewes
O Ia: Maj. v. Redern, Hptm. v. Harbou, Hptm. Bulcke, Hptm. Wagner, Oblt. Poten
O Ib: Maj. v. Bartenwerffer, Oblt. Boehm, Oblt. v. Wallenberg
O Ic: Hptm. Frhr. v. dem Bussche-Ippenburg, Oblt. v. Rosenberg-Gruszczynski
O II: Maj. Bauer, Hptm. Geyer
O.T.: Hptm. Koeppen

Nachrichten-Abteilung (Intelligence Department)
Chef: Obstlt. Hentsch
Sekt. Ia: Hptm. v. Hepke
Sekt. Ib: Maj. v. Rauch, Hptm. Hessig
N. II O: Hptm. v. Cochenhausen, Oblt. Oßwald, Oblt. v. Rothkirch u. Panthen
N. II a (*Fremde Heere*—Foreign Military Forces): Maj. v. Klüber
N. Gz.Offz.: Hptm. König
III b (Nachrichtenwesen–Military Intelligence[2]): Maj. Nicolai
Geh. N.D.: Hptm. v. Rohrscheidt, Hptm. Neuhof, Hptm. Stotten, Hptm. Ernst
Büro-Offz.: Hptm. Kolaczek

Politische Abteilung (Political Department)
Obstlt. v. Dommes, Hptm. Janensch

Generalquartiermeister: Gen. Lt. v. Stein
Chef d. St. des Generalquartiermeisters: Gen. Maj. v. Voigts-Rhetz
Adj.: Hptm. Frhr. v. Hammerstein-Equord, Hptm. v. Holleuffer, Hptm. v. Schleicher

---

[2] Assignment of military intelligence to IIIb was done for historical reason: During the Franco-Prussian War section b of the 3rd Department, dealing with the French Army, also assumed responsibility over military intelligence. During all restructurings of the Great General Staff between 1871 and 1914 the 3rd Department always remained the "French Department." (Nicolai, 1921), p. 478.

Generalintendant (General Responsible for Supplies):
Gen. Maj. v. Schoeler
Stabsoffz.: Hptm. Ketzler
Adj.: Hptm. v. Oertzen
Chef des Feldeisenbahnwesens (Chief Railroad): Obstlt. Gröner
Eisenbahn-Abt.: Maj. v. Natzmer, Maj. v. Velsen, Maj. Frhr. v. Oldershausen, Maj. v. Kirchbach, Hptm. v. Stockhausen, Hptm. v. Dewitz gen. v. Krebs, Hptm. Koppen, Hptm. v. Stuckrad, Hptm. Kretzschmann, Hptm. Fleck, Hptm. v. Boetticher
Chef des Feldmunitionswesens (Chief Field Munitions Service)
Gen. Lt. Sieger
Chef des Feldsanitätswesens (Chief Field Medical Service)
General-Stabs Arzt d. Armee Prof. Dr. v. Schjerning

Under direct command of the GHQ:
Zeppelin air ships: VII, VIII, IX, Hansa, Victoria Luise, Sachsen
Parseval air ship: IV
3. (Hptm. Grzybowski) and 4. (Hptm. Prien) schw. Küstenmörser-Bttr. (30,5 cm Mrs. β-Gerät), from 17.8. with 2. Army
2. (42 cm Mrs. γ-Gerät, Hptm. Becker) and 3. (42 cm Mrs. M-Gerät, Hptm. Erdmann) kurze Marine-Kanonen-Bttr. (42 cm Mrs.), used in Liège
All reserve foot artillery regiments, except: II./Res. Fuß-Art. Regt. 9 (with 2. Army), I. and II. / bayer. Res. Fuß-Art. Regt. 2 (Hauptreserve Metz), Res. Fuß-Art. R. 14 (Hauptreserve Straßburg) and: II. / Res. Fuß-Art. R. 1, II. / Res. Fuß-Art. R. 4 (Hauptreserve Königsberg)

"STRATEGIC RESERVE"

Marine-D. (mobilized: 23.08.14, fielded mid-October. Starting from 28 November: 1. Marine-Div. with 3 brigades)
Kdr.: N.N., later Admiral von Schroeder
Ia: Oberst von Hülsen
1. Landw. Esk. X. A. K
Marine Inf. Brig. (Gen.Maj. v. Wichmann): Marine I. R. 1, Marine I. R. 2, later also: Marine I. R. 3.
Matrosen Art. Brig. used as infantry (Kapitän z. S. Herr): Matrosen Art. Rgt. 1, Matrosen Art. Rgt. 2
1. Landw. Esk. X. A. K.
2. / Landw. Feld-Art. Abt. X. A. K.
2. Seew. Pi. Kp.

IX. Reservekorps (covering force for Schleswig-Holstein, so called "Nord-Armee" Army of the North)

Kdr. Gen.: Gen. d. Inf. v. Boehn
Chef: Oberst v. Stolzmann
Ia: Maj. v. Klewitz
Ic: Hptm. Witting
Ib: Hptm. Albrecht
Id: Hptm. Lund

II. 2. G. Fuß-Art. R. (10 cm Kann.)
4., 1. Res., and 2. Res. / G. Pi. Btl., 4. / Pi. Btl. 28

17. R.D.
Kdr.: Gen. Lt. Wagener
Ia: Hptm. v. Rosenberg-Lipinsky
Res. H. R. 6
81. Inf. Brig. (Oberst v. Lewinsky): I. R. 162, I. R. 163
33. Res. Inf. Brig. (Gen. Lt. Dernen): hanseat. Res. I. R. 75, hanseat. Res. I. R. 76,
Res. Feld-Art Rgt. 17
4./ Pi. Btl. 9

18. R.D.
Kdr.: Gen. d. Inf. Gronen
Ia: Hptm. Würz
Res. H. R. 7
34. Res. Inf. Brig. (Oberst v. Busse): Res. I. R. 31, Res. I. R. 90
35. Res. Inf. Brig. (Gen. Lt. Frhr. v. Ompteda): Res. I. R. 84, Res. I. R. 86, Res. Jg. Btl. 9
Res. Feld-Art Rgt. 18
1., and 2. Res. / Pi. Btl. 9

1. Landw. D. (belongs to. "Nord-Armee," 27.8. to 8. Armee)
Kdr.: Gen. Lt. Frhr. v. d. Goltz
Ia: Hptm. Göldner
33. Mixed Landw. Brig. (Gen. Maj. v. Oertzen): Landw. I. R. 75, Landw. I. R. 76, 2. Landw. Esk. G. Kav., 1. Landw. Esk. IX. A. K., 1. Landw. Bttr. IX. A. K.,
34. Mixed Landw. Brig. (Gen. Lt. v. Pressentin): Landw. I. R. 31, Landw. I. R. 84, 3. Landw. Esk. G. Kav., 2. Landw. Esk. IX. A. K., 2. Landw. Bttr. IX. A. K.,
37. Mixed Landw. Brig. (Gen. Lt. v. Meyer): Landw. I. R. 73, Landw. I. R. 74, 2. Landw. Esk. X. A. K., II. Landw. Feld-Art. Abt. X. A. K.,
38. Mixed Landw. Brig. (Gen. Lt. v. Kotze): Landw. I. R. 77, Landw. I. R. 78, 2. Landw. Esk. X. A.K.

Gen.Kdo. Mobile Landw. Truppen (covering force for Silesia, under comm. AOK 8)

Kdr. Gen.: Gen. d. Inf. v. Woyrsch
Chef: Obstlt. Heye
Ia: Maj. Kundt
Ic: Hptm. Benecke
Ib: Hptm. Loeschebrandt-Horn

3. Landw. D.
Kdr.: Gen. Lt. Frhr. v. König
Ia: Hptm. Steuer
Landw. Kav. Rgt. 1

17. Mixed Landw. Brig. (Gen. Lt. v. Grumbkow): Landw. I. R. 6, Landw. I. R. 7
18. Mixed Landw. Brig. (Gen. Maj. Neven du Mont): Landw. I. R. 37, Landw. I. R. 46
17. Ers. Brig. (Gen. Lt. Rieß v. Scheuernschloß): E. Btl. I. R. 17, E. Btl. I. R. 18, E. Btl. I. R. 19, E. Btl. I. R. 20, E. Btl. I. R. 77
Feld-Art. E. Abt. 20, Feld-Art. E. Abt. 41, 1., and 2. Landst. Bttr. V. A. K.
Ers. Kp. Pi. Btl. 5

4. Landw. D.
Kdr.: Gen. Lt. v. Wegerer
Ia: Hptm. Sehmsdorf
Landw. Kav. Rgt. 2, Ers. K. R.
22. Mixed Landw. Brig. (Gen. Maj. Sachs): Landw. I. R. 11, Landw. I. R. 51
23. Mixed Landw. Brig. (Oberst v. Mutius): Landw. I. R. 22, Landw. I. R. 23
21. Ers. Brig. (Gen. Lt. v. Busse): E. Btl. I. R. 21, E. Btl. I. R. 22, E. Btl. I. R. 23, E. Btl. I. R. 24, E. Btl. I. R. 78
Feld-Art. E. Abt. 6, Feld-Art. E. Abt. 57, 1., and 2. Landst. Bttr. VI. A. K.
Ers. Kp. Pi. Btl. 6

SIX NEW RESERVE CORPS (ORDERED BY WAR MINISTER ON 16 AUGUST 1914)

Ordered to be operationally ready 10 October, except Bavarian 6th Reserve division, the divisions did not have brigade staffs.

A huge change in the structure resulted in no infantry brigades being formed. Thus, there were initially no brigade commanders, but only one infantry comander—with the rank of a colonel or a major-general, very likely a reactivated "z.D." officer—for each division. This one officer had to direct the tactical use of four infantry regiments and two rifle battalions without the support of a brigade staff; under the given circumstances this was an almost impossible task. Also, there was a lack of artillery. Since only one field artillery regiment was allocated to each division, there was no brigade organization. Therefore, the artillery brigade commander and artillery officer, who were the primary consultants to the division commander in artillery matters, were also lacking.

For the most part, the troops were volunteers and reservists as well as older officers who were retired from the active, reserve or Landwehr forces. Based on perceived requirements, these formations received an extremely short period of training, as little as eight weeks. In this deplorable state, the young troops sent into the field had to immediately participate in the heaviest fighting imaginable, namely the battles in Flanders in the autumn of 1914.

XXII. Reservekorps (Berlin)

Kdr. Gen.: Gen. d. Kav. v. Falkenhayn (Eugen, brother of the war minister)

43. R.D. (Berlin)
Res. Jg. Btl. 15 (Potsdam)
Res. Kav. Abt. 43 (Berlin)

Res. I.R. 201 (Berlin), Res. I.R. 202 (Berlin), Res. I.R. 203 (Spandau), Res. I.R. 204 (Potsdam)
Res. Feld-Art. Rgt. 43 [3 Abt.] (Jüterbog)

44. R.D. (Brandenburg)
Res. Jg. Btl. 16 (Gr. Lichterfelde)
Res. Kav. Abt. 44 (Potsdam)
Res. I.R. 205 (Frankfurt a.O.), Res. I.R. 206 (Brandenburg), Res. I.R. 207 (Prenzlau), Res. I.R. 208 (Braunschweig)
Res. Feld-Art. Rgt. 44 [3 Abt.] (Brandenburg)

XXIII. Reservekorps (Stettin)

Kdr. Gen.: Gen. d. Kav. v. Kleist

45. R.D. (Stettin)
Res. Jg. Btl. 17 (Lübben)
Res. Kav. Abt. 45 (Demmin)
Res. I.R. 209 (Stettin), Res. I.R. 210 (Stettin), Res. I.R. 211 (Pr. Stargard), Res. I.R. 212 (Altona)
Res. Feld-Art. Rgt. 45 [3 Abt.] (Kolberg und Belgard)

46. R.D. (Schwerin)
meckl. Res. Jg. Btl. 18 (Ratzeburg)
meckl. Res. Kav. Abt. 46 (Ludwigslust)
meckl. Res. I.R. 213 (Schwerin), meckl. Res. I.R. 214 (Rostock), hann. Res. I.R. 215 (Hannover), hann. Res. I.R. 216 (Celle)
meckl. Res. Feld-Art. Rgt. 46 [3 Abt.] (Güstrow)

XXIV. Reservekorps (Magdeburg)

Kdr. Gen.: N.N.

47. R.D. (Magdeburg)
Res. Jg. Btl. 19 (Naumburg)
Res. Kav. Abt. 47 (Halberstadt)
Res. I.R. 217 (Magdeburg), Res. I.R. 218 (Minden), Res. I.R. 219 (Detmold), Res. I.R. 220 (Paderborn)
Res. Feld-Art. Rgt. 47 [3 Abt.] (Minden)

48. R.D. (Frankfurt a.M.)
Res. Jg. Btl. 20 (Bückeburg)
Res. Kav. Abt. 48 (Paderborn)
hess. Res. I.R. 221 (Darmstadt), hess. Res. I.R. 222 (Gießen), hess. Res. I.R. 223 (Frankfurt a.M.), Res. I.R. 224 (Erfurt)
Res. Feld-Art. Rgt. 48 [3 Abt.] (Hannover)

XXV. Reservekorps (Posen)
Kdr. Gen.: Gen. d. Inf. v. Scheffer-Boyadel

49. R.D. (Posen)
Res. Jg. Btl. 21 (Hirschberg)
Res. Kav. Abt. 49 (Torgau)
Res. I.R. 225 (Glogau), Res. I.R. 226 (Liegnitz), Res. I.R. 227 (Rawitsch), Res. I.R. 228 (Schweidnitz)
Res. Feld-Art. Rgt. 49 [3 Abt.] (Magdeburg)

50. R.D. (Breslau)
Res. Jg. Btl. 22 (Oels)
Res. Kav. Abt. 50 (Züllichau)
Res. I.R. 229 (Breslau), Res. I.R. 230 (Brieg), Res. I.R. 231 (Halle), Res. I.R. 232 (Torgau)
Res. Feld-Art. Rgt. 50 [3 Abt.] (Sprottau)

XXVI. Reservekorps (Cassel)
Kdr. Gen.: Gen. d. Inf. v. Hügel

51. R.D. (Cassel)
Res. Jg. Btl. 23 (Goslar)
Res. Kav. Abt. 51 (Cassel)
Res. I.R. 233 (Meiningen), Res. I.R. 234 (Cassel), Res. I.R. 235 (Coblenz), Res. I.R. 236 (Köln)
Res. Feld-Art. Rgt. 51 [3 Abt.] (Cassel)

52. R.D. (Cöln)
Res. Jg. Btl. 23 (Marburg)
Res. Kav. Abt. 52 (Darmstadt)
Res. I.R. 237 (Trier.), bad. Res. I.R. 238 (Karlsruhe), bad. Res. I.R. 239 (Mannheim), bad. Res. I.R. 240 (Rastatt)
Res. Feld-Art. Rgt. 52 [3 Abt.] (Karlsruhe)

XXVII. Reservekorps (Dresden)
Kdr. Gen.: Gen. L. v. Carlowitz

53. R.D. (Dresden)
sächs. Res. Jg. Btl. 25 (Dresden)
Res. Kav. Abt. 53 (Königsbrück)
sächs. Res. I.R. 241 (Dresden), sächs. Res. I.R. 242 (Döbeln), sächs. Res. I.R. 243 (Dresden), sächs. Res. I.R. 244 (Chemnitz)
sächs. Res. Feld-Art. Rgt. 53 [3 Abt.] (Dresden)

54. R.D. (Stuttgart)
sächs. Res. Jg. Btl. 26 (Freiberg)
württ. Res. Kav. Abt. 52 (Ludwigsburg)

sächs. Res. I.R. 245 (Leipzig), württ. Res. I.R. 246 (Stuttgart), württ. Res. I.R. 247 (Stuttgart), württ. Res. I.R. 248 (Stuttgart)
württ. Res. Feld-Art. Rgt. 54 [3 Abt.] (Ulm)

bayer. 6. R.D. (Munich, to be operationally ready 18 October 1914)
bayer. Res. Kav.R. 6 (München)
12. bayer. Res. Inf. Brig.: bayer. Res. I.R. 16 ("Regiment List" München), bayer. Res. I.R. 17 ("Regiment Großmann" Augsburg),
14. bayer. Res. Inf. Brig.: bayer. Res. I.R. 20 ("Regiment Weiß" Nürnberg), bayer. Res. I.R. 21 ("Regiment Braun" Fürth)
bayer. Res. Feld-Art. Rgt. 6 [3 Abt.] (München)
bayer. Res. Fuß-Art. Btl. 6 (München)

1. ARMEE (A.H.Qu.: GREVENBROICH)

Ob.Bef.: Gen. Oberst. v. Kluck
Chef: Gen. Maj. v. Kuhl
O.Qu.: Oberst v. Bergmann
Ia: Obstlt. Grautoff
Ic: Maj. v.d. Hagen
Ib: Hptm. v. Alten
Id: Hptm. Scultetus
Bba.: Hptm. Bührmann
kdt.: Maj. Renner

Pi. Rgt. 18
Feld-Flieg. Abt. 12

10. Mixed Landw. Brig. (Oberst v. Lenthe): Landw. I.R. 12, Landw. I.R. 52, 1. Landw. Esk III.A. K., 1. Landst. Bttr. III. A. K.

11. Mixed Landw. Brig. (Oberst v. der Schulenburg): Landw. I.R. 20, Landw. I.R. 35, 1. Landw. Esk G. K, 2. Landst. Bttr. III. A. K.

27. Mixed Landw. Brig. (Gen. Lt. Dallmer): Landw. I.R. 53, Landw. I.R. 55, 2. Landw. Esk VII. A. K.,

II. Armeekorps

Kdr. Gen.: Gen. d. Kav. v. Linsingen
Chef: Oberst Frhr. v. Hammerstein-Gersmold
Ia: Maj. Mengelbier
Ic: Hptm. Ludloff
Ib: Hptm. v. Bock und Polach
Id: Hptm. Müller

I. / Fuß-Art. R. 15 (s.F.H.)
Feld-Flieg. Abt. 30

3. I.D.
Kdr.: Gen. Lt. v. Trossel
Ia: Hptm. Graf v. Poninski
D. R. 3
5. Inf. Brig. (Gen. Maj. Frhr. Treusch v. Buttlar-Brandenfels): G. R. 2, G. R. 9
6. Inf. Brig. (Gen. Maj. Nieland): F. R. 34, I. R. 42
3. Feld-Art. Brig. (Gen. Maj. v. Stamford): Feld-Art Rgt. 2, Feld-Art Rgt. 38
1./ Pi. Btl. 2

4. I.D.
Kdr.: Gen. Lt. v. Pannewitz
Ia: Maj. Klette
D. R. 12
7. Inf. Brig. (Gen. Maj. v. Runckel): I. R. 14, I. R. 149
8. Inf. Brig. (Gen. Maj. v. Schmettau): I. R. 49, I. R. 140
4. Feld-Art. Brig. (Gen. Maj. Krafft): Feld-Art Rgt. 17, Feld-Art Rgt. 53
2., and 3./ Pi. Btl. 2

III. Armeekorps

Kdr. Gen.: Gen. d. Inf. v. Lochow
Chef: Obstlt. v. Seeckt
Ia: Maj. v. Wetzell (transfered to mobilization department of the Great General Staff on 1 August)
Ic: Hptm. v. Lindequist
Ib: Hptm. v. Behr
Id: Hptm. v. Perthes

I. / 2. G. Fuß-Art. R. (s.F.H.)
Feld-Flieg. Abt. 7

5. I.D.
Kdr.: Gen. Lt. Wichura
Ia: Maj. v. Westhoven
3./ H. R. 3
9. Inf. Brig. (Gen. Maj. v. Doemming): G. R. 8, I. R. 48
10. Inf. Brig. (Gen. Maj. Sontag): G. R. 12, I. R. 52
5. Feld-Art. Brig. (Oberst v. Lotterer): Feld-Art Rgt. 18, Feld-Art Rgt. 54
1./ Pi. Btl. 3

6. I.D.
Kdr.: Gen. Maj. Herhudt v. Rhoden
Ia: Maj. v. Viereck
2./ H. R. 3

11. Inf. Brig. (Gen. Maj. v. Wachter): I. R. 20, F. R. 35
12. Inf. Brig. (Gen. Maj. v. Gabain): I. R. 24, I. R. 64
6. Feld-Art. Brig. (Gen. Maj. v. Kleist): Feld-Art Rgt. 3, Feld-Art Rgt. 39
2., and 3./ Pi. Btl. 3

IV. Armeekorps

Kdr. Gen.: Gen. d. Inf. Sixt v. Arnim
Chef: Gen. Maj. v. Stocken
Ia: Maj. v. Mantey
Ic: Hptm. Kriegsheim
Ib: Hptm. Metz
Id: Hptm. Hinze

I. / Fuß-Art. R. 4 (s.F.H.)
Feld-Flieg. Abt. 9

7. I.D.
Kdr.: Gen. Lt. Riedel
Ia: Hptm. v. Schenkendorff
St., and 3./ H. R. 10
13. Inf. Brig. (Gen. Maj. v. Schüßler): I. R. 26, I. R. 66
14. Inf. Brig. (Oberst v. Oven): I. R. 27, I. R. 165
7. Feld-Art. Brig. (Gen. Maj. Stumpff): Feld-Art Rgt. 4, Feld-Art Rgt. 40
1./ Pi. Btl. 4

8. I.D.
Kdr.: Gen. Lt. Hildebrandt
Ia: Maj. Lämmerhirt
2./ H. R. 10
15. Inf. Brig. (Gen. Maj. Reichenau): F. R. 36, I. R. 93,
16. Inf. Brig. (Gen. Maj. v. Jarotzky): I. R. 72, I. R. 153
8. Feld-Art. Brig. (Gen. Maj. Bothe): Feld-Art Rgt. 74, Feld-Art Rgt. 75
2., and 3./ Pi. Btl. 4

III. Reservekorps

Kdr. Gen.: Gen. d. Inf. v. Beseler
Chef: Oberst Meister
Ia: Maj. v. Tschischwitz
Ic: Hptm. v. Heeringen
Ib: Hptm. v. Bogen
Id: Hptm. Muff

5. R.D.
Kdr.: Gen. Lt. v. Voigt
Ia: Hptm. v. Brunn

Res. D. R. 2
9. Res. Inf. Brig. (Oberst Briese): Res. I. R. 8, Res. I. R. 48
10. Res. Inf. Brig. (Gen. Lt. Stumpff): Res. I. R. 12, Res. I. R. 52, Res. Jg. Btl. 3
Res. Feld-Art Rgt. 5
4./ Pi. Btl. 3

6. R.D.
Kdr.: Gen. Lt. v. Schickfus und Neudorff
Ia: Maj. v. Holleben
Res. U. R. 3
11. Res. Inf. Brig. (Oberst v. Jacobi): Res. I. R. 20, Res. I. R. 24
12. Res. Inf. Brig. (Gen. Maj. Wachsmuth): Res. I. R. 26, Res. I. R. 35
Res. Feld-Art Rgt. 6
2., and 3. Res/ Pi. Btl. 3

IV. Reservekorps

Kdr. Gen.: Gen. d. Art. v. Gronau
Chef: Obstlt. v. d. Heyde
Ia: Obstlt. Czettritz
Ic: Hptm. Osius
Ib: Hptm. Hellwig
Id: Hptm. Koch

7. R.D.
Kdr.: Gen. Lt. Graf v. Schwerin
Ia: Hptm. Arens
bayer. schw. Res. Reiter Rgt. 1
13. Res. Inf. Brig. (Oberst v. Dresler u. Scharfenstein): Res. I. R. 27, Res. I. R. 36
14. Res. Inf. Brig. (Gen. Maj. v. Wienkowski): Res. I. R. 66, Res. I. R. 72, Res. Jg. Btl. 4
Res. Feld-Art Rgt. 7
2., and 3./ Pi. Btl. 2 and 4./ Pi. Btl. 4

22. R.D.
Kdr.: Gen. Lt. Riemann
Ia: Hptm. v. Rundstedt
Res. Jg. z. Pf. R. 1
43. Res. Inf. Brig. (Oberst v. Lepel): Res. I. R. 71, Res. I. R. 94, Res. Jg. Btl. 11
44. Res. Inf. Brig. (Gen. Lt. v. Mühlenfels): Res. I. R. 32, Res. I. R. 82
Res. Feld-Art Rgt. 22
1., and 2. Res/ Pi. Btl. 4

2. ARMEE (A.H.Qu.: MONSCHAU [MONTJOIE])

Ob.Bef.: Gen. Oberst. v. Bülow
Chef: Gen. Lt. v. Lauenstein

O.Qu.: Gen. Maj. Ludendorff
Ia: Obstlt. Matthes
Ic: Maj. Graf Scheck v. Wittenau
Ib: Hptm. Baron de la Motte-Fouqué
Id: Hptm. Thilo
Bba.: Hptm. Brause
kdt.: Hptm. Brinckmann

II. and III. / Fuß-Art. R. 4 (21 cm Mrs.)
I. and II. / Fuß-Art. R. 9 (21 cm Mrs.)
II. / Res. Fuß-Art. R. 9 (10 cm Kan.)
1. (Hptm. Neumann) and 5. (Hptm. Scharf) schw. Küstenmörser-Bttr. (30.5 cm Mrs. β -Gerät), 3., and 4. Bttr. (30.5 cm β-Gerät) from 17. August
Pi. R. 24, Pi. R. 25
Feld-Flieg. Abt. 23

25. Mixed Landw. Brig. (Gen. Lt. v. Glasenapp): Landw. I. R. 13, Landw. I. R. 16, 1. Landw. Esk. VII. A. K., Landst. Bttr. VII A. K.

29. Mixed Landw. Brig. (Oberst v. Rothenberg-Lipinsky): Landw. I. R. 28, Landw. I. R. 29, 1. Landw. Esk. VIII. A. K., Landst. Bttr. VIII. A. K.

Garde-Korps

Kdr. Gen.: Gen. d. Inf. Frhr. v. Plettenberg
Chef: Obstlt. Graf v. d. Schulenburg
Ia: Maj. v. Thaer
Ic: Hptm. v. Bock
Ib: Hptm. v. Arnim
Id: Hptm. v. Bose

I. / 1. G. Fuß-Art. R. (s.F.H.)
Feld-Flieg. Abt. 1

1. G.D.
Kdr.: Gen. Lt. v. Hutier
Ia: Hptm. v. Schweinitz
Leib G. Hus. Rgt.
1. G. Inf. Brig. (Gen. Maj. v. Kleist): 1. G.-R. z. F., 3. G.-R. z. F.,
2. G. Inf. Brig. (Gen. Maj. Schach v. Wittenau): 2. G.-R. z. F., 4. G.-R. z. F.
1. G. Feld-Art. Brig. (Gen. Maj. Frhr. v. Buddenbrock): 1. G. Feld-Art Rgt., 3. G. Feld-Art Rgt.
1./ G. Pi. Btl.

2. G.D.
Kdr.: Gen. Lt. v. Winckler
Ia: Maj. v. d. Hagen
2. G. U. R.

3. G. Inf. Brig. (Oberst v. Petersdorff): G. Gren. R. 1 (Alexander), G. Gren. R. 2 (Elisabeth)
4. G. Inf. Brig. (Gen. Maj. v. Gontard): G. Gren. R. 2 (Franz), G. Gren. R. 4 (Augusta)
2.G. Feld-Art. Brig. (Gen. Maj. Trimborn): 2. G. Feld-Art Rgt., 4. G. Feld-Art Rgt.
2., and 3./ G. Pi. Btl.

VII. Armeekorps

Kdr. Gen.: Gen. d. Kav. v. Einem gen. v. Rothmaler
Chef: Oberst v. Wolff
Ia: Maj. v. Caprivi
Ic: Hptm. Knuth
Ib: Hptm. Henke
Id: Hptm. Fellinger
kdt.: Hptm. Kroeger

I. / Fuß-Art. R. 7 (s.F.H.)
Feld-Flieg. Abt. 18

13. I.D.
Kdr.: Gen. Lt. v. d. Borne
Ia: Hptm. v. Platen (Axel)
St., and 3./ U. R. 13
25. Inf. Brig. (Gen. Maj. v. Unruh): I. R. 13, I. R. 158
26. Inf. Brig. (Oberst v. Brauchitsch): I. R. 15, I. R. 55,
13. Feld-Art. Brig. (Oberst v. Klipfel): Feld-Art Rgt. 22, Feld-Art Rgt. 58
1./ Pi. Btl. 7

14. I.D.
Kdr.: Gen. Maj. Fleck
Ia: Hptm. v. Bock (Franz-Karl)
3./ U. R. 16
24. Inf. Brig. (Oberst v. Massow): I. R. 16, I. R. 53
79. Inf. Brig. (Gen. Maj. Schwarte): I. R. 56, I. R. 57
14. Feld-Art. Brig. (Oberst v. Campe): Feld-Art Rgt. 7, Feld-Art Rgt. 43
2., and 3./ Pi. Btl. 4

IX. Armeekorps

Kdr. Gen.: Gen. Lt. v. Quast
Chef: Obstlt. Sydow
Ia: Maj. Auer v. Herrenkirchen
Ic: Hptm. Mende
Ib: Hptm. v. Platen
Id: Hptm. Feige

I. / Fuß-Art. R. 20 (s.F.H.)
Feld-Flieg. Abt. 11

17. I.D.
Kdr.: Gen. Lt. v. Bauer
Ia: Hptm. v. Voß
St., and 3./ D. R. 16
33. Inf. Brig. (Gen. Maj. v. Lewinski): I. R. 75, I. R. 76
34. Inf. Brig. (Gen. Maj. v. Kraewel): Gren. R. 89, Füs. R. 90
17. Feld-Art. Brig. (Gen. Maj. v. Ditfurth): Feld-Art Rgt. 24, Feld-Art Rgt. 60
1./ Pi. Btl. 9

18. I.D.
Kdr.: Gen. Lt. v. Kluge
Ia: Maj. v. Gellhorn
1., and 2./ D. R. 16
35. Inf. Brig. (Gen. Maj. Hunaeus): I. R. 84, Füs. R. 86
36. Inf. Brig. (Gen. Maj. Frhr. v. Troschke): I. R. 31, I. R. 35
18. Feld-Art. Brig. (Gen. Maj. Bloch v. Blottnitz): Feld-Art Rgt. 9, Feld-Art Rgt. 45
2., and 3./ Pi. Btl. 9

X. Armeekorps

Kdr. Gen.: Gen. d. Inf. Emmich
Chef: Oberst Frhr. v. d. Wenge
Ia: Maj. Kirch
Ic: Hptm. Krall
Ib: Hptm. v. Stülpnagel
Id: Hptm. v. Winterfeld

II. / Fuß-Art. R. 20 (s.F.H.)
Feld-Flieg. Abt. 21

19. I.D.
Kdr.: Gen. Lt. Hoffmann
Ia: Maj. v. Dommes
3./ H. R. 17
37. Inf. Brig. (Gen. Maj. v. Scheliha): I. R. 78, I. R. 91
38. Inf. Brig. (Oberst v. Oertzen): I. R. 73, I. R. 74
19. Feld-Art. Brig. (Gen. Maj. Heygster): Feld-Art Rgt. 26, Feld-Art Rgt. 62
1./ Pi. Btl. 10

20. I.D.
Kdr.: Gen. Lt. Schmundt
Ia: Maj. v. Wiarda
St., and 3./ H. R. 17
39. Inf. Brig. (Oberst v. L'Estocq): I. R. 79, I. R. 164
40. Inf. Brig. (Gen. Maj. v. Lindequist): I. R. 77, I. R. 92
20. Feld-Art. Brig. (Oberst Rüstow): Feld-Art Rgt. 10, Feld-Art Rgt. 46
2., and 3./ Pi. Btl. 10

Garde-Reservekorps

Kdr. Gen.: Gen. d. Art. v. Gallwitz
Chef: Oberst v. Bartenwerffer
Ia: Maj. v. Haeften
Ic: Hptm. Landfried
Ib: Hptm. Crantz
Id: Hptm. Weste

II. /1. G. Fuß-Art. R. (s.F.H.)
Feld-Flieg. Abt. 45

3. G.D.
Kdr.: Gen. Lt. v. Bonin
Ia: Hptm. v. Wulffen
G. Res. U. R.
5. G. Inf. Brig. (Gen. Maj. v. Below): 5. G.-R. z. F., G. Gren. Rgt. 5
6. G. Inf. Brig. (Gen. Maj. v. Friedeburg): G. Füs. Rgt., Lehr-Inf. Rgt.
3. G. Feld-Art. Brig. (Gen. Maj. Graf v. Schweinitz u. Krain): 5. G. Feld-Art Rgt., 6. G. Feld-Art Rgt.
1./ Pi. Btl. 28

1. G.R.D.
Kdr.: Gen. Maj. v. Albrecht
Ia: Maj. v. Knauer
G. Res. Drag. Rgt.
1. G. Res. Inf. Brig. (Gen. Maj. Frhr. v. Langermann u. Erlencamp): 1. G. Res. Rgt., 2. G. Res. Rgt., G. Res. Jg. Btl.
15. Res. Inf. Brig. (Oberst v. Below): Res. I. R. 64, Res. I. R. 93, G. Res. Schtz. Btl.
G. Res. Feld-Art. Brig. (Oberst Mertens): 1. G. Res. Feld-Art. Rgt., 3. G. Res. Feld-Art. Rgt.
2,. and 3. / Pi. Btl. 28

VII. Reservekorps

Kdr. Gen.: Gen. Lt. v. Zwehl
Chef: Obstlt. Hesse
Ia: Maj. v. Lösecke
Ic: Hptm. v. Stülpnagel (Otto)
Ib: Hptm. Degenkolb
Id: Hptm. Schönheinz

13. R.D.
Kdr.: Gen. Lt. v. Kühne
Ia: Hptm. Frhr. v. Rotberg
Res. H. R. 5
25. Res. Inf. Brig. (Gen. Lt. v. Harbou): Res. I. R. 13, Res. I. R. 56
28. Res. Inf. Brig. (Gen. Maj. Neuhauß): Res. I. R. 39, Res. I. R. 57, Res. Jg. Btl. 7
Res. Feld-Art Rgt. 13
4./ Pi. Btl. 7

14. R.D.
Kdr.: Gen. Lt. v. Unger
Ia: Hptm. v. Bredow
Res. H. R. 8
28. Inf. Brig. (Oberst Frhr. v. Ziegesar): Füs. R. 39, I. R. 159
27. Res. Inf. Brig. (Gen. Lt. Sunkel): Res. I. R. 16, Res. I. R. 53,
Res. Feld-Art Rgt. 14
1., and 2./ Pi. Btl. 7

X. Reservekorps

Kdr. Gen.: Gen. d. Inf. Graf v. Kirchbach
Chef: Oberst Marquard
Ia: Maj. Frhr. v. Ledebur
Ic: Hptm. Dunst
Ib: Hptm. Weyland
Id: Hptm. Baare

2. G.R.D.
Kdr.: Gen. Lt. Frhr. von Süßkind
Ia: Hptm. v. Wolff
Res. U. R. 2
26. Res. Inf. Brig. (Oberst Roeßler): Res. I. R. 15, Res. I. R. 55
38. Res. Inf. Brig. (Gen. Maj. Weese): Res. I. R. 77, Res. I. R. 91, Res. Jg. Btl. 10
Res. Feld-Art. Rgt. 20
4. / Pi. Btl. 10

19. R.D.
Kdr.: Gen. Lt. v. Bahrfeld
Ia: Hptm. v. Blomberg
Res. D. R. 6
37. Res. Inf. Brig. (Oberst v. Winterfeldt): Res. I. R. 73, Res. I. R. 78
39. Res. Inf. Brig. (Gen. Lt. Friedrich Prinz v. Sachsen-Meiningen, Herzog zu Sachsen): Res. I. R. 74, Res. I. R. 92, III./ Res. I. R. 79
Res. Feld-Art. Rgt. 19
1., and 2. Res./ Pi. Btl. 10

H.K.K. 2

Kdr. Gen.: Gen. Lt. v. d. Marwitz
Chef: Maj. Hoffmann v. Waldau
Ib: Hptm. v. Bülow

Jg. Btl. 3, Jg. Btl. 4, Jg. Btl. 7, Jg. Btl. 9, Jg. Btl. 10.

2. K.D.
Kdr.: Gen. Maj. Frhr. v. Krane

Ia: Hptm. Frhr. v. d. Osten gen. Sacken
Ib: Hptm. Janssen
5. Kav. Brig. (Oberst v. Arnim): D. R. 2, U. R. 3
8. Kav. Brig. (Gen. Maj. Frhr. Thumb v. Neuburg): K. R. 7, H. R. 12
Leib-Hus. Brig.: Leib-Hus. R. 1, Leib-Hus. R. 2
MG-Abt. 4
reit. Abt. / Feld-Art. Rgt. 35

4. K.D.
Kdr.: Gen. Lt. v. Garnier
Ia: Hptm. Brüggemann-Ferno
Ib: Hptm. Blankenhorn
3. Kav. Brig. (Oberst Graf v. der Goltz): K. R. 2, U. R. 9
17. Kav. Brig.: (Gen. Maj. Graf v. Schimmelmann) D. R. 17, D. R. 18
18. Kav. Brig. (Oberst v. Printz): H. R. 15, H. R. 16
G. MG-Abt. 2
reit. Abt. / Feld-Art. Rgt. 3

9. K.D.
Kdr.: Gen. Maj. Graf v. Schmettow (Eberhard)
Ia: Maj. Herwarth v. Bittenfeld
Ib: Hptm. Braemer
13. Kav. Brig. (Oberst Seiffert): K. R. 4, H. R. 8
14. Kav. Brig. (Oberst v. Heuduck): H. R. 11, U. R. 5
19. Kav. Brig. (Oberst Frhr. v. Zedlitz u. Leipe): D. R. 19, U. R. 13
MG-Abt. 7
reit. Abt. / Feld-Art. Rgt. 10

3. ARMEE (A.H.Qu.: PRÜM)

Ob.Bef.: Gen. Oberst. Frhr. v. Hausen
Chef: Gen. Maj. v. Hoeppner
O.Qu.: Gen. Maj. Leuthold
Ia: Maj. Hasse
Ic: Maj. v. Schmalz
Ib: Hptm. Looff
Id: Hptm. v. Weise
Bba.: Hptm. Pramann

III. / Fuß-Art. R. 1 (21 cm Mrs.)
Feld-Flieg. Abt. 22

47. Mixed Landw. Brig.: Landw. I. R. 104, Landw. I. R. 106, 1., and 2. Landw. E. XIX A. K., Landst. Bttr. XIX A. K.

XI. Armeekorps

Kdr. Gen.: Gen. Lt. v. Plüskow
Chef: Oberst v. Sauberzweig
Ia: Maj. v. Brandenstein
Ic: Hptm. v. Plessen
Ib: Hptm. v. Vahlkampf
Id: Hptm. Kaupisch

I. / Fuß-Art. R. 18 (s.F.H.)
Feld-Flieg. Abt. 28

22. I.D.
Kdr.: Gen. Maj. Dieffenbach
Ia: Hptm. Caracciola
St., and 1. Halb-Regt. K. R. 6
43. Inf. Brig. (Gen. Maj. v. Hülsen): I. R. 82, I. R. 83
44. Inf. Brig. (Gen. Maj. Nordbeck): I. R. 32, I. R. 167
22. Feld-Art. Brig. (Gen. Maj. Gronau): Feld-Art Rgt. 11, Feld-Art Rgt. 47
1./ Pi. Btl. 11

38. I.D.
Kdr.: Gen. Lt. Wagner
Ia: Maj. Sydow
2. Halb-Regt. K. R. 6
76. Inf. Brig. (Gen. Maj. v. Versen): I. R. 71, I. R. 95
83. Inf. Brig. (Gen. Maj. Frhr. v. Hanstein): I. R. 94, I. R. 96
38. Feld-Art. Brig. (Gen. Maj. Krahmer): Feld-Art Rgt. 19, Feld-Art Rgt. 55
2., and 3./ Pi. Btl. 11

XII. Armeekorps (1. K.S.)

Kdr. Gen.: Gen. d. Inf. d'Elsa
Chef: Obstlt. v. Eulitz
Ia: Maj. v. Loeben (Georg)
Ic: Hptm. Schroeder
Ib: Hptm. v. Loeben (Paul)
Id: Hptm. Bahrdt

I. / Fuß-Art. R. 19 (s.F.H.)
Feld-Flieg. Abt. 29

23. I.D.
Kdr.: Gen. Lt. Frhr. v. Lindemann
Ia: Maj. v. Hingst
H. R. 20
45. Inf. Brig. (Gen. Maj. Lucius): sächs. Leib-Gren. Rgt. 100, Gren. R. 101
46. Inf. Brig. (Gen. Maj. v. Watzdorff): Sächs. Schtz. Rgt. 108, I. R. 182

32. Feld-Art. Brig. (Gen. Maj. Fincke): Feld-Art Rgt. 12, Feld-Art Rgt. 48
1./ Pi. Btl. 12

32. I.D.
Kdr.: Gen. Lt. Edler v. d. Planitz
Ia: Hptm. Graf Vitzthum v. Eckstädt (Alexander)
H. R. 18
63. Inf. Brig. (Gen. Maj. v. Gersdorff): I. R. 102, I. R. 103
64. Inf. Brig. (Gen. Maj. Morgenstern-Döring): I. R. 177, I. R. 178
32. Feld-Art. Brig. (Gen. Maj. Schramm): Feld-Art Rgt. 28, Feld-Art Rgt. 64
2., and 3./ Pi. Btl. 12

XIX. Armeekorps (2. K.S.)

Kdr. Gen.: Gen. d. Kav. v. Laffert
Chef: Obstlt. Frotscher
Ia: Maj. Hoffmann
Ic: Hptm. Stäcker
Ib: Hptm. Schubert
Id: Hptm. Graf Vitzthum v. Eckstädt (Eckhardt)

II. / Fuß-Art. R. 19 (s.F.H.)
Feld-Flieg. Abt. 24

24. I.D.
Kdr.: Gen. Lt. Krug v. Nidda
Ia: Maj. Kretzschmar
U. R. 18
47. Inf. Brig. (Gen. Maj. Frhr. v. Falkenstein): I. R. 139, I. R. 179
48. Inf. Brig. (Gen. Maj. Kaden): I. R. 106, I. R. 107
24. Feld-Art. Brig. (Oberst Baeßler): Feld-Art Rgt. 77, Feld-Art Rgt. 78
1./ Pi. Btl. 22

40. I.D.
Kdr.: Gen. Lt. Götz v. Olenhusen
Ia: Maj. Gysae
H. R. 19
88. Inf. Brig. (Gen. Maj. Bärensprung): I. R. 104, I. R. 181
89. Inf. Brig. (Gen. Maj. v. Seydewitz): I. R. 133, I. R. 134
40. Feld-Art. Brig. (Gen. Maj. Devrient): Feld-Art Rgt. 32, Feld-Art Rgt. 68
2., and 3./ Pi. Btl. 22

XII. Reservekorps (K.S.)

Kdr. Gen.: Gen. d. Art. v. Kirchbach
Chef: Obstlt. v. Koppenfels
Ia: Maj. v. Watzdorf

Ic: Hptm. Frhr. v. Friesen
Ib: Hptm. Diemer
Id: Hptm. Klose

23. R.D.
Kdr.: Gen. Lt. v. Larisch
Ia: Hptm. v. Zanthier
sächs. Res. Hus. Rgt.
45. Res. Inf. Brig. (Gen. Lt. v. Sydow): sächs. Res. I. R. 100, sächs. Res. I. R. 101, sächs. Res. Jg. Btl. 12
46. Res. Inf. Brig. (Gen. Lt. Hempel): sächs. Res. I. R. 102, sächs. Res. I. R. 103
sächs. Res. Feld-Art. Rgt. 23
4./ Pi. Btl. 12

24. R.D.
Kdr.: Gen. Lt. v. Ehrenthal
Ia: Hptm. Saxe
sächs. Res. Ul. Rgt.
47. Res. Inf. Brig. (Gen. Lt. Ullrich): sächs. Res. I. R. 104, sächs. Res. I. R. 106, sächs. Res. Jg. Btl. 13
48. Res. Inf. Brig. (Gen. Lt. Wilhelm): sächs. Res. I. R. 107, sächs. Res. I. R. 133
sächs. Res. Feld-Art. Rgt. 24
1., and 2./ Pi. Btl. 12

4. ARMEE (A.H.Qu.: TRIER)

Ob.Bef.: Gen. Oberst. Albrecht, Herzog von Württemberg
Chef: Gen. Lt. Frhr. v. Lüttwitz
O.Qu.: Oberst Weidner
Ia: Maj. v. Werder
Ic: Maj. Bronsart v. Schellendorff
Ib: Hptm. Humser
Id: Hptm. Frhr. v. Fritsch
Bba.: Hptm. Muff

II. and III. Fuß-Art. R. 7 (21 cm Mrs.)
Pi. R. 30
Feld-Flieg. Abt. 6

49. Mixed Landw. Brig. (Gen. Maj. v. Hartmann): Landw. I. R. 116, Landw. I. R. 118, 2., and 3. Landw. Esk. XI A. K., 1. Landw. Esk. XVIII A. K., 2. Landst. Bttr. XVIII A. K.

VI. Armeekorps
Kdr. Gen.: Gen. d. Inf. v. Pritzelwitz
Chef: Obstlt. v. Derschau
Ia: Maj. v. Pommer-Esche

Ic: Hptm. v. Taysen
Ib: Hptm. Spemann
Id: Senftleben
kdt.: Hptm. Gudowius

III. / Fuß-Art. R. 6 (s.F.H.)
Feld-Flieg. Abt. 13

11. I.D.
Kdr. Gen. Lt. v. Webern
Ia: Maj. Graf York v. Wartenburg
Jg. Rgt. z. Pf. 11
21. Inf. Brig. (Gen. Maj. v. Drabich-Waechter): Gren. R. 10, Füs. R. 38
22. Inf. Brig. (Oberst Seydel): Gren. R. 11, I. R. 51
11. Feld-Art. Brig. (Gen. Maj. v. Bischoffshausen): Feld-Art Rgt. 6, Feld-Art Rgt. 42
1./ Pi. Btl. 6

12. I.D.
Kdr.: Gen. Lt. Châles de Beaulieu
Ia: Hptm. v. Miaskowski
U. R. 12
24. Inf. Brig. (Gen. Maj. v. der Heyde): I. R. 23, I. R. 62
78. Inf. Brig. (Gen. Maj. Vollbrecht): I. R. 63, I. R. 157
12. Feld-Art. Brig. (Gen. Maj. Zietlow): Feld-Art Rgt. 21, Feld-Art Rgt. 57
2., and 3./ Pi. Btl. 6

VIII. Armeekorps

Kdr. Gen.: Gen. Lt. Tülff v. Tschepe u. Weidenbach
Chef: Oberst v. Cramon
Ia: Maj. van den Bergh
Ic: Hptm. Reuter
Ib: Hptm. Mackowsky
Id: Hptm. Kühlenthal
kdt.: Hptm. Witte

III. / Fuß-Art. R. 9 (s.F.H.)
Feld-Flieg. Abt. 10

15. I.D.
Kdr.: Gen. Lt. Riemann
Ia: Maj. Henz
K. R. 8
29. Inf. Brig. (Gen. Maj. v. Mückwitz): I. R. 25, I. R. 161
80. Inf. Brig. (Gen. Maj. Frhr. Reitz v. Frentz): I. R. 65, I. R. 160
15. Feld-Art. Brig. (Gen. Maj. v. Woyna): Feld-Art Rgt. 59, Feld-Art Rgt. 83
1./ Pi. Btl. 8

16. I.D.
Kdr.: Gen. Lt. Fuchs
Ia: Maj. v. Stülpnagel (Edwin)
H. R. 7
30. Inf. Brig. (Gen. Maj. v. Pfuel): I. R. 28, I. R. 68
31. Inf. Brig. (Gen. Maj. Wellmann): I. R. 29, I. R. 69
16. Feld-Art. Brig. (Gen. Maj. Beckmann): Feld-Art Rgt. 23, Feld-Art Rgt. 44
2., and 3./ Pi. Btl. 8

XVIII. Armeekorps

Kdr. Gen.: Gen. d. Inf. v. Schenck
Chef: Obstlt. v. Blücher
Ia: Maj. Frhr. v. Stoltzenberg
Ic: Hptm. Halm
Ib: Hptm. v. Roques (Franz)
Id: Hptm. Bruckmann

I. / Fuß-Art. R. 3 (s.F.H.)
Feld-Flieg. Abt. 27

21. I.D.
Kdr.: Gen. Maj. v. Oven
Ia: Maj. v. Tschudi
U. R. 6
41. Inf. Brig. (Gen. Maj. v. der Esch): I. R. 87, I. R. 88
42. Inf. Brig. (Gen. Maj. Elstermann v. Elster): Füs. R. 80, I. R. 81
21. Feld-Art. Brig. (Gen. Maj. Scherbening): Feld-Art Rgt. 27, Feld-Art Rgt. 63
1./ Pi. Btl. 21

25. I.D.
Kdr.: Gen. Maj. Kühne
Ia: Maj. Faupel
D. R. 6
49. Inf. Brig. (Gen. Maj. v. Uthmann): hess. Leib-G. I. R. 115, I. R. 116
50. Inf. Brig. (Gen. Maj. Frhr. v. Speßhardt): I. R. 117, I. R. 118
25. Feld-Art. Brig. (Gen. Maj. Freise): Feld-Art Rgt. 25, Feld-Art Rgt. 61
2., and 3./ Pi. Btl. 21

VIII. Reservekorps

Kdr. Gen.: Gen. d. Inf. Frhr. von und zu Egloffstein
Chef: Oberst Buchholtz
Ia: Maj. Bethcke
Ic: Hptm. Zimmermann
Ib: Hptm. v. Roques (Karl)
Id: Hptm. Schaller

15. R.D.
Kdr.: Gen. Lt. v. Kurowski
Ia: Hptm. v. Morsbach
Res. U. R. 5
30. Res. Inf. Brig. (Oberst v. Bermuth): Res. I. R. 25, Res. I. R. 69
32. Res. Inf. Brig. (Gen. Maj. Scholz): Res. I. R. 17, Res. I. R. 30
Res. Feld-Art. Rgt. 15
4./ Pi. Btl. 8

16. R.D.
Kdr.: Gen. Lt. Mootz
Ia: Hptm. Pfeiffer
bayer. schw. Res. Reiter. Rgt. 2
29. Res. Inf. Brig. (Gen. Lt. Schumann): Res. I. R. 29, Res. I. R. 65
31. Res. Inf. Brig. (Gen. Lt. v. Ditfurth): Res. I. R. 28, Res. I. R. 68
Res. Feld-Art. Rgt. 16
1., and 2. Res./ Pi. Btl. 8

XVIII. Reservekorps

Kdr. Gen.: Gen. Lt. v. Steuben
Chef: Oberst v. Studnitz
Ia: Maj. v. Berenhorst
Ic: Hptm. Frhr. v. Neubronn u. Eisenburg
Ib: Hptm. Zeitz
Id: Hptm. Held

21. R.D.
Kdr.: Gen. Lt. v. Rampacher
Ia: Hptm. Schröder (Karl)
Res. D. R. 7
41. Res. Inf. Brig. (Gen. Lt. v. Mey): Res. I. R. 80, Res. I. R. 87
42. Res. Inf. Brig. (Gen. Lt. v. Quidtmann): Res. I. R. 81, Res. I. R. 88
Res. Feld-Art. Rgt. 21
4./ Pi. Btl. 11

25. R.D.
Kdr.: Gen. Lt. Torgany
Ia: Hptm. v. Unruh
Res. D. R. 4
49. Res. Inf. Brig. (Oberst v. Helldorff): Res. I. R. 116, Res. I. R. 118
50. Res. Inf. Brig. (Oberst v. Bassewitz): Res. I. R. 168, Res. I. R. 83
Res. Feld-Art. Rgt. 25
1., and 2. Res./ Pi. Btl. 11

H.K.K. 1

Kdr. Gen.: Gen. Lt. Frhr. v. Richthofen
Chef: Obstlt. v. Raumer
Ib: Hptm. Simon
Jg. Btl. 11, Jg. Btl. 12 (1. sächs.), Jg. Btl. 13 (sächs.)

G.K.D.

Kdr.: Gen. Maj. v. Storch
Ia: Hptm. Niemann
Ib: Hptm. Graf Wolfskehl v. Reichenberg
1. G. Kav. Brig. (Oberst v. Baerensprung): Rgt. Gardes du Corps, G. K. R.
2. G. Kav. Brig. (Gen. Maj. Graf v. Rothkirch u. Trach): 1. G. U. R., 3. G. U. R.
3. G. Kav. Brig. (Oberst Frhr. v. Senden): 1. G. D. R., 2. G. D. R.
reit. Abt. 1. G. Feld-Art. Rgt.
1. G. MG-Abt., G. Jg. Btl., G. Schtz. Btl.

5. K.D.

Kdr.: Gen. Maj. v. Ilsemann
Ia: Maj. Buchfink
Ib: Hptm. Henning
9. Kav. Brig. (Gen. Maj. Rusche): D. R. 4, U. R. 10
11. Kav. Brig. (Oberst v. Wentzky u. Petersberg): Leib-Kür. Rgt. 1, D. R. 8
12. Kav. Brig. (Gen. Maj. Graf v. Pfeil u. Klein-Ellguth): H. R. 4, H. R. 6
reit. Abt. Feld-Art. Rgt. 5
MG-Abt. 1

H.K.K. 4

Kdr. Gen.: Gen. Lt. Frhr. v. Hollen
Chef: Obstlt. Frhr. v. Brandenstein
Ib: Hptm. Frhr. v. Willisen

Jg. Btl. 5, Jg. Btl. 6

3. K.D.

Kdr.: Gen. Lt. v. Unger
Ia: Hptm. Lamotte
Ib: Hptm. Graf v. Brandenstein-Zeppelin
16. Kav. Brig. (Oberst Kleemann): Jg. Rgt. z. Pf. 7, . Rgt. z. Pf. 8
22. Kav. Brig. (Oberst v. Wurmb): D. R. 5, H. R. 14
25. Kav. Brig. (Oberst v. Glasenapp): hess. Garde-Drag. Rgt. Nr. 23, hess. Leib-Drag. Rgt. Nr. 24
reit. Abt. Feld-Art. Rgt. 11
MG-Abt. 2

6. K.D.

Kdr.: Gen. Lt. Graf v. Schmettow
Ia: Hptm. v. Werner

Ib: Hptm. Klewitz
28. Kav. Brig. (Oberst v. Selchow): Leib-Drag. R. 20, D. R. 21
33. Kav. Brig. (Gen. Maj. v. Etzel): D. R. 9, D. R. 13
45. Kav. Brig. (Gen. Maj. v. Hofacker): H. R. 13, . Rgt. z. Pf. 13
reit. Abt. Feld-Art. Rgt. 8
MG-Abt. 6

5. ARMEE (A.H.Qu.: SAARBRÜCKEN)

Ob.Bef.: Gen. Lt. Wilhelm, Kronprinz des Deutschen Reiches und von Preußen
Chef: Gen. Lt. Schmidt v. Knobelsdorff
O.Qu.: Gen. Maj. Rogalla v. Bieberstein
Ia: Maj. v. Heymann
Ic: Maj. Ehrhardt
Ib: Hptm. Matthiaß
Id: Hptm. Wahl
Bba.: Hptm. Steinbömer

I. and II. / Fuß-Art. R. 6 (21 cm Mrs.)
II. and III. / Fuß-Art. 12 (21 cm Mrs.)
Pi. R. 20, Pi. R. 29
Feld-Flieg. Abt. 25

2. Landw. D.
Kdr.: Gen. Lt. Franke
Ia: Hptm. v. Strube
9. bayer. Mixed Landw. Brig. (Gen. Maj. Kießling): bayer. Landw. I. R. 6, bayer. Landw. I. R. 7, 1. Landw. Esk. bayer. III. A. K., 1. Landst. Bttr. Bayer. III. AK
13. Mixed Landw. Brig. (Gen. Maj. Saenger): Landw. I. R. 26, Landw. I. R. 27, Landw. Esk. IV. A. K., 1., and 2. Landst. Bttr. IV. A. K.
43. Mixed Landw. Brig. (Gen. Lt. v. der Lippe): Landw. I. R. 32, Landw. I. R. 83, 1. Landw. Esk. XI. A. K., 1., and 2. / excess Landw. Bttr. XI. A. K.
45. sächs. Mixed Landw. Brig. (Gen. Maj. v. Bosse): sächs. Landw. I. R. 100, sächs. Landw. I. R. 102, sächs. Landw. Esk. XII. A. K., sächs. Landst. Bttr. XII. A. K.
53. württ. Mixed Landw. Brig. (Gen. Maj. v. Oßwald): württ. Landw. I. R. 124, württ. Landw. I. R. 125, württ. 3. Landw. Esk. XIII. A. K., württ. Landst. Bttr. XIII. A. K.

V. Armeekorps

Kdr. Gen.: Gen. d. Inf. v. Strantz
Chef: Obstlt. v. Kessel
Ia: Maj. Dove
Ic: Hptm. Foerster
Ib: Hptm. Wachenfeld
Id: Hptm. Klug
kdt.: Hptm. Lüders

I. / Fuß-Art. R. 5 (s.F.H.)
Feld-Flieg. Abt. 19

9. I.D.
Kdr.: Gen. Lt. v. Below
Ia: Maj. Föhrenbach
U. R. 1
17. Inf. Brig. (Gen. Maj. Melms): I. R. 19, I. R. 58
18. Inf. Brig. (Gen. Maj. Falckenheiner): G. R. 7, I. R. 154
9. Feld-Art. Brig. (Gen. Maj. Müller): Feld-Art Rgt. 5, Feld-Art Rgt. 41
1./ Pi. Btl. 5

10. I.D.
Kdr.: Gen. Lt. Kosch
Ia: Maj. Aubert
Jg. Rgt. z. Pf. 1
19. Inf. Brig. (Gen. Maj. Liebeskind): G. R. 6, I. R. 46
20. Inf. Brig. (Gen. Maj. Frhr. v. der Horst): I. R. 47, I. R. 50
10. Feld-Art. Brig. (Gen. Maj. Frhr. v. Watter): Feld-Art Rgt. 20, Feld-Art Rgt. 56
2., and 3./ Pi. Btl. 5

XIII. Armeekorps (K.W.)

Kdr. Gen.: Gen d. Inf. v. Fabeck
Chef: Obstlt. v. Loßberg
Ia: Maj. Reinhardt
Ic: Hptm. v. Brandenstein
Ib: Hptm. Friese
Id: Hptm. Deutelmoser

I. / Fuß-Art. R. 13 (s.F.H.)
Feld-Flieg. Abt. 4

26. I.D.
Kdr.: Gen. Lt. Wilhelm, Herzog v. Urach, Graf von Württemberg
Ia: Maj. Wöllwarth
U. R. 20
51. Inf. Brig. (Gen. Maj. v. Stein): G. R. 119, I. R. 125
52. Inf. Brig. (Gen. Maj. v. Teichmann): I. R. 121, F. R. 122
26. Feld-Art. Brig. (Gen. Maj. v. Mohn): Feld-Art Rgt. 29, Feld-Art Rgt. 65
1./ Pi. Btl. 13

27. I.D.
Kdr.: Gen. Lt. Graf v. Pfeil und Klein-Ellguth
Ia: Maj. Frhr. von Stotzingen
U. R. 19
53. Inf. Brig. (Gen. Maj. v. Moser): G. R. 123, I. R. 124

54. Inf. Brig. (Gen. Maj. Langer): I. R. 120, I. R. 127
27. Feld-Art. Brig. (Gen. Maj. v. Bernhard): Feld-Art Rgt. 13, Feld-Art Rgt. 49
2., and 3./ Pi. Btl. 13

XVI. Armeekorps

Kdr. Gen.: Gen. d. Inf. v. Mudra
Chef: Oberst v. Borries
Ia: Maj. Frhr. v. Esebeck
Ic: Hptm. v. Größnitz
Ib: Hptm. Koethe
Id: Hptm. v. Brauchitsch
Kdt.: Hptm. Lübcke

I. / Fuß-Art. R. 10 (s.F.H.)
Feld-Flieg. Abt. 2

33. I.D.
Kdr.: Gen. Lt. Reitzenstein
Ia: Maj. Ludwig
Jg. Rgt. z. Pf. 12
66. Inf. Brig. (Oberst Heuer): I. R. 98, I. R. 130
67. Inf. Brig. (Gen. Maj. Brosius): I. R. 135, I. R. 144
33. Feld-Art. Brig. (Gen. Maj. Merling): Feld-Art Rgt. 33, Feld-Art Rgt. 34
1./ Pi. Btl. 16

34. I.D.
Kdr. Gen. Lt. Heinemann
Ia: Hptm. v. Greiff
U. R. 14
68. Inf. Brig. (Gen. Maj. v. Estorff): I. R. 67, I. R. Königs I. R. 145
86. Inf. Brig. (Gen. Maj. Miesitschek v. Wischkau): I. R. 30, I. R. 173
34. Feld-Art. Brig. (Gen. Maj. v. Müller): Feld-Art Rgt. 69, Feld-Art Rgt. 70
2., and 3./ Pi. Btl. 16

V. Reservekorps

Kdr. Gen.: Gen. d. Inf. v. Gündell
Chef: Obstlt. v. Stockhausen
Ia: Maj. Hasse (Otto)
Ic: Hptm. Sichting
Ib: Hptm. Franke
Id: Hptm. Hemmerich

9. R.D.
Kdr.: Gen. Lt. v. Guretzky-Cornitz
Ia: Hptm. Frhr. v. Mirbach

Res. D. R. 3
17. Res. Inf. Brig. (Oberst Schrötter): Res. I. R. 6, Res. I. R. 7
19. Res. Inf. Brig. (Gen. Lt. v. Wyszecki): Res. I. R. 19, Res. Jg. Btl. 5
Res. Feld-Art. Rgt. 9
4./ Pi. Btl. 5

10. R.D.
Kdr.: Gen. Lt. v. Wartenberg
Ia: Hptm. Kewisch
Res. U. R. 6
77. Inf. Brig. (Gen. Maj. v. Dewitz): F. R. 37, Res. I. R. 155
18. Res. Inf. Brig. (Gen. Maj. Glahn): Res. I. R. 37, Res. I. R. 46
Res. Feld-Art. Rgt. 10
1., and 2. Res./ Pi. Btl. 5

VI. Reservekorps

Kdr. Gen.: Gen. d. Inf. v. Goßler
Chef: Oberst v. Rath
Ia: Maj. Hecker
Ic: Hptm. v. Stünzner
Ib: Hptm. Beck
Id: Hptm. Schwantes

11. R.D.
Kdr.: Gen. Maj. Surén
Ia: Hptm. Franck-Lindheim
Res. H. R. 4
23. Inf. Brig. (Oberst v. Götzen): I. R. 22, Res. I. R. 156
21. Res. Inf. Brig. (Oberst v. Gallwitz gen. Dreyling): Res. I. R. 10, Res. I. R. 11
Res. Feld-Art. Rgt. 11
4./ Pi. Btl. 6

12. R.D.
Kdr.: Gen. Lt. Frhr. v. Lüttwitz
Ia: Hptm. v. Kahlden
Res. U. R. 4
22. Res. Inf. Brig. (Gen. Maj. v. Leyser): Res. I. R. 23, Res. I. R. 38, Res. Jg. Btl. 6
23. Res. Inf. Brig. (Gen. Maj. Frhr. v. Wilmowski): Res. I. R. 22, Res. I. R. 51
Res. Feld-Art. Rgt. 21
1., and 2. Res./ Pi. Btl. 6

6. ARMEE (A.H.Qu.: St. AVOLD)

Ob.Bef.: Gen. Oberst. Rupprecht, Kronprinz von Bayern
Chef: Gen. Maj. Krafft v. Dellmensingen

O.Qu.: Gen. Maj. v. Hartz
Ia: Maj. Ritter Mertz v. Quirnheim
Ic: Maj. Hassenstein
Ib: Maj. Ritter v. Xylander
Id: Maj. Hierl
Bba.: Hptm. Haußer
kdt.: Maj. Benzien

II., and III. / Fuß-Art. R. 18 (21 cm Mrs.)
II. / bayer. 3. Fuß-Art. R. (21 cm Mrs.)
2. schw. Küstenmörser-Bttr. (30,5 cm Mrs. β-Gerät, Hptm. v. Theobald)
1. kurze Marine-Kanonen-Bttr. (42 cm Mrs. γ-Gerät, K.S. Hptm. Solf)
Pi. R. 19, bayer. Pi. R.
Feld-Flieg. Abt. 5

Bayer. E.D.
Kdr.: Gen. d. Inf. Ritter v. Benzino
Ia: Maj. Schmitt (Konstantin)
1. bayer. Mixed Ers. Brig. (Gen. Maj. Grüber): bayer. Brig. Ers. Btl.1, bayer. Brig. Ers. Btl. 2, bayer. Brig. Ers. Btl. 3, bayer. Brig. Ers. Btl. 4, Kav. Ers. Abt. München, 1. bayer. Feld-Art. Ers. Abt., 4. bayer. Feld-Art. Ers. Abt., 2. Ers. / bayer. Pi. Btl. 1
9. Bayer. Mixed Ers. Brig. (Gen. Maj. Krieger): bayer. Brig. Ers. Btl. 9, bayer. Brig. Ers. Btl. 10, bayer. Brig. Ers. Btl. 11, bayer. Brig. Ers. Btl. 12, Kav. Ers. Abt. Nürnberg, 8. bayer. Feld-Art. Ers. Abt., 10. bayer. Feld-Art. Ers. Abt., 1. Ers. / bayer. Pi. Btl. 3

4. E.D.[3]
Kdr.: Gen. Lt. v. Werder
Ia: Maj. v. Wittich
9. Mixed Ers. Brig. (Gen. Maj. Trip): Brig. Ers. Btl. 9, Brig. Ers. Btl. 10, Brig. Ers. Btl. 11, Brig. Ers. Btl. 12, Kav. Ers. Esk. III. A. K., Feld-Art. Ers. Abt. 18, Feld-Art. Ers. Abt. 39, 2. Ers. / Pi. Btl. 3
13. Mixed Ers. Brig. (Gen. Maj. Quade): Brig. Ers. Btl. 13, Brig. Ers. Btl. 14, Brig. Ers. Btl. 15, Brig. Ers. Btl. 16, Kav. Ers. Esk. IV. A. K., Feld-Art. Ers. Abt. 40, Feld-Art. Ers. Abt. 75, 1. Ers. / Pi. Btl. 4
33. Mixed Ers. Brig. (Gen. Lt. Melior): Brig. Ers. Btl. 33, Brig. Ers. Btl. 34, Brig. Ers. Btl. 35, Brig. Ers. Btl. 36, Brig. Ers. Btl. 81, Kav. Ers. Esk. IX. A. K., Feld-Art. Ers. Abt. 45, Feld-Art. Ers. Abt. 60, 1. Ers. / Pi. Btl. 9

8. E.D.
Kdr.: Gen. d. Kav. v. Hausmann
Ia: Maj. v. Lengerke
29. Mixed Ers. Brig. (Gen. Lt. Kosch): Brig. Ers. Btl. 29, Brig. Ers. Btl. 30, Brig. Ers. Btl. 31, Brig. Ers. Btl. 32, Brig. Ers. Btl. 80, Brig. Ers. Btl. 86, Kav. Ers. Esk. VIII. A. K., Feld-Art. Ers. Abt. 23, Feld-Art. Ers. Abt. 44

---

[3] E.D. means "Ersatz Division"

51. Mixed Ers. Brig. (Gen. Maj. v. Steinhardt): Brig. Ers. Btl. 51, Brig. Ers. Btl. 52, Brig. Ers. Btl. 53, Brig. Ers. Btl. 54, Kav. Ers. Esk. XIII. A. K., Feld-Art. Ers. Abt. 29, Feld-Art. Ers. Abt. 65
41. Mixed Ers. Brig. (Gen. Maj. v. Grolmann): Brig. Ers. Btl. 41, Brig. Ers. Btl. 42, Brig. Ers. Btl. 49, Brig. Ers. Btl. 50, Kav. Ers. Esk. XVIII. A. K., Feld-Art. Ers. Abt. 25, Feld-Art. Ers. Abt. 27, 1. Ers. / Pi. Btl. 21

10. E.D.
Kdr.: Gen. d. Inf. Frhr. v. Gayl
Ia: Hptm. Adolph
25. Mixed Ers. Brig. (Gen. Maj. Biß): Brig. Ers. Btl. 25, Brig. Ers. Btl. 26, Brig. Ers. Btl. 27, Brig. Ers. Btl. 28, Brig. Ers. Btl. 79, Kav. Ers. Esk. VII. A. K., Feld-Art. Ers. Abt. 22, Feld-Art. Ers. Abt. 43
37. Mixed Ers. Brig. (Gen. Lt. Baron Digeon v. Monteton): Brig. Ers. Btl. 37, Brig. Ers. Btl. 38, Brig. Ers. Btl. 39, Brig. Ers. Btl. 40, Kav. Ers. Esk. X. A. K., Feld-Art. Ers. Abt. 46, Feld-Art. Ers. Abt. 62, 1. Ers. / Pi. Btl. 10
43. Mixed Ers. Brig. (Gen. Lt. Frhr. v. Willisen): Brig. Ers. Btl. 43, Brig. Ers. Btl. 44, Brig. Ers. Btl. 76, Brig. Ers. Btl. 83, Kav. Ers. Esk. XI. A. K., Feld-Art. Ers. Abt. 47, Feld-Art. Ers. Abt. 55, 3. Ers. / Pi. Btl. 11

1. bayer. Mixed Landw. Brig. (Gen. Maj. Eichhorn): bayer. Landw. I. R. 1, bayer. Landw. I. R. 2, 1. Landw. E. bayer. I. A. K., 1. Landst. Bttr. Bayer. I. AK, 1. Landst. Pi. Kp. Bayer. I. A. K.

2. bayer. Mixed Landw. Brig. (Gen. Maj. v. Lachemair): bayer. Landw. I. R. 3, bayer. Landw. I. R. 12, 2. Landw. E. bayer. I. A. K., 2. Landst. Bttr. Bayer. I. AK, 2. Landst. Pi. Kp. Bayer. I. A. K., 1. / Fuß-Art. R. 16

5. bayer. Mixed Landw. Brig. (Gen. Maj. Wening): bayer. Landw. I. R. 4, bayer. Landw. I. R. 5, 1. Landw. E. bayer. II. A. K., 1. Landst. Bttr. Bayer. II. AK

I. bayer. Armeekorps

Kdr. Gen.: Gen. d. Inf. Ritter v. Xylander
Chef: Oberst Frhr. Nagel zu Aichberg
Ia: Maj. Hemmer
Ic: Hptm. Leeb
Ib: Hptm. Frhr. v. Berchem
Id: Hptm. Deuringer

II. / bayer. 1. Fuß-Art. R. (s.F.H.)
bayer. Feld-Flieg. Abt. 1

1. bayer. I.D.
Kdr.: Gen. Lt. Ritter v. Schoch (Albert)
Ia: Maj. Kaspar
Ch. R. 8
1. bayer. Inf. Brig. (Gen. Maj. Rauchenberger): bayer. Inf. Leib-Rgt., bayer. I. R. 1
2. bayer. Inf. Brig. (Gen. Maj. Ritter v. Endres): bayer. I. R. 2, bayer. I. R. 16

1. bayer. Feld-Art. Brig. (Gen. Maj. Frhr. v. Stein): bayer. Feld-Art Rgt. 1, bayer. Feld-Art Rgt. 7
1., and 3./ bayer. Pi. Btl. 1

2. bayer. I.D.
Kdr.: Gen. Lt. Ritter v. Hetzel
Ia: Maj. Graf v. Holstein aus Bayern
Ch. R. 4
3. bayer. Inf. Brig. (Gen. Maj. Schoch, Emil): bayer. I. R. 3, bayer. I. R. 20
4. bayer. Inf. Brig. (Gen. Maj. Schoch, Karl): bayer. I. R. 12, bayer. I. R. 15
2. bayer. Feld-Art. Brig. (Gen. Maj. Usselmann): bayer. Feld-Art Rgt. 4, bayer. Feld-Art Rgt. 9
2./ bayer. Pi. Btl. 1

II. bayer. Armeekorps

Kdr. Gen.: Gen. d. Inf. Ritter v. Martini
Chef: Obstlt. Stängl
Ia: Maj. Schraudenbach
Ic: Maj. Graf v. Luxburg
Ib: Hptm. v. Griesheim
Id: Hptm. List

I. / bayer. 1. Fuß-Art. R. (s.F.H.)
bayer. Feld-Flieg. Abt. 2

3. bayer. I.D.
Kdr.: Gen. Lt. Ritter v. Breitkopf
Ia: Maj. Trautmann
Ch. R. 3
5. bayer. Inf. Brig. (Gen. Maj. Danner): bayer. I. R. 22, bayer. I. R. 23
6. bayer. Inf. Brig. (Gen. Maj. Clauß): bayer. I. R. 17, bayer. I. R. 18
3. bayer. Feld-Art. Brig. (Oberst Held): bayer. Feld-Art Rgt. 5, bayer. Feld-Art Rgt. 12
1., and 3./ bayer. Pi. Btl. 2

4. bayer. I.D.
Kdr.: Gen. Lt. Graf v. Montgelas
Ia: Maj. Seißer
Ch. R. 3
7. bayer. Inf. Brig. (Gen. Maj. Henigst): bayer. I. R. 5, bayer. I. R. 9
5. bayer. Res. Inf. Brig. (Gen. Maj. Mark): bayer. Res. I. R. 5, bayer. Res. I. R. 8
3. bayer. Feld-Art. Brig. (Gen. Maj. Burkhard): bayer. Feld-Art Rgt. 2, bayer. Feld-Art Rgt. 11
2./ bayer. Pi. Btl. 2

III. bayer. Armeekorps

Kdr. Gen.: Gen. d. Kav. Frhr. v. Gebsattel
Chef: Obstlt. Braun

Ia: Maj. Frhr. Kreß v. Kressenstein
Ic: Hptm. Hörauf
Ib: Hptm. Eberth
Id: Hptm. Kriebel

I. / bayer. 3. Fuß-Art. R. (s.F.H.)
bayer. Feld-Flieg. Abt. 3

5. bayer. I.D.
Kdr.: Gen. Lt. Ritter v. Schoch
Ia: Maj. Ritter v. Reichert
Ch. R. 7
9. bayer. Inf. Brig. (Gen. Maj. Jäger): bayer. I. R. 14, bayer. I. R. 21, bayer. Res. Jg. Btl. 2
10. bayer. Inf. Brig. (Gen. Maj. v. Heydenaber): bayer. I. R. 7, bayer. I. R. 19
5. bayer. Feld-Art. Brig. (Gen. Maj. Paul): bayer. Feld-Art Rgt. 6, bayer. Feld-Art Rgt. 10
1., and 3./ bayer. Pi. Btl. 3

6. bayer. I.D.
Kdr.: Gen. Lt. Ritter v. Höhn
Ia: Maj. Schmitt (Paul)
Ch. R. 2
11. bayer. Inf. Brig. (Gen. Maj. Lang): bayer. I. R. 10, bayer. I. R. 13
12. bayer. Inf. Brig. (Gen. Maj. v. Kirschbaum): bayer. I. R. 6, bayer. I. R. 11
6. bayer. Feld-Art. Brig. (Gen. Maj. Ritter v. Eyßling): bayer. Feld-Art Rgt. 3, bayer. Feld-Art Rgt. 8
2./ bayer. Pi. Btl. 3

XXI. Armeekorps

Kdr. Gen.: Gen. d. Inf. v. Below (Fritz)
Chef: Oberst v. Haxthausen
Ia: Maj. Völckers
Ic: Hptm. v. Massow
Ib: Hptm. Wäninger
Id: Hptm. v. Kluge
kdt.: Hptm. Richter

II. Fuß-Art. R. 3 (s.F.H.)
Feld-Flieg. Abt. 8

31. I.D.
Kdr.: Gen. Lt. v. Berrer
Ia: Maj. Riedel
U. R. 7
32. Inf. Brig. (Gen. Maj. v. Behr): I. R. 70, I. R. I. R. 174
62. Inf. Brig. (Gen. Maj. Maschke): I. R. 60, I. R. 137, I. R. 166
31. Feld-Art. Brig. (Gen. Maj. Glokke): Feld-Art Rgt. 31, Feld-Art Rgt. 67
1./ Pi. Btl. 27

42. I.D.
Kdr.: Gen. Lt. v. Bredow
Maj. Bürkner
D. R. 7
59. Inf. Brig. (Gen. Maj. v. Wurmb): I. R. 97, I. R. I. R. 138
65. Inf. Brig. (Gen. Maj. v. Kehler, 18.8. verwundet) : I. R. 17, I. R. 131
42. Feld-Art. Brig. (Oberst Krahmer): Feld-Art Rgt. 8, Feld-Art Rgt. 15
2., and 3./ Pi. Btl. 27

I. bayer. Reservekorps

Kdr. Gen.: Gen. d. Inf. Ritter v. Fasbender
Chef: Oberst v. Lossow
Ia: Maj. Lenz
Ic: Maj. Frhr. v. Riedel
Ib: Hptm. Baur
Id: Hptm. Preitner

1. bayer. R.D.
Kdr.: Gen. Lt. Göringer
Ia: Maj. Ruith (Adolf)
bayer. Res. Kav. Rgt. 1
1. bayer. Res. Inf. Brig. (Gen. Maj. Frhr. v. Reitzenstein): bayer. Res. I. R. 1, bayer. Res. I. R. 2
2. bayer. Res. Inf. Brig. (Gen. Maj. Ritter v. Graf): bayer. Res. I. R. 3, bayer. Res. I. R. 12
bayer. Res. Feld-Art Rgt. 1
1. Res./ bayer. Pi. Btl. 1

5. bayer. R.D.
Kdr.: Gen. d. Inf. Frhr. Kreß v. Kressenstein
Ia: Maj. Ruith (August)
bayer. Res. Kav. Rgt. 5
9. bayer. Inf. Brig. (Gen. Lt. Hurt): bayer. Res I. R. 6, bayer. Res. I. R. 7
11. bayer. Inf. Brig. (Gen. Maj. Reuter): bayer. Res. I. R. 10, bayer. Res. I. R. 13, bayer. Res. Jg. Btl. 1
bayer. Res. Feld-Art Rgt. 5
1., and 3./ bayer. Pi. Btl. 2

H.K.K. 3

Kdr.: Gen. d. Kav. Ritter v. Frommel
Chef: Maj. v. Meiß
Ia: Maj. Graf v. Podewils-Dürniz

1. bayer. Jg. Btl., 2. bayer. Jg. Btl.

Bayer. K.D.
Kdr.: Gen. Lt. v. Stetten
Ia: Maj. Graf v. Tattenbach

Ib: Hptm. Jahreiß
1. bayer. Kav. Brig. (Gen. Maj. v. Staudt): bayer. 1. schw. Reiter Rgt., bayer. 2. schw. Reiter Rgt.
4. bayer. Kav. Brig. (Oberst Frhr. v. Crailsheim): bayer. U. R. 1, bayer. U. R. 2
5. bayer. Kav. Brig. (Gen. Maj. v. Hößlein): 1. Ch. R., 6. Ch. R.
reit. Abt. bayer. Feld-Art. R. 5
bayer. MG-Abt. 1

7. K.D.
Kdr.: Gen. Lt. v. Heydebreck
Ia: Maj. Frhr. v. Rotberg
Ib: Hptm. Prausnitzer
26. Kav. Brig. (Gen. Maj. Herzog Norbert v. Württemberg): D. R. 25, D. R. 26
30. Kav. Brig. (Oberst v. Graevenitz): D. R. 15, H. R. 9
42. Kav. Brig. (Gen. Maj. v. Koscielski): U. R. 11, U. R. 15
reit. Abt. Feld-Art. R. 5
MG-Abt. 3

8. K.D.
Kdr.: Gen. Lt. Graf v. d. Schulenburg
Ia: Maj. Tillmanns
Ib: Hptm. v. Schwerdtner
23. Kav. Brig. (Gen. Maj. v. der Decken): sächs. Garde Reiter Rgt., U. R. 17
38. Kav. Brig. (Gen. Maj. Weinschenk): Jg. Rgt. z. Pf. 2, Jg. Rgt. z. Pf. 6
40. Kav. Brig. (Gen. Maj. Frhr. v. Luttitz): sächs. Carabiniers Rgt., U. R. 21
reit. Abt. Feld-Art. R. 12
MG-Abt. 8

7. ARMEE (A.H.Qu.: STRAßBURG)

Ob.Bef.: Gen. Oberst. v. Heeringen
Chef: Gen. Lt. v. Hänisch
O.Qu.: Gen. Maj. v. Zieten
Ia: Obstlt. Frhr. v. Blomberg
Ic: Maj. v. Hahnke (Oskar)
Ib: Hptm. Kaupisch
Id: Hptm. v. Theobald
Bba.: Hptm. Thränhardt

Feld-Flieg. Abt. 26

Garde Ersatz Division
Kdr.: Gen. Lt. v. Twardowski
Ia: Hptm. v. Marklowski
1. Mixed G. Ers. Brig. (Gen. Lt. v. Harbou): G. Brig. Ers. Btl. 1, G. Brig. Ers. Btl. 2, G. Brig. Ers. Btl. 3, G. Brig. Ers. Btl. 4, Brig. Ers. Btl. 5, Brig. Ers. Btl. 6, Kav. Ers. Esk. G. K., 1. G. Feld-Art. Ers. Abt., 2. G. Feld-Art. Ers. Abt.

5. Mixed Ers. Brig. (Gen. Maj. v. Eberhardt): Brig. Ers. Btl. 5, Brig. Ers. Btl. 6, Brig. Ers. Btl. 7, Brig. Ers. Btl. 8, Kav. Ers. Esk. II. A. K., Feld-Art. Ers. Abt. 38, Feld-Art. Ers. Abt. 53, 1. Ers. / Pi. Btl. 2
17. Mixed Ers. Brig. (Gen. Lt. Rieß v. Scheuernschloß): Brig. Ers. Btl. 17, Brig. Ers. Btl. 18, Brig. Ers. Btl. 19, Brig. Ers. Btl. 20, Brig. Ers. Btl. 77, Kav. Ers. Esk. V. A. K., Feld-Art. Ers. Abt. 20, Feld-Art. Ers. Abt. 41

XIV. Armeekorps

Kdr. Gen.: Gen. d. Inf. Frhr. v. Hoiningen, gen. Huene
Chef: Obstlt. v. Brauchitsch
Ia: Maj. v. Lettow-Vorbeck
Ic: Hptm. Thümmel
Ib: Hptm. v. Sydow
Id: Hptm. v. Oppeln-Bronikowski
kdt.: Hptm. Fischer

II. / Fuß-Art. R. 14(s.F.H.)
Feld-Flieg. Abt. 20

28. I.D.
Kdr.: Gen. Lt. v. Kehler
Ia: Maj. Henning auf Schönhoff
Jg. Rgt. z. Pf. 5
55. Inf. Brig. (Oberst v. Olszewski): bad. Leib-Gren. R. 109, G. R. 110
56. Inf. Brig. (Gen. Maj. Freyer): F. R. 40, I. R. 111
28. Feld-Art. Brig. (Gen. Maj. Fabarius): Feld-Art Rgt. 14, Feld-Art Rgt. 50
2., and 3./ Pi. Btl. 14

29. I.D.
Kdr.: Gen. Lt. Isbert
Ia: Maj. Helfritz
D. R. 22
57. Inf. Brig. (Gen. Maj. v. Trotta gen. Treyden): I. R. 113, I. R. I. R. 114
58. Inf. Brig. (Gen. Maj. Stenger): I. R. 112, I. R. 142
84. Inf. Brig. (Gen. Maj. v. Zaborowski): I. R. 169, I. R. 170
29. Feld-Art. Brig. (Oberst Hamann): Feld-Art Rgt. 30, Feld-Art Rgt. 76
1./ Pi. Btl. 14

19. E.D.
Kdr.: Gen. Lt. Müller
Ia: Maj. Ritter and Edler Herr v. Berger
21. Mixed Ers. Brig. (Gen. Lt. v. Busse): Brig. Ers. Btl. 21, Brig. Ers. Btl. 22, Brig. Ers. Btl. 23, Brig. Ers. Btl. 24, Brig. Ers. Btl. 78, Kav. Ers. Esk. VI. A. K., Feld-Art. Ers. Abt. 6, Feld-Art. Ers. Abt. 57
45. Mixed Ers. Brig. (Gen. Maj. Frhr. v. Bodenhausen): Brig. Ers. Btl. 45, Brig. Ers. Btl. 46, Brig. Ers. Btl. 63, Brig. Ers. Btl. 64, sächs. Kav. Ers. Esk. XII. A. K., Feld-Art. Ers. Abt. 28, Feld-Art. Ers. Abt. 48, 1. Ers. / Pi. Btl. 12

47. Mixed Ers. Brig. (Gen. Maj. Schönberg): Brig. Ers. Btl. 47, Brig. Ers. Btl. 48, Brig. Ers. Btl. 88, Brig. Ers. Btl. 89, sächs. Kav. Ers. Esk. XIX. A. K., Feld-Art. Ers. Abt. 32, Feld-Art. Ers. Abt. 77, 1. Ers. / Pi. Btl. 22

XV. Armeekorps

Kdr. Gen.: Gen. d. Inf. v. Deimling
Chef: Obstlt. Wild
Ia: Maj. Meister
Ic: Hptm. Fischer
Ib: Hptm. v. Kalm
Id: Hptm. v. Schickfus u. Neudorff
kdt. Hptm. Starke

II. / Fuß-Art. R. 10(s.F.H.)
Feld-Flieg. Abt. 3

30. I.D.
Kdr.: Gen. Lt. v. Eben
Ia: Maj. Frhr. v. Nettelbladt
Jg. Rgt. z. Pf. 3
60. Inf. Brig. (Gen. Maj. v. Altrock): I. R. 99, I. R. I. R. 143
85. Inf. Brig. (Oberst Nagel): I. R. 105, I. R. 136
30. Feld-Art. Brig. (Oberst Goeden): Feld-Art Rgt. 51, Feld-Art Rgt. 84
1./ Pi. Btl. 15

39. I.D.
Kdr.: Gen. Lt. Frhr. v. Watter
Ia: Maj. Frhr. v. Bernewitz
D. R. 14
61. Inf. Brig. (Gen. Maj. v. Frankenberg u. Ludwigsdorf): I. R. 126, I. R. I. R. 132, Jg. Btl. 8
82. Inf. Brig. (Gen. Maj. Sommerfeld): I. R. 171, I. R. 172, Jg. Btl. 14
39. Feld-Art. Brig. (Gen. Maj. Erythropel): Feld-Art Rgt. 66, Feld-Art Rgt. 80
2., and 3./ Pi. Btl. 15

XIV. Reservekorps

Kdr. Gen.: Gen. d. Art. v. Schubert
Chef: Obstlt. Bronsart v. Schellendorff (Bernhard)
Ia: Maj. Brüggemann
Ic: Hptm. Buchrucker
Ib: Hptm. Riedel
Id: Hptm. v. Bose

26. R.D.
Kdr.: Gen. d. Inf. Frhr. v. Soden
Ia: Hptm. Frhr. Seutter v. Lötzen
württ. Res. D. R.

51. Res. Inf. Brig. (Gen. Lt. Wundt): Res. I. R. 180, Res. I. R. 121
52. Res. Inf. Brig. (Gen. Lt. v. Auwaerter): Res. I. R. 119, Res. I. R. 120
Res. Feld-Art. Rgt. 26
4. Res./ Pi. Btl. 13

28. R.D.
Kdr.: Gen. Lt. v. Pavel
Ia: Maj. Frhr. v. Coburg
Res. D. R. 8
55. Res. Inf. Brig. (Gen. Lt. v. Sieg): Res. I. R. 49, Res. I. R. 109, Res. Jg. Btl. 8
56. Res. Inf. Brig. (Gen. Maj. v. Hammerstein-Equord): Res. I. R. 110, Res. I. R. 111, Res. Jg. Btl. 14
Res. Feld-Art. Rgt. 28
und 2. Res./ Pi. Btl. 13

8. ARMEE (A.H.Qu.: MARIENBURG)

Ob.Bef.: Gen. Oberst. v. Prittwitz u. Gaffron
Chef: Gen. Maj. Graf v. Waldersee (Georg)
Adj.: Hptm. Zippert
O.Qu.: Oberst Grünert
O.Qu II.: Oberst v. Groddeck
Abt. Chef.: Oberst Graf v. Posadowsky-Wehner
General d. Pi.: Gen. Maj. Kersten
Ia: Obstlt. Hoffmann
Ic: Maj. Drechsel
Ib: Hptm. v. Vollard-Bockelberg
Id: Hptm. Mierzinsky
Bba.: Hptm. Sperr
kdt.: Maj. v. Eggling

Feld-Flieg. Abt. 16, Luftschiff Zeppelin Z5 (Posen), Luftschiff Schütte-Lanz (Liegnitz)

3. R.D.
Kdr.: Gen. Maj. v. Morgen
Ia: Maj. Frantz
Res. D. R. 5
5. Res. Inf. Brig. (Gen. Maj. Hesse): Res. I. R. 2, Res. I. R. 9,
6. Res. Inf. Brig. (Gen. Maj. Krause): Res. I. R. 34, Res. I. R. 49
Res. Feld-Art. Rgt. 5
2. Res./ Pi. Btl. 2

1. K.D.
Kdr.: Gen. Lt. Brecht
Ia: Hptm. v. Stephany
Ib: Hptm. Frhr. v. Gienanth
1. Kav. Brig. (Oberst v. Glasenapp): K. R. 3, D. R. 1

2. Kav. Brig. (Gen. Maj. Frhr. v. Kap-herr): U. R. 12, Jg. Rgt. z. Pf. 9
41. Kav. Brig. (Gen. Maj. v. Hofmann): K. R. 5, U. R. 4
reit. Abt. Feld-Art. R. 1
MG-Abt. 5

6. Mixed Landw. Brig. (Gen. Maj. Krahmer): Landw. I. R. 34, Landw. I. R. 49, 1., 2., and 3. Landw. Esk. II A. K., Landst. Feld-Art. Bttr. II A. K.

70. Mixed Landw. Brig. (Gen. Maj. Breithaupt): Landw. I. R. 5, Landw. I. R. 18, 2., and 3. Landw. Esk. XVII A. K., 1., 2., and 3. Landw. Esk. XX. A. K., 1., and 2. Landst. Bttr. XVII A. K.

I. Armeekorps

Kdr. Gen.: Gen. Lt. v. François
Chef: Oberst Frhr. Schmidt v. Schmidtseck
Ia: Maj. v. Massow
Ic: Hptm. Jarosch
Ib: Hptm. Schubert
Id: Oblt. Karmann
kdt.: Hptm. Gempp

I. / Fuß-Art. R. 1 (s.F.H.)
Feld-Flieg. Abt. 14

1. I.D.
Kdr.: Gen. Lt. v. Conta
Ia: Maj. v. Graberg
U. R. 8
1. Inf. Brig. (Gen. Maj. v. Trotha): Gren. R. 1, I. R. 41
2. Inf. Brig. (Gen. Maj. Paschen): Gren. R. 3, I. R. 43
1. Feld-Art. Brig. (Gen. Maj. Moewes): Feld-Art Rgt. 16, Feld-Art Rgt. 52
1./ Pi. Btl. 1

2. I.D.
Kdr.: Gen. Lt. v. Falk
Ia: Hptm. Goedel
Jg. Rgt. z. Pf. 10
3. Inf. Brig. (Gen. Maj. Mengelbier): Gren. R. 4, I. R. 44
4. Inf. Brig. (Gen. Maj. Boeß): F. R. 33, I. R. 45
2. Feld-Art. Brig. (Gen. Maj. Fouquet): Feld-Art Rgt. 1, Feld-Art Rgt. 37
2., and 3./ Pi. Btl. 1

XVII. Armeekorps

Kdr. Gen.: Gen. d. Kav. v. Mackensen
Chef: Obstlt. v. Dunker
Ia: Maj. Graf v. Schwerin

Ic: Hptm. Graf v. Stillfried u. Rattonitz
Ib: Hptm. v. Bartenwerffer
Id: Hptm. v. Kalckreuth
kdt.: Hptm. Weste

I. / Fuß-Art. R. 11 (s.F.H.)
Feld-Flieg. Abt. 17

35. I.D.
Kdr.: Gen. Lt. Henning
Ia: Maj. Engelien
Jg. Rgt. z. Pf. 4
70. Inf. Brig. (Gen. Maj. Schmidt v. Knobelsdorff): I. R. 21, I. R. I. R. 61
87. Inf. Brig. (Gen. Maj. v. Hahn): I. R. 141, I. R. 176, Jg. Btl. 2 (until 21.8. to 1. K.D.)
35. Feld-Art. Brig. (Gen. Maj. Uhden): Feld-Art Rgt. 71, Feld-Art Rgt. 81
1./ Pi. Btl. 17

36. I.D.
Kdr.: Gen. Lt. v. Heineccius
Ia: Maj. v. Winnng
H. R. 5
69. Inf. Brig. (Gen. Maj. v. Engelbrechten)**:** I. R. 129, I. R. 175
71. Inf. Brig. (Oberst v. Dewitz): G. R. 5, I. R. 128
36. Feld-Art. Brig. (Gen. Maj. Hahndorff): Feld-Art Rgt. 36, Feld-Art Rgt. 72
2., and 3./ Pi. Btl. 17

XX. Armeekorps

Kdr. Gen.: Gen. d. Art. v. Scholtz
Chef: Oberst Hell
Ia: Maj. Kunhardt v. Schmidt
Ic: Hptm. Waenker v. Dankenschweil
Ib: Hptm. Erfurth
Id: Hptm. Fusban
kdt. Hptm. Volkmann

II. / Fuß-Art. R. 5 (s.F.H.)
Feld-Flieg. Abt. 15

37. I.D.
Kdr.: Gen. Lt. v. Staabs
Ia: Maj. v. Gazen gen. Gaza
D. R. 11
73. Inf. Brig. (Gen. Maj. Wilhelmi): I. R. 147, I. R. 151, Jg. Btl. 1
75. Inf. Brig.: (Gen. Maj. v. Böckmann) I. R. 146, I. R. 150, Jg. Btl. 2
37. Feld-Art. Brig. (Gen. Maj. Buchholz): Feld-Art Rgt. 73, Feld-Art Rgt. 82
1./ Pi. Btl. 26

41. I.D.
Kdr.: Gen. Maj. Sontag
Ia: Maj. Weniger
D. R. 10
72. Inf. Brig. (Gen. Maj. Schaer): I. R. 18, I. R. I59
74. Inf. Brig. (Gen. Maj. Reiser): I. R. 148, I. R. 152
41. Feld-Art. Brig. (Gen. Maj. Neugebauer): Feld-Art Rgt. 35, Feld-Art Rgt. 79
2., and 3./ Pi. Btl. 26

I. Reservekorps
Kdr. Gen.: Gen. Lt. v. Below (Otto)
Chef: Oberst v. Griesheim
Ia: Maj. Keller
Ic: Hptm. Fleck
Ib: Hptm. Tybusch
Id: Hptm. Müller (Ludwig)

1. R.D.
Kdr.: Gen. Lt. v. Förster
Ia: Hptm. Heinersdorf
Res. U. R. 1
1. Res. Inf. Brig. (Gen. Maj. Barre): Res. I. R. 1, Res. I. R. 3
72. Res. Inf. Brig. (Gen. Maj. Licht): Res. I. R. 18, Res. I. R. 59, Res. Jg. Btl. 1
Res. Feld-Art. Rgt. 1
4./ Pi. Btl. 2

36. R.D.
Kdr.: Gen. Maj. Kruge
Ia: Hptm. Boelcke
Res. H. R. 1
69. Res. Inf. Brig. (Gen. Maj. v. Homeyer): Res. I. R. 21, Res. I. R. 61, Res. Jg. Btl. 2
70. Res. Inf. Brig. (Gen. Maj. Vett): I. R. 54, Res. I. R. 5
Res. Feld-Art. Rgt. 36
1. Res./ Pi. Btl. 2

FESTUNGS-GOUVERNEMENT-STÄBE (FORTRESS COMMANDS)

Festung Königsberg (including Feste Boyen, Lötzen)
Gouv.: Gen. Lt. v. Pappritz
Chef: Obstlt. Nehbel
Ia: Maj. Jahn
Ib: Hptm. Friedrichs
Festungs-Flieger Abt. 5
Festungs-MG Abt. 1, Res. MG Abt. 1, 17 Ersatz- und Festungs-MG Kompanien

1. Landw. Brig.: Landw. I. R. 3, III. / Landw. I. R. 4
13 ½ Ers. Btlne. von Regimenter des I. and XX. A. K.
3 ½ Ersatz Eskadronen from I. and XX. A. K.
I. / G. Res. Fuß-Art. R. (21 cm Mrs.), I. Res. Fuß-Art. R. 4 (10 cm Kan.)
6 battalions and 8 batteries Ers., Landw. and Landst. Art.
2 battalions and 6 companies Ers., Landw., and Landst. Pi.

Landw. D. Königsberg (Hauptreserve Königsberg)
Kdr.: Gen. Lt. Brodtrück
Ia: N.N.
Res. D. R. 1, E. Kav. Rgt. I. A. K.
9. Landw. Brig.: Landw. I. R. 24, Landw. I. R. 48
Ers. Brig. Königsberg: E. I. R. 1, E. I. R. 2
Landst. Brig. Königsberg: Landsturm-Btl. Königsberg 1, Landsturm-Btl. Königsberg 2, Landsturm-Btl. Königsberg 3, Landsturm-Btl. Königsberg 4
II. / Res. Fuß-Art. R. 1 (21 cm Mrs.), II. / Res. Fuß-Art. R. 4 (10 cm Kan.)
4. / Pi. Btl. 1

2. Mixed Landw. Brig. (Oberst Frhr. v, Lupin): Landw. I. R. 3, Landw. I. R. 33, 1., and 2. Landw. E. I. A. K. Landw. Feld-Art. Abt. I. A. K.

Feste Boyen
Kdt.: Oberst Busse
Ia: N.N.
Festungs-Flieg. Abt. 7
11 Festungs-MG Kompanien
E. R. 147, IV./Landw. I. R. 18, 2 ½ Bataillone Landsturm, Festungs-MG Abt. 2, batteries Fuß-Artillerie (Fortress-artillery), 2 Landsturm batteries XX. AK, E. Esk. D. R. 11

Festung Thorn
Gouv.: Gen. Lt. v. Dickhuth-Harrach
Chef: Obstlt. Wachs
Ia: Maj. v. Thadden
Ib: Hptm. Schmidt

Festungs-MG Abt. 5,
II. / Res. Fuß-Art. 15

35. R.D. (Hauptreserve Thorn)
Kdr.: Gen. Maj. v. Schmettau
Ia: Hptm. Mertens
bayer. Schw. Res. Reiter Rgt. 3
5. Landw. Brig.: Landw. I. R. 2, Landw. I. R. 9
20. Landw. Brig.: Landw. I. R. 19, Landw. I. R. 107
E. Abt. Feld-Art. Rgt. 35
E. Abt. Feld-Art. Rgt. 81

Festung Graudenz
Gouv.: Gen. Lt. v. Zastrow
Chef: Obstlt. Wilckens
Ia: Maj. Stapf
Ib: Hptm. Liebmann

Festungs-MG Abt. 3, Festungs-MG Abt. 4
II. / Res. Fuß-Art. R. 17 (21 cm Mrs.)

Festung Posen
Gouv.: Gen. Lt. Koch v. Hernhaußen
Chef: Obstlt. Lequis
Ia: Maj. Merkel
Ib: Hptm. Heller

Festungs-Flieger Abt. 4
Festungs-MG Abt. 6, 2 x Res. Festungs-MG Abt.

18. Landw. D. (Hauptreserve Posen)
Kdr.: N.N.
Ia: N.N.
E. / Jg. Rgt. z. Pf. 1
Res. MG-Abt. 5
19. Landw. Brig.: Landw. I. R. 47, Landw. I. R. 72, Landw. I. R. 133
Feld-Art. E. Abt. 17, Feld-Art. E. Abt. 56
2. Res. / Pi. Btl. 1, 2. Res. / Pi. Btl. 26
I. / Res. Fuß-Art. R. 5 (10 cm Kan.), II. / Res. Fuß-Art. 6 (21 cm Mrs.)

Festung Breslau
Gouv.: Gen. Lt. Schalscha v. Ehrenfeld
Ia: Maj. Huebner

Festung Cöln
Gouv.: Gen. Lt. v. Wandel
Chef: Obstlt. Frhr. v. Salmuth
Ia: Maj. Budde
Ib: Hptm. Geyer

Festungs-MG Abt. 7

Festung Mainz
Gouv.: Gen. d. Inf. v. Kathen
Chef: Obstlt. Scherenberg
Ia: Maj. Füßlein
Ib: v. Nolte

Festungs-MG Abt. 8

Festung Germersheim
Gouv.: Gen. Lt. Ritter v. Fischer
Chef: Obstlt. Hierthes
Ia: Hptm. Voith

1. bayer. Landw. D. (Hauptreserve Germersheim, mobilized 21 August 1914)
Kdr.: N.N.
Ia: N.N.
E. / 2. G. U. R., 1. Landw. Esk. bayer. II. A. K.
bayer. 13. Landw. Brig.: bayer. Landw. I. R. 8, bayer. Landw. I. R. 10, bayer. Festungs-MG Abt. 4
bayer. 14. Landw. Brig.: bayer. Landw. I. R. 1, bayer. Landw. I. R. 2, württ. Landw. I. R. 122, bayer. Festungs-MG Abt. 5
bayer. Landst. Bttr. Landau
1. Landw. Pi. Kp. Bayer. I. A. K., 1. Landw. Pi. Kp. Bayer. II. A. K.

Festung Straßburg i. E. (including Feste Kaiser Wilhelm II, Mutzig)
Gouv.: Gen. Lt. v. Eberhardt
Chef: Obstlt. v. Böckmann
Ia: Maj. Mohs
Ib: Hptm. Hosse

Festungs-MG Abt. 9 (Straßburg), Festungs-MG Abt. Mutzig

30. R.D. (Hauptreserve Straßburg)
Kdr.: Gen. Lt. v. Knoerzer
Ia: Hptm. v. Schäfer
Res. H. R. 9
60. Res. Inf. Brig. (Gen. Lt. v. Hopffgarten): Res. I. R. 60, Res. I. R. 99
bayer. 3. Res. Inf. Brig. (Gen. Maj. v. Langhaeuser): bayer. 4. Res. I. R., bayer. 15. Res. I. R.
bayer. 10. Res. Inf. Brig. (Gen. Lt. Müller): bayer. Res. I. R. 11, bayer. Res. I. R. 14
bayer. 5. Ers. Brig. (Gen. Maj. Graf v. Zeck auf Neuhofen): bayer. E. I. R. 2, bayer. E. I. R. 4, 2., and 12. Bayer. Feld-Art. E. Abt.
Res. Fuß-Art. R. 14
1./ Pi. Btl. 15

Oberrhein-Befestigungen
Gouv.: Gen. Lt. v. Bodungen
Ia: Hptm. v. Loewenfeld

55. Mixed Landw. Brig. (Gen. Lt. v. Frech): Landw. I. R. 40, Landw. I. R. 109, 1., and 2. Landw. E. XIII. A. K., Landw. Feld-Art. Abt. XIV. A. K., Ers. Feld-Art. Abt. XXI. A. K.

60. Mixed Landw. Brig. (Gen. Maj. v. Heidborn): Landw. I. R. 60, Landw. I. R. 99, Landw. E. XIV. A. K.

55. Mixed E. Brig.: Brig. Ers. Btl. 55, Brig. Ers. Btl. 56, Brig. Ers. Btl. 57, Brig. Ers. Btl. 58, Brig. Ers. Btl. 82, Brig. Ers. Btl. 84, Kav. Ers. Abt. XIV. A. K., Feld-Art. Ers. Abt. 14, Feld-Art. Ers. Abt. 76

verst. bad. Landw. I.R. 110, 2. Landw. Esk. XIV. A. K., Ers. Feld-Art. Abt. XXI. A. K.

Festung Metz
Gouv.: Gen. d. Inf. v. Oven
Chef: Obstlt. Fischer
Ia: Maj. Madlung
Ib: Hptm. v. Westernhagen
Ic: Hptm. Verstl

Festungs-MG Abt. 12, Festungs-MG Abt. 13, Festungs-MG Abt. 14, Festungs-MG Abt. 15

33. R.D. (Hauptreserve Metz)
Kdr.: Gen. Maj. Bausch
Ia: Hptm. v. Ditfurth
Res. H. R. 2
66. Res. Inf. Brig. (Gen. Maj. Rehbach): Res. I. R. 67, Res. I. R. 130, Res. I. R. Metz
bayer. 8. Inf. Brig. (Gen. Maj. Riedl): bayer. I. R. 4, bayer. I. R. 8
E. Abt. Feld-Art. R. 33, E. Abt. Feld-Art. R. 34, E. Abt. Feld-Art. R. 69, E. Abt. Feld-Art. R. 70
I., and II. / bayer. 2. Res. Fuß-Art. R. (s.F.H.)

Festung Diedenhofen (Thionville)
Gouv.: Gen. Maj. v. Lochow
Ia: Hptm. Obkircher

Festungs-MG Abt. 11

Festung Ulm
Gouv.: Gen. Lt. v. Gerok
Chef: Obstlt. Launhardt
Ia: Hptm. Wittmer

Festung Berlin
Gouv.: Gen. Oberst. v. Kessel
Ia: Maj. v. Schwarzkoppen

APPENDIX G

BIOGRAPHICAL NOTES

This appendix contains short biographical notes on some of the major military leaders in imperial Germany between 1871 and 1914. We did not include all commanding generals in order to keep this appendix relatively short and concise. It is also not our intent to show any officer's career path from the imperial Army to the Wehrmacht or to trace the Wehrmacht élite to the War Academy of the Prussian Army—although such continuity certainly exists.

The Ranglisten only list officers by their last names and provide first names only if there were officers of the same family name and the same rank listed in the same year. Thus, it is particularly difficult to trace officers from aristocratic families that simultaneously supplied more than one member to the armed forces. This can lead to confusion if the text only refers to Moltke or to Generals v. d. Planitz or Graf v. Waldersee. Additionally, for some officers there is a great deal of literature available that gives a wealth of information. For other officers, no biographies exist at all, making it very difficult to establish facts such as birthday and date of death. The following notes are therefore not intended to serve as detailed and complete biographies but will give the reader an oververview of the person concerned based upon the available literature. These notes are of particular interest, because it is possible to trace, which career paths tended to lead an individual to key appointments later. Many individuals had a series of names. The name by which they were commonly known is in italics.

Albedyll, Emil v.

Emil Heinrich Ludwig von Albedyll, born 1 April 1824 in Liebenow, Pomerania; died 13 June 1897 in Potsdam.

- Started his military career as ordnance officer during the campaign against Denmark in 1848 where he participated in the battles of Schleswig, Düppel and Fredericia.
- On promotion to Rittmeister in 1858, he was transferred to the Department for Personal Matters in 1862.
- In 1864, Albedyll was promoted to Oberstleutnant and aide de camp and served during the 1864 campaign against Denmark in the General Headquarters.
- After the Franco-Prussian War, he became the first head of the newly founded military cabinet and maintained this position until 1888. He was one of the most influential officers of the Kaiserreich. He pulled strings behind the scenes and was the responsible advisor for the staffing of almost all positions in the army.
- In 1888, he became Commanding General of the VII Army Corps in Münster and retired in 1893.

Bauer, Max

Max Hermann Bauer, born 31 January 1869 in Quedlinburg; died 6 May 1929 in Shanghai.

- After earning his Abitur in 1888, he began studying law, but had to give up his studies because of the sudden financial problems of his father.
- Bauer joined Foot Artillery Regiment 2 as an officer candidate on 12 October 1888 and was promoted to Sekondelieutenant in January 1890.
- He served in foot artillery regiments in Danzig, Swinemünde and Metz before he joined the Artillerie-Prüfungskommission (Artillery Testing Committee) in January 1899. He remained there until September 1902.
- After this posting to the Artillerie-Prüfungskommission, he became a battery commander in Foot Artillery Regiment 7 located in Köln-Wahn until 1907. Subsequent to that he was transferred to the Great General Staff as a heavy artillery specialist.
- Major Bauer was one of the very few officers who was formally transferred (not just posted) to the Great General Staff without having graduated from the War Academy. Due to his experience and his service at the Artillerie-Prüfungskommission, he was exactly the expert on heavy artillery issues the General Staff needed after Schlieffen demanded more and heavier artillery to crush the French fortress belt.
- In the General Staff, Bauer analyzed the Russian forts and their performance in the Russo-Japanese War.
- He wrote a confidential analysis of the siege of Port Arthur and came to the conclusion that Port Arthur was crushed after the Japanese bombarded it with 28cm heavy guns.
- Together with Ludendorff, he pushed for the development of the super-heavy artillery and used unofficial channels to the Krupp factory to initiate the secret development of 42cm artillery pieces (See Chapter 14 on artillery doctrine).
- Upon mobilization, Major Bauer became O II of the Operations Department of the OHL.
- He managed the destruction of the Belgian forts at Liège in August 1914 with 30.5cm Skoda guns and 42cm Krupp guns.
- During the war, Bauer served as a kind of technical advisor to the OHL and was responsible for the development of flame-throwers and for the further development of gas shells.
- He was awarded the Pour le Mérite on 16 December 1916.
- After the war, Oberst Bauer was involved with several extremely right-wing volunteer units (Freikorps). Due to his participation in the Kapp-Lüttwitsch putsch, a warrant was issued for his arrest.
- In 1923, he accepted an invitation from Leon Trotsky to go to Moscow, where he supported the Soviet government with the building of weapons plants.
- Bauer paved the way for the secret cooperation between the Reichswehr and the Red Army to develop tanks, airplanes, and heavy artillery under concealment.
- Although Bauer was pardoned for his participation in the Kapp-Lüttwitz putsch, he continued working abroad and designed chemical weapons in Spain and artillery pieces for SIG in Switzerland. He travelled to China in 1927 to support Chiang Kai-Chek as a military advisor.
- Bauer died from typhus in 1929 in a British military hospital in Shanghai.

Bernhardi, Friedrich v.

Friedrich Adolf Julius von Bernhardi, born 22 November 1849 in St. Petersburg, Russia; died 11 December 1930 in Kunnersdorf, Silesia.

- Descended from an aristocratic Estonian family, Bernhardi was born in St. Petersburg and moved to Germany with his family in 1851.
- Bernhardi joined Husaren-Regiment Landgraf Friedrich II. von Hessen-Homburg (2 Kurhessisches) Nr. 14 in Kassel as an officer candidate and became a Sekondelieutenant in that regiment.
- During the Franco-Prussian War, Bernhardi served with Husaren-Regiment 14 and was honored for his bravery by leading the victory parade through the Arc de Triomphe in Paris.
- From 1875 until 1878, he completed studies at the War Academy and successfully graduated as a General Staff officer.
- In 1879, he joined the Topographical Department of the Great General Staff and was sent to Greece from 1882 until 1886 to carry out topographical tasks for the Greek government.
- Upon his return he was appointed as the Ia for the 15th Infantry Division.
- From 1891 until 1894, he became the military attaché in the Swiss capital of Bern.
- After returning from this diplomatic posting, he was appointed as Commander of the 1. Badisches Leib-Dragoner- Regiment Nr. 20.
- From 1898 until 1901, he headed the Military History Department of the Great General Staff and began work on the history of the wars of Frederick the Great. In this position Bernhardi pointed out similarities between the invasion of Saxony by Frederick the Great at the outset of the Seven Years War and the necessary violation of the Belgian neutrality during a German offensive on France. Bernhardi paved the way for Schlieffen to justify the necessary invasion of Belgium in order to bypass the French fortress belt.
- During this period, he also became a well-recognized author of military history and strategic theory. He was involved in the very polemic debate with the historian Hans Delbrück about the different approaches between strategies of attrition and annihilation.
- In 1901, he became Commander of the 30 Cavalry Brigade in Strasbourg and then took command of the 7th Division in Magdeburg in 1904. Eventually he became the Commanding General of the VII Army Corps in Münster.
- In 1909, Bernhardi resigned to focus on his new career as an author on military issues. He developed into a very influential author on cavalry issues. As such, Bernhardi took very conservative positions.
- In 1911 and 1912, he travelled around the world and held presentations concerning his theories and books in Eastern Asia, Egypt, and the United States.
- In 1912, he published the pivotal books *On Current War* (Vom heutigen Kriege), a title that was reminiscent of Clausewitz's famous book *On War* (Vom Kriege). He also published *Germany and the Coming War* (Deutschland und der nächste Krieg). Publishing these books in the shadow of the second Moroccan crisis, Bernhardi was quoted as the typical aggressive and militaristic German general staff officer, particularly by British sources. Bernhardi was supported by the Pan-German League in his theories about Germany as a future leading world power (Weltmacht).
- On mobilization in 1914, Bernhardi was recalled to duty and appointed as interim Commander of the V Army Corps in support of General der Infanterie v. Strantz—Strantz became commander of the Strantz Group (Armee-Abteilung Strantz) formed from the left wing of the Fifth Army in the Verdun area at the same time.

- Bernhardi served in a couple of different appointments particularly on the Eastern Front, where he was awareded the Pour le Mérite on 20 August 1916 for his performance in crushing the Russian Brusilov offensive.
- Appointed as Commanding General of the Corps Staff for Special Assignments Nr. 55 (Generalkommando zur besonderen Verendung 55), he completed several assignments and missions before he retired again on 23 November 1918.

Boguslawski, Albert v.

Albert Karl Friedrich Wilhelm von Boguslawski, born 24 December 1834 in Berlin; died 7 September 1905 in Berlin.

- Boguslawski joined the Prussian Army as officer candidate in 1852 and was commissioned as a Sekondelieutenant in 1854.
- He campaigned with the 3. Niederschlesisches Infanterie-Regiment Nr. 50 in all three unification wars: 1864, 1866, and 1870–71. During the Franco-Prussian War he served as a company commander of the 12th company, Infantry Regiment 50.
- In the 1880s, he became the Commander of the Colbergsches Grenadier-Regiment Graf Gneisenau (2. Pommersches) Nr. 9, and later of Füsilier-Regiment Fürst Karl Anton von Hohenzollern (Hohenzollernsches) Nr. 40.
- He was promoted to Generalmajor in 1890 and retired to z.D. in 1891.
- Boguslawski was a well-known military writer; a traditionalist, who opposed Sigismund v. Schlichting's reform attempts.
- Later he was promoted charakterisierter Generalleutnant.

Bronsart v. Schellendorff, Paul

Paul Leopold Eduard Heinrich Anton Bronsart von Schellendorff, born 25 January 1832 in Danzig; died 23 June 1891 at Schettnienen estate (*Gut Schettnienen*).

- Other members of the Schellendorff family also reached general's rank in the army. Here the focus is on Paul v. Schellendorff because of his role as War Minister.
- After attending a Gymnasium in Danzig, he was educated in the Kadettenanstalt in Kulm and the Hauptkadettenanstalt in Groß-Lichterfelde. He joined the Kaiser Franz Garde-Grenadier-Regiment Nr. 2 as a Sekondelieutenant and later became adjutant of the Fusilier battalion of Garde-Landwehr-Regiment Nr. 4.
- After successfully attending the War Academy from 1 October 1855 through 31 July 1858, Bronsart v. Schellendorff joined the Great General Staff in 1861.
- After a sequence of General Staff appointments (II Army Corps) and troop positions (Commander, Grenadier-Regiment König Friedrich Wilhelm IV. (1. Pommersches) Nr. 2 1864–1865), he joined the Great General Staff again and became a lecturer at the War Academy.
- During the Franco-Prussian War, he served as a department head in the General Headquarters.
- On 1 September 1870, he was sent to Sedan to lead the negotiations with the French army about the surrender and the capture of the Emperor Napoléon III.
- After the war, Bronsart v. Schellendorff was promoted to Oberst and became Chief of Staff, Guard Corps.
- In 1876, he was promoted to Generalmajor and took command of the 1 Guard Brigade in 1876.
- In 1881, Bronsart v. Schellendorff became Commander of the 1st Guard Division and was promoted to Generalleutnant.

- On 11 March 1883, he was appointed to the position of War Minister. During his term he was responsible for introducing a new infantry rifle, the Model 88 repeating rifle firing cordite powder. Due to several technical faults the model 88 rifles became a political issue.
- On 8 April 1891, Bronsart v. Schellendorff was relieved and appointed Commanding General of I Army Corps. Only a few weeks later he died at his estate at Schettnienen in East Prussia.

Bülow, Karl v.

Karl Wilhelm Paul v. Bülow, born 24 March 1846 in Berlin; died 31 August 1921 in Berlin.

- In 21 December 1864, Bülow joined 2 Garde-Regiment zu Fuß as an officer candidate and fought with the regiment in the 1866 war.
- Graduating from the War Academy in 1869, he served during the Franco-Prussian War as a Hauptmann in the General Headquarters.
- After a normal sequence of General Staff and troop appointments, Bülow was made the Commander of the 4. Garde-Regiment zu Fuß from 27 January 1894 until 5 February 1897.
- Then Bülow was transferred to the War Ministry and was promoted to Generalmajor on 22 March 1897 and served as Director of the Central Department (Zentral-Departement ZD).
- After promotion to Generalleutnant on 22 May 1900, Bülow became Commander of the 2nd Guard Division on 18 April 1901.
- After a short term in the General Staff as General Quartermaster, Bülow became Commanding General of III Army Corps on 18 April 1903 and was promoted to General der Infanterie on 15 September 1904.
- During his term as commanding general, Bülow earned a reputation as a skilled trainer.
- In 1905, Bülow was one of the potential candidates to succeed Schlieffen as Chief of the Great General Staff. Schlieffen, however, had rejected Bülow as a "strategist of frontal battles."
- He kept this position until he took over the III Army Inpection in Berlin on 1 October 1912. When promoted to the rank of Generaloberst, he was mobilized as Commander, Second Army in 1914.
- As Commander, Second Army he played a crucial role in the Marne Battle. After the war, the Schlieffen disciples in the Reichsarchiv held Bülow responsible, together with Hentsch, for pushing the First Army into the withdrawal from the Ourcq.
- Having been appointed Feldmarschall on 27 January 1915, Bülow suffered a heart attack on 4 April 1915 from which he never fully recovered. On 22 June 1916, he was retired z.D.
- Bülow died in 1921. Hentsch and Moltke died during the war, so all three "scapegoats" of the Marne disaster were dead and could not defend themselves when the debate on the Marne Battle started in the early 1920s. This paved the way for the Schlieffen apologists supporting Groener and Freytag-Loringhoven to build-up the Schlieffen-plan legend.

Einem, Karl v.

Karl Wilhelm Georg August Gottfried von Einem, born 1 January 1853 in Herzberg in the Harz; died 7 April 1934 in Mülheim.

- Einem joined the 2. Hannoversches Ulanen-Regiment Nr. 14 in Verden as an officer candidate on 3 August 1870 and spent the entire Franco-Prussian War on campaign with the regiment. Having been promoted to Sekondelieutenant on 12 December 1870, he was awarded the Iron Cross 2nd Class for exceptional bravery.

- Coming back from France he served as a regimental adjutant from 1873 until 1876. From 1876 until 1880, he served as the brigade adjutant in the 8 Cavalry Brigade in Erfurt.
- After a tour of duty as a squadron commander, Einem graduated from the War Academy and was transferred to the Great General Staff.
- He took command of the Kürassier-Regiment von Driesen (Westfälisches) Nr. 4 in Münster from 1893 until 1895 and was appointed Chief of Staff of the VII Army Corps on 18 October 1895. In this role he was responsible for the preparation of the expedition to China in 1900.
- During this period the Kaiser recognized the organizational talent of Einem and appointed him as the successor to War Minister Heinrich v. Goßler in 1903. Einem reorganized the field artillery during his term as War Minister by upgrading the field guns Model 96 with a recoil mechanism and introduced machineguns into the infantry.
- In 1907, Einem took legal steps against Karl Liebknecht (the Socialist) who was convicted and sentenced to one and a half years of fortress prison for high treason.
- In 1909, he returned to Münster as Commanding General of the VII Army Corps, where he succeeded Bernhardi. Einem led the corps at the Marne Battle and succeeded Generaloberst v. Hausen as Commander of the Third Army, a post that he held until the end of the war.
- After the war, Einem engaged himself in several right wing veterans' associations before he died in 1934 in Mülheim a.d. Ruhr.

Falkenhayn, Erich v.

Erich v. Falkenhayn, born 11 September 1861 in Burg Belchau near Graudenz; died 8 April 1922 in Lindstedt close to Potsdam.

- Having been educated at the Kadettenanstalt Culm and then in the Hauptkadettenanstalt Lichterfelde, he joined the Oldenburgisches Infanterie-Regiment Nr. 91 as a Sekondelieutenant in 1880.
- After graduating from the War Academy he was transferred to the Great General Staff in 1893 and served from 1896 until 1903 as a military advisor in China. It was in China where he took over the position of a Chief of Staff of the East-Asian Expeditionary Forces and came into contact with Alfred v. Waldersee.
- After several troop commands in Germany, he became the Prussian War Minister in 1913.
- After the Marne disaster, he followed the younger Moltke as Chief of General Staff. He was responsible for the First Battle of Ypres and subsequently for the German attack on Verdun. Hindenburg replaced him on 29 August 1916.
- After being dismissed as Chief of the General Staff, he assumed command over the Ninth Army and successfully led the campaign against Romania.
- In May 1917, he took command of the Turkish and German forces in Palestine (Pasha II, Yildirim) where he failed against the British forces under Edmund Allenby. The British took Jerusalem on 9 December 1918.
- On 3 March 1918, Falkenhayn took command of Tenth Army, which carried out occupational tasks in White Russia (today Belarus) after the Brest-Litovsk peace treaty. Falkenhayn, probably correctly saw the command over this weakened occupational force as degrading as the Kaiser had not given him command of one of the armies participating in the spring offensive on the Western Front in 1918. Nevertheless, he held his position in Russia until June 1919.

Freytag-Loringhoven, Hugo Frhr. v.

Hugo Friedrich Philipp Johann Freiherr von Freytag-Loringhoven, born 20 May 1855 in Copenhagen; died 19 October 1924 in Weimar.

- The descendant of an aristocratic Latvian family, his father was the Russian Consul-General to Denmark.
- He joined the Russian army and was educated as a Russian officer, but he transferred to the German army.
- After joining the German army, he successfully graduated from the War Academy and started a career as a General Staff officer.
- From 1893 until 1895, he served a first term in the Great General Staff; then from1898 to 1901, he was with the Military History Department.
- From 1910–1914, Freytag served as Senior Quartermaster V and was responsible for both military history departments. Generalmajor v. Redern succeeded him upon his retirement on 1 April 1914. Like Verdy du Vernois, Freytag turned out to be one of most influential military historians of the German army.
- He was the Commander of the 17th Reserve Division from April until December 1916 and promoted to Generalleutnant.
- He was awarded the civilian version of the Pour le Mérite for arts and science, which was regarded as a kind of second-class Pour le Mérite, in 1916.
- He assumed the role of Chief of Staff of the Replacement General Staff (stellvertretende Generalstab) in December 1916 after Moltke's death and held this position until the end of the war.
- Freytag edited a selection of Schlieffen's offical writings in the volume on Official Writings (Dienstschriften) and on The General Staff Rides East (Große Generalstabsreisen Ost). Unfortunately, the latter was never published.
- He continued his career as a military historian after the war. He edited Schlieffen's writings in the volume on Cannae that made him one of the leading members of the Schlieffen school after the war.

Goltz, Colmar v.d.

Wilhelm Leopold *Colmar* Frhr. v. d. Goltz, born 12 August 1843 in Bielkenfeldt, Eastern Prussia; died 19 April 1916 in Baghdad.

- After earning his Abitur, Goltz joined Infanterie-Regiment von Boyen (5. Ostpreußisches) Nr. 41 as an officer candidate in Königsberg, East Prussia in 1861 and went through regular officer's training.
- Attending the War Academy from 1864 until 1866, he served with his regiment in the 1866 war and was severly wounded at the Battle of Trautenau.
- In 1867, Goltz joined the Great General Staff and served in the Franco-Prussian War as General Staff officer in the staff of Prince Friedrich Karl, who commanded the Prussian Second Army.
- Going through a sequence of troop and general staff appointments after the war, he served in the Military History Department of the Great General Staff and became a teacher of military history at the War Academy from 1878 until 1883.
- In 1883, he published, *From Roßbach to Jena and Auerstedt* where he criticized the deterioration of the Prussian Army after Frederick the Great and used the analogies to issue a indirect criticism of contemporary imperial Germany.

- From 1883 until 1895, he was sent to Turkey and reorganized the Ottoman army, where he was promoted to Feldmarschall of that army and was elevated to the noble title of Pasha. After 1895, Goltz was known as v. d. Goltz Pasha.
- Upon his return, Goltz became a divisional commander and then Commanding General of the I Army Corps in Königsberg before he was promoted to Prussian Fedlmarschall and retired to z.D. in 1913.
- In 1905, Goltz was one of the potential candidates to succeed Schlieffen as Chief of the Great General Staff together with Generals v. Bülow and v. Beseler. Schlieffen refused Goltz and Bülow for professional reasons.
- On 7 July 1909, Goltz was the subject of a discussion between the Kaiser and the Director of the Civilian Cabinet, Rudolf v. Valentini, on whether or not he was a potential candidate to become Reichskanzler. In the end, the Kaiser preferred Theobald v. Bethmann Hollweg.
- Again working as a military advisor in Turkey between 1909 and 1911, v. d. Goltz Pasha reorganized the armament of the Ottoman army and made sure that it was equipped with the latest models of German rifles, machineguns, and Krupp artillery pieces. Goltz also arranged the refurbishment of the Turkish forts protecting the Dardanelles.
- Upon mobilization, Goltz was disappointed that he did not receive a command position. Between 23 August and 28 November 1914, he served as Governor General of the Imperial German Government in Belgium before he was sent to Turkey again where he was supposed to have replaced the head of the German Military Mission, General Liman v. Sanders. Sanders took command of the Fifth Ottoman Army.
- A short time later, Goltz became Commander of the First Ottoman Army in Constantinople and then of the Sixth Ottoman Army in Mesopotamia, where he died on 19 April 1916 from typhus.

Goltz, Rüdiger v.d.

Gustav Adolf Joachim *Rüdiger* Graf v. d. Goltz, born 8 December 1865 in Züllichau; died 4 November 1946 in Kinsegg, an estate close to Bernbeuren.

- He joined the 1.Garde-Regiment zu Fuß as an officer candidate on 3 March 1885.
- He successfully graduated from the War Academy and went through a sequence of general staff and troop appointments.
- Another Goltz, Generalleutnant Frhr. v.d. Goltz was mobilized in 1914 as Commander of the 1st Landwehr Division.
- As commander of the 3 Cavalry Brigade prior to 1914, he served with his brigade in the newly formed 4th Cavalry Division in HKK 2, commanded by Generalleutnant v. d. Marwitz. During the Marne Battle, Rüdiger v.d. Goltz was seriously wounded.
- After commanding several different brigades on both Western and Eastern Fronts, he was promoted to Generalmajor in 1916 and took command of the 37th Infantry Division in June 1917 and the 12th Landwehr Division in February 1918. This formation was later renamed the Baltic Division (Ostsee-Division). With the Baltic Division, he successfully fought Red Guards during the Finnish Civil War together with the Finnish general Carl Gustaf Emil Mannerheim and was awarded the Pour le Mérite for his performance on 15 May 1918.
- Later he supported Mannerheim as military advisor during the build-up of the new Finnish army.
- On 1 February 1919, he became the Military Governor in Libau in Latvia and took command of the VI Reserve Corps, which was involved in the civil war in the Baltic. Goltz supported the build-up of the Iron Division, a right-wing voluntary formation (Freikorps) of around

16,000 men, which was heavily involved in the civil war. Heinz Guderian, the renowned founder and leader of the German armored forces in the Second World War served in the Iron Division as Ib from April until August 1919. His troops, together with the Iron Division, were responsible for the summary execution of several thousand Latvian people under martial law. As a result Goltz was forced to resign from his command on 12 October 1919.

- Back in Germany, Goltz took a position against the Weimar Republic and supported the Kapp-Lüttwitz putsch in 1920 by mobilizing a couple of hundred members of the former Iron Division for street-fights in Berlin.
- In the 1920s and 1930s, Goltz founded and chaired several nationalistic associations and was one of the founders of the Harzburg Front that paved the way for the Nazis to seize power in 1933.

Goßler, Heinrich v.

Heinrich Wilhelm Martin von Goßler, born 29 September 1841 in Weißenfels, Saxony; died on 10 January 1927 in Berlin.

- He started his career as officer candidate in the Grenadier-Regiment Kronprinz (1. Ostpreußisiches) Nr. 1 in 1860. He was promoted to Sekondelieutenant in 1861.
- Goßler served in 1866 and 1870–71 with the Grenadier-Regiment Nr. 1. During the Franco-Prussian War, he served as company commander.
- In July 1871, Goßler was posted to the War Ministry. In October 1872, he temporarily worked in the Army Department (1. Armee-Abteilung A1).
- He transferred back to the troops where he served as a company commander in Grenadier-Regiment König Friedrich Wilhelm IV. (1.Pommersches) Nr. 2, until 1878 and was then transferred again to the Army Department of the War Ministry. On promotion to Oberstleutnant, he headed the department from 1885 and was a member of the committee responsible for the examination of officer candidates at the same time.
- Goßler was one of the very few top-ranking officers who had no general staff training.
- In 1888, Goßler became commander of the 3. Garde-Regiment zu Fuß and was promoted to Oberst.
- In 1891, he became commander of the 43 Infantry Brigade in Kassel and was promoted to Generalmajor.
- In October, he was appointed Director of the General War Department (Allgemeines Kriegs-Departement AD), which was the most important step on the way to becoming Minister of War. At the same time Goßler was appointed to become a member of the National Defense Committee (Landesverteidigungskommission) and a number of further high-level committees.
- Goßler was promoted to Generalleutnant in 1895 and took command of the 25th Infantry Division (Hesse) in Darmstadt.
- Upon the resignation of Bronsart v. Schellendorff, he became his successor as Minister of War in 1896.
- Having been promoted General of the Infantry, Goßler was retired to z.D. on 15 August 1903.

Groener, Wilhelm

Karl Eduard *Wilhelm* Groener, born 22 November 1867 in Ludwigsburg (Württemberg); died 3 May 1939 in Potsdam.

- Joined Infanterie-Regiment Alt-Württemberg (3. Württembergisches) Nr. 121 as a Fahnenjunker after earning his Abitur in 1884.

- He served in this regiment until he joined the War Academy in 1896.
- After successfully passing the War Academy, a sequence of General Staff and troop assigments followed, until he took over the Railroad Department of the Great General Staff on 1 October 1911.
- Upon mobilization, he became Chief of Railroads in the OHL. For his performance in this appointment, he was promoted to Generalmajor and rewarded with the Pour le Mérite on 11 September 1915.
- When transferred to the War Ministry, he ran into a conflict with Ludendorff and was transferred to the Eastern Front as commander of the 33rd Infantry Division in 1917.
- In December 1917, he commanded the XXV Reserve Corps and took over the I Army Corps at the start of 1918, before becoming Chief of General Staff of the Army Group v. Eichhorn (Heeresgruppe Eichhorn).
- After Ludendorff's dismissal, he followed him into the position of First Quartermaster General on 26 October 1918.
- Groener established a positive and trusted relationship with Friedrich Ebert from the Social Democratic Party and helped to lead Germany through the revolution into the newly founded Weimar Republic.
- During the Weimar Republic, he served several terms as Minister of the Army (Reichswehrminister) under various chancellors, before he finally retired in 1932.

Haeseler, Gottlieb Graf v.

Gottlieb Ferdinand Albert Alexis Graf v. Haeseler, born 19 January 1836 in Potsdam; died 25 October 1919 in Harnecop, northeast of Berlin.

- After being educated at the Knight's Academy in Brandenburg and the residential Internatsgymasium Pädagogium in Halle-Saale, Graf Haeseler joined the cadet corps and began his military service as a Sekondelieutenant in 1853 with the Husaren-Regiment von Zieten (Brandenburgisches) Nr. 3.
- In 1860, he became an adjutant to the Prussian Prince Friedrich Karl Nikolaus v. Preußen, who was the Commanding General of the III Army Corps.
- In this role, Haeseler served in the Danish War of 1864, the war of 1866, and the Franco-Prussian War. In 1866 and 1867, he served for a short term as a squadron commander in the Husaren-Regiment Königin Wilhelmina der Niederlande (Hannoversches) Nr. 15.
- After the peace with France he served as Senior Quartermaster of the German occupation forces in France and became Commander of Ulanen-Regiment Graf Haeseler (2. Brandenburgisches) Nr. 11 between 1873 and 1879. The name "Graf Haeseler" was assigned to the regiment by the Kaiser on 18 May 1903 upon Haeseler's retirement.
- Beginning in 1879, Haeseler headed the Military History Department of the Great General Staff.
- In 1880, he became Commander of 12 Cavalry Brigade and was promoted to Generalmajor in 1881.
- In 1883, Haeseler became the Commander of 31 Cavalry Brigade and in 1886, together with his promotion to Generalleutnant, he was appointed, in quick succession, Commander 20th Infantry Division then 6th Infantry Division.
- In 1889, Haeseler became Senior Quartermaster in the Great General Staff and served as Commanding General of the newly formed XVI Army Corps in Metz between 1890 and 1903.

- Promoted to General der Kavallerie in 1890, Haeseler became Generaloberst in 1903 upon his retirement to z.D. and was made a Feldmarschall in 1905.
- After his retirement, Graf Haeseler became member of the Prussian Herrenhaus, supported the build-up of vocational schools and became involved in the Boy Scout movement in Germany.
- Since he was already 78 years old, in 1914 he was not mobilized for an active command, but he was allowed to join the XVI Army Corps as an observer—the corps he had commanded for so many years.
- Gottlieb Graf v. Haeseler was one of the most distinguished, although at times eccentric, military leaders in Germany before 1914.

Hahnke, Wilhelm v.

Wilhelm Gustav Karl Bernhard von Hahnke, born1 October 1833 in Berlin; died 8 February 1912 in Berlin.

- Hahnke was educated in the cadet corps and joined the Kaiser Alexander Garde-Grenadier Regiment Nr. 1 in 1858 as a Sekondelieutenant.
- As a captain and company commander, he was transferred to the Königin Elisabeth Garde-Grenadier Regiment Nr. 3.
- Still a company commander during the 1864 war, he went on to serve in the headquarters (HQ) of the Prussian Crown Prince, becoming aide de camp to Duke Ernest II of Saxe-Coburg-Gotha prior to the Franco-Prussian War.
- During the war he served again in the HQ of the Crown Prince.
- From 1872 until 1881, he held several different different General Staff officer's positions and became Generalmajor, Commander of the 1 Guard Infantry Brigade and Commandant of Potsdam in 1881.
- In 1886, he took command of the 1st Guard Infantry Division before he was appointed Chief of the Military Cabinet in 1888, a position he held until his retirement to z.D. in 1901.
- On 1 January 1905, he was promoted to Feldmarschall and became general aide de camp (*Generaladjutant*) to the Kaiser.

Hammerstein-Equord, Kurt Frhr. v.

Kurt Gebhard Adolf Philipp Freiherr von Hammerstein-Equord, born 26 September 1878 in Hinrichshagen, Mecklenburg; died 24 April 1943 in Berlin.

- After his education in the Kadettenanstalt Plön and in the Hauptkadettenanstalt Lichterfelde, he joind the 3. Garde-Regiment zu Fuß and was promoted to Sekondelieutenant on 15 March 1898.
- Kurt v. Schleicher, the later Reichskanzler, started his military career in the same regiment and was promoted Sekondelieutenant in 1900. Both men were close friends.
- Hammerstein successfully passed the War Academy 1907–1910 and was transferred to the deployment department of the Great General Staff in 1911.
- Upon mobilization, Hauptmann v. Hammerstein served with the OHL where he served as adjutant to the Quartermaster General, Generalleutnant v. Stein.
- After carrying out several different General Staff appointments during the war, he managed to join the Reichswehr where he served on the staff of his father-in-law, General v. Lüttwitz.
- Refusing active participation in the Kapp-Lüttwitz putsch, he had a successful career in the Reichswehr.

- On 1 October 1929, he became head of the Truppenamt, the covert successor organization of the General Staff, which had been forbidden by the Versailles Treaty.
- Hammerstein was highly appreciated by Reichwehrminister Groener as well as by Reichskanzler Heinrich Brüning, which paved the way for his further career.
- On 1 November 1930, Hammerstein became Chef der Heeresleitung. In this position he was responsible for the issue of the basic tactical manual H.Dv. 300/1, which was a pivotal text for the German army throughout the entire Second World War.
- He also secretly designed the massive build-up program the Wehrmacht followed starting in 1935.
- After Hitler seized power on 30 January 1933, Hammerstein, as an ardent anti-Nazi, was more or less forced to retire. This was granted by Reichspräsident v. Hindenburg on 31 January 1934.
- When the Second World War began, Hammerstein was re-activated again, but dismissed by Hitler once more on 24 September 1939 because of his "negative attitude towards National-Socialism." He continued his resistance to the Nazis right up until his death from cancer in 1943.

Heeringen, Josias v.

Josias v. Heeringen, born 9 March 1850 in Cassel; died 9 October 1926 in Berlin.

- After going through the regular officer's career and after graduating from the War Academy, Heeringen became a Major in the War Ministry in 1887.
- In 1898, he became Director of the Central Department (Zentral Department ZD), dealing with administrative affairs. In this position he was promoted to Generalmajor.
- In 1901, he became Commander of the 22nd Infantry Division and was promoted to Generalleutnant.
- In 1906, he became General der Infanterie and Commanding General of II Army Corps.
- From 1909 until 1913, Heeringen served as War Minister, succeeded by Falkenhayn.
- He was then appointed General Inspector of the II Army Inspection in Berlin and was mobilized as Commander Seventh Army in Southern Alsace in 1914.
- In the opening days of August 1914, he played a crucial role for the combined Sixth and Seventh Armies, during which time he won the counterproductive victory at Mulhouse.
- From 1916 until 1918, he was Commander of the Coastal Defense and retired in 1918 as a Generaloberst.
- From 1918 until 1926, Heeringen was President of the Kyffhäuserbund, a right-wing veterans association with considerable political influence in the Weimar Republic.

Hentsch, Richard

Richard Hentsch (born 18 September 1869 in Cologne; died 13 February 1918 in Bucharest)

- He joined the Kgl. Sächs. 4. Infanterie-Regiment Nr. 103 as an officer candidate in 1888.
- After being promoted to Sekondelieutenant in 1890, he studied at the War Academy and joined the Great General Staff in 1899.
- From 1912–1914, he acted as the Ia to the Saxon XIX Army Corps and transferred back to the 2nd department of the Great General Staff on 1 July 1914.
- Upon mobilization, he joined Tappen in the Operations Department and became the scapegoat for the Marne disaster, having been employed as a messenger, shuttling back and forth beween OHL and the army staffs during the climax of the battle and finally triggering the withdrawal.

- He was transferred to the Austrian General Staff. In July 1915, he became Senior Quartermaster (Oberquartiermeister) of the Mackensen Army Group in the east (Heeresgruppe Mackensen).
- On 12 September 1915, he was promoted Oberst.
- On 1 March 1917, Hentsch became Chief of General Staff of the Military Administration in Romania and was awarded the Pour le Mérite on 23 September 1917.
- He died on 13 February 1918 from complications following a gallbladder operation.
- Although an official hearing conducted by Ludendorff in 1917 officially exculpated him from blame for the Marne, he was never free of the shadows the episode cast.
- Because Moltke and Hentsch died in 1916 and 1918 respectively, they were easily made scapegoats for the Marne disaster after the war.

Hindenburg, Paul v.

Paul Ludwig Hans Anton von Beneckendorff und von Hindenburg, born 2 October 1847 in Posen; died 2 August 1934 at Neudeck estate (Gut Neudeck), Eastern Prussia).

- Educated at the Kadettenanstalt Wahlstatt (close to Liegnitz, in today's Poland) and the Hauptkadettenanstalt Lichterfelde, in 1865, he became a Page to Queen Elisabeth, the widow of King Friedrich Wilhelm IV.
- In April 1866, he joined the 3. Garde-Regiment zu Fuß as a Sekondelieutenant and served with the regiment in 1866. Hindenburg participated in the Battle of Königgrätz.
- Serving with that regiment again in the France-Prussian War, Hindenburg represented his regiment during the German Kaiser's proclamation in the Hall of Mirrors at Versailles Palace on 18 January 1871.
- After attending War Academy training from 1873 until 1876, he was transferred to the Great General Staff in 1877 and promoted to Hauptmann the same year.
- In 1881, he became the Ia of the 1st Infantry Division in Könisberg.
- In 1888, Hindenburg was one the officers officially holding wake at the publicly exhibited corpse of Kaiser Wilhelm I.
- In 1890, Hindenburg joined the War Ministry and headed the 2nd Infantry department.
- In 1893, he took command of Oldenburgisches Infanteriey-Regiment Nr. 91 in Oldenburg and was promoted to Oberst.
- Chief of Staff of the VIII Army Corps from 1896, Hindenburg became commander of the 28th Infantry Division in Karlsruhe in 1900 and was promoted to Generalleutnant.
- In 1905, Hindenburg became Commanding General of the IV Army Corps in Magdeburg, was promoted General der Infanterie, and was retired to z.D. in 1911.
- Hindenburg moved to Hanover in 1911 and volunteered for a new command upon mobilization. On 22 August, he was appointed Commander of the Eighth Army, with Ludendorff accompanying him as his Chief of Staff.
- Awarded the Pour le Mérite for his performance at Tannenberg, Hindenburg received the Great Cross of the Iron Cross (Großkreuz des Eisernen Kreuzes) on 9 December 1916 and the Star of the Iron Cross, on 25 March 1918. This medal was also called the Hindenburgstern, as it was exclusively designed for him.
- Through the victory at Tannenberg and the following victories over the Russian army at the Masurian Lakes and during the winter battle in Masuria, Hindenburg backed by Ludendorff, became the mythical hero of the German army; the only man who could prevent the country from losing the war. Together with Ludendorff, he designed the third OHL (the first OHL was built by Moltke, the second one by Falkenhayn) as almost

a dictatorship, mobilizing all personal and industrial resources of the country to conduct total war.

- On 9 November 1918 it was Hindenburg who pushed the Kaiser to exile at Doorn in The Netherlands to make way for peace negotiations with the Allies. Hindenburg was finally retired by the Weimar President Ebert on 25 June 1919, two weeks before the demobilization ended.
- The Hindenburg myth persisted even after the end of the war. He was elected Reichspräsident at the age of 77 on 26 April 1925. The British Prime Minister, David Lloyd George, called him a very sensible old man; in fact, he acted as a kind of Ersatz-Kaiser for Germany.
- After some prosperous years, Hindenburg was confronted with the the political turmoil of the 1929 economic crisis. Leading the country through an increasing abuse of the presidential powers, and based upon the Emergency Act (Article 48) of the Weimar Constitution, Hindenburg paved the way for Hitler. He disliked Hitler as a brown proletarian, but who promised to be the only politician to bring about a kind of stability in 1933.
- Hindenburg died one and a half years after he lent his reputation to Hitler during the Day of Potsdam on 21 March 1933.

Hohenborn, Adolf Wild v.

Adolf Wild v. Hohenborn, born 8 July 1860 in Cassel; died 25 October 1925 in Malsburg-Hohenborn.

- He attended the University of Cassel where he befriended the future Kaiser Wilhelm II.
- He joined Infanterie-Regiment von Wittich (3. Kurhessisches) Nr. 83 in Cassel as a Fahnenjunker in 1878 and was promoted to Sekondelieutenant in 1880.
- Transferred to 1. Lothringisches Regiment Nr. 130 in Metz, then after further university study, was posted to Brandenburgisches Jäger Bataillon Nr. 3 in Lübben in 1886.
- After training, he joined the Great General Staff as a Major in Berlin in 1899.
- He served as Chief of Staff, 1st Guard Infantry Division for six years beginning in 1900, then was promoted to Oberstleutnant and transferred to XIII Army Corps in Stuttgart, again as Chief of Staff.
- The Kaiser raised him to the nobility in 1900.
- Given command of 2. Badisches Grenadier-Regiment Kaiser Wilhelm I. Nr. 110 as an Oberst in 1909, and the following year posted as Commander, Königin Elisabeth Garde-Grenadier-Regiment Nr. 3 in Berlin.
- After command of 3 Guard Infantry Brigade and promotion to Generalmajor he was serving on the Great General Staff at the outbreak of war. He briefly commanded 30th Infantry Division and was Chief of Staff of Eighth Army for a short time before returning to General Staff duties in Berlin.
- He was promoted to Generalleutnant and became Falkenhayn's successor as Minister of War from 21 January 1915 until 29 October 1916, when he was dismissed due to open criticism of Hindenburg and Ludendorff.
- Certain troop commanding appointments followed, including Commander of XVI Army Corps. Post-war he was gazetted z.D. in 1919 with the rank of General der Infanterie.

Hülsen-Haeseler, Dietrich Graf v.

Dietrich Graf von Hülsen-Haeseler, born 13 February 1852 in Berlin; died 14 November 1908 in Donaueschingen.

- After his education in the cadet corps, Haeseler joined Kaiser Alexander Garde-Grenadier Regiment Nr. 1 as a Sekondelieutenant.
- After successfully graduating from the War Academy in 1881, he was transferred to the Great General Staff in 1882.
- In 1889, he became aide de camp to the Kaiser.
- In 1894, he was elevated to Graf (count) and transferred as military attaché to the German embassy in Vienna.
- In 1895, he became an Oberst and took command of the Garde-Füsilier Regiment in 1897.
- In the autumn of 1897, he was promoted commander of the 2 Guard Infantry Brigade and was appointed Chief of Military Cabinet in 1901.
- Graf Hülsen-Haeseler died from a heart attack in 1908 during a party after a hunting trip, when the Kaiser forced him to dance in female clothes until he was exhausted.

Kaltenborn-Stachau, Hans v.

Hans Karl Georg von Kaltenborn-Stachau, born March 1836 in Magdeburg; died 16 February 1898 in Braunschweig.

- Educated in the cadet corps he joined Infanterie-Regiment Prinz Louis Ferdinand von Preußen (2. Magdeburgisches) Nr. 27 as a Sekondelieutenant in 1854.
- Completing the War Academy between 1857 and 1860, Kaltenborn joined the Topographical Department of the Great General Staff in 1861.
- During the Danish War of 1864, he served in the railroad line commission in Altona. Soon after the war he was transferred to the staff of the VI Army Corps in December 1864.
- During the war of 1866, he served with the VI Army Corps and became commander of the 5th company in the Infanterie-Regiment Großherzog v. Sachsen (5. Thüringisches) Nr. 94 in 1868.
- In 1869, he became a general staff officer with VII Army Corps and went to war in 1870 with that headquarters.
- After the war he went through the regular sequence of troop and staff positions before he became Commander of 2 Guard Infantry Brigade and interim Commander of the 3rd Infantry Division.
- In 1888, he took command of 2nd Guard Infantry Division and was promoted to Generalleutnant.
- Appointment as War Minister followed on 4 October 1890. The army was increased in size by 70,000 men in the 1893 build-up during his tour of duty.
- On 12 October 1893, Kaltenborn resigned from his position and was retired to z.D.

Krafft v. Dellmensingen, Konrad v.

Konrad Krafft v. Dellmensingen, born on 24 November 1862 in Laufen; died 22 February 1955 in Seeshaupt at the Starnberg lake south of Munich.

- Educated in the Bavarian cadet corps, he became an officer candidate in the field artillery in 1881.
- After several troop positions, he graduated from the Bavarian War Academy and joined the Bavarian General Staff.
- In 1908, v. Dellmensingen became an Oberst and was posted to the Bavarian Ministry of War.
- In 1911, he became Commander of the 11 Bavarian Field Artillery Brigade.
- In 1912, v. Dellmensingen was appointed Chief of General Staff of the Bavarian Army.

- Upon mobilization, he became Chief of General Staff of the Sixth Army. The Bavarian Crown Prince Rupprecht commanded this army, and it was comprised of all the Bavarian formations fielded in 1914. To this day there is a debate about whether this army had the task of acting as the left wing in a giant pincer movement, which was to have broken through the French fortress belt south of Verdun.
- From 1915 until 1917, v. Dellmensingen was the Commander of the German Alpine Corps (Deutsches Alpenkorps) and fought at Verdun, in Romania, and in the Italian Alps at the river Isonzo.
- In October 1917 at the 12th Battle of Isonzo, he played a major role in breaking through the Italian frontline and pushing Italy close to surrender. For this he was awarded the Grand Cross of the Bavarian Military Max-Josef Order, and he also received the Pour le Mérite the following year.
- In contrast to the Prussian Schlieffen disciples, v. Dellmensingen always argued the case for success by means of a frontal breakthrough, which led to intense controversies in the 1920s.
- After the war, v. Dellmensingen became involved in anti-monarchy plots in Bavaria, but nothing came of them. Subsequently, he was better known as an historian and writer on military subjects.

Kuhl, Dr. Hermann v.

Dr. phil. *Hermann* Josef von Kuhl, born 2 November 1856 in Koblenz; died 4 November 1958 in Frankfurt a.M.

- After his Abitur, he first studied philosophy and German literature and then completed his studies by earning his Ph.D. (Dr. phil.).
- On 1 October 1878, he joined the 5. Westfälisches Infanterie-Regiment Nr. 53 in Cologne as an officer candidate and became a Sekondelieutenant on 16 February 1889.
- Before he successfully passed the War Academy in 1896, he served at the Bezirkskommando in Wesel and in the Grenadier-Regiment König Friedrich Wilhelm I. (2. Ostpreußisches) Nr. 3 in Königsberg.
- Joining the Great General Staff in 1898, he was promoted to Major and soon became a department head. In the General Staff, he worked together with Hindenburg and also very closely with Ludendorff.
- Moltke the Younger regarded him as one of the best future military leaders. He was elevated to the nobility on the occasion of the 25th anniversary of the ascent of the Kaiser to the throne on 16 June 1913.
- At the 1914 mobilization, he served as Chief of General Staff of Kluck's First Army.
- Between 1914 and 1916, he was Chief of General Staff of the First, Twelfth, and Sixth Armies—all on the Western Front. He was appointed Chief of General Staff of Army Group Crown Prince Rupprecht (Heeresgruppe Kronprinz Rupprecht) on 28 August 1916 soon after Hindenburg and Ludendorff took over the OHL. Awarded the Pour le Mérite upon his change to the Army Group Crown Prince.
- On 10 November 1919, he was promoted General der Infanterie and then retired. He died in 1958 at the age of 102.

Ludendorff, Erich

Erich Friedrich Wilhelm Ludendorff, born 9 April 1869 in a small village close to Posen; died 20 September 1937 in Munich.

- After his training in the Kadettenanstalt in Plön and in the Hauptkadettenanstalt in Groß-Lichterfelde, he joined the Infanteie-Regiment Herzog Ferdinand von Braunschweig (8.Westfälisches) Nr. 57 in Wesel in 1882. In 1887, he was transferred to the Marine Battalion (See-Bataillon) of the imperial German Navy and served on several ships, before he was posted to the War Academy in 1890.
- During his studies at the War Academy, he developed a strong interest in Russia and learned Russian. After graduation, he was sent in 1894 to St. Petersburg to support the military attaché in the German embassy in Russia.
- After returning to Germany, he went through the typical sequence of general staff and troop officer's positions.
- After a term as a lecturer at the War Academy, Ludendorff joined the Great General Staff in 1908 and soon became head of the deployment department. Ludendorff was an important member of the younger Moltke's staff in reviewing and adapting the Schlieffen Doctrine (we prefer doctrine instead of plan).
- Ludendorff designed the coup de main on Liège, which was inevitable if the violation of the neutral territory of the Netherlands was to be avoided. He created the plan of funneling the First and Second Army through this extremely tight bottleneck around the Maastricht appendix of the southern Netherlands. To guarantee the success of this coup, Ludendorff was one of the advocates of the development of super-heavy artillery.
- On promotion to Oberst in 1913, he was transferred out of the General Staff and was made Commander of the Niederrheinisches Füsilier-Regiment Nr. 39 in Düsseldorf. After Ludendorff's final dismissal in 1918, the Kaiser assigned the honorary name "General Ludendorff" to this regiment.
- On 22 April 1914, Ludendorff was promoted Generalmajor and made commander of 85th Infantry Brigade in Strassbourg.
- Upon mobilization, he became Senior Quartermaster of the Second Army and personally managed the coup de main on Liège, which had been threatening to fail.
- Awarded the Pour le Mérite, he was sent to East Prussia on 22 August 1914 to become Chief of General Staff of Hindenburg's Eighth Army.
- Winning the battle of Tannenberg against massive Russian superiority, gave the duo of Hindenburg-Ludendorff the aura of invincibility. The duumvirate led a couple of very successful campaigns at the Eastern Front until the summer of 1915—always in fierce opposition to Falkenhayn, who wanted to put the strategic emphasis on the Western Front.
- After Falkenhayn's dismissal upon the bloody failure at Verdun and the resource-consuming Somme battle, the duumvirate left their Supreme Command East (Oberkommando Ost—abbreviated: Oberost) to build the 3rd OHL starting from 29 August 1916.
- This 3rd OHL was now regarded as a kind of military dictatorship, designed to mobilize all industrial and human resources of Germany for a victory in a total war.
- After the failed spring offensive 1918 and the disastrous result of the battle at Amiens, Ludendorff pushed the imperial government towards a cease-fire agreement with the Allies.
- After rapidly losing power and influence in October, Ludendorff was dismissed on 26 October 1918, thus breaking up the duumvirate.
- After the war, Ludendorff liaised with Hitler and supported Hitler's attempted coup in Munich on 9 November 1923.

- After that Ludendorff started to develop a very different writing career. Under the influence of his wife, he lost himself in conspiracy theories and cabalistic historical research.
- Ludendorff died in 1937 in Munich.

Lyncker, Moritz Frhr. v.

Moritz Freiherr von Lyncker, born 30 January 1853 in Spandau; died 20 January 1932 in Demnitz.

- He joined the Kaiser Franz Garde-Grenadier Regiment Nr. 2 in 1870 as an officer candidate and served in France with the regiment.
- Seriously wounded in the battle of Gravelotte, he became a Sekondelieutenant in 1872 and attended the War Academy between 1878 and 1881.
- After a first term in the Great General Staff, he became company commander in the 1. Garde-Regiment.
- After completing a series of General Staff officer's appointments and a short term as Adjutant to Crown Prince Friedrich, he became a battalion commander in the Garde-Füsilier Regiment and then was appointed Commander of Königin Elisabeth Garde-Grenadier Regiment Nr. 3.
- In 1901, he was promoted to Generalmajor and took command of 1st Guard Infantry Brigade and simultaneously, Commandant of the city of Potsdam in 1902.
- In 1905, he was promoted to Generalleutnant and given command of 19th Infantry Division. Upon the sudden death of Count Hülsen-Haeseler, he became Chief of the Military Cabinet in 1908 and continued in that role until July 1918, when he became President of the Imperial Military Court (*Reichsmilitärgericht*).
- Lyncker retired in 1919.

Mackensen, August v.

Anton Ludwig Friedrich *August* v. Mackensen, born 6 December 1849 in Dahlenberg, Saxony; died 8 December 1945 in Burghorn, close to Celle.

- Educated in the Realgymnasium der Franckeschen Stiftung in Halle, Mackensen had to leave the school at Easter 1868 at the end of Unterprima as he was pressured by his father to learn farming.
- First disqualified for military service during his Musterung, he managed to join the 3. Niederschlesisches Infanterie-Regiment Nr. 50 in Lissa in the province of Posen in 1869 as One-Year-Volunteer. After his year of service, Mackensen started to study agricultural economics.
- During the Franco-Prussian War, Mackensen was mobilized as a reserve officer candidate. He was awarded the Iron Cross 1st Class in October 1870. After the war, he resumed his studies but joined his former regiment again in 1873 as a career officer.
- After going through a sequence of troop functions, Mackensen was transferred to a General Staff appointment in 1880 without ever having attended the War Academy. In 1882, he joind the Great General Staff.
- In 1891, he became First Adjutant to the Chief of General Staff, Count Schlieffen.
- In 1898, Mackensen became aide de camp, and in 1903 he was appointed General Adjutant to the Kaiser. At the same time he was elevated to the nobility.
- In 1898, Mackensen founded the *Deutsche Gesellschaft für Heereskunde* (German Society for Military Science); after the war Mackensen became Honorary President of the Gesellschaft.

- After his term as a regimental commander of the 1. Leib-Husaren-Regiment Nr. 1, Mackensen became Commander of the newly formed Leib-Husaren Brigade in Danzig-Langfuhr in 1903. The Kaiser granted him the permanent right to wear the uniform of the 1.Leib-Husaren-Regiment Nr. 1.
- Before the war, Mackensen was the Commanding General of the XVII Army Corps in Danzig as a General der Kavallerie and led his corps through the Battle of Tannenberg and the subsequent Battle of the Masurian Lakes.
- In November 1914, he became Commander of the newly formed Ninth Army and then of the Eleventh Army on 16 April 1915. In this role, he, together with his Chief of Staff, Generalmajor von Seeckt, was responsible for the successful breakthrough at Gorlice-Tarnów on 1–3 May 1915.
- After formation of Army Group Mackensen, he became a Feldmarschall upon the recapture of Lemberg in Galicia. In autumn 1915, his army group led the successful campaign against Serbia.
- During the last two years of the war, Mackensen served as Military Governor of Serbia.
- Like Hindenburg, Mackensen became a symbol of the old monarchy. And, as a dedicated follower of the old monarchy, he found it difficult to identify himself with the Weimar Republic. Although he had a certain dislike for the proletarian National-Socialist party, he developed a personal affection and admiration for Adolf Hitler and allowed the Nazis to use him for propaganda issues.
- For his role, he was rewarded with a grant of 350,000 Marks and the Brüssow estate close to Prenzlau, which comprised 1,231 hectares of land.

Marschall, Ulrich Frhr. v.

Veit *Ulrich* Gustav Gotthold Freiherr von Marschall, born 19 May 1863 in Erlebach, Thuringia; died 8 May 1923 in Erlebach.

- He joined 1. Badisches Leib-Grenadier-Regiment Nr. 109 in 1881 as an officer candidate.
- He left the regiment as company commander in 1902 to be transferred to the Intendance Department (2. Intendantur-Abteilung Z2) of the War Ministry in Berlin.
- In 1908, he transferred to the Military Cabinet and was promoted to Major on 18 July 1905. He worked as a departmental head in the Military Cabinet starting in1912.
- He became Chief of the Military Cabine and aide de camp to the Kaiser on 27 July 1918 until the Military Cabinet was disbanded on 26 October 1918.
- Marschall was married to Adelheid v. Goßler, a daughter of the former War Minister v. Goßler.

Marwitz, Georg v. d.

Johannes *Georg* v. d. Marwitz, born 7 July 1856 in Stolp; died 27 October 1929 in Wundlichow.

- After being educated in the cadet corps, Marwitz joined the 2. Garde-Ulanen-Regiment in Berlin as a Sekondelieutenant in 1875.
- He attended the War Academy from 1883 until 1886, and successfully graduated. After a series of appointments alternating between command of troops and the General Staff, he became Commander of the 3. Garde-Ulanen-Regiment in 1900.
- After five years as a regimental commander, he was made Chief of General Staff to XVIII Army Corps in Frankfurt am Main in 1905.

- After that he took command of the 1 Guard Cavalry Brigade in Berlin and was promoted to Generalmajor in 1908.
- On 2 March 1911, Marwitz became Commander of the 3rd Division in Stettin and was promoted to Generalleutnant on 20 March 1911.
- On 11 November 1912, he became Inspector General (Generalinspekteur) of the cavalry.
- In 1914, he was mobilized as Commander of HKK 2 and was responsible for the disastrous combat at Haelen on 12 August. On 23 December 1914, HKK 2 was disbanded and Marwitz became Commanding General of the newly formed XXXVIII Reserve Corps on the Eastern Front. He successfully participated in the Winter battle in Masuria with the corps.
- Later this corps became known as Beskidenkorps and joined the successful operations against the Russian Army in spring 1915. On 7 March 1915, Marwitz was awarded the Pour le Mérite.
- After a lengthy period of sick leave during late summer and autumn 1915, Marwitz became Commanding General of the VI Army Corps in the west, but was soon transferred back to the Eastern Front with his corps to help counter the Russian Brusilov-Offensive.
- On 6 October, Marwitz was appointed General Adjutant to the Kaiser. He took command of the Second Army in the west in December 1916.
- Successfully beating back the British tank attack at Cambrai in November 1917, Marwitz took command of the Fifth Army until the end of the war.
- At the end of the war, Marwitz retired into private life.

Moltke, Helmuth Graf v.

Helmuth Karl Bernhard Graf v. Moltke, called Moltke the Elder, was born on 26 October 1800 in Parchim and died on 24 April 1891 in Berlin.

- After the family moved to Denmark, Moltke joined the Danish cadet corps in Copenhagen in 1811 and was promoted to Sekondelieutenant in the Danish army in 1818.
- After four years of service, he applied for dismissal to join the Prussian army, where he successfully attended and passed the War Academy in 1826.
- At the War Academy, Clausewitz discovered his talent and acted as his mentor until Moltke joined the General Staff in 1833.
- After an educational journey through the Orient in 1835, the Turkish Sultan asked Moltke to serve as a military advisor to the Turkish Army, which Moltke did until 1839.
- After his stint in Turkey, he served as Adjutant to the Prussian Prince Karl Heinrich in Rome.
- Completing several terms in General Staff and troop general staff positions, he became Adjutant to the later Emperor Friedrich III in 1856 and was promoted to Generalmajor in 1857, when he was asked to head the Great General Staff. He was officially confirmed as Chief of General Staff in 1858.
- Moltke optimized the mobilization strategy of the Prussian army and worked out the operations plans for the wars of 1864 and 1866, where the largely unknown Chief of General Staff achieved a breakthrough at the battle of Königgrätz.
- As the strategic planner behind the Franco-Prussian War, he developed a mystic aura of military genius.
- Promoted to Feldmarschall and elevated to the title of Graf on 28 October 1870, Moltke remained in his position until his retirement on 9 August 1888.

Moltke, Helmuth v.

Helmuth Johannes Ludwig von Moltke, also known as Moltke the Younger, was born 25 May 1848 in Gersdorf; died 18 June 1916 in Berlin.

- During the Franco-Prussian War, he served as a Fähnrich and then Sekondelieutenant in the Grenadier-Regiment König Wilhelm I. (2. Westpreußisches) Nr. 7, where he was awarded for exceptional bravery during the battle of Weissenburg.
- After the war, he was transferred to 1. Garde-Regiment zu Fuß, where he met the later Emperor Wilhelm II.
- Moltke successfully attended and passed the War Academy between 1875 and 1878 and joined the Great General Staff in 1880.
- In 1882, he became second adjutant to his uncle, the elder Moltke. In 1888, he was promoted to Major and became First Adjutant.
- After his uncle passed away, he was appointed as one of the personal aides-de-camp to the Kaiser in April 1891. From that moment on, he belonged to the imperial entourage and had daily access to the Kaiser.
- In 1893, he became Commander of the Schlossgarde-Kompanie and in 1896, he was promoted to Oberst and took command of Kaiser Alexander Garde-Grenadier-Regiment Nr. 1.
- In 1899, he became a Generalmajor and Commander of the 1 Guard Brigade and Military Commander (Stadtkommandant) of the city of Potsdam.
- In 1902, as a Generalleutnant, he became commander of the 1st Guard Division and was transferred as Quartermaster General to the Great General Staff in 1904.
- Because Moltke had never commanded an army corps, he was not regarded as a suitable Chief of General Staff by many traditional generals. The Chief of the Military Cabinet strongly opposed his appointment. Nevertheless, after Schlieffen's retirement he became Chief of General Staff due to his trusted, personal relationship to the Kaiser.
- After the Marne battle, he was replaced by Falkenhayn and had to take the position of a Chief of Staff of the Replacement General Staff (stellvertretender Generalstab) that was left behind in Berlin after mobilization.
- Moltke passed away in 1916 after suffering a stroke.

Planitz, Ernst Rudolf Edler v. d.

Ernst Rudolf Max Edler von der Planitz, born 4 July 1836 in Altenburg (Reuß); died 10 November 1910 in Potsdam.

- He was a descendant of the Thuringian line of an old Saxon aristocratic family. While most of the Planitzes served in the Saxon Army, Ernst Rudolf joined the Prussian Army.
- He joined the 1. Brandenburgisches Dragoner-Regiment Nr. 2 in 1855 as an officer candidate. He successfully attended the War Academy from 1861 until 1864.
- Ernst Rudolf v. d. Planitz was promoted to Rittmeister and became a squadron commander in Dragoner-Regiment von Arnim (2.Brandenburgisches) Nr. 12 in 1866.
- In 1869, he joined the Great General Staff and served in different General Staff positions during the Franco-Prussian War. After this he was finally assigned to the General Staff of Second Army.
- After the war, he became a squadron commander in Husaren-Regiment Kaiser Franz Joseph von Österreich, König von Ungarn (Schleswig-Holsteinisches) Nr. 16 and took command of the regiment in 1877.
- In 1882, Planitz was promoted to Oberst.

- He took command of 28 Cavalry Brigade in 1885.
- After being promoted to Generalmajor, he was appointed Commander of 2 Guard Cavalry Brigade in 1888.
- In the 1889 Kaisermanöver, Planitz commanded the cavalry division of XV Army Corps, became Commander of the Guard Cavalry Division, and was promoted to Generalleutnant the same year.
- In 1894, Planitz became Inspector of the 2 Cavalry Inspection and became Inspector General of the Cavalry on 1 April 1898.
- Ernst Rudolf v. d. Planitz was one of the most traditional and conservative cavalry leaders of the Prussian Army, advocating the role of battle cavalry and cavalry mass charges until the end of his military career.

Planitz, Karl Paul Edler v. d.

Karl Paul Edler von der Planitz, born 20 September 1837 in Hohengrün, Saxony; died 19 August 1902 in Hosterwitz, Saxony.

- He also was a descendant of the Saxon line of an old aristocratic family.
- He joined an artillery regiment of the Saxon Army in 1856 as a Sekondelieutenant and was transferred to the Saxon General Staff in 1861.
- Karl Paul v. d. Planitz served in the Danish War in 1864 as a General Staff officer of the troops, which the Germanic Confederation had sent to Holstein.
- In 1866, Planitz served with the Saxon Army and fought against Prussia.
- In 1867, he was appointed an adjutant to the Saxon Crown Prince Albert.
- In 1869, Planitz became a battery commander and served with the General Staff of the Maas Army in the Franco-Prussian War. In this position and as an artillery specialist, he helped to organize the siege of Paris.
- After the Frankfurt Peace Treaty, he was transferred to the Great General Staff and was posted to the Saxon General Staff in 1872–73.
- After completing these General Staff assignments, Planitz became Saxon Military Plenipotentary in Berlin, and then was transferred back to Dresden to become Chief of the Saxon General Staff; he was promoted to Generalmajor in 1888.
- In 1889, Planitz took command of 45 Infantry Brigade (1 Saxon) in Dresden.
- When promoted to Generalleutnant, Planitz was appointed to Saxon Minister of War in 1891.
- Having been appointed to Governor of the Imperial Fortress of Mainz in 1893, he was promoted to General der Infanterie and retired to z.D. in 1896.

Poseck, Maximilian v.

Maximilian von Poseck, born 1 October 1865 in Rastatt; died 18 November 1946 in Berge.

- Poseck was educated in the cadet corps and joined the 1. Badisches Leib-Dragoner-Regiment Nr. 20 as a Sekondelieutenant on 14 April 1885.
- In 1903, he was promoted Rittmeister and appointed Squadron Commander of 5th Squadron Westfälisches Dragoner-Regiment Nr. 7 in Saarbrücken.
- In 1905, Poseck was promoted to Major and became Adjutant to the Inspector General of the Cavalry—in those days Generalleutnant Ernst Rudolf v. d. Planitz.
- Later Poseck became Chief of Staff to the Inspector General of the Cavalry.
- Having been promoted to Oberstleutnant, Poseck took command of the 1. Brandeburgisches Dragoner-Regiment Nr. 2 in Schwedt on the river Oder on 27 January 1912—the

Kaiser's birthday. On 22 March 1914, he was promoted to Oberst in this position and served with his regiment upon mobilization.

- The Dragoner-Regiment 2 served with 5 Cavalry Brigade, 2nd Cavalry Division of HKK 2.
- When the HKKs received corps staffs in the autumn of 1914, Poseck was appointed Chief of Staff of HKK 2 and moved in the same role to HKK 1 on the Eastern Front after HKK 2 was disbanded in December 1914.
- On 21 January 1918, Poseck became Commander of the Guard Ersatz Division, was promoted to Generalmajor and led this division during the spring offensive on the Western Front.
- Leading this division back to Germany after the armistice, he organized its demobilization that was then absorbed by the Reichswehr.
- On promotion to Generalleutnant, Poseck became Cavalry Inspector of the Reichswehr on 1 October 1920 and was promoted General der Kavallerie on 1 January 1925.
- Serving as Calvalry Inspector Poseck worked hard to rehabilitate the reputation of the cavalry that had become stained during the war.
- On 30 September 1926 Poseck was retired.

Roon, Albrecht Graf v.

Albrecht Theodor Emil Graf von Roon, born 30 April 1803 in Pleushagen near Kolberg; died 23 February 1879 in Berlin.

- After being educated in the Kadettenanstalt in Kulm and in the Hauptkadettenanstalt in Groß-Lichterfelde, he joined the Infanterie-Regiment Graf Schwerin (3. Pommersches) Nr. 14 as a Sekondelieutenant in 1821.
- He successfully studied at the War Academy between 1824 and 1827 and joined the topographical department of the General Staff in 1833.
- After completing several tours of duty in troop and General Staff positions, he was promoted to Oberst in 1851 and Generalmajor in 1856, becoming commander of 14th Infantry Division in 1858.
- After supporting Prince Wilhelm during the constitutional crisis, he was appointed War Minister in 1859 and Navy Minister two years later.
- Together with Moltke and Bismarck, Roon promoted the modernization of the Prussian army that made the victories in the Unification Wars of 1864–1871 possible.
- As a reward for his performance, he was awarded the Pour le Mérite in 1870 and the noble title of Graf on 16 June 1871.
- He was promoted to the rank of Feldmarschall upon his retirement on 9 November 1873.

Rundstedt, Gerd v.

Karl Adolf *Gerd* von Rundstedt, born 12 September 1875 in Aschersleben; died 12 February 1953 in Hanover.

- After completing the Oberrealschule in 1890, he was educated at the Kadettenanstalt Oranienstein and at the Hauptkadettenanstalt in Groß-Lichterfelde.
- On 22 March, he joined Infanterie-Regiment von Wittich (Kurhessisches) Nr. 83 in Cassel and was promoted to Sekondelieutenant on 17 June 1893.
- After completing the War Academy in 1907, he was transferred to the Great General Staff in 1907 on probational terms and confirmed as a General Staff Officer with his promotion to Hauptmann in 1909.
- He acted as Generalmajor v. Kuhl's Adjutant in the Great General Staff in 1914.

- During the Great War, he filled various General Staff officer's positions on the Western Front and in Turkey.
- After the war, he continued his career in various General Staff and command appointments in the Reichswehr before he was promoted to General der Infanterie in 1932, when he took over the command of the Reichswehrgruppenkommando I in Berlin.
- Having a positive attitude towards Hitler, he continued his career after 1933.
- Rundstedt became the chief planner of the invasion of Poland in 1939 and later served as commander of army groups in France and at the beginning of the campaign against the Soviet Union.
- Due to differences with Hitler, he was dismissed by the end of 1941, but received a grant of 250,000 Mark to show that his dismissal was honorable.
- Reactivated in 1942, he became the Supreme Commander West (Oberbefehlshaber West) in France and planned the defense of the Atlantikwall.
- After the successful Allied landing in Normandy on 6 June 1944, he again came into conflict with Feldmarschall Keitel and Hitler, when he advocated an end to the war.
- Hitler dismissed him on 2 July 1944, but called him again to take the lead of the Honor Court of the Wehrmacht (Ehrenhof der Wehrmacht), which pursued the co-conspiratorsof the plot of 20 July 1944.
- Rundstedt appreciated this chance for rehabilitation. He made it possible for Roland Freisler's notorious Volksgerichtshof to sentence many officers who had participated in that attempted coup. This was only possible by dismissing them from the army first and submitting them subsequently to the jurisdiction of the Volksgerichtshof.
- Rundstedt was reinstalled as Supreme Commander West in September 1944 and commanded during the Battles of Arnhem, Metz, and the Bulge in December 1944.
- As a British prisoner of war, Rundstedt was tried by the international court in Nuremberg for war crimes, but was released in 1949 before being sentenced due to his age and heart problems.
- He died in 1953.

Scharnhorst, Gerhard v.

Gerhard Johann David v. Scharnhorst, born 12 November 1755 in Bordenau, close to Hanover; died 28 June 1813 in Prague.

- Joined a cavalry regiment of the army of Hanover in 1778 and promoted to Sekondelieutenant in an artillery regiment in 1782.
- He served as lecturer at the Hanover military academy.
- Scharnhorst gathered his first war experience as a battery commander in the campaigns against France 1793–1795.
- He transferred as an *Oberstlieutenant* to the Prussian army in 1801.
- Elevated into the nobility in 1804, Scharnhorst became the Chief of Staff in General v. Rüchel's troops and later in the army of the Duke of Brunswick.
- Wounded during the battle of Jena in 1807, he later received the Pour le Mérite for his performance at Preussisch-Eylau.
- Promoted to the position of a Chief of General Staff, Scharnhorst headed the military reorganization committee that prepared the beaten Prussian army for the successful conduct of the Liberation Wars against Napoleon.
- Wounded in the battle of Gross-Görschen on 2 May 1813, he was awarded the Iron Cross 1st Class but died a couple of weeks later due to poor medical care of his wounds.

Scherff, Wilhelm v.

Wilhelm Karl Friedrich Gustav von Scherff, born 6 February 1834 in Frankfurt a.M.; died 16 April 1911.

- He joined the Prussian Army as an officer candidate in 1852 and successfully attended the War Academy between 1856 and 1859.
- He served as Adjutant to the Commander of the Prussian Occupation Brigade in Schleswig-Holstein between 1860 and 1866.
- Scherff served as a General Staff officer during the campaign 1866 and 1870–71 and joined the Great General Staff after the Franco-Prussian War.
- From 1873 until 1878, he taught military history at the War Academy.
- In 1879, Scherff served in Bulgaria as a member of the border adjustment committee, adjusting the borders in the Balkans after the Russo-Turkish War of 1877–78.
- Upon his return, he became Commander of the Infanterie-Regiment von Horn (3. Rheinisches) Nr. 29.
- In 1882, Scherff became Chief of General Staff of XI Army Corps.
- In 1883, he became Commander of 41 Infantry Brigade in Mainz; in 1888, he took command of the 33rd Infantry Division in Strasbourg and was promoted to Generalleutnant.
- In the mid 1890s, Scherff retired to z.D.
- Scherff was a well-known military writer; a traditionalist, who opposed Sigismund v. Schlichting's reform attempts.

Schëuch, Heinrich

Heinrich Schëuch, born 21 June 1846 in Schlettstadt (Alsace); died 3 September 1946 in Bad Kissingen.

- He went to school in Colmar and was educated in a Kadettenanstalt.
- He joined Infanterie-Regiment "Prinz Wilhelm" (4. Badisches) Nr. 112 as a Portepee-Fähnrich and was promoted Sekondelieutenant there.
- After a couple of troop assignments, he became Adjutant to the Director of the Armee-Verwaltungs-Departement BD of the War Ministry and was promoted to Hauptmann. Schëuch did not complete a General Staff officer's training.
- After serving as a company commander in the 7. Rheinischen Infanterie-Regiment Nr. 69, he was transferred to the War Ministry again to work in 9. Ersatzwesen-Abteilung A9 and in 1. Kassen-Abteilung B1.
- As Director of the Zentral Department ZD of the War Ministry, he was mobilized to the OHL in August 1914 working on ammunition supply issues. On 8 August, Walther Rathenau, the chairman of the board of the AEG (Allgemeine Electricitäts-Gesellschaft, one of the biggest industrial conglomerates of this time), contacted Schëuch and explained to him that Germany had only very few reserves of raw materials. In particular, the gunpowder reserves would only last for about six months.
- On 16 May 1916, he took command of the 29th Infantry Brigade and was promoted to Generalmajor.
- On 13 January 1917, Schëuch became commander of the 33 Infantry Division and was promoted to Generalleutnant.
- In August 1917, Schëuch became Director of the Kriegsamt, a central authority within the War Ministry created in 1916 with the introduction of the Hindenburg program. Major task of the Kriegsamt was the central management of raw materials and industrial resources and manufacturing capacities.

- Schëuch was awarded the Pour le Mérite on 8 April 1918 and became Director of the Central Department of the War Ministry during the War.
- Schëuch was the last Minister of War in 1918–19. He took the tough job of managing the demobilization of the beaten German army during the turmoil of the revolution.

Schlichting, Sigismund v.

Wilhelm Lorenz *Sigismund* von Schlichting, born 3 October 1829 in Berlin; died 22 October 1909 in Herischdorf.

- Sigismund's father was General of the Infantry, Eduard Karl Lorenz von Schlichting, Director of the War Academy.
- Educated at the Kadettenanstalt in Wahlstatt and in the Hauptkadettenanstalt in Groß-Lichterfelde, he joined Grenadier-Regiment König Wilhelm I. (2. Westfälisches) Nr. 7 on 22 April 1847.
- Schlichting did not attend the War Academy but studied at the universities of Bonn and Göttingen.
- He was promoted Hauptmann in 1861, serving in both the 1866 war and the Franco-Prussian War.
- After the 1866 war, he was promoted to Major and joined the Great General Staff.
- During the Franco-Prussian War, he was a battalion commander in the 4. Oberschlesisches Infanterie-Regiment Nr. 63 and was awarded the Iron Cross II Class.
- After the war he became Chief of Staff of the VII Army Corps from 1872 until 1874 and was then appointed Commander of Königin Elisabeth Garde-Grenadier-Regiment Nr. 3 on 27 October 1874.
- In 1878, he became Chief of Staff of the Guard Corps.
- On 1 June 1885, he was made Commander of the 1st Guard Division.
- From 9 August 1888 until 1895, he was Commanding General of the XIV Army Corps in Karlsruhe.
- Schlichting was one of the modern German military thinkers of his day and was the mastermind behind the 1889 infantry manual.
- On 2 January 1896, he was retired to z.D. and appointed à la suite of 1. Badisches Leib-Grenadier-Regiment Nr. 109.
- Schlichting died in 1909.

Schlieffen, Alfred Graf v.

Alfred Graf v. Schlieffen, born 28 February 1833 in Berlin; died 4 January 1913 in Berlin.

- After being educated by the Herrnhuter Brüdergemeine (Moravian Church), he earned his Abitur at the Joachimsthaler Gymnasium in Berlin and started to study law.
- Soon after, he joined an infantry regiment of the Prussian Army as a OYV. Then he soon changed to the cavalry. He became an active officer, graduated from the War Academy, and joined the Great General Staff in 1863.
- Schlieffen went through the Unification Wars in several troop general staff positions.
- From 1876 until 1884, Schlieffen was commander of the 1. Garde-Ulanen-Regiment in Potsdam and returned to the Great General Staff as a department head in 1884.
- In 1888, he became General Quartermaster and followed Waldersee in 1891 as Chief of the General Staff. Retired to z.D. at the end December 1905 and was promoted to Feldmarschall in 1911.

- Immediately after his retirement, he wrote his operative study about a war with France, later known generally as the Schlieffen Plan. He passed this study on to his successor in early 1906. This study was later considered to be Schlieffen's operational and strategic legacy to the German Army. In 1920 after the lost war, Schlieffen disciples in the Reichsarchiv even went so far as to call this study a "sure recipe of victory," one which the younger Moltke unfortunately failed to carry out correctly.
- Schlieffen had the reputation of being highly intelligent but extremely sarcastic. Schlieffen's critique of decisions during maneuvres or war games were feared and could be personally crushing.

Seeckt, Hans v.

Johannes Friedrich Leopold v. Seeckt (Hans ist the short form of Johannes), born 20 April 1866 in Schleswig; died 27 December 1936 in Berlin.

- After his Abitur, Seeckt joined the Kaiser Alexander Garde-Grenadier-Regiment Nr. 1 in 1885 as an officer candidate and underwent regular officer's training.
- He completed general staff training at the War Academy from 1893–1896 and graduated as best in his class.
- After following the normal sequence of General Staff appointments and troop commands, Seeckt was an Oberstleutnant and Chief of Staff of the III Army Corps in 1914.
- In March 1915, he became Chief of General Staff of the newly formed Eleventh Army under the command of Generaloberst v. Mackensen on the Eastern Front and was one of the intellectual fathers of the decisive breakthrough victory at Gorlice-Tarnów. He was awarded the Pour le Mérite for his performance and promoted to Generalmajor in June 1915.
- When the Army Group Mackensen was formed, he remained Mackensen's chief of staff and fought the successful campaign against Serbia in autumn 1915.
- During the Russian Brusilov offensive in 1916, he was transferred as Chief of General Staff to the Austrian (k.u.k.) Seventh Army under General v. Pflanzer-Baltin and later transferred to the Army Group (called Heeresfront in the Austrian army) of Archduke Karl—later Archduke Joseph.
- In December 1917, he succeeded Friedrich Bronsart v. Schellendorff as military advisor to the Turkish Minister of War, Enver Pasha, and served as de facto Chief of General Staff of the Turkish army.
- After the 1918 armistice, he first served as Chief of General Staff of the border protection forces in eastern Germany and then became a member of the German delegation at Versailles.
- On 1 October 1919, Seeckt became the first head of the Truppenamt, the covert successor organization of the General Staff in the Reichswehr, a function that had been expressly forbidden under the terms of the Versailles Treaty.
- In 1920, Seeckt became Chef der Heeresleitung—de facto commander of the Reichswehr and supported the Weimar government during the crisis years until 1924.
- Seeckt formed the small 100,000-man army of the Reichswehr into a cadre army that could be rapidly mobilized or changed into a much bigger force. He promoted the idea of an élite force with a very small but extremely well-educated and prepared officer corps of only 4,000 officers. Seeckt's aim was to preserve within the Reichswehr the quintessential spirit of the old German army.

- He pushed secret cooperation with the Soviet Union and prepared the build-up of air force and armored formations that followed in the 1930s. He also created a huge system of mobilization preparations that would enable the rapid build-up of forces if needed in the event of war.
- Although Seeckt's plan for a huge build-up of force, the so called Große Plan from 1925, provided the blueprint for the later arms build-up that Hitler executed, he was no supporter of the Nazi movement.

Tappen, Gerhard

Dietrich *Gerhard* Emil Theodor Tappen was born 3 July 1866 in Essens; died 28 May 1953 in Goslar.

- He transferred from head of the 2nd Department to Chief of the Operations Department of the OHL upon mobilization. He was a confidant of Moltke.
- Tappen stood in as Chief of General Staff of Seventh Army in spring 1915 and was awarded the Pour le Mérite on 11 September 1915.
- He filled several General Staff and command appointments during the war.

Verdy du Vernois, Julius v.

Adrian Friedrich Wilhelm *Julius* Ludwig von Verdy du Vernois, born July 1832 in Freystadt; died 30 September 1910 in Stockholm, Sweden.

- He was the descendant of a Huguenot French aristocratic family that had immigrated to Prussia in 1780 and were then hired by the Prussian court.
- He joined the Kadettenhaus in Potsdam in 1844, changed to Groß-Lichterfelde later, where he met Alfred v. Waldersee and developed a close friendship with him.
- He joined Infanterie-Regiment Graf Schwerin (3. Pommersches) Nr. 14 as a Sekondelieutenant on 27 April 1850 in Berlin and moved with the regiment to Thorn, where he married his wife in 1855.
- He successfully completed the War Academy from 1855–1857 and joined the Military History Department of the Great General Staff from 1858 until 1860. He then transferred to the Topographical Department in 1860 and in 1861 was posted as Ic to the General Staff of the IV Army Corps in Magdeburg. From there he went to the HQ of the Russian forces in Warsaw from 1863 until 1865. Due to his excellent performance, the Czar invited him to visit Moscow and St. Petersburg.
- Returning to Germany he was sent on a journey through the southern German states to gather information about their war preparations. His reports were so excellent that the King asked him for a personal report and Moltke became his mentor.
- During the 1866 war he was promoted to Major and served on the General Staff of the Second Army led by the Crown Prince. He thereby gained the trust and personal friendship of the prince, who later became Kaiser Friedrich III. After the war, he acted as one of the authors of the official publication of the Military History Department concerning the 1866 war.
- During the Franco-Prussian War, Verdy served as the youngest departmental head in the Great General Staff and in the General Headquarters.
- After the war, Verdy became chief of staff of I Army Corps in Königsberg, was promoted to Generalmajor and took command of 62 Infantry Brigade in Strasbourg in 1878.

- From 1879 until 1883, he was director of the General War Department (Allgemeines Kriegs-Departement AD), which was the most important department of the War Ministry. He was promoted to Generalleutnant on 15 November 1881.
- After this promotion, he took command of 1st Infantry Division in Königsberg, where Hindenburg worked for him as Ia officer.
- Returning to Strasbourg as a fortress governor from 1887 until 1889, Verdy was responsible for pushing forward the refurbishment of the Strasbourg fortress belt.
- On 23 April 1888, he was promoted to General der Infanterie. He became War Minister on 8 April 1889 with the recommendatiaon of the Chief of General Staff, Alfred v. Waldersee.
- Although Verdy's term lasted only one and a half years, he was responsible for a major arms build-up. During his term the XVI and XVII Army Corps were created, together with Infantry Regiments 140–145, Field Artillery Regiments 33–36 and the Railroad Brigade.
- On 4 October 1890, he retired to z.D. at the age of 58 to start his new career as a well-recognized author of numerous books and articles on military history, tactics and strategy.

Waldersee, Alfred Graf v.

Alfred Heinrich Karl Ludwig Graf v. Waldersee, born 8 April 1832 in Potsdam; died 5 March 1904 in Berlin.

- Waldersee was promoted to Sekondelieutenant in 1850 after being educated in several Kadettenanstalten.
- In 1866, he was Adjutant to the Great Headquarters and joined the Great General Staff soon after the war, having successfully graduated from the War Academy.
- In 1870, he was sent as military attaché to the Prussian embassy in Paris, where he gathered secret information that turned out to be valuable to Moltke for the strategic planning against France.
- During the Franco-Prussian War, he served first as aide de camp to the Prussian King and then as chief of staff in the army of Grand-Duke Friedrich Franz II.
- After the war, he first went back to the embassy in Paris and then became Chief of Staff of the X Army Corps in Hanover.
- In 1874, he married an American wife: Marie Esther Lee.
- In 1882, he became Quartermaster General in the Great General Staff and took step-by-step control from the elder Moltke, who had personally selected Waldersee.
- Officially following Moltke as Chief of General Staff in 1888, the Kaiser dismissed him in 1891. Waldersee had dared to let the Kaiser's side lose in the Kaisermanöver of 1891.
- Waldersee then became Commanding General of the IX Army Corps in Altona.
- In 1898, he took over the Third Army Inspection and was promoted to the rank of Feldmarschall in 1900.
- Due to the attitude of Waldersee and the fact that he was appointed to be Commander of the Expeditionary Forces going to China to counter the Boxer Rebellion, the title Feldmarschall was satirically, but discreetly, rendered Weltmarschall (translatable as world marshal).
- After returning from China in 1901, he again took over the Third Army Inspection and died in 1904.

Waldersee, Georg Graf v.

Georg Graf v. Waldersee was born in 1860; died in 1932. He was a nephew of the Chief of General Staff Feldmarschall Alfred Graf v. Waldersee. The Waldersee family was directly descended from Leopold I, Prince of Anhalt-Dessau (1676–1747)—the so-called "*Alte Dessauer*."

- Upon mobilization, he became Chief of General Staff of the Eight Army defending East Prussia.
- When the commander of the army, Generaloberst v. Prittwitz and Gaffron was dismissed and replaced by Hindenburg on 22 August 1914, Waldersee was also retired to z.D. in favor of Ludendorff, who became Chief of General Staff Eighth Army in his place. Generaloberst v. Prittwitz and Gaffron was dismissed because of his orders to withdraw behind the river Vistula and to sacrifice East Prussia to the advancing Russian steamroller.

Wetzell, Georg

Georg Wetzell, born 5 March 1869 in Nieder-Erlenbach; died 3 January 1947 in Augsburg.

- He joined 1. Lothringisches Pionier-Bataillon Nr. 16 in Metz as an officer candidate on 1 October 1889 and was promoted to Sekondelieutenant on 22 August 1891.
- In 1898, he transferred to the infantry and joined 5. Lothringisches Infanterie-Regiment Nr. 144. After successfully completing the War Academy in 1903, he was transfered to the Great General Staff.
- After holding several General Staff officer's positions, he was eventually the Ia of III Army Corps before he was transferred to the mobilization department of the Great General Staff on 1 August 1914.
- He was posted back to III Army Corps on 9 March 1915, before being appointed Chief of the Operations Department of the OHL in August 1916 as Tappen's successor.
- When Hindenburg and Ludendorff took over, he was awarded the Pour le Mérite on 11 December 1916.
- At the end of September 1918, he became Chief of Staff of Fifth Army.
- After the war, he managed to be retained within the Reichswehr and retired on 31 October 1927 as charakterisierter General der Infanterie.
- From 1930–1935, he worked as military advisor in China.

Wrisberg, Ernst v.

Ernst August Ludwig Konrad v. Wrisberg, born 2 August 1862; died 1 April 1927.

- One of the military managers, who successfully planned and conducted the 1914 mobilization.
- He graduated from the War Academy after completing the course of officer training in the infantry.
- From 1897 until 1898, he served as a member of the Military History Department of the Great General Staff.
- As head of the General War Department from 25 March 1915, he was promoted to Generalmajor on 6 November 1915.
- In 1917, he first commanded an infantry brigade and then the 18th Reserve Division on the Western Front. He was awarded the Pour le Mérite to honor his performance in planning and conducting the 1918 spring offensive.

BIBLIOGRAPHY

Abrams, L. (1992). *Worker's Culture in Imperial Germany.* London: Routledge.

Albisetti, J. (2006). Education. In R. Chickering, *Imperial Germany a Historiographical Companion* (pp. 244–271). Westport Connecticut: Greenwood Press.

Aldenhoff, R. (1996). Agriculture. In R. Chickering, *Imperial Germany a Historiographical Companion*. Westport Connecticut: Greenwood Press.

Alten, G. (1903). *Neue Kanonen?* Berlin: E.S. Mittler & Sohn.

Alten, G. v. (1913). *Handbuch für Heer und Flotte–Enzyklopädie der Kriegswissenschaften und verwandter Gebiete.* Vol. 5. Berlin: Deutsches Verlagshaus Bong & Co. Berlin, Leipzig, Wien.

Alten, G. v. (1911). *Handbuch für Heer und Flotte – Enzyklopädie der Kriegswissenschaften und verwandter Gebiete.* Vol. 1. Berlin: Deutsches Verlagshaus Bong & Co. Berlin, Leipzig, Wien.

Altgelt, D. C. (1921). Feldsanitätswesen. In M. Schwarte, *Der Weltkampf um Ehre und Recht.* Vol 6, none given: Publisher's Syndicate.

Applegate, C. (2008). Culture and the Arts. In J. Retallack, *Imperial Germany 1871–1918.* Oxford: Oxford University Press.

Balck, W. G. (1921, May-June). *Die Wegnahme des Sperrforts Manonviller. Artilleristische Monatshefte*, 100–117.

Bald, D. (1982). *Der deutsche Offizier—Sozial- und Bildungsgeschichte des deutschen Offizierkorps im 20. Jahrhundert.* Munich: Bernard & Graefe Verlag.

Bartsch, R. v. (1907). *Deutsche Soldatenleben.* Minden, Westfallen: Wilhelm Kohler.

Berghahn, V. (1994). *Imperial Germany 1871–1914.* Providence: Berghan Books.

Berlin, H. (1904). *Handbuch der Waffenlehre—Für Offiziere aller Waffen zum Selbstunterricht, besonders zur Vorbereitung für die Kriegsakademie.* Berlin: E.S. Mittler.

Bernhardi, F.G. v. (1907). *Organisation und Ausbildung der Kavallerie für den nächsten Krieg.* Berlin: E.S. Mittler & Sohn.

Bernhardi, F.G. v. (1910). *Reiterdienst. Kritische Betrachtungen über Kriegstätigkeit, Taktik, Ausbildung und Organisation unserer Kavallerie.* Berlin: E.S. Mittler & Sohn.

Bernhardi, F.G. v. (1927). *Denkwürdigkeiten aus meinem Leben nach gleichzeitigen Aufzeichnungen und im Lichte der Erinnerungen.* Berlin: E.S. Mittler & Sohn.

Bessel, R. (2006). Mobilizing German Society for War. In R. Chickering, & S. Förster, *Great War, Total War* (pp. 437–452). Washington DC: Cambridge University Press.

Bethmann-Hollweg, T. v. (1919). *Betrachtungen zum Weltkriege.* Vol. I. Berlin: Verlag Reimar Hobbing.

Blackbourn, D. (2003). *History of Germany 1780–1918.* Malden: Blackwell.

Blanke, R. (1993). *Orphans of Versailles.* Lexington Kentucky: University Press of Kentucky.

Blau, E.-G. (1934). *Die operative Verwendung der Kavallerie im Welrkrieg 1914–1918" part one "Friedensvorbereitungen."* Munich: C.H. Becksche Verlagsbuchhandlung.

Bloem, W. (2004). *The Advance from Mons 1914.* Solihull: Helion.

Blumentritt, G. (1959). *Militärisches Schulsystem und Hochschule* (Vol. 12, 1959). Wehrkunde.

Bloem, W. (1916). Vormarsch. Leipzig: Grethlein & Co.

Boguslawski, A. v. (1903). *Taktische Folgerungen aus dem Burenkrieg und der Gruppenangriff.* Berlin: E.S. Mittler & Sohn.

Bolitho, H. (Ed.) (1938). Further Letters of Queen Victoria: from the archives of the house of brandenburg-prussia. London, UK: Thorton Butterwood Ltd.

Bond, B. J. (1965). *Doctrine and training in the British cavalry.* London.

Brennfleck, M. A. (1939). *Das Königlich Bayerische 2. Feldartillerie-Regiment Horn.* (M. A. Brennfleck, Ed.) Munich: Major a.D. Joseph Karl Brennfleck.

Brose, E. D. (2001). *The Kaiser's Army.* New York, New York, USA: Oxford University Press.

Buchholz, F. (2009). Gab es einen Schlieffenplan? *Gesellschaft für Heereskunde.*

Budde, H. (1904). *Die französischen Eisenbahnen im deutschen kriegsbetriebe 1870–71.* Berlin: E.S. Mittler & Sohn.

Bundesminister der Verteidigung. (1987). *HDv 100/100 Truppenführung (TF).* Bonn: MOD.

Busche, H. (1998). Formationgesichte der deutschen Infanterie im Ersten Weltkreig. *Manuscript*, 375.

Byern, H. (1905). *Anhaltspunkte für die Ausbildung des Schützen, der Rotte und der Gruppe.* Berlin: E.S, Mittler & Sohn.

Carter, M. (2010). *George, Nicholas and Wilhelm: three royal cousins and the road to world war I.* New York City, New York, USA: Alfred A. Knopf.

Chef der Heeresleitung (v. Hammerstein-Equord). (1933). *H.Dv. 300/1 Truppenführung.* Berlin: Verlag von E.S. Mittler & Sohn.

Chickering, R. (2004). *Imperial Germany and the Great War, 1914–1918.* Cambridge: Cambridge University.

Chickering, R. (2007). *The Great War and Urban Life in Germany.* New York: Cambridge University press.

Chickering, R. (2008). Militarism and Radical Nationalism. In J. Retallack, *Imperial Germany 1871–1918.* Oxford: Oxford University Press.

Chinn, G. M. (1951). *The Machine Gun—History, Evolution and Development of Manual, Automatic and Airborne Repeating Weapons.* Vol. I. Washington DC: US Government printing office.

Clark, C. (2008). Religion and Confessional Conflict. In J. Retallack, *Imperial Germany 1871–1918.* Oxford: Oxford University Press.

Clausewitz, C. v. (1832). *Vom Kriege–hinterlassenes Werk"* (Three volumes). Berlin: Dümmler's Verlagsbuchhandlung.

Clausewitz, C. v. (1989). *On War-translated by Michael Howard and Peter Paret.* Princeton: Princeton University Press.

Clemente, S. E. (1992). *For King and Kaiser.* Westport: Greenwood Press.

Cochenhausen, O. v. (1928). *Ein Handbuch für den Truppenführer und seine Gehilfen.* Berlin: E. S. Mittler & Sohn.

Confino, A. (1997). *The Nation as a Local Metaphor.* Chapel Hill: The University of North Carolina Press.

Creveld, M. van (1994). *Supplying War.* Cambridge: Cambridge University Press.

Cron, H. (1935). *Die Entwicklung des deutschen Heeres von seinen Anfängen bis auf unsere Tage" part I.* Fürstenwalde: Verlag für Militärgeschichte und Deutsches Schrifttum.

Cron, H. (1937). *Geschichte des Deutschen Heeres im Weltkriege 1914–1918.* Berlin: Geschichte des Deutschen Heeres im Weltkriege 1914–1918.

Cron, H. (2002). *Imperial German Army 1914–1918.* Solihull, UK: Helion and Co.

Dupuy T.N. (1977) *A Genius For War: The German Army and General Staff 1807–1945* London, UK: MacDonald and Jane's.

Dürr, V. (1985). The Fatal Symbiosis: Prussia and Imperial Germany. In H. H. Dürr, *Imperial Germany.* Madison, Wisconsin: University Of Wisconsin Press.

Davis, B. J. (2000). *Home Fires Burning.* Chapel Hill North Carolina: University Of North Carolina Press.

Delbrück, H. (1975). *History of the Art of War within the Framework of Political History*. Vol. 1. Greenwood, Ct.: Greenwood Press.

Demeter, K. (1963). *Das deutsche Offizierkorps in Gesellschaft und Staat 1650–1945.* Frankfurt a.M.: Bernard & Graefe Verlag.

Department, D. U. (n.d.). *Northwest Europe 1914*. Retrieved 8-December 2008, from http://www.dean.usma.edu/history/web03/atlases/great_20war/great_20war_20_20pages/great_20war_20map_2003new.htm

Deuringer, K. (1929). *Die Schlacht in Lothringen und in den Vogesen 1914.* (Bayer. Kriegsarchiv, Ed.) Munich: Max Schick.

Deutscher Offizier Bund. (Berlin). *Stellenbesetzung der höheren Führer und Generalstabsoffiziere bei Beginn des Weltkrieges, supplement to Ehren-Rangliste des ehemaligen Deutschen Heeres.* 1926: E.S. Mittler & Sohn.

Donson, A. (2010). *War in the Fatherless Land.* Cambridge, Massachusetts, USA: Harvard University Press.

EB.com. (2011). Retrieved 17 December 2011, from Encyclopedia Britannica: http://www.britannica.com/EBchecked/topic/268949/Hohenzollern-dynasty.

Echevarria II, A. J. (2000). *After Clausewitz.* Lawrence, KS: University Press of Kansas.

Einem, Karl (1933). *Erinnerungen eines Soldaten.* Leipzig.

English Monarchs. (2004). Retrieved 23 May 2012, from http://www.englishmonarchs.co.uk/haemophilia.html.

Exner, M. (1897). *Der Weg zum Einjährig-Freiwillinen.* Leipzig: Verlagbuchhandlung.

Förster, S. (1985). *Der doppelte Militarismus.* Stuttgart: Franz Steiner Verlag.

Förster, S. (2006). The Armed Forces and Military Planning. In R. Chickering, *Imperial Germany a Historiographical Companion* (pp. 454–488). Westport Connecticut: Greenwood Press.

Fairbairn, B. (2008). Economic and Social Developments. In J. Retallack, *Imperial Germany 1871–1918*. Oxford: Oxford University Press.

Falkenhayn, E. v. (16 August 1916). *Kriegsministerium M.J. 3531/14, AI geheim), Militärarchiv PH 1/3.* Berlin: Kriegsministerium.

Feuchtwanger, E. (2001). *Imperial Germany 1850–1918.* London: Routledge.

Fife., R. H., jr. (1916). *The German Empire Between Two Wars.* Chautauqua: Chautauqua Press.

Fischer, F. (1968). *Germany's Aims in the First World War.* NewYork: W. W. Norton & Company.

François, H. v. (1910). *Verwaltungs-Generalstabsreisen. Nur für den Dienstgebrauch bestimmt.* Berlin: Reichsdruckerei.

Frevert, U. (2004). *A Nation in Barracks.* Oxford: Berg.

Freytag-Loringhoven, Frhr. v. (1913). *Generalfeldmarschall Graf Alfred v. Schlieffen – Gesammelte Schriften* (Vol. 1). Berlin: E.S. Mittler & Sohn.

Freytag-Loringhoven, Frhr. v. (1901–1903). *Studien über Kriegführung auf Grundlage des Nordamerikanischen Sezessionskrieges in Virginien* (Three volumes). Berlin: E.S. Mittler & Sohn.

Freytag-Loringhoven, Frhr. v., (1907). *Das Exerzier-Reglement für die Infanterie vom 29. Mai 1906 kriegsgeschichtlich erläutert.* Berlin: E.S. Mittler & Sohn.

Friedag, B. (1914). *Führer durch Heer und Flotte 1914.* Berlin: Verlagsbuchhandlung Alfred Schall.

Frobel, G. v. (1909). Das neue Exerzier-Reglement für die Kavallerie. *Beiheft zum Militär-Wochenblatt 4. Und 5. Heft 1909.*

Frobel, G. v. (1901). Militär-Wochenblatt Heft 3. *Militär-Wochenblatt Heft 3.*

Generalinspektion der Kavallerie. (1914). *Gesichtspunkte für den Aufklärungsdienst nur für den Dienstgebrauch!* Berlin: Reichsdruckerei.

General-Inspektion des Militär-Erziehungs- und Bildungswesen (1912). *Leitfaden für den Unterricht in der Taktik auf den Königlichen Kriegsschulen.* Berlin: E.S. Mittler & Sohn.

Generalstab des Feldheeres. (1918). *Lüttich–Namur.* Oldenburg: Gerhard Stalling.

Generalstab des Heeres 7. Abt. (1939). *Der Handstreich auf Lüttich vom 3. Bis 7. August 1914.* Berlin: E.S. Mittler.

Geyer, M. (1984). German strategy in the age of machine warfare, 1914–1945. In P. Paret, *Makers of Modern Strategy—from Macchiavelli to the nuclear age.* Princeton: Princeton University Press.

Green, A. (2004). *Fatherlands.* New York: Cambridge University Press.

Green, A. (2004). Political and Diplomatic Movements, 1850–1870. In J. Sperber, *Germany 1800–1870*. Oxford, United Kingdom: Oxford University Press.

Griepenkerl, O. (1901). *Taktische Unterrichtsbriefe – Zur Vorbereitung für das Kriegsakademie-Examen, taktische Übungsritte, Kriegsspiel und Manöver.* Berlin : E.S. Mittler.

Groß, G. P. (2008). There Really Was a Schlieffen Plan. *War in History*.

Groß, G. P. (2006). There was a Schlieffen Plan. In M. F. (Ed.), *Der Schlieffenplan – Analysen und Dokumente.* Paderborn: Ferdinand Schöningh.

Großer Generalstab. (1914). *Anhaltspunkte für den Generalstabsdienst.* (G. G. (Ed.), Ed.) Berlin: Großer Generalstab.

Großer Generalstab. (1914). *Taschenbuch für den Generalstabsoffizier (geheim).* Berlin: E.S. Mittler.

Großer Generalstab, Abtheilung für Kriegsgeschichte I. (1900). *Moltkes Taktisch-strategische Aufsätze aus den Jahren 1857 bis 1871.* Berlin: E.S. Mittler und Sohn.

Großer Generalstab, Krieggeschichtliche Abteilung I. (1903). *Kriegsgeschichtliche Einzelschriften – Erfahrungen außereuropäischer Kriege der neuesten Zeit. Aus dem südafrikanischen Kriege 189–1901 (Vol. 32).* Berlin: E.S. Mittler.

Großer Generalstab, Krieggeschichtliche Abteilung I. (1867). *Der Feldzug von 1866.* Berlin: Mittler und Sohn.

Großer Generalstab, Krieggeschichtliche Abteilung I. (1874–1881). *Der Krieg 1870–71.* Berlin: E.S. Mittler.

Großer Generalstab, Kriegsgeschichtliche Abteilung I. (1911). *Moltke Militärische Werke Volume IV (Kriegslehren), part 1 "Die operativen Vorbereitungen zur Schlacht".* Berlin: E.S. Mittler & Sohn, Berlin.

Groener, W. G. (1931). *Der Feldherr wider Willen.* Berlin: E. S. Mittler & Sohn.

Guderian Generaloberst a. D., H. (1951). *Erinnerungen eines Soldaten.* Heidelberg: Kurt Vowinckel Verlag.

Höhn, R. (1959). *Sozialismus und Heer.* Bad Homburg: Verlag Dr. Gehlen.

Hackl, O. (1989). *Die Bayerische Kriegsakademie 1867–1914.* Munich: C.H. Beck'sche Verlagsbuchhandlung.

Hafenader, R. (2008). *German Colonial Cartography.* Munich: Bundeswehr University Munich.

Haffner, S. /. (1982). *Das Wunder an der Marne—Rekonstruktion der Entscheidungsschlacht des Ersten Weltkriegs.* Bergisch-Gladbach: Gustav Lübbe Verlag.

Harrell, J. L. (1983). *Regimental Steins.* Frederick Maryland: The Old Soldier Press.

Hausen, G. F. (1920). *Erinnerungen an den Marnefeldzug 1914.* Leipzig: K. F. Koehler Verlag.

Kriegsministerium (1904). *Heerodnung des Deutsches Reiches.* Berlin: E.S. Mittler & Sohn.

Hein. (1901). *Das kleine Buch vom Deutschen Heere.* Kiel: Lipsius & Tischer.

Henningsen, N. (none given). *Wie Lüttich fiel.* Köln: Verlag Hermann Schffstein.

Herr, U. et. al. (2012). *Die deutschen Generale sowie Kriegsministerien und Generalstäbe von 1871 bis 1914.* Vienna: Militaria-Verlag.

Herr U. et.al. (2008). *The German Infantry from 1871 to 1914.* Vienna Austria: Verlag Militaria.

Herwig, H. H. (1997). *The First World War Germany and Austria Hungary 1914–1918.* London: Arnold.

Herwig, H. (2009). *The Marne, 1914.* NY, USA: Random House.

Hewitson, M. (2008). Wilhelmine Germany. In J. Retallack, *Imperial Germany 1871 – 1918* (pp. 40–60). Oxford: Oxford University Press.

Heydenreich, W. (1906). *Das moderne Feldgeschütz.* Leipzig: G.J. Göschensche Verlagsbuchhandlung.

Hilger, H. (1905). *Die Länder und Staaten der Erde.* Berlin: Berann Hilger Verlag.

Hoehn, G. v. (1913). *Führungstechnik der Artillerie des Feldheeres.* Munich: Theodor Riedel's Buchhandlung,.

Hoenig, F. (1890). *Untersuchungen über die Taktik der Zukunft entwickelt aus der neuesten Kriegsgeschichte.* Berlin: E.S. Mittler & Sohn.

Holmes, T. M. (2008). All Present and Correct: The Verifiable Army of the Schlieffen Plan. *War in History*, 98–115.

Holmes, T. M. (2003). Classical Blitzkrieg: The Untimely Modernity of Schlieffen's Cannae Programme. *Journal of Military History; Jul 2003, 67* (3), 745–771.

Horne, J., & Kramer, A. (2001). *German Atrocities, 1914.* New Haven, Connecticut: Yale University press.

Horsetzky, A. v. (1905). *Feldzüge in Europa.* Vienna: L. W. Seidel & Sohn.

Howard, B. E. (1906). *The German Empire.* London: Macmillan.

Howard, M. (1984). Men against fire: The doctrine of the offensive in 1914. In P. Paret, *Makers of Modern Strategy—from Macchiavelli to the nuclear age.* Princeton: Princeton University press.

Hutcheson, J. (2005). *The Encyclopeida of World War I: a political, social, and military history* (Vol. 1). (S. C. Tucker, Ed.) Santa Barbara, CA, USA: ABC-CLIO, Inc.

Israel, B. (2009, October 12). *Discover Magazine.* Retrieved 23 May 2012, from http://blogs.discovermagazine.com/80beats/2009/10/12

Janke, T. (2011). Landwehrmänner und Reservisten. In T. a. Loch, *Wie die Siegessäule nach Berlin kam* (pp. 48–5). Freiburg i.Br.: Rombach Verlag.

Jany, C. (1967). *Die Königlich Preußische Armee und das Deutsche Reichsheer 1807–1914 vol 4, 2nd edition.* Osnabruck: Biblio Verlag.

Königlich Bayerisches Kriegsministerium. (1906). *Exerzier-Reglement für die Infanterie. D.V. Nr. 158.* Munich: Münchner Buchgewerbehaus M. Müller & Sohn.

Kaiserliches Statistisches Amt. (1914). *Statistik des Deutschen Reichs.* Berlin: Mittler & Sohn.

Kayser, O. (1942). Das AOK 7 während der Kämpfe in den Reichslanden (August – September 1914).

Kim, D. (2009). *Soldatenleben in Württemberg 1871–1914: Zur Sozialgeschichte des deutschen Militärs.* Paderborn: Schöningh.

Kitchen, M. (1968). *The German Officer 1890–1914.* Oxford: Clarendon Press.

Kluck, A. v. (1926). *Der Marsch auf Paris und die Schlacht am Ourcq.* Berlin: Walter de Gruyter & Co.

Koenig, M. A. (3 August 2010). Royal Musings.

Krüger, F. K. (1915). *Government and Politics of the German Empire.* Yonkers: World Books Company.

Krafft v. Dellmensingen, K. (1931). *Kritischer Streifzug durch die Studien des Generalleutnants a.D. Wilhelm Gröner über den Weltkrieg—Das Oberkommando in den Reichslanden im Sommer 1914.* Munich: Max Schick.

Krafft, M. (1903). *Handbuch für die Vorbereitung zur Kriegsakademie.* Berlin: E.S. Mittler.

Krafft, M. (1910). *Die Aufgaben der Aufnahmeprüfung 1910 für die Kriegsakademie – Besprechungen und Lösungen–3. Nachtrag zur 2. Auflage des Handbuchs für die Vorbereitung zur Kriegsakademie.* Berlin: E.S. Mittler.

Krafft, M. (1912). *Die Aufgaben der Aufnahmeprüfung 1920 für die Kriegsakademie – Besprechungen und Lösungen–5. Nachtrag zur 2. Auflage des Handbuchs für die Vorbereitung zur Kriegsakademie.* BERLIN: E.S. Mittler.

Kramer, A. (1997). Wackes at War: Alsace-Lorraine and the failure of German national mobilization. In J. Horne editor, *State, society and mobilization in Europe during the First World War.* New York, New York: Cambridge University Press.

Kraus, J. (2012). *Handbuch der Verbände und Truppen des deutschen Heeres 1914–1918. Part VI: Infanterie, Volume 2: Reserve- und Landwehr-Infanterie.* Vienna.

Kriegsministerium. (1909). *Das Königlich Preußische Kriegsministerium, 1. März 1809–1. März 1909.* Berlin: War Ministry.

Kriegsgeschichtliche Abteilung der Luftwaffe. (1939). *Mobilmachung, Aufmarsch und erster Einsatz der deutschen Luftstreitkräfte im August 1914.* Berlin: E.S. Mittler & Sohn.

Kriegsministerium. (1913). *Anhang (supplement) zum Exerzier-Reglement für die Feldartillerie D.V.E. Nr. 414a.* Berlin: E.S. Mittler & Sohn.

Kriegsministerium. (1911). *Anlage 1 zum Exerzier-Reglement für die Fußartillerie.* Berlin: E.S. Mittler & Sohn.

Kriegsministerium. (1904). *D.V.E. No. 44 Exerzier-Reglement für die Maschinengewehr-Abteilungen.* Berlin: E.S. Mittler & Sohn.

Kriegsministerium. (1909). *D.V.E. Nr.: 240, Schießvorschrift für die Infanterie.* Berlin: E.S. Mittler & Sohn.

Kriegsministerium. (1908). *D.V.E. Nr.: 323, Schießvorschrift für die Fußartillerie.* Berlin: E.S. Mittler & Sohn.

Kriegsministerium. (1914). *D.V.E. Nr.: 416, Schießvorschrift für die Feldartillerie.* Berlin: E.S. Mittler & Sohn.

Kriegsministerium. (1909). *D.V.E. Nr.:342, Schießvorschrift für die Kavallerie.* Berlin: E.S. Mittler & Sohn.

Kriegsministerium. (1909). *Exerzier-Regiment für die Kavallerie.* Berlin: E.S. Mittler & Sohn.

Kriegsministerium. (1907). *Exerzier-Reglement für die Feldartillerie D.V.E. Nr. 414.* Berlin: E.S. Mittler & Sohn.

Kriegsministerium. (1906). *Exerzier-Reglement für die Infanterie D.V.E. Nr. 130.* Berlin: E.S. Mittler & Sohn.

Kriegsministerium. (1899). *Exerzir-Reglement für die Feldartillerie.* Berlin: E.S. Mittler & Sohn.

Kriegsministerium. (1889). *Exerzir-Reglement für die Infanterie 1889.* Berlin: E.S. Mittler.

Kriegsministerium. (1812). *Exerzir-Reglement für die Infanterie der Königlich Preußischen Armee.* Berlin: Georg Decker.

Kriegsministerium. (1847). *Exerzir-Reglement für die Infanterie der Königlich Preußischen Armee.* Berlin: Decker'sche Geheime Ober-Hofdruckerei.

Kriegsministerium. (1895). *Exerzir-Reglement für die Kavallerie.* Berlin: E.S. Mittler & Sohn.

Kriegsministerium. (1876). *Exerzir-Reglement für die Kavallerie vom 5. Juli 1876.* Berlin: Verlag der Königlichen Geheimen Ober-Hofbuchdruckerei R. v. Decker.

Kriegsministerium. (1908). *Felddienst-Ordnung.* Berlin: E.S. Mittler & Sohn.

Kriegsministerium. (1907). *Bericht über die Aufklärungsübung 1905 geheim!* Berlin: Reichsdruckerei.

Kriegsministerium. (1911). *"D.V.E. Nr. 130b IV. Teil des Exerzier-Reglements für die Infanterie.* Berlin: E.S. Mittler & Sohn.

Kriegsministerium. (1819). *Rang- und Quartierliste der Königlich Preußischen Armee für das Jahr 1819.* Berlin: Wilhelm Dieterei.

Kriegsministerium. (1838). *Rang- und Quartierliste der Königlich Preußischen Armee für das Jahr 1838.* (G. Kriegs-Kanzlei, Ed.) Berlin: E.S. Mittler & Sohn.

Kriegsministerium. (1851). *Rangliste 1851 Rang- und Quartierliste der Königlich Preußischen Armee und Marinefür das Jahr 1851.* (G. Kriegs-Kanzlei, Ed.) Berlin: E.S. Mittler & Sohn.

Kriegsministerium. (1914). *Rangliste 1914.* Berlin: E.S. Mittler & Sohn.

Kriegsministerium. (1905). *Vorschrift über die Ergänzung der Offiziere des Friedensstandes nebst Dienstordnung für die Ober-Militär-Prüfungskommission.* Berlin: E.S. Mittler & Sohn.

Kriegsministerium. (1871). *Rang- und Quartierliste der Königlich Preußischen Armee und Maine für das Jahr 1870–71, Stand vom 01.10.1871.* Berlin: E.S. Mittler und Sohn.

Kriegsministerium, K.B. (1914). *Militär-Handbuch für das Königreich Bayern nach dem Stande vom 16. Mai 1914 (47. Auflage).* (A. f. Angelegenheiten, Ed.) Munich: Drucksachen-Verlag des Kriegsministerium, gedruckt im Kriegsministerium.

Kriegsministerium, K.S. (1914). *Rangliste der Königlich Sächsischen Armee für das Jahr 1914 (nach dem Stande vom 20. Dezember 1913).* (A. f. Angelegenheiten, Ed.) Dresden-Neustadt: Druck von C. Heinrich.

Kuhl, H. v. (1921). *Der Marnefeldzug 1914.* Berlin: E. S. Mittler & Sohn.

Kuhl, H. v. (1929). *Movements and Supply of the German First Army during August and September 1914.* Fort Leavenworth: The Command and Gen. Staff School Press.

Kybitz, W. (1939). *Ludendorffs Handstreich auf Lüttich.* Munich: Ludendorffs Verlag.

Lau, K. M. (1921). Die Heeresverpflegung. In M. Schwarte, *Der Weltkampf um Ehre und Recht* (Vol. 7). none given: Publisher's Syndicate.

Lehmann, G. (1905). *Die Mobilmachung von 1870–71.* Berlin: E.S. Mittler & Sohn.

Lerman, K. A. (2008). Bismarckian Germany. In J. Retallack, *Imperial Germany 1871–1918*. Oxford: Oxford University Press.

Lindenau, O. v. (1902). Was lehrt uns der Burenkrieg für unseren Infanterieangriff? *Beiheft zum Militär-Wochenblatt Heft 3*.

Linnenkohl, H. (1996). *Vom Einzelschuß zur Feuerwalze—Der Wettlauf zwischen Technik und Taktik im Ersten Weltkrieg*. Bonn: Bernard & Graefe Verlag.

Ludendorff, E. (1933). *Mein militärischer Werdegang*. Munich: Ludendorffs Verlag.

Lundström, R. (2009, May). message traffic between Richard Lundström and the author. San Antonio Texas.

Müller-Loebnitz, W. O. (1939). *Die Führung im Marne-Feldzug 1914*. Berlin: E. S. Mittler & Sohn.

Macky, R. W. (1991). *The Zabern Affair 1913–1914*. Lanham, MD: University Press of America.

Marengo. (2009, May 19). *The Royal Articles*. Retrieved 20 May 2011, from http://www.theroyalarticles.com

Martin, A. G. (1936). *Mother Country Fatherland*. London: McMillan & Co.

Martinez, V. (2011). *An Unusual Journey Through Royal History* (Vol. 1). Chapel Hill, NC, USA: Who Dares Wins Publishing.

Martinzez, V. (2011). *An Unusual Journey Through Royal History* (Vol. 2). NC, USA: Who Dares Wins Publishing.

Massie, R. K. (1992). *Dreadnought—Britain, Germany and the Coming of the Great War*. London: Pimlico.

Mattuschka, E. G. (1979). *Organisationsgeschichte des Heeres von 1890 bis 1918 in Militärgeschichtliches Forschungsamt (1980) Handbuch zur deutschen Militärgeschichte 1648–1939 (Vol 3)*. Munich: Bernard & Graefe Verlag.

McLean, R. R. (2007). *Royalty and Diplomacy in Europe, 1890–1914*. New York City, New York, USA: Cambridge University Press.

McManners, J. (2001). *The Oxford History of Christianity*. Oxford: Oxford U. Press.

Model, H. (1968). *Der deutsche Generalstabsoffizier*. Fankfurt a.M.: Bernard & Graefe Verlag.

Moltke, E. v. (1922). *Generaloberst Helmuth von Moltke—Erinnerungen, Briefe, Dokumente 1877–1916*. Stuttgart: Der kommende Tag.

Mombauer, A. (2003). *Helmuth von Moltke and the Origins of the First World War*. Cambridge: Cambridge University Press.

Mommsen, W. J. (1995). *Bürgerstolz und Weltmachtstreben 1890–1918*. Berlin: Propyläen-Verlag.

Mommsen, W. J. (1995). *Imperial Germany 1867–1918*. London: Arnold.

Moncure, J. (1993). *Forging the King's Sword*. New York: Peter Lang.

Mummenhoff. (1907). *Die modernen Geschütze der Fußartillerie, Teil II*. Leipzig: G.J. Göschensche Verlagsbuchhandlung.

Nöll v. d. Nahmer, R. (1968). *Bismarcks Reptilienfonds*. Mainz: Hase and Koehler Verlag.

Naujoks, E. (1968). *Bismarcks auswärtige Pressepolitik und die Reichsgründung*. Wiesbaden: Franz Steiner Verlag.

Neiberg, M. (2011). *Dance of the Furies*. London, England: Belknap press.

Nicolai, W. O. (1921). Nachrichten wesen und Aufklärung. In M. Schwarte, *Der Weltkampf um Ehre und Ruhm*. Leipzig: Johann Ambrosius Barth.

Opfell, O. S. (2001). *Royalty Who Wait: the 21 heads of formerly regnant houses of Europe*. Jefferson, NC, USA: McFarland & Company, Inc.

Ortenburg, G. (1990). *Waffe und Waffengebrauch im Zeitalter der Einigungskriege*. Koblenz: Bernard & Graefe Verlag.

Ortenburg, G. (1992). *Waffe und Waffengebrauch im Zeitalter der Millionenheere*. Bonn: Bernard & Graefe Verlag.

Packard, J. M. (1998). *Victoria's Daughters*. New York City, New York, USA: St. Martin's Griffin.

Pelet-Narbonne, G. z. (1908). *v. Löbvell's Jahresberichte über das Heer und Kriegswesen XXXIV. Jahrgang 1907*. Berlin: E.S. Mittler & Sohn.

Perris, H. (1912). *Germany and the German Emperor.* New York: Henry Holt & Co.

Pflugk-Hartung, D.J. v. (1896). *Die Heere und Flotten der Gegenwart, Band I Deutschland.* Berlin: Verlag Schall & Grund.

Poseck, M. v. (1921). *Die deutsche Kavallerie in Belgien und Frankreich 1914.* Berlin: E.S. Mittler & Sohn.

Poseck, M. v. (1921). *The German Cavalry 1914 in Belgium and France* (Reprinted in 2007 ed.). (M. J. Howe, Ed.) Sandhurst: The Naval and Mlitary Press.

Pounds, N. (1996). Historical Geography. In R. Chickering, *Imperial Germany a Historiographical Companion*. Westport Connecticut: Greenwood Press.

Price, M. (2009, October). *Science AAAS.* Retrieved 23 May 2012, from http://news.sciencemag.org/sciencenow/2009/10/08-02html.

Rüdt von Collenberg, L. (1922). *Die deutsche Armee von 1871–1914.* (1914). *Die deutsche Land- und Seemacht und die Berufspflichten des Offiziers.* Berlin: Mittler u. Sohn.

Reichenau, G. (1902). *Stahlgeschoß und Schutzschild—Eine neue Phase in der Entwicklung des Feldgeschützes.* Berlin: Vossische Buchhandlung.

Reichsarchiv. (1928). *Das deutsche Feldbahnwesen-Erster Band: Die Eisenbahnen zu Kriegsbeginn.* Berlin: E.S. Mittler & Sohn.

Reichsarchiv. (1930). *Der Weltkrieg 1914–1918—Kriegsrüstung und Kriegswirtschaft"* (Supplement volume). Berlin: E.S. Mittler & Sohn.

Reichsarchiv. (1926). *Der Weltkrieg 1914–1918* (Vol. 4) *Der Marne-Feldzu—Die Schlacht.* Berlin: E.S. Mittler & Sohn.

Reichsarchiv. (1925). *Der Weltkrieg 1914–1918* (Vol. 1) *Die Grenzschlachten im Westen.* Berlin: E.S. Mittler & Sohn.

Reichsarchiv. (1926). *Der Weltkrieg 1914–1918* (Vol. 3) *Der Marne-Feldzug—Von der Sambre zur Marne.* Berlin: E.S. Mittler & Sohn.

Reichswehrministerium (1923). *H.Dv. 487 Führung und Gefecht der verbundenen Waffen.* Berlin: Verlag Offene Worte.

Reichswehrministerium, C. d. (1923). *H.Dv. 487 Führung und Gefecht der verbundenen Waffen.* Berlin: Verlag Offene Worte.

Retallack, J. (1996). *Germany in the Age of Kaiser Wilhelm II.* London: MacMillan.

Ritter, G. (1956). *Der Schlieffenplan.* Munich: Oldenbourg Verlag.

Rochs, D. H. (1921). *Schlieffen—Ein Lebens- und Charakterbild für das deutsche Volk.* Berlin: Vossische Buchhandlung.

Rohl, J. M. (1998). *Purple Secret: Genes, 'Madness' and the Royal Houses of Europe.* Great Britain: Bantam Press.

Rossiter, C. (2002). *Constitutional Dictatorship.* Edison New Jersey: Transaction.

Royal Musings. (12 November 2008). Retrieved 20 May 2012 from http://royalmusingsblogspotcom.blogspot.com/search?q=saxe-coburg-gotha

Rushton, A. R. (2008). *Royal Maladies: Inherited Diseases in the Ruling Houses of Europe.* Victoria, British Columbia, Canada: Trafford Publishing.

Sacher, H. (1911). *Oldenburg.* (K. Knight, Ed.) Retrieved 20 January 2012, from New Advent: http://www.newadvent.org/cathen/11237b.htm

Scarlata, P. S. (2008). *The German Gewehr 88 'Commission' Rifle.* Woonsocket, RI: Mowbray.

Schössler, D. (2009). *Clausewitz–Engels–Mahan: Grundriss einer Ideengeschichte militärischen Denkens.* Münster: Lit-Verlag.

Schäfer, T. v. (1927). *Schlachten des Weltkrieges* (vol. 19) *Tannenberg.* Oldenburg: Verlag Gerhard Stalling.

Scherff, W. v. (1904). *Gewehr und Gelände im heutigen Angriffskampf.* Berlin: E.S. Mittler.

Schlichting, G. d. (1897–1899). *Taktische und strategische Grundsätze der Gegenwart, 3 volumes.* Berlin: E.S. Mittler & Sohn.

Schlieffen, A. Graf v. (January 1909). Der Krieg in der Gegenwart. *Deutsche Revue.*

Schlieffen, A. Graf v. (1913). *Gesammelte Schriften* (Vol. 1). Berlin: E. S. Mittler & Sohn.

Schmid, J. (2011). *Die Dialektik von Angriff und Verteidigung—Clausewitz und die stärkste Form des Kriegführens.* Wiesbaden: VS-Verlag.

Schmidt, R. H. (1923). Die Nachrichtenmittel. In M. Schwarte, *Der Weltkampf um Ehre und Ruhm* (Vol. 7). Leipzig: Publisher's Syndicate.

Schmidt-Richberg, W. (1979). *Die Regierungszeit Wilhelms II. in: Militärgeschichtliches Forschungsamt (Ed.) Handbuch zur deutschen Militärgeschichte 1648–1939.* Munich: Bernard & Graefe Verlag.

Schroeder, K. O. (1923). Die Etappe. In M. Schwarte, *Der Weltkampf um Ehre und Recht* (Vol. 7). Leipzig: Publisher's Syndicate.

Schwarz, D. H. (1962). *Gefechtsformen der Infanterie und ihre Entwicklung in Mitteleuropa.* Munich: self.

Senior, I. (2012). *Home Before the Leaves Fall.* Oxford.

Shafritz, J. M. (1990). *Words on War.* New York: Prentice-Hall.

Shaser, A. (2008). Gendered Germany. In J. Retallack, *Imperial Germany 1871–1918.* Oxford: Oxford University Press.

Shaw, K. (1999). *Royal Babylon: the alarming history of European royalty.* New York, NY, USA: Broadway Books.

Sheldon, J. (2009, 22-April). Email. San Antonio.

Sheldon, J. (2010). *The German Army at Ypres 1914.* Barnsley, South Yorkshire, England: Pen and Sword Books.

Sheldon, J. (2005). *The German Army on the Somme.* Barnsley: Pen and Sword Books.

Sheldon, J. (2008). *The German Army on Vimy Ridge.* Barnsley: Pen and Sword Books.

Showalter, D. E. (1991). *Tannenbrg: Clash of Empires.* Hamden Connecticut: Archon Book.

Showalter, D. E. (2004). *The Wars of German Unification.* London: Hodder Education.

Showalter, D. (2000). From Deterrence to Doomsday Machine: The German Way of War, 1890–1914. *The Journal of Military History, Vol. 64, No. 3.*

Sigel, G. (1900). *Deutschlands Heer und Flotte.* Akron: The Werner Co.

Silverman, D. P. (1972). *Reluctant Union.* University Park: Pennsylvania State University Press.

Smith, W. D. (1996). Colonialism and Colonial Empire. In R. Chickering, *Imperial German,y A Historiographical Companion*. London: Greenwood Press.

Solf, F. M. (1920). *Zwei Kriegsjahre einer 42cm Batterie.* Stuttgart: Chr. Belser'sche Verlagsbuchhandlung.

Spears, E. (2000). *Liaison 1914.* London: Cassel & Co.

Staatsbürger Bibliothek. (1913). *Das Landheer.* M. Gladbach: Volksverein Verlag.

Stachelbeck, C. (2012). *Militärische Effektivität im Ersten Weltkrieg—Die 11. Bayerische Infanteriedivision 1915–1918,* Munich: Ferdinand Schöningh Verlag.

Stein, G. v. (1921). *A War Minister and His Work.* London: Skeffington & Son.

Stein Hans-Peter (1984) *Symbole und Zeremoniell in deutschen Streitkräften.* Herford und Bonn: Mittler.

Stoneman, M. R. (2006, 12 19). Wilhelm Groener, Officering, And The Schlieffen Plan. *Graduate School of Arts and Sciences of Georgetown University*. Washington, DC, USA.

Storz, D. (2012). *Deutsche Militärgewehre, Band 2: Schußwaffen 88 und 91.* Vienna: Militaria Verlag.

Storz, D. (1992). *Kriegsbild und Rüstung vor 1914.* Herford et. Al. : E.S. Mittler & Sohn.

Strachan, H. (2003). *The First World War.* New York: Viking.

Strachan, H. (2001). *The First World War volume 1: To Arms.* New York: Oxford University Press.

Stubbs, T. N. (2004). *Imperial German Military Officer's Helmets & Head Dress 1871–1918.* Altgen: Schiffer.

Sußdorf, W. (1921). Das Feldkraftfahrwesen. In Schwarte, Max, *Der Weltkampf um Ehre und Recht* (Vol. 6). Leipzig: Publisher's Syndicate.

Tettau, F. v. (1910). *Der russisch-japanische Krieg – amtliche Darstellung des russischen Generalstabes* (Vol. 5). Berlin: E.S. Mittler & Sohn.

Thöny, E. (none given). *Militaer.* Munich: Verlag Albert Langen.

The General Staff. (1918). *Handbook of the German Army in the War.* Nashville: Imperial War Museum and Battery Press.

Tice, K. K. (2010, December). The Triumphs, Tragedies, and Scandals of the Daughters-in-Law of Kaiser Vilhelm II. *European Royal History Journal*.

Times, N. Y. (1871, 21-July). Conventions with Baden and Hesse. *New York Times*.

Tipton, F. B. (1996). Technology and Industrial Growth. In R. Chickering, *Imperial Germany a Historiographical Companion* (pp. 62–96). Westport Connecticut: Greenwood Press.

Tschischwitz, v. G. (1940). *General von der Marwitz.* Berlin: Steiniger Verlage.

Turinetti, James D.; O'Connor, John Albert. (2006). *Imperial Germany Headgear.* Fairfield Ohio: self.

U.S. Army War College. (1917). *Notes on the German Army in the War.* Washington: Government Printing Office.

Unruh, K. (1986). *Langemarck—Legende und Wirklichkeit.* Koblenz: Bernard & Graefe Verlag.

Urach, Herzog v. (1905). *Vepflegung einer Kavallerie-Division im Felde.* No publisher given.

Van der Kiste, J. (2003). *The Georgian Princesses.* Stroud, Gloucestershire, Great Britain: Sutton Publishing.

Velsen, S. v. (1921). Das Militärbahnwesen. In M. Schwarte, *Der Weltkampf um Ehre und Recht* (Vol. 6). none given: Publisher's Syndicate.

Verhey, J. (2000). *The Spirit of 1914.* Cambridge: Cambridge Press.

Verhey, J. (2008). War and Revolution. In J. Retallack, *Imperial Germany 1871–1918*. Oxford: Oxford University Press.

Waldersee, Graf v. (1927). *Von Kriegführung, Politik, Persönlichkeiten und ihrer Wechselwirkung aufeinander.* Deutscher Offiziers Bund.

Wallach, J. L. (1967). *Das Dogma der Vernichtungsschlacht.* Frankfurt a. M.: Bernard & Graefe Verlag.

Wandt, H. (1921). *Etappe Gent.* Berlin: Buchverlag der Freien Presse.

Wawro, G. (1998). *The Austro-Prussian War.* New York: Cambridge University.

Wehler, H.-U. (1985). *The German Empire.* New York: Berg.

Kriegsministerium. (1888). *Deutsche Wehrordnung 1914.* Berlin: Mar Galle Verlag.

Wenninger, R. G. (1913). *Wert oder Unwert der Kavallerie? in: Deutsche Revue Nr. 38.*

White, D. S. (1996). Regionalism and Particularism. In R. Chickering, *Imperial Germany A Historiographical Companion*. Westport Connecticut: Greenwood Press.

Widder, W. M. (2002, Sept–Oct). Auftragstaktik and Innere Führung: Trademarks of German Leadership. *Military Review.*

Wikipedia. (2009 1–March). *Orthographische Konferenz von 1901*. Retrieved 2009, 14-April from http://de.wikipedia.org/wiki/Orthographische_Konferenz_von_1901.

Wurtzbacher, L. (1921). Die Versorgung des Heeres mit Waffen und Munition. In M. Schwarte, *Der Weltkampf um Ehre und Recht* (Vol. 6). none given: Publisher's Syndicate.

Xylander, R. R. (1935). *Deutsche Führung in Lothringen 1914.* Berlin: Junker und Dünnhaupt Verlag.

Zuber, T. (2007). *Ardennes 1914: The Battle of the Frontiers.* Charleston: The History Press.

Zuber, T. (2002). *Inventing the Schlieffen Plan.* New York: Oxford University.

Zuber, T. (2010). *The Mons Myth: A Reassessment of the Battle.* Stroud: The History Press.

Zuber, T. (1999). The Schlieffen Plan Reconsidered. *War in History*.

Zwehl, General der Infanterie a.D., H. (1923). *Generalstabsdienst in Frieden und Krieg.* E.S. Mittler.

QUALITY REFERENCE BOOKS ARE THE BUILDING BLOCKS OF AN ADVANCED COLLECTION

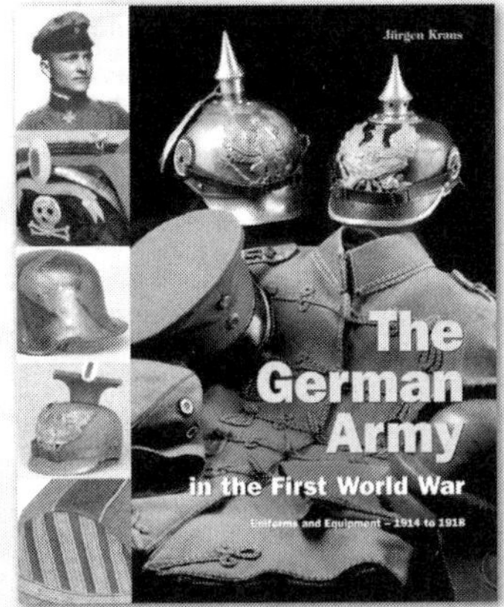

ISBN: 978-3-9501642-6-8 $ 140

The German Army – in the First World War

Author: Jürgen Kraus

640 pages, approx. 1400 photographs and illustrations, linen-bound with a book jacket. Format: 29.5 × 25 cm

This superbly illustrated 640 page volume presents a comprehensive picture of the uniforms and equipment of the German Army in the First World War. More than 1400 magnificent colour photographs illustrate the full range of clothing and insignia, from lowly private to lofty field marshal. This book includes not only detailed descriptions of all the garments worn in the German Army during the war, but also of the special uniforms and insignia of each branch of service. This fascinating collection of photographs of original pieces is supplemented by 400 contemporary wartime photographs showing clearly how they were actually worn. Together they illustrate the external changes in the German Army between 1914 and the end of the war. The collection of the Bayerisches Armeemuseum in Ingolstadt was photographed for the first time for this book, along with some important artefacts from the Wehrgeschichtliches Museum in Rastatt. Despite the camouflage function of the field-grey uniform, it still reflected the structure of the German Army in the various contingents and branches of service.

ISBN: 978-3-902526-33-5 $ 140

Only available in GERMAN

Die feldgraue Uniformierung des deutschen Heeres 1907–1918

Author: Jürgen Kraus

2 Textbände mit Schuber: 1150 Seiten + 70 ganzseitige Farbtafeln, Hardcover-Band mit Schutzumschlag. Format: 26,5 × 18,5 cm

Auf der Grundlage jahrelanger Quellenforschungen behandelt dieses zweibändige Werk nahezu lückenlos die gesamte feldgraue Uniformierung des deutschen Heeres von den ersten Entwicklungen bis zum Ende des Ersten Weltkriegs. Durch seinen wissenschaftlichen Aufbau kann die vorliegende Arbeit als absolutes Quellenwerk und bleibendes Standardwerk zur feldgrauen Uniformierung des deutschen Heeres im Ersten Weltkrieg bezeichnet werden.

Im ersten Teil der Arbeit werden alle Bekleidungsstücke einzeln in ihren Veränderungen, die oft durch die knappe Rohstofflage im Krieg bedingt waren, ausführlich beschrieben und durch klare Illustrationen veranschaulicht. Der zweite Teil behandelt, geordnet nach Waffengattungen, detailliert die Uniformierung der einzelnen Truppen und Behörden des Heeres. Die vorliegende Arbeit kann als absolutes Quellenwerk und bleibendes Standardwerk bezeichnet werden. Insgesamt 70 ganzseitige Farbtafeln führen dem Leser die Systematik der feldgrauen Uniform in übersichtlicher Form vor Augen.

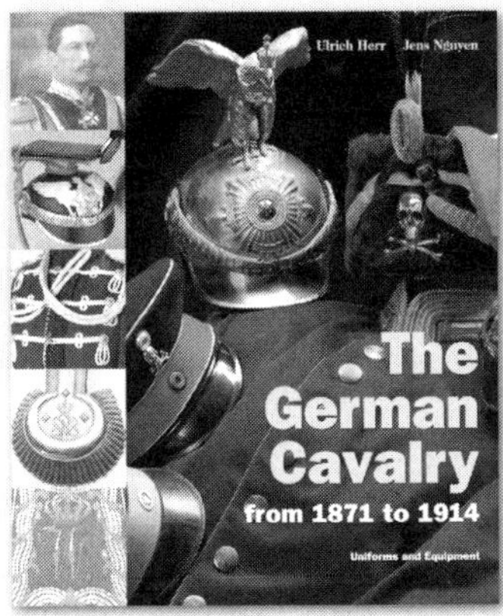

ISBN: 978-3-902526-07-6 $ 140

The German Cavalry – from 1871 to 1914

Author: Ulrich Herr, Jens Nguyen

640 pages, approx. 1500 photographs and illustrations, linen-bound with a book jacket. Format: 29,5 × 25 cm

With its traditions and diversity the German cavalry represented the most colourful branch of service of the German Empire. To an extent never seen before, this **640 page, magnificently illustrated book** shows the uniforms, equipment and armament of the entire German cavalry from the **foundation of the Empire in 1871** to the eve of the **First World War in 1914**. Brilliant colour photographs give the reader a graphic picture of the **splendid headgear** of cuirassiers, Saxon 'Schwere Reiter', dragoons, Bavarian chevaulegers, hussars, uhlans and mounted Jäger. Numerous photographs of original specimens document the different branches of the service and the state contingents of the German Empire. The mode of wearing individual **uniforms and items of equipment** is illustrated by contemporary black and white photographs. Based on still extant sources such as clothing regulations or military decrees, the book endeavours to document modifications and alterations to different items of equipment over a period of 43 years. Not only the collector can learn a wealth of new aspects, the military historian can also gain a valuable overview due to the **well structured and systematic** arrangement of the book.

www.militaria.at

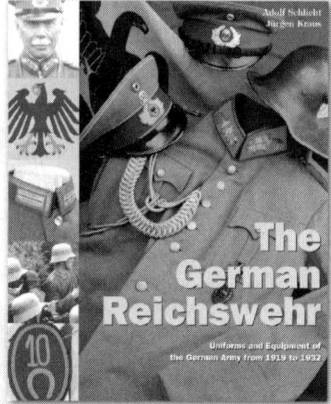

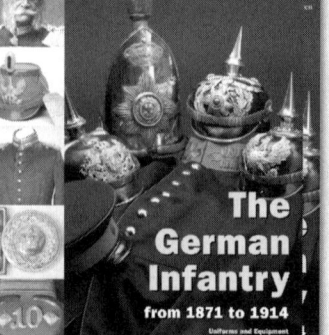